INSIDERS' GUIDE® TO

TUCSON

SEVENTH EDITION

MARY PAGANELLI VOTTO

INSIDERS' GUIDE

GUILFORD, CONNECTICUT
AN IMPRINT OF GLOBE PEQUOT PRESS

All the information in this guidebook is subject to change. We recommend that you call ahead to obtain current information before traveling.

INSIDERS' GUIDE ®

Editor: Amy Lyons
Project Editor: Heather Santiago
Text Design: Sheryl Kober
Maps: XNR Productions, Inc. © Morris Book Publishing, LLC

ISSN 1529-3459
ISBN 978-0-7627-7324-4

Printed in the United States of America
10 9 8 7 6 5 4 3 2 1

Tucson

All photos licensed by Shutterstock.com.

Page 1: A rustic chair poses before the warm, welcoming walls of an adobe in Tucson.

Page 2 (top left): The vibrant buildings of La Placita in downtown Tucson; (top right) Dusk splashes San Xavier Mission with color; (bottom) Hot air balloons in an array of patterns and colors stand out against a brilliant blue sky.

Page 3 (top): The city of Tucson nestled against the Catalina Mountains; (bottom left) A rope of delicious green and fiery red chili peppers; (bottom right, upper) The hardy petals of a rosette-shaped succulent plant; (bottom right, lower) Relaxed but alert, a coyote surveys the area from a comfortable distance.

Page 4 (top): An artfully landscaped walkway at the Arizona Sonora Desert Museum; (bottom) The breathtaking and wild landscape of Sabino Canyon in Tucson.

CONTENTS

Directory of Maps

ABOUT THE AUTHOR

A graduate of Vassar College and the New School Culinary Arts Program, **Mary Paganelli Votto** is a food writer, photographer, editor, recipe tester, and chef. She moved to Tucson from New York City in 2001 and enjoys the wide-open spaces, natural beauty, and terrific weather in southern Arizona. Mary is the author of *From I'itoi's Garden: Tohono O'odham Food Traditions,* a full-color reference and cookbook written with Tohono O'odham elders and community members. Mary is also an adjunct professor of culinary arts at Tohono O'odham Community College, tests recipes for Canyon Ranch, and contributes food and entertainment articles to *Tucson Lifestyle* magazine.

ACKNOWLEDGMENTS

Thank you, thank you to my wonderful husband, Ernie, and my fabulous son, Eric—for being there, for all your support, for visiting all of Tucson's new attractions, partying downtown, and eating at lots and lots of great restaurants all over the city. I couldn't do it without you! Also thanks to all who shared ideas for this edition of the guidebook: Debbie Graves, Tristan Reader and Karen Wyndham, Susan Lobo, Terrol Dew Johnson, Ellen Rauch, Kate Reynolds for all her earlier contributions, David Berryman for the Bisbee input, the Pinal Historical Society, and Uncle Losh and Janie Spalla for a real insiders' tour of Lake Havasu City.

Tucson & Surrounding Area

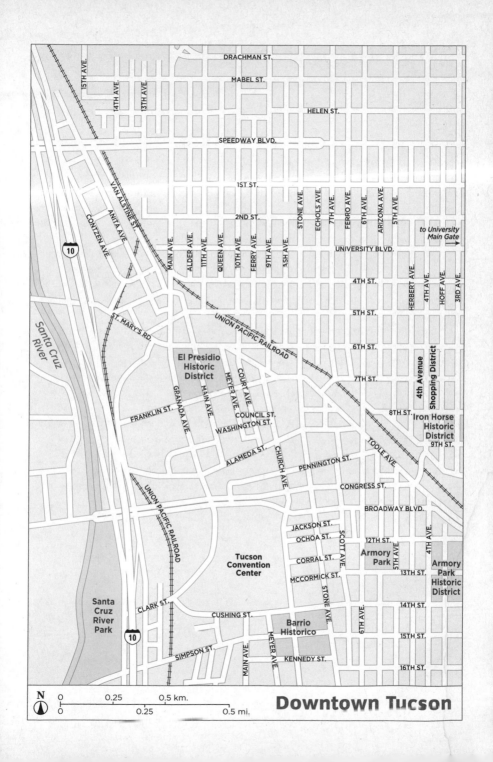

Downtown Tucson

INTRODUCTION

Welcome to Tucson—the Old Pueblo!

One of the "themes" you'll notice as you read through this guidebook is diversity. Tucson is a diverse city—in culture, in history, in recreation, in business, in dining, in lodging, in entertainment, in education, in the arts . . . the list goes on and on. There are many reasons for such diversity.

Maybe it all started when a settlement was established in the name of Spain just a stone's throw from where Native American tribes had lived for centuries.

Perhaps it's because so many people here are from someplace else—places like Milwaukee, Mexico, or Montreal—and they've all brought with them their talents and interests.

Maybe it's the University of Arizona with its mix of people and ideas from all over the world, as well as its outstanding programs in everything from space exploration to creative writing to music to medicine.

Of course the amazing weather has something to do with our diversity. With more than 350 days of sunshine a year, folks can enjoy all sorts of outdoor activities except playing on a beach (but Tucson does have more than its fair share of places to swim and splash).

Tucson's colorful history—over the years we've lived under five different flags—certainly has something to do with it. Tucson has been a sleepy pueblo, a wild and woolly Western town, a midsize Air Force city, and a sophisticated university town.

The best guess would be that all of these factors (and a handful of others that aren't quite so apparent) make Tucson—Tucson. You'll soon see that Tucson is a great place to visit or live, with lots of exciting activities, fascinating landscapes, and amazing wildlife.

Discovering Tucson's many hidden treasures is what makes living and visiting here fun, and you'll find many such gems described in these pages. As with any city as diverse and growing as Tucson, there is lots to see and do.

So grab this *Insiders' Guide* and explore the Old Pueblo. We're glad you're here.

HOW TO USE THIS BOOK

Maybe you're visiting Tucson on a family vacation or business trip. Perhaps you've just relocated to Tucson or plan to soon. Or maybe you're a "snowbird"—the term Southwesterners use for winter visitors who take flight from the snow states to spend all or most of the winter in our inviting city. No matter why you're here or for how long, you'll find this the most thorough and interesting guide available for the city and surrounding areas.

The Tucson area is alive with unique and fascinating flora and fauna; with a multitude of outdoor recreation offerings; with restaurants, attractions, nightlife, and lodgings to suit any taste and budget; and with sports for everyone from basketball fans to birders to bicyclists. We'll tell you how to get there, what you'll see, how much it will cost, and impart some Insiders' tips, special Close-ups and well-founded opinions to help you choose wisely among the vast array of things to do, see, and experience in Tucson. The city proper comprises only 125 square miles. Therefore, much of what you'll see and do in Tucson is located in the metropolitan area of Pima County that surrounds the city of Tucson. So even though we say "Tucson" on this book's cover and throughout its pages, keep in mind that we are really referring to a metropolitan area of approximately 500 square miles that extends from one mountain range to another. Like most Southwestern cities, Tucson has developed outward rather than upward. You'll find very few high-rises here, but you will find a lot of land to traverse getting from one attraction on the far east side, for example, to another "way out west." With our help you will get there, and it will be worth the trek.

Each chapter of this book covers a specific topic (or combines related topics). We think we've covered every subject that would be of interest and value to any traveler or newcomer. It's easy to zero in on Restaurants if sating your appetite is on your mind, or on our Golf chapter if you're longing to hit the links. If you're just arriving to Tucson, turn to our Getting Here, Getting Around chapter and find out how to get where you're going in town—without breaking any rules of the road along the way. Read the Natural World chapter, and you'll soon know as much as Tucsonans do about the fascinating cacti, our summer monsoons, and the four mountain ranges that surround Tucson. If you're looking for a magazine, newspaper or how to find National Public Radio, dial in to the Media chapter. And don't skip the History chapter if you want to know the origin of Tucson's name and lots more about this historic city.

Within each chapter, the information typically is subdivided to help you easily find a specific type of cuisine, a place to shop for Native American jewelry or pottery, or a weekend or day trip out of town. Places are listed alphabetically within each chapter or subsection of a chapter.

NOTE: Unless otherwise indicated, all listings are in Tucson proper.

Scattered throughout the various chapters are special Insiders' tips (indicated by an 🛈) for quick insights. The tips are our way of sharing our insider information. You will also find lengthy Close-ups profiling truly unique aspects of the area's lifestyle and culture.

You'll also find listings accompanied by the ✳ symbol—these are our top picks for attractions, restaurants, accommodations, and everything in between that you shouldn't miss while you're in the area. You want the best this region has to offer? Go with our **Insiders' Choice.**

Finally, if you're moving to the Tucson area or already live here, be sure to check out the blue-tabbed pages at the back of the book. There you will find the **Living Here** appendix that offers sections on relocation, media, child care, education, worship, health care, and retirement.

If we'd included everything in the Tucson area, this book would be far too weighty to travel with you in a glove compartment, briefcase, or backpack. The philosophy of *Insiders' Guides* is to cover the best of what a city has to offer and show you the hidden treasures that are here. And while we have made every effort to be accurate and to include all the highlights of Tucson, we're only human. If you find mistakes in our book, if you disagree with something we've said, if you'd like to recommend additions or changes in future editions, or if you'd like to compliment us on a job well done, we would appreciate hearing from you: *Insiders' Guide to Tucson*, PO Box 480, Guilford, CT 06437 or you may e-mail us at: editorial@GlobePequot.com.

AREA OVERVIEW

Double rainbows, spectacular sunsets, hot yellow sun and cool pale moon in the same azure sky, towering saguaro and purple mountains majesty, over 350 days of perfect weather—this is Tucson, and it doesn't get much better than this! The city's personality is a combination of great climate, modern metropolitan area, artsy college town, incredible landscapes, ethnic and cultural diversity, upscale resorts, high-tech business, and the Old West.

Many people on their first visit to Tucson are pleasantly surprised by what they find. Shaped by the images of old Western films and television shows, newcomers often expect to see cowboys strutting dusty streets, rattlesnakes under every rock, and townsfolk traveling by buckboard and stagecoach. What they find instead is a bustling city with seasonal bumper-to-bumper traffic, a tall gleaming skyline, and a thoroughly modern, but easygoing, lifestyle.

Tucsonans take great pride in our colorful history and its many cultural influences. Mexico is just 60 miles to the south, and with Tucson's large Hispanic population, its influences are everywhere—from architecture to dining, entertainment to street names.

The Native American population is a small percent, but the Tohono O'odham and Pascua Yaqui tribes have been here for centuries, and their influence impacts Tucson in numerous ways from art to music.

Casual and *laid-back* are words that are often used to describe Tucson. You'll find that the lifestyle here is relaxed and sophisticated. There are many terrific hidden treasures in this town alongside the more obvious natural and man-made wonders. Exploring and discovering the secrets and history of Tucson is part of what makes living here special. There's something for everyone.

GEOGRAPHICALLY SPEAKING

Metro Tucson covers approximately 500 square miles reaching from one mountain range to another and sits at 2,389 feet above sea level. The city limits of Tucson cover about 156 square miles. The mountain ranges that surround the area (the Catalinas to the north, the Rincons to the east, the Tucsons to the west, and the Santa Ritas to the far south) contribute to Tucson's wonderful climate. Our location is another contributing factor—the city lies in a zone that receives more sunshine (about 350 days per year) than any other region of the US.

The city of Tucson is located in the center of eastern Pima County at the intersection of I-10 and I-19. Pima County was created in 1864 and included approximately all of southern Arizona acquired from Mexico by the Gadsden Purchase. The county now covers over 9,000 square miles and encompasses not only Tucson but also the separate towns of Marana, Oro Valley, Sahuarita, and South Tucson as well as several unincorporated areas, including Green Valley.

The average rainfall is 12 inches per year, but that doesn't mean we average an inch a month, as ongoing drought conditions have drastically affected rainfall levels. The summer months bring the monsoon season (see the Natural World chapter), and even in December or January, rainfall can be quite heavy. The months in between tend to be hot and very dry, with nary a drop of measurable rainfall. But with an average temperature that hovers near the perfect 81 degrees, Tucson is attractive to many folks from less-mild climes.

POLITICS & THE PEOPLE

Tucson is proud of its multicultural heritage (the region has flown the flags of Spain, Mexico, the Confederacy, the Union, and the US) and diversity (census figures show Tucson is home to several hundred ancestry groups and is one of the largest cities in the country in number of Native Americans). Family friendly, Tucson attracts people from all walks of life and income. Next Generation Consulting ranked Tucson 16th on a list of the best places for young professionals to live and work, among cities with a population of more than 500,000.

The median age of a Tucson resident is 33.2, but you'll find all kinds of people here: silver-haired retirees, middle-income families, ranchers, professors, university students, artists, and recent immigrants from all over the world. All are attracted to Tucson for the same reason: its terrific quality of life.

The area is home to two major Indian reservations: the Pascua Yaqui Tribe on 1.87 square miles with about 6,000 members, and the Tohono O'odham Nation on 4,453 square miles with nearly 24,000 members. Each is self-governing, with its own laws and officials. Both nations operate gaming casinos that pour millions of dollars back into their communities in the form of jobs, scholarships, improved health care, and housing.

The city of Tucson operates under a council/manager type of government. This means that both the mayor and city council members are elected by the people to make decisions, and a city manager is appointed by the council to help carry out those decisions. There are six councilpersons, in addition to the mayor, all chosen in citywide elections. The Pima County Board of Supervisors has five elected members (by district) and also appoints a county manager to oversee implementation of laws.

As a nod toward the idea of allowing citizens to have their say, the mayor and council created the Livable Tucson Vision Program, an ongoing effort to develop and implement key goals for the city in areas that include transportation, responsive government, safety and health, education, growth and preservation, and improving the lifestyle of everyone with better jobs, clean air, plentiful water, and more equal opportunities.

GROWTH & DEVELOPMENT

What started out as a small presidio evolved first into a series of barrios multiplying slowly across the valley and then into a spread-out, medium-size city. Tucson has gone from being a slow-paced, small town to a bustling city. Attractive to families and retirees alike with its great climate and relatively low cost

Close-up

Gabrielle Giffords

January 8, 2011, will always be remembered as a dark day in Tucson's history. That is the day our congresswoman, Gabrielle Giffords, known to all as Gabby, was shot by alleged gunman Jared Lee Loughner.

A third-generation Tucsonan, from 2000 to 2005 Gabby represented Tucson in the Arizona legislature, where she was the youngest woman ever elected to the Arizona state Senate. Elected to Congress in 2007 to represent Congressional District 8, she is the third woman in Arizona history to be elected to the US Congress.

Although tragic, the shooting brought out the best of Tucson.

Police, firemen, and medical staff rushed to the scene to help. Top surgeons at Tucson's hospitals worked night and day to save Gabby and the other wounded. The city came together to offer support, love, and care, placing flowers, notes, and teddy bears at impromptu memorials at the shooting site, the hospital, and Gabby's midtown office. Candlelight vigils brought Tucson's citizens together at this time of great sorrow.

But instead of wallowing in grief and anger at this senseless tragedy, Tucson rallied and came closer together, showing the rest of the country and the world that out of tragedy you can build a stronger community.

President Barack Obama visited our small city, shining a light on the multicultural threads that make this a special place and focusing on the good that Tucsonans one and all chose to pursue in the wake of this tragedy.

Ron Barber, Gabby's district director, himself injured in the shooting, organized a concert from his hospital bed to benefit a new organization: the Fund for Civility, Respect, and Understanding. The concert brought top singers and songwriters, such as Jackson Brown, Alice Cooper, Graham Nash, and David Crosby to Tucson's Convention Center, where they were joined by over 4,000 Tucsonans helping to heal the city's wounds through music.

A park (the Cañada del Oro Christina Taylor Green Memorial River Park) and sculpture were dedicated to Christina Taylor Green, the littlest victim. The sculpture, titled *Freedom's Steadfast Angel of Love*, is a replica of similar statues placed at Ground Zero in New York, the Pentagon, and the Flight 93 crash site, and is the first angel to be made of wreckage from all three 9/11 sites—reminding us that in tragedy we all stand together.

We salute the fallen—Gabe Zimmerman, Judge John M. Roll, Christina Taylor Green, Dorothy Morris, Phyllis Schneck, and Dorwan Stoddard. We cherish their memories and contributions to our community.

We thank the brave—the police officers, emergency medical technicians, firefighters, staff at Tucson's hospitals, and especially Daniel Hernandez Jr. for surely saving Gabby's life.

We hope for Gabby's recovery and for her return to public service, to her family, and to Tucson.

We remember that from tragedy can grow strength and community.

of living, Tucson is practically bursting at the seams.

> **i** Created in 1949, the Economic and Business Research Center—a part of the University of Arizona's Eller College of Management—provides Arizona's business community with scads of information on economic, demographic, and business trends. Statistics buffs will love all the data on their website, http://ebr.eller.arizona.edu.

The Tucson region is considered one of the most affordable places to live in the Sun Belt and the West, as ranked by the Association of Applied Community Researchers' 2009 cost of living index. Add the wonderful weather and laid-back lifestyle, and you get a very popular relocation spot. In November 2006 the population of Pima County reached 1 million and is projected to continue increasing at a steady pace. *Sunset Magazine's* March 2010 issue named Tucson among the "20 Best Towns of the Future."

Median income for a family of four in Tucson is $57,500, according to the US Department of Housing and Development's 2009 statistics, and despite the generally slow growth nationwide, Tucson is projected to be the 23rd-fastest growing major market in the US, according to the Nielsen Claritas 2010 survey of major markets. In May 2010 *Forbes Magazine* ranked Tucson as one of the 20 most innovative cities in America. The housing market is still in a state of flux—in August 2010 the Tucson Association of Realtors showed the average housing sale price as $186,562, with a median sales price of $150,750.

By far the fastest growing area in metropolitan Tucson is the northwest, outside the city limits, in the towns of Oro Valley and Marana. The areas southeast of town and toward the western edge are also expanding rapidly, with new housing developments, master-planned communities, and major retailers moving in. Nevertheless, Tucson retains its slow pace and Western attitude despite it all, and there are still plenty of wide-open spaces, giant saguaros, and cougars roaming residential neighborhoods to remind us that this is still the West.

TUCSON'S CHALLENGES

The biggest challenges confronting Tucson in the face of its rapid growth are transportation, development, and conservation. All are critical issues that fuel debate countywide. At issue: how to keep intact the things that make Tucson special but allow development that will foster economic growth and not compromise the natural beauty of the area. It's an issue that many small cities wrestle with, and these are natural growing pains. The good news is that the city and the good citizens of Tucson are not standing still but are facing the challenges of growth and development with the typical forward thinking and independent spirit that make Tucsonans and Tucson special.

TRANSPORTATION

The lack of a citywide transportation system and the deterioration of major roadways and neighborhood streets continue to be matters of great concern. The Tucson Department of Transportation oversees the maintenance and reconstruction of nearly 4,400 lane miles of streets. The department is also responsible for hundreds of drainage structures, public art pieces, street lights and signs, and traffic signs and signals in Tucson.

Road congestion and traffic gridlock have increased exponentially, especially with the influx of visitors during the winter season. The implementation of a Regional Transportation Authority and Regional Transportation Committee to review and make recommendations is a good start in the desperately needed effort to improve Tucson's roadways.

The battle continues over the development of freeways, and voters have rejected plans for a light-rail system several times. Getting across town from any direction at rush hour is a challenge and, at some major intersections, dangerous. The current roadway system was developed in the 1920s, and it looks like it. Although the city has implemented several strategic plans, including upgrading major thoroughfares and paving side streets, the problem is a big one, which will require foresight, planning, major funding, and citizen support to solve.

LAND USE PLANNING & CONSERVATION

Tucson continues to experience rapid growth, with retirees and others pinpointing this desert paradise as their new home. As a result, much of the desert landscape is being mowed down and destroyed, even though the Sonoran Desert has been identified by The Nature Conservancy as one of the top eco-regions worldwide, deserving of special conservation attention. Both those who have lived here for decades and those who have moved here recently recognize the importance of preserving the unique desert landscape that makes this place special. It's all about choices and trade-offs. It's one thing to be passionate about protecting our environment, but quite another to achieve success. For example, if we use water to grow cotton, that water can't be used to drink. If we use fire to help a forest protect itself, we generate air pollution downwind as the fire burns. Recycling newspapers causes water pollution. Details are always debatable, but what is clear is that trade-offs stand at the center of environmental debate, and the issues are highly complex. How can we protect desert land while continuing to encourage growth?

Local environmental and conservation agencies and organizations like Native Seeds/SEARCH, the Audubon Society, Sierra Club, and The Nature Conservancy are working with city and county governments and developers to address these vital concerns.

Clean air is an absolute must wherever you choose to live. Tucson, like any other growing city, faces issues of pollution. Approximately 60 percent of Tucson's air pollution, such as particulate matter (soot) and carbon monoxide, comes from on-road vehicles.

i In August 2010 the Tucson region was ranked the nation's number-one Alternative Energy Industry Leader by *Business Facilities* magazine. The American Lung Association's 2010 *State of the Air* report ranked Tucson as sixth in cleanest year-round particle pollution.

Tucson, like many cities in the Southwest, is vehicle-oriented. The state has imposed gas additives in the metro areas of Arizona during winter (October through March). Although this has helped some, it has not drastically reduced the amounts of pollutants in the air. There is a strong push by city leaders to encourage other means of transportation such as city buses, car pools,

Tucson Vital Statistics

Population (2009 estimate): Pima County 1,020,200; Tucson 543,566

Area & altitude: 156 square miles; 2,389 feet

Nickname: The Old Pueblo

Average temperatures: July: High 99/Low 74, January: High 63/Low 37

Average number of sunny days per year: 350

Average precipitation: 12 inches

Tucson founded: 1775

Arizona achieved statehood: 1912

Major colleges & universities: University of Arizona, Pima Community College, University of Phoenix

Major area employers: Raytheon Missile Systems, University of Arizona, State of Arizona, US Army Intelligence Center and Fort Huachuca, Davis-Monthan Air Force Base, Tucson Unified School District

Military base: Davis-Monthan Air Force Base

Major airport: Tucson International Airport

Public transportation: Sun Tran bus service

Driving laws: Children under age 5 must ride in car seats. Drivers and front-seat passengers must wear seat belts. Arizona has some of the strictest DUI laws in the nation.

Alcohol laws: Arizona law prohibits anyone younger than age 21 to purchase or consume alcoholic beverages. The purchase, service, or consumption of liquor is prohibited from 2 to 6 a.m. Mon through Sat and from 2 to 10 a.m. on Sun.

Daily newspapers: *The Arizona Daily Star*

and bicycles. The acceptance of these alternative forms of transportation is slow and in small numbers, despite the many days when commuters notice the haze that hangs over the city.

A proactive approach to clean air is the city's Trees for Tucson project. As part of Tucson Clean and Beautiful (a city-operated project), trees that thrive in the desert—meaning without needing a lot of water—are planted all over the city. With the help of Tucson Electric Power Company, thousands of trees have been planted in yards and parks and also along roadways.

The city, through various departments, operates several environmental projects, including Adopt-a-Park, where groups and individuals can help maintain not just parks but also streets, washes, and other areas; and Waste Reduction Education, where schoolchildren learn ways to reduce, reuse, and recycle. Tucson Clean and Beautiful offers

Weekly newspapers: *Tucson Weekly*, Thursday

Sales tax: State tax is 5.6 percent; city tax is 9.1 percent

Chamber of commerce:

Tucson Metropolitan Chamber of Commerce
(520) 792-2250
www.tucsonchamber.com

Visitor center:

Metropolitan Tucson Convention & Visitors Bureau
100 S. Church Ave.
(520) 624-1817, (888) 288-2766
www.visittucson.org

Weather: The National Weather Service's local forecast line is (520) 881-3333, or check www.wrh.noaa.gov/tucson.

Daylight saving time: The State of Arizona does not observe daylight saving time. Tucson is on mountain standard time half the year and on Pacific time when other parts of the country are on daylight saving time.

Important dates in history:

1775—The city is established by Spanish soldiers as a walled presidio, the Presidio of San Augustin de Tucson.
1821—Tucson becomes part of Mexico when Mexico wins independence from Spain.
1853—Tucson becomes a part of the US because of the Gadsden Purchase.
1880—The Southern Pacific Railroad reaches Tucson.
1885—University of Arizona established.
1912—Arizona becomes the 48th state.

Famous Tucsonans: Linda Ronstadt, singer; Kerri Strug, gymnast; Stewart K. Udall, former secretary of the interior; Barbara Kingsolver, author

other programs about recycling throughout the community. Local communities and grants sponsor much of this great community work.

ECONOMIC CLIMATE

Tucson has always had a reputation for being a low-wage town, yet people are willing to work for less money just to stay in this fast-growing, sun-drenched Southwestern city. Slow but steady growth is projected for the region. Statistics compiled by the *Arizona Daily Star* in April 2011 showed that of Arizona's top 200 employers, 91 reported adding jobs in 2010, while most industry sectors showed decreases or no change. The mining and agriculture industries showed an increase of 13.5 percent. Call centers, one of Tucson's larger employers, posted a 9 percent increase. Most of the shrinkage occurred in construction and contracting

(9 percent loss), resorts (-6 percent) education (-5 percent) and real estate and financial services (-4 percent). But all the news is not negative. In August 2009 *Business Facilities* magazine ranked Tucson number six in its list of the top 10 metro areas for aerospace/defense manufacturing, and Tucson's average annual earnings per worker are $40,260 (an increase of 1.8 percent over 2009).

According to the chamber of commerce, with more than 1,200 companies employing over 50,000 people in the high-tech industries of southern Arizona, Tucson has become a leader in the new knowledge-based economy. Raytheon Missile Systems leads off as the largest single employer in the city, with over 11,000 employees. The University of Arizona is second, with over 10,000 local employees.

Companies like Raytheon Missile Systems, IBM, Amplimed, DILAS Diode Lasers, OZ Optics, Sion Power Corporation, and Arizona Center for Innovation do business here. Tucson's highly educated workforce has led to a high level of underemployment. Middle-management positions are difficult to come by and have a fairly low turnover. These usually pay a fairly low starting wage compared to other major metro areas—usually in the low to mid $30,000s. Highly skilled positions in the aerospace and optics industries command a more competitive wage, but hourly positions in the hospitality and service industries are fairly low. Thus Tucson finds itself with an increasing wage gap; in fact, Arizona has the fourth-highest income gap in the nation. To attract young professional families who will contribute to the community socially and economically, Tucson must actively pursue and attract companies that will pay nationally competitive wages.

> **i** The nonprofit Planetary Sciences Institute (PSI; www.psi.edu) is one of many innovative and growing small businesses in Tucson. Founded in 1972, PSI focuses on exploring the solar system through NASA missions, field work, and science education. In 2010, according to the Arizona Daily Star, PSI received more than $7 million in grants and contracts, added 9 employees, and generated an additional $1.5 million in revenue.

Tucson Regional Economic Opportunities (TREO)—a partnership of Pima County, the City of Tucson, and the business community—has targeted specific kinds of industrial clusters for relocation to the area, which has resulted in the creation of thousands of jobs in recent years. These include jobs in aerospace, bio-industry, optics, environmental technologies, and information technology and teleservices. Aerospace is the largest cluster, according to TREO statistics.

The area has become one of the top five locations in the country for teleservices operations and is becoming known as Optics Valley due to the more than 100 innovative optics businesses that have sprouted up in the area. Travel and tourism is an important segment of Tucson's employment scene.

Tucson's proximity to the Mexican border has always had an impact on the region's economy. Tucson was ranked seventh by *Hispanic* magazine in its list of top 10 cities. Since the passage of the North American Free Trade Agreement in January 1994, Tucson's status as a gateway to Mexico and South America has only been enhanced, positioning the area to export its expertise in industrial equipment, telecommunications, electronics, and financial services.

The military, too, has always had a strong presence here, and Davis-Monthan Air Force Base is home to the 355th Fighter Wing, the nation's only A-10 training facility. The base hires plenty of civilians, as well as pouring hundreds of thousands of dollars into the local economy.

The University of Arizona has been instrumental in Tucson's high-tech growth, establishing the Science and Technology Park on the southeast side of the metropolitan area just off I-10 near Houghton Road. The site is self-sustaining, with its own water wells, a railroad spur, sewage treatment plant, power plant, a gray water system to recycle water for toilets and landscaping, a recreation center, and cafeteria. This complex was built by IBM in the late 1970s and employed 5,000 people at its peak. When IBM pulled out much of its operation in 1989 and 1990, it left behind about 1,000 workers

and a $13 million state-of-the-art, 345-acre complex of 12 buildings.

In 1994 the University of Arizona acquired the site (considered the largest real estate deal ever in Tucson), establishing the Science and Technology Park. This networked, 2-million-square-foot technology campus is the sixth-largest university-related research park in the US. It's home to three Fortune 500 companies: IBM, Raytheon, and Citigroup.

TOURISM

Tourism is a billion-dollar-a-year industry in Tucson. It accounts, directly or indirectly, for one out of 10 jobs in the area and adds more than $2.3 billion per year to the local economy (source: Pima Association of Governments). Restaurants, hotels, tourist sites, and the like are obvious employers. But other companies that benefit from all the tourists include grocery stores, food suppliers, and printing companies. The list goes on and on.

There are really several types of tourists who visit Tucson: those who come for one of the hundreds of conventions held here every year, those who come for family vacations, and of course those who come to escape winter—the proverbial "snowbirds." This last group is made up largely of retirees who "move" here from the Midwest and Northeast for at least half the year to escape winter. Some rent homes; many stay in their RVs (see the Campgrounds & RV Parks and Retirement chapters). According to Metropolitan Tucson Convention and Visitor Bureau statistics, the following states account for most of our visitors: California, Colorado, Texas, Illinois, Washington, Minnesota, New York, North Carolina, and Oregon. Welcome all!

Top 10 Employers in Southern Arizona

1. Raytheon Missile Systems
2. University of Arizona
3. State of Arizona
4. Davis-Monthan Air Force Base
5. Wal-Mart Stores
6. Tucson Unified School District
7. US Army Intelligence Center, Fort Huachuca
8. Pima County
9. City of Tucson
10. Carondelet Health Network

Source: *Arizona Daily Star,* 2011

Thousands of visitors come to see the area's natural wonders, such as Saguaro National Park (about 740,000 people per year), Arizona-Sonora Desert Museum (over 470,000 per year), Reid Park Zoo (about 445,000 people per year), Old Tucson Studios (about 196,000 people per year), and Mount Lemmon (about 188,000 people per year). But annual events attract their share of crowds as well. The Pima County Fair normally draws over 250,000 people each year and generates millions for the community. The Fiesta de los Vaqueros Rodeo draws about 11,000 people, and its parade—the world's longest nonmotorized parade—sees an estimated 60,000 people line the streets. Baseball's spring training pumps millions into the economy.

After their first taste of all that Tucson has to offer, many folks go back home, pack their bags, and return for good. There haven't been any specific studies to track these people, but tourism ultimately affects Tucson's economy in this roundabout way as well.

DOWNTOWN REVITALIZATION

The downtown is undergoing a major renaissance. After numerous attempts to revitalize the area through the much-maligned Rio Nuevo plan and many independent ventures, life has started to seep back into the area with funky lofts, lots of renovations of historic buildings, new construction, many new hip restaurants, galleries, tree-lined streets, a streetcar route, and improved parking alternatives. Today hundreds of events are presented in downtown Tucson each year, including outdoor movies, club crawls, art walks, folk festivals and weekly downtown walks, runs, and special events (see the Arts & Culture, Nightlife, and Festivals & Events chapters).

Business owners in the area have also formed the Downtown Tucson Alliance (520-837-6504; www.downtowntucson.org), a nonprofit group charged with the mission of improving business conditions that has done much to promote businesses and fund events downtown. The alliance publishes the *Downtown Tucsonan* and promotes area businesses through a variety of events and activities. *Zocalo,* a free magazine devoted to downtown happenings (see the Media chapter), has also helped publicize the exciting developments in this area.

i **The 222-acre Solar Park on S. Rita Road and I-10 (at the University of Arizona's Science and Technology Park) is one of the world's most efficient photovoltaic systems. Dedicated in April 2011, the system consists of 36 giant solar panels, each about the size of an IMAX screen, that will generate enough electricity to power 500 homes.**

SUNNY DAYS AHEAD

The future is bright for Tucson. If we continue to work together and respect our history and natural resources, we can continue to be the place where the Old West meets the New West in a positive and progressive manner.

GETTING HERE, GETTING AROUND

Tucson's rapid growth has had a major impact on all areas of transportation in town. In 2010, there were over 3.5 million passenger arrivals and departures from the Tucson International Airport. The downtown train depot has been restored to its 1941 look with original terrazzo floor and replica of the original ticket counter. Although controversy continues about expansion of the road and freeway system, major thoroughfares are being upgraded, widened, and beautified with public art. A light-rail system is still a dream of many in town, as is commuter rail service to Phoenix.

Planes, trains, cars, and buses will all bring you to Tucson, but when you get here, you really need to have a car. Although there is a bus system, it can be pretty slow going and won't take you to all the attractions in town, not to mention the many not-to-be-missed side trips just a few hours away.

As the second-largest city in Arizona, Tucson is a busy place. But unlike most large cities, there are just two freeways here, and mainly they just circle the city. Although this makes for a much prettier in-town driving atmosphere, it can result in some traffic congestion and tie-ups, especially in prime season (October through May), when visitors and snowbirds flock here to take advantage of the great weather.

Before we tell you the ins and outs and tricks of getting around the metro area, we'll tell you the ways to get here. (Just about the only mode of transportation you can't take to get to the Old Pueblo is a boat.) And we'll tell you how best to get from your arrival point to where you're going in Tucson.

GETTING HERE

By Air

Tucson International Airport is the major air artery into the city. Located just 10 miles south of downtown Tucson off Valencia Road, it's an easy ride from here to just about any part of town. There are also three private airfields serving the Tucson area: the executive terminal of the Tucson International Airport (and just adjacent to it), Ryan Airfield to Tucson's southwest, and Marana Northwest Regional Airport in Marana.

TUCSON INTERNATIONAL AIRPORT
7250 S. Tucson Blvd.
(520) 573-8100
www.flytucsonaiport.com
Many major domestic airlines serve Tucson International Airport, and those that don't can probably get you into Phoenix, a short flight or less-than-two-hour bus or car ride away. **US Airways** (800-428-4322) and **Southwest Airlines** (800-435-9792) are the

two major airlines with frequent flights in and out of Tucson, but other major carriers like **American** (800-433-7300), **Delta** (800-221-1212), **Continental** (800-525-0280), and **United** (800-241-6522) also provide service to Tucson. Eight airlines provide nonstop service to 15 destinations with connections worldwide. If you're flying to or from a foreign country, you'll go through US Customs in the international wing of the airport.

There are some real pluses to arriving at Tucson International Airport. Flights rarely are encumbered by weather delays. The airport is fairly small and uncongested compared to behemoths like Phoenix, Los Angeles, or Chicago, so flight delays are not as common. And passengers can usually get into and out of the airport with ease and minimal hassles.

A free cell phone waiting area is available on Airport Drive just west of the airport entrance.

The airport has both short-term and long-term parking lots, the former very close to the terminal for ease of lugging your luggage or finding an arriving traveler, but even the long-term lot is within walking distance. The short-term lot charges $1 per half hour and $12 per day. The long-term lot charges $1 per half hour then $1.50 per hour and $9 for the day. The garage with 605 spaces offers hourly and daily rates. If you're parking long-term, you'll probably save money at one of the private parking lots just outside the airport, which will shuttle you to and from the terminal. Several of these lots are on Tucson Boulevard, the main road into the airport, and cost about $4 a day. The Park 'N Save lot on Corona Drive between S. Tucson Boulevard and S. Country Club (520-573-8400) is fenced, covered, and lighted, with 24-hour security.

Ground transportation—taxis, shuttles, limos, or hotel vehicles—will drop you off or pick you up right in front of the terminal, and the locations are well marked with signs as you step out of the terminal's lower (baggage) level.

Airport passengers have several choices for ground transportation. **Sun Tran,** Tucson's public bus system, provides service to and from the airport, so check with the terminal information centers or Sun Tran (520-792-9222) for information. Many hotels provide complimentary airport transportation for their guests, so either ask when you make your hotel reservation or stop at the hotel reservation board in the lower terminal level for direct phone service to some hotels. Although you may have a tough time finding a taxi anywhere else in Tucson, they're plentiful at the airport. They have a flag drop rate that includes the first mile plus a per-mileage charge after that (unless you're going beyond 25 miles of the airport, in which case it would be a flat fee). Expect to pay about $25 between the airport and central Tucson. Taxi fares include baggage and extra persons going to the same location. **Arizona Stagecoach** (520-889-1000; www .azstagecoach.com) operates a door-to-door van service to and from the airport. You can call them in advance for information or go to the company's reservation desk in the terminal's lower level.

Many car rental agencies are located in or close to the airport. If they're off the grounds, they'll have shuttles to and from the terminal. They include **Alamo** (520-573-4740), **Avis** (520-294-1494), **Budget** (520-573-8475), **Dollar** (520-573-4000), **Enterprise** (520-573-5250), **Hertz** (520-573-5201), and **National** (520-573-8050). It's obviously best to reserve your car before your trip to Tucson, but if you didn't, merely walk up to one of the car rental counters in the building adjacent to the terminal and see if anything's available.

If you want the luxury of limousine service, several in Tucson will transport you to or from the airport. Information on this service is available at the airport as well as later in this chapter.

i Easy Pay stations that take credit and debit cards are located outside baggage claim areas and near elevators in the parking garage.

EXECUTIVE TERMINAL
TUCSON INTERNATIONAL AIRPORT
7081 S. Plumer Ave.
(520) 573-8128, (800) 758-1874
www.flytucsonairport.com
Operated by the Tucson Airport Authority and connected to Tucson International Airport, the executive terminal is the busiest of the three private fields, primarily because of its proximity to the airport and the city. Open 24 hours, it has access and facilities for all kinds of aircraft, from two-seaters to million-dollar jets. Aircraft services available include fuel, overnight parking, a weather briefing room, and lavatory clean-out, but no aircraft maintenance or repair services. (These are available at neighboring businesses, as is flight instruction.) There's a pilots lounge in the terminal with Wi-Fi, plus car rentals and taxi and limo services. The terminal can also reserve cars and make hotel accommodations. At this airport there are no landing fees for privately owned aircraft, but commercial (cargo or for-hire) craft flying operation 135 or 121 will pay a fee per thousand pounds of the aircraft's maximum gross landing weight capability. The UNICOM number is 122.95.

Those in the know say this is a popular spot for the rich and famous (or infamous) to land and step out of their aircraft into a waiting limousine without curious observers ever seeing them.

RYAN AIRFIELD
9700 W. Ajo Way
(520) 883-2921 (maintenance),
(520) 883-9800 (general information)
www.flytucsonairport.com
Ryan Airfield, also operated by the Tucson Airport Authority, lies at the western end of Valencia Road, where it intersects with Ajo Highway in a fairly remote area about 15 miles from Tucson International. Services here include fuel, rental cars, overnight parking at daily and monthly rates, and a restaurant open daily. Maintenance, repair, and lessons are available at private businesses adjacent to the airfield. There are no landing fees. Tower hours are 6 a.m. to 8 p.m. There is no UNICOM, but radio frequencies are 125.8 for air and 118.2 for ground control.

MARANA NORTHWEST REGIONAL
   AIRPORT
11700 W. Avra Valley Rd., Marana
(520) 682-2999, (800) 264-2266
www.tucsonaero.com
Marana Northwest Regional Airport, operated by and located in the town of Marana, about 5 miles west of I-10, and may be most convenient to residents of Tucson's northwest. Services are provided by Tucson Aeroservice Center and include fuel, overnight parking at fees depending on aircraft size, car rental available with advance notice, a restaurant, and a pilots lounge (with showers). There are no landing fees, and a private fixed-based operator on-site provides maintenance, repair, lessons, and charter flights. UNICOM is 122.875

i Tucson's airport was originally located on the current Tucson Rodeo Grounds on S. 6th Avenue, where Randolph E. Fisher made the first landing on November 20, 1919. Originally named Fishburn Field, the airport was renamed the Tucson Municipal Flying Field in 1923 and moved to its current site on S. Tucson Boulevard in 1948.

Charter Services

If you prefer private to commercial flying and don't have your own wings, several companies operate charter and aircraft rental services. They'll take you to other cities for business or pleasure or on flights of fancy, such as over the Grand Canyon or whale watching in Mexico's Sea of Cortez. **Double Eagle Aviation** (520-294-8214; www.2-eagle.com) is conveniently located near the Executive Terminal and offers a wide range of services for charter and private flying. **Tyconic** (520-883-4823) is based at Ryan Airfield and offers flight instruction and aircraft rentals. Operating out of Marana Northwest Regional Airport, **Tucson Aeroservice Center** (520-682-2999; www.tucsonaero.com) has full charter services. All three service Mexico and Canada as well as the US. Located at the Tucson International Airport, **Tucson Helicopter Charters** (800-615-1655; www.tucsonhelicoptercharters.com) offers a variety of helicopter sightseeing tours.

By Train

AMTRAK
400 N. Toole Ave.
(520) 623-4442, (800) 872-7245
www.amtrak.com
Tucson's Amtrak station is downtown, in the refurbished 1941 historic train depot at the northwest corner of 4th and Toole Avenues. The station is open Tues, Thurs and Sat from 6 p.m. to 1:30 a.m., and Sun, Wed and Fri from 7:30 p.m. to 3 a.m., primarily corresponding to trains' arrivals and departures. Amtrak's Sunset Limited passes through eastbound to Orlando, Florida, and westbound to Los Angeles several days a week. The Texas Eagle portion of the line will get you to San Antonio or Chicago. Strangely, Amtrak does not service Phoenix directly but instead stops in Maricopa, about 30 minutes outside Phoenix. Talk continues about light-rail services and commuter service to Phoenix, which would be based at the station.

Parking is available at the station and nearby on the street, but none of it is secured or advisable for the long term. The safest bet for long-term parking is a nearby city garage. Ground transportation from the train station is convenient because it's located downtown and only a stone's throw from Sun Tran's Ronstadt Transit Center at Pennington Street and 6th Avenue. Beyond the city bus, you're likely to find taxicabs either at the train station or the bus transit center. For a rental car, you'll need to call one for a pickup; none are within walking distance of the train station or in the immediate downtown area.

By Bus

GREYHOUND
471 W. Congress St.
(520) 792-3475
www.greyhound.com
If you follow the old saying "Leave the driving to us," you'll be arriving or departing Tucson by Greyhound bus.

Greyhound serves all points north, south, east, and west of Tucson, including Nogales and several other cities in Mexico. For example, you can get to or from Las

Vegas, Los Angeles, Texas, or Phoenix from Tucson. For the convenience of airline travelers, Greyhound also has several trips a day from its Tucson terminal to its terminal 1 mile from the Phoenix airport. The Tucson station is located at Congress and I-10.

By Car

If you're driving to Tucson from points west, such as California or western Arizona, you'll probably be traveling east along I-8, which meets up with I-10 just south of Casa Grande and about 70 miles north of Tucson. From that point, I-10 east will take you southward right into Tucson. If you're driving from points north like Flagstaff or Phoenix, I-10 eastbound will deposit you in Tucson. If you'd rather take the scenic route than the fast route, exit I-10 early and head for Sacaton or Coolidge, which will take you to Highway 87 and past the Casa Grande Ruins National Monument, then connect with I-10 again.

Mexico is about the only point south of Tucson, so if you're coming from that direction you must be coming across the border, in which case I-19 will carry you north into downtown Tucson. Or take the scenic path, Highway 82 north to Highway 83 north, which will connect with I-10 east of Tucson, then take that west to the city. Traveling from the east, such as from New Mexico, the major route into Tucson is I-10 westbound. This part of I-10 goes through some lovely country, including farmlands around Willcox, Arizona, and a boulder-laden area called Texas Canyon.

If you're traveling from Colorado or northeastern Arizona and its fascinating Indian reservation spots like Canyon de Chelly National Monument or Window Rock, the fast option is to take I-40 east into Flagstaff, then go south along I-17 and I-10 to Tucson. For scenic routes, there are many choices, including Highway 77, which goes through the White Mountains and eventually becomes Oracle Road into Tucson, or US 191, a very scenic road winding through forestlands that eventually connects with I-10 east of Tucson.

GETTING AROUND

OK, you've arrived. Now how do you find your way from one end of the 500-square-mile valley that's metropolitan Tucson to the other, and all points in between? Well, it won't be by boat or by fast transit (like trains), but it could be by car, bus, taxi, or limousine. Here's how to find and use the various forms of in-town transportation and how to get around the streets if you're the driver.

Navigating the Streets

In one sense Tucson is fairly easy to navigate by car. If you get to know the four mountain ranges that are strategically located at the four compass points, you'll be able to ascertain north from south and east from west from nearly any spot in the city. At the very least, learn to recognize the Santa Catalinas and you'll know where north is. And much of Tucson, especially the central area, is laid out in a grid system with streets 1 mile apart and running directly north–south or east–west.

But there are more than a few chinks in this plan, which can confuse even longtime Tucsonan drivers. For example, there are the streets that inexplicably change their name somewhere midstream, or natural obstacles such as washes, rivers, or mini-mountains (and man-made obstacles such as an Air Force base) that simply won't let a street pass through or over them. There are streets that go in any direction but straight and twist and turn until you're almost dizzy trying to stay on course. And then there are the myriad strange names for streets, many of them Spanish—as tricky to read as to pronounce.

To find your way easily through the maze of Tucson streets, we strongly suggest latching onto a good street map and never letting go. Several helpful maps are available in the *Official Destination Guide* published by the Metropolitan Tucson Convention & Visitors Bureau and available free at the visitor center on 110 S. Church Ave. in downtown Tucson. The rental car company maps are particularly easy to follow and cover most major roads and intersections; pick one up free at any rental car agency. For super detail, Rand McNally has a page-by-page street guide as well as a laminated Easy-Finder version. Another wise piece of advice is to plot out your trip in advance, especially if you're driving to some obscure street that may sound like several other streets.

Keep in mind that many Tucson street names include Spanish words that mean street, way, or place. Among them are *calle, camino, placito, via, avenida,* and *paseo.* Street names can be frustrating to newcomers, but with patience you'll get as proficient at deciphering (or ignoring) them as Tucsonans are.

Downtown Tucson continues its efforts at renovation, resulting in changes to street parking, ramp access, street access, and even possible direction changes. For up-to-the-minute details, check the City of Tucson website (www.knowyourwaydowntown .info) or contact the **Regional Transportation Authority** (520-770-9410; www.rta mobility.com), the organization that oversees all these projects.

Main Thoroughfares

Our primer on land travel begins with the two biggest arteries, the two interstates or freeways. I-10 comes down from Phoenix heading east (which actually seems like south) into Tucson and skirts the western side of the city. Near downtown, it curves abruptly and actually begins heading directly east, then brushes the very southern part of the metro area to points east, including eventually New Mexico. The other freeway is I-19, which begins about where I-10 curves to go east. From there I-19 heads directly south past Green Valley and eventually to Mexico. (The signs on I-19 give distances in kilometers, not miles.)

Construction and widening on I-10 is ongoing and affects several on-ramps and access points into the city. Be sure to check the local paper (if you live in town) or the Arizona Department of Transportation for up-to-the-minute information on which exits are closed. Their website (www.i10tucson district.com/29toP.html) provides details.

The interstates are handy if you're traveling to Phoenix, New Mexico, or Mexico or along the western or far southern parts of the metro area. Beyond that, drivers must tolerate surface streets and lots of stop-and-go traffic, even to get from, say, the far northwest to the east or from the foothills to downtown.

So if the interstates won't get you to where you're going, you might want to know about some of the major streets that cross town. Starting up north, Ina Road will take drivers from the far west, actually I-10 and beyond, all the way to the mountains in the east, but it changes names—first to Skyline Road and then to Sunrise Drive. River Road is another west-to-east option, but it terminates well before the interstate on the west and goes only to Sabino Canyon Road on the east. Nonetheless, it's a good route, albeit curvy in spots, and comes with views. Other major east–west streets are Grant Road, Speedway Boulevard, Broadway Boulevard, 22nd Street, Golf Links Road, Ajo Way, Irvington Road, and Valencia Road, all of which run parallel to one another and are major byways lined with all manner of commercial enterprises.

Major north–south streets, beginning on the west side, include Oracle Road, Stone Avenue, Campbell Avenue, Alvernon Way, Swan Road, Craycroft Road, Kolb Road, and Houghton Road. Some of these streets end abruptly, usually because of natural or man-made barriers. Swan and Craycroft Roads, for example, are stopped in the south by the Air Force base. Tucson International Airport is the southern terminus for streets like Park and Campbell Avenues (which for part of its route is called Kino Boulevard).

A Road by Any Other Name . . .

Quirks are common with Tucson's streets. For example, 22nd Street, a major east–west thoroughfare, changes to Starr Pass Boulevard west of I-10; 5th Street becomes 6th Street and then St. Mary's Road and finally Anklam Road as you travel west. Pima Street turns into Elm Street near the Arizona Inn. And there's a Pantano Road and a Pantano Boulevard, and they run next to each other, so who knows which is which. Of all the street quirks in Tucson, however, the strangest may well be the place where Wilmot Road becomes Tanque Verde Road and Grant Road becomes Kolb Road, and they all intersect and go off in different directions. This is a very busy area to boot. Again, consult your trusty map and plan ahead.

And if you're looking for any rhyme or reason to the use of terms such as street or avenue or boulevard, forget it. Many roads are tagged with boulevard, but you may never see one along its length. The use of numbered roads can be confusing also: We have 5th Street and 5th Avenue and 6th Street and 6th Avenue, for example, and often they intersect. Just remember that in the case of numbered roads, the avenues run north–south and the streets run east–west.

Rules & Warnings

You won't be on Tucson streets long before you notice that most of the main ones have a left turn lane down the center, indicated by yellow lines. This is a fairly easy concept even for newcomers—turn left from the center turn lane. At intersections with a green arrow for left turns, pay attention. The turn signal usually, but not always, comes after, not before, the green light.

And if that's confusing, try figuring out the address numbering system in Tucson. We'll explain it but make no guarantees that it makes sense or that you'll get it. First, the point of origin for addresses in Tucson is Stone Avenue and Broadway Boulevard. In other words, Stone Avenue is the dividing line for east versus west streets and Broadway Boulevard for north and south streets (everything north of Broadway is called north something street, and so forth). That's not terribly difficult, but read on. When you are on an east–west street looking for an east address, you'll find odd building numbers on the north side of the street and even addresses on the south side. But once you cross Stone Avenue and are in the west streets, the exact opposite is true—the odd numbered addresses are on the south side and the even on the north.

> **i** Construction on major and in-town roadways continues throughout Pima County. For a list of all current and future roadway improvements, check www.roadprojects.pima .gov, which lists all road projects with detailed links to each one and provides a map of closures.

And guess what happens to the north–south streets? When you're north of Broadway Boulevard, the odd address numbers are on the west and the even on the east. But south of Broadway Boulevard, the switch takes place and odd numbers are on the east side of the street and even on the west. And making matters worse is the fact that only about every third building (at best) in Tucson even has a visible address number. Finding your destination and driving at the same time can be a real challenge.

Another caution about Tucson streets pertains to rainstorms. We have them infrequently, but they can be fierce. In a flash, a simple dip in the roadway or a low spot where a wash or arroyo crosses the road will fill up with rushing water and can careen vehicles downstream with no warning. So when you see a Do Not Cross When Flooded sign, heed the warning.

As a final caution for driving Tucson's streets, be aware that many downtown streets are one-way, even though they may be two-way streets beyond downtown. Stone Avenue, for example, becomes strictly southbound as it goes through downtown, while Congress Street is westbound and Broadway Boulevard becomes eastbound during their downtown paths. Again, refer to the trusty street map before you turn on the ignition.

Parking

Driving and parking—you can't have one without the other, so here's the mostly good news on parking your vehicle in the Tucson environs. With two primary exceptions, parking is usually very accessible and free. Nearly every business and major attraction has ample parking, and there's almost never a charge. The two notable exceptions are downtown Tucson and the university, where people congregate, buildings dominate, and land for parking is scarce. So if you're attending one of the many events or attractions in either of these areas, you'll probably have to hunt for an available space and pay once you find it. Both areas have metered street parking, but it's not easy to get. Both also have numerous pay parking garages and lots at hourly rates with daily rate specials. Metered parking and some university garages are free on weekends. The university publishes an annual campus parking map, which is also available online (www.parking.arizona.edu), and a guide to downtown parking is available at the city Department of Transportation website (www.parkwise.tucsonaz.gov).

Rental Cars

The major national car rental agencies are represented here, and most are located at the airport (see the listing for the Tucson International Airport previously in this chapter) but also have additional locations around town. It's often possible to rent a vehicle in Tucson and drop it off in Phoenix (or vice versa) without the typical steep drop-off charge, which is a big help if you're using the Phoenix airport. As is true in most large cities, you'll find a number of car rental companies that aren't the "biggies"—they're local but usually offer the same types of vehicles and rates as the national agencies. Some of these are operated out of car dealerships. Check the Yellow Pages under "Auto Renting" and "Auto Leasing" for the many car rental options in Tucson.

If you're renting a vehicle and plan to travel south of the border, however, be advised that you're unlikely to find any rental vehicle that you can take to Mexico. (If the border town of Nogales, Mexico, is your destination, you can easily park in the US and walk a block or two to the border crossing and into Nogales. Check out the Day Trips & Weekend Getaways chapter for all the details on going to Mexico.)

Riding the Bus

Tucson has only one form of public transit: the **Sun Tran** bus system (520-792-9222; www.suntran.com). It'll get you to and from many places, but it's by no means as frequent or as comprehensive as bus transportation in major cities in other areas of the country. Tucson buses travel mostly within the city limits, even though much of Tucson lies beyond the city. Here are some of the bus basics.

For starters, let's talk about where the buses stop. They only stop at designated bus stops, of which there are over 2,000, indicated by signs. The sign will tell you which route (by number and name) stops there and whether an express bus also stops there. Many stops are covered, which is good news if you're a summer rider or just don't want to wait in the fierce sun, and most are wheelchair accessible.

Sun Tran has several features that make it a usable system for the disabled. Many

Sun Tran buses are lift-equipped for wheelchairs and are marked with the international wheelchair symbol on the door. Some buses accommodate people who have difficulty stepping up. Sun Tran produces special guides for people with vision disabilities, operates **TTY/TDD phone service** (520-628-1565), and accommodates guide dogs. If you're in need of special assistance, chances are Sun Tran can accommodate you. Tucson has a special on-call transit service for the disabled, called **SunVan,** at (520) 798-1000.

Sun Tran also caters to drivers who want to park and ride and bike riders. There are about two dozen locations where you can park a car for free and then take a bus to your destination. They're listed in the *Sun Tran Ride Guide*. For bike riders, Sun Tran buses are equipped with bike racks on the front (although they only carry two, so it's first-come, first-served) at no extra charge. They also rent monthly bike lockers (you need your own lock) at designated locations and have bike racks at designated bus stops.

> **i** Send a scenic e-card of Tucson to friends and family while you're here. There's a great selection of free images on the Metropolitan website at www.visitTucson.org/phototour.

Once you've figured out how to find a bus stop, you'll need to know how to get where you want to go. It can be complicated, so your best bet is to call **Sun Tran** (520-792-9222), and they'll give you specific instructions (in Spanish if needed). Or go to their website's trip planning page for an interactive guide. You can also pick up a *Ride Guide,* which you can get just about anywhere, including grocery stores and libraries. The guide tells you everything you always

Close-up

Useful Information

Whether you're here for a vacation or a business trip, there is so much to see and experience in Tucson. No matter how much (or little) planning you've done, there's nothing harder than coming to a new city and trying to find your way around, especially if you don't have a lot of time on your hands. Here are some great local sources that will help you get the best from your trip and give you a sense of what's happening at the moment.

VISITOR INFORMATION

Metropolitan Tucson Convention & Visitors Bureau
*100 S. Church Ave., Tucson
(520) 624-1817, (888) 288-2766
www.visittucson.org
Located in the colorful Plaza Placita, the center offers free maps, guides, pamphlets, and brochures for everything in town. The extremely helpful staff can answer questions, suggest walking tours and itineraries, and tell you about any special events taking place in town.

City of Tucson
http://cms3.tucsonaz.gov
The city's website will give you a great overview of the city, with visitor information, a live city cam, events, maps, and even job listings.

Pima County
www.pima.gov
The county site offers general county government information and a great page of links to Tucson attractions.

wanted to know about Sun Tran. Another option is to go to one of the three transit centers, which have information booths as well as covered waiting areas, restrooms, and telephones. They're also major transfer points for buses. The **Tohono Tadai Transit Center** is located on Stone Avenue just north of Wetmore Road; the **Roy Laos Transit Center** is at Irvington Road and S. 6th Avenue; and the **Ronstadt Transit Center** is downtown at Pennington Street and 6th Avenue.

Fees

To ride the bus you'll need exact change or a fare pass. The regular non-express route fare for ages 6 to adult is $1.50. Kids younger than 5 with an adult ride free; seniors, disabled, and low-income riders carrying a special ID pay 50 cents. Transfers are free for non-express routes, but you need to request one when you first get on the bus. It's good for two hours in the same direction. In other words, it won't work for a return trip.

If you're a regular rider, the passes may be the way to go. There are several varieties,

MAGAZINES

Tucson Guide

A superhelpful quarterly publication that covers events, restaurants, festivals and fiestas, theater, arts, shopping, golf, and dining. Special sections highlight regional attractions. The "101 Things to Do" is an eclectic guide to lots of unusual and interesting activities and attractions in town, a real keeper.

Tucson Lifestyle

The upscale monthly magazine covers the city beautifully with features, city and dining guides, event calendars, day and weekend trip ideas, and more. Watch for the "Newcomers" edition published annually and bursting with useful information.

NEWSPAPERS

The Arizona Daily Star

www.azstarnet.com

The major daily morning paper in town. The Friday section, "Caliente" covers the week's activities from music and art to hiking, bicycling, festivals, stargazing, shopping, dining, movies, and special events. It's got it all. Daily events are covered in the Community Calendar in section B of the paper and on the Web at www.azstarnet .com/entertainment.

EXCLUSIVELY ON THE WEB

www.dotucson.com

This helpful local website offers listings of events, attractions, dining, and nightlife.

such as a monthly pass and an economy pass for seniors and qualified low-income riders, as well as monthly express passes, university passes, and booklets of rides. Passes are available at lots of places, including Sun Tran, so call or refer to the *Ride Guide* for where to get one. They're also available by mail and online at www.suntran.com.

Hours & Special Events

Sun Tran buses generally operate from about 5:15 a.m. to 10:45 p.m. Mon through Fri and from about 6:15 a.m. to 7 p.m. on Sat, Sun, and holidays. Not all of the bus routes operate all these hours, however, so check the schedule or call Sun Tran.

Even though Sun Tran may not exactly cover the land and may not operate buses every 10 minutes (or even close to that), it does have a number of special runs that make it easy to get to some major events like football and rodeo.

Catching the Cat

Folks who attend or work at the University of Arizona have another transit option—the university's Cat Tran shuttle, its name taken from the school's Wildcat nickname. It operates Mon through Fri from 6 a.m. to 6:30 p.m. The NightCat operates Mon through Fri from 6 p.m. to 12:30 a.m. but not usually during semester breaks or on school holidays. It's free to riders showing the appropriate ID, and route maps are available at the university. The website (www.parking.arizona.edu) offers a full schedule and route maps, or call (520) 626-7275.

Taxis & Van Services

This isn't New York, Los Angeles, or Chicago, folks, so hailing a taxi isn't even in the vocabulary here. About the only places you can expect to see a taxi ready to take on a passenger are the airport, bus and train stations, and possibly major event venues, such as the Tucson Convention Center. And except for the airport, even these locations aren't a sure bet. So plan on calling for a taxi if you need one.

Tucson has fewer than a dozen taxicab companies, plus several private transportation services operating on-call vans. Taxi rates aren't regulated in Arizona, so they vary widely—we recommend shopping around. Most taxis use a flag drop rate plus mileage charge for shorter trips and a flat fee for longer ones, such as from Tucson to Green Valley. Extra charges usually are not levied for more than one passenger going to the same destination. Several taxi companies can accommodate Spanish-speaking passengers, including Fiesta Taxi and Yellow Cab. Several also have wheelchair-accessible cabs available, including Allstate Cab Company and Yellow Cab. The major taxi companies serving the area are **VIP Taxi Company** (520-881-2227) and **Yellow Cab** (520-624-6611).

As an alternative to taxis, several companies operate private van or car services. Some accommodate either individual passengers or groups, while others are strictly for groups. They typically have flat rates per hour or by destination and may offer tours, special services to businesses, and other limousine-like services. These companies include **Maximum Transportation Service** (520-293-2233), **Diamond Transportation** (520-825-8888), **Ms. Transportation** (520-327-4674), and **Safe Ride** (800-797-7433).

Limousines

If luxury is your lifestyle or if you just want to be pampered on occasion, Tucson has plenty of limousine services—about two dozen. They'll drive you in everything from town cars to Hummers, and some also have vans and minicoaches. The more vehicle and the more amenities you desire, the more it will cost. Some have special rates to and from the Tucson and Phoenix airports. Check the phone book's Yellow Pages under "Limousine" for all the options, but here are a few: **Paradise Limousine** (520-884-7605), **Tucson Town Cars** (520-884-5997), and **Sunset Limousine** (520-573-9418).

HISTORY

A s the oldest continually inhabited region in the Northern Hemisphere, Tucson (pronounced *TOO-sahn*) has been home to an astounding variety of cultures and peoples dating back as early as the first century AD. The name Tucson is actually a derivation of the Tohono O'odham word *stjukshon* (pronounced *chuk-son*) that translates literally as "spring at the foot of dark mountain" and referred to the Tohono O'odham's original settlement at the foot of the volcanic mountain Sentinel Peak. This area, inhabited for an estimated 3,000 years, is considered the city's birthplace.

Today Tucson is a unique blend of old and new, a city that embraces its diverse cultural heritage and cherishes its natural wonders. Here is a brief look into its fascinating past.

EARLY TUCSONANS

In 1997 archaeologists uncovered the largest Southwest settlement of the Late Archaic period along the Santa Cruz River. The settlement dated back to the Cienega phase (800 BC to AD 150). The Cienega were farmers in a time dominated by nomadic hunters and gatherers. They grew corn, beans, squash, and tobacco. They traded with others throughout the Southwest for shells and other trinkets that they used in making jewelry. The settlement's 171 pit dwellings, storehouses, and communal structures are believed to have been occupied between 760 and 200 BC, several centuries before the better-known Mogollon, Anasazi, and Hohokam cultures.

The Hohokam occupied an area along the Santa Cruz River (known then as the Rio de Santa Maria) near what is now downtown Tucson from AD 600 to 1450. They irrigated and farmed the area for 700 years. The Hohokam were a dominant culture in

the Southwest and built 200 miles of canals around Phoenix to irrigate their crops. They also settled the Tucson area's riverbanks. *Hohokam* is a Tohono O'odham word meaning "those who have vanished," and anthropologists still debate the reason for their disappearance. Some have suggested that the Hohokam may have been the ancestors of the Tohono O'odham, who currently live in the area.

i The book *Papago Woman*, by noted anthropologist Ruth M. Underhill and first published in 1936, offers a fascinating glimpse into the culture of the Papago (now known as the Tohono O'odham) people. Written as an autobiography of Chona, born around 1846 on the Tohono O'odham Nation, this beautifully written, lyrical book tells the story her life and people.

Other Native American tribes followed the Hohokam into the area, settling along the Santa Cruz River and farming the valley. The Tohono O'odham clustered at the foot of Sentinel Peak (now known as "A" Mountain, named for the large whitewashed "A" on its flank that represents the University of Arizona).

SPANISH DISCOVERY

When Jesuit Padre Eusebio Francisco Kino, "the Priest on Horseback," who served as a missionary for the Catholic Church in Spain, arrived in the area from Mexico in 1692, the Tohono O'odham were thriving in a village at the base of Sentinel Peak, farming the fertile valley of the then-flowing Santa Cruz River. Kino, an explorer, cartographer, and scientist, established a mission in the valley. He taught agricultural techniques and introduced Christianity to the Tohono O'odham people.

Father Kino established a number of missions in the Southwest, including Mission San Jose de Tumacacori, south of Tucson near Tubac, and San Xavier del Bac, "the White Dove of the Desert," located 19 miles south of what is now downtown. San Xavier still stands today (see the Attractions chapter). A statue honoring Kino on horseback now graces Kino Boulevard near the Lewis C. Murphy Overpass in Tucson. Duplicate statues stand in the Mexican city and state of Magdalena and Sonora, and in Italy, which was Kino's homeland.

Present-day Tucson was officially founded on August 20, 1775, when Hugo O'Conor, an Irishman who served in the Spanish army, established the walled Presidio de San Agustin in what is now downtown Tucson. Plans for the presidio included a 12-foot adobe wall for defense against the Apaches. Construction was slow going: By November 1779, the walls were only 4 feet tall.

The walls didn't discourage neighboring Apaches, who launched several attacks on the presidio in the ensuing years. With their failure, however, the Apaches and the Spanish settlers formed a peace that would last until the 1830s.

The Spanish army completed the presidio in 1783. It consisted of a walled garden and more than 20 buildings, including a two-story convent, a chapel, barracks for soldiers, stables, and a granary. The presidio covered about 12 acres and included the area outlined by modern-day Church Street on the east, Washington Street on the north, Main Avenue on the west, and Pennington Street on the south—basically the heart of today's downtown business district. Some historians believe it's the only walled city in our nation's history, and it's from this structure that Tucson gets its nickname, "the Old Pueblo."

MEXICAN RULE

Spain's claim to Tucson ended in 1821 when Mexico gained its independence. For the 65 European settlers in the presidio, it only meant changing their flag—life went on as usual. Farming, sheep and cattle ranching, and trapping in the mountains continued with limited contact with the outside world. What did change was residential development outside the walls of the presidio. Lacking a seaport for the transportation of goods in the early 1800s, the area depended on the Mexican port of Guaymas some 300 miles to the south, from which goods were transported by wagon, creating a new business for "freighters" in the Old Pueblo.

A US TERRITORY

Tucson gained its rough-and-tumble reputation during the early part of the 19th century. When the US signed the Gadsden Purchase in 1853, some 30,000 square miles of Arizona and the Southwest became part of the New Mexico Territory and thus part of the US. But Tucson remained a Mexican garrison until March 1856, when the Mexican army packed up and left. It wasn't until November that US dragoons rode into town and raised the US flag atop the Miles Mercantile Store. For the next few years, Anglos and American goods began arriving in the area. This was the start of a long and rich cultural mix that thrives today.

i Be sure to visit the replica of Tucson's original adobe-walled fortress, the Presidio Wall, on the corner of North Church and West Washington Streets. The site includes a 20-foot-tall lookout tower (*torreón*) and 10-foot-high adjoining walls. There's a tiny museum inside with interpretive information, displays, and artifacts.

In 1858 the Butterfield Overland Route brought the first stagecoaches to Tucson, making it one of 16 stations in Arizona. By 1860 the city's non-Indian population had grown to more than 600, but many were rough characters who had been chased out of California. Tucson quickly gained a reputation as a lawless Western town. Street fights were daily events, and most people carried weapons. Because there was no jail, a plaza whipping post was established to dish out punishment.

The outbreak of the Civil War called Federal troops back East from all over the frontier. Their departure left the settlers defenseless against the Apaches, who had resumed their attacks in the 1830s. Tucson, surrounded by its adobe walls, became one of a few territorial refuges for miners and ranchers in the area. Citizens didn't seem too particular about which side—the Union or the Confederacy—provided protection. When 200 mounted Confederate soldiers arrived from Texas in February 1862, Tucsonans greeted them happily. Soon word came that 2,000 California volunteers would arrive from Yuma, so the Texans retreated home. On May 20, 1862, Union Col. Joseph R. West took possession of Tucson with nary a protest from anyone.

By the time President Lincoln gave Arizona territorial status in 1863 and named Prescott the capital, Tucson's reputation for gambling, prostitution, and filthy streets was common reading in Eastern newspapers. But despite the lawlessness, Tucson had garnered enough political clout by 1867 to force a vote to change the territorial capital from Prescott to Tucson. The Old Pueblo was the capital for 10 years until the power of northern mining interests helped return the title to Prescott.

During this decade Tucson fast became a genuine "city" and a bustling business and transportation crossroads. The population in 1869 was 3,200. By 1872 a public school had been built. Tucson had two flour mills, four livery stables, and two hotels. Other businesses that thrived included two breweries and numerous saloons. Roulette wheels spun 24 hours a day until 1905.

Just before Tucson became the "Sodom of the Southwest," a new arrival brought some much-anticipated civilization. The first Southern Pacific Railroad train arrived in March 1880. Now goods from the East could be brought in faster and cheaper.

Construction materials were a big item, and Tucson's architecture took on the look of sophisticated homes back East. Adobe was no longer the material of choice. You can still see some of these homes today near and around the railroad tracks. Home tours in these historic neighborhoods take place every spring (see the Festivals & Events and Attractions chapters).

> **i** Follow the turquoise line, also known as the Presidio Trail, for a fascinating journey back in time. The self-guided walking tour takes you through downtown Tucson to all major historic landmarks. Grab a free map from the visitor center at La Placita, or download a copy at www.tucsonpresidiotrust.org. The map is chock-full of fascinating information about Tucson's early days.

The railroad brought other touches of civilization. All kinds of new folks moved in. That same year (1880) also brought the area's first hospital. The Sisters of St. Joseph de Carondelet established St. Mary's Hospital and Sanitarium. A modern St. Mary's Hospital exists today, not far from the site of the original.

The influx of white settlers led to intensified attacks on the surrounding area by the Apaches. US troops constructed Fort Lowell to protect Tucson and nearby ranchers. The raids ended in 1886 when Geronimo, the last great Apache leader, surrendered. The fort was deactivated in 1891. Remnants still stand in Fort Lowell Park in what is now central Tucson. The "fort" is listed on the National Register of Historic Places.

The city's first telephone rang in 1881, and gas-operated streetlights were turned on for the first time in Tucson on March 20, 1882. Suddenly Tucson was a bit less "Wild West." Ironically, that same night Wyatt Earp, avenging his brother Morgan's death in Tombstone earlier that week, shot and killed Frank Stilwell at the Tucson railroad station. Another modern innovation sprang up in 1882: water pipes! Citizens wondered: What could be next?

BUILDING A UNIVERSITY

In 1885 the Thirteenth Territorial Legislature granted Tucson $25,000 to establish a university—the first in a territory that had no high schools. Politicians believed the university would bring economic benefits, but their other purpose was to appease Tucsonans for moving the capital to Prescott. But locals were still more interested in becoming the territorial capital, and, after all, a university might have a negative influence on the city's gambling.

The story of how all this came about is legendary in Arizona. The city's territorial legislators left for Prescott to force a vote to return the capital to Tucson. But in an unfortunate chain of events, inclement weather delayed them. When the legislators finally arrived, they found that a vote had already been held and Prescott had already won. Tucson was tossed money for a university as a consolation prize. This did not go over well with the locals. When the delegates returned to Tucson, they were pelted with rotten fruit and vegetables.

> **i** In 1870 Tucson was the territorial capital, with 3,224 people. The capitol building was a dirt-floored series of rooms on Ochoa Street, just off Stone Avenue. The population of Pima County was 5,716.

The city fathers convinced a pair of wealthy gamblers and a saloon owner to donate land for the university, which they did—with a catch. The school had to be situated as far away from downtown gambling saloons as possible—to keep any high-minded influences away from the gamblers. The chosen spot was 3 miles across the desert. In 1891 "Old Main," as it's known today, opened its doors to 32 students and 6 faculty members. Today more than 34,000 students are enrolled at the University of Arizona, and the campus, once in the middle of the desert, now lies in the heart of the city.

A NEW ERA & A NEW STATE

By 1886 Geronimo and his band of renegade Chiricahua Apaches had been exiled to Florida, ending the official Indian Wars (of almost 30 years) with the "Blue Coats" in this part of the West. That was the beginning of the demise of "Wild West" Tucson. In 1896 the first mule-driven streetcars started running, and the following year the first "horseless carriage" sputtered down the dirt streets. By 1906 the mules were replaced with electric streetcars, making a 3-mile loop from downtown to the university.

On a territorial level, Arizona's battle for statehood was driven by lawmakers in the capital, which was finally relocated to Phoenix in 1889. The battle ended on February 14, 1912, when President Taft made Arizona the 48th state. Tucson's population at the time was 13,125.

Along with the new status in the country came a new frontier—flight. Aviation came to Tucson on February 17, 1910, when barnstorming pilot Charles Hamilton flew his biplane a mere 900 feet above the ground to thrill spectators. In 1915 Katharine Stinson, a 19-year-old daredevil pilot, delivered the first airmail to the city. But these were just tastes of what was to come. The aviation age formally arrived in Tucson when the city built the nation's first municipal airport in 1919. In 1927 Charles Lindbergh dedicated the Davis-Monthan Field, which had evolved from that early aviation effort. By the 1930s the US Army Air Corps was using Davis-Monthan Field; they finally took it over completely in 1940. With a state charter and the generosity of 25 local businessmen (each pitched in a $1,000 loan), the Tucson Airport Authority was established in 1948 to operate the municipal airport. TAA still oversees all operations at Tucson International Airport.

By 1920 the city's population had grown to 20,292, and the first of many resort hotels had been built to draw Easterners to Arizona's warm, dry climate. Many came to these elaborate resorts hoping that the climate would cure tuberculosis. In 1931 gasoline-powered buses replaced the electric trolley cars, just like a "real" city.

Hollywood discovered Tucson in 1939, when movie producers built what became Old Tucson Studios as a set for the epic movie *Arizona* (see the Attractions chapter). Since then, hundreds of movies, television shows, and commercials have been made in and around town.

Tucson's population boomed during World War II with the many people who were seeking military employment at Davis-Monthan Field, which had become a military base for training pilots to fly B-17 bombers. After the war, when Davis-Monthan Field became a US Air Force base, it continued providing employment opportunities, both military and civilian (see the chapter on Davis-Monthan Air Force Base).

By 1950 the population was 55,454 in the city and 118,034 in the metropolitan area. The increase in population is attributed to the return of many servicemen and their families to Tucson after the war, as well as the advent of air-conditioning. In the 1960s and 1970s the city focused on developing the arts. In 1967 the Arizona Theatre Company was founded here as the state's only professional resident theater company. The state's only opera company, the Arizona Opera Company, was founded in 1972 and based in Tucson. Three years later the new Tucson Museum of Art was built near the original presidio in downtown Tucson.

During the 1980s high-tech businesses began moving to Tucson, led by aviation-related companies. The metropolitan area's population grew a whopping 22.6 percent to 431,988 in 1993. During this period Madison Avenue advertising agencies began using the saguaro-studded desert to sell everything from cars to beer to jeans to credit cards. The constant romantic image of the West in print and TV ads spurred growth in Arizona's population as many Easterners left their homes to discover the new "promised land."

The '90s brought continued growth and a housing boom, with the population for Pima County reaching one million. At the dawn of the 21st century, Tucson continues its growth while preserving its unique desert landscape and friendly, small-city feel. Its perfect climate, fascinating history, and incredible desert and mountain landscape keep people visiting and relocating here. Tucson offers a unique combination of sleepy '50s town and bustling metropolis. With the University of Arizona, several symphonies, dance companies and theaters, spectator sports and international bicycling tours in town, along with a huge number of award-winning restaurants, Tucsonans have the best of all worlds.

ACCOMMODATIONS

You'll find just about every kind of place to stay in Tucson—gorgeous mansions, antique adobes, quaint bed-and-breakfasts, luxury spas and resort hotels, and even some old-fashioned dude ranches. Whatever your pleasure, you'll find it here. When making your travel plans, keep in mind that peak season here is between October and April, when the weather is magnificent. February is a particularly popular month with several major conventions in town, so be sure to make reservations well in advance. Summer (May through September) brings some of the best rates and some of the hottest weather.

Visitors who wish to be pampered have a choice of several resorts and spas. You'll pay handsomely for facilities that offer a totally upscale experience, but many feel it's worth the extra cost (most of the resorts do offer fantastic summer rates). Noted for their "elite status" among resorts and spas are Canyon Ranch, Miraval, Starr Pass Marriott, Loews Ventana Canyon Resort, Westward Look Resort, and many more. You may even spot a famous person or two during your stay.

OVERVIEW

Many Tucson lodgings follow the two-room guest-suite trend geared toward business and family travelers. These accommodations typically have a separate bedroom and living room with a kitchen and two televisions. A continental breakfast is often included (we'll try to let you know which places offer this most welcome amenity). Please note, when we use the word spa at a hotel, we are talking about whirlpools, hot tubs, and the like—as opposed to the spa services you can get at several of the resorts.

For those who prefer to stay at a bed-and-breakfast, we have a separate section in this chapter. Many of the local bed-and-breakfasts are in historic neighborhoods, and the houses' histories are as interesting and colorful. Several others are found on the perimeter of town, surrounded by the desert. Whichever you might choose, be assured that the owners will be able to tell you all about the history of their home and the surrounding area.

If you want a more unique experience without the "hotel" atmosphere, a guest ranch may be what you are looking for. Some offer true "cowboy" adventures, with horseback riding and cookouts. Others are more like summer camp, with swimming, tennis, volleyball, and horseshoe tossing, but, unlike camp, offer plenty of pampering. Some ranches have rooms with individual kitchens and telephones, while others offer only the basics for those wanting to escape material trappings.

Most establishments offer the choice of smoking or nonsmoking accommodations as well as rooms that are wheelchair accessible. We've tried our best to note when an accommodation is not the norm. However, we suggest that if you have special needs or requests, you convey them to the accommodation when making your reservations.

We'll note a local number, a toll-free reservation telephone number when available, and a price range symbol (see Price Code).

Price Code

The following price codes indicate the cost of a one-night, double-occupancy stay during peak season. While peak season usually runs from October to April, February brings the highest rates due to all the events that are happening during that month. The price guidelines are therefore most applicable for this very busy month. Rates can be considerably lower during all other months and if you book well ahead of time. The codes do not include a hotel/motel tax within the city limits or a hotel/motel tax in Pima County. Virtually everyone accepts credit cards (we only note the ones that do not), but pets are another story, so it is best to call.

$	Less than $115
$$	$115 to $145
$$$	$145 to $175
$$$$	$175 to $215
$$$$$	More than $215

$$$$$

The Arizona Inn, Resorts & Spas, 45

Best Western Royal Sun Inn, Hotels & Motels, 34

Canyon Ranch Health Resort, Resorts & Spas, 45

Desert Diamond Casino and Hotel, Hotels & Motels, 36

Doubletree Tucson Hotel at Reid Park, Hotels & Motels, 36

Embassy Suites Williams Center, Hotels & Motels, 36

Hampton Inn & Suites, Hotels & Motels, 38

Hilton El Conquistador Golf & Tennis Resort, Resorts & Spas, 46

Hilton Garden Inn—Tucson Airport, Hotels & Motels, 38

Hotel Arizona, Hotels & Motels, 39

La Zarzuela, Bed-and-Breakfast Inns, 53

The Lodge at Ventana Canyon, Resorts & Spas, 46

Loews Ventana Canyon Resort, Resorts & Spas, 47

Marriott University Park, Hotels & Motels, 41

Miraval—Life in Balance, Resorts & Spas, 47

Omni Tucson National Golf Resort and Spa, Resorts & Spas, 48

Radisson Suites Tucson Hotel, Hotels & Motels, 41

Rancho de la Osa Guest Ranch, Guest Ranches, 43

Ritz-Carlton Dove Mountain, Resorts & Spas, 48

Sheraton Tucson, Hotels & Motels, 42

Starr Pass Marriott Resort and Spa, Resorts & Spas, 49

Tanque Verde Ranch, Guest Ranches, 44

The Westin La Paloma Resort, Resorts & Spas, 49

Westward Look Resort, Resorts & Spas, 49

White Stallion Ranch, Guest Ranches, 44

$$$$

Best Western InnSuites Catalina Foothills, Hotels & Motels, 34

Clarion Hotel Tucson Airport, Hotels & Motels, 34

Courtyard by Marriott Airport, Hotels & Motels, 35

HOTELS & MOTELS

Tucson is home to numerous hotels and motels, from small cozy inns, suite hotels, and luxury penthouses to standard motels, and you'll find most major chains here. Most offer free continental-style breakfasts, a morning paper, and a variety of amenities, from heated pools and spas to tennis courts.

BEST WESTERN INNSUITES CATALINA
FOOTHILLS $$$$
6201 N. Oracle Rd.
(520) 297-8111, (800) 554-4535
www.bestwestern.com

Located 5 miles east off I-10 at the Orange Grove Road exit in the near northwest side of town, this facility offers 159 one- or two-room suites with refrigerator, microwave oven, coffeemaker, hair dryer, free Wi-Fi, and free HBO. The larger suites have a kitchenette and separate living room, which is ideal for extended stays. Included in the price are a complimentary full breakfast, morning newspaper, and an afternoon social hour at the poolside cafe. You can also enjoy the pool and spa area, 2 lighted tennis courts, and the fitness center. There is a complimentary airport shuttle.

BEST WESTERN ROYAL SUN
INN & SUITES $$$$$
1015 N. Stone Ave.
(520) 622-8871, (800) 545-8858
www.bestwestern.com

Centrally located, this hotel has 59 rooms, including 20 suites with whirlpool tubs. All rooms feature a coffee/tea maker, hair dryer, iron, ironing board, vanity mirror, refrigerator, 27-inch television, DVD player, and high-speed Internet access. Additional amenities include a fitness center, outdoor heated pool and spa, and a full-service restaurant and lounge. Complimentary full, hot breakfast and two-for-one drink specials are offered to hotel guests only.

CASINO DEL SOL RESORT, SPA
AND CONFERENCE CENTER $$$
5655 W. Valencia Rd.
(520) 838-6698, (800) 344-9435
www.casinodelsol.com

Luxury is the word at this upscale high-rise resort hotel, part of the Casino del Sol complex and due to open in November 2011. Owned by the Pascua Yaqui tribe, the hotel is just 15 minutes from Tucson International Airport and downtown Tucson.

The hotel features 215 luxurious rooms and suites with complimentary Wi-Fi, 55-inch flat-screen HDTV, in-room coffee station, walk-in travertine tile showers with rain-down shower heads, digital alarm clock/radio with docking station, refrigerator, and complimentary wireless Internet. For the ultimate in luxury, Sky Level rooms also feature bathrobes and slippers, a Jacuzzi tub, and fresh flowers.

An 18,000-square-foot ballroom, 5 meeting rooms, a boardroom for 12, and a conference center that holds up to 2,000 make this a top pick for conferences and meetings. Top-notch amenities include a huge outdoor pool surrounded by palm trees, fire pits, a spa, and a fitness center. Dining options include a steak house, international buffet, sushi restaurant, and super pool bar.

CLARION HOTEL TUCSON
AIRPORT $$$$
6801 S. Tucson Blvd.
(520) 746-3932, (800) 526-0550
www.clarionhotel.com

A half mile from the airport, the hotel's 194 units include cable TV, direct-dial phones, and refrigerators. Also available are a heated pool, spa, coin laundry, fitness center, continental breakfast, and complimentary beverages in the evening. The hotel offers transfers to the airport. The dining room offers 3 meals a day; you'll find some of the city's better hotel dining here.

COMFORT INN SUITES $$$
7007 E. Tanque Verde Rd.
(520) 298-2300, (866) 890-1399
www.comfortsuites.com

About half of the 90 rooms here are studio suites, with a microwave oven, refrigerator, king-size bed or two double beds, sleeper sofa, cable with HBO, free Wi-Fi, and free local calls. Each stay includes a complimentary breakfast bar and weekday social hour. You can hang out at the pool or relax in the outdoor spa. Located in the heart of the Eastside Restaurant Row, you have your choice of dining—everything from New Southwest and steaks to a flurry of chain restaurants. For those with business on their minds, this hotel offers a 750-square-foot meeting room that can hold up to 45 people, voice mail and dataport lines, and access to a full-service gym nearby.

COURTYARD BY MARRIOTT AIRPORT $$$$
2505 E. Executive Dr.
(520) 573-0000, (800) 321-2211
www.marriott.com

These spacious 149 rooms and suites offer everything you'll need when not lounging by the landscaped courtyard and pool or in the lovely lobby. A spa, fitness room, laundry rooms, restaurant, and lounge are all on-site. Courtyard has an airport shuttle and 2 conference rooms that can accommodate up to 40 people each. The on-site business center offers free Wi-Fi.

COURTYARD BY MARRIOTT— WILLIAMS CENTER $$$$
201 S. Williams Blvd.
(520) 745-6000, (800) 321-2211
www.marriott.com

This midtown spot is right across the street from the busy Williams Center business complex. It's also located right in the heart of town, so families and nonbusiness travelers can easily get to all the attractions with a minimum of fuss. You'll find a pool, a spa, an exercise area, and an in-house bistro offering breakfast and dinner. You'll also find plenty of other good eats just minutes away (you may not even need to use your car), and getting downtown is just a matter of catching Broadway Boulevard a half block away and heading west for about 5 minutes.

DAYS INN $$$
222 South Freeway
(520) 791-7511, (800) 329-7466
www.daysinn.com

Just off I-10 west of downtown Tucson, this inexpensive facility has 122 rooms and offers guests a free continental breakfast, large pool, laundry, and meeting room that can hold 950 guests. Days Inn offers a number of discounts to government, military, and AARP members. Free Wi-Fi.

i One of Tucson's first hotels, the Spanish colonial–style Ghost Ranch Lodge at 801 W. Miracle Mile was originally designed by famed architect Josias Josler. Although the property has been converted to senior housing, the original neon sign (rumored to have been designed by artist Georgia O'Keeffe) is still in place.

DESERT DIAMOND CASINO
AND HOTEL $$$$$
7350 S. Nogales Hwy.
(520) 294-7777
www.desertdiamondhotel.com

If you like high-tech hotels, then the Desert Diamond is for you. Everything is state-of-the-art, high-end luxury, and you're only steps away from a casino, gift shop, several restaurants, and the Monsoon nightclub. The hotel, opened in late 2007, is owned, operated, and governed by the Tohono O'odham nation. Each of the spacious 149 rooms and suites is tastefully appointed, with your choice of 1 king- or 2 queen-size beds. You'll find an in-room safe and refrigerator, a desk, and a flat-screen plasma TV (the executive suites have 42-inch TVs and a wet bar). The casino operates several restaurants, including a 24-hour grill and a steak house that serves top-of-the-line beef. Meeting space is plentiful, with various screens and flexible divisions, all changeable by the flick of a finger. Outside you can play in the moon-shaped pool, relax in the oversize Jacuzzi, or sit by the fire pit on cool evenings. The hotel and casino are located about a mile from the airport, so it's easy to get in and out. One more bonus—you won't pay any taxes here. The price you see is what you pay.

DOUBLETREE TUCSON HOTEL
AT REID PARK $$$$
445 S. Alvernon Way
(520) 881-4200, (800) 222-8733
http://doubletree1.hilton.com

This 10-story, 295-room is centrally located to attractions, shopping, the university, and business districts and is across the street from Del Urich and Randolph Park Golf Courses, as well as beautiful Reid Park, where you'll find plenty to do (see the Parks & Recreation chapter). You also get freshly baked chocolate chip cookies upon arrival! The resort-style hotel has 3 tennis courts, a pool, a spa, 2 restaurants, a lounge, and a fitness center.

For business travelers, rooms for meetings and banquets can accommodate between 10 and 1,200 people.

EMBASSY SUITES WILLIAMS
CENTER $$$$$
5335 E. Broadway Blvd.
(520) 745-2700, (800) 362-2779
http://embassysuites1.hilton.com

Each of Embassy Suites' 142 suites has a private bedroom and separate living room with sleeper sofa, kitchen, microwave, refrigerator, and coffeemaker. Two telephones with dataports and voice mail, as well as in-room movies on 2 TVs, help you keep in touch with the outside world. A complimentary beverage and cooked-to-order breakfast are included. The lounge offers billiards and a TV for when you're not enjoying the outdoor pool, spa, or fitness center. Among the business services is free transportation within 5 miles of the hotel, which includes the University of Arizona and Davis-Monthan Air Force Base.

> **i** Take the family out for an evening of stargazing at Loews Ventana Canyon Ranch. The free programs, offered year-round on Wednesday and Saturday nights, are open to the public. A University of Arizona astronomer is there to help. Times vary, so call ahead (520-299-2020). Ask for the concierge.

EMBASSY SUITES TUCSON—
PALOMA VILLAGE $$$$
3110 E. Skyline Dr.
(520) 352-4000
www.embassysuites.com

This 119-room all-suite hotel, opened in 2007, is especially appealing to families, golfers, and business travelers. All suites feature either a king- or 2 queen-size beds and a 32-inch plasma TV. Each morning you'll eat a cooked-to-order breakfast inside or on a patio with a lovely mountain view. A coin laundry, ATM, and high-speed Internet access are among the features you'll enjoy when not working out in the state-of-the-art fitness center or relaxing by the heated pool. Lots of restaurants are close by, and many golf courses are also easily reached. Three meeting rooms are available; the largest can accommodate 150 people. Outdoor event space and catering are available.

EXTENDED STAY AMERICA TUCSON $
5050 E. Grant Rd.
(520) 795-9510, (800) EXT-STAY
(398-7829)
www.extendedstayhotels.com
This midtown motel is ideal for business travelers or those looking for a no-frills long-term stay. Located across the street from Tucson Medical Center, each room has free local phone calls and voice mail, cable TV, a full kitchen complete with utensils, and access to wireless Internet for a small fee. Fax and mail delivery are perks for the business traveler. Laundry facilities are also available. You have your choice of 1 queen bed, 1 king bed, or 2 double beds. Although there isn't a restaurant on-site, you'll find a great choice of restaurants literally minutes away.

THE FOUR POINTS BY SHERATON $$$$
7060 S. Tucson Blvd.
(520) 746-0271, (800) 368-7764
www.starwoodshotels.com
This is the closest hotel to Tucson International Airport (you can watch planes coming

and going from the pool), with 149 rooms, free cable, free Wi-Fi, heated pool, spa, and 24-hour exercise facility. A perk for the business traveler: For an additional fee, the hotel can arrange for audio, video, and computer equipment in its conference suites. The hotel is also just minutes from the casino and the Pima Air and Space Museum. A full-service restaurant serves 3 meals a day.

FOUR POINTS BY SHERATON
   TUCSON UNIVERSITY PLAZA $$$$
1900 E. Speedway Blvd.
(520) 327-7341, (800) 843-8052
www.starwoodhotels.com/fourpoints
.com
Located at the busy intersection of Speedway Boulevard and Campbell Avenue, across from the University of Arizona and down the street from the University Medical Center. You'll find 150 rooms, a pool, a dining room that serves breakfast and dinner, a lounge with a big-screen TV, underground parking, room service, and a variety of convention and banquet services.

GRANT INN $
1365 W. Grant Rd.
(520) 622-7791, (866) 285-3281
www.grantinn.com
This hotel is conveniently located just off I-10 at the Grant Road exit, making it accessible to downtown, the Arizona-Sonora Desert Museum, Old Tucson Studios, and just about any other attraction in town. A large separate building on the grounds is the site for yearly trade shows.

Guests will welcome the pool and spa, in-room refrigerator, microwave, hair dryer, laundry, and free Wi-Fi. The restaurant and bar are great places to gather after a long, hard day of whatever you've been doing.

ACCOMMODATIONS

HAMPTON INN AIRPORT   **$$$$**
6971 S. Tucson Blvd.
(520) 889-5789, (800) HAMPTON
(426-7866)
http://hamptoninn1.hilton.com
With 126 rooms, Hampton Inn also offers suites with a separate bedroom and living room, as well as your choice of executive suites and standard rooms. All rooms have coffeemakers, hair dryers, refrigerators, microwaves, and irons and ironing boards for those last-minute touch-ups before your big meeting. Enjoy the heated pool, fitness center, spa, in-room movies and cable on the 25-inch TVs, and hot breakfast. The hotel also offers an airport shuttle and laundry valet services. The businessperson can take advantage of the business center, in-room voice mail, and free Wi-Fi.

HAMPTON INN & SUITES   **$$$$$**
5950 N. Oracle Rd.
(520) 618-8000, (800) HAMPTON
(426-7866)
http://hamptoninn1.hilton.com
Choice is the word when you stay at this near northwest hotel. You have a choice of a king suite, a king room, or a guest room (where you can choose 2 double beds if that's more to your liking). Some suites include a full kitchen (cooking utensils included) with a dining area and a separate living room. Business travelers will be delighted with the free local calls and business center, high-speed and wireless Internet access, access to fax and photocopying equipment, a fitness center, and meeting rooms. Families can take advantage of the swimming pool, the spa, free cable TV, guest laundry on premises, and the fact that kids younger than 18 stay free when accompanied by parents. In the

morning, all can enjoy a complimentary continental breakfast.

HILTON GARDEN INN—
  TUCSON AIRPORT   **$$$$$**
6575 S. Country Club Rd.
(877) 219-5888, (520) 741-0505
http://hiltongardeninn1.hilton.com
Opened in 2008, this 3-story, 125-room hotel features the customary swimming pool, but this one is surrounded by a winding "river," where you can float on a raft, enjoying the ambience. Families will appreciate the convenience of a refrigerator, microwave oven, coffeemaker, HDTV, and freshly prepared daily breakfast. Businesspeople will find a business center, meeting rooms with outdoor terrace, high-speed Internet access and Wi-Fi, and secure remote printer. An on-site fitness center and evening room service round out the package.

HOLIDAY INN EXPRESS
  AIRPORT   **$$$$**
2548 E. Medina Rd.
(520) 889-6600, (800) 465-4329
www.hiexpress.com
Conveniently located near the airport, this 3-story hotel has 98 rooms with free high-speed Internet, hair dryer, iron and ironing board, voice mail, speaker phone, coffeemaker, microwave, refrigerator, pay-per-view movies, and cable TV. Your room comes with a complimentary newspaper, and you get freshly baked cookies daily. A free buffet breakfast bar is available every morning. The hotel also has a business center, which may be rented as a meeting room for an additional charge and can accommodate 10 people. It includes a computer with free high-speed Internet access, color printer,

and dry-erase board. Those of you with furry friends will be pleased to know that pets are allowed with a $50 refundable deposit.

HOLIDAY INN—PALO VERDE
TUCSON AIRPORT $$$$
4550 S. Palo Verde Rd.
(520) 746-1161, (800) 315-2621
www.hitucsonairport.com

This 6-story Holiday Inn near the airport has 301 guest rooms with 53 suites, easy access to most parts of town, and a complimentary shuttle within a 5-mile radius of the hotel. Unlike at other places in town, no continental breakfast is served, but a full-service menu is offered at the in-house restaurant, where kids eat free. Plus you can enjoy a drink or two in the bar. You'll also find a pool, a whirlpool, and a 24-hour fitness center.

Both regular rooms and suites are available. The suites come with a kitchenette, and all rooms have an ironing board, iron, refrigerator, microwave, and hair dryer. This is a favorite for many local groups for business or family gatherings, thanks to several meeting rooms. You'll also see plenty of military folks, as this hotel is just a few minutes from Davis-Monthan Air Force Base.

HOTEL ARIZONA $$$$$
181 W. Broadway Blvd.
(520) 624-8711, (800) 845-4596
www.thehotelaz.com

In the center of downtown Tucson, this 307-room complex hosts a number of major convention events while still offering individual travelers a homey experience. A heated pool and restaurant are within this high-rise (you'll get some of the greatest views of the city in the topmost floors). The hotel has lots of meeting rooms that accommodate 10 to 1,000 people. The Tucson Convention Center is just across the street, as are local, state, and federal government buildings. The Arts District is just a short walk away.

*HOTEL CONGRESS $
311 E. Congress St.
(520) 622-8848, (800) 722-8848
www.hotelcongress.com

Established in 1919, this brick-and-marble building was constructed to provide accommodations to Southern Pacific Railroad passengers traveling through Tucson. Its 40 rooms on the second-floor overlook the Downtown Arts District.

One of the many colorful stories about the hotel involves the infamous John Dillinger gang, which was captured here in 1934. Today the hotel's first floor caters to Tucson's artists and writers with The Cup cafe (see the Restaurants chapter) and the locally popular Club Congress, featuring live bands and disc jockeys (see the Nightlife chapter). This is not just a historic hotel—it's an experience.

Hotel Congress is in the heart of downtown and also operates a youth hostel.

HYATT PLACE TUCSON AIRPORT $$$$
6885 Tucson Blvd.
(520) 295-0405, (888) 492-8847
www.hyattplacetucsonairport.com

If you need to stay near the airport during your visit, this suite hotel is conveniently located right at Tucson International Airport. There are 120 suites, with valet service, complimentary airport shuttle, 42-inch flat-screen TV, complimentary Wi-Fi, refrigerator, wet bar, and coffeemaker. What more could you need?

INN SUITES—HOTEL TUCSON CITY CENTER $

475 N. Granada Ave.
(520) 622-3000, (800) 842-4242
www.innsuites.com

You can get just about anywhere easily from this downtown-area hotel, located just off the I-10 Broadway exit. You'll have your choice of room styles here. You can pick a studio with either a king bed or 2 queens; an executive/family suite with a choice of beds, a sleeper sofa, and a separate living room; or pop for the Presidential Suite with its large spa and extra space. All suites have a microwave, a refrigerator (with complimentary water), and a coffeemaker (with tea or coffee). You can get pretty, too, with the in-room hair dryer. You'll also find free Wi-Fi and a complimentary breakfast and social hour.

This hotel has some of the larger meeting rooms in town. With 13 in all, you can hold everything from a huge wedding in the ballroom (capacity 1,500 people) to a class in one of the smaller facility rooms.

LA POSADA LODGE & CASITAS $$

5900 N. Oracle Rd.
(520) 887-4800, (800) 810-2808
www.laposadalodge.com

This 3-story adobe-style hotel with teal doors is conveniently located right on busy Oracle Road. All rooms face a serene landscaped inner courtyard with gated pool and spa. The lodge offers 60 deluxe guest rooms in the main lodge and 12 courtyard casitas. The rooms are decorated in various styles, from funky pastel with Jetsons' chairs and lava lamps to sophisticated Southwestern. Eight of the private casitas have front and back patios. Each guest room has a coffeemaker and coffee, hair dryer, iron and ironing board, satellite TV, work desk, and

free Wi-Fi. Open-air walkways connect all the floors, along with an elevator. The hotel also features an on-site hair salon and the upscale Miguel's restaurant (see the Restaurants chapter).

LA QUINTA INN AND SUITES TUCSON AIRPORT $$$

7001 S. Tucson Blvd.
(520) 573-3333, (800) 531-5900
www.lq.com

Located 1 block from the airport, this facility offers 143 rooms and 8 two-room suites with separate sitting and sleeping areas, double vanities, microwave, refrigerator, desk, and speaker phones. All rooms have computer-friendly dataport phones and free Wi-Fi to make your business travel easy. You can also take advantage of the heated swimming pool, spa, exercise facility, meeting rooms for up to 75 people, guest laundry, and same-day dry-cleaning service. The complimentary continental breakfast offers a choice of cereals, fruit, pastries, bagels, and juices.

One nice extra: If you pay for just one night's weekday rate, you can leave your automobile at the hotel for up to 7 nights for free (the hotel will transport you to the airport).

MARRIOTT RESIDENCE INN $$$

6477 E. Speedway Blvd.
(520) 721-0991, (800) 331-3131
www.marriot.com/tusaz

Ideal for those who plan to be here for just a little longer, this modern accommodation offers your choice of 128 suites—studio suites have queen beds and sleeper sofas; the Penthouse Suites have a loft, bedroom, and sleeper sofas. Some have fireplaces.

Both a complimentary buffet breakfast and social hour are part of your stay. Other perks include local restaurant dinner delivery and an on-site fitness center. You can also enjoy the Monday through Thursday evening barbecues (in season); the outdoor pool and spa; a sport court ideal for volleyball, basketball, or other sports; and an on-site inexpensive laundry room (1-day dry-cleaning service is also available). Pets are welcome for an additional fee.

And while there isn't a restaurant on-site, you're just minutes from the Eastside Restaurant Row and its plethora of dining choices.

MARRIOTT UNIVERSITY PARK $$$$$
880 E. 2nd St.
(520) 792-4100, (866) 596-7897
www.marriott.com
This 9-story atrium hotel, which features 250 guest rooms and several suites, is near the main gate of the University of Arizona, on the corner of Tyndall Avenue and Second Street. The hotel also has a concierge floor, for those who may need a haven during the relocation process. All rooms are specially equipped with high-speed Internet, workspaces, and voice mail. The Saguaro Grill is in the atrium, and the hotel also has an outdoor pool, whirlpool, and fitness center. It's just seconds from restaurants and shopping. The Marriott is a perfect choice for parents visiting their young scholars at the university.

PALO VERDE INN SUITES $
5251 S. Julian Dr.
(520) 294-5250, (800) 997-5470
www.paloverdeinn.com
Just off the I-10 exit at Palo Verde Road, these 153 rooms and 20 two-room suites are just minutes from Tucson International Airport (ask about the hotel's shuttle service) and include a coffeemaker, free Wi-Fi, and free HBO. You'll appreciate the complimentary hot breakfast, outdoor heated swimming pool, and spa.

QUALITY INN $$
7411 N. Oracle Rd.
(520) 575-9255, (800) 456-4000
www.qualityinn.com
Most of the 91 suites and 65 studios have kitchenettes, and suites feature king- or queen-size beds. The hotel also has a putting green, pool, whirlpool, and courtyard for relaxing. Every morning you can expect a free continental breakfast. This hotel offers free Wi-Fi.

QUALITY INN AIRPORT $$$$
2803 E. Valencia Rd.
(520) 294-2500, (800) 424-6423
www.qualityinn.com
A 98-room facility just blocks from the airport, Quality Inn offers all the usual amenities, such as outdoor pool and spa, free airport shuttle, free high-speed Internet, cable TV, and hot complimentary deluxe breakfast bar. Some suites are available, as are meeting rooms. You get a free newspaper on weekdays.

RADISSON SUITES TUCSON HOTEL $$$$$
6555 E. Speedway Blvd.
(520) 721-7100, (800) 333-3333
www.radisson.com
Each of these 299 two-room suites includes an extra-large bathroom, 2 vanities, 2 TVs, 2 telephones, a refrigerator, and a coffeemaker. Two Presidential Suites have fireplaces, dining rooms, and hydro tubs. On the grounds guests can use the oversize heated pool or fitness room. Meeting planners, take note of the 14,000 square feet of meeting space.

ACCOMMODATIONS

RAMADA LIMITED   **$$$**
665 North Freeway
(520) 622-6491, (800) 272-6232
www.ramada.com
Just off I-10 at St. Mary's Road near down-town, Ramada Limited offers in-room movies and video games, free high-speed Internet, same-day dry cleaning, guest laundry facilities, and a heated swimming pool. All of the 132 rooms have a microwave and refrigerator. You'll find a free continental breakfast, as well as meeting space.

**SHERATON TUCSON HOTEL
  & SUITES**   **$$$$$**
5151 E. Grant Rd.
(520) 323-6262, (800) 325-3535
www.sheraton.com
With 216 deluxe rooms—108 of which are suites—this is a midtown favorite. It's a great place to relax after a hard day of sightseeing or business meetings, thanks to the outdoor pool and hot tub. You'll also find a fully equipped fitness center. Get a good night's rest on the Sheraton Sweet Sleeper beds. You can dine at the on-site restaurant Fire+Spice—an Arizona Grill. Rooms also offer complimentary high-speed wireless and wired Internet access.

VARSITY CLUBS OF AMERICA   **$**
3855 E. Speedway Blvd.
(520) 318-3777, (800) 438-2929
www.diamondresorts.com
Located a short 2 miles east of the University of Arizona, this hotel is also just minutes from great golf and tennis, outstanding shopping, and many fine restaurants (the in-house restaurant, the Stadium Sports Grill, is filled with university Wildcat decorations). Offering luxury suites, the Tucson branch of Varsity

Clubs of America is a favorite of alumni and many other visitors to the university. Spacious suites with limited-cooking kitchens, a heated swimming pool, a workout center, and a business center are just a few of the amenities that attract visitors.

VISCOUNT SUITE HOTEL   **$$**
4855 E. Broadway Blvd.
(520) 745-6500, (800) 527-9666
www.viscountsuite.com
Locally owned and operated, this 4-story atrium hotel includes 216 elegant 2-room suites with TVs, telephones, dataports, free wireless Internet, and a living room with a desk. The hotel has a pool, spa, cafe, restaurants, and laundry facilities.

**WINDMILL INN AT ST. PHILIP'S
  PLAZA**   **$$**
4250 N. Campbell Ave.
(520) 577-0007, (800) 547-4747
www.windmillinns.com
Windmill Inn at Campbell Avenue and River Road offers 122 two-room suites with a wet bar, microwave, desk, 3 phones, wireless Internet access, 2 remote-controlled TVs, and refrigerator. Each morning you'll awake to complimentary coffee, a free continental breakfast with make-your-own waffles, eggs, bacon, and omelets, and a daily newspaper. The hotel also offers a free best-seller lending library, guest laundry facilities, meeting rooms for up to 300 people, and an outdoor pool and spa. Bicycles are provided so that guests can explore the nearby Rillito River Park. Stay here and you'll be near some taste-bud temptations: Look for the Sunday farmers' market in the adjacent St. Philip's Plaza (good shopping, too!).

GUEST RANCHES

A really unique way to experience Tucson is by staying at one of its guest ranches, some of which are still working cattle ranches. You can horseback ride, hike, bird-watch, take roping lessons, and even attend a rodeo at these restored luxury ranches.

C.O.D. RANCH $$
PO Box 241, Oracle 85623
(520) 615-3211, (800) 896-9161
www.codranch.com

Thirty-five miles north of Tucson at an elevation of 5,000 feet in the Coronado National Forest, C.O.D. Ranch offers a cool getaway from the city's heat and hustle. Juniper and mesquite trees fill the grounds and keep the casitas and rooms cool and comfortable.

All rates include 3 meals and snacks, served on-site. Most casitas have queen-size beds and private bath; some have full kitchens and fireplace.

Activities include hiking in the surrounding forest, mountain biking, swimming in the heated pool, horseback riding, guided nature walks, wagon rides, and great bird-watching. You are also welcome to relax in the beautifully restored Main House, which was built in the late 1880s.

C.O.D. Ranch is a great place for a group outing; a wedding can be turned into a weekend event, with guests staying not just for the ceremony but for other planned activities as well. A two-night minimum stay is required.

i For an up-to-the-minute list of US dude ranches, head over to www.duderanch.org. A list of Arizona dude ranches can be found at www.azdra.com.

RANCHO DE LA OSA GUEST RANCH $$$$$
PO Box 1, Sasabe 85633
(520) 823-4257, (800) 872-6240
www.ranchodelaosa.com

Just north of the Mexican border about an hour southwest of Tucson, Rancho De La Osa ("ranch of the she-bear") is a bit of a drive but well worth it. You'll pass through some amazing desert country before you discover this gem of a guest ranch with an amazing history: Father Eusebio Francisco Kino and his followers built an adobe mission outpost on the ranch, which is still standing and is reputed to be the second-oldest building in Arizona. Pancho Villa was said to have fired shots at the hacienda during the Mexican Revolution, and there's a cannon ball to prove it!

A guest ranch since the 1920s, there are only 18 rooms, lovingly and simply furnished, each with a private bath and some with a wood-burning fireplace. There's a pool, hot tub, and corrals. Activities include horseback riding, road biking, bird-watching, and hiking.

There is a social cocktail hour around 6 every evening. Three gourmet meals are served in the historic Hacienda dining room, on the private outdoor courtyard, or under the stars at a cookout. All meals are included in the room rate. Satellite TV and complimentary Wi-Fi are available in the Cantina.

Be prepared for serenity and isolation; there are no cars, no stores, and no in-room TVs—in fact, no noise other than birdsong and whistling wind. None of life's stresses intrude here.

✳TANQUE VERDE RANCH $$$$$
14301 E. Speedway Blvd.
(520) 296-6275, (800) 234-DUDE (3833)
www.tanqueverderanch.com

This ranch is in the foothills of the Rincon Mountains on the far east side near Saguaro National Park East and Tanque Verde Falls. Established as a cattle ranch in the 1880s and transformed into a dude ranch in the 1920s, this 640-acre facility offers individual Western casitas, 3 swimming pools (including 1 indoors), gourmet dining, 5 tennis courts, a health spa, and more than 150 horses (Arizona's largest riding stable) for daylong pack trips through the Sonoran Desert. Hiking enthusiasts will also be happy to note that nearby trails can take you to pools of cool mountain water.

Three meals a day are included in your cost. You'll be surprised at the array of choices included in the rate. Weekly activities may include a Southwestern barbecue with a cowboy entertainer/singer, line dancing, and lectures on horse sense and desert wildlife. Parents will appreciate the children's program for ages 4 to 11.

Tanque Verde Ranch is open year-round.

i **If you're staying at or just visiting the magnificent Tanque Verde Ranch, don't miss one of Tucson's most scenic trails. The Douglas Spring Trailhead, part of Saguaro Park East is located at the very eastern end of Speedway Boulevard just before you reach Tanque Verde Ranch. This gorgeous trail is easily accessible for all ages and abilities; you can walk just a little way and get a feel for the desert landscape or trek all the way to the spectacular Bridal Wreath Falls.**

WHITE STALLION RANCH $$$$$
9251 W. Twin Peaks Rd.
(520) 297-0252, (888) 977-2624
www.wsranch.com

Step back into movie history at White Stallion Ranch. Located on 3,000 acres of secluded desert near the Tucson Mountains and Saguaro National Park West, the site served as the location for the filming of many scenes from the TV show *High Chaparral*. Many other Western flicks have been shot here as well.

A working cattle ranch, the White Stallion was purchased by the True family in 1965 and has been catering to guests ever since. The house itself was built circa 1939 by David Young, a homesteader. Happily, the True family has retained much of the original look and feel of the old place, with some of the same furniture and accessories from the house.

Dining is as big as the ranch itself. Happy hour with complimentary hors d'oeuvres is served nightly and every Thursday is steak night. Recreation choices are abundant, although the emphasis is as it should be—on horseback riding. You'll enjoy a heated swimming pool, indoor hot tub, table tennis, sport court, tennis courts, shuffleboard, billiards, horseshoe courts, hiking (remember the ranch borders Saguaro National Park West), moonlight bonfires with a cowboy singer, and even astronomy programs with a large telescope. If that's not enough, they have a fitness center with gym and sauna, a movie theater, and a kids' recreation room. A weekly rodeo showcases roping, riding, and steer wrestling. Take some time to explore the petting zoo of miniature horses, deer, emus, and pygmy goats.

Indoors, if you're not hanging out in the large library, you may want to try the saloon on a stool created from a real saddle.

RESORTS & SPAS

For true self-indulgence, treat yourself to a stay at one of Tucson's luxurious resort hotels or world-renowned spas. Gorgeous views, incredible landscaping, championship golf and tennis facilities, and superb restaurants are just some of the terrific amenities available at these top-notch resorts. There are lots of styles to choose from, from 21st-century modern to historic; you won't be disappointed.

✳THE ARIZONA INN $$$$$
2200 E. Elm St.
(520) 325-1541, (800) 933-1093
www.arizonainn.com

This historic hotel, listed on the National Register of Historic Places, not only has a four-diamond lodging rating but is also a local jewel. Built in 1930 by Isabella Greenway, a community leader and Arizona's first congresswoman (1933–1936), and now run by her great-grandson, the first-class inn sits on 14 acres of gardens surrounded by vine-covered walls. The 95 rooms are classy and quiet in one of the city's nicer neighborhoods but still close to everything. The grounds are lush with older established trees, shrubbery, and lots and lots of colorful flowers. Clay tennis courts, outdoor swimming pool, fountains, indoor/outdoor dining, a library in the main sitting room, and a piano lounge add to the inn's elegant atmosphere. It's been listed as one of *Travel + Leisure*'s top 500 hotels in the world. Even if you decide not to stay here, at least stop by for a visit just to view the magnificent grounds and decor.

CANYON RANCH HEALTH RESORT $$$$$
8600 E. Rockcliff Rd.
(520) 749-9000, (800) 742-9000
www.canyonranch.com

If a total health and fitness vacation experience is what you want or need, look no farther than Canyon Ranch. The world-famous 70-acre complex offers beautifully landscaped grounds, the desert just a step away, and some outrageous views of the surrounding mountains. Besides deluxe accommodations and 3 gourmet meals a day, the Health and Healing Center has health professionals and full-time physicians who offer more than 50 fitness classes daily. Or you can consult directly with any of the spa's nutritionists, exercise physiologists, movement therapists, and psychologists. Also offered are activities such as boxercise, Tai Chi, yoga, squash, and racquetball. Then treat yourself to a massage, herbal wrap, cleansing facial, or other body treatments. Canyon Ranch offers special Health and Healing packages that range from 4- to 7-night stays. No tobacco or alcohol products are allowed at the facility. Also, children must be at least 14 years old to participate in any activities or use the facilities.

i The deluxe Canyon Ranch Health Resort was once the Double U Ranch, a dude ranch that was popular from the 1930s right up to the 1970s. Originally a working cattle ranch, a portion of the original ranch was bought by Canyon Ranch founder Mel Zuckerman, then refurbished and opened as Canyon Ranch. When the ranch opened in 1979, a room cost $85 per night.

ESPLENDOR RESORT AT RIO RICO $$$
1069 Camino Caralampi, Rio Rico
(520) 281-1901, (800) 288-4746
www.esplendor-resort.com

You'll find the magnificent Esplendor Resort in Rio Rico, about 40 minutes south of Tucson. With a distinct European feel, the resort sits atop a hill with a lovely view of the surrounding mountains. The 179 rooms are decorated with Mexican tiles and rustic furnishings, and many have private terraces. A central courtyard houses a pool, sauna, and Jacuzzi. A ballroom and outdoor terrace offer great spaces for weddings or conferences. Golf can be had at the neighboring top-rated 18-hole Robert Trent Jones Sr.–designed golf course. A full service dining room has one of the best views in town, with private curtained banquettes for a romantic touch.

✳HACIENDA DEL SOL GUEST
RANCH RESORT $$$
5601 N. Hacienda del Sol Rd.
(520) 299-1501, (800) 728-6514
www.haciendadelsol.com

This resort opened in 1929 as a preparatory school for girls. When it was turned into a guest resort in the mid-1930s, it became the favorite spot for Hollywood types like Clark Gable, Joseph Cotton, and Spencer Tracy. From the 1950s to 1970s, it operated as a private club, and then it was reopened to the public in 1983. The 30 rooms and 3 casitas sit on 34 acres in the Catalina foothills.

Each room is individually decorated, but the general decor and construction follow the 1930s Art Deco style. The guest lobby has a lovely library, bridge tables, and a cozy fireplace. Outdoor activities include horseshoes, tennis, croquet, and horseback riding.

The Grill at Hacienda del Sol is open for dinner daily and Sunday brunch (see the Restaurants chapter). The Terraza Lounge offers lunch and dinner.

HILTON EL CONQUISTADOR
GOLF & TENNIS RESORT $$$$$
10000 N. Oracle Rd.
(520) 544-5000, (800) 325-7832
www.hiltonelconquistador.com

The Hilton is one of the largest golf and tennis resorts in the West, with 3 golf courses, 2 pro shops, and more than 30 lighted tennis courts, plus horseback riding. With 428 rooms (each with a view of either the desert/mountains or the pool area), 100,000 square feet of meeting space, and 5 restaurants—4 right in the hotel and one at El Conquistador Country Club, located not far away—this resort attracts locals and tourists alike.

Golfers can choose to try the challenging 9-hole Pusch Ridge course or venture over to the 18-hole championship course at the El Conquistador Country Club, just 10 minutes down the road. Hiking, jogging, a fitness center, and spa services can round out your stay. Ask the concierge for a list of planned weekly activities.

THE LODGE AT VENTANA
CANYON $$$$$
6200 N. Clubhouse Ln.
(520) 577-1400, (800) 828-5701
www.thelodgeatventanacanyon.com

This 600-acre private golf resort and lodge has 50 guest suites with a private balcony/patio, a spiral staircase to the 2-bedroom loft, and a complete kitchen. Nestled in the Ventana Canyon area of the Santa Catalina Mountains, the two 18-hole golf courses have won *Golf Magazine*'s Silver Medal Award and *Links* magazine's Best of Golf

Award. The fitness center is open around the clock, and the 12 lighted tennis courts, saunas, spas, and swimming center with its baby pool give guests plenty to do. The resort also has 7,000 square feet of flexible meeting space. The Catalina Room and Ventana Bar & Grill offer panoramic views of the mountain range, golf course, and the desert creatures that make their homes around the resort.

LODGE ON THE DESERT $$$$
306 N. Alvernon Way
(520) 320-2000, (877) 498-6776
www.lodgeonthedesert.com

You'd never guess as you drive down busy Alvernon Way (just off 5th Street) that just over the adobe walls lies a peaceful, elegant resort—the Lodge on the Desert. Originally a private residence, this beautiful in-town resort has been serving guests since 1936 and in that time has earned a reputation for great service, private getaways, and old-world charm.

Its midtown location is ideal for whatever you've got planned—golfing, tennis, shopping, sightseeing, dining, a game at nearby UA—you name it. If you'd rather spend your day right at the lodge, you can swim in the heated pool.

The adobe-like casitas are charmingly decorated with Mexican tiles and furniture and high-beamed ceilings. Some have wood-burning fireplaces, and one even has its own indoor heated pool. All are easily accessible to the beautiful grounds replete with ocotillo and other desert plants, palms, flower gardens, and lush lawns.

The elegant in-house restaurant serves 3 meals a day. You should plan to spend one special evening there.

LOEWS VENTANA CANYON
RESORT $$$$$
7000 N. Resort Dr.
(520) 299-2020, (800) 234-5117
www.loewshotels.com

On 93 acres above Tucson, this 398-room golf and tennis resort lies exactly where the Sonoran Desert and the Santa Catalina Mountains meet. The views here are splendid.

For the athlete in you, try one of the 8 lighted tennis courts, the 2 Tom Fazio–designed PGA championship golf courses, fitness center, hiking, biking, horseback riding, 2 pools, or a waterfall plunge. When you're all done, grab a massage or a facial at the spa. Shops, croquet, and a hair salon are also found right at the resort.

The resort boasts a total of 48,000 square feet for business visitors.

Five restaurants offer something for your every mood—casual fare at the Canyon Cafe, five-diamond dining at the Ventana Room, poolside meals at Bill's Grill, the Cascade Lounge for snacks and drinks, and the Flying V, located at the Spa and Tennis Center, for a taste of the Southwest and a terrific view of the city.

Each of the elegant 398 rooms is decorated to reflect the natural world outside your patio. The bathrooms are a vacation unto themselves. We recommend a long soak in the two-person bathtub. Room service is available 24 hours a day.

MIRAVAL—LIFE IN BALANCE $$$$$
5000 E. Via Estancia Miraval
(520) 825-4000, (800) 232-3969
www.miravalresorts.com

Staying at Miraval, ranked one of the top spas in the nation, is more than a few nights at a resort. Miraval offers an entire new experience. Here not only will you come away relaxed but also will be enriched by learning to live "mindfully." That is, learning to live for the moment.

Located in the high desert north of the city, Miraval offers guests individual programs to increase their overall well-being. Through yoga, Tai Chi, the Quantum Leap (where you climb a 35-foot pole and take a giant step into the air), horseback riding, fitness programs, swimming, and other recreational activities, you will see yourself in a whole new light. Take an equine therapy class on specially trained horses to gain self-insight. Programs are individualized through the help of experts. There are 117 hacienda-style guest rooms and suites on 400 acres that include a Zen garden and labyrinth.

World-class personal services add a special touch. Try a seaweed wrap, a manicure, and a wonderful hot stone massage (only one of several types of massages offered).

Meals at Miraval are an integral part of the process. Both gourmet and healthful, the menu has everything from smoothies to elegant dinners. Desserts are as beautiful as they are good for you. Wine and beer are available.

Having won rave reviews from *Condé Nast Traveler, Travel + Leisure, Vogue,* and *Harper's Bazaar* (just to name a few), Miraval is a favorite of locals and celebrities (think Oprah!) from around the world. Miraval—Life In Balance is an experience not to be missed.

OMNI TUCSON NATIONAL GOLF RESORT AND SPA $$$$$
2727 W. Club Dr.
(520) 297-2271, (800) 528-4856
www.omnitucsonnational.com

Offering 279 rooms (some are suites or villas), this boutique golf resort is nestled in the foothills of the far northwest side. The four-star European-style spa and fitness center and the two 18-hole championship PGA golf courses (see the Golf chapter) are outstanding. You'll also enjoy an infinity pool, 2 whirlpools, a sauna, a power walk area, and tennis.

Splurge on cocktails poolside at the Cabana Bar, or sink your teeth into a juicy steak at Bob's Steak and Chop House. For upscale pub fare, try the Legends Bar and Grill. The resort's fine location is just a short drive to many other great choices in dining.

RITZ-CARLTON DOVE MOUNTAIN $$$$$
15000 N. Secret Springs Dr., Marana
(520) 572-3000
www.ritzcarlton.com/dovemountain
One of Tucson's newest luxury resorts, the very ritzy Ritz-Carlton Dove Mountain opened in Marana, just north of Tucson, in December 2009. Nestled against the Tortolita Mountains, the resort features 209 rooms, including 44 individual and casita suites. Rooms are decorated with mesquite furnishings, and you'll sleep soundly on 400-thread-count linens by Frette and 100 percent goose-down pillows. Every room has wireless Internet access, a 42-inch TV, iPod docking station, and fully automated minibar. A complimentary overnight shoeshine will keep you looking dapper. Amenities include a 27-hole golf course with a 45,000-square-foot clubhouse and a 17,000-square-foot spa and fitness center. The full-service spa houses 14 indoor/outdoor treatment rooms, a Vichy shower, and a full-service salon for mani/pedis and blowouts. Three swimming pools, evening stargazing, and personalized

tours of nearby ancient Indian petroglyphs round out the experience. Meeting and wedding planners and guests love the more than 44,000 square feet of indoor/outdoor function space. Dining options include the upscale Core Kitchen and Wine Bar (see the Restaurant chapter), a pub, a Latin grill, and Cayton's at the golf club. No expense has been spared to make this a top hotel destination for locals as well as visitors.

STARR PASS MARRIOTT RESORT AND SPA $$$$$
3800 W. Starr Pass Blvd.
(520) 792-3500, (800) 535-4028
www.starrpassmarriott.com

This luxury 6-floor, 575-room resort (the largest in Tucson) is nestled against the Tucson Mountains in Tucson Mountain Park. Close to downtown (about 5 miles from the convention center) yet in the midst of hiking trails and saguaros, the hotel features a 20,000-square-foot spa with 23 treatment rooms, private lap pool, and Jacuzzis. Every room has a patio or balcony and comes with high-speed Internet, a flat-screen TV, minibar, and coffeemaker. Multiple dining options cover breakfast, lunch, and dinner, including a poolside bar and grill, Southwestern lobby bar, and southern Italian sit-down restaurant. The hotel also offers 88,000 square feet of indoor and outdoor event space, a real plus for the downtown area. Guests have access to the 27-hole Arnold Palmer Signature Starr Pass Golf Course (see the Golf chapter). The views are magnificent.

i Many resort hotels offer special rates on rooms and spa services for Tucson residents (be sure to ask when you make a reservation) and host special events throughout the year.

THE WESTIN LA PALOMA RESORT $$$$$
3800 E. Sunrise Dr.
(520) 742-6000, (800) 937-8461
www.westinlapalomaresort.com

This 487-room resort (some of the suites come with wood-burning fireplaces and sunken hot tubs) offers a 27-hole Jack Nicklaus Signature golf course, which was named one of the top 75 resort courses in the country by *Golf Digest*. If golf isn't your favorite physical activity, La Paloma also has a Red Door Spa, 12 tennis courts, indoor racquetball, 3 swimming pools, a 177-foot waterslide and waterfalls, an aerobics center, Nautilus room, and children's play area. One of the pools even has a swim-up bar for drinks and sandwiches.

Top-rated Janos restaurant and sister J Bar offer scrumptious Southwestern fare (see the Restaurants chapter). An 18,000-square-foot ballroom, 18 meeting rooms, and lovely landscaping make it a great place for weddings, conventions, and reunions.

WESTWARD LOOK RESORT $$$$$
245 E. Ina Rd.
(520) 297-1151, (800) 722-2500
www.westwardlook.com

Nestled at the base of the Santa Catalina Mountains on 80 lush acres in the Sonoran Desert, Westward Look was built in 1912 as a private residence. You can see the original sitting room—which has a huge stone hearth, exposed beam and ocotillo branch ceiling, and period furnishings—just off the resort's lobby.

This resort offers 244 luxurious rooms with great city or mountain views from cozy private terraces. You can dine on New American Sonoran cuisine in Gold (see the

Restaurants chapter) or on casual South-western fare in the Lookout Bar and Grille.

Don't pass up a stroll around the lovely landscaped grounds, with tinkling fountains, shade and citrus trees, a Zen-style labyrinth, and an herb, butterfly, and chef's edible garden framed by amazing views.

Tennis is the sport of choice at Westward Look. The 10 championship Laykold courts (4 are clay) have helped the resort earn the honor of being named one of the "Top 50 Tennis Resorts" for more than 20 years by *Tennis Magazine.* Other awards include a AAA Four-Diamond Award and *Wine Spectator's* Award of Excellence..

Golf isn't neglected, with a 27-hole Jack Nicklaus Signature course garnering a spot in *Golf Digest's* "Top 75 Resort" courses.

Resort guests have many additional options, including 5 pools, a top-rated spa, horseback riding, a wellness center and fitness club, 16 meeting rooms, and 20,000 square feet of meeting space. Small pets are allowed for a fee.

BED-AND-BREAKFAST INNS

There are lots and lots of great bed-and-breakfasts of all kinds in Tucson, from historic mansions downtown to cozy adobes in the desert; it's a great way to stay here. We can't possibly cover all of them, so we feature some of the more unique spots in town.

ADOBE ROSE INN $$
940 N. Olsen Ave.
(520) 318-4644, (800) 328-4122
www.aroseinn.com
A historic 1933 adobe home, the centrally located Adobe Rose Inn offers 6 rooms, including a suite and casita. The private Atanacia Room has a striking 6-foot green,

blue, and gold stained-glass window, a kiva-style fireplace, high-beamed ceiling, brick floor, and separate entrance. The romantic Sam Hughes Room also features a kiva fireplace, oak floors, and a deep soaking tub—aaah! All rooms have wireless Internet. There are quaint courtyards with bistro tables and evening candlelight, a fountain, and lovely landscaping that includes cactus gardens and potted flowering plants. The whole property is surrounded by thick adobe walls, which make this a private, quiet in-town getaway. The inn also has a pool and a spa, and it serves a delicious breakfast. It's been chosen by BedandBreakfast.com as one of the five best undiscovered inns for romance. This is a great choice for visiting parents, because the university is only a couple of blocks away.

i Tucson is home to over 120 bed-and-breakfast inns, according to the Metropolitan Tucson Convention & Visitors Bureau. A full listing of those in Tucson and southern Arizona can be found at www.listbb.com.

ALTA VISTA BED AND BREAKFAST $$
11300 E. Broadway Blvd.
(520) 647-3037, (800) 947-3037
www.altavistabedandbreakfast.com
Hosts Peter and Gaila Smith invite you to their desert oasis near Saguaro National Park East. Voted as having the "most scenic view" by *Inn Traveler Magazine,* the Alta Vista is perched high on a hill with amazing views of the Santa Catalina Mountains to the north and the Rincon Mountains in the east.

The two lovely rooms invite you to kick off your shoes and stay awhile. The White Wicker Room's king-size bed and kiva-style fireplace are complemented by a private bathroom with a shower, satellite dish, television and DVD player, microwave, and refrigerator. The king lodgepole bed in the Santa Fe Room welcomes guests ready for a good night's sleep by the fireplace, while daylight brings wonderful views of the Catalinas. A full homemade breakfast is served in the dining room. Customized spa packages are also available.

CASA TIERRA ADOBE BED AND BREAKFAST INN $$$
11155 W. Calle Pima
(520) 578-3058, (866) 254-0006
www.casatierratucson.com

Located on 5 acres of secluded Sonoran Desert on the western side of the Tucson Mountains, this rustic adobe hacienda offers spectacular views of the mountains and is surrounded by beautiful desert dotted with saguaro cacti. Casa Tierra ("earth house") features more than 50 arches and entryways with vaulted brick ceilings and an interior arched courtyard. The area is only minutes from the Arizona-Sonora Desert Museum, Saguaro National Park West, and Old Tucson Studios. The 3 rooms and 2-bedroom suite include private baths, small refrigerators, microwaves, patios, and private entrances. In the morning you will be treated to a full vegetarian breakfast, along with home-baked goods, fresh-ground coffee, and a variety of herbal teas. The site is great for birding and hiking or just plain relaxing in the hot tub.

CAT MOUNTAIN LODGE $$
2740 S. Kinney Rd.
(520) 505-4769
www.catmountainlodge.com

Located on the far western edge of the city, this eco-friendly B&B (solar panels, gray-water harvesting) offers 4 spacious rooms, each with a private bath and sitting area opening onto a central courtyard. Two of the rooms are wheelchair accessible, and 1 room is dog friendly. Located on more than 13 acres, Cat Mountain Lodge offers easy access to major attractions, including Saguaro Park West, Old Tucson Studios, and the Arizona-Sonora Desert Museum (see the Attractions chapter). Room fees include breakfast or lunch at neighboring Coyote Pause Cafe. Stargazers will love the telescopes outside the courtyard in Spencer's Observatory.

CATALINA PARK INN $$
309 E. 1st St.
(520) 792-4541, (800) 792-4885
www.catalinaparkinn.com

This 1927 mansion near the University of Arizona is your chance to vacation in true elegance. The 6 guest rooms have been lovingly decorated with antiques, and all include a phone, TV, and private bath. Some rooms also have private porches. The rest of the house, with its mahogany doors, is just as beautiful as the rooms. Take some time to enjoy the native landscaping. Breakfast is delicious, with freshly made pancakes, baked goods, fresh fruit, cereals, and coffee or tea, served in the gorgeous dining room—it's one of the prettiest rooms in the house.

DESERT DOVE BED & BREAKFAST $$
11707 E. Old Spanish Trail
(520) 722-6879, (877) 722-6879
www.desertdovebb.com

This territorial-style adobe is on 4 acres nestled in the foothills of the Rincon Mountains. The great porches, polished colored concrete floors, and open trusses in the great room, along with the antiques and collectibles, give this B&B a truly unique feel. There are 2 spacious guest rooms decorated with antiques and collectibles, each with a private entrance, private bathroom, queen-size bed, and seating area. Amenities include Wi-Fi, bathrobes, and hair dryers. There's no swimming pool, but an outdoor hydrotherapy spa with lovely views of the mountains does just fine. A homemade breakfast in the country kitchen with its 1927 wood-burning stove is served on vintage tableware.

DUNN'S WAY BED AND
BREAKFAST $$$$
4975 W. Via Scaramuzzo
(520) 629-9694
www.dunnswaybb.com

Perched high in the Tucson Mountains, you'll enjoy spectacular city and mountain views from the patio and guest suites at this well-appointed, award-winning B&B owned by Smithie and Jim Dunn. A cozy great room welcomes you to this homey spot where 2 light and airy private guest suites feature full private baths and patios, refrigerator, microwave, cable TV, phone, and complimentary newspaper. Dunn's Way is especially noted for excellent customer service.

A delicious full-service breakfast is served in the dining room from 8 to 9 a.m., or you can choose to enjoy an in-room continental breakfast. Closed mid-May to mid-Sept.

✳EL PRESIDIO BED AND
BREAKFAST INN $$
297 N. Main Ave.
(520) 623-6151, (800) 349-6151
www.bbonline.com/az/elpresidio

For historic Victorian ambience near downtown, consider this 1880s adobe mansion, listed on the National Register of Historic Places. It's a vacation for all the senses. Eyes and noses are enraptured by the beauty and fragrances of the gardens; ears and fingers

revel at the gentle music and cool current of the fountains. Taste buds are treated to a full breakfast; the menu changes but often has stuffed French toast, bacon, fruit, and juice. Four luxury suites have private baths, TVs, wireless Internet, and phones. El Presidio is within walking distance of the Tucson Museum of Art and the city's historic Presidio District.

HACIENDA DEL DESIERTO BED
AND BREAKFAST $$$
11770 Rambling Trail
(520) 298-1764, (800) 982-1795
www.tucson-bed-breakfast.com

This Spanish-style hacienda sits on 16 acres in the Rincon Mountain foothills near Saguaro National Park East. There are 3 rooms able to accommodate up to 4 people each. Each room has a queen-size bed and hide-a-beds as well as a private bath, kitchenette, TV/DVD player, telephone, and private entrance. In addition, a large casita has 2 bedrooms, a full kitchen, living room, bath, and a private outdoor spa. A business center with Wi-Fi access, computers, and printer is available. You'll find shady porches, great views, and a courtyard with fountains and flowers.

Breakfast includes fruit, cereal, hard-boiled eggs, homemade muffins, coffee, and juice. Take a walk on the 0.8-mile nature trail to work it all off.

THE JEREMIAH INN BED AND
BREAKFAST $$
10921 E. Snyder Rd.
(520) 749-3072, (888) 750-3072
www.jeremiahinn.com

Located in the eastern foothills near Sabino Canyon, this 3.3-acre desert retreat offers 5 rooms in a contemporary Santa Fe–style home. Two rooms adjoin to create a suite. All rooms include a queen-size bed, private bath, TV, telephone, and outside entrance. Guests can enjoy nearby golf or horseback riding or take a dip in the pool or spa after a breakfast of a special entree, fruits, and juices served in the dining room, poolside, or in your room. Children age 6 and under stay free and have access to a super game and toy closet and library. This is a very kid-friendly place that even serves chocolate milk.

LA POSADA DEL VALLE $
1640 N. Campbell Ave.
(520) 885-0883, (877) 775-8355
www.thejoeslerhistoricinn.com
Tucson's first bed-and-breakfast, this elegant 1929 adobe mansion, designed by noted Tucson architect Josias Joesler, is surrounded by gardens and orange trees. Across the street from University Medical Center, the inn has 6 guest rooms with private baths and entrances. Each room's furnishings are inspired by individual Southwestern themes. The living room has views of the Catalina Mountains. In the morning expect a hearty country breakfast. Free Wi-Fi and cable TV are available as well.

i If you're looking for a bed-and-breakfast in town (or anywhere in Arizona), check in with the Arizona Association of Bed & Breakfast Inns. This professional association lists over 50 inns that have met their strict standards for inclusion. Go to www.arizona-bed-breakfast.com. For statewide reservations, the Arizona Trails Bed & Breakfast Reservation Service will set you up at any of hundreds of state-inspected B&Bs, inns, hotels, and ranches. Call (888) 799-4284 or go to www.arizonatrails.com.

LA ZARZUELA $$$$$
455 Camino de Oeste
(888) 848-8225
www.zarzuela-az.com
With its stunning desert setting, this 5-casita bed-and-breakfast is the perfect rendezvous for romance. Each brightly painted and well-appointed casita features a private bath, private entryway, patio, and mountain view. In addition, all have refrigerators, coffeemaker, hair dryer, TV, video and CD player. You'll find a shaded and welcoming patio, a negative-edge pool, and spa. La Zarzuela offers full concierge and travel planning services, from flight reservations to picnic lunches. A full gourmet breakfast with home-baked goodies is served daily, and the 4-course Sunday brunch tops everything. On Sunday the host puts on an organ recital.

This is a perfect desert oasis for couples or groups up to 50 people, but bear in mind that town is a good half-hour drive away.

PEPPERTREES BED AND
** BREAKFAST INN** $$
724 E. University Blvd.
(520) 622-7167, (800) 348-5763
www.peppertreesinn.com
You might not expect Victorian mansions in the Old West, but this 1905 inn is just that. It's an oasis of tranquility near the main gate of the University of Arizona and is within walking distance to shops, museums, and restaurants. The name comes from 2 large California peppertrees that once dominated the front of the inn. (They were lost to one of many summer monsoons some years back.)

The inn comprises 4 distinct homes. The East Wing House offers 2 queen-bedded rooms with sitting rooms, private baths, and full kitchen. The Casita is a king-size suite decorated with a Mexican theme and includes a private entrance, full kitchen, sitting room, king-size bed, and private tiled bathroom. Two private guesthouses (Sunrise and Sunset) have private patios, and separate entrances.

A gourmet organic breakfast, prepared by acclaimed pastry chef (and owner) Jill McCormick, is served daily, usually in the lovely gardens.

ROCKING M RANCH $$
6265 N. Happy Trail
(520) 744-2457, (888) 588-2457
www.rockingmranch.net
If you travel with your horse, Rocking M Ranch may be the spot for you. On 10 acres adjacent to miles of trails within Saguaro National Park West, this bed-and-breakfast has 5 covered corrals with automatic water for keeping your horse ready for a ride at nearby stables or on open trails (no stallions, please). Rocking M has 4 rooms available. Two rooms have a queen-size bed and private bath. The remaining 2 rooms share a bath; queen or twin beds are available. During the week a continental breakfast is served, and on weekends a full breakfast with eggs, toast, fresh fruit, and coffee begins the day. There is also a no-breakfast option. A boot-shaped pool and heated spa round out the luxuries.

THE ROYAL ELIZABETH BED & BREAKFAST INN $$$$
204 S. Scott Ave.
(520) 670-9022, (877) 670-9022
www.royalelizabeth.com
At this Victorian treasure right in the heart of the Old Pueblo, Anglophiles will love the meticulously renovated 1878 mansion crafted out of adobe. Six spacious guest rooms are beautifully furnished with period antiques, along with satellite TV, wireless Internet, and a refrigerator. A heated pool and outdoor spa, home theater, and lounge round out the amenities. Personalized service sets this wonderful desert oasis apart. A 2-course gourmet breakfast is served daily. You'll be pampered with fresh fruit and healthy options to get a good start to your day. Beverages are available throughout the day.

SAM HUGHES INN BED AND BREAKFAST $
2020 E. 7th St.
(520) 861-2191
www.samhughesinn.com
Sam Hughes Inn is a 1931 California mission–style bed-and-breakfast with a red-tiled roof, original oak floors, and Art Deco architectural details. Just 2 blocks from the University of Arizona, this is a historic property located in the National Historic District of Tucson, which also bears the name of a famous early settler: Sam Hughes, an alderman and brother of the governor of the territory of Arizona. You can sleep in Tombstone, Nogales, and Santa Fe without leaving town! The 4 rooms (2 with private entrances) are decorated with antique and contemporary Southwestern furnishings. All come with a private bath, minifridge, hair dryer, and shower robes. A great room with fireplace offers cable TV and a library. Free Wi-Fi is available. In the morning you'll be treated to a delicious full breakfast in the dining room or outside, weather permitting.

THE SUNCATCHER BED & BREAKFAST $$$
105 N. Avenida Javelina
(520) 885-0883, (877) 775-8355
www.suncatchertucson.com

Owned by Janos Siess (former manager of the top-ranked Cafe Des Artistes restaurant in New York City), this elegant and newly remodeled bed-and-breakfast is furnished with antique Spanish colonial pieces and original period artworks. Four rooms—the Suncatcher, Sonoran, Oriental, and Vaqueros—are located poolside with private entrances and offer king beds, wireless Internet, satellite TV, luxury robes, and hairdryers. For a daily fee, horses are welcome, too, and are treated just as luxuriously with Bermuda and alfalfa at no extra cost. Riding trails in Saguaro National Park are accessible right out the front gate, or they can stretch their legs in the Olympic-size arena on-site. An award-winning gourmet breakfast is served daily. Heated pool and spa are just steps away from each room. Free Wi-Fi is available throughout the property.

CAMPGROUNDS & RV PARKS

The best thing about camping in the Tucson area is that, no matter where the campground, it's probably close to, if not surrounded by, some of southern Arizona's most fascinating attractions. The second-best thing is that camping around here offers something to suit just about everyone's taste—from low-lying desert dotted with cacti to high mountains covered with conifer forests and from backcountry camping to fairly posh RV resorts.

In this chapter we cover all the public campgrounds and several of the best private sites close to Tucson, as well as a number of the best camping areas in each direction away from Tucson—except east. Tucson's east—actually the Rincon Mountains—only offers backcountry camping, and it's accessible only by hiking or horseback. (But if that's your style, contact the Saguaro National Park's Rincon Mountain District at 520-733-5153 for details on these campsites and the required permits.) We only include an RV park if it also accommodates the "old-fashioned" type of camper—in a tent. So if you're strictly an RVer, check our Retirement chapter, the Tucson Convention & Visitors Bureau, or the Yellow Pages for additional offerings. And we hasten to add that rates are subject to change and seem to do so quite often.

OVERVIEW

To get the most out of this chapter, you should use it hand in hand with several other chapters of the book, especially the Natural World, Attractions, and Parks & Recreation chapters. The Natural World chapter, for example, contains lots of additional environmental information on the areas in which you're camping, such as Madera Canyon, the Tucson Mountains, and Mount Lemmon. It can also familiarize you with the unusual flora and fauna you're likely to see no matter where you set up your tent or RV. The Attractions chapter gives details on the many sites you may want to visit from your campground base. And because many of the campgrounds are in or near parklands,

the Parks & Recreation chapter will give you a more complete picture of what awaits you in and around these camping areas.

If you're a first-time camper or RVer in Tucson, there are two things you should keep in mind when using the campground descriptions in this chapter. Below the name of the campground is an address or city where it's located. The city listed is the city closest to the camping area. For example, Bog Springs Campground is listed as Green Valley, Arizona; while the campground is near Green Valley, it's also a ways away in the Santa Rita Mountains. So consider the "city" indicator just a general description of the location.

Our second piece of advice relates to the 520 area code. This chapter contains a number of campgrounds that are far enough from the Tucson metro area to be considered long distance by phone, even though they're still in the 520 area code. So be aware that in some cases you'll have to dial the area code even if you're calling from Tucson, and it will be a long-distance call. Although a recording will tell you the error of your ways if you dial only the seven-digit phone number, it may not be helpful enough to tell you the way to correct it—but now you know how.

Now you're ready to dive into the fun part of this chapter—our picks of some of the best places to pitch your tent or park your RV in and around Tucson. So pack up your gear, supplies, and sunscreen, and get ready for your adventure in the great outdoors.

BOG SPRINGS
FSR 70, Green Valley
(520) 281-2296
www.fs.fed.us

At the western side of the steep Santa Rita Mountains and about 30 minutes south of Tucson—not counting the extra time it might take to traverse up the Forest Service road for 13 miles—sits this 15-acre campground in and operated by the Coronado National Forest. The campground lies just below Madera Canyon, one of the premier birding spots in the Southwest. You'll drive past plenty of century plants, yuccas, and barrel and prickly pear cacti, and if it's spring or fall, they may be in full bloom or showing off their colorful fruits. You'll also wind through pecan groves and across grassland sprinkled with mesquite trees.

At the campground's 5,200-foot elevation, you'll be surrounded by junipers, oaks, and sycamores and hear the soft tumbling of Madera Creek. The many hiking trails leading into the Santa Ritas and the elevation make this a popular spot, especially in summer.

If you're in an RV, keep in mind that the limit is 22 feet and the campground loops, though paved, are steep and twisting. There are 13 tent or RV sites with no hookups at $10 per night per vehicle. Near the campground entrance are several shaded picnic areas with grills, as well as restrooms but no showers. Bog Springs is open all year for 14-day stay limits. Winter nights at this elevation can get quite cold, but summertime camping can be a comfortable diversion from temperatures on the valley floor below. It's a popular place, and spaces cannot be reserved in advance.

If you happen to run out of some basic supplies or food, Madera Canyon even has a small store or two, but it's iffy whether they'll be open (although more likely in summer). Many trails take off from here up toward the Mount Wrightson Wilderness—more than 70 miles of them throughout the mountain range. Or you can save your hiking shoes for another time and simply hike around Madera Canyon and along the creek. Another option is to take the bus tour to the Smithsonian Astrophysical Observatory at the top of Mount Hopkins from the observatory's ground-level visitor center. And nearby you'll find attractions like the Titan Missile Museum and the outstanding golf courses of Green Valley.

To get to Bog Springs, take I-19 south from Tucson to exit 63 (Continental Road/Madera Canyon) and head east on FSR 70 for about 13 miles.

ADVENTURE BOUND CACTUS COUNTRY RV RESORT
10195 S. Houghton Rd.
(520) 574-3000, (800) 777-8799
www.abtucson.com
If you're looking for the amenities of a resort but still want to bunk in your own tent or RV, Cactus Country RV may be the spot. This private RV complex covers 3 acres on Tucson's far southeast, close to the Santa Rita Mountains, the Santa Rita Golf Club, and the Pima County Fairgrounds. You can stay for a day, week, month, or a season and have access to electricity, heaters, air-conditioners, cable TV, restrooms, dump station, heated pool, whirlpool, shuffleboard, recreation room, and laundry facilities.

And all of this is in a serene desert setting surrounded on all four sides by state land. Cactus Country sits on a hill from which you can see not only the nearby Santa Ritas but also the Rincon and Santa Catalina Mountains to the north and unobstructed sunset views to the west. The resort offers mature vegetation, paved roads, and gravel-covered spaces.

Of the 265 sites, many of which are tree-shaded, 260 are for RVs at $38 a day and 5 are for tents at $22 a day. You'll pay less per day for longer term stays. Many of the extras listed above require an additional fee. Cactus Country is open year-round, and the busiest time is January through March.

From Tucson, take I-10 east, exit at Houghton Road, and go north about 0.25 mile.

CATALINA STATE PARK CAMPGROUND
11570 N. Oracle Rd.
(520) 628-5798
www.azstateparks.com/CATA/index.html

The closest campground to Tucson is also one of the best. Located in the Santa Catalina Mountains on Tucson's northwest, Catalina State Park covers 5,500 acres at elevations ranging from 2,650 to 3,000 feet. There are plenty of nature trails in the park and, for the more serious hiker, trails extending up the mountains into the national forest. Highlights of the park include Romero Canyon with its falls and clear pools shaded by sycamore and oak trees, ruins of the pit houses left by Hohokam Indians, and the nearby Pusch Ridge Wilderness, home to desert bighorn sheep. And from this location nearly every attraction in and around Tucson is less than an hour's drive away.

Spacious campsites pleasantly arranged amid groves of mesquite trees await road-weary travelers. There are 120 sites, 95 with water and electric hookups. Facilities include wheelchair-accessible restrooms with showers. Fees vary seasonally, the area is open year-round, and the maximum stay is 14 nights. Keep in mind that summer camping here will really feel like summer due to the campground's desert terrain and elevation. Reservations are not accepted, so it's best to show up early in the day (between 8 and 10 a.m.) during the busy winter season for a campsite. Catalina State Park is about 9 miles north of the city limits on Highway 77 (Oracle Road).

CRAZY HORSE RV CAMPGROUNDS
6660 S. Craycroft Rd.
(520) 574-0157, (800) 279-6279
www.crazyhorserv.com
The owner calls this "a good old down-to-earth RV park with dust." (He means the kind of desert dust a crazy horse would kick up or, in the absence of such an animal, a windy desert day.) In other words,

it's comfortable with all the basics but not fancy. The basics consist of 152 sites for RVs, full hookups (electric, water, and sewage), restrooms, showers, a laundry room, and a pool that is heated seasonally. The main road is paved, but the spaces aren't, and trees are few, which no doubt contributes to the dust in the air. Crazy Horse welcomes both kids and pets but does have rules about noise in an attempt to keep the park as peaceful as the surrounding desert.

The daily fee of $28.50 for one to two people is all-inclusive; weekly, monthly, and seasonal rentals are available as well. Crazy Horse is open all year, but the peak season is January 15 to March 15.

Located in the southeast of Tucson 0.5 mile north of I-10 and Craycroft Road, Crazy Horse is close to the Pima Air and Space Museum on Valencia Road and no more than 60 minutes away from any other attraction in the metro area. A truck stop and convenience store are close by.

GILBERT RAY CAMPGROUND
Kinney Road, Tucson Mountain Park
(520) 883-420 (Jan–Mar), (520) 887-6000
www.pima.gov/nrpr/camping
Of the two units of Saguaro National Park (east and west), the west unit is the only one with a nearby campground. On the west side of the Tucson Mountains and not very far from downtown Tucson is the vast 20,000-acre Tucson Mountain Park, where this campground is located. Its proximity to Tucson and to some great attractions means that this popular campground, though large, often sports the full sign (it's first-come, first-served). In addition to Saguaro National Park, both the Arizona-Sonora Desert Museum and Old Tucson Studios are nearby. So is the 6-mile Bajada

Loop Drive, where you'll see Indian petroglyphs. Wildlife is abundant here despite the number of humans around. You'll see the typical varieties of thorny vegetation, lots of birdlife, and probably a coyote or mule deer or two. An excellent visitor center can give you a complete orientation to the park and its trails and sights.

Operated by Pima County Natural Resources Parks and Recreation Department, the campground has 130 sites, with individual 30-amp hookups. There are wheelchair-accessible restrooms and a dump station but no showers. Volunteer attendants are on duty during regular business hours in the winter season but usually not during the slower summer season, when campers are on the honor system to pay at the lock box. The fees are $10 for tenters and $20 for RVs per night for a maximum of 7 days, no credit cards accepted.

The easiest way to get here is to take Ajo Way west to Kinney Road and then head north to the campground. The scenic route is Speedway Boulevard to Gates Pass Road, then south on Kinney Road. RVers must take the easy way—RVs are not permitted on Gates Pass Road.

LAKEVIEW
Highway 83, Sonoita
(520) 378-0311
www.fs.fed.us/r3/coronado/forest/
recreation
Fishing might be the reason you choose this campground, but the camping is also superb. It's located almost at the Mexico border at 133-acre Parker Canyon Lake, where the cottonwoods, willows, and marsh grass—not to mention the sight of water—might fool you into thinking you're not in Arizona. It's not recommended for swimming (algae and

reeds would slow your progress across the lake), but bring your fishing gear along and see if you can land any of the lake's rainbow trout, largemouth bass, sunfish, or catfish for a tasty dinner. Lakeside there's a store, a marina, and boats for rent. Pets are allowed on leash only.

Operated year-round by the Sierra Vista Ranger District of the Coronado National Forest, the 65 campsites on 50 acres in the shadow of the hulking Huachuca Mountains accommodate either tents or RVs, with a 32-foot limit. There are restrooms but no showers, dump station, or RV hookups. Maximum stay is 14 nights at $10 a night per campsite.. At an elevation of 5,400 feet, summer nights will be heavenly and winter nights on the cool side.

i **If you love camping out but miss some of the comforts of home, consider renting the rustic adobe cabins in historic Kentucky Camp in the Santa Rita Mountains just 9 miles north of Sonoita. Built in 1904 as the headquarters of the Santa Rita Water and Mining Company, the camp houses five century-old adobe buildings. You can rent the 10-room headquarters building or the cabin as part of the Forest Service's "Room with a View" program. Watch for white-tailed deer, coatimundis, pronghorns and coyotes, which all make their home here. Call (877) 444-6777 to make a reservation.**

The easiest way to get here from Tucson is to take I-10 east to the Patagonia/Sonoita exit and then head south on Highway 83 for about 25 miles to Parker Canyon Lake.

MOUNT LEMMON

Tucson's own "sky island," Mount Lemmon is also the region's most diverse outdoor recreation area. Along 25 miles of steep and curving roadway up to a 9,000-foot elevation, sights and sounds include full-blown pine forests, see-forever views, biking, skiing, fishing, picnicking, hiking, wildlife watching, and camping. For Tucsonans it's akin to making a short drive to Canada. So it's a very popular place year-round. In summer it's an escape from the heat down below, in fall a spectacular foliage show, in winter a test of winter driving skills and a close place to hit the ski slopes, and in spring a blooming treat for the senses. Designated a scenic byway in 2005, the drive is sublime.

There are several Forest Service–maintained campgrounds. And for the brave among you, wilderness camping is permitted on Mount Lemmon 0.25 mile or more away from campgrounds. All of the Coronado National Forest campgrounds, including those on Mount Lemmon, have a 14-day stay limit. For information on any of the four campgrounds, call (520) 749-8700 or check www.fs.fed.us/r3/coronado. Here are some details on the most popular sites.

MOLINO BASIN

Despite its location in the Santa Catalina Mountains, this campground is actually closed during the summer months (late April through the end of September) due to the heat (no, that isn't a typo). That's because its southern exposure, even at an elevation of 4,500 feet, makes it warmer than, say, Catalina State Park on the northern slope of the same mountain range. Conversely, the same conditions make wintertime camping here quite pleasant at an elevation that normally would be uncomfortably cold.

Close-up

Mount Lemmon Rules

Here are some things you should know to keep your Mount Lemmon experience safe and rule abiding.

- Bears live here, too, and they're attracted to food, so keep yours well covered and hidden—that means tightly sealed and in your car or one of the bear barriers.

- Your own pets must be on a leash.

- You can fish at Rose Canyon Lake, but you can't get a license on the mountain, so get one before you come.

- If a summer is particularly dry, the Forest Service may temporarily ban all fires, so have a backup for your charcoal-broiled steaks or hot dogs.

- Gas up your vehicle in Tucson—there are no stations on the mountain.

- At the top in the village of Summerhaven, you'll find a few stores and restaurants.

- Trail maps for the mountain are available at the Sabino Canyon Visitors Center (on Sabino Canyon Road), so get them before you begin your trek up the mountain.

- Some of the campgrounds have daily fees, and all have a 14-day stay limit.

- Most important, keep our precious environment clean and undisturbed—a good thing to remember no matter where you're camping.

Molino Basin is the first of several campgrounds on Mount Lemmon operated by the Catalina Ranger District of the Coronado National Forest. About 10 miles up the highway from Tucson, it nests in a deep V between two granite ridges. This is a great area to get the kids treasure hunting for "jewels"—the sandy washes in this basin composed of metamorphosed granite are rich in silvery mica flakes and tiny burgundy "sand rubies," better known as garnets. The area offers great scenic views, rock climbing, and hiking. You'll even spot a few saguaros, which generally don't grow above 3,500 feet.

The Catalina Highway (or Mount Lemmon Highway) begins at Tanque Verde Road about 5 miles east of Sabino Canyon Road. In late 1997 the USDA Forest Service instituted a recreational fee for the Santa Catalina Mountains, which includes Mount Lemmon. If you're camping or otherwise recreating, it costs $5 a day per vehicle, $10 a week, or $20 for an annual pass; often in addition to your campground fees. You can purchase passes at the booth at Milepost 5.5 just before Molino Basin 24 hours a day, 7 days a week. Other places to buy the Mount Lemmon passes are the Tucson Convention & Visitors Bureau in La Placita Village downtown and several Walgreens, Chevron gas stations, and CVS drugstores along E. Tanque Verde Road. Visit www.fs.fed.us/r3/coronado/forest/passes/fees/purchase_locations.shtml.

The campground covers 65 acres and has over 30 sites for tents and RVs up to 22 feet for a daily fee of $10, plus you must have a Mountain Pass ($5) to access certain areas. Check with the fee station at Milepost 5.1. There are restrooms but little else, so be sure to have drinking water on hand. Campsites cannot be reserved in advance, but Molino does have a reservable group site. Go to www.recreation.gov to make a reservation.

Just 2 miles north of Molino, you'll find the Gordon Hirabayashi area. Formerly an internment camp for Japanese Americans, who helped build the Mount Lemmon Highway during their captivity, this site has 12 units with restrooms but no hookups or water for a $10 per vehicle nightly rate. This area is open year-round. Nearby you'll find an interpretive nature trail with photos and remnants of the old camp.

GENERAL HITCHCOCK

At Milepost 12 and an altitude of 6,000 feet, General Hitchcock is the smallest Mount Lemmon campground; open year-round. The 11 picturesque campsites are not recommended for RVs. Fees are $10 a day but can't be reserved in advance. There are restrooms but no water, showers, or hookups.

ROSE CANYON

If the idea of lakeside camping and casting for your dinner appeals to you, this is the campground to choose. Only about a block from the campground, the 7-acre Rose Canyon Lake is stocked with several varieties of trout and surrounded by tall green pines. The campground is at Milepost 17.2, with paved loops winding through a number of campground sections and ending at the lake's parking lot. It's only open

from mid-April to mid-October, and this oasis at 7,100 feet is very popular with Tucsonans escaping summer's heat. Campsites for tents and RVs number 74. You'll find wheelchair-accessible restrooms and water but no showers, no hookups, and no RVs longer than 22 feet. There is a per-day rate on a first-come, first-served basis. A 1-day-use group site can be reserved by calling (877) 444-6777.

> **i** Dr. Gordon Hirabayashi was one of only three Japanese Americans to challenge the constitutionality of internment and a curfew imposed on Japanese American citizens. Convicted by the US Supreme Court, he served his sentence at an internment camp in the Coronado National Forest doing hard labor. Ultimately his conviction was overturned, and in 1999 the Coronado National Forest named a new recreation site at the old internment camp after its most famous inmate to honor him and other resisters of conscience who were imprisoned there.

SPENCER CANYON

The highest of the mountain's campsites is at Milepost 21.7 at an elevation of 8,000 feet and is only open mid-April to mid-October. It has 60 campsites for tents and RVs shorter than 22 feet, restrooms, and water but no hookups or showers. The fee is $18 a day, first-come, first-served, no reservations.

The campground is laid out in 4 levels, connected by all-weather roads. Keep in mind that activity at this altitude can be a real strain for lowlanders and confirmed couch potatoes. But if hiking and rock climbing are not your cup of tea, the village of Summerhaven is nearby, along with a few shops, restaurants, and probably a cup of tea that *will* suit you.

✳PATAGONIA LAKE STATE PARK
Highway 82, Patagonia
(520) 287-6965
www.patagonia-lake.com

Patagonia Lake, not far from Arizona's southern border, offers fun on the water as well as a nicely laid-out campground. The 265-acre lake features fishing, boating, a sandy beach, a store, a marina with boat rentals, and even a high pedestrian bridge with a scenic view. Although rainbow trout are stocked in the lake in winter, you're more likely to hook bass, sunfish, crappies, and catfish in this warmwater fishery. The lake also offers southern Arizona campers a rare treat—waterskiing and windsurfing are allowed here (but only during summer and only on weekdays). As you might guess, Patagonia Lake is a very popular spot for water-deprived folks in this area.

Situated on one of the gentle slopes above the lake, the year-round campground has picnic areas, restrooms, and wheelchair-accessible showers. Of the 118 campsites, 34 have hookups and 12 are boat accessible only. Fees vary, the RV limit is 35 feet, and there is a maximum stay of 14 days. Campsites cannot be reserved in advance.

To get here from Tucson, take I-10 east to Highway 83, go south to Highway 82, and continue south 7 miles past the town of Patagonia. Nearby is Patagonia-Sonoita Creek Preserve, a 312-acre wildlife sanctuary of The Nature Conservancy that's open to the public. The border town of Nogales, Mexico, is only about 40 minutes away.

PEPPERSAUCE
FR 38, Oracle
(520) 749-8700
www.fs.fed.us/r3/coronado/forest/
recreation/camping/sites/peppersauce
.shtml

This is a superb campground for several reasons, not the least of which is the story (or perhaps tall tale) of how its name originated. The story goes that prospector Alex McKay, who was hooked on pepper sauce—hot sauce—lost a bottle of it in the wash and was upset for the rest of his days at the campsite. And whether you believe that or not, once you see this spot you will surely believe that it's a sight to behold.

Start out in Oracle, which is about 20 miles north of Tucson, and head east-southeast on Mount Lemmon Road, or FR 38. (This is the north side of the Catalinas, not the more famous and traversed Mount Lemmon Highway that goes from Tucson to Mount Lemmon.) After the pavement ends, you'll pass through dry desert laden with ocotillo, cholla, and barrel cacti for about 5 miles. Suddenly you'll top out on a hill, and a few hundred yards below you'll gaze upon a grove of giant sycamores shading the Peppersauce Campground. The roots of this giant green canopy are nourished from Peppersauce Springs, a short distance up the wash, or arroyo, from the campground. This cool retreat from the surrounding heat makes for a great summer camp experience, but it is open all year. It probably comes as no surprise that Peppersauce is a very popular spot.

Peppersauce is operated by the Catalina Ranger District of the Coronado National Forest. There are 19 campsites with tables and fire grills at a daily rate of $10 per vehicle. Trailers are not recommended. Restrooms and water are available but hookups are not, and the stay limit is 14 days. A group campsite with maximum capacity of 10 cars and up to 35 people is also available at Peppersauce for $50 a night. Tents and cars only, no RVs. You can make a reservation by calling (877) 444-6777 or visiting www .recreation.gov.

ℹ️ Looking for top-notch camping gear? Head to Summit Hut for a great selection. Call (800) 499-8696 for locations.

PICACHO PEAK STATE PARK
I-10, exit 219, Picacho
(520) 466-3183
www.azstateparks.com/parks/PIPE/index
.html
Once you see the rocky pinnacle 40 miles north of Tucson known as Picacho Peak, you'll always recognize its dramatic and distinct shape from afar. Along its slope is a state park of the same name. (And speaking of names, the word *peak* could easily have been left out, since that's what *picacho* means in Spanish.) Rising 1,500 feet above the desert floor, the peak is thought to be 22 million years old—four times as old as the Grand Canyon. It is also the site of the westernmost battle of the Civil War, fought between a dozen Union and 16 Confederate soldiers. Rains permitting, in mid-March the

park explodes with traffic-stopping displays of wildflowers—acres of golden, purple, and magenta blooms. Within the 4,000-acre park are 7 miles of hiking trails and a scenic drive.

Rest assured that, even though Picacho borders the very busy I-10 connecting Phoenix and Tucson, the campground is far enough removed—about 2 miles west of the freeway—that noise doesn't intrude. Campers have access to 86 electric sites, and the maximum stay is 14 nights. The year-round campground has a visitor center with restrooms and a gift shop. The city of Casa Grande is about 20 minutes away if you have the unstoppable urge to outlet shop or if you need any major services or supplies. At only 2,000 feet, camping is comfortable here in winter but a bit warm in summer.

Drive west from Tucson on I-10 about 40 miles to exit 219—you can't miss it.

✳VOYAGER RV RESORT
8701 S. Kolb Rd.
(520) 574-5000, (800) 424-9191
www.voyagerrv.com
Located on the far southeast side, this RV resort park might as well be a city. With over 1,576 spaces, 150 acres, 24-hour security, a 9-hole golf course, 2 heated pools, saunas, spas, classes, and entertainment, many people make this their permanent home. Daily, weekly, monthly, and annual rates are available.

RESTAURANTS

One of the great things about Tucson is the wide variety of restaurants you'll find here, from cowboy steak houses and retro diners to award-winning resort fare and ethnic cuisine. Tucsonans are very proud of the great variety and quality of their restaurants. Although Sonoran Mexican food and mesquite-grilled steaks continue to play a role on the menu, visitors and residents of the Old Pueblo do not subsist on tortillas and T-bones alone.

OVERVIEW

Tucson is home to gastropubs, bistros, and cafes, Asian cuisine from pho to Thai to Malaysian, and eclectic mom-and-pops serving up ethnic delights from Bosnia, Hawaii, Jamaica, and Peru, just to name a few. Fine dining is alive and well, with continental, American, Southwestern, French, and Italian in the mix. The university area offers all sorts of possibilities including cupcakeries, sushi and Indian restaurants, brewpubs, Greek spots, coffeehouses, all-American burger joints, and pizza parlors to keep hungry students (and you) well fed for months.

Downtown is hopping with renovated historic buildings morphing into restaurants of all shapes and sizes, offering cuisines from global to Thai, steak to New York pizza.

Dress for the most part is Tucson casual—comfortable chic for upscale and resort hotels and very casual for most others.

We've divided the restaurants by cuisine, but many of them could easily be placed in more than one category. You may want to scan the entire chapter to get a full view of what the area has to offer. Not included in these pages are national restaurant chains, which are rapidly moving into town.

Along with descriptions of the food and the ambience of the establishment, we've added information on the history of the eatery or the building in which it is housed. We'll also advise you about parking for places near the university or downtown, and the necessity for reservations, and we'll recommend signature dishes or favorite entrees. Bon appétit!

Also, please note that many restaurants in town have a different menu and different hours during summer (some even close for a couple of weeks in summer).

Price Code

The following dollar-sign codes indicate what you will pay for a dinner for two, excluding appetizers, cocktails, dessert, tips, and taxes. You can assume that most restaurants take major credit cards; we only make note of those that do not.

$	Less than $15
$$	$15 to $30
$$$	$30 to $50
$$$$	More than $50

Lani's Luau, Eclectic Eats, $, 81

Le Buzz Caffe, Coffee & Tea Houses, $, 77

Le Rendez-vous, French, $$$, 84

Lil Abner's Steakhouse, Steak Houses, $$$, 96

Lindy's Diner on 4th, Burgers, Sandwiches & Such, $, 73

Little Anthony's Diner, All-American, $$, 69

Lodge on the Desert, Contemporary, $$, 80

Luxor Cafe, Greek & Middle Eastern, $$, 85

Mama's Pizza and Heros, Pizza, $, 94

Mariscos Chihuahua, Seafood, $$, 95

Maynards Market and Kitchen, Fine Dining/Get It & Go, $–$$, 83, 84

McMahon's Prime Steakhouse, Steak Houses, $$$, 96

Melt. A Sandwich Joint, Burgers, Sandwiches & Such, $, 73

Metropolitan Grill, Contemporary, $$, 80

Miguel's at La Posada, Mexican/Latin, $$$, 92

Mi Nidito Cafe, Mexican/Latin, $$, 92

New Delhi Palace, Indian, $$, 87

Nimbus Brewery, Breweries & Brewpubs, $, 71

Noblehops Gastropub, Breweries & Brewpubs, $$, 71

Om Modern Asian Kitchen, Asian, $$, 70

Opa!, Greek & Middle Eastern, $, 86

Pasco Kitchen & Lounge, Cafes & Bistros, $$, 76

Pat's Drive In, Burgers, Sandwiches & Such, $, 73

Pinnacle Peak Steakhouse, Steak Houses, $$, 96

Primo, Italian, $$$–$$$$, 88

Raging Sage, Coffee & Tea Houses, $, 77

Rincon Market, Get It & Go, $$, 84

Rosa's, Mexican/Latin, $$, 92

Sabine's Cafe Passe, Coffee & Tea Houses, $, 78

Saffron Indian Bistro, Indian, $, 87

Sakura, Asian, $$$, 70

Sam Hughes Place Championship Dining, Steak Houses, $$, 97

Sauce, Pizza, $, 94

The Sausage Deli, Burgers, Sandwiches & Such, $, 73

Seri Melaka, Asian, $$, 70

Seven Cups Tea Room, Coffee & Tea Houses, $, 78

Taqueria Pico de Gallo, Mexican/Latin, $, 93

Tasteful Kitchen, Healthy, Vegetarian & Alternative, $$, 87

Tavolino, Italian, $$, 88

Tohono Chul Tearoom, Cafes & Bistros, $$, 76

Tony's Italian Style Deli, Butcher Shop, & Restaurant, Get It & Go, $, 85

Tucson McGraw's Cantina and Steak House, Steak Houses, $$, 97

Vila Thai Fine Dining, Asian, $$, 71

Vivace Restaurant, Italian, $$$, 89

Whole Foods Market, Get It & Go, $$, 85

Yoshimatsu Healthy Japanese Food, Healthy, Vegetarian & Alternative, $, 87

Zachary's, Pizza, $, 94

Zemam's, Eclectic Eats, $, 81

Zin Burger Wine and Burger Bar, Burgers, Sandwiches & Such, $$, 74

ALL-AMERICAN

BOBO'S $
2938 E. Grant Rd.
(520) 326-6163
www.bobostucson.com
It ain't fancy, just home cooking in a tiny roadside diner, but it sure is good. Especially breakfast, which is served all day. If you're in the mood for real home fries, fresh eggs over easy, and a slab of ham, this is the place for you. Delicious pancakes are bigger than your head—try the blueberry banana. (*NOTE:* Real maple syrup lovers should bring their own.) Hot coffee and the daily paper will start your day off right. Open every day for breakfast and lunch until 2 p.m.

i Both *Tucson Lifestyle* and *Tucson Guide* publish handy free dining guides throughout the year. You'll find them scattered around town at restaurants, shops, and at the Metropolitan Tucson Convention & Visitors Bureau.

✳GRILL $
100 E. Congress St.
(520) 623-7621
The Grill is a favorite hangout for the young, artsy downtown crowd. The interior is a honest-to-goodness old-fashioned diner, complete with a semicircular counter and booths, an eclectic menu, and 24-hour service. You can get typical diner fare, such as fluffy pancakes, terrific burgers, and American tuna melts and the best malted milkshake in town, but the Grill is much more than a diner. You'll find pastas, vegan and vegetarian specialties, and funky sandwiches here to go with the hipster downtown crowd. And ask about the Haystack!

Downtown parking is limited, but you can use either metered spaces (free on weekends) or one of several pay lots within walking distance.

GUS BALON'S $
6027 E. 22nd St.
(520) 747-7788
If you're looking for honest, all-American food, Gus Balon's is the place. All the breads are homemade, the eggs are fried in butter, and every day more than 20 homemade pies are on the menu. Kids can enjoy a jelly omelet or a good ole pb&j sandwich, but *the* thing to order here are the humongous homemade cinnamon rolls, made from scratch daily.

Grown-ups might like to try a breakfast special or a baked ham sandwich. This homey local breakfast favorite even garnered a mention in famous food writers Jane and Michael Stern's book *Roadfood: The Coast to Coast Guide to 800 of the Best Barbeque Joints, Lobster Shacks, Ice Cream Parlors, and Highway Diners and Much, Much More.*

Gus's is open until 3 p.m.; closed on Sunday.

HUNGRY FOX RESTAURANT $
4637 E. Broadway Blvd.
(520) 326-2835
www.thehungryfox.com
The Hungry Fox looks like a cozy country kitchen, with antiques and reproduction pieces on high shelves that run along the walls. The room is bright and cheerful, just like the waitstaff.

Eggs are the things to order here. Boiled, fried, poached, scrambled, basted—you name it and they can do it. They are all double yolked, so you get two, two, two eggs in one! You can read all about it on the menu, where a helpful guide, "How eggs are prepared and how to order them," explains all the options.

Open for breakfast and lunch 7 days a week, the Hungry Fox closes at 2 p.m.

LITTLE ANTHONY'S DINER $$
7010 E. Broadway Blvd.
(520) 296-0456
www.littleanthonysdiner.com
Little Anthony's is Tucson's original retro diner. This '50s-style eatery is located at the rear of the Gaslight Theatre, another entity owned by the same family (see the Arts & Culture chapter), and is relatively easy to find.

There will be no surprises here: big juicy burgers (the names are rock 'n' roll related), tasty sandwiches, thick shakes and malts, and even wet fries (french fries served with brown gravy on the side). Pizza, actually Grandma Tony's pizza, another restaurant owned by the same folks, rounds out the menu. If these standards don't appeal, you can always order from the section of the menu titled "Things Elvis Wouldn't Eat"; you'll have to stop in to see just what those things are!

The waitstaff is young and friendly, with plenty of energy. Kids get a kick out of the DJ spinning those Golden Oldies at dinnertime while the grown-ups wax nostalgic over all the '50s memorabilia hanging on the walls.

It's a great place to take the kids for a relatively quick something-for-everybody meal. Little Anthony's is open for lunch and dinner on weekdays and adds a breakfast shift on Sat and Sun.

ASIAN

AN DEL SOL $$
5655 W. Valencia Rd. (in Casino del Sol)
(520) 838-7177
www.casinodelsol.com/andelsol
It may seem strange to go to a casino for sushi, but this upscale, clean space offers one of the biggest selections in town along with an extensive Chinese dinner menu. The restaurant is one of several popular Asian restaurants owned by local entrepreneur Qwang C. An. Sushi lovers who have traveled far and wide for this delicacy claim Mr. An has a winner here, too. You'll find standard sushi and sashimi along with unusual fusion sushi prepared expertly and quickly at the sushi bar. Unusual offerings include the ahi tuna stacked with mozzarella and tomatoes, and the White Mountains, a unique combination of escolar tuna, blue cheese, and wasabi wrapped in thinly sliced beets. Chinese selections include the familiar chop suey, pan-fried noodles, chow mein, and fried rice, along with Peking and pressed duck. Open daily.

COM TAM THUAN KIEU
VIETNAMESE RESTAURANT $
1990 W. Orange Grove Rd.
(520) 638-7912
There are over 211 entree and appetizer choices at this family-friendly restaurant right next to the wonderful Lee Lee Asian Market (see the Shopping chapter). The decor is minimal here but the food is plentiful, fresh, and delectable. Most people order the traditional pho soups, fresh spring rolls, and amazing iced coffee with sweetened condensed milk, but go off the beaten path and select some of the more unusual Vietnamese specialties available here. The crepe appetizer is big enough for two. A thin, crisp,

coconutty shell is studded with scallions and filled with bean sprouts, shrimp, and thinly sliced beef and served with fresh mint and lettuce leaves. Grab a handful of bright green chopsticks from the handy container right on the table and dig in. Other interesting choices include broken-rice dishes and vermicelli bowls. Ask your server or the friendly diners at the next table for advice. Open daily.

✳GINZA SUSHI $$
5425 N. Kolb Rd.
(520) 529-8877
www.ginzatucson.com

Up in the foothills of the Catalina Mountains, Ginza puts out some super sushi and other Japanese specialties. Dark paneling, soothing music, and a great sushi bar helmed by owner Jun Arai make this the go-to sushi destination. Lunch features bento boxes and sashimi specials for reasonable prices, great with a tall glass of iced matcha green tea. Unusual offerings include *yamamoito,* a starchy mountain potato served shaved and icy cold, and *nattou,* the fermented sticky soybeans that are definitely an acquired taste for non–Japanese nationals. The fish here is super fresh, and Jun San (born in Nagano, Japan) is a master at slicing them just right for his signature rolls, sashimi platters, and sushi specials (check the board for new ones daily). Open for lunch Tues through Sat, dinner Mon through Sat.

OM MODERN ASIAN KITCHEN $$
1765 E. River Rd.
(520) 299-7815
www.om-az.com

You may see other Oms around the country, but this is Tucson's own Om! Sleek and contemporary, Om offers global Asian cuisine with a modern twist. You'll find pulled-pork spring rolls, lamb samosas, and sesame fries, along with sushi on the appetizer menu. Soups include a familiar miso alongside a red curry sweet potato bisque. Hunan black pepper shrimp come with an Asian-style couscous, while pork sliders are served with a side of kimchi slaw. It's all mixed up here, but it works. Leave room for dessert—hot pineapple cheesecake is a winner. Open daily for lunch and dinner.

SAKURA $$$
6534 E. Tanque Verde Rd.
(520) 298-7777
www.sakuratucson.com

You'll find an interesting combination at Sakura, which is both a sushi bar/teppan-style restaurant and a sports bar. The rooms are separate, but whichever side you choose, we're sure you'll enjoy yourself.

Decorated in traditional Japanese style, the dining rooms offer a show with your dinner: The trained chefs dazzle diners with flashing knives and fire right at the table as they prepare fresh seafood or New York steak teppan-style dinners. Kids will enjoy the show. Prices here are fairly steep, and the show sometimes is better than the food.

The sports bar is a favorite with Eastsiders, offering TVs, dining, and dancing. Open daily.

SERI MELAKA $$
6133 E. Broadway
(520) 747-7811
www.serimelaka.com

If you want to experience Malaysian cuisine, this is the place to come. Warm and welcoming, and family run, this is where you'll find terrific Malay dishes alongside familiar Chinese fare. Try the chili crab, a traditional

Malay favorite. Giant king crab legs (or whole Dungeness crabs if you call 48 hours in advance) are deep-fried and added to a magnificent sauce made with loads of ginger, garlic, and chilies. The tapioca dessert, *buburchacha*, is a unique dish made with giant tapioca pearls, sweet potato, corn, and coconut milk. Try it.

VILA THAI FINE DINING $$
9 E. Congress Ave.
(520) 882-8143
www.vilathai.com
Owner Vila Jarrell is passionate about her food and Thai culture and has poured her heart and soul into her restaurant. An outdoor alley that leads into the space has been converted into a super lounge complete with comfy couches, a bar, and live music. It's a great place to try starters, unusual mixed drinks, and Thai wines only available here. Inside, the slightly cramped quarters are packed with fans of Vila's signature cuisine—large portions of hot and spicy Thai favorites. The winner here is smoky pad thai with fresh noodles. Numerous special events, wine tastings, and art and musical evenings take place weekly. Parking can be tricky here, but metered parking is free after 5 p.m. and several paid garages are in the area. Open 7 days a week.

BREWERIES & BREWPUBS

GENTLE BEN'S BREWING CO. $$
865 E. University Blvd.
(520) 624-4177
www.gentlebens.com
Located in the heart of the university area, Gentle Ben's is just 2 blocks from the main gate. A downstairs beer garden and an upstairs deck complete with fountains and flowering vines make it a great spot for a bite and a beer.

The restaurant offers great salads, several different burgers, and great brewhouse sandwiches. You'll also find pasta and numerous Southwest specialties.

While you wait for your meal, enjoy a stroll past the glass-enclosed vats of the brews ranging from Red Cat Amber Ale to Tucson Blonde. Some beers are seasonal, and the menu explains each type of beer.

Parking is at a premium. Note that the metered angle parking along the 3 blocks in this area is back-in only!

NIMBUS BREWERY $
3850 E. 44th St.
(520) 745-9175
www.nimbusbeer.com
Ben Franklin once said, "Beer is living proof that God loves us," and the owners of Nimbus Brewery have adopted this philosophy (the quote is part of their logo).

In a warehouse district off S. Palo Verde Road, Nimbus Brewery is a little tricky to find: On 44th Street, head east off of Palo Verde Road and then continue to where 44th Street dead-ends. There, in a large converted warehouse, you'll find the brewery. The atmosphere is very casual.

Food is limited to appetizers, burgers, and sandwiches, which are served at lunch and dinner daily. Live music is featured on weekends. Nimbus beers, which are brewed in small 10-gallon batches, are the only local brews sold at other beer parlors.

✳NOBLEHOPS GASTROPUB $$
1335 W. Lambert Ln.
(520) 797-4677
http://noblehopspub.com

A huge bar (no surprise!) anchors this hip gastropub, offering 28 beers on tap and over 150 unique bottled beers sourced from local breweries and funky underground bottlers. It all comes to the taps from a windowed keg room filled with barrels. But it's not just about the suds here; the food is top-notch and way above typical brewpub fare. You can choose from outdoor patios, a lounge, and a private dining room, and, of course, you can always eat at the bar. Open daily.

BURGERS, SANDWICHES & SUCH

✳BEYOND BREAD $
3026 N. Campbell Rd.
(520) 322-9965
www.beyondbread.com

Fantastic sandwiches, pastries, cookies, and bread fill this busy cafe and bakery. Daily specials like fresh tomato, basil, and mozzarella on a focaccia; a huge 3-layer turkey club made with real turkey; and ripe brie and rare roast beef on a baguette are only a few of the more than 20 sandwich choices. There's also soup served right in a bread bowl if you have a hearty appetite, and hot breakfast items like cinnamon raisin French toast. The sandwiches are fresh and enormous, the coffee is freshly brewed, and the place is packed. The good news is that you can sample the bread, served alongside a crock of sweet butter, while you wait. Lines are out the door at lunch, so plan accordingly. Additional locations are at 6260 E. Speedway Blvd., Monterey Village (520-747-7477), and 421 W. Ina Rd. (520-461-1111).

BOB DOBBS $
2501 E. 6th St.
(520) 325-3767
www.bobdobs.net

You won't find any ads for Bob Dobbs. One of Tucson's best-kept secrets, this local sports bar is reputed to have the best burger in town—the Bob Burger. A huge bun with two 4-ounce patties (made with a special mix of garlic, Worcestershire, and soy), it's topped with cheddar and comes with tomato and lettuce on the side. Bob's is right next to Rincon Market on 6th Street.

EEGEE'S $
21 locations
www.eegees.com

The story behind eegee's is the American dream come true. In the early '70s, two college students were looking for a way to earn some money when one of them remembered the Italian ices he had loved as a child in New York City. They came up with a recipe for lemon ice, sold the ices from a used vending truck, and the rest, as they say, is history.

The lemon ices remain the mainstay of the menu (there's nothing like an ice-cold eegee's on a hot summer's day). Other flavors are offered monthly. Hot and cold sandwiches, called grinders, are available as well as salads. Open for lunch and dinner daily, there are 21 eegee's locations throughout the Tucson area.

FROGS ORGANIC BAKERY $
7109 N. Oracle Rd.
(520) 229-2124
www.frogsorganicbakery.com

Five-star chef Jean-Luc Labat, a native of France, makes super sandwiches using homemade organic breads made right in the on-site bakery. You can build your own or go for the classic croque monsieur, a melty mouthful of thinly sliced ham, creamy béchamel, and nutty Emmental cheese on pain de miel. Warm open-faced sandwiches are for hearty appetites; made on organic whole-wheat bread, they come piled with roasted chicken, sautéed veggies, or pastrami. You can even request gluten-free bread for a nominal extra charge. If you want to make your own sandwich at home, get a batch of buttery croissants or a crusty artisan bread to go. If you want dessert, the choices are mouthwatering: pastries, pies, tarts, cakes—it's all here! Breakfast and lunch are served, too. Closed Mon.

LINDY'S DINER ON 4TH $
431 N. 4th Ave.
(520) 207-2384
www.lo4th.com

Don't be afraid. Lindy's may look a little scary but the burgers are worth it, so go on in. Big and super juicy, they are grilled to perfection. Get the Lindy's original, just meat, cheddar, lettuce, tomato, and Lindy's special sauce. That's all you need. Gluttons can go for the triple Lindy: three layers of beef plus bacon, onion rings, fried eggs, lettuce, tomato, onion, mayo, mustard, and ketchup. Are you game? Adam Richman of television's *Man v. Food* took it on and won. See how you do. Open daily.

MELT. A SANDWICH JOINT $
5056 E. Broadway
(520) 326-6358
www.melttucson.com

The space may be small but the sandwiches here are big—and tasty. Especially the signature Philly cheesesteak. Thin-sliced rib eye steak, grilled onions, peppers, and gooey American cheese are all stuffed into an Italian roll. What's not to like? The owner here is from Philly, so he should know. There are 21 (yes, 21!) other sandwich choices here. There's even one for breakfast. Lunch never looked so good. Open Mon through Sat. P.S.: A cupcake bakery is right next door in case you're hungry for dessert.

There are lots of terrific farmers' markets all over town where you'll find fresh produce, farm eggs, local honey, grass-fed beef, and local specialties ranging from emu oil to jams, breads, cakes, and salsas—depending on who's there. For listings see the weekend "Caliente" section of the *Arizona Daily Star*.

PAT'S DRIVE IN $
N. Grande Avenue at W. Niagara Street
1202 W. Niagara St.
(520) 624-0891

Pat's chilidogs are known citywide, especially by those folks who were teenagers in Tucson during the '50s and '60s. It was a great place to take a date after a school dance or a movie. Today Pat's still serves inexpensive, good food for lunch and dinner daily. Great care is taken to ensure customers get the kind of food they remember. And just because the dogs are the highlight here, don't shun Pat's burgers, fries, or onion rings. All have been named favorites in area polls year after year. Parking can be tricky. There are a few spaces right on the lot, or you can try parking on a side street.

THE SAUSAGE DELI $
2334 N. 1st Ave.
(520) 623-8182
www.sausagedeli.com

RESTAURANTS

University students and faculty flock to this tiny eatery for some of its most unusual sandwiches, made with quality cold cuts, cheeses, and breads (but no sausage). The Susie Sorority is turkey with Havarti on whole wheat with tons of mayo, tomato, and sprouts; the Artichoke Reuben uses chokes instead of sauerkraut to top off the hot corned beef. The regular Reuben is called the Reuben Goldburger. All sandwiches can be served submarine style. Lunch specials come with a choice of chips or one of the deli salads. Beer, sodas, juices, tea, and lemonade are available. Party subs come as long as 3 feet. Sausage Deli is open Mon through Sat from 10 a.m. to 5 p.m.

**ZIN BURGER WINE AND
  BURGER BAR** $$
1865 E. River Rd.
(520) 299-7799
www.foxrestaurantconcepts.com/
zinburger.html

Are you a burger fan? If you are, rush over to Zin Burger, *the* place in town for upscale burgers and fries. With lines out the door, you'll have to plan your evening—they don't take reservations. The Kobe burger, a zinfully tender burger topped with Vermont cheddar and wild mushrooms, is to die for. Hand-cut fries will cost you extra, but they're worth it, hot and crispy. Feel like gilding the lily? Double truffle fries served with truffle aioli and truffle oil will do it. Signature cocktails, 20 wines by the glass, and 12 beer selections will make everything go down easy. Leave room for dessert—shakes, floats, banana cream pie, and the famous Bars of Zin will definitely take you over the edge. Another location is at 6390 E. Grant Rd. (520-298-2020).

CAFES & BISTROS

THE ABBEY EAT + DRINK $$
6960 E. Sunrise Dr.
(520) 299-3132
www.theabbeytucson.com

Looking for a casual spot with great views of the Catalina Mountains? The Abbey is the place to go. This popular neighborhood restaurant offers a cozy interior, patio dining, and an outdoor bar. The menu features comfort foods with an extra punch: The juicy burger comes on an English muffin with homemade onion jam, turkey pot pie arrives in its own cast-iron skillet, and the grilled cheese features whipped brie and pesto—you get the idea. The ambience is welcoming and kid friendly. Lots of foothills families and well-heeled couples hang out here for great food and camaraderie. Open Tues through Sun for dinner and happy hour.

CAFE À LA C'ART $
150 N. Main St.
(520) 628-8533
www.cafealacarttucson.com

Located in the lovely courtyard at the Tucson Museum of Art, this delightful cafe offers great salads, sandwiches, and homemade pastries. You can eat on the patio or inside. Try the popular spinach salad or the tasty salmon club on focaccia with aioli. Open Mon through Fri from 11 a.m. to 3 p.m. and select Sundays for special museum events.

CAFFE MILANO $
47 W. Congress St.
(520) 628-1601
www.caffemilano.us

For an authentic taste of Italy, head here. Run by real Italians from Milano, this cozy cafe with bistro tables is a great spot for lunch or dinner. Try the grilled focaccia sandwiches filled with real imported proscuitto, hand-made mozzarella, and pesto. There are lots of other lunch choices here, along with a great selection of Italian fashion and lifestyle magazines. Dinner options include an authentic lasagna Bolognese and veal *scaloppine di vitello al limone. Mangia!*

Don't miss the wonderful cold espresso poured over vanilla ice cream for dessert. Open for lunch Mon through Fri and dinner Thurs through Sat.

Want a great bistro lunch without the price tag? Make a reservation at Al Bistro. Hidden within the Art Institute of Tucson, this little gem with only 36 seats is the working restaurant for Al's culinary students. With an ever- changing menu, the students work both the front and the back of the house in full view through the big window into the kitchen. You'll see what it's really like to work the line in this hands-on teaching environment. The food is super, the students are engaging, and the price is right—just over $10 gets you a 3-course tasting menu. Reservations are critical; the bistro is only open Tues through Thurs from 11:30 a.m. to 12:30 a.m. when classes are in session. Call (520) 318-2726 to make a reservation.

THE CUP $$
Hotel Congress
311 E. Congress St.
(520) 798-1618
www.hotelcongress.com

For a true sense of downtown Tucson, spend an hour or so at The Cup. Whether it's for breakfast, lunch, or dinner, you will see the full spectrum of the downtown scene, from the city movers and shakers to those who are just passing through.

Featured on the Food Network, this cozy eclectic cafe serves up a fine and feisty menu for breakfast, lunch, tea, and dinner. Looking for a hearty breakfast? Try Eggs and Gunpowder and you'll get a bowl filled with roasted red potatoes, topped with 2 eggs, and crowned with chorizo and jack cheese. Add a side order of mouth-tingling spicy pinto beans. The lunch menu offers a variety of salads, pasta, tofu, and Mexican-style dishes, while dinner spans the culinary globe with quesadillas and nachos, chicken satay, and *katmandu*—seasonal vegetables in a rich banana curry, served with coconut quinoa and garnished with banana chips and black sesame seeds. Don't miss the homemade pies and super chocolate chip cookies for dessert.

Parking is typical of downtown—some metered spots, a few pay lots, and very few spaces in back of the building.

✳THE DISH $$
3131 E. 1st St.
(520) 326-1714
www.dishbistro.com

Also a Food Network pick, The Dish is an elegant, sophisticated restaurant serving up delicious gourmet food. Hard to find, it's located inside the Rum Runner Wine and Cheese Company, Tucson's largest wine store. (See the Shopping chapter.)

The menu is divided into Small Dishes, Green Dishes, Deep Dishes, and Big Dishes. Several evening specialties always include a fresh fish and a meat entree as well as a soup of the day. And here's an Insiders' tip: Sit at the lovely bar and you can order a giant bowl of mussels and a glass of wine for only $11.50 (Tues, Wed, and Thurs only).

Dinner is served Tues through Sat, and reservations are strongly suggested.

HUB RESTAURANT AND ICE CREAMERY $$
266 E. Congress St.
(520) 207-8201
www.hubdowntown.com

Soaring ceilings, brick walls, and funky lighting make this a downtown hot spot. Once home to a taxi company, the space is open, airy, and fun (ask about the ship's ropes on the walls). A comfort-food menu offers corned beef sandwiches, burgers, wings, salads, and entrees like roast pork and roast chicken with super roasted fingerling potatoes. The main thing to order here is the ice cream—especially the addictive salty caramel in a cone or cup (three scoops, please!). Open daily for lunch and dinner.

PASCO KITCHEN & LOUNGE $$
820 E. University Blvd.
(520) 882-8013
http://pascokitchen.com

Pasco is a culinary oasis located on busy University Boulevard amid breweries and pizza joints. The best seats in the house are on the side patios around the quiet, peaceful Geronimo Plaza. The small menu features well-thought-out and -executed dishes all the way from appetizer to dessert. Most ingredients are locally sourced, including grass-fed meats. The Asian salad is a tasty toss of mizuna greens, fresh orange segments and crunchy wontons with a toasty sesame dressing. Most of the menu items are offered in half portions so you can try lots of things. Leave room for dessert, because the chocolate-filled beignets should not be missed. Pasco attracts a pre- and post-theater crowd and lots of foodies from all over town.

TOHONO CHUL TEAROOM $$
Tohono Chul Park
7366 N. Paseo Del Norte
(520) 797-1222
www.tohonochulpark.org

Sitting on the patio at Tohono Chul Tearoom, you'll forget that just a little more than a block away lies one of Tucson's busiest intersections, Ina and Oracle Roads. That's because the restaurant is set amid the quiet serenity of Tohono Chul Park, a little oasis of desert in the ever-expanding city (see the Attractions chapter).

You have a choice of 2 patios that are divided by the indoor dining area. On the larger patio you'll find views of the park and some bird-watching. The smaller patio offers the serene sounds of a trickling fountain. The menu is well balanced, including such favorites as chicken salad, quesadillas, club sandwiches, and, for dessert, sorbet and more.

Breakfast and lunch are served daily, as is tea. At tea you'll be offered a choice of teas and little teacakes, scones, and pastries. After your meal, take a minute to browse through the gift shop, where you'll find hundreds of handcrafted and imported items.

COFFEE & TEA HOUSES

BENTLEY'S HOUSE OF COFFEE AND TEA $
730 E. Speedway Blvd.
(520) 795-0338
www.bentleyscoffeehouse.com

A popular roosting spot for UA grad students, Bentley's is a comfy place for singles or families with kids. Lots of tables, lights, and plug-ins make it great for work; a kids' play area is fun for the younger set. An eclectic menu includes bagels, salads, baked potatoes, soups, and a large selection of coffee drinks, teas, chai, and more. Bentley's is open daily until 8 p.m..

CHANTILLY TEA ROOM $
5185 N. Genematas Dr,
(520) 622-3303
www.chantillytearoom.com
Looking for some respite during a busy day? How about a cup of soothing tea and a bite to eat? Chantilly is the place. This charming little boîte offers lunch, luncheon teas, and a full afternoon tea Tues through Sat from 11 a.m. to 3 p.m. Salads, soup, quiche, and a full selection of specialty teas and desserts are offered here. Reservations are strongly suggested. Open Tues through Sat.

THE EPIC CAFE $
745 N. 4th Ave.
(520) 624-6844
www.epic-cafe.com
Located on the corner of 4th Avenue and University Boulevard, the Epic has been named the "best cafe for everything" by readers of *Tucson Weekly*.

In addition to lattes, espresso, and other coffee drinks, the Epic has an eclectic array of food from soup to nuts, with lots of vegan and vegetarian-friendly choices. Desserts are changed frequently and are always the perfect way to end a meal here.

The Epic is open 6 a.m. to midnight daily. Parking can be found on 4th Avenue or University Boulevard.

GLASS ONION CAFE $
990 W. River Rd.
(520) 293-6050
www.glassonioncafe.net
This friendly little coffeehouse is located in a shopping center on the west side of town.

If you love the Beatles, you will be at home here. Owner Jen MacDonald has papered the walls with Beatles memorabilia and it spills over onto the menu. Sandwiches, salads, drinks, and desserts are all named after Beatles songs and lyrics—see if you can recognize them all. Live music happens Thursday, Friday, and select Saturdays. Open daily.

LE BUZZ CAFFE $
9121 E. Tanque Verde Rd., # 125
(520) 749-3903
www.lebuzzcaffe.com
Without a doubt, Le Buzz has some of the best pastries in Tucson. This tiny cafe is popular with the bicycling crowd, eager to fill up on carbs after cycling Mount Lemmon, and after you eat here you'll see why. Flaky fruit tarts, buttery croissants, crumbly scones, and giant frosted cinnamon rolls are just some of the delicious goodies to come out of the kitchen. They also offer a full breakfast menu, light lunch, and dinner on select evenings. Open daily.

RAGING SAGE $
2458 N. Campbell Ave.
(520) 320-5203
www.ragingsage.com
Great coffee and terrific homemade desserts make this tiny coffee shop popular. You'll find lots of people hunched over computers or reading one of the many complimentary newspapers stacked around the place. They use only shade-grown coffee beans to brew up deep, dark, rich java. Non–coffee drinkers will find chai, herbal teas, and Italian sodas on the menu, too. The espresso brownies are the best in town. There's a tiny outdoor seating area. Open daily.

✳SABINE'S CAFE PASSE $
415 N. 4th Ave.
(520) 624-4411
www.cafepasse.com
If you're looking to rest after shopping 4th Avenue (see the Shopping chapter), head on in to Sabine's. The cozy coffee shop offers several inside seating areas (all with Wi-Fi) and 2 lovely outdoor patios. All the food here is homemade. Owner Sabine Blaes, originally from Germany, brings a passion for pastry and good coffee to 4th Avenue java lovers. Coffee drinks of all kinds and flavors are extremely popular here, as are vegan and vegetarian-friendly sandwiches and salads. Don't pass up a slab of Sabine's Black Forest cake—it's her family recipe. Open daily.

i In 1912 the Old Pueblo boasted 26 eating establishments, including hotel restaurants, cafes, Mexican restaurants, and the Canton Noodle Shop.

SEVEN CUPS TEA ROOM $
2516 E. 6th Ave.
(520) 881-4072
www.sevencups.com
Tea lovers will adore this beautiful oasis on busy 6th Avenue. The dark wood lacquer tables were hand-carved in China, and soft lighting comes from Chinese lanterns—a perfect setting to unwind from a hectic day and sip some wonderful teas. And this place is serious about tea. They import numerous varieties directly from China and prepare them in traditional ways—no dipping the tea bag in hot water here. Loose, fresh tea leaves are steeped slowly for full flavor and body by a certified Chinese tea master. Open daily.

CONTEMPORARY

DAKOTA CAFE & CATERING CO. $$
6541 E. Tanque Verde Rd.
(520) 298-7188
www.dakotacafeandcatering.com
An innovative mix of New American and Southwestern cooking makes the Dakota a favorite Trail Dust Town dining spot (see the Shopping chapter). Colorful walls are decorated with paintings by local artists, a heavy wooden bar adds a touch of the past, and the small dining room is divided into two areas, which add coziness to the modern atmosphere. You can also dine on the patio. The menu always features a fish of the day as well as appetizers, soups, and salads. The restaurant has a full bar, and espresso and desserts are prepared on the premises daily.

Dress is casual. Lunch and dinner are served Mon through Sat, brunch on Sun. Catering is available. Parking can be found on the perimeter at Trail Dust Town.

DOWNTOWN KITCHEN + COCKTAILS $$
135 S. 6th Ave.
(520) 623-7700
www.downtownkitchen.com
Award-winning master chef Janos Wilder has brought global cuisine to Tucson. Downtown (as it's referred to by insiders) features an unusual menu to match its funky decor. Casual and friendly, the well-trained servers will be happy to explain the menu and describe their favorite dishes. Be adventurous and try everything. From green papaya salad to soba noodles to peanut yam soup, you never know what's going to be on the menu. There are eclectic touches everywhere, like the funky plastic

chairs, boulder sculpture, and casual-chic colored ceramic place settings (commissioned from a local ceramics company). Much of the interior is a celebration of downtown Tucson, including the hand-painted mural behind the bar and the old fire map near the back door. Local musicians play live music on select nights.

✳FLYING V BAR AND GRILL $$$
Loews Ventana Canyon Resort
7000 N. Resort Dr.
(520) 529-7936
www.loewshotels.com
A lovely spot in the Catalina foothills, the outdoor patio looks over the golf course, waterfall, and mountains. The indoor seating area features a super bar, comfy chairs, and a fireplace. Don't miss the tableside guacamole, prepared by "guac-amolieres" who expertly fillet fresh avocados and combine them with your favorite ingredients (onion, garlic, jalapeño, tomatoes, cilantro) in a giant volcanic rock molcajete. Best eaten with the signature frozen prickly pear margarita.

47 SCOTT $$
47 N. Scott Ave.
(520) 624-4747
www.47scott.com
In case you couldn't tell, this tiny restaurant is located at 47 Scott Avenue, smack in the middle of downtown. And it's a good thing the name and the address are the same, because it's not easy to find and it's even harder to park. Scott is a little side street that you might pass by in the blink of an eye, but don't. You can shell out a few bucks to park in the paid garage right across the street from the entrance and then have a nice leisurely lunch. The narrow space is low-ceilinged and

spare with a small outdoor patio. The small menu is pleasing with a selection of comfort foods, from grass-fed burgers couched in a soft bun to pork belly and catfish. The soups are super here. Go for the bowl and not the tiny cup and enjoy seasonal freshness in every spoonful. The creamy spinach asparagus with a house-made flan is a real winner; pair it with the addictive grilled crusty bread and olive oil. Open for lunch Mon though Fri, dinner Mon through Sat.

THE GRILL AT HACIENDA
** DEL SOL** $$$$
Hacienda del Sol Guest Ranch Resort
5601 Hacienda del Sol Rd.
(520) 299-1501
www.haciendadelsol.com
Continental cuisine, elegant Spanish colonial decor, and panoramic views of Tucson and the Catalina Mountains are the hallmarks of this award-winning restaurant. The seasonal menu features classic dishes with a Southwestern flair. The chef's tasting menu will give you a terrific sense of it all. Tapas are also served at the bar and patio dining areas. And don't miss the amazing desserts.

A terrific Sunday brunch offers fresh-baked pastries, fresh fruit, freshly squeezed orange juice, and coffee or tea served with a buffet with carving stations and an omelet bar. Enjoy dinner in the dining room or at the patio bar Terraza del Sol, with its great view of the sunset. Dinner is offered daily, and brunch is served on Sun starting at 9:30 a.m.

JANOS AND J BAR $$$$
Westin La Paloma
3770 E. Sunrise Dr.
(520) 615-6100
www.janos.com

Janos and J Bar restaurants feature French-inspired Southwestern cuisine. Produce is the very freshest, purchased from Arizona farmers, and seafood is flown in from around the world, including the Sea of Cortez. The menu is constantly evolving, reflecting seasonal and local ingredients.. You never know what you'll find on the menu here, but it is guaranteed to be beautifully presented, and like nothing you've ever had before. Go with lots of friends so you can try everything on the menu, and leave room for dessert; you won't regret the calories!

Here's a tip: Janos offers a special summer tasting menu that's highly affordable and a great way to taste the terrific cuisine without breaking the bank. Watch the local paper for dates. There are also prix fixe special tasting menus available so you won't have to miss anything. Antiques, colorful walls, and high ceilings all add to the ambience.

J Bar has a lovely outdoor patio for alfresco dining, and the menu here is more casual. It's a great place for a super specialty drink; their margarita is reputed to be the best in town, and the nonalcoholic *liquado del dia* features a different blend of fruits and juices every day.

Janos and J Bar are open Mon through Sat for dinner only. Reservations are recommended.

JONATHAN'S CORK $$$
6320 E. Tanque Verde Rd.
(520) 296-1631
www.jonathanscork.com
A Tucson original, chef Jonathan Landeen has been serving up award-winning Southwestern fare since 1994. You'll find a full bar, an extensive wine list, a patio, and 5 cozy dining rooms with beehive fireplaces

and terrific Southwestern decor at Jonathan's. Specialties include ostrich served charbroiled, blackened, or sautéed with a selection of sauces; selected game meats; and grilled Baja shrimp marinated in a variety of herbs and spices. Steak and prime rib are house specialties. Don't skip the famous mud pie for dessert. Jonathan's is open daily for dinner; reservations are recommended.

LODGE ON THE DESERT $$
306 N. Alvernon Way
(520) 320-2000
www.lodgeonthedesert.com
The chef here, Ryan Clark, a graduate of the CIA, was selected by the American Culinary Foundation as one of the top junior chefs in the nation. He may look like a kid, but he's won major accolades and culinary contests around town for his consistently innovative and delicious food. Housed in the Lodge on the Desert Hotel, the intimate restaurant features New American cuisine. The menu changes seasonally. Try the sweet pepper rellenos, local peppers stuffed with shrimp and cheese, deep fried, and sauced with a chipotle coulis. They're a great twist on the standard fare. Sangria from the tap will douse the flames.The interior is charming, decorated in pseudo Mexican hacienda style with tin chandeliers and wood-beamed ceilings. Open for breakfast, lunch, and dinner.

METROPOLITAN GRILL $$
7892 N. Oracle Rd.
(520) 531-1212
www.metrorestaurants.com
This contemporary grill is owned by Metro Restaurants, a local group. It's beautifully decorated with an open feel—you'll enjoy the comfortable atmosphere as much as the food. Appetizers, entrees, pizzas, and house

specialties are wood-fired or spit-roasted. The bar features nightly specials. Cigars are sold and can be smoked in the bar area only.

Metropolitan Grill is in a shopping plaza at the corner of Oracle and Magee Roads. Open for lunch and dinner daily. Reservations are recommended for dinner.

ECLECTIC EATS

*ALISAH RESTAURANT $
5931 N. Oracle Rd.
(520) 887-5305
www.alisahrestaurant.com
What do Tucson and Bosnia have in common? Chef Alisah! He has brought his hearty home cooking to Tucson, and we say thank you. The lamb stew just may bring tears of joy to your eyes. "It reminded me of the stew my grandma used to make," said one grateful customer. There's nothing fancy here, just good, hearty food made with lots of love. Everything is made from scratch, from the cheese to the sausages to the bread. Top picks are the *cevapi* (beef sausages), *gulas* (beef goulash), and *sarma* (stuffed cabbage leaves) but the real winner is the whole roasted lamb offered as a special dinner every two weeks on Wednesday. Reservations for the lamb roast are a must; it sells out way in advance, so put Chef Alisah on your speed dial. Alisah is tucked away on the side of a building, so keep your eyes peeled for the sign. Open daily.

CEE DEE JAMAICAN KITCHEN $
1070 N. Swan Rd.
(520) 795-3400
www.jamaicanrestauranttucson.com
"Don't you worry 'bout a thing, 'cause every little thing's gonna be all right," to quote a famous Jamaican who surely must have

been singing about the food at Cee Dee. This tiny space with lots of Jamaican accents (think flags, posters) packs them in with homemade curries, fricassees, and stews. You can sit at the teeny bar, squeeze into a booth, or take out some of Tucson's finest Jamaican fare. Moist jerk chicken is bathed in herbs and spices, and curried goat is thick and rich. A slice of rum cake or a scoop of potato pudding will keep you full till the next day. Homemade drinks like sorrel punch along with Jamaican bottled and canned drinks (try the Irish Moss peanut punch) round out the menu. Open Tues through Sun for lunch and dinner.

LANI'S LUAU $
2532 S. Harrison Rd.
(520) 886-5828
www.lanisluau.webs.com
Lani's was the first to bring Hawaiian cuisine to the Old Pueblo. Serving up traditional plate lunches—heaps of food piled on a plate—Lani's has lots to choose from. Try the pork luau, pork steamed in a taro leaf, or for a taste of everything, go for the *laulau* plate filled with the most traditional Hawaiian flavors: tender, smoky marinated kalua-style pork, lomi lomi salmon, and poke (a raw fish salad) all served with rice or poi (a mash made from the taro plant). Dessert? Shaved ice, of course, or *malasadas,* Hawaii's own doughnuts. Closed Sun and Mon.

ZEMAM'S $
2731 E. Broadway
(520) 323-9928
www.zemams.com
Do you like eating with your fingers? If so, you'll love Zemam's, a tiny little Ethiopian cafe where instead of napkins, all the dishes come with a spongy bread (called *injera*)

used to sop up luscious sauces. Try the *doro wat* (spicy chicken), spinach *wat* (spinach and cottage cheese), and any number of thick meat and vegetable stews. Extremely casual; bring your own bottle. Open Tues through Sun for lunch and dinner.

i If you're an adventurous cook looking for unusual ingredients, don't miss the 17th Street Market (520-792-2588; www.seventeenthstreet market.com), a huge warehouse space full of every ethnic ingredient possible from Asian to Middle Eastern plus fresh produce, live fish, meat, and tons of frozen things you probably won't even recognize. Located at 830 E. 17th St. Call for directions; it's hidden away and tricky to find.

FINE DINING

✳ACACIA $$
3001 E. Skyline Dr.
(520) 232-0101
Acacia offers upscale dining with a fabulous view of Tucson. High above town in the foothills, Chef Albert Hall goes out of his way to procure the very freshest, pesticide-free, organic ingredients, especially the salmon—sourced all the way from Scotland. This commitment to freshness is reflected in the seasonal menu, which features well-executed classics with fresh, clean flavors. Signature dishes include house-made gnocchi with roasted red peppers, sweet peas, and Gorgonzola cream, a cioppino packed with shellfish in a rich, spicy broth, and that famous salmon, bronzed with a pecan mustard glaze. Open daily; a full brunch is offered Sat and Sun starting at 10 a.m.

ANTHONY'S IN THE CATALINAS $$$$
6440 N. Campbell Ave.
(520) 299-1771
www.anthonyscatalinas.com
A longtime Tucson favorite, Anthony's is continental dining at its best. Nestled at the base of the magnificent Santa Catalina Mountains, it offers you terrific city and mountain views. Anthony's award-winning wine list is considered one of the finest in the world, with over 1,700 selections. Start with a steaming bowl of rich French onion soup topped with melted gruyère, next a classic roast duckling. Beef lovers will swoon over the incredible chateaubriand served with a red wine sauce and a heavenly béarnaise sauce. Leave room for the ethereal soufflés. Open for dinner daily.

THE ARIZONA INN $$$
2200 E. Elm St.
(520) 325-1541
www.arizonainn.com
Casual elegance is the way to describe the ambience in the dining room at this historic inn in central Tucson. The signature breakfast is eggs Benedict and for lunch the classic chilled vichyssoise, but you can also find an eclectic mix of entrees at lunch and dinner. The weekly tasting menu offers signature dishes.

The views of the beautiful grounds are legendary. The Arizona Inn dining room is open for breakfast, lunch, and dinner daily and offers brunch on Sat and Sun.

CORE KITCHEN AND WINE BAR
AT THE RITZ-CARLTON DOVE
MOUNTAIN $$$
15000 N. Secret Springs Dr., Marana
(520) 572-3000
www.ritzcarlton.com

The ultra-luxe Ritz-Carlton resort (see Accommodations chapter) in far north Marana is home to the upscale Core. The drive is lovely, along winding roads with beautiful vistas of city and mountains. Once you arrive, the very accommodating valets will park your car and escort you down the winding staircase to Core. Choose from patio, barside, banquette, or table seating in the open dining area, decorated in shades of soothing beige with a view of the mountain. The menu features American cuisine sprinkled with Sonoran Desert influences and ingredients. For starters, a prickly pear grilled quail, accompanied by quail egg and iceberg lettuce wedge draped with blue cheese dressing. A specialty of the house is the buffalo tenderloin with mesquite noodles and a three-chili aioli. Breakfast and dinner are served daily. Reservations suggested.

GOLD $$$$
Westward Look Resort
245 E. Ina Rd.
(520) 297-1151
www.westwardlook.com
The award-winning Gold Room at Westward Look Resort has a stunning view of the Tucson valley whether you dine in or eat on the lovely outdoor terrace. Winner of *Mobil Travel Guide*'s Four-Star Award, AAA's Four-Diamond Award, and *Wine Spectator*'s Award of Excellence, the signature cuisine is a fusion of Southwestern, pan-Asian, and European culinary styles, accented with herbs and produce from the on-site chef's garden. You'll find a variety of dishes on the seasonal menu and an excellent wine list.

Well-prepared food coupled with incredible views and impeccable service make this a good choice for any occasion. Open daily for breakfast, lunch, and dinner.

MAYNARDS MARKET AND
KITCHEN $-$$
400 N. Toole Ave.
(520) 545-0577
www.maynardsmarkettucson.com
Housed in the historic railway station, Maynard's is *the* dining destination for hip food lovers. Inside dark paneling, soft lighting, and a long row of windows and draperies make for an intimate and cozy dining experience. For a more open and less formal experience, opt for the market table. Great for groups, a large pine table is surrounded by chairs in the middle of the market, featuring to-go foods and lots of local items, from soaps to grass-fed beef. The casual outdoor patio is a popular spot too; referred to as the Plaza, it's right on the train tracks and often features live music. Wherever you choose to sit, you can sample the seasonal menu. Steamed mussels with pommes frites or the artisan cheese plate are great openers. An aged New York strip, daily fresh fish, and a layered vegetable terrine baked to order are just a few of the entree choices. The wine list includes boutique and natural wines, all from the adjacent market. Open daily.

FRENCH

GHINI'S FRENCH CAFFE $
1803 E. Prince Rd.
(520) 326-9095
www.ghiniscafe.com
Ghini's offers a taste of France at a petite price. This small cafe is open for breakfast and lunch only. Ghini's has omelets, sandwiches, salads, and desserts from the adjacent bakery.

The omelets are made with 3 eggs and stuffed with such goodies as potatoes, onions, cheeses, bacon, garlic, and herbs

Provençal. Salads are fresh; both the salade nicoise and wilted spinach salad stand out among several flavorful choices. Chef Ghini's favorite is the eggs Provençal (she confesses to eating them every day). Sides include homemade pâté maison, scalloped potatoes, and French onion soup. And if you're in the mood for just a sweet treat and a latte, Ghini's is happy to accommodate you. The restaurant is open for breakfast and lunch Tues through Sun.

LE RENDEZ-VOUS $$$
3844 E. Fort Lowell Rd.
(520) 323-7373
www.lerendez-vous.com
Winning accolades from food critics, dining at Le Rendez-vous is not just a meal but a total "experience." From the impeccable service to the extensive wine list to the fabulous menu offerings, this midtown restaurant brings France to the heart of the Sonoran Desert.

Start with the escargots and then leisurely wend your way through Les Potages, Les Salades, Les Poissons, and Les Viandes to Les Desserts. All are served in a romantic, intimate atmosphere.

The front door to the restaurant is not directly on Fort Lowell Road. You can park in the attached lot. Le Rendez-vous serves lunch and dinner Tues through Fri and dinner only on weekends.

GET IT & GO

AJ'S FINE FOODS $-$$
La Encantada
2805 E. Skyline Drive
(520) 232-6380
www.ajsfinefoods.com

Upscale, expensive, and full of great food and drink, AJ's is gourmet to the max. Owned by grocery entrepreneur Eddie Basha, AJ's offers top-of-the-line meats, seafood, a wine cellar, sushi bar, and cafe—all under one roof. Don't feel like cooking? There's a huge selection of prepared entrees. Need some fancy table linens? Fresh flowers for the centerpiece? You'll find all that here and more, along with knowledgeable and helpful staff. Open daily.

MAYNARDS MARKET AND KITCHEN $-$$
400 N. Toole Ave.
(520) 545-0577
www.maynardsmarket.com
You'll find lots of foods to go along with dozens of local items, including olive oil, honey, and tamales, at this bright, airy market in the historic railway station downtown. The grab-and-go menu includes hot items like lasagna, quiche, and pot pies along with sandwiches, salads, and soups. You can even pick up a bottle of wine, all from boutique and local wineries, to sip as you sup. Open daily.

RINCON MARKET $$
2513 E. 6th St.
(520) 327-6653
www.rinconmarket.com
The Rincon Market has been a neighborhood grocery store since 1928. In addition to groceries, Rincon Market has a salad bar, deli sandwiches, baked goods, and a wonderful prepared-meal take-out section. The offerings change on a daily basis, but at any given time you will have a choice of lasagna, tamale pie, dolmas, stuffed cabbage, and an assortment of salads and side dishes. The market's roasted chicken is a favorite of harried mothers all over town: The

well-seasoned chickens are cooked daily on a rotisserie. The result is homemade taste without the homemade mess.

Wine and beer are available, and there is a butcher in the grocery store offering quality meats and seafood. The market is open daily.

TONY'S ITALIAN STYLE DELI, BUTCHER SHOP & RESTAURANT $
6219 E. 22nd St.
(520) 747-0070
www.tonysitaliandelitucson.com

This Eastside deli is small but filled to the rafters with Italian goodies. The refrigerator counter holds fresh mozzarella, strings of Italian and German sausages, cold cuts, pepperoncini, and marinated artichokes. There are plenty of deli sandwiches on the menu. Try the Rocky, which is stuffed with mortadella, prosciutto, and provolone and drizzled with oil and vinegar. Or indulge in the house specialties of veal saltimbocca or spaghetti carbonara. For a quick family-style dinner, pick up a Bucket of Spaghetti and Meatballs, which can feed from 2 to 28 people. There are also pans of lasagna. Both come with garlic rolls. They also do catering.

Tony's is open Mon through Sat from 9 a.m. to 8 p.m.

i Several local stores cater to vegetarian palates. Aqua Vita (2801 N. Country Club Rd.; 520-293-7770) and the Food Conspiracy Co-op (412 N. 4th Ave.; 520-624-4821) carry a wide selection of organic produce and frozen vegetarian entrees. For additional resources, check out www.vegansource.net.

WHOLE FOODS MARKET $$
3360 E. Speedway Blvd.
(520) 795-9860
www.wholefoodsmarket.com

Whole Foods is a gourmet market and so much more—butcher shop, fishmonger, health food store, sandwich shop, bakery, and deli. The list of items you can get here seems endless.

But if you're in a hurry and still want something with homemade flavor, stop in at any one of the markets and pick up a salad to go, veggie lasagna, baked chicken, and a killer brownie from the bakery. Your choice of beverages is wide: everything from juices and bottled water to beers from around the world. You're bound to find something to please your palate. Whole Foods is open daily. An additional Tucson location is at 7133 N. Oracle Rd. (520-297-5394).

GREEK & MIDDLE EASTERN

LUXOR CAFE $$
3699 N. Campbell Ave.
(520) 325-3771

Craving Middle Eastern cuisine? Take your magic carpet to Luxor, where you can feast on traditional and delicious dishes from a creamy homemade hummus and deep-fried lamb kibbe to slow-cooked lamb shanks and chicken kebabs. A basket of warm pita bread is on every table. A hookah lounge and belly dancers make for an exotic experience. Open for lunch and dinner daily.

ATHENS ON 4TH AVENUE $$
500 N. 4th Ave.
(520) 624-6886

Owned by real Greeks, this longtime 4th Avenue restaurant serves up traditional Greek cuisine. Start with the creamy *taramosalata* dip with pita bread or the Pikilia combination plate with stuffed grape leaves and *kefaloritiri* cheese. *Avgolemono* soup, lemony broth with rice, is a terrific and refreshing starter. Entrees include the standard spanakopita, moussaka, and pastitsio; but go out on a limb and try some of the house specialties: sautéed sweetbreads or seafood stew. Enjoy a glass of Greek dessert wine and a baklava on the enclosed patio for dessert. Open Mon through Sat, dinner only.

OPA! $
2990 N. Campbell Ave., #130
(520) 327-2841
Tucson Greeks looking for a taste of home head to Opa! Flaming cheese, spanikopita, gyros, kebabs, Greek salad (of course!), and baklava are all prepared by Athens-born chef Andreas Andoniadis in a sleek, contemporary eatery tucked into a strip mall on Campbell Avenue. Murals and photos along with Greek music will make you feel like you're in the sunny Aegean instead of the Sonoran Desert. Lift a glass of Greek beer or wine and shout *opa!* Open daily for lunch and dinner.

HEALTHY, VEGETARIAN & ALTERNATIVE

BLUE WILLOW RESTAURANT, BAKERY & GALLERY $$
2616 N. Campbell Ave.
(520) 327-7577
www.bluewillowtucson.com
The first part of the name comes from the antique china pattern of star-crossed lovers (their story is on the menu, and the pattern is repeated throughout the restaurant). The second part comes from the nifty cards, posters, and trinkets that are sold in the front shop. On busy days the wait never seems long because the store has so many fun things to look at and play with.

Crepes, omelets, and quiche are the mainstays of the menu. Croissants are excellent, too. Sandwiches, soups, and salads complete the menu. The patio is famous for remaining cool on hotter days; it's tented with netting held up by little balloons.

Expect a wait, especially on weekend mornings. There's a small parking lot and limited free parking on the street. The Blue Willow serves breakfast, lunch, and dinner 7 days a week.

DELECTABLES $$
533 N. 4th Ave.
(520) 884-9289
www.delectables.com
Dining at Delectables is, well, delectable! Open for lunch and dinner 7 days a week, this 4th Avenue staple is still wowing diners of all followings (food followings, that is). You'll find all sorts of choices here: enchiladas, quiche, pasta, an assortment of salads and sandwiches, and lots of yummy desserts, along with vegan and vegetarian options like vegan puttanesca pasta and vegetarian spinach manicotti.

The atmosphere here is casual, and you have your choice of eating in the cool, open dining room or on the patio, where you'll be able to watch 4th Avenue at its best. Parking can be a problem on the "Avenue." Patience usually pays off when you're looking for a spot along the street.

GOVINDA'S $$
711 E. Blacklidge Dr.
(520) 792-0630
www.govindasoftucson.com
Located just off N. 1st Avenue—between Glenn Avenue and Fort Lowell Road—in the

Chaitanya Cultural Center, Govinda's serves meals buffet style, and all are consistently good. Dine indoors or on the outdoor patio and enjoy waterfalls, fountains, gardens, and exotic birds that add serenity to your dining experience.

Lunch and dinner are served Tues through Sat; brunch is offered on Sun. Thurs is vegan only.

✳TASTEFUL KITCHEN   **$$**
722 N. Stone Ave.
(520) 250-9600
www.thetastefulkitchen.com
If you can find it, this tiny, unpretentious, and low-key spot offers some of the tastiest raw, vegan, and vegetarian dishes in town. Sister owners Keanne and Sigret Thompson make everything here from scratch. The best way to get a real sense of the food is to choose the multi-course prix fixe menu. It changes seasonally and includes refreshing just-squeezed juices in between each course and fabulous desserts—do not pass up the gluten-free orange almond cake, moist and delicious. Located in a somewhat barren part of Stone Avenue near Economy Restaurant Supply, there is no sign, so it's best to call for directions and make a reservation while you're at it. Open Wedn through Sun, dinner only.

YOSHIMATSU HEALTHY JAPANESE
  FOOD   **$**
2660 N. Campbell Ave.
(520) 320-1574
www.yoshimatsuaz.com
A restaurant with the guts to put the word *healthy* in its name has a lot to live up to, and Yoshimatsu succeeds. The funky interior features unusual Japanese pop art and a separate sushi bar. You'll find a reasonably priced menu with a wide variety of noodle soups, curries, bento combos, tempura, rice, and sushi. Open for lunch and dinner 7 days a week.

INDIAN

NEW DELHI PALACE   **$$**
6751 E. Broadway Blvd.
(520) 296-8585
New Delhi Palace, a top pick of *Tucson Weekly* readers, specializes in vegetarian and nonvegetarian Indian food. The bread is baked to order in tandoori ovens, and the owner takes pride in the authentic masalas and curries. For the vegetarian, a good bet is the Bengan Bharta, gently seasoned roasted eggplant. Nonvegetarians will delight in any one of the curries, especially satisfying when washed down with one of many varieties of cold beer served from the full bar. New Delhi is open daily for lunch and dinner.

SAFFRON INDIAN BISTRO   **$**
7607 N. Oracle Rd., Oro Valley
(520) 743-9100
www.tucsonindianrestaurant.com
Sophisticated and sleek, Saffron offers new Indian cuisine in a modern setting. But you'll still find your favorites here; samosas and pakoras, biryanis and naan, tandoori and tikka masalas are all on the menu, served up on beautiful geometric plates and bowls. The airy, high-ceilinged space is light and offers a lovely view of the mountains from large, open windows. Professional servers glide across the floor whisking plates away and replenishing drinks. The all-you-can-eat lunch buffet served daily is a great introduction to the variety of Indian-inspired dishes served here. Open daily.

ITALIAN

CARUSO'S $$

434 N. 4th Ave.
(520) 624-5765
www.carusoitalian.com

Caruso's may well be one of the city's oldest restaurants. In fact, the Zagona family has been serving great southern Italian-American food to Tucsonans at the same location for more than 50 years!

The food is hearty, the ambience charming and very Italian, and the prices reasonable. The Lasagna al Forno, made with homemade noodles and baked to perfection, is a house specialty, and all your Italian favorites are served. Your waitperson can help you choose from the wines offered, which are available by the glass or the bottle. You may dine indoors or on the patio.

Caruso's is a great place to dine after a long day of shopping on 4th Avenue. The restaurant is open Tues through Sun for lunch and dinner. No reservations are accepted. You'll find limited parking on the street.

GAVI $$

Piazza Gavi
5415 N. Kolb Rd.
(520) 577-1099

Softly lit interior, fireplace, 2 outdoor patios, pizza oven, espresso bar, and comfy couches—you can stay here all day. The menu features contemporary Italian cuisine with giant bowls of steaming pasta, lasagna, platters of meat and fish, baskets of bread, pizzas, humongous salads, and enormous desserts.

Gavi has developed a reputation for Italian dinners that offer something more than the usual fare; the servings are large and

come piping hot. Open for breakfast, lunch, and dinner. Closed Sun.

PRIMO $$$–$$$$

Starr Pass Marriott Resort and Spa
3800 W. Starr Pass Blvd.
(520) 792-3500
www.primo.jwstarrpassmarriott.com

Housed in the gorgeous Starr Pass Marriott Resort hotel on the far west side of town (see the Accommodations chapter), Primo offers Italian-inspired cuisine. You can eat indoors in the well-appointed dining room or outside on the beautiful patio with its amazing views of the city. The ever-changing seasonal menu offers antipasti (including pizza), pasta, fish, meat (from sustainable and organic sources), and various sides (try the sautéed greens with garlic). Don't get too full—desserts are tasty, too. Open Tues through Sun for dinner.

Looking for Italian ingredients? Head to Roma Imports. Hidden away on a tiny side street, this huge warehouselike space offers all you can possibly want from pasta to frozen items like meatballs and lasagna. And if you don't feel like cooking, they make sandwiches, too. Located at 627 S. Vine Ave.; (520) 792-3173; www.romaimports.com. Open Mon through Sat. Call for directions.

*TAVOLINO RISTORANTE
   ITALIANO $$

2890 E. Skyline Dr.
(520) 531-1913
www.tavolinoristorante.com

Get ready for some of the best authentic Italian food in town—chef Massimo Tenino is the real thing, showcasing the homey, delicious cuisine of northern Italy in a spacious, open location. The homemade linguine alla

Bolognese is perfection, with a rich meaty sauce that perfectly coats the strands of rich egg pasta. The lasagna is saucy, with beef, veal, and pork lightly layered with mozzarella and Parmesan cheese. And don't pass up the traditional pesto, a beautiful marriage of fresh basil, virgin olive oil, and Parmesan. The Ravioli di Zucca, a house specialty, is stuffed with butternut squash and napped with a sauce of brown butter and sage. A wood-fired oven sends out pizzas and roasted meats, but pasta is definitely the star. A close rival is the amazing Bonet dessert—a chocolate custard topped with crushed amaretti cookies and a sinful bitter caramel sauce.

Open for lunch and dinner. Reservations are essential; they book up early. Closed Sun and part of Aug.

VIVACE RESTAURANT $$$
St. Philip's Plaza
4310 N. Campbell Ave.
(520) 795-7221
www.vivacetucson.com
While it is an Italian restaurant, with osso buco, polenta, and pastas on the menu, it may better be classified as New Italian for its innovative preparations. For lunch Vivace has pastas, sandwiches, salads, and various house specialties. Vivace's dinner menu offers several selections. Start with artichokes and escargot baked in Gorgonzola cheese and garlic butter for an appetizer, and then try artichoke–goat cheese cannelloni. Vivace has a full bar with an extensive choice of wines by the bottle or the glass. You can dine outside on the lovely patio. Vivace is open for lunch and dinner Mon through Sat. We suggest reservations.

MEXICAN/LATIN

CAFE POCA COSA $$
110 E. Pennington St.
(520) 622-6400
www.cafepocacosatucson.com
Chef/owner Suzana Davila has transformed the ground floor of this rather bleak downtown garage space at E. Pennington and N. 6th Avenue into a sleek, comfortable restaurant. Davila creates interesting dishes inspired by different regions of her native Mexico. The menu, listed on a tiny chalkboard, changes daily, but you can always choose the Plato Poca Cosa, which showcases the specials. Closed Sun and Mon.

CASA VICENTE $
375 S. Stone Ave.
(520) 884-5253
www.casavicente.com
In the mood for some flamenco music? A steaming platter of paella? Head to Casa Vicente, where the kitchen is hopping and the music is lively. Start with tapas, those tiny finger-licking-good appetizers Spain is known for. You'll find a great selection here, over 26 hot and cold choices, from a traditional Spanish frittata to menudo cooked with garbanzos. If you want paella, you need to call at least two hours in advance and bring four hungry friends. Try the Paella Negra, black rice flavored with squid ink and brimming with seafood. Ask about the specials of the day, and don't forget to order a large pitcher of sangria.

There's live music every night. Flamenco performances are on Fri and Sat. Open for dinner Tues through Sun, lunch Tues through Sat. Summer hours vary.

DON PEDRO'S PERUVIAN BISTRO $
3386 6th Ave., #120
(520) 209-1740
http://donpedrosperuvianbistro.com
This out-of-the-way spot in South Tucson is drawing raves from people who have actually lived and eaten in Peru. "Delicious" and "authentic," they enthuse! Start with the national drink of Peru, the classic Pisco Sour, a sweet/sour concoction that comes to you frothy and delightfully cold. Those in the know pick the Peruvian specialties: *antichucos* (kebabs), *papas rellenos* (deep-fried potatoes stuffed with ground meat, raisins, and spices), *chaufa* (fried rice), *lomo saltado* (stir-fried vegetables and meat), and *cebiche* (marinated raw fish). Open daily.

EL CHARRO CAFE $$
311 N. Court Ave.
(520) 622-1922
www.elcharrocafe.com
Regularly voted Best Mexican Restaurant by the *Tucson Weekly* readers' poll, the original El Charro Cafe is a Tucson treasure. In the historic downtown El Presidio district, the building at N. Court Avenue is an 1896 adobe on the National Historic Register. The business is the nation's oldest Mexican restaurant continuously operated by the same family (since 1922), and the food reflects the tradition.

The menu includes *topopo jalisciense,* a signature chimichanga, *carne seca,* and baked fish tacos. *Carne seca* (marinated dried beef) is a house specialty. Try it in the famous, huge chimichanga. For some more unusual items, choose from Carlotta's Creations, which feature interesting combinations of flavors and ingredients. If you just can't decide, they do have a tasting plate, or you can choose from several combination platters that will give you a little bit of everything. They even have their own cookbook, so you can make your favorites at home. The original location downtown (Court Avenue) has the most charm; other locations are at 6310 E. Broadway Blvd. (520-745-1922); 7725 N. Oracle Rd., Oro Valley (520-229-1922); 15920 S. Rancho Sahuarita (520-325-1922); and 6910 E. Sunrise Dr., Ventana (520-514-1922).

All locations are open for lunch and dinner 7 days a week.

i For a taste of Mexico all in one place, head to Mercado San Agustin at 100 Avenido del Convento at W. Congress Street. Part of a lovely renovation in this southeast corner of town, the Mercado is home to La Estrella Bakery, Dolce Pastello, Sonoran Sno Cones, and Taqueria el Pueblito, as well as retail shops. Check www.mercadosanagustin.com for details.

EL GUERO CANELO #1 $
5201 S. 12th Ave., South Tucson
(520) 295-9005
www.elguerocanelo.com
It's not at all fancy—in fact, it's just a step above a taco stand—but this south-side favorite offers an extensive menu of home-style Sonoran dishes, from giant burros and overstuffed tacos to menudo (served Sat and Sun only). Order at the window and serve yourself condiments (lime wedges, cucumbers, shredded cabbage, salsas, and hot sauces). Open daily until midnight for breakfast, lunch, and dinner. This area is somewhat isolated and can be intimidating at night, so consider breakfast or lunch for your first visit. There are two other locations in town, but they have none of the charm of the original.

EL MINUTO CAFE $$
354 S. Main Ave.
(520) 882-4145
www.elminutocafe.com

This longtime downtown landmark is known for its carne seca and refried beans. While many restaurants in town serve low-fat cooking, El Minuto has stuck with the traditional methods—maybe not heart healthy, but certainly worth falling off the diet wagon for.

The dining area is decorated with Mexican curios, chili strings, and hand-painted flowered trim on the turquoise and pink walls. Serapes are used for curtains. Eat indoors or sip a Mexican beer as you soak up the historical ambience of the neighboring barrio from the patio at the downtown location.

Located across from the Tucson Convention Center, it's a great place to stop before or after an event. There will be a wait on weekends, so get there early. While you wait, take a short walk to the shrine, El Tiradito, next door. Closed Sun.

EL MOLCAJETE MEXICAN FOOD $
663 S. Plumer Ave.
(520) 623-8886

A true Insiders' spot, this mom-and-pop Mexican restaurant is a hidden treasure. Open only for breakfast and lunch, it's a favorite with locals. They, and you, come for the terrific homemade soups, fresh guacamole, the best green corn tamales in town, and the homey, friendly atmosphere. Don't come here if you're looking for fancy food; this is homemade Mexican comfort food. Open 7 days a week until 3 p.m.

EL TORERO $$
231 E. 26th St.
(520) 622-9534

Finding this longtime south-side favorite might be a little difficult, but we'll give you an Insiders' tip: As you head south on 4th Avenue, watch for a mural of a bullfighter, then make the next right onto 26th Street. The second building from the corner is El Torero.

The first things that will catch your eye in this brightly lit restaurant are the long wooden bar, high ceilings, and thick adobe walls. The place may seem a bit noisy, but don't let that change your mind. Even on busy nights, you'll be seated quickly at one of the many tables, and you won't notice the noise.

Anything you order will be tasty, but try the carne seca plate. You'll get a heap of seasoned shredded beef with Mexican rice and refried beans. A warm flour tortilla accompanies the meal. To eat this in true Mexican style, tear off a piece of the tortilla (making sure you cover it up again to keep it soft and warm), and plop on some carne seca, a dollop of beans, and some salsa. La Bandera (red, green, and white enchiladas) is another favorite, as is the topopo salad, a corn tortilla slathered with beans and topped with a mountain of lettuce, avocado, tomatoes, and your choice of cheese, chicken, or shrimp. It really doesn't need any dressing, but there is vinaigrette available on request.

El Torero is open every day except Tuesday for lunch and dinner. Although a parking lot is adjacent to the restaurant, it's better to park on the street.

JOHN JACOB'S EL PARADOR $$
2744 E. Broadway Blvd.
(520) 881-2744
www.elparadortucson.com

You might wonder if a Mexican restaurant with a non-Mexican owner could survive the competition in Tucson. But that's exactly what the Jacob family has done, and done well, since 1946.

The food is unique. Try the ceviche or taquitos appetizer, then choose from fajitas, tamales, chiles rellenos, and a carne seca chimichanga with pico de gallo.

Lush plants and a skylight give the feeling of eating in a tropical paradise. Several private dining rooms can be used for meetings or special functions, and El Parador also provides catering services.

The restaurant is open daily for lunch or dinner, and on Sunday a brunch is served. Stop in the Cantina, El Parador's bar, at happy hour on weekday afternoons. Friday and Saturday nights feature a nightclub with live music.

MIGUEL'S AT LA POSADA $$$
La Posada Lodge & Casitas
5900 N. Oracle Rd.
(520) 887-3777
www.laposadalodge.com

Miguel's introduces Nuevo Latino cuisine to Tucson. Housed in the La Posada Lodge & Casitas (see Accommodations chapter), this lovely open and airy restaurant features an unusual and inventive menu. Chilies of all kinds—chipotle, serrano, poblano, pequin, and more—make a showing on the menu in every category. Homemade salsas grace each table along with multicolored chips for dipping. Mexico meets Italy in the flatiron-grilled filet mignon, which pairs olive oil and garlic with cilantro and Tabasco chilies. The chicken a la brasa in a mole verde comes with a creamy Oaxacan green chili rice. The menu also features fresh seafood dishes like cabrilla and bacon-wrapped Guaymas prawns.

You can sit in the dining room near the fireplace or on the patio and enjoy pool or mountain views. A comfortable semicircular bar with bamboo chairs is a great spot for a drink. Open daily.

MI NIDITO CAFE $$
1813 S. 4th Ave.
(520) 622-5081
www.minidito.net

The wait at Mi Nidito on many evenings can be as long as 45 minutes. Serving Tucson since 1952, Mi Nidito has been voted the best Mexican food in several newspaper polls for many years. Just ask President Clinton. It was here at Mi Nidito that he lunched while in town.

The decor hasn't changed much over the years, nor has the food, a standard take on Sonoran cuisine. Mexican tile, white-washed walls, and a fake palm tree in the back of the restaurant are not unlike decor in restaurants on the other side of the border. The large and crispy flautas are topped with lettuce, guacamole, sour cream, and a sprinkling of Mexican farmer cheese. The menudo is classic. The chiles rellenos and the burro deluxe are also filling and hearty.

Mi Nidito is open for lunch and dinner every night except Mon and Tues.

ROSA'S $$
1750 E. Fort Lowell Rd.
(520) 325-0362
www.rosasmexicanfoodaz.com

When Rosa opened her restaurant years ago, patrons could watch her as she cooked meals, waited tables, and kept a watchful eye on her children, who were often at the restaurant when not in school. Today those very same children are grown and continuing the tradition their mom began so long ago.

The refried beans at Rosa's are truly traditional and are some of the best in all of Tucson. The enchiladas, tacos, burritos, chimichangas, and chiles rellenos are all made in the traditional manner as well. The daily sopas (soups) are delicious. If you're not sure which menu item to pick, try one of the family's special combination plates. Don't miss the fabulous salsa, smooth and spicy. Top your meal off with some sopapillas (fry bread) with honey or the almendrado, a unique pudding topped with almond sauce.

Rosa's is open for lunch and dinner 7 days a week.

i Tamales and empanadas can be had at two Tucson stores. The Tucson Tamale Company (2545 E. Broadway Blvd.; 520-305-4760) serves up meat, vegetarian, vegan, and dessert tamales from its small storefront. You can buy them here or at lots of farmers' and local markets. Mamma Llamas Gourmet Empanadas offers just that at 2418 E. Craycroft Rd. (520-564-4994; www.mammallamas.com). Flaky pastry surrounds a variety of fabulous fillings. Get them to go or at the farmers' markets around town.

TAQUERIA PICO DE GALLO $
2618 S. 6th Ave.
(520) 623-8775
Raised from relative obscurity by a review in *Gourmet* magazine, this tiny taqueria in South Tucson has kept its modest digs and low-key attitude. The only change is that you can now use credit cards to pay for some of the tastiest Mexican food in town. Don't pass up the fabulous shrimp tacos served with homemade corn tortillas or a

huge steaming bowl of tortilla soup full of shredded chicken, cheese, and avocado. The whole fried fish is a stunner. Daily combination plates feature whatever's fresh from the sea or the market. Dessert has to be the big plastic cup of fresh fruit the restaurant is named for, pico de gallo: slices of coconut, papaya, pineapple, jicama, and oranges, sprinkled with lime juice and chili pepper. No reservations; open daily for lunch and dinner.

PIZZA

BROOKLYN PIZZA $
534 N. 4th Ave.
(520) 622-6868
www.brooklynpizzacompany.com
Brooklyn Pizza may be the only solar-powered pizza parlor in the country.

The decor might be called funky. There are a dozen mismatched '50s Formica-topped tables. The walls are painted a deep yellow and covered with artwork. And the music is everything from '50s hits to alternative rock.

A favorite with students, the pizzas come with lots of topping choices, including artichoke hearts, chicken, eggplant, feta cheese, ground beef, meatballs, ricotta, and spinach.

You can also have pasta with marinara sauce, garlic knots, cheese, or any of the pizza toppings. The hero sandwiches are imaginative. Try the Florentine or the Vatican Veggie.

The restaurant serves lunch and dinner daily and has late-night hours. Beer and wine are available. Brooklyn Pizza delivers to just north of 6th Street, with a minimum order; it will even deliver beer.

*EMPIRE PIZZA AND PUB $
137 E. Congress Ave.
(520) 882-7499
www.empirepizzapub.com

Rejoice! True New York–style pizza has finally come to Tucson courtesy of Empire. The front of the house is dedicated to takeout, lots and lots of slices (hooray) with toppings from pineapple (!) to BBQ chicken to the good old classic—just plain cheese and sauce. Customers line up here to eat slices while standing on the sidewalk or get pizza to go, but you can also sit on the tiny front patio and watch the downtown come to life or head to the back, where a lovely high tin-ceiling bar area offers drinks and beers on tap. Perch on a stool and enjoy your slice along with a cold one. Open daily for lunch and dinner.

MAMA'S PIZZA AND HEROS $
7965 N. Oracle Rd.
(520) 297-3993
www.mamasfamous.com

With three generations of Mama's children working in the restaurants, you can rest assured that whatever you order will be just like Mama made. The family-size pizza is big enough for a family of four plus any number of relatives and friends who might stop by unannounced. Mama's also serves some great sandwiches. Additional Tucson locations are at 6996 E. 22nd (520-750-1919); 4500 E. Speedway Blvd. (520-319-8856); and 50 S. Houston (520-751-4600). All Mama's are open for lunch and dinner every day.

SAUCE $
Casas Adobes Plaza
7117 N. Oracle Dr.
(520) 297-8575
www.foxrestaurantconcepts.com/sauce

Have a craving for crispy crust pizza? Sauce is the place. Yummy pizzas come topped with pepperoni and cremini mushrooms, rosemary potato, spinach, feta and olive tapenade, or the unlikely prosciutto and melon combo. People chow 'em down in an instant. You can also choose from several tasty salads and lasagna. Wine and beer are available as thirst quenchers. Open for lunch and dinner daily from 11 a.m. Additional Tucson locations are at 5285 E. Broadway Blvd. (520-512-1122) and 2990 N. Campbell Ave. (520-795-0344).

ZACHARY'S $
1019 E. 6th St.
(520) 623-6323

Zachary's has a reputation for cold beers and humongous pizzas. The beers come from all over the world. In fact, Zachary's had a large beer selection long before it became trendy. Dress is very casual, and families are welcome.

Pizzas are 2 inches thick and come loaded with toppings, including the standards as well as broccoli, artichoke hearts, fresh tomatoes, jalapeños, spinach, prosciutto, and pineapple. The Big Z is the house specialty. Meat lovers will want to try the T Rex, which comes with pepperoni, sausage, and ham. For veggie lovers, the staff recommends the Uptowner. The salad dressings are homemade. Due to the size of the pizzas, the wait once you've ordered can be almost an hour, especially on nights when there is a UA game. Zachary's is open every day.

SEAFOOD

BLUEFIN SEAFOOD BISTRO $$

7053 N. Oracle Rd.
(520) 531-8500
http://bluefintucson.com

A sister restaurant to Kingfisher (see below), this classy seafood bistro is tucked away in the middle of Casas Adobes Plaza. Brick walls and banquette seating are the setting for some super seafood. Oysters, clams, shrimp, clam chowder, and ceviche are just for starters. Specialties include crab cakes, fish-and-chips with house-made tartar sauce, and the grilled salmon melt. Patio dining is available as well. Open daily for lunch and dinner.

*KINGFISHER $$$$

2564 E. Grant Rd.
(520) 323-7739
www.kingfishertucson.com

Kingfisher bills itself as an American grill, but the accent is on seafood in every way, shape, and form. Diners can select 15 varieties of oysters flown in daily from the Northwest, the East Coast, and other briny places. And if you don't know one oyster from another, your knowledgeable waitperson will explain the subtle differences.

Fresh fish specials change daily; all are cooked with attention to detail and are free of heavy sauces. Salmon is a staple, but that's not to say the steaks and other entrees aren't good here. The kitchen grills up a pretty mean steak. The award-winning wine list is large and varied enough to find a suitable match for any choice of entree.

The decor is modern but cozy. Reservations are suggested. Lunch is served Mon through Fri, and dinner daily.

MARISCOS CHIHUAHUA $$

1009 Grande Ave.
(520) 623-3563
www.mariscoschihuahua.com

Cheap, cheap, cheap and tasty, this local chain offers market-fresh seafood and shrimp from the Sea of Cortez. The head on whole fried fish is a wonder to behold. It arrives crispy and flaky on a giant platter along with tortillas and a giant bottle of ranch dressing; ignore the eyeballs and dig in. There's lots of shrimp here: fried or sautéed with garlic and oil are winners. The Seven Seas soup is a must, a rich broth swimming with all sorts of sea creatures. Don't expect a fancy place—you'll find simple tables and chairs and a unique, colorful ocean decor. Other locations are at 356 E. Grant Rd. (520-884-3457); 3901 S. 6th Ave. (520-741-0361); 435 W. Irvington Rd. (520-294-3194); 999 N. Swan Rd. (520-881-2372); 4185 W. Ina Rd. (520-572-2523); and 2902 E. 22nd St. (520-326-1529). All locations are open daily.

STEAK HOUSES

CHAD'S STEAKHOUSE & SALOON $$

3001 N. Swan Rd.
(520) 881-1802
www.chadssteakhouse.com

Local beef lovers adore Chad's. Old-fashioned and low-key, it's all about the beef here. Steak, prime rib, and all the fixin's are what's on the menu. Go for the rib eye rare; the charred pink meat is juicy and corn fed. A giant baked spud, split and topped with melted butter and sour cream, will add to your cholesterol count but it sure tastes good! Salad dressings are homemade and dinner comes with warm bread and cowboy beans. Yee-haw! Open for lunch and dinner daily.

EL CORRAL $$

2201 E. River Rd.
(520) 299-6092
www.traildusttown.com

El Corral has long been a Tucson tradition when it comes to where to take out-of-town visitors for prime rib. There's not an evening any day of the week or season of the year when the outside patio isn't comfortably filled with people waiting for a table. Don't be dissuaded by the wait: It's reasonable, even in peak season. You'll have just enough time for a beer, wine, or highball or two from the bar.

El Corral's claim to fame is prime rib, but the ribs are also a great choice. The prime rib comes in several cuts and sizes, and the ribs come as a full or half rack. Sides include the usuals, such as choice of potatoes or pilaf, but Insiders know that the tamale pie is the way to go. This fluffy, soft corn bread is slightly sweet and studded with mild green chilies and kernels of corn. The ambience here is totally Tucson—casual, comfortable, and slightly rustic Southwestern. Several dining rooms and close tables add comfort instead of a crowded feeling. You'll see diners in their Sunday best and others who look like they just stepped off the golf course. Service is also a plus—quick, knowledgeable, and friendly.

El Corral serves only dinner nightly and does not take reservations.

LIL ABNER'S STEAKHOUSE $$$

8501 N. Silverbell Rd.
(520) 744-2800

Old-timers in Tucson can remember when the drive out to Lil Abner's Steakhouse was a trek. The road was dark, narrow, and winding, but it was always a treat once you arrived. Today the ride doesn't seem so long due to all the development in this part of Tucson and the wider, well-lit road, and there is still a treat at the end. Lil Abner's has some of the best mesquite-grilled steaks around. And the atmosphere is about as cowboy as you can get. Dinner on the patio means beautiful desert views, especially at sunset; the smell of your dinner on the grill; and the twang of Western music, which is offered Fri and Sat.

Other entree selections include beef ribs, pork ribs, and chicken, all cooked on the grill of course. Sides include your choice of cowboy beans or potatoes. All meals come with a small salad.

Lil Abner's serves dinner nightly.

MCMAHON'S PRIME STEAKHOUSE $$$

2959 N. Swan Rd.
(520) 327-7463
www.metrorestaurants.com

Voted the best steak house in Tucson by local magazines, McMahon's is famous for its USDA prime aged beef and fresh seafood. Try one of the dry-aged steaks, rare, with a side of creamed spinach, mashed potatoes, and a Caesar salad. Seafood specialties include lobster tails. You'll also find great appetizers, desserts, and over 25,000 wines. Open for lunch and dinner daily.

✳PINNACLE PEAK STEAKHOUSE $$

6541 E. Tanque Verde Rd.
(520) 296-0911
www.traildusttown.com

If you have a friend who has horrible taste in ties, bring him (or her) to Pinnacle Peak. Anyone who walks in sporting a tie will promptly be the center of attention as the waitresses begin clanging cowbells and all action stops. Then, snip! snip! A waitress cuts off the tie and hangs it from the ceiling where it joins hundreds of others. Yep, this place takes casual dress to a whole new level.

Located in Trail Dust Town on Tanque Verde Road, Pinnacle Peak is a Tucson tradition for big mesquite-grilled steaks. A range of steak is offered, from the smaller 1-pound T-bone to the monster 2-pound porterhouse. Ribs, barbecue chicken, and fish are also available. Sides include the cowboy staples of beans, taters, salad, and bread. Try the apple cobbler for dessert, if you have room that is, and then enjoy a stroll through Trail Dust Town. The shops here are unique, and the kids may want to ride the scale-model train that runs the perimeter (see the Shopping and Kidstuff chapters).

Pinnacle Peak is open nightly for dinner, but expect a wait (especially on weekends); they don't take reservations.

SAM HUGHES PLACE CHAMPIONSHIP DINING $$
446 N. Campbell Ave.
(520) 747-5223
www.championshipdining.com
Part sports bar, part sophisticated restaurant, Sam Hughes Place offers "a menu of American favorites," including seafood, salads, and sandwiches, but beef is the thing here, brought in fresh daily and cut in-house. Choose from sterling silver–grade 21-ounce bone-in rib eye, 15-ounce bone-in New York strip, 10-ounce filet mignon, and the gargantuan 23-ounce porterhouse, all accompanied by a giant baked potato with sour cream, butter, bacon, and chives. While you wait for your entree, feast your eyes on the 23 high-definition TVs (usually showing sports) in the main dining room. If you have to use the loo, you won't miss a thing—there are 4 more TVs in the restrooms. Open daily.

TUCSON MCGRAW'S CANTINA AND STEAK HOUSE $$
4110 S. Houghton Rd.
(520) 885-3088
www.tucsonmcgraws.com
For a steak with a view, put on your spurs and head to Tucson McGraw's. This Tucson original has been in business since 1984, a time when there were only 6 lights and everybody knew their neighbors on Houghton Road. Perched on top of a hill, McGraw's has one of the best views in town of the mountains, sunsets and spectacular lightening storms. The place is just right for a laidback dinner of old fashioned cowboy grub. Owner Lex McGraw knows how to rustle up some good food and locals bring their out-of-town guests here for a taste of how food in the West used to be: plain, simple and hearty. Starters like his home made Texas chili and thick-cut beer battered onion rings whet the appetite for a big, juicy steak grilled over mesquite wood for that signature smokiness. Choose from rib eye, tri tip, sirloin and New York strip. BBQ ribs, chicken and seafood round out the menu. Tuesday nights are Steak Night, with top sirloin offered at a bargain price. So sit back, sip a frosty brew or an icy Margarita and enjoy the view. Lunch and dinner served daily.

NIGHTLIFE

You'll find a lot happening here: great music, from classical to folk to rock and, of course, country, along with dance clubs, cafes and pubs, and outdoor movies. Tucson has it all!

If nightlife to you means live music, you'll find a full slate in town, including rock, country, jazz, alternative, dance, blues, and acoustic performances. The major live music clubs are clustered along 4th Avenue and Congress Avenue, but other venues can be found in all parts of town. You'll also find plenty of cafes, pubs, and bars that offer open mics and live music. Many restaurants offer jazz, piano, acoustic guitar, and strolling mariachis on select nights and weekends. Tucson Weekly publishes a full listing every Thursday (see the Media chapter).

The downtown is undergoing a renaissance with hip clubs, hot restaurants, and lots of special events that keep things hopping. 2nd Saturdays Downtown (www.2ndsaturdaysdowntown.com) brings a lively urban street fest to Congress Avenue, with live music, street vendors, special events, and discounts at select restaurants. This free event takes place the second Saturday of every month.

Club Crawl (http://clubcrawl.ning.com) takes you all over 4th Avenue and downtown with more than 80 bands and musical acts performing on 25 outdoor stages and inside select clubs You can access all the fun with a low-cost wristband available in advance or at the door.

For the cinema crowd, in addition to the handful of "regular" movie houses, you'll find the Loft, which shows artsy foreign films, and the Screening Room, specializing in independent productions and the works of local producers. Free outdoor movies are shown weekly from May to October at Plaza Placita (www.cinemaplacita.com).

Other nightlife options include numerous theatrical productions, ballets, operas, symphonic music presentations, and poetry readings at various venues, from coffeehouses to bookstores. (See the Arts & Culture chapter for more specific information.)

A FEW GROUND RULES

In the state of Arizona, you must be 21 years of age to consume alcohol, and Tucson's clubs won't let you in the door without a picture ID. Cabs don't really roam the streets here, but if you need one, the clubs are more than happy to call one for you. Arizona's drunk driving laws are very strict and strongly enforced with random roadblocks—especially on holiday weekends—so it's better to pay the money for a cab than spend a night in jail.

Credit card acceptance varies. Cover charges often depend on the popularity of the entertainment and whether or not the band playing is an out-of-town act. Our best advice if you're strapped for cash, or if you just don't believe in paying for entertainment, is to call before you head out the door.

The following listings are broken down into general categories, but nothing in Tucson is written in stone. In any given week, a club could have bands playing rock one night, blues the next, and reggae the following evening. And unless we tell you otherwise, these clubs have full bars.

EASY LISTENING

THE ARIZONA INN
2200 E. Elm St.
(520) 325-1541
www.arizonainn.com
One of the city's most elegant and historic spots, the Arizona Inn's classy Audubon Lounge offers overstuffed chairs and sofas where you can listen to a pianist play. (For more information on the Arizona Inn, check the Accommodations chapter.)

LOEWS VENTANA CANYON RESORT
7000 N. Resort Dr.
(520) 299-2020
www.loewshotels.com
The comfortable Cascade Lounge with big picture windows overlooking the pool area and a huge fireplace offers live music (duos, trios, big bands, and easy listening) on Fri until 8 p.m. and Sat until 11 p.m. Settle into one of the comfy couches or chairs, nurse a drink (their prickly pear margarita and homemade lemonade are fantastic), and enjoy the sweet sounds in grand style.

MCMAHON'S PRIME STEAKHOUSE
2959 N. Swan Rd.
(520) 327-2333
www.metrorestaurants.com

This popular, upscale steak house has live music nightly in the piano lounge. You'll find a pianist performing a wide repertoire of jazz, show tunes, oldies, and standards from 6 to 9 p.m. daily. Full bar service and restaurant menu are available in the lounge.

i For all the skinny on Tucson nightlife, check http://tucson.metromix.com. This website has searchable listings and ratings of bars and clubs, music and movies along with reviews and recommendations.

CAFES

EPIC CAFE
745 N. 4th Ave.
(520) 624-6844
www.epic-cafe.com
This casual, funky cafe offers live music and a variety of open-mic nights. A great place to hang out, with high ceilings, great acoustics, and an eclectic crowd, you also get a great view of the Old Pueblo Trolley at night. Performances are spotty, so call first to see who's on the bill. There's free Wi-Fi, too! Open daily.

THE GLASS ONION
1990 W. River Rd.
(520) 293-6050
www.glassonioncafe.net
Small and cozy, this Beatles-themed cafe on the northwest side of town hosts local singers and songwriters Thursday, Friday, and select Saturday nights. Stop by to hear some of Tucson's own and grab a bite while you're there. All the menu items here are named after Beatles songs.

CLUBS

CLUB CONGRESS
311 E. Congress St.
(520) 622-8848
www.hotelcongress.com

This eclectic club, in the historic Congress Hotel, has risen to the forefront of the downtown night scene. And although it's a favorite of the younger, not-so-tragically hip crowd, older folks can kick up their heels on the dance floor without sticking out like sore thumbs. Club Congress claims to have been "inventing Tucson nightlife since 1985." You'll find lots of live music (local and national) and special events in this funky downtown setting. Weekly events include a '80s dance night. You'll also find considerably calmer live music in the lobby/bar on select weeknights.

i Club Congress was named "One of the Best Bars in America" by *Esquire* magazine, one of only two bars in the Southwest to make it onto the list.

DV8
5851 E. Speedway
(520) 885-3030

DV8 is one of Tucson's hippest clubs. Get ready for hip-hop, R&B, '80s, '90s, and today's music. The bartenders are friendly and the drinks cheap. Foosball and billiards will keep nondancers busy. Open Tues through Sat.

LEVEL BAR AND LOUNGE
St. Philip's Plaza
4280 N. Campbell Ave.
(520) 615-3835
www.leveltucson.com

A hot spot for the upscale, well-dressed, and well-heeled, Level is a small but hip spot for seeing and being seen. A cozy dance floor, flat-screen televisions, curtained VIP room, sleek wooden bar, and outdoor patio with a fire pit brings them in all night long. Dress codes are strictly enforced—you won't find shorts or work boots on this well-turned-out crowd. Open Wed through Sat until 2 a.m.

MONSOON AT DESERT DIAMOND CASINO
I-19 and Pima Mine Road at exit 80
(520) 294-7777
www.desertdiamondcasino.com

The classy Monsoon Nightclub offers a huge dance floor and all types of music. Call or check their website to see what's coming up.

✳SAPPHIRE LOUNGE
61 E. Congress St.
(520) 624-9100
www.sapphiretucson.com

The *it* place to be on Congress, this 3-story club has 2 hardwood dance floors, cool blue lighting, sexy waitresses, and a very hip vibe. The upper-level outdoor patio and lounge has fab views of the downtown skyline, a bar, and flaming torches. Friday nights local DJs broadcast live from the rooftop during happy hour from 5 to 9 p.m.

i While you're on Congress Street visiting all the clubs, stop in at one of Tucson's oldest music stores—the amazing, the eclectic, the crammed-to-the-ceiling Chicago Music Store (130 Congress St.; 520-622-3341). Filled to the brim with everything musical from instruments to sheet music, they sell, rent, trade, and buy. The staff can find anything from a kid's bongo set to a concertina in this huge store. They're open Mon through Sat.

THE SHELTER
4155 E. Grant Rd.
(520) 326-1345
Open since 1994, Shelter bills itself as a go-go boot–wearing, martini-drinking, swanky, groovy lounge. The crowd is very eclectic. They sip drinks at the bar or in booths while a strange collection of tunes plays on the stereo, and the television runs classic flicks such as '60s James Bond movies. There are DJs on the first Sunday of every month and pool tables, but the draw here is the ambience and the cocktails. Drinks are serious business here: Bartenders only offer top-of-the-line libations and never use prefab mixes or disperse alcohol from a gun. Open daily 3 p.m. to midnight.

VAUDEVILLE
110 E. Congress St.
(520) 622-3535
www.myspace.com/vaudeville
downtowntucson.com
Velvet curtains screen the view from the street, but don't be intimidated—go on in. With great lighting and sound, you'll find all sorts of gigs from local musicians to touring acts on the stage at this downtown spot. Open daily until 2 a.m.

THE WILDCAT HOUSE
1801 N. Stone Ave.
(520) 622-1302
www.thewildcathouse.com
Named for the Arizona Wildcats, this cavernous, low-lit club packs 'em in for all sorts of dance nights, including R&B, hip-hop, and Tejano. Peopled mostly by a younger crowd, the 3 bars keep the drinks coming, and the large-screen TVs are usually on the sports channel. Happy hour is Mon, Tues, Wed, and Fri from 4 to 8 p.m. If you get hungry from all

that dancing, they have an extensive menu of bar food, steaks, salads, sandwiches, and excellent burgers. It's located at the northwest corner of Stone and Lester. There is a cover charge on weekends for live music. Open Mon through Sat.

ZEN ROCK
121 E. Congress St.
(520) 306-8116
www.zenrocktucson.com
Don't let the husky bouncer at the door intimidate you! DJs are spinning cool tunes on the inside and it's worth a visit. You'll find high ceilings, low lighting, and sleek furnishings here along with 2 levels for dancing, VIP concierge service, and private VIP seating areas. The club attracts an edgy, urban crowd that dances to Top 40 tunes.

BARS

THE BUFFET BAR AND CROCK POT
538 E. 9th St.
(520) 623-6811
www.thebuffetbar.com
The oldest bar in Tucson, this spot should not be missed on your nightlife prowls of the downtown. Look for the neon sign on 9th Street off of 4th Avenue. Mentioned in *Playboy* and *Esquire* and given the dubious distinction of Tucson's Best Dive bar by *Tucson Weekly*, the Buffet offers cheap brews, drunken hot dogs (they're boiled in beer), and the oldest barmaid in Tucson (rumor has it she's over 80, but don't ask—real ladies don't tell). Opens at 6 a.m. daily!

CHE'S LOUNGE
350 N. 4th Ave.
(520) 623-2088
www.cheslounge.com

Not much to look at, this friendly neighborhood bar on 4th is not out to impress. No cover, dollar beers, excellent bartenders, and a terrific jukebox make this a great place to hang out. Live entertainment most weekends.

FAMOUS SAM'S
3010 W. Valencia Rd.
(520) 883-8888
www.famoussams.com

If you're looking for a dark spot with ice-cold beer, great background music, lots of TVs, and friendly service, Famous Sam's is the place (or should we say places, as there are now multiple Famous Sam's scattered throughout the city). Sam's started over 25 years ago with one little bar on the east side of town. It quickly became "famous" for killer hot pastrami sandwiches and a friendly, casual atmosphere. Today any one of the Sam's offers much the same (happily, the pastrami sandwiches are still very good, while the menu has been expanded some). These are great sports bars. Evening drink and food specials can be found, although each entity may have different daily specials. Live entertainment is also found at some of the bars on weekends. See website for additional locations.

THE HUT
304 N. 4th Ave.
(520) 623-3200
www.facebook.com/thehuttucson

You'll find tropical drinks and live music 7 nights a week at the hopping Hut. Look for the giant tiki head (rescued from a local minigolf park) that marks the entrance to this drinker's paradise, with its huge bar and outdoor patio. Belly up to the grass-skirted bar for a drink and listen to a wide variety of musicians, from local crooners to top area bands.

O'MALLEY'S
247 N. 4th Ave.
(520) 623-8600
www.facebook.com/pages/
omalleys-on-fourth-tucson-az

With a very large bar, late-night snacks, and a separate club for live bands, this is a popular weekend college hangout. Live music is featured Tues, Thurs, Fri, and Sat, but O'Malley's sees business all week long. Patrons are drawn in by the airy high ceilings (the building was once home to a highly successful lumber company), outside patio, and several pool tables. On weekends don't be surprised to see people waiting in line to get in. O'Malley's charges a cover when there's a band.

PLUSH
4th Avenue and 6th Street
(520) 798-1298
www.plushtucson.com

A great atmosphere with comfy couches, deep-red walls, and big windows that look out on the 4th Avenue scene, Plush offers live music ranging from jazz to alternative, Southwestern, country, rock, and blues.

THE RED ROOM AT THE GRILL
100 E. Congress St.
(520) 623-7621
http://redroomtucson.blogspot.com

You'll find live music weekends starting at 10 p.m. at the Grill's eclectic Red Room. No cover, ever! This funky diner is the only thing in Tucson that's open 24/7. Grab some grub (see the Restaurants chapter) and a drink from the full bar, and settle in for a night of unique entertainment.

THE SHANTY
401 E. 9th St.
(520) 623-2664

This place has been packing them in for over 30 years, so much so that many of today's patrons are children (and even some grandchildren) of earlier generations.

There are several reasons for the continued popularity of the Shanty. One is its location—just blocks from the UA and right in the heart of the 4th Avenue/downtown scene. Another is the large selection of imported beers. The third is the casual atmosphere where students and professors can meet and mingle. Summer nights find the patio abuzz with activity.

SKY BAR
536 N. 4th Ave.
(520) 622-4300
www.skybartucson.com

At the only solar-powered bar in Tucson (maybe even in the country?), head inside to the casual, open, airy bar or, better yet, head upstairs to the outdoor astronomy bar for a look at the stars. Nightly astronomy shows and deep-space images projected from the club's own telescope make for an enchanted evening. Open-mic nights, live music, and game nights along with special events pack them in nightly here.

JAZZ

CUSHING STREET BAR & RESTAURANT
198 W. Cushing St.
(520) 622-7984
www.cushingstreet.com

Step back in time at this wonderful downtown bar and cafe housed in a historic landmark. There's a fabulous wooden bar complete with a brass foot rail, floor-to-ceiling cabinets, and antiques. A limited menu of comfort foods (homemade soups, salads, meat, and potatoes) is just fine. Come for the ambience and the great bar, where the bartenders can make just about anything. (Don't believe it? Ask for a German chocolate cake and see what you get.) There's live jazz every Saturday night and concerts take place during the summer in the beautiful enclosed outdoor patio. Call for a schedule. Open Tues through Sat; there's a cover charge for special musical events.

i Solar Culture Gallery at 31 E. Toole Ave. (520-884-0874; www .solarculture.org) is a funky venue that brings eclectic performing artists to the Old Pueblo. This long, narrow space will remind you of a boho living room, with rows of mismatched chairs, unusual art, and a small stage. All events start at 9 p.m. and tickets are sold the night of the show.

THE GRILL
Hacienda del Sol Guest Ranch Resort
5601 N. Hacienda del Sol Rd.
(520) 529-3500
www.haciendadelsol.com

Friday and Saturday you'll find live Latin jazz music on the outdoor patio, where you can sip delicious drinks, indulge in tasty appetizers, or order a complete dinner while you enjoy the high-energy rhythms at one of Tucson's premier historic hotels.

RIC'S CAFE
5605 River Rd.
(520) 577-7272
www.ricscafeonline.net

Friday and Saturday nights at Ric's you'll find delightful contemporary jazz performed by a variety of professional musicians. You can sit under the softly lit palms at the bistro tables and enjoy both the music and dinner in the lovely outdoor courtyard.

MARIACHI/LATIN

BAR ¡TOMA! AT EL CHARRO CAFE
311 N. Court Ave.
(520) 622-1922
Mariachi music fills the courtyard weekends at this downtown bar and restaurant known for its Mexican cuisine. The restaurant opens at 10 a.m. Mon through Sun. Enjoy the funky cowboy-hatted fountain while you listen to the bouncy, upbeat tunes.

✳CASA VICENTE
375 S. Stone Ave.
(520) 884-5253
www.casavicente.com
Do you like flamenco dancing? Reserve your Friday and Saturday nights for live flamenco performances at this casual, delightful Spanish restaurant. The dancers are gorgeous, intense, and hot, hot, hot! There's a cover charge of $5 on top of your meal to view the dancers as they stomp on the center stage to live guitar music and castanets. You'll want to sign up for lessons *immediatamente* (tango and milonga lessons are offered Wed night)—olé!

EL PARADOR
2744 E. Broadway Blvd.
(520) 881-2744
www.elparadortucson.com
Every Friday and Saturday night the leafy large entry area is hopping with a live salsa band. Salsa lovers 21 and over can join in the fun for a mere $7 cover charge. Don't miss the salsa lessons for $5.

LA FUENTE
1749 N. Oracle Rd.
(520) 623-8659
www.lafuenterestaurant.com
You'll find authentic mariachi music at La Fuente Thursday through Sunday year-round. The talented singers roam the restaurant and perform onstage right up until closing.

ROCK & BLUES

BOONDOCKS LOUNGE
3306 N. 1st Ave.
(520) 690-0991
www.boondockslounge.com
You can't miss this place—a giant wine bottle sits in front of the building. This funky club has 2 bars, a dance floor, and several pool tables. Live music runs every day but Wednesday, with a variety from rock to blues. It's dark, and the crowd varies depending on who's playing. This is a great little place to shoot some pool on an off night or hear some of Tucson's best local bands. You'll pay a cover to get in the door when there is a band.

THE CHICAGO BAR
5954 E. Speedway Blvd.
(520) 748-8169
www.chicagobartucson.com
With bands 7 nights a week, this has been one of Tucson's most popular spots since its beginnings as a blues club in 1972. A widely mixed crowd packs the place almost every night. The dance floor is well used (as are the pool tables), and Tucson's most popular bands play this venue, including rock, metal, reggae, blues, and R&B. There is a cover for most shows.

FROG & FIRKIN
874 E. University Blvd.
(520) 623-7507
www.frogandfirkin.com
This is a real college hangout, and live music begins blasting out of the doors around 6 p.m. on select weeknights and weekends. The Frog is always packed—indoors and out—with kids downing beers and enjoying traditional pub fare and pizza.

RIALTO THEATRE
318 E. Congress St.
(520) 740-1000
www.rialtotheatre.com
The historic Rialto Theatre hosts some of the biggest names in town, with live performances from punk to salsa to rockabilly. It's quite a scene.

GAY & LESBIAN BARS

AIN'T NOBODY'S BIZNESS
2900 E. Broadway Blvd., Ste. 118
(520) 318-4838
www.thebiztuc.com
This popular little pub is primarily a lesbian bar, but lots of straight people come here just for the great DJ music. There's a bar and a dance floor (which is always packed). People in the know refer to this place as The Biz.

IBT'S
616 N. 4th Ave.
(520) 882-3053
www.myspace.com/ibtstucson
If you're looking for the young, hip, gay crowd, head to IBT's (It's 'bout Time). Located downtown on 4th Avenue, they've got it all here: dancing, drinks, drag shows, live DJs, jazz night, outside patio bar, friendly bartenders, an automatic teller machine, video games, human Jenga, bingo for fun, patio barbecues, and more. Open daily.

WOODY'S BAR
3710 N. Oracle Rd.
(520) 292-6702
http://mywoodysaz.com
This friendly spot on the west side of town has a nice vibe. There's a bar, flat-screen TVs, DJs, and occasional live music. A spacious outdoor patio and grassy lawn is home to barbecues and casual conversation. Karaoke, Havana Night, a chilidog buffet, and more take place throughout the week, so come on down. Special events include an annual Jell-O wrestling fund-raiser. Open daily.

MAKE 'EM LAUGH

LAFF'S COMEDY CLUB
2900 E. Broadway Blvd.
(520) 323-8669
www.laffstucson.com
In the tradition of New York comedy clubs, Tucson's nightspot for a good chuckle is open Thurs through Sat. A full bar and menu is available. The club hosts both touring and local up-and-coming comics. There is a cover charge.

CASINOS

AVA AMPHITHEATER AT CASINO DEL SOL
5655 W. Valencia Rd.
(800) 344-9435
www.casinodelsol.com
This huge 5,000-seat amphitheater with lawn and reserved seating plays host to a variety of concerts and events during the year. Past shows have featured Sheryl Crow, Van Halen, Luis Miguel, Tony Bennett, and Toby Keith.

DIAMOND CENTER AT DESERT DIAMOND CASINO

I-19 and Pima Mine Road at exit 80
1100 W. Pima Mine Rd., Sahuarita
(520) 294-7777
www.desertdiamondcasino.com

The 2,400-seat Diamond Center at this state-of-the-art casino run by the Tohono O'odham Nation has a whole slew of acts throughout the year, from boxing and comedians to singers and rock groups. Recent acts have included Cyndi Lauper and Wayne Newton. Call or check their website to see what's coming up.

ROOTIN' TOOTIN' GOOD TIMES

CACTUS MOON

5470 E. Broadway Blvd.
(520) 748-0049
www.cactusmoon.net

This hot Top 40 country music dance club does not offer live music, but it does offer nonstop country hits, line dancing, a Friday happy hour (starting at 5 p.m.), and a variety of drink specials. If you're a little unsure of your dancing capabilities, line dance lessons are offered on Wednesday, Thursday, and Saturday nights. All this can be yours for a low cover. The Moon doesn't shine Mon or Sun.

*THE MAVERICK

6622 E. Tanque Verde Rd.
(520) 298-0430
www.tucsonmaverick.com

The Maverick is one of the true country bars in town. Bands are pure country, and dancing is as much a part of the scene here as the drinking. It's been said the Maverick is the kind of place a country gal can walk into

alone and not feel intimidated. You can even take dance lessons on select nights.

The dance floor is smooth and can get quite crowded on nights when the bar offers 2-for-1 drink specials. Service is great, as are the drinks and food (you'll also be pleased with the reasonable prices). Live music 4 nights a week. Open Tues through Sat.

THE RIVER'S EDGE LOUNGE

4635 N. Flowing Wells Rd.
(520) 887-9027

The River's Edge Lounge has karaoke 5 nights a week. Rowdy and raucous, with a dance floor and several bars, it's usually packed and pulsing with energy. Beer's the beverage of choice here. Open until 2 a.m.

BREWING UP A STORM

GENTLE BEN'S BREWING CO.

865 E. University Blvd.
(520) 624-4177
www.gentlebens.com

Located 1 block west of the UA main gate, Gentle Ben's Brewing Company is Tucson's favorite place for fresh microbrews, food, and fun. Ben's is 2 stories of an award-winning brewery, a full-service restaurant, and 2 neighborhood bars. It's a great place for lunch, dinner, special occasions, private parties, catering, and partying. This continues to be a favorite of the college crowd, basically because of its prime location. Lunch and dinner are served daily. (See the Restaurants chapter.)

NIMBUS BREWERY

3850 E. 44th St.
(520) 745-9175
www.nimbusbeer.com

This converted warehouse may be a bit tricky to find. From Palo Verde Road, turn east on 44th Street and continue to its very end. There you'll find a very casual, wide-open brewpub. Weekend evenings will find music and special events. If you get hungry, you can chow down on a selection of beer-battered appetizers, chicken fingers, burgers, or the (in)famous fried bologna sandwich. Pool tables are also available.

BARRIO BREWING
800 E. 16th St.
(520) 791-2739
To find this place, look for the giant white grain silo on the southeast corner of Toole Avenue and 16th Street, or better yet, call for detailed directions—it isn't easy to find even with your iPhone mapping app! Housed in a converted warehouse in a funky part of town, this great bar features 12 microbrews on tap. An extensive menu features the usual bar favorites including crispy loaded potato skins, fries, and wings, plus burgers, sandwiches, salads, and more. Go for the "beer sponges," giant soft pretzels served warm from the oven.

ALTERNATIVE CINEMA

Tucson has two theaters that offer foreign, art, and independent films. The University of Arizona also presents a number of films and documentaries at various locations on campus, and when it does, the shows are usually well advertised in the local newspaper calendar sections.

THE LOFT CINEMA
3233 E. Speedway Blvd.
(520) 795-7777
www.loftcinema.com

With 3 screens, this is where you can satisfy your urge for foreign and art films, including a regular midnight screening of *The Rocky Horror Picture Show* on Saturday. Become a member and get super discounts and free popcorn.

THE SCREENING ROOM
127 E. Congress St.
(520) 622-2262
www.azmarc.org
A small, 90-seat theater with an art gallery in the lobby, the Screening Room is known for independent productions, both from local producers and internationally known filmmakers. The theater, in the heart of the downtown Arts District, sponsors a week-long film festival every April that screens everything from full-length films to short documentaries (see the Festivals & Events chapter). Ticket prices vary.

i Attention all film buffs! Do not miss Tucson's greatest video store, Casa Video. Located at 2905 E. Speedway and open 9 a.m. to 1 a.m. every day, this store has one of the most incredible collections of videos in town, if not the country. You'll find classics, foreign, documentaries, and wonderful theme collections (Favorite Directors, Oscar Winners). You could spend days here just exploring and you won't go hungry; bags of freshly popped popcorn are free to all. Call (520) 326-6314 or visit their website at www.casavideo.com.

IN THE STARS

For a more mellow way to spend an evening, Tucson offers great stargazing opportunities.

You can take a drive to the outer limits of the city and do your own, or try one of these more formal (and more up-close) looks at the stars. (See the Attractions chapter for more about both observatories.)

FLANDRAU—THE UA SCIENCE CENTER AND PLANETARIUM
Cherry Street and University Boulevard
(520) 621-7827
www.flandrau.org
You can catch a glimpse of the stars from the observatory's 16-inch telescope Wed through Sat from 7 to 10 p.m. A knowledgeable guide will explain in detail what you are seeing. The stargazing is free.

KITT PEAK NATIONAL OBSERVATORY
Highway 386
(520) 318-8726
www.noao.edu
The Kitt Peak National Observatory is open to the public daily from 9 a.m. to 3:45 p.m., except Thanksgiving, Christmas, and New Year's Day. Guided tours are offered daily at 10 a.m., 11:30 a.m., and 1:30 p.m.; group tours are available by appointment. Guided tours last approximately 1 hour and are led by trained docents who know the history and interesting facts regarding each telescope. Normally the tours go to the following telescopes: 10 a.m., the world's largest solar telescope; 11:30 a.m., the 2.1-meter telescope; and 1:30 p.m., the 4-meter Mayall Telescope (this tour lasts 90 minutes). Tour locations are subject to change due to maintenance and safety issues. Visitor center admission is free. Prices for guided tours vary; children under 6 are free.

You can also stargaze at Kitt Peak at night with the reservation-only Nightly Observing Programs. Hours for the popular stargazing programs vary throughout the year based on sunset times and space is limited. The nighttime stargazing is not available from July 15 through September 1. (See the Attractions chapter for details.)

A few suggestions that will make your visit more enjoyable. Wear warm clothing to tolerate the 15- to 20-degree temperature difference (Kitt Peak's elevation is 6,875 feet). Also wear walking shoes, as you'll traverse steep paths on your way to the scopes. It is recommended that those with cardiac, respiratory, or other health problems notify the visitor center ahead of time.

i For a wonderful evening under the stars, head downtown to colorful La Placita Village, 110 S. Church Ave., for a free outdoor movie. Held at 7:30 p.m. every Thurs from May through October, this series of great classic films ranges from *Dr. Strangelove* to *Lolita*. You can grab a bite at one of the many tiny eateries, take-out shops, and cafes or bring your own. Call (520) 326-5282 or check www.cinemalaplacita.com for more information.

MOUNT LEMMON SKYCENTER OBSERVATORY
(520) 626-8122
http://skycenter.arizona.edu
For an amazing view of the cosmos, head up Mount Lemmon to UA's SkyCenter Observatory for the Sky Night program. The 5-hour program starts in the late afternoon and includes an orientation, light meal, and sunset viewing.

Once darkness falls, you will head up to the observatory dome area for additional briefing on stars and constellations followed by a viewing of the magnificent heavens through the 32-inch Schulman telescope, the largest dedicated public telescope in the Southwest. Wear warm clothing—you will be at 9,157 feet and it can be cold, even when it's super hot in town. Start times vary throughout the year. There is a per-person fee, and reservations are required.

The program is held nightly, and although you can make a reservation 24 hours in advance, it's best to reserve a spot a week in advance if possible, as the number of participants is limited to 20. Children must be 7 or older. The SkyCenter is located just outside Summerhaven, about an hour and a half drive from downtown. *NOTE:* You do not need to pay the Mount Lemmon access fee if you are going to the observatory.

SHOPPING

The best thing about shopping in Tucson is exploring the hundreds of small shops that carry items uniquely Southwestern. And most folks who visit here or live here are looking for just that—things Western, Mexican, cowboy, or American Indian. In this chapter we emphasize the gifts, clothes, food, art, and home furnishings that people want to see and buy when they come to Tucson.

We also have malls, and we do have major department stores that are every bit as complete as those in cities of the East and West Coasts.

If you're not quite sure what "Southwestern" or regional specialty items are, here are a few tips. Chiles are big (as in popular) here and come in all forms and shapes, from the many varieties of fresh ones ready to be added to a recipe to the dried ones hanging on strings, known as *ristras*. Hanging a ristra on your door is said to bring good luck. Local shops carry Native art from many nations: Zuni fetishes, O'odham baskets, Hopi kachina dolls, and Navajo textiles. The truly local Native art is primarily O'odham baskets and Pascua Yaqui masks.

Popular items from south of the border include mesquite furniture, characterized by thick natural wood and intricate carvings, Talavera pottery, stoneware, iron and tin ornaments, wool rugs, and colorful blankets. Much of the food considered regional has its origins in Mexico as well, such as tortillas and salsas. Tucson also has some food specialties that grow locally, including pecans, pistachios, mesquite honey, citrus fruits, and sweets made from cacti.

With this briefing on regional specialties, you're ready to put on your walking shoes and explore the shopping scene in Tucson.

NATIVE AMERICAN

Below we highlight some of the shops dealing in Native American arts and crafts, but check other categories, such as "Malls, Plazas, and Shopping Centers," "Shopping Districts," and "Southwestern Shops," for more places to find these popular regional items.

BAHTI INDIAN ARTS
4330 N. Campbell Ave., Ste. 73
(520) 577-0290
www.bahti.com
This store on the north side of charming St. Philip's Plaza offers fine Indian arts and crafts. You'll find rugs, pots, sand paintings, weavings, kachinas, fetishes, sculpture, and baskets by contemporary Southwest Indian artists. The shop also has books, tapes, and CDs on and by Native Americans.

DESERT RAIN GALLERY
Main Street, Sells
(520) 383-4966
www.tocaonline.org

This tiny gallery on the Tohono O'odham Nation is operated by the nonprofit organization Tohono O'odham Community Action. Exquisite baskets hand-woven by members of the basket cooperative, books about Tohono O'odham culture, traditional-music CDs, locally made jewelry and pottery, and traditional O'odham foods and ribbon dresses are available here. Closed Sat and Sun; call ahead for hours.

Weaving History

The Tohono O'odham are renowned for their exquisite baskets, woven by hand from a variety of native plants. They are so finely made that some can actually hold water. Baskets were also used for cooking and were prized as trading items. They can range in size from 1 inch to several feet high and feature designs that incorporate spiritual as well as natural themes. Some lovely examples can be viewed at the Arizona-Sonora Desert Museum. The best place to purchase an authentic basket is through the Tohono O'odham Basketweavers Organization (520-383-4966), on the Tohono O'odham Reservation in Sells, about an hour outside Tucson. You can also view and purchase baskets at their online gallery at www.tocaonline .org. The distinctive look, incredible craftsmanship, and smell of grass and desert air make for more than a wonderful souvenir.

DESERT SON
4759 E. Sunrise Dr.
(520) 299-0818
www.desertson.com

This shop specializes in Southwest Indian items such as art, pottery, vases, kachinas, Navajo rugs, sand paintings, and jewelry. Desert Son is closed on Sun.

GALLERY WEST
6420 N. Campbell Ave.
(520) 529-7002
www.indianartwest.com

Serious collectors will appreciate the museum-quality antique Native American art here, including rugs, weavings, baskets, pottery, and beadwork. Gallery West is closed on Sun (and Mon during summer).

GREY DOG TRADING COMPANY
2970 N. Swan Rd.
(520) 881-6888
www.greydogtrading.com

You'll find Grey Dog in the lovely Plaza Palomino, along with its selection of Hopi kachinas, Pueblo pottery, Zuni fetishes, Navajo weavings, jewelry, baskets, and sand paintings. The store is closed on Sun.

MAC'S INDIAN JEWELRY
2400 E. Grant Rd.
(520) 327-3306

This shop boasts a large selection of well-priced Native American jewelry but also has kachinas, pottery, rugs, carvings, and sand paintings. It's closed on Sun.

MORNING STAR TRADERS
2020 E. Speedway Blvd.
(520) 881-2112
www.morningstartraders.com

Morning Star Traders offers baskets, pottery, Navajo rugs, kachinas, and a large selection of old and new jewelry in a charming Spanish Colonial Revival building. Closed Sun.

SAN XAVIER MISSION SHOPS
1959 E. San Xavier Rd.

While visiting the historic San Xavier Mission, you'll have a chance to shop for items pertaining to the mission in the on-site gift shop as well as specialty shops located in the plaza across from the mission that carry items such as pottery, art, and baskets representing Southwest Indians, particularly the Tohono O'odham, on whose reservation the mission resides.

TURQUOISE SKIES
4410 S. Mission Rd.
(520) 578-1673
www.turquoiseskies.com

It's a bit off the beaten path and seems forlorn all by itself, but Turquoise Skies is across the street from 2 huge adult RV and mobile home communities. The store sells items by Navajo, Hopi, and Zuni Indians and over 35 other tribes, including rugs, jewelry, baskets, and kachinas. It's closed Sun and Mon.

GOURMET FOOD & SPIRITS

Tucson offers a number of specialty food items that are great for both chowing down and gift giving—goodies such as tortillas and other Mexican favorites, medjool dates, locally grown pistachios, prickly pear cactus candies, and all manner of Mexican and Southwestern flavorings. Here are some of the best spots for finding food items for which Tucson is famous, as well as some of the more unusual places to go for other taste treats.

✳AJ'S FINE FOODS
La Encantada
2805 E. Skyline Dr.
(520) 232-6340
www.ajsfinefoods.com

You'll find lots of terrific gourmet fare here along with a sushi bar, cafe, wine cellar, and boulangerie. Prepared foods to go include super salads all made in-house, pastas, pizzas, and more. It's expensive, but you get what you pay for. The produce section is a work of art. Open daily.

ALEJANDRO'S TORTILLA FACTORY
5330 S. 12th Ave.
(520) 889-2279

The retail part of this wholesale operation offers customers not only tortillas but also bagged spices and prepared foods such as tacos, tortas, and pastries. They also serve burritos with a variety of fillings, including chorizo. Menudo is available daily.

CARAVAN MIDDLE EASTERN MARKET
28217 N. Country Club Rd.
(520) 323-6808

This store stocks Middle Easter ingredients of all kinds: Egyptian rice, Israeli couscous, coffees, teas, nuts, canned foods, frozen meats, delicious pastries, and some of the best olives in town. Open daily.

EL RIO BAKERY
901 N. Grande Ave.
(520) 624-4996
www.elriobakery.com

Located in a heavily Hispanic area west of downtown and I-10, El Rio has great Mexican baked goods plus some traditional ones. Here you'll find *pan de huevo* (egg bread), empanadas, pan dulce, *cochinitos* (gingerbread pigs, a favorite), delicious Mexican cookies, and tortillas. El Rio also has some prepared take-out food such as burritos with *machaca* and beans, plus a small selection of grocery items.

EUROPEAN MARKET & DELI
4500 E. Speedway Blvd.
(520) 512-0206
www.europeanmarketanddeli.com
Folks hungry for items from Russia and other Eastern European countries always find a treat here. The market carries 30 kinds of sausage in addition to vodka, dried fish, canned goods, bakery items, and a variety of candies and chocolates. Lunch and dinner are served all day, too.

5TH STREET DELI AND MARKET
5071 E. 5th St.
(520) 325-3354
www.5thstreetdeli.com
This is the only kosher deli and butcher in town, offering fresh meats along with a variety of other market items, including bagels, of course. The deli offers smoked fish, fresh salads, knish, sandwiches, corned beef, and pastrami, among other items. It's closed Sun and on Jewish holidays.

G&L IMPORT EXPORT
4828 E. 22nd St.
(520) 790-9016
Tucsonans need not go to the Far East to find anything Asian—it's all right here at this large store specializing in Asian imports. It's filled with Japanese, Chinese, and Middle Eastern food products in bottles, boxes, cans, and bags, including soy sauces, pastas, wines, seasonings, and vegetables. There's also a large selection of cooking tools such as woks, tea utensils, strainers, chopsticks, and even a few Asian furnishings and accessories.

INDIA DUKAAN
2754 N. Campbell Ave.
(520) 321-0408
This shop offers a wide variety of Indian foods, from papadums to rice of all kinds. You'll find unusual condiments, spices, curries, naan, dals, sweets, nuts, frozen dinners, and ayurvedic medicines along with a library of original "Bollywood" videos and DVDs to rent. Not sure how to cook up these fragrant ingredients? There's a selection of cookbooks, too. Open daily.

LA BUENA MEXICAN FOODS
234 E. 22nd St.
(520) 624-1796
You'll find great Mexican food prepared daily here, such as flour and corn tortillas, taco shells, green corn and red chili tamales, plus the ingredients to make your own, such as masa and nixtamal. The store has fresh menudo daily.

LA MESA TORTILLAS
7823 E. Broadway Blvd.
(520) 298-5966
www.lamesatortillas.com
La Mesa makes fresh, delicious whole wheat, original, corn, and jalapeno tortillas daily. Other offerings include burros with a variety of fillings and tamales by the dozen. Lunch is served from 11 a.m. to 2 p.m. Other locations are at 2112 E. Pima St. (520-777-6172) and 3923 E. Grant Rd. (520-623-9703). The stores are closed on Sun.

i Super-luxe Canyon Ranch Health Resort uses La Mesa tortillas for all its sandwich wraps.

LEELEE ORIENTAL MARKET

1990 W. Orange Grove Rd.

(520) 638-8328

This massive, sparkling-clean Asian market is a welcome addition to the Northwest part of town. One of 3 stores in Arizona, they carry products from just about every Asian country. Aisles are organized by region, and you'll find fresh produce, fresh fish and meats, and bazillions of fascinating canned, dried, and frozen products—plan to spend the whole day. You're likely to see some of Tucson's top chefs hovering in the aisles. Open daily.

RINCON MARKET

2513 E. 6th St.

(520) 327-6653

www.rinconmarket.com

This corner market and deli in central Tucson is almost an institution and a favorite of locals. The store specializes in spit-roasted chicken and has other deli delights as well, plus a complete market with butcher shop and fishmonger. You can take your deli food to go or dine inside or on the outdoor patio.

ROMA IMPORTS

627 S. Vine Ave.

(520) 792-3173

www.romaimports.com

If you're cooking Italian and want authentic ingredients, shop at Roma's, where you'll find pastas, cheeses, sauces, sausages, pancetta, prosciutto, biscotti, cannoli, tiramisu, olive oils, sun-dried tomatoes, olives, and lots more, all imported or made on-site. You can also get a great sandwich, specials, and salads to eat in or take out. If you want to eat Italian at home without cooking, Roma's offers frozen lasagna, meatballs, soups and sauces, all microwave or oven ready. The

shop is closed on Sun. Make sure to get directions; it's hard to find.

RUM RUNNER WINE AND CHEESE COMPANY

3131 E. 1st St.

(520) 326-0121

www.rumrunnertucson.com

Wines and cheeses are definitely the specialty of this upscale shop, but it carries other things as well, such as homemade deli items, gift baskets, breads, and regional food products. The wine selection is one of the best in the area. The shop also has a full-service bistro and wine bar. The new location is just down the street from the old.

17TH STREET FARMERS' MARKET

830 E. 17th St.

(520) 792-2588

www.seventeenthstreetmarket.com

This huge market is hidden away on 17th Street between Euclid and Park. It's stuffed with every ethnic ingredient imaginable. They also have tons of fresh organic produce, a huge selection of seafood (some swimming in tanks), and fresh meats. You can spend days roaming the aisles here. Closed Sun.

TANIA'S TORTILLAS AND MEXICAN FOOD

2856 W. Drexel Rd.

(520) 883-1595

For a selection of prepared food that's as large as any Mexican restaurant's menu, stop by Tania's. This tiny shop has soups, red and green chilies, *machaca,* carne asada, menudo, flour tortillas, and lots more.

TED'S COUNTRY STORE

2760 N. Tucson Blvd.

(520) 325-3122

This place is like a homey old-time country corner store that has an updated style and an upscale selection of products. They have a great wine selection, a deli with sandwiches made to go, and regional food products such as spices, jellies, and honey. You'll also find the basics here. Closed Sun.

VIRO'S REAL ITALIAN BAKERY
8301 E. 22nd St.
(520) 885-4045
If you have a hankering for Italian baked goods like those sold in ethnic neighborhoods back East, try Viro's. Along with all kinds of breads, Viro's has sweets such as biscotti, panettone, and *pizzelles*. The bakery is closed Mon.

WHOLE FOODS MARKET
3360 E. Speedway Blvd.
(520) 795-9844
www.wholefoodsmarket.com
This chain of upscale organic grocery stores carries lots of regional and local specialty products in addition to their normal grocery items. You'll find locally made prickly pear juice and syrup, Tucson-made salsas, homegrown olives, Arizona pistachios and pecans, wines and beers from local vineyards and microbreweries, along with cotton clothing, hats, unusual gift items, and Southwestern-themed kitchenware. If they don't have it, they'll go out of their way to order it for you. An additional location is at 7133 N. Oracle Rd. (520-297-5394).

GROWING THINGS (OR DESERT FLORA)

In this section we concentrate on nurseries that specialize in things that grow in the desert, which are popular items not only for folks who live here but also for visitors who

want to take a bit of Mother Nature's unusual desert life back home.

B&B CACTUS FARM
11550 E. Speedway Blvd.
(520) 721-4687
www.bandbcactus.com
On Tucson's far east side, B&B features more than 600 species and varieties of cacti and succulents from all over the world in its greenhouses and outdoor displays. You'll find desert-garden kits, container cactus gardens, Mexican pottery, and hanging baskets for the patio. Take your camera along, and you can photograph some amazing blooms. B&B packs plants for traveling and shipping and also has mail-order selections. The nursery is closed Sun and Mon.

BACH'S GREENHOUSE CACTUS NURSERY
8602 N. Thornydale Rd.
(520) 744-3333
www.bachs-cacti.com
Located in the far northwest, Bach's has hundreds of species of cacti to choose from. Whether you're looking for a cactus for your home or yard or an unusual one for a gift, you'll surely be able to find it here. The nursery sells planted cacti gardens and will pack your selections. Bach's is closed on Sun.

DESERT SURVIVORS
1020 W. Starr Pass Blvd.
(520) 884-8806
www.desertsurvivors.org
This is a favorite spot for locals for two reasons: Desert Survivors has a great selection of desert "greenery," and it's a vocational rehab and early intervention program, so your purchase helps these people maintain active and productive lives. Although you

won't find cacti here, you will find nearly everything else that grows in these parts, including trees, yucca plants, agave, and succulents. The nursery is open year-round, Tues through Sun, and has very popular semiannual sales in April and October.

✳NATIVE SEEDS/SEARCH
3061 N. Campbell Rd.
(520) 622-5561, (866) 622-5561
www.nativeseeds.org
As unusual as the store's name is what it sells—seeds and more seeds. This nonprofit shop is heaven for the desert gardener. The shelves are lined with thousands of seeds, some of which are endangered species. And if Native Seeds doesn't have what you want, it can probably be ordered (hence the "SEARCH" in the name). The mission is to preserve and promote the traditional crops, seeds, and farming methods that have sustained native peoples throughout the American Southwest and northern Mexico. (Native Seeds/SEARCH also maintains a conservation farm in Patagonia.) If you're looking for the unusual, such as blue speckled tepary beans or blue corn, or the more common desert lupine, sunflower, or evening primrose seeds, you'll find them here, along with baskets, jewelry, and lots of food products including all kinds of dried chilies, bean soup mixes, mesquite meal, and salsas. You'll also find a great selection of books about gardening and the Southwest. Native Seeds is open daily.

TANQUE VERDE GREENHOUSES
10810 E. Tanque Verde Rd.
(520) 749-4414
This desert nursery on the far east side has 6 large greenhouses with thousands of plants and hundreds of varieties of cacti and succulents. The selection includes euphorbia from Africa, mammillaria from Mexico, and organ pipes from Arizona. You can buy a ready-to-go dish garden of cacti or have one custom designed. Employees carefully pack the cacti for air or road travel or mail them (fully guaranteed) if you prefer. If you don't have a green thumb but still want a cactus memento, the greenhouses also have sweet treats made from cacti, such as candies and jellies. Closed Sun.

MEXICAN IMPORTS

For locals and visitors who don't want to make the trek south of the border for authentic Mexican goods, Tucson has plenty to offer right here. We list some of the more popular ones, but check in other sections of this chapter because nearly every mall or shopping plaza has a store carrying some items imported from Mexico. One of the best spots is the Lost Barrio shopping district on S. Park Avenue, where most of the shops specialize in Mexican imports. Mexican products that seem to be very popular stateside include Mexican (or Spanish) colonial furniture, pigskin furniture (called *equipale*), rugs, blankets, hand-blown glassware, framed mirrors, tin and metal light fixtures and lamps, pottery, stoneware, religious statuary, Talavera (the brilliantly painted ceramics made in the city of Puebla), and colorful wooden animals made in Oaxaca.

ANTIGUA DE MEXICO
3235 W. Orange Grove Rd.
(520) 742-7114
Mexican goods offered here include equipale furniture, glassware, carved wood furniture, lighting fixtures, stone fountains and statuary, clay pottery, tin items, folk art, and sterling silver jewelry.

AZTECA MEXICAN IMPORTS
1111 S. Kolb Rd.
(520) 290-0024

You may not see a sign proclaiming that it's Azteca, but you will see a huge collection of pottery, fountains, and chimineas at this outdoor location just north of 22nd Street. Open daily.

BORDERLANDS OUTLET STORE
309 E. 7th St.
(520) 622-3476

Chock-full of wonderful Talavera pottery, tiled mirrors, glass, furnishings, Mexican paper flowers, and unusual knickknacks, this rustic shop offers a multitude of imported products in all price ranges. Open daily.

LA BUHARDILLA
2360 E. Broadway Blvd.
(520) 622-5200

In English it means "the attic," and finds here include colonial and Spanish baroque furniture, wrought iron, pottery including Talavera, silver, and paintings. The store also carries hand-carved wooden doors and materials for restoring or building haciendas. La Buhardilla is closed Sun and Mon.

LA CASA MEXICANA
204 S. Park Ave.
(520) 624-1420

This shop in the Lost Barrio shopping district specializes in handcrafted Mexican-style furniture and accessories. They custom build furniture and fashion tile-topped tables and ironwork. Closed Sun.

QUE BONITA
6934 E. Tanque Verde Rd.
(520) 721-1998
www.quebonitafurniture.com

This shop specializes in Old Mexico and Santa Fe furniture and boasts a large showroom with new arrivals weekly. There's also an extensive selection of Southwestern decorative accessories, pottery, and Zapotec rugs. The shop has a unique collection of southwestern clothing and jewelry too. Closed Sun.

SOUTHWESTERN SHOPS

A chapter on shopping in Tucson just wouldn't be complete without a section devoted to regional, or Southwestern, items. Tucsonans and visitors are always interested in things grown or made in the Southwest—chilies (whether real or artificial), salsas, sweets made from cacti, locally grown pecans and pistachios, minerals, turquoise, and Mexican and American Indian arts and crafts. Here are some ideas of where to look, but many more are included in other sections of this chapter.

CACTUS CARDS & GIFTS
5975 W. Western Way Circle
(520) 883-5930

If you happen to be visiting the many attractions on the western side of the Tucson Mountains, you'll be near this shop that offers lots of southwestern goods, from T-shirts to sweets and cards to pottery and souvenirs. Closed Sun.

WESTERN WEAR

Both real cowboys and wannabes have a good choice of Western wear in Tucson, from hats and chaps to bolo ties and belt buckles.

ARIZONA HATTERS
2790 N. Campbell Ave.
(520) 292-1320
www.arizonahatters.com

This store carries a large selection of name-brand hats, including Stetson, Resistol, and Milano, for both men and women, plus a selection of men's Western shirts and belts. They'll custom-fit and shape the hat of your choice.

BOOT BARN
6701 E. Broadway Blvd.
(520) 731-3422
www.bootbarn.com
Claiming to "dress the West for less," this store also claims to have the biggest selection of boots, hats, clothes, and accessories for the whole family. (Employees speak Spanish.) The huge selection of straw and felt hats includes names such as Resistol and Stetson, plus they'll steam and shape your hat for free. The collection of boots represents practically every size and color imaginable, from cowhide to exotic leathers. Additional locations are at 3776 S. 16th Ave. (520-622-4500) and 3719 N. Oracle Rd. (520-888-1161).

BOOT BUNKHOUSE
5126 E. Pima St.
(520) 322-9044
Off the beaten track between Swan and Craycroft, this old-time family-owned shop specializes in boots of all kinds: Western, hiking, work, hunting, and uniform. Not only is there a huge selection to choose from, but they are also famous for their sizes, which range from 3 to 17 and AAAA to EEE. They sell accessories, wallets, belts, straw hats, and T-shirts as well. Personalized service is superb. Owner Chuck Siegfried promises, "We're about service; we get you what you want." Open Mon through Sat.

COWTOWN BOOTS
5190 N. Casa Grande Hwy.
(520) 888-0290
www.cowtownboots.com
If you can figure out how to get here, you can choose from about 10,000 pairs of boots for both men and women made by Cowtown Boot Company, Durango, Dingo, and others. It also carries Western clothing for children and adults. It's located on the eastside frontage road of I-10 just north of the Ruthrauff Road exit.

MALLS, PLAZAS & SHOPPING CENTERS

Tucson has malls and an abundance of plazas and shopping centers—sometimes it seems like there's one at every intersection. We cover a number of the more unusual ones here.

BROADWAY VILLAGE
E. Broadway Boulevard at Country Club Drive
(no phone number)
Built in 1932, this Joesler-designed Mission-style complex was one of Arizona's first shopping centers. You can still see parts of the original whitewashed adobe brick and inlaid tile structure that today surrounds a brick courtyard with trees all around. The plaza is home several shops including Zocalo offering handmade Mexican furnishings, Avenue Boutique with clothing and jewelry, and Bon, featuring home and garden accessories.

CASAS ADOBES PLAZA
N. Oracle and Ina Roads
(no phone number)
www.casasadobesplaza.com

When this Spanish-style plaza was built in the 1940s, it was a shopping hub out in the boonies. Today it's at a busy intersection, but strolling here can still be pleasant. The plaza also houses a boutique, beauty salons, footwear, eyewear, and linen shops, a Whole Foods Market, Maya Palace, and Chico's. For food there's Sauce, Wildflower Grill, and Bluefin Seafood Bistro.

CROSSROADS FESTIVAL
Grant and Swan Roads
(no phone number)
This plaza meanders from Swan Road around the corner and east along Grant Road for the equivalent of several blocks. It's an eclectic mix ranging from upscale apparel stores to discount hair salons and everything in between. It houses a major grocery store, a bank, a cupcake shop, jewelry and gift shops, fine apparel stores, Bed, Bath & Beyond for housewares, and Mrs. Tiggy Winkle's Toys (see the Kidstuff chapter). If you're looking for the only Tucson jeweler that carries Tiffany products or a certified Rolex watch dealer, Marshall's Artistry in Gold is the spot. Several restaurants are here, including the very popular Good Egg and Buddy's Grill. There's also the Grand Cinemas Crossroads movie theater, which offers discounted recently released movies, but you'll need to hunt for it because it's hidden in back.

EL CON MALL
3601 E. Broadway Blvd.
(520) 795-9958
www.shopelcon.com
El Con was Tucson's first mall and occupies a large parcel of what is now very valuable land in a central Tucson location. Although spread out, it's all one level and therefore not as overwhelming as the many more modern malls. It's home to JCPenney, Ross, Burlington Coat Factory, In-N-Out Burger, Home Depot, and Target. You'll also find a Century 20 theater complex and a small food court. The mall is easily accessible by bus.

> **i** El Con Mall stands on the grounds of what was one of Tucson's most gorgeous hotels, the El Conquistador resort hotel, which was demolished in 1959 to make room for the mall. The original copper dome from the roof of the old hotel now rests atop Joel's Pottery at the Casa Blanca shopping center at 208 W. Rudasill Rd. in northwest Tucson. If you love historical trivia, mall owner Nick Genematas (520-297-7222) has photos of the craning and removal of the dome. He also claims there is a .45-caliber slug hole in the bottom of the dome—we'll let him tell the story of how it got there.

EL MERCADO
Wilmot Road at Broadway Boulevard
(no phone number)
Designed to resemble a Spanish open-air *mercado* (market), this plaza features a number of unusual shops plus salons and restaurants. Here you'll find a store with all kinds of delicious handmade chocolates and Maya Palace. The El Charro Cafe is an offshoot of El Charro, Arizona's oldest Mexican restaurant (see the Restaurants chapter).

FOOTHILLS MALL
Ina Road and La Cholla Boulevard
(520) 219-0650
www.shopfoothillsmall.com
Foothills Mall is distinguished by its wide Saltillo tile corridors and architectural features that give it the feeling of a village

mercado. An upscale outlet and entertainment mall, it houses a Saks Fifth Avenue outlet, Barnes and Noble, Levi's, Old Navy, and Dress Barn outlets, among others. For food there are several sit-down restaurants, a brewery, and a food court with several vendors. For entertainment, the mall has a 15-screen movie theater and GameWorks Studio. There are plenty of special events and entertainment at the mall as well. It's a pleasant place to shop, be entertained, or just people watch.

JOESLER VILLAGE
River Road and Campbell Avenue
(no phone number)
Named for Josias Joesler, Tucson's premier architect, this upscale shopping plaza on the northwest corner of this intersection is home to boutiques, clothing stores, several galleries, and a number of casual and sophisticated restaurants.

☀LA ENCANTADA
2905 E. Skyline Dr.
(520) 299-3556
www.laencantadashoppingcenter.com
Big, beautiful, and full of wonderful stores, this lovely outdoor mall sits at the crest of Campbell Avenue at Skyline. Open courtyards, fountains, balconies, and gardens make this a great spot to stroll and shop. Shops include Tucson's only Crate & Barrel, Williams-Sonoma, and Pottery Barn. You'll also find specialty clothing and stores like Bebe, Brooks Brothers, and Cole Haan, and a phenomenal Apple retail store. Upscale restaurants offer options from barbecue to northern Italian; AJ's Fine Foods has gourmet groceries. Spend the day.

PARK PLACE
5870 E. Broadway Blvd.
(520) 745-7575
www.parkplacemall.com
This attractive mall is built on all one level in a close-in Eastside location. The large stores are Sears, Macy's, and Dillard's, which are accompanied by more than 100 shops and restaurants plus a movie theater. For books there's Borders Books and Music; for moviegoers, a huge 20-plex theater. The information booth is located just inside the mall's main entrance, which is at the center of the building on the south side facing Broadway Boulevard. Park Place is wheelchair accessible and rents strollers. There's also a kids' playground at the food court.

PLAZA PALOMINO
2970 N. Swan Rd.
(no phone number)
www.plazapalomino.com
This is one of the loveliest places to shop in Tucson, although it definitely leans toward upscale. Elegant shops, galleries, and restaurants constructed of adobe with Spanish-tiled roofs surround a tiled courtyard with fountains, foliage, and singing birds. Plaza Palomino is located near the Fort Lowell historic district, full of old Spanish charm and a peaceful break from hectic malls. You'll find a number of boutiques, jewelry, art, and home decor shops, and several restaurants with patio seating so you can enjoy the surroundings. Shops include clothing at La Contessa; Native American arts and crafts at Grey Dog Trading; and jewelry, art, and Western-style furniture at Appaloosa in the Woods. It's also host to a great farmers' market on Saturday.

THE RIVER CENTER
5605 E. River Rd.
(no phone number)
At the base of the Catalina foothills, River Center is a pretty setting for its 2 dozen shops and restaurants, including a branch of the Pima County Library. A fountain, outdoor dining, and views of the city lights below add to the ambience. In addition to a major drugstore, you'll find boutiques, the Green Monkey, an upscale consignment shop, a beauty salon, and several small businesses. Restaurants include Ric's Cafe, with outdoor dining.

ST. PHILIP'S PLAZA
River Road at Campbell Avenue
(520) 529-2775
www.stphilipsplaza.com
Set in a Joesler-designed Mexican-style plaza, this is an upscale shopping center in a pleasant (but congested) location. The plaza itself is a series of Spanish-style brick courtyards, which make for a picturesque stroll with shade trees, lovely tiled fountains, and gardens. One of Tucson's finest beauty salons and day spas, Gadabout, is located here (they have several other locations, too). Shops include the hip Changes. There are art galleries, jewelry stores, and several of Tucson's top eateries. Also located at St. Philip's is Windmill Inn, an all-suite hotel. Watch for special doings that take place here, such as outdoor concerts and a Sunday farmers' market.

TRAIL DUST TOWN
6541 E. Tanque Verde Rd.
(520) 296-4551
www.traildusttown.com
To find this hidden shopping and entertainment area, look for a 3-story stack of boulders with a small covered wagon on top. Trail Dust Town offers regional items in a handful of small shops that line a bricked courtyard, complete with gazebos, grass areas, colorful flowers, and plenty of shady spots and benches for people watching. You'll see facades and memorabilia of the Old West all around—a bank, apothecary store, jail, barbershop, hotel, saloon, train depot, wagon parts, posters, and signs. The real stores include Wild West Hot Sauce, and AZ Gold. Trail Dust Treasures features Southwestern gifts and novelties, while Dad Pfeenerbar's Old Time Photos will deck you out in Western wear and snap your photo. There's also a chocolate shop and the very fascinating General Store, which sells everything from old-time candy and nostalgia items to fine totem poles. For fun, take a ride on the train that circles the shopping area or on the carousel. And kids and grown-ups alike enjoy the Wild West stunt shows that take place periodically. Dining options here include the cowboy steak house Pinnacle Peak and Dakota Cafe, with patio dining and Southwestern-style food (see the Restaurants chapter).

TUCSON MALL
4500 N. Oracle Rd.
(520) 293-7330
www.tucsonmall.com
We're not talking megamall like the ones in Chicago or Minneapolis, but this is certainly Tucson's largest. Its 2 levels contain more than 200 department stores and specialty shops, including Dillard's, JCPenney, Sears, H&M, Forever 21, Gap, Guess?, Footlocker, Lane Bryant, Eddie Bauer, Victoria's Secret, Disney Store, and a number of shops specializing in gifts, jewelry, home furnishings, athletic wear, and shoes. There's something

here to suit anyone's taste and budget. Kids (and adults) will enjoy riding the dragons, horses, and reindeer on the carousel, while indoor fountains add a bit of tranquility to the frenzied shopping. The food court has more than a dozen food booths and plenty of inside seating to accommodate famished shoppers. Next to the food court is Arizona Avenue, a row of shops specializing in regional items from Indian and Mexican rugs to pottery to food. Don't miss the See's Candies Store and your free sample. There's also a colorful children's play area. The mall has strollers and wheelchairs (free) available as well as TDD phones. And just across Stone Avenue on the mall's east side is a major Sun Tran bus transit center.

SHOPPING DISTRICTS

They can't really be classified as malls, plazas, or shopping centers, so we've labeled them shopping districts—areas around town that have a concentration of commercial establishments, mostly retail shops, that shouldn't be overlooked. These are places where you'll get a taste of Tucson history and culture along with your purchases.

Downtown

Also known as the Tucson Arts District, the downtown area is a hub of cultural, social, and commercial activity, bounded roughly by Cushing Street on the south, Granada Avenue on the west, Franklin Street on the north, and Scott Avenue on the east. You'll find an amazing array of shops, many of them quite unusual—everything from plumbing supplies to tattoo parlors—along with galleries and eateries. The main thoroughfare bisecting this area is Congress Street, where many of the stores are concentrated. As with

many downtown areas, however, the shops here tend to come and go. Nonetheless it's worth exploring this eclectic area for the unusual and for the experience. A focus of the city's downtown renovation efforts, this area is undergoing a renaissance. Things not to miss include the historic **Hotel Congress** (311 E. Congress; 520-622-8848), the eclectic shop **Got All Your Marbles** (220 E. Congress; 520-628-1433), with jewelry and accessories made with marbles; **Chicago Store** (130 E. Congress; 520-622-3341), stuffed to the brim with instruments of all shapes and sizes; and the historic *Fox Theatre (17 W. Congress; 520-624-1515). **Santa Theresa Tile Works** (440 N. 6th Ave.; 520-623-1856) offers ceramic works of art. **Flanagan's Celtic Corner** (222 E. Congress; 520-623-9922), sells just about everything Celtic, from glassware to coats of arms, and the **Sacred Machine Museum** (245 E. Congress; 520-777-7403) showcases the unusual art of Daniel Martin Diaz (see the Arts & Culture chapter). The colorful **La Placita Village** (110 S. Church) is home to the **Tucson Visitors Center** (open daily) and several shops, cafes, and restaurants. A great time to visit is during the Club Crawl or 2nd Saturdays Downtown events (see the Nightlife chapter).

This area is accessible by Sun Tran bus, and parking is available on the street or in public lots or garages.

LOST BARRIO
200 S. Park Ave.
(no phone number)
A barrio that became a warehouse district is now a shopping district—one of the most interesting in Tucson if you're in the market for imports. Located on the southwest corner of Park Avenue and 12th Street, these warehouse buildings along a 2- to 3-block

Close-up

4th Avenue Should Be on Your List

A great shopping and people-watching destination is 4th Avenue. This historic district runs for 6 blocks along 4th Avenue south from University Boulevard to 9th Street. It's a real mix of funky, fun, and eclectic shops, galleries, boutiques, restaurants, and unusual secondhand stores. Free street parking is available all along the Avenue and the side streets, or you can take the Sun Tran bus.

A great way to start your tour of the area is to hop on the restored trolley car at 4th Avenue and 8th Street and ride it all the way to 1 block from the University of Arizona's main gate (about 10 minutes). This fun, old-fashioned ride will give you a bird's-eye view of what there is to see and do along the Avenue! It runs Fri evening, Sat noon to midnight, and Sun noon to 6 p.m. for $1 one way (and only 50 cents for seniors and kids 6 to 12; it's free for younger ones). The all-day fares are cheap, too: $2.50 for adults and $1.25 for kids over 6.

Once you disembark, take a leisurely stroll and wander in and out of the more than 100 shops that line 4th Avenue. Thrift shopping here may be about the best in the city. You can buy, sell, or trade everything from bicycle parts and washers to old lace and vintage clothing. If you're going to a shindig and need a costume, 4th Avenue can outfit you. Other old stuff you'll find here includes furniture, jewelry, antique dolls, vintage musical instruments, and funky sunglasses. Even if you're not in the market for old things, you'll take a trip down memory lane at secondhand stores like **The Other Side, Kanella's,** and **How Sweet It Was.** Don't miss the amazing solar panels at the corner of 4th Avenue and 5th Street that supply shade to the parking lot and power to **Brooklyn Pizza** and **Sky Bar.**

In need of a grass skirt, Hawaiian lei, a costume, or bolo tie? You'll probably be able to find them all somewhere along 4th Avenue. Care for some light? You'll find dragon's blood–scented candles at the **Rustic Candle** company. **Creative Ventures** craft mall showcases the clever wares of many local artisans and crafters. **Del Sol International Shop** has a huge array of Mexican products, from glassware and jewelry to clothing and rugs. The unique **Book Stop** book shop here shouldn't be missed; it has a huge collecton of used, rare, and out-of-print books (see listing in this chapter). You'll also find one-of-a-kind jewelry, ceramics, glass and metal shops, unusual bookstores (including Antigone Books, profiled in this chapter), art galleries, and lots more on this Avenue.

There's no shortage of places to stop or shop for food: coffeehouses; sweet shops; the **Food Conspiracy,** a natural grocery and specialty foods store; **Caruso's,** featuring Italian food; **La Indita Restaurant,** combining Mexican and Indian tastes; **Chocolate Iguana; Delectables;** the always popular **Delectables; Brooklyn Pizza Company;** the **Sky Bar** for the outdoor patio and upstairs astronomy bar; and even **Dairy Queen.**

And if all of this isn't enough to satisfy your shopping urge, twice a year 4th Avenue closes to traffic and puts on a huge street fair with hundreds of booths offering a mind-boggling array of arts and crafts, food, entertainment, and other types of fun. You'll find 4th Avenue guides at many of the shops on the Avenue. For more information call the **4th Avenue Merchants Association** at (520) 624-5004 or (800) 933-2477 or visit their website: www.fourthavenue.org.

area aren't fancy, but they're packed full of furniture and accessories in wood, iron, metal, stone, fabric, and glass. Much of it is from Mexico, but you'll also find work from Native American, African, and other cultures, and nearly everything is warehouse-priced. Stores here include La Casa Mexicana (520-624-1420), Old Brazil (520-461-1063), and Colonial Frontiers (520-622-7400). Some of the shops will also provide custom work in wood, iron, and upholstery. If you want to experience a bit of Nogales, Mexico, without crossing the border, this may be the spot, but not on Sunday. Parking is free on the street.

OLD TOWN ARTISANS
201 N. Court Ave.
(520) 623-6024, (800) 782-8072
www.oldtownartisans.com

This 1850s restored adobe structure fills an entire city block in the heart of the historic El Presidio neighborhood. Reputedly the original buildings on this site were dwellings and shops for early settlers. In keeping with Spanish tradition, the exterior wall was built on the property line with a central courtyard inside. Today the buildings surrounding the courtyard are shops offering Southwestern folk art, American Indian tribal art, and imports from Mexico. Many of the items are handmade by some of Tucson's finest artisans, yet it's all reasonably priced. If you're looking for regional items, you'll find one of the best collections all in one spot here. Old Town Artisans also houses La Cocina (Spanish for "kitchen") and its delightful patio garden. While shopping, ask for a walking-tour map and visit all the nearby sites reflecting Tucson's history and culture. You can park at meters on surrounding streets or in nearby public lots.

University Area

Although there's shopping almost all around the university, the most concentrated area is on University Boulevard extending about 2 blocks west from the main gate at Park Avenue. As one might expect, the shops and businesses here are student-oriented, but they also appeal to most anyone. Besides, it's an interesting place to watch university life.

Among the shops on this street are **Cry Babay Couture, Pitaya, American Apparel, Urban Outfitters,** and **Landmark Clothing and Shoes,** which carries popular brands such as Bass, Teva, Polo, Timberland, and Birkenstock. The shopping area just wouldn't be complete without a store selling everything University of Arizona, from clothing and hats to school supplies and calendars, and it's got that in the **Arizona Bookstore.** The eateries in this area, many with outdoor seating facing the street, offer a varied selection of food and refreshments with a view. There's the popular **Gentle Ben's** (see the Restaurants and Nightlife chapters), several gourmet pizza places, and eclectic restaurants and bars. For a comprehensive listing go to www.maingatesquare.com.

The Old Pueblo Trolley runs down the center of University Boulevard and connects with the 4th Avenue shopping district. (See this chapter's Close-up.) Metered parking is available on University Boulevard.

BARGAIN & OUTLET SHOPPING

Tucson has a number of places devoted to outlet shopping and other bargain merchandise. And if you want even more choices, head to Casa Grande, Arizona, about an hour north of Tucson.

BUFFALO EXCHANGE

2001 E. Speedway Blvd.

(520) 795-0508

www.buffaloexchange.com

This is the place for great bargains on gently used clothing and accessories. You can bring in items for trade or cash on the spot, or just browse the clean and hardly used clothing on the racks. Open daily. Additional locations are at 6170 E. Speedway Blvd. (520-885-8392) and 250 E. Congress Ave. (520-882-2939).

LITTLE TRADERS

6216 E. Speedway Blvd.

(520) 881-8438

www.littletraders.com

This consignment shop sells everything for kids: clothes (preemie to boys size 12 and girls size 16), books, toys, and equipment. They also have maternity clothes and books. Open daily.

NORDSTROM RACK

4320 North Oracle Road

http://shop.nordstrom.com

Nordstrom's has finally made it to Tucson! The 33,000 plus square foot store, scheduled to open in October of 2011, will offer clearance items including clothes accessories and shoes. Located on the corner of North Wetmore Road and West Oracle Roads in The Corner shopping plaza.

OLD PUEBLO TRADERS

6228 E. Broadway

(520) 747-0800

www.oldpueblotraders.com

You might want to head to this store, known locally as OPT, when your sore feet won't make it to another shopping spot, but you desperately need a comfy pair of Hush Puppies or Grasshoppers. OPT is like a warehouse of clothes and shoes for women, the latter including hard-to-find sizes. Brands you'll find here, in addition to the aforementioned shoes, include Koret, Sasson, Jantzen, Playtex, and Easy Spirit.

PRELOVED CHICA CLOTHING BOUTIQUE

102 E. 31st St.

(520) 303-8523

www.fortindelasflores.org

This cute boutique sells gently used clothing, jewelry, and accessories. All proceeds support Fortin de las Flores, a membership organization that provides a variety of services to low-income women including job search assistance, food, and toiletries. Call for hours.

> **i** To find the best bargains in Tucson, go to www.tucsononthecheap.com for up-to-the-minute info on deals and freebies all over town, from dining to shopping to fitness to gas.

TANQUE VERDE SWAP MEET

4100 S. Palo Verde Rd.

(520) 294-4252

www.tanqueverdeswapmeet.com

Put on your walking shoes and grab a hat and a jug of water so you'll be all set for a morning or evening of swap meeting. It's called the Tanque Verde Swap Meet because it started out on the corner of Tanque Verde and Grant Roads in the days when there used to be enough land to accommodate it. It moved but retained its name.

There's plenty of parking and dust, but buyers can find some good bargains and interesting items here. Most days you'll even find vendors selling some great produce from Mexico such as tomatoes, watermelons, limes, peppers, avocados, and mangos. The swap meet is open from 3 to 11 p.m. Thurs and Fri; 7 a.m. to 11 p.m. Sat. On Sun hours are from 7 a.m. to sundown.

VF FACTORY OUTLET
3754 S. 16th Ave.
(520) 882-2718
www.vffo.com

Compared to more modern outlet centers, VF Factory Outlet is small. But that may be a blessing for folks who don't want to walk a mile to shop. There are no more than a dozen indoor stores, carrying apparel, accessories, luggage, housewares, and party and paper products. Brand names include Vanity Fair, Wrangler, Lee, Healthtex, and Jantzen. It's a bit tricky to get to, however, so look for the Palo Verde Inn on S. Julian Drive—you'll see the outlet building almost adjacent to it.

BOOKS, ETC.

Although Tucson has its share of national bookstore chains, which are often located in malls, you'll also find many other bookstores, both new and used, all around the metro area. Here are just a few of the more notable ones.

ANTIGONE BOOKS
411 N. 4th Ave.
(520) 792-3715
www.antigonebooks.com

This shop in the 4th Avenue shopping district offers books by and about women and has a unique selection of nonsexist books for children. Antigone Books also has music, cards, and T-shirts on related topics.

ARIZONA BOOKSTORE
845 N. Park Ave.
(520) 622-4717
www.arizonabookstore.com

University of Arizona and Pima College students frequent this store because it buys and sells college textbooks. They also have a great selection of UA items, as well as school and engineering supplies, computer books and software, and technical and general interest books. Validated parking is available.

BOOK STOP
214 N. 4th Ave.
(520) 326-6661
www.bookstoptucson.com

Specializing in used, rare, and out-of-print books, this eclectic bookstore has a little bit of everything, from general fiction paperback and hardcovers to fascinating Native American and Arizona history books to a unique children's book collection with lots of classic titles. With over 100,000 volumes stuffed into floor-to-ceiling shelves, bookworms will love this place.

✳BOOKMAN'S
1930 E. Grant Rd.
(520) 325-5767
www.bookmans.com

The 3 Bookman's locations account for over 50,000 square feet of fabulous new and used books. The 20,000-square-foot shop on Grant Road is a favorite of locals and university students because it's centrally located, an interesting place, open until 10 p.m., and full of great used materials. You'll find both hardbound and paperback used books here on nearly any subject and new books on subjects of local interest, such as the desert and hiking. They also deal in used CDs, videos, and software and have a great selection of old and rare magazines, as do the other two locations in town: 3733 W. Ina Rd. (520-579-0303) and 6230 E. Speedway Blvd. (520-748-9555).

CLUES UNLIMITED
3146 E. Fort Lowell Rd.
(520) 326-8533
www.cluesunlimited.com
This specialty bookstore stocks over 10,000 titles in mystery and detective fiction, including the latest releases, hard-to-find and unusual titles, collectors' editions, and signed firsts. They also offer an extensive backlist and ship anywhere in the US and overseas. One nice feature: They offer home delivery service in Tucson. Open Mon through Sat.

KID'S CENTER
1725 N. Swan Rd.
(520) 322-5437
www.e-kidscenter.com
You'll find a great selection of children's books for all ages here, from baby classics like *Pat the Bunny* to the ever-popular *Magic Treehouse* series and chapter books for the older set. Kids love to hang out in this comfortable and welcoming store, which also carries a range of games and toys for all ages. Kids ages 1 to 10 can sign up for the Birthday Club and get a discount coupon.

MOSTLY BOOKS
6208 E. Speedway Blvd.
(520) 571-0110
www.mostlybooksaz.com
This general bookstore has thousands of terrific new and used books covering all topics, including fiction, recovery, and children's, along with hundreds of used audiobooks. They also have a large selection of greeting cards and gifts.

SINGING WIND BOOKSHOP
700 W. Singing Wind Rd., Benson
(520) 586-2425
OK, so it's not in Tucson. But you should not miss this amazing store. You'll find it off exit 304 in Benson, at the end of Singing Wind Road. Owned by the feisty and extremely knowledgeable Winn Bundy, the place is a treasure trove of books about the Southwest and Americana. The vast collection includes travel guides, fiction, nonfiction, photography, anthropology, poetry, religion, and more, all organized in Winn's unique style. There's a great children's reading room. The store also hosts special musical events and readings; call to find out the schedule. Cash or check only; open daily.

TUCSON'S MAP AND FLAG CENTER
3239 N. 1st Ave.
(520) 887-4234
www.mapsmithus.com
This is the top source in town for maps, from street atlases of Tucson and Phoenix to topographical maps and charts. The center has travel maps of Mexico, plus an excellent selection of travel guides for the entire planet. If it has to do with geography or topography, you'll probably find it here, but not on Sunday, when the store is closed.

FASHIONS

You'll find lots of fashionable clothing stores in Tucson in plazas, malls, and shopping centers all around town. Here we offer some of the more eclectic and unusual stores in town, which cater to every taste.

CELE PETERSON'S
St. Philip's Plaza
(520) 323-9413
www.celepetersons.com

Cele Peterson's is practically a Tucson fashion institution, having opened the first store in 1931. The store carries sophisticated but pricey clothing for women in both dressy and casual styles. The shop has a large collection of Pandora and Yolanta jewelry. It's closed on Sun.

CHANGES
4300 N. Campbell Ave.
(520) 577-8055
Tres chic. Changes offers lots and lots of casual and sophisticated clothing for all occasions, accessories, shoes, and jewelry. Located in St. Philip's Plaza.

CHICO'S
7003 N. Oracle Rd.
(520) 797-1200
www.chicos.com
Part of a national chain, you'll find these women's clothing stores in the Casas Adobes and Crossroads Festival shopping centers. With a motto of "easy wear, easy care," clothes here are stylish and comfortable and cater to a variety of tastes and sizes. You'll also find all kinds of accessories here, from jewelry to shoes.

Extremely helpful staff can assist you with putting together an outfit for casual or fancy occasions. An additional location is at 5870 E. Broadway Blvd. (520-325-2422).

FIRENZE BOUTIQUE
2840 E. Skyline Blvd.
(520) 299-2992
Located in a small shopping plaza in the foothills, Firenze sells Giorgio Armani clothes, accessories, and shoes for both men and women. The boutique is open daily.

MAYA PALACE
El Mercado
6332 E. Broadway Blvd.
(520) 748-0817
www.mayapalacetucson.com
This unusual fashion store for women has 2 locations. They specialize in fashions and accessories from around the world, along with a selection of handcrafted gift items. If you're looking for a unique, exotic, brightly colored outfit in flowing fabrics such as cotton, rayon, and silk, this is the place to shop. The salespeople are friendly and will help you coordinate a total look, right down to the jewelry. Open daily. The Casas Adobes Plaza location is at 7057 N. Oracle Rd. (520-575-8028).

PICANTE BOUTIQUE
2932 E. Broadway Blvd.
(520) 320-5699
The accent here is on comfortable women's cotton and natural fiber, easy care–easy wear clothing. You'll also find jewelry from glittery to tribal to funk, hand-painted silk and batik scarves, and an unusual collection of ethnic shawls from Mexico, Guatemala, and Bolivia. Closed Sun.

OUTDOORS & RECREATION

In addition to national chain stores offering outdoor and recreation gear and clothing, Tucson has a few specialty stores that cater to the outdoor lifestyle.

AUDUBON NATURE SHOP
300 E. University Blvd.
(520) 629-0510
www.tucsonaudubon.org
Affiliated with the Tucson Audubon Society, this shop in the university area has a wide

selection of natural history books and gifts. Book subjects include astronomy, geology, birds (of course), mammals, insects, reptiles, plants, and oceans. It also has educational materials and children's books on nature subjects and supplies for birders and hikers, such as binoculars, field guides, and hiking maps. For gift giving or for personal use, you'll find games, greeting cards, maps, tapes, and records, all with a nature theme. And for your feathered friends, you'll find bird feeders. The shop is closed on Sun.

SUMMIT HUT
5045 E. Speedway Blvd.
(520) 325-1554, (800) 499-8696
www.summithut.com
This is a local favorite for all kinds of outdoor equipment and advice, including a great selection of books and pamphlets on outdoor and southern Arizona subjects. In addition to all the outdoor stuff for sale, Summit Hut also rents gear such as tents, packs, sleeping bags, and climbing boots. And if you need a present for someone who's into nature, it has T-shirts and cards and funky gift items. Another location is at 605 E. Wetmore Rd. (520-888-1000).

YESTERYEAR'S TREASURES

Tucson has some great antiques shops and secondhand stores. Antiques fairs, shows, and auctions take place here year-round with great prices and wide variety. You'll find everything from furniture and kitchenware to glass and toys. The main "antiques district" is on Grant Road between Campbell Avenue and Craycroft Road. You can pick up a free antiques guide at most of the antiques stores in town—just ask.

i The Freecycle Web Network, started in Tucson in 2003, is a Web-based community swap program. You can donate your used items or find something you need. Visit freecycle .org. You'll have to create an account, but it's free.

AMERICAN ANTIQUE MALL
3130 E. Grant Rd.
(520) 326-3070
www.americanantiquemall.com
Voted the "Best of Tucson," this is the largest antiques mall in the city and offers everything from A to Z. You'll find pre-Columbian artifacts, vintage clothing, glassware, turn-of-the-20th-century pottery, Navajo rugs, artwork, and more right in the heart of the antiques district. Closed Sun and Mon.

THE ANTIQUE PRESIDIO
3024 E. Grant Rd.
(520) 323-1844
www.antiquepresidio.com
Packed floor to ceiling with goodies, this huge, multiroomed antiques store has a wide selection of everything from funky furs to vintage clothes and hats to rows of many-colored Pyrex kitchenware to a fair share of kitsch, including a large collection of goofy salt and pepper shakers. A mixed bag of wooden furniture might delight refinishers out there. Check the website for discount coupons before you go. Open daily.

CANYON STATE COLLECTIBLES
5245 E. Pima St.
(520) 795-1922
Whether you're hunting for movie and movie-star memorabilia or political and military collectibles, Canyon State probably has it. It also offers sports cards, old jewelry,

collector plates, old toys and dolls, postcards, animation art, stamps, coins, Native American jewelry and artifacts, and Hummels, Royal Doultons, and Lladros. Lots and lots of amazing goods are found here. The store is closed on Sun and Mon.

CHRISTINE'S ANTIQUE SHOP & DOLL COLLECTION
4940 E. Speedway Blvd.
(520) 323-0018
http://christinesantiquestucson.com
Nearly every square inch of this large store is crammed full of old things, including glassware, lamps, furniture, dolls, dollhouse miniatures, and antique linens. It's fascinating and a real find for doll collectors. Closed Sun.

MUSEUM SHOPS

Many of Tucson's major attractions and museums also have gift shops where you'll find lots of unique Southwestern, Mexican, and other gift items. Here are some of the more outstanding ones.

ARIZONA-SONORA DESERT MUSEUM GIFT SHOP
2021 N. Kinney Rd.
(520) 578-3008
www.desertmuseum.org
You'll find everything you ever wanted with a Sonoran Desert motif at this terrific shop. T-shirts, hats, books about desert and plant life created exclusively for the museum, desert artifacts and collectibles, jewelry, cards, stuffed animals—you name it, they've got it! Open daily.

TOHONO CHUL PARK GIFT AND MUSEUM SHOPS
7366 N. Paseo del Norte
(520) 742-6455
www.tohonochulpark.org
This lovely park is home to 2 shops bursting with a wonderful collection of gifts and collectibles. Lovely one-of-a-kind pottery by local artists, traditional and native crafts, unique gift items like saguaro cactus cookie cutters, hummingbird ceramic tiles, wind chimes, regional specialty food items, books, plants, and much, much more. The shops are open daily.

TUCSON BOTANICAL GARDENS GIFT SHOP
2150 N. Alvernon Way
(520) 326-9686
www.tucsonbotanical.org
Plant lovers will find all sorts of goodies here, such as botanical books, wildflower seeds, whimsical garden art, and unusual jewelry. The shop is open daily.

TUCSON MUSEUM OF ART SHOP
140 N. Main Ave.
(520) 624-2333
www.tucsonmuseumof art.com
This elegant shop carries all sorts of work by regional artists, including beautiful blown-glass bowls and pitchers, Mexican-style tiled mirrors, jewelry by local artists, painted furniture, and a wonderful selection of cards, prints, and books from around the world. Closed Mon.

ATTRACTIONS

There is so much to see and do in Tucson. You'll find it all here: sophisticated art museums and galleries, cowboy ghost towns, an internationally renowned desert museum, and spectacular natural wonders like Colossal Cave, Saguaro National Park, and Sabino Canyon. There are many hidden treasures here, too, like tiny shrines, historic buildings, and hummingbird gardens. We cover lots of them in this chapter, but it's just the tip of the iceberg. Plan to take a lot of time in Tucson to do justice to the many amazing natural and man-made attractions in and outside of town. (See the Kidstuff chapter for activities geared more toward the younger set.)

Price Code

The following price codes indicate what you will pay per adult for general admission. If an attraction is free, it will not have a price code. If the attraction offers free admission on certain days, it will be indicated in the listing.

$....................Less than $5
$$ ....$5 to $10
$$$ .... $10 to $20
$$$$ .... More than $20

ARIZONA HISTORY MUSEUM &
HISTORICAL SOCIETY $–$$
949 E. 2nd St.
(520) 628-5774
www.arizonahistoricalsociety.org

The Tucson branch of the Arizona Historical Society is actually 3 museums, with the main one near the UA campus on 2nd Street. Its other locations are the Downtown History Museum and the Fort Lowell Museum. (The last is covered separately in this chapter.)

Main Museum

Entering the historical society's lovely old building is to take a walk through Arizona's history. Permanent exhibits include authentically decorated period rooms depicting life in the Arizona Territory, artifacts from Arizona's frontier life and its Native American populations, and a full-scale re-creation of underground mining. Numerous temporary exhibits focus on specific times or topics in Arizona's past. And for anyone doing research on nearly anything pertaining to Arizona or Tucson, the historical society maintains an excellent library, which includes rare and unique maps and photos, that's open to the public. Docent tours are offered by appointment, and the museum is wheelchair accessible. There's also a gift shop, Arizona Mercantile, specializing in authentic Southwestern arts and crafts and books. The historical society conducts special events and lectures year-round. Admission is $5 for adults, $4 for seniors and students 12 to 18 years of age, and free for children under 12. Admission is free on the first Saturday of the month. Hours are 10 a.m. to 4 p.m. Mon through Sat. The library is open from noon to 4 p.m. Tues through Fri and from 10 a.m.

ATTRACTIONS

to 1 p.m. on the first Sat of the month. Parking is available at the multistory garage at Euclid Avenue and 2nd Street, where there is a special section set aside for visitors to the historical society; watch for a small sign at the entrance. Take your parking ticket to the society for validation and your parking is free.

Downtown
The society's Downtown History Museum (520-770-1473) is located at 140 N. Stone Ave. in the historic Wells Fargo Bank Building. This museum specializes in the history of downtown Tucson and offers a variety of permanent and rotating exhibits. It's open Tues through Fri from 10 a.m. to 4 p.m. Admission is $3 for adults, $2 for seniors and children 12 to 18. Admission is free on first Friday of the month.

✴ARIZONA-SONORA DESERT MUSEUM $$$
2021 N. Kinney Rd.
(520) 883-2702
www.desertmuseum.org
This fabulous "museum" is actually a combination zoo, museum, and botanical garden. Here you will learn everything you ever wanted to know about the Sonoran Desert. Exhibits re-create desert habitats of all varieties of plants and animals.

Allow yourself at least 3 hours. The natural landscape is re-created so realistically that you find yourself eye-to-eye with mountain lions, prairie dogs, Gila monsters, hawks, and hummingbirds. Every inch of this mostly outdoor museum is packed full of fascinating plant and animal life. One exhibit features nocturnal desert dwellers. Another gives visitors an underwater view of beavers, river otters, and fish. A walk-through cave leads to a fine collection of rare and beautiful regional gems and minerals. And you'll see all varieties of reptiles and spiders safely tucked away behind glass. In the hummingbird aviary, one of the museum's most popular spots, hundreds of tiny birds hover about, showing off their colors and flying skills. All during your walk you'll find volunteers giving fascinating demonstrations about the creatures and plant life of the desert.

From late October through mid-April, the Desert Museum offers unique raptor free-flight demonstrations that showcase hawks, falcons, owls, and other birds. Showtimes are typically at 10:30 a.m. and 1:30 p.m., but call first to check.

The museum is clean, meticulously cared for, and exquisitely laid out to give the best views possible of the plants and animals. It's wheelchair accessible and stroller friendly, and both are available for free. The museum also has excellent eateries; shops that shouldn't be missed for natural history books, native crafts, bird feeders, and much more; and an art gallery of artists' Sonoran Desert interpretations in a variety of media.

It's open daily from 8:30 a.m. to 5 p.m. (*Note:* no entry after 4:15 p.m.) Oct through Feb and 7:30 a.m. to 5 p.m. Mar through Sept. From June through Aug, the museum is open Sat until 10 p.m. There are shade ramadas, drinking fountains, and restrooms in several locations, but be prepared to protect yourself from the sun, especially in summer. Admission prices vary seasonally; children under 6 are free. Discount coupons are usually easy to find at the Tucson Convention & Visitors Bureau, in the Tucson Attractions Passport booklets (available at the visitors bureau), in local publications, and in some stores and banks.

The museum is located on the west side of the Tucson Mountains, about 14 miles from downtown Tucson, and can be reached via either Ajo Way or Speedway Boulevard. RVers must take the Ajo Way route to Kinney Road.

i You can go behind the scenes at the Desert Museum through a variety of specialty tours. The Winged Wonders tour takes you into the hummingbird aviary before the museum opens (6:45 a.m.) for an insiders' view of these amazing tiny creatures Mon through Thurs. If you like slightly larger creatures, consider the Walk on the Wild Side, led by one of the museum's mammalogy and ornithology keepers. You'll visit the museum's Riparian Corridor, Cat Canyon, and Sheep Mountain and even get to feed the animals—carefully! This tour is available only on Thurs at 10:30 a.m.; no children under 12. Each tour is $35 plus regular admission price. Reservations are a must; find more information at www.desert museum.org.

ARIZONA STATE MUSEUM $
Park Avenue and University Boulevard
1013 E. University Blvd.
(520) 621-6302
www.statemuseum.arizona.edu
Enter the main gate of the University of Arizona campus and you face a lovely tree-lined street bordered by some exquisite old buildings. Two of these are the Arizona State Museum's north and south buildings. As the oldest and largest anthropology museum in the Southwest, its collections are recognized as some of the world's most significant resources for the study of Southwestern cultures. Included are 100,000 artifacts from archaeological excavations of the Hohokam,

Mogollon, and Anasazi cultures; more than 25,000 ethnographic objects documenting the cultures of both historic and living American Indians; the largest collection of Southwest Indian pottery; and 175,000 historic and contemporary photographic images.

Through the museum's exhibits, visitors discover the wonders of ancient civilizations and the contributions of living Native American cultures. Anyone with an interest in the Southwest will also appreciate the museum's library of 70,000 volumes (open to the public Mon through Thurs from 10 a.m. to 3 p.m.), including many rare titles. In the gift shop browsers or buyers will find an excellent selection of pottery, kachina dolls, rugs, carvings, jewelry, baskets, cards, posters, and books.

Hours are Mon through Sat 10 a.m. to 5 p.m. Admission is $5 for adults; 18 and under are free. Both buildings are wheelchair accessible. Metered street parking is available to the west of the main gate on University Boulevard, 2nd Street, and 1st Street; several pay parking lots located in the same area will cost no more than a few dollars and are free on weekends.

ASARCO MINERAL DISCOVERY CENTER $$
I-19 and Pima Mine Road, Sahuarita
(520) 625-8233
www.mineraldiscovery.com
Folks who are interested in minerals or copper mining will see and learn all about them at this attraction 15 miles south of Tucson. Dubbed the largest man-made attraction in southern Arizona, visitors have a choice of seeing just the Mineral Discovery Center, which is free, or also taking the open-pit mine tour, for which a fee is charged for

anyone older than age 4 ($5 for kids age 5 to 12, $8 for adults, and $6 for seniors).

The Mineral Discovery Center has a variety of hands-on exhibits about mining and minerals, from how ore deposits are formed and how they are discovered and mined to how the land is reclaimed after mining. A multimedia theater has presentations on mining, mineral resources, and reclamation. There's also a display of historic and present-day mining equipment. The tour takes visitors by air-conditioned bus to an operating open-pit copper mine nearby. You'll see how the land is excavated, the massive machinery that mills the earth and extracts and processes the minerals, and the reclamation process designed to restore the landscape.

Tours take about an hour, and flat shoes are recommended because some walking will be required. Call ahead if you need arrangements for wheelchair access. The center is open Tues through Sat from 9 a.m. to 5 p.m. Tour times vary seasonally, so call ahead. Reservations are recommended; call (520) 625-8233. It's operated by ASARCO Inc., a worldwide mining company whose copper operations are based in Tucson.

BIOSPHERE 2 $$$
Highway 77 at Mile Marker 96.5
32450 S. Biosphere Rd.
(520) 838-6200
www.b2science.com
Named by Time-Life Books as one of the 50 must-see man-made wonders of the world, Biosphere 2 (the earth itself is Biosphere 1) sits at an elevation of 4,000 feet on over 35 acres of land in Oracle just off Highway 77. The Biosphere truly has to be seen to be believed. Funded by billionaire Edward Bass's Philecology Foundation to the tune of $150 million and built in 1987, the main structure (the Biosphere) is 92 feet tall at its highest point and has 6,500 windows that enclose 7.2 million cubic feet.

The Biosphere itself contains 5 ecologically distinct areas (biomes), including a rain forest, a 700,000-gallon saltwater ocean, a savannah, a marsh, and a fog desert. Two acres of machinery below the surface power it all. In 1991, with great fanfare, 8 people were sealed into the Biosphere for 2 years to see if they could survive in a closed system. Today the facility is managed by the University of Arizona and used for a wide variety of scientific research projects. Open to the public, tours are available daily and begin with a 13-minute movie followed by an hourlong walking tour through this unique science facility. Wear comfortable shoes; bottled water only is allowed on the tour itself.

A cafe and outdoor picnic area are also available. The Biosphere is open daily from 9 a.m. to 4:30 p.m. except Christmas and Thanksgiving Day. Tours start at 9:30 a.m.; the last tour is at 4 p.m. Prices vary: adults, $20; seniors 62 and over, $18; children 6 to 12, $13. Discount coupons are often available at the visitors bureau and in local publications.

To get here take Oracle Road north about 15 miles and watch for the sign pointing to Biosphere 2.

i For a true Insiders' point of view on living in the Biosphere, pick up a copy of Tucsonan Jane Poynter's book, *The Human Experiment: Two Years and Twenty Minutes Inside the Biosphere*. In this interesting memoir, she shares the scary day-to day-realities and inner politics of living in the hermetically sealed pseudo world—this is the stuff the tour guides don't tell you!

CASINO OF THE SUN
7406 S. Camino de Oeste
(520) 883-1700, (800) 344-9435
www.casinosun.com

CASINO DEL SOL
5655 W. Valencia Rd.
(520) 838-6506, (800) 344-9435
www.casinodelsol.com

The Pascua Yaqui Tribe was one of the last Native American peoples to gain federal recognition by the US Congress. In 1964 the tribe was deeded about 200 acres of desert land southwest of Tucson and acquired an additional 590 acres in 1988. Today about 13,000 members of the tribe live in the area, which also houses the tribe's casinos, a source of revenue and employment for tribal members. Casino of the Sun, built in 1989, boasts casino games, slot machines, live-action card room, blackjack, video poker, and more. There are over 500 games to choose from.

The tribe's second casino, Casino Del Sol, built in 2001, offers live entertainment in an outdoor amphitheater (see the Nightlife chapter) and has 22,500 square feet of gaming space, featuring nearly 1,000 multi-denominational slot machines, plus live blackjack and poker. Casino Del Sol has several dining options, including a fine-dining sushi restaurant, several casual and quick restaurants, and a bar/lounge in the center of the gaming floor. Players clubs are available at both locations. The casinos are open every day except on certain days during the Holy Week of Easter.

As with casinos all across the US, these places really draw the crowds, particularly on weekends. Parking is free, with plenty of wheelchair-accessible spots. From Tucson go west on Valencia Road about 5 miles past

I-10—you won't miss the signs pointing the way. Both casinos are open 24/7.

COLOSSAL CAVE MOUNTAIN PARK $$
16721 E. Old Spanish Trail, Vail
(520) 647-7275
www.colossalcave.com

This attraction is one of the most unusual and fascinating in southern Arizona. Colossal Cave was formed somewhere between 12 million and 20 million years ago by the welling up of hot sulfur–laden brine. It is the largest dry, or dormant, cave in the US. The cave has a fascinating history: It was used by prehistoric peoples around AD 900 for shelter and storage, and in the 1800s train robbers used it as a hideout.

The tour route is 0.5 mile long and takes about 50 minutes. It's led by a guide who relates the cave's history, legends, and geology. You'll walk down and back up about 6 stories (and some 360 steps) to see amazing stalactites, stalagmites, flowstone, and other formations, not to mention a few prehistoric markings. It's always 70 degrees and dry in the cave. Unfortunately, this is not an attraction for people who are in wheelchairs or who have difficulty walking.

Tours are given daily year-round. They're not prescheduled, but the wait is 30 minutes at most. Part of the 2,000-acre Colossal Cave Mountain Park, there are lots of other things to do here. You can visit the 120-year-old La Posta Quemada Ranch; browse in the terrific gift shop that has rocks, minerals, and unusual souvenirs; take a horseback ride along the historic stagecoach route; or just enjoy the spectacular view from the stone terrace. The La Posada Quemada Ranch Museum on the grounds has a great exhibit all about the cave.

The cost is $11 for those 13 and older, $6 for ages 6 to 12, and free for younger ones. You will also pay a fee of $5 per car just to enter the park. Summer hours, in effect March 16 through September 15, are 8 a.m. to 5 p.m. daily. To get here from Tucson, take scenic Old Spanish Trail for about 17 miles or I-10 east to exit 279 and then north for about 6 miles.

i Colossal Cave Park is home to numerous species of bats—some rare and endangered. Townsend's big-eared bat (listed as threatened in Arizona), the cave myotis, and the big brown bat species bear their young right in the cave. Ask your tour guide for more details.

DAVIS-MONTHAN AIR FORCE BASE
Craycroft and Valencia Roads
(520) 228-4717
www.dm.af.mil

You can read all about Davis-Monthan Air Force Base, located on Tucson's south side, in our separate chapter of the same name. Tours of the AMARC storage facility on base are operated by Pima Air and Space Museum and embark from that site, 6000 E. Valencia Rd. (There will be a security check of the bus before it enters the grounds.) The 1-hour tour goes through the base, including down the flight line for a view of the array of planes using the 14,000-foot runway, but it focuses on the intriguing aircraft storage facility (or "boneyard"). Photos are allowed. If you're at all interested in the military or in vintage and modern aircraft, we highly recommend the base tour. (*NOTE:* Everyone over age 16 will need a government-issued photo ID.) Details are in the Davis-Monthan Close-up.

DESERT DIAMOND CASINO/NOGALES HIGHWAY
7350 S. Nogales Hwy.
(520) 294-7777, (866) 332-9467

DESERT DIAMOND CASINO/I-19
1100 W. Pima Mine Rd.
Exit 80 off I-19, Sahuarita
(520) 294-7777, (866) 332-9467
www.ddcaz.com

Casinos are hot in Tucson, bringing in revenue for several indigenous tribes. The Desert Diamond Casinos, with 3 locations (2 in Tucson and 1 in Why, Arizona) are among the largest moneymakers. Owned and operated by the Tohono O'odham Nation, they have over 1,200 employees.

Opened in 1993, the original Desert Diamond Casino on Nogales Highway hosts more than 1,000 fast-paced slot machines, blackjack, poker, a large bingo center, and keno. The casino also offers a full-service bar, grill, and a 24-hour snack bar for late-night munchies.

The location at Pima Mine Road just south of Tucson opened in 2001. The Santa Fe–style architecture, fountains, exhibits of Native American crafts, and open plazas are a delight just to wander through even if you're not into gambling. The complex is home to the upscale Agave Restaurant as well as lunch and dinner buffets, a grill, and a sports bar. The gaming area looks like it has descended from outer space and features 500 slot machines plus live blackjack and keno. The 2,400-seat Diamond Center serves as a venue for live acts (see the Nightlife chapter). Open 24/7; you must be 21 to enter the gaming area.

FLANDRAU—THE UA SCIENCE CENTER AND PLANETARIUM $$

Cherry Avenue and University Boulevard
(520) 621-7827
www.flandrau.org

A science center, observatory, planetarium, and mineral museum, Flandrau houses several exciting areas in one easy-access facility.

The science center exhibits feature an asteroid cave and the Mars Wall, the largest 3-D scaled map of the Martian surface, part of the "Mars, Up Close and Personal" exhibit. Home to the largest public-viewing telescope (16 inches) in southern Arizona, the observatory is open year-round and offers free viewings Wed through Sat evenings.

Planetarium shows are available by reservation only for school and youth groups on weekdays from 10 a.m. to 3 p.m., shows are open to the general public Thurs and Fri evenings from 6 p.m. to 9 p.m., and Sat and Sun during regular visiting hours. The planetarium also hosts very popular laser shows for a separate admission fee.

Downstairs the Mineral Museum, home to one of the finest university-owned collections, features a fascinating display of Arizona minerals, gems, and specimen rocks. And finally, Flandrau has a wonderful science store featuring science kits, posters, puzzles, star charts, books, toys, games, and more—all designed to make learning about science fun.

Admission is $7.50 for adults, $5 for kids 4 to 15. On weekends and after 1 p.m. on weekdays, Flandrau visitors can park for free along Hawthorne Street (north of the Science Center). There is a parking fee at the Cherry Avenue Garage near McKale Center all day on weekdays, but the garage is free on weekends. Flandrau is open 7 days a week; hours vary.

FORT LOWELL MUSEUM $

2900 N. Craycroft Rd.
(520) 885-3832
www.arizonahistoricalsociety.org

This small museum, a branch of the Arizona Historical Society, is located in the pleasant surroundings of Fort Lowell Park, once the site of a Hohokam Indian village. Centuries later a cavalry fort was erected here. From 1873 to 1891 soldiers were stationed at Fort Lowell to protect Tucson settlers from Indian raids. The museum is actually a reconstruction of the commanding officers' quarters. Here you'll find period furnishings, a photographic story of the 75 former occupants of Fort Lowell, and frontier artifacts. It's open Wed through Sat from 10 a.m. to 4 p.m. Adults pay $3 entrance fee. Seniors and students are admitted for $2. Kids under 12 get in free.

GARDEN OF GETHSEMANE

W. Congress Street and Bonita Avenue
(520) 791-4873, ext. 0

This little gem is tucked away behind a gate in a small downtown park at the corner of Congress Street and Bonita Avenue. Called the Garden of Gethsemane, the park contains life-size carvings of the Last Supper, the Crucifixion, and the Holy Family, along with several smaller shrines. The carvings were created by Spanish sculptor Felix Lucero, who vowed to do the work as a tribute to God when his life was spared on a WWI battlefield. A restful and contemplative place in the midst of heavy traffic, the garden is open daily from 8 a.m. to 3:30 p.m. and there's no admission fee. The garden may be reserved for special occasions.

Close-up

Unique Spots in Town

Tucson is home to so many hidden treasures; these are unique and worth a stop:

History of Pharmacy Museum
The College of Pharmacy at the University of Arizona
1703 E. Mabel St.
(520) 626-1427
www.pharmacy.arizona.edu/museum
The weirdest thing here is a wad of John Dillinger's gum (yes, really!). The rest of the collection takes up 4 floors of the pharmacy building and includes over 60,000 bottles; 18 show globes (the symbol of the profession of pharmacy) of various shapes, sizes, and colors over 100 years old; original drug containers; books; and artifacts from Arizona circa 1880–1950, including several large drug store fixtures from Arizona's territorial days. Open Mon through Fri 8 a.m. to 5 p.m. Free admission.

Jewish History Museum
564 N. Stone Ave.
(520) 670-9073
www.jewishhistorymuseum.org
Housed in the restored first synagogue built in the Arizona Territory, this museum is dedicated to collecting and preserving the Jewish experience in the Southwest. The museum hosts special events, speakers, and numerous special exhibitions. A treasure trove of information, it is also home to a collection of oral histories. Open Wed through Sun, 1 p.m. to 5 p.m., closed seasonally during part of the summer. Admission is $5, under age 12 are free.

Postal History Foundation
920 N. 1st Ave.
(520) 623-6652
www.postalhistoryfoundation.org/

HISTORIC OLD PUEBLO

The downtown area of Tucson is home to historic homes, museums, specialty shops, and some of the oldest and most interesting architecture in town, ranging from adobes to ornate mansions. The downtown is also known as the Tucson Arts District, with a number of eclectic galleries, funky restaurants, and sophisticated shops. After all, this is the area of town where Tucson began.

Here you'll find remnants of the original presidio wall, look up at the striking mosaic tile dome of the Pima County Courthouse juxtaposed against Tucson's few high-rises, and wander along narrow streets lined with colorful restored adobes. It's a unique combination of old and new.

Unlike many bustling downtowns, Tucson's downtown area retains a sleepy, low-key atmosphere. You won't find hordes of

This Tucson jewel opens a door into the fascinating world of Western postal history. Inside, you'll find a library containing 30,000 books and US Post Office publications, a collector stamp sales office, a museum with turn-of-the-20th-century fittings, and a working post office. The library has been honored for its noteworthy architecture and is open to anyone wanting a quiet place to study. The museum claims to have over a million stamps, and staff operates an extensive youth education program. The coolest thing about this museum is the volunteers, who love showing people around. Few Tucson residents are even aware of the existence of this museum—shhhhh. Open Mon through Fri from 8 a.m. to 3 p.m. Free admission.

Southern Arizona Transportation Museum
Downtown Train Depot
414 N. Toole Ave.
(520) 623-2223
www.tucsonhistoricdepot.org
Housed in the beautifully restored 1942 historic train depot, this small museum focuses on the history of the railroad in southern Arizona, which roared into town in 1880. You can check out Locomotive No. 1673, which had a starring role in the movie Oklahoma! and is one of only 8 mogul-type steam engines in the country. It's permanently parked in the back of the depot near the tracks. Call to check museum hours. Free admission.

Steward Observatory Mirror Lab
(520) 626-8792
933 N. Cherry Ave.
http://mirrorlab.as.arizona.edu
Hidden beneath the UA football stadium, the Mirror Lab is busy at work producing the world's largest telescope mirrors. You'll get to go behind the scenes to see the amazing spin-casting process that creates these mirrors. Tours are 90 minutes long and are offered Tues through Fri at 1 p.m. and 3 p.m. Admission for adults is $15, $8 for students age 7 to 22; participants must be over age 7. Closed-toe shoes are required, as are reservations.

tourists thronging the shops or pouring into the museums. It's relaxing and invigorating with lots of interesting sights to see around every corner. Take your time, carry lots of water, and just stroll through this unique part of Tucson's past and present.

Streets in these neighborhoods weren't created with car traffic in mind, so it's best to tour through history the old-fashioned way:

on foot. There are 4 distinct districts, each with its own attractions.

One is defined by what once was the old presidio wall, which today is bounded by Pennington Street, Church Avenue, Washington Street, and Main Avenue and represents over 130 years of the city's architectural history. This area offers more than 2 dozen attractions, including the Gardes Footbridge; the Pima County Courthouse; and other historic houses open to the public, including the Stevens House and the Edward Nye Fish House. In the center of the more modern Tucson Museum of Art lies the Plaza of the Pioneers, honoring Tucson's early citizens.

Just to the north is the second area to tour, the El Presidio Historic District, bounded by Washington and 6th Streets and Granada and Church Avenues. Although some of the old mansions here are still private residences, they're worth just walking by. You'll also find several, like the territorial-style 1907 Manning House and Steinfeld Mansion, that have been converted into offices but still hold their allure. And be sure to take a peaceful break in the Alene Dunlop Smith Memorial Garden on the east side of Granada Avenue.

Downtown and Barrio Historico comprise the third area to tour, which is south of the presidio wall district and bounded by Simpson Street, Church Avenue, Congress Street, and Granada Avenue. Here you'll find the lovely 1880s town house, Sanmaniego House, now a restaurant, El Tiradito, the wishing shrine; and the lovely Cushing Street Bar & Grill. Just to the east of the barrio area is the Church Avenue District, extending to 5th Avenue. This area encompasses the lovely Temple of Music and Art; the former Carnegie Library, now housing the Children's Museum; and St. Augustine Cathedral, one of central Tucson's most striking structures, dating from 1896. At the northeast corner of this area, you'll find the old Congress Hotel and the renovated historic Southern Pacific Railroad Depot, now operated by Amtrak.

INTERNATIONAL WILDLIFE
MUSEUM $$
4800 W. Gates Pass Rd.
(520) 617-1439
www.thewildlifemuseum.org

Both kids and their parents have an opportunity to see and often touch more than 400 kinds of mounted animals from around the world here. Bighorn sheep, for example, are perched along a large boulder display, showing how they live and interact in the mountains around the Sonoran Desert. Another display graphically shows the huge size difference among bears, from the smallest black bear to the grizzly. The nocturnal area depicts desert creatures of the night. Other species on display include reptiles, insects, and birds. Visitors can also watch award-winning nature films in the 100-seat theater, learn about wildlife through interactive computer displays, or shop for unique gifts from around the world.

Except for major holidays, the museum is open Mon through Fri from 9 a.m. to 5 p.m., Sat and Sun 9 a.m. to 6 p.m., and is wheelchair accessible. Admission is $8 for adults, $6 for seniors and students, $3 for kids 4 to 12, and free for younger ones.

It's located 5 miles west of I-10 via Speedway Boulevard to Gates Pass Road.

KARTCHNER CAVERNS STATE
PARK $$$
Highway 90, Benson
(520) 586-4100 (information line),
(520) 586-2283 (reservations)
www.pr.state.az.us
Discovered by two cavers in 1974 and kept secret for many years, this amazing natural attraction is now part of an extensive park area. Guided tours of the Throne Room (all ages welcome) and Big Room (children under 7 not permitted) are available seasonally year-round and are led by knowledgeable rangers.

You will enter through hermetically sealed doors developed to maintain the humidity levels in these magnificent wet caves and preserve them in their original state. You won't find garish colored lights, just natural phenomena more amazing than you can imagine. It's a tough tour for kids— there's no touching and lots of walking and talking—and no strollers or baby backpacks are allowed. However, kids will enjoy the trails, nature walks, and the great interactive discovery center.

Reservations are required; make them well in advance, as tours book up early. Fees vary, but you will pay a park entrance fee per vehicle as well as a separate fee to tour the caves. (See the Parks & Recreation chapter for more details.) The park is located 9 miles south of I-10, off Highway 90 at exit 302.

i For an unusual and fun way to tour Tucson, try an hour or two on a battery-powered Segway. Roll With It offers several tours of the downtown area, ranging from 1-hour rides to several hours on the Presidio Trail. Everyone gets a lesson first. For more information call (520) 749-5325 or visit www.tucsonrollwithit.com.

KITT PEAK NATIONAL OBSERVATORY
Highway 386
(520) 318-8726, (520) 318-8200
www.noao.edu
Visit the world's largest collection of optical telescopes at Kitt Peak. At an elevation of 6,875 feet above the Sonoran Desert floor, Kitt Peak is in the Quinlan Mountains, which are part of the Tohono O'odham Indian Reservation, on land leased to the federal government. The location is so appealing to astronomers because it's under some of the finest night skies in the world.

To see this amazing collection of observatories (one of which is 18 stories tall) and telescopes, start at the Kitt Peak Visitor Center and learn the history of optical astronomy and the role Kitt Peak has had in shaping astronomical research. Then take a 1-hour guided tour (10 a.m., 11:30 a.m., and 1:30 p.m.) to see the facilities and learn how astronomers use telescopes to unlock the mysteries of the universe. At the National Solar Observatory exhibit gallery, you'll be able to watch astronomers operate the world's largest solar telescope. All of this takes place daily (except Thanksgiving, Christmas Eve and Day, and New Year's Day) from 9 a.m. to 4 p.m. There's no admission charge, but donations are suggested.

For a totally different experience and the chance to actually view the skies through some of the equipment, visit Kitt Peak at night or plan your daytime visit so you can stay until dark. But be aware that reservations are a must for the nighttime program (the limit is 34 people). Called the Nightly Observing Program, it's conducted nightly by tour guides and costs $48 for adults or $44 for students, active military, seniors, and anyone younger than 18. It lasts for three and a half hours, but you must arrive one hour before sunset, so the starting time varies. (To limit the effect of bright lights at night, drivers are escorted down the peak using only parking lights for about a mile.) The stargazing program uses the visitor center telescope dome, which is equipped with binoculars and a state-of-the-art 16-inch telescope to view planets, the birth and death of stars, nebulae, and galaxies. Keep in mind that temperatures are 10 to 20 degrees cooler than in Tucson, so on winter nights it will actually be frigid. Also be aware that walking paths to several of the telescopes are steep and may pose a problem for people with cardiac and respiratory troubles.

There are no food or gas facilities at Kitt Peak. Public restrooms are adjacent to the parking lot, while wheelchair-accessible restrooms are in the visitor center. Kitt Peak is 56 miles southwest of Tucson, a 90-minute drive, via Ajo Way (Highway 86) to Highway 386, which is Kitt Peak Road.

i Just 22 miles east of Kitt Peak is a giant moonlight collector. Yes, you read it right—moonlight! Created by Richard and Monica Chapin to pursue research about the healing powers of moonlight, the structure (officially called the Interstellar Light Collector) is 52 feet high and 60 feet across, and weighs 25 tons. It contains hundreds of rotating mirrors that can reflect moonlight onto large and small areas, similar to a laser. If you want to bask in the moonlight or learn more about this fascinating project, call (520) 323-3446 for a tour.

**MINI-TIME MACHINE MUSEUM
OF MINIATURES** $$
4455 E. Camp Lowell Rd.
(520) 881-0606
www.theminitimemachine.org
This museum really has to be seen to be believed. Thousand of miniatures, from antique kewpie dolls to glass frogs, along with dollhouses and room boxes, are displayed in several themed rooms (Enchanted Realm, History Gallery, and Exploring the World).

Start with the Enchanted Realm, which is anchored by a fantastical tree surrounded by glass cases filled with displays of all kinds featuring fairies, wizards, elves, witches, and

goblins. The exhibits here are all from the private collection of Pat Arnell, who amassed these treasures over many years of collecting and creating. Many of the houses and room boxes were actually created by Pat for competitions and workshops. A prodigious collector, her collection of period dollhouses from as early as the 1700s is incredible to view with period furnishings, kitchens, and detailed decor.

One of the most interesting display areas is devoted to architectural scale models and international houses, including a replica of a Craftsman-style house by architects Greene & Greene and a miniature Japanese kitchen. You can wander for hours and days in these miniature worlds—each visit unearths a new miniature treasure. It's an amazing collection that Tucson is privileged to be home to. Thank you, Pat!

Guided group tours are available if you want more details about collecting and the history of miniatures. Open Tues through Sat from 9 a.m. to 4 p.m. Closed major holidays. General admission is $7.

＊MISSION SAN XAVIER DEL BAC
1950 W. San Xavier Rd.
(520) 294-2624
www.sanxaviermission.org
Also referred to as the White Dove of the Desert, this incredible structure, built between 1777 and 1797, is a wondrous sight to behold. At this, the oldest Catholic church in the US, the full name means "mission for the Saint Francisco Xavier at the place where the water appears." (The reference is to the place where the underground Santa Cruz River rose to the surface.) But you need not know the correct way to say it or what it means to appreciate the splendor of

this luminous white structure rising out of the desert floor on the land of the Tohono O'odham Indians.

Pronounced *Sahn-hav-yair,* for 2 centuries it has stood as a symbol of religion brought to Native Americans by missionaries traveling from Mexico. It was the O'odham who became the skilled masons and laborers who erected the domed, vaulted, and arched building of fired bricks, stone, and lime mortar (or stucco) under the direction of missionary priests who had seen great edifices in Spain and Italy. From Father Kino's initial work on the foundation in 1700, it took 97 years before the church was opened for services, and even then it was not actually completed. (Look closely and you'll see that the east bell tower has never been completed.)

Today it remains the parish church of the O'odham of the San Xavier District of the Tohono O'odham Nation. But by the thousands, people of all faiths come through the mission's old dark doors of mesquite wood to appreciate its beauty and the labor of love it so obviously took to construct it.

Six generations of the same family have worked to maintain the mission's exterior, using a mixture of sand, lime, and cactus juice for stucco. An interior restoration taking 6 years and $2 million (mostly donated) was completed to mark the mission's 1997 bicentennial. An international team of experts refurbished 54 polychrome wall paintings and 44 statues, many made in Mexico more than 200 years ago, as part of their task. Nearly every area of the baroque-style interior is covered with elaborate paintings and sculpture created by unknown artists. Throughout the small rooms of the mission there are photos, documents, and artifacts showing its history. A gift shop, craft store,

museum, and refreshments are available on the premises.

The mission is open to visitors daily from 7 a.m. to 5 p.m., and Masses are held at various times. Admission is free, but donations are welcomed. It's located 19 miles south of downtown Tucson via I-19. Words can't adequately describe the mission; it must be seen.

i Written by local author and renowned anthropologist Bernard "Bunny" Fontana, the book *A Gift of Angels: The Art of Mission San Xavier del Bac* provides over 200 lush photographs and a thorough history of the fascinating art found in this historic church.

MOUNT LEMMON SKI VALLEY SKYRIDE $$$$
Mount Lemmon
(520) 576-1321 (live), (520) 576-1400 (recorded information)
www.skithelemmon.com
Many chapters in this book discuss Mount Lemmon, Tucsonans' playground in the sky in the Santa Catalina Mountains. All along the 30-mile ride to the top, activities include hiking, picnicking, camping, fishing, climbing, and just enjoying the diverse scenery and topography as it changes from desert to pine forest through 5 distinct vegetative zones. At the highway's end, just past the village of Summerhaven, lies Ski Valley, but you need not be a skier to enjoy the lift, or skyride, to the summit. The 30-minute round-trip ride of about 1 mile operates year-round both weekdays and weekends. It departs at the base of the ski area at an 8,200-foot elevation and travels to 9,157 feet with spectacular views of the valley

below and mountains as far away as Globe and Phoenix. At the base you'll find a gift shop, mountainside patio where snacks and beverages are served, and a restaurant. For folks who'd rather glide down the slopes than ride, this is a complete ski area—the southernmost in the US—with 22 ski runs at beginner, intermediate, and expert levels; equipment rental shop; and ski school (see the Parks & Recreation chapter).

If you're taking the skyride for pleasure, the ticket prices vary seasonally. The Mount Lemmon, or Catalina, Highway begins at Tanque Verde Road about 5 miles east of Sabino Canyon Road. For road conditions (weather or construction delays), call (520) 547-7510. Although there is a per-car user fee for Mount Lemmon, the fee does not apply if you're going to Ski Valley.

OLD PUEBLO TROLLEY $
4th Avenue and 8th Street
(520) 792-1802
www.oldpueblotrolley.org
Don't miss a ride on Tucson's historic Old Pueblo Trolley. Introduced in 1906 (when trolleys replaced Tucson's mule-drawn streetcars), trolleys ferried passengers until 1930, when they were replaced by buses. Sixty years later (in 1990), thanks to the efforts of volunteers who restored cars and lines of track, trolley service started again. The wood-paneled interiors, velvet seats, and live engineer make for a great trip into the past on several antique cars from Japan (1953), Belgium (1930s), and Portugal. The trolley currently takes passengers on a 1-mile journey through some of the most historic and diverse areas of Tucson. It runs between Tyndall Avenue and 4th Avenue and 8th Street, and riders can catch it at either end and hop off along the way. At the end of the

line on 8th Street, there's a car barn where you might see other trolleys being restored. An extension in the works will run from 4th Street, go west on Congress Street, and south on 5th Avenue, turn east on Broadway, and then head north again to reconnect at 4th Avenue for the return trip. The trolley operates Fri from 6 to 10 p.m., Sat from noon to midnight, and Sun from noon to 6 p.m. Kids younger than 6 ride free, kids 6 to 12 and seniors pay 75 cents, and adults pay $1.25 for a one-way trip. All-day fares are only $3 for adults and $2 for kids 6 to 12. Sunday all fares are 25 cents one-way.

OLD TOWN ARTISANS
201 N. Court Ave.
(520) 623-6024, (800) 782-8072
www.oldtownartisans.com
This unique marketplace in a historic 1850s adobe is one of the highlights of the downtown area. Tucked away in the El Presidio Historic District, it is now home to galleries and all sorts of shops offering pottery, glass, Southwestern and Native American jewelry, clothing, accessories, and much more. This is a great place to shop. You'll also find a lovely patio with tables, a restaurant, and a coffee bar (see also our Shopping chapter).

OLD TUCSON STUDIOS $$$
201 S. Kinney Rd.
(520) 883-0100
www.oldtucson.com
To see a slightly hokey re-creation of a Western town in the 1880s, Hollywood style, head on out to Old Tucson Studios. This Tucson-area attraction started out in 1939 as an elaborate set for the movie *Arizona* and was eventually turned into a frontier town replica for the public. Old Tucson Studios suffered a serious fire in 1995 and some of the original

structures and memorabilia were destroyed, but it has been rebuilt and expanded. All the buildings in this town are meticulously constructed and adorned to reflect the Old West, and you'll really feel taken back in time as you saunter by or enter saloons, dance halls, a jail, a general store or mercantile, corrals, stables, and wooden sidewalks. But there's lots more to do here than soak up the atmosphere and dream about the famous movie stars who may have stood on the same spot. Activities range from historical to modern day—gunfight shows, stagecoach rides, saloon revues, a gun museum, an antique Reno locomotive exhibit, gold panning, amusement rides, petting farms, magic shows, shops, and restaurants.

Admission prices vary, but it's free for kids age 4 and under. Discount coupons are easy to find at the Tucson Convention & Visitors Bureau, some grocery stores and banks, and other locations. Old Tucson Studios' hours vary seasonally; they are closed Thanksgiving and Christmas Day. Of the two ways to get here from Tucson—west on either Ajo Way or Speedway Boulevard to Kinney Road—the Ajo Way route is easiest to travel. The other route leads to Gates Pass Road through the Tucson Mountains, which offers breathtaking views and scenery but is a narrow cliff-hugging road often referred to as "white-knuckle pass." RVers must take Ajo Way to Kinney Road.

i The first movie to be filmed at Old Tucson Studios was the 1939 western *Arizona,* starring William Holden. In the 1970s, the television shows *Little House on the Prairie* and *Gunsmoke* were filmed here.

PIMA AIR AND SPACE MUSEUM $$
6000 E. Valencia Rd.
(520) 574-0462
www.pimaair.org
History and aircraft buffs, along with everyone else, will be enthralled by this indoor and outdoor museum displaying one of the largest collections in the world of vintage and current flying machines. Visitors will see everything from an exact full-scale replica of the Wright flyer, the first machine to fly, to the fastest, the SR-71 Blackbird, a sleek machine that flies at more than 2,000 miles per hour (or Mach 3-plus, in flying lingo). You'll see just about every type of aircraft flown by the US military branches over the years, plus many types of private and commercial aircraft, including an Air Force One plane used by Presidents Kennedy and Johnson. Visitors can go inside many of the larger aircraft and see navigation equipment, gunnery bays, and cargo holds. Throughout the museum, interpretive exhibits inform visitors about the aircraft and about aviation's past, present, and future. The museum has a space artifacts gallery containing early space items such as mock-ups of the X-15 and Mercury space capsule. The museum also houses the Challenger Space Center, which is open to the public daily for tours.

Be sure to visit the 390th Memorial Museum (520-574-0287; www.390th.org), housed on the grounds of the Air and Space Museum. This museum-within-a-museum is dedicated to the members of the 390th Bombardment Group, which was active in World War II from 1943 through 1945. Exhibits include a fully restored B-17G Flying Fortress, along with photographs and a library that maintains 80,000 wartime records on microfiche. Open 10 a.m. to 4 p.m. daily except Thanksgiving and Christmas; entry is free with paid admission to the Air and Space Museum.

The Air and Space Museum is open daily except Thanksgiving and Christmas from 9 a.m to 5 p.m., but there's no admittance after 4 p.m. Kids 6 and under get in free; admission prices vary seasonally, with discounts for seniors and military personnel. Wheelchair accommodations and tours are available. Pima Air and Space Museum is also the place from which to take a bus tour of Davis-Monthan Air Force Base and its aircraft boneyard, AMARC. (See the separate Davis-Monthan listing in this chapter.)

i The *Tucson Attractions Passport* booklet gives you two-for-one admissions and other savings at lots of area attractions. You can buy your passport on the Web at www.visittucson.org or pick one up at the visitor center. You can save hundreds of dollars, and the passport's good for a year.

REID PARK ZOO $$
1100 S. Randolph Way
(520) 791-4022
www.tucsonzoo.org
Among the 400 exotic animals you'll see at the zoo is the strange-looking, long-nosed giant anteater, an animal for which Reid Park Zoo has the most successful captive breeding program in the world. But you'll see lots more at this terrific small-scale zoo: bears, llamas, tortoises, giraffes, zebras, elephants, and lions, plus several types of exotic and more common birds, reptiles, and fish. All the animals live in environments approximating their natural habitat. Maybe you'll even be lucky enough to be in town when one of the female residents has just given birth. (The

zoo staff is great about announcing these arrivals and will gladly let you know.)

To help visitors learn about the animals, there are a few roving interpretive stations as well as docents leading impromptu tours. On weekends the zoo offers several special events. The zoo has a gift shop, wheelchair-accessible restrooms, a restaurant, snack bars, and free parking. All of this takes place in the middle of centrally located Reid Park, where the facilities and fun include walking and biking paths, picnic ramadas, swimming pools, tennis courts, a lake with pedal boats for rent, a formal rose garden, and a band shell.

The zoo is open 9 a.m. to 4 p.m. Sept through May, and 8 a.m. to 3 p.m. June through Aug, except Christmas and Thanksgiving. Try to go early, because the morning is the best time to see the animals being active. Admission prices are $7 for those age 15 and older, $5 for seniors, $3 for kids 2 to 14, and free for younger kids. All children younger than 14 must be accompanied by an adult.

SABINO CANYON RECREATION
  AREA $$
5900 Sabino Canyon Rd.
(520) 749-2861, (520) 749-2327 (tram reservations)
www.sabinocanyon.com
One of Tucson's most popular and spectacular natural attractions, Sabino Canyon is not to be missed. Located on the extreme eastern border of the Sonoran Desert, the area is visited by over 1 million people a year. You'll see incredible rock cliffs, running streams, and terrific views of the Catalina Mountains, along with many varieties of cactus and other indigenous plants. The best way to experience the canyon is to take a 45-minute

Close-up

Public Art Treasures

Keep your eyes peeled as you travel throughout town, as there are numerous public art projects, big and small, sprinkled around, from bridges and sculptural bus stops to gorgeous murals and tile work. Some of the more notable include the amazing Diamondback Bridge conceived by Simon Donovan that spans Broadway west of Euclid Avenue. Just look up as you drive on Broadway Boulevard heading downtown—you can't miss it.

The enormous mural on the sound barrier wall dividing Barrio Anita from I-10 is another visual pleasure. Commissioned by the Arizona Department of Transportation and designed by artists Joshua Sarantitis and William Wilson, it features tile mosaics as well as painted images depicting neighborhood people and barrio life. There are two sections located on N. Contzen Avenue just off Speedway Boulevard and I-10.

Smaller in scale, but equally interesting, is the mural on the side of an old adobe home at 555 Meyer Ave. between 16th and 17th Streets. Created by Franklin, it's a great example of "primitive art" a la Grandma Moses with its burro, street scene, and angels. And for gorgeous tile work, check out the lovely wall sprouting ceramic saguaro flowers on 10th Avenue between 36th and 37th Streets.

shuttle-bus narrated tour, offered 365 days a year, weather permitting. You can also hike, bike, picnic, or just walk through this pristine desert landscape. The park is open every day, 24 hours a day. Entry fee is $5 per vehicle, or you can buy an annual pass for $20 also good for Mount Lemmon and Madera Canyon. (See the Parks & Recreation chapter for additional details.) The visitor center is open daily 8:30 a.m. to 4:30 p.m. Tram tours take place on a variable schedule daily and cost $8 for adults, $4 for kids over age 2.

TITAN MISSILE MUSEUM $$
I-19 and Duval Mine Road, Sahuarita
(520) 625-7736
www.titanmissilemuseum.org
This museum is a National Historic Landmark because it displays the only remaining Titan II missile that wasn't dismantled after the cold war ended and the Strategic Arms Limitation

Treaty took effect. For more than 20 years, from the mid-1960s to the mid-1980s, this nuclear Titan II was on 24-hour alert ready for launching from its underground silo. This site near Green Valley was transformed into a museum and is operated by the Arizona Aerospace Foundation.

Except for the propellants and nuclear warhead, the missile and its huge launching arena are just as they were years ago. Some of the displays are above ground, while others are 35 feet underground, so walking shoes are required to descend the 55 steps. (People in wheelchairs or those who have difficulty walking can arrange to use the elevator.) Underground, you'll walk through the 200-foot-long cableway to the silo containing the Titan II missile and see the launch control center. Aboveground, you'll get another look at the missile through the glass covering where the massive 750-ton roll-back silo door is partially open. You'll also see the rocket engine that propelled the 330,000-pound missile from launch to an altitude of 47 miles in just 2.5 minutes, plus the reentry vehicle, a favorite subject of photographers (picture taking is allowed).

Guided tours are offered daily beginning at 9 a.m., with the last tour at 4:30 p.m. They take 1 hour and start on the half hour. No reservations are taken, except for large groups. The museum is open daily (except Thanksgiving and Christmas) from 9 a.m. to 5 p.m. Kids 6 and under are free, ages 7 to 12 are $6, and adults are $9.50, with discounts for seniors and military personnel. To get here, take I-19 south to exit 69 west, then go past La Canada Drive to the museum's entrance.

i If you're a real adventurer, sign up for the 4.5–hour special Top to Bottom tour at the Titan Missile Museum. You'll visit never-before-seen areas, like the actual launch duct and the pump rooms. You must be at least 18, be able to climb a 15-foot ladder, and fit through holes 2 feet in diameter to go on this tour. Reservations are necessary, and tours are limited to 6 people. Call the museum for details, (520) 625-7736.

TOHONO CHUL PARK $$
7366 N. Paseo del Norte
(520) 742-6455
www.tohonochulpark.org
Step into this 49-acre oasis, and you'll forget that the sights and sounds of the bustling city are a mere stone's throw away. Tohono Chul, meaning "desert corner" in Tohono O'odham, envelops visitors with its solitude and beauty. Named "One of the Great Botanical Gardens of the World" by Travel & Leisure Magazine, it's a wonderful place to experience and learn about the nature, art and culture of the Sonoran Desert.

Nature trails of 0.25 and 0.75 miles, shaded by lush palo verde trees, meander through gardens, pools, exhibits, and washes. Rabbits, lizards, and Gambel's quail scurry around, while hummingbirds and many other varieties of birdlife fly overhead in this "aviary without walls." Plant life native to the desert surrounds the trails, much of it labeled with their common and scientific names, so you'll actually be able to identify these strange-looking growing things. Several gardens on the grounds include the hummingbird garden, designed to attract these small hovering birds, and the ethnobotanical garden, showing crops grown by early Indian settlers and introduced by Spanish and Anglo arrivals.

The park's Exhibit House is a 1937 restored adobe building with art and cultural exhibits, and the La Galeria gift shop. Another building, a hacienda-style former residence, provides a lush plant-filled courtyard and patios for relaxing or a meal, snack, or afternoon tea replete with scones, jam, and cream in the Tea Room. There's also a gift shop, La Fuente, adjacent to the Tea Room. At the La Entrada Greenhouse you can ask questions about desert plants and gardens and purchase native plants. The park conducts a variety of tours and holds special events like the Wildflower Festival in spring and the night-blooming cereus event in early summer. (See the Natural World chapter to read about this unusual flower and other desert flora you'll see at the park.)

Admission to this desert preserve is $8 for adults, $5 for seniors and military, $3 for students, $2 for children ages 5 to 12, and free for kids under 5. Free parking is available. The wheelchair-accessible grounds are open daily from 8 a.m. to 5 p.m. The gift shop hours vary. You'll find Paseo del Norte at the first stoplight on Ina Road just west of Oracle Road.

✳TUCSON BOTANICAL GARDENS $$
2150 N. Alvernon Way
(520) 326-9686
www.tucsonbotanical.org
One of Tucson's treasures, this small but exquisite in-town garden presents a complete primer on the amazing plants that thrive in southern Arizona. Its 5.5 acres offer a shady and peaceful spot to view and learn about plants indigenous to the area plus some that normally would grow only in the tropics if not for the environment and care provided by the Tucson Botanical Gardens staff.

Walking paths and garden oases are surrounded by cacti of all types, native trees, wildflowers, flowering plants that attract birds, and even plants imported from tropical climates. Although the gardens are open year-round with plenty to see, there are specific times of the year that certain garden areas thrive. For example, the herb garden is prolific April through June, the wildflower garden blooms March through May, cactus plants show their colorful blooms April through August, and the Native American crops garden has its yield May through August. The folks at the botanical gardens will tell you what's in bloom if you call. They'll also tell you what special events are coming up, such as herb or plant sales held during the year. There's a gift shop with books and other items focusing on southern Arizona's flora and even a picnic area where visitors can bring their own refreshments and dine among the cypress, citrus trees, and roses. A small cafe is open in the Xeriscape Garden on specific days offering salads, sandwiches, coffee, and juices.

Tucson Botanical Gardens is open from 8:30 a.m. to 4:30 p.m. except on New Year's Day, July 4, Thanksgiving, and Christmas. Admission is $8 for ages 12 and older; children 4 to 12 are $4, and kids 3 and under are free.

TUCSON MUSEUM OF ART
** AND HISTORIC BLOCK $$**
140 N. Main St.
(520) 624-2333
www.tucsonmuseumofart.com
The cornerstone of this historic arts district is the contemporary Tucson Museum of Art, home to 6,000 pieces of art in its permanent collection, a gift shop, and one of the loveliest courtyards in town, with sculpted benches, fountains, and a chic cafe. The rest of the block consists of 4 historic homes dating from the 1800s. Each one has a colorful history and contains fascinating period exhibits. Docent-led tours are available October through April (call for specific times); they are free with the price of museum admission. The museum is open 10 a.m. to 5 p.m. Tues through Sat and noon to 5 p.m. on Sun. Closed Mon and major holidays. Admission is $8 for adults; children under 12 are free. Senior and student admissions are discounted. Admission is free on the first Sunday of the month. (See the Arts & Culture chapter for additional information.)

UNIVERSITY OF ARIZONA
** MINERAL MUSEUM $$**
Cherry Avenue and University Boulevard
1601 E. University Blvd.
(520) 621-4227
www.uamineralmuseum.org

In the basement of the Flandrau Science Center and Planetarium (described previously in this chapter) is the university's Mineral Museum. Rock hounds or other folks interested in gems and minerals will appreciate this small but excellent exhibit of more than 2,000 rock and gem samples, some of which are rare and most of which were excavated in Arizona. Call for admission prices and hours.

WHIPPLE OBSERVATORY TOUR $$
Mt. Hopkins Road, Amado
(520) 670-5707
http://cfa-www.harvard.edu/facilities/
flwo/visit_center.html
It's customary to associate the Smithsonian Institution with our nation's capital, so most folks are surprised to find the Smithsonian linked with Arizona. But that renowned organization does have a facility south of Tucson—the Fred Lawrence Whipple Observatory on the top of Mount Hopkins in the Santa Rita Mountains. A number of telescopes and meteorological instruments are located on a half-mile ridge at 7,600 feet, while the mountain's summit at 8,550 feet houses the world's fourth-largest multiple-mirror telescope. The latter is a joint project of the Smithsonian and the University of Arizona.

At the base of the mountain stands the Whipple Observatory visitor center (open Mon through Fri), which also happens to be a lovely area with walking trails, desert flora, and picnic tables. From there it's 10 miles up the mountain to the observatory on a narrow switchback road. Although the road can be traversed, at its end drivers will discover a locked gate, so the only way to visit the

observatory is by taking a tour, which the observatory conducts by bus. From mid-Mar through Nov, public tours are operated on Mon, Wed, and Fri starting at the more down-to-earth visitor center, which opens at 8:30 a.m. weekdays.

The tour begins at 9 a.m. with a video presentation, after which the bus travels up the mountain, returning at 3 p.m. Tour-takers should be aware of the elevation, which can pose a problem to people with certain health problems. Also, some uphill walking, stair climbing, and standing for 15 to 20 minutes are required during the tour. And if you're squeamish about narrow mountain roads with few guardrails, it's best to pass on the tour and learn about the observatory at the visitor center. Reservations are a must for the tour, and only 30 people can be accommodated. Children younger than age 6 are not permitted because of the tour's duration. And even if you have a reservation, it's best to call whenever weather conditions are poor, as the tour could be canceled. Bring a lunch, because you'll only find a soft-drink machine and drinking water at the top. They do have picnic tables. And don't forget sunglasses, a hat, and possibly even a jacket—the summit is 15 to 20 degrees cooler than down below. The tour fee is $7 for adults and $2.50 for kids ages 6 to 12.

Finding the visitor center is a bit tricky, but you won't be disappointed, even if your plans don't call for a tour. From I-19 south take exit 56 (Canoa Road) to the east-side frontage road; head south for 3 miles to Elephant Head Road, then turn right onto Mt. Hopkins Road and drive 7 miles to the visitor center.

KIDSTUFF

Kids thrive in Tucson, with its fresh air, sunny skies, beautiful parks, and wildlife galore. There aren't many places left where you can see coyotes, hawks, owls, quail, snakes, and javelinas all right in your own backyard. You'll find lots and lots of things to do here indoors and out. One-of-a-kind museums, stargazing, cowboy towns, kid-friendly art, music, theater, and many more unique hidden treasures are here for children of all ages.

YESTERDAY, TODAY & TOMORROW

The following attractions transport kids into the past or the future as well as show them the world around them today. They're mostly educational, but that will be our little secret. Your kids will be having too much fun to realize they're actually learning something.

ARIZONA HISTORY MUSEUM & HISTORICAL SOCIETY, MAIN MUSEUM $-$$
949 E. 2nd St.
(520) 628-5774
www.arizonahistoricalsociety.org
Say "We're going to the historical society" to your kids, and you'll probably hear a loud groan. But say "Let's go see what an old Tucson fort was like," and the response should be an enthusiastic "Yeah!" The society, which is actually a museum, is fun for kids as well as adults. Youngsters can climb aboard a restored stagecoach; see a replica of El Presidio, a fort that was Tucson's first settlement; hunker down inside a traditional brush hut; view a Tohono O'odham Indian village; try on serapes; and lots more. One favorite is the

mine display, complete with a walk-through underground mine tunnel, that shows how early settlers here drilled for gold and silver. It's history with a fun slant.

The historical society is smack in the midst of the university area, so street parking can be tough. However, you can park free at the big garage at the northeast corner of Euclid Avenue and Second Street, about 1.5 blocks from the society; just be sure to get your ticket validated by the receptionist before you leave the museum to head for your vehicle. Hours are 10 a.m. to 4 p.m. Mon through Sat. Admission is free for anyone under 12. (See the Attractions chapter for more adult-oriented features of the historical society.)

BIOSPHERE 2 $$$
Highway 77 at Mile Marker 96.5
3240 S. Biosphere Rd.
(520) 838-6200
www.b2science.com
Kids love the surreal, futuristic structures of Biosphere 2, the world's largest

glass-enclosed ecological laboratory. It used to be that researchers lived inside for years, so visitors could only tour the outside and peek in. Now visitors can actually go inside and see how the crews lived and how this miniature of our own biosphere, Earth, runs. The main tour starts with the "human habitat" where the scientists lived. From there you go through an airlock into the wilderness areas, including a steamy tropical savanna. A wooden trail travels along the 40-foot ocean cliff where you can look down into the million-gallon tropical ocean. A special kids' area teaches them about sound, light, and conservation. The on-site University of Arizona research program offers kid-friendly programming and hands-on activities. This is a better bet for older kids (over 6). Toddler types might find it frustrating, because beyond viewing the fascinating architecture, there isn't too much for younger kids to do and not all areas are accessible via stroller. High-energy kiddies can run around the extensive grounds (250 acres).

There's also a shop, a snack bar, and daily guided tours. Only the exterior grounds and not the guided tours of Biosphere 2 are accessible by stroller, wheelchair, and walker.

Admission is fairly steep, but kids younger than 5 are admitted free. Discounts are available for AAA members, seniors, and college students, plus you can usually get discount coupons at lots of local places, including in the newspaper or from the Tucson Convention & Visitors Bureau. No pets are permitted, and no food or drink except for bottled water is allowed on the premises. Biosphere 2 is about 45 minutes north of downtown Tucson on Oracle Road. Open daily from 9 a.m. to 4 p.m.; closed Thanksgiving and Christmas Day. (See the Attractions chapter for more information.)

COLOSSAL CAVE MOUNTAIN PARK $$
16721 E. Old Spanish Trail, Vail
(520) 647-7275
www.colossalcave.com

The dry cave at this extensive park about 30 minutes east of Tucson is a great family destination. The 45-minute guided tours take you deep into the cave, once home to ancient peoples and desperados. Strollers are not permitted, but kids 5 and older will enjoy the spooky shadows and stories. A park admission fee of $5 per car plus guided cave tour admission fees apply. (See the Attractions chapter for additional information, including fees and hours.)

There are no eating facilities here, so be sure to fill up or take your own snacks. If you're not into spelunking, the on-site museums have several kid-friendly exhibits. You can also pan for gold and gemstones and visit Henry and Big Nasty, 2 resident desert tortoises. There are daily trail rides available for an additional fee. The park also sponsors many family-friendly weekend events; check the newspaper or website for a schedule.

FLANDRAU—THE UA SCIENCE CENTER AND PLANETARIUM $$
Cherry Avenue and University Boulevard
1601 E. University Blvd.
(520) 621-7827
www.flandrau.org

Located on the University of Arizona campus, Flandrau is a real kid-pleaser. This is a science center, an observatory, a planetarium, and a mineral museum all wrapped into one! The Science Center exhibits feature a cool asteroid cave and the amazing 3-D Mars Wall. The planetarium also hosts amazing laser shows for a separate admission fee.

The Mineral Museum housed downstairs holds case upon case of fascinating

Close-up

Docent Program for Kids

Do your kids love animals? Are they interested in the desert world that surrounds them? If so, they might be the perfect candidates for the Junior Docent program at the fabulous Arizona-Sonora Desert Museum (see this chapter's listing and the Attractions chapter for information on the museum). This unique program offers kids ages 13 to 18 a chance to work behind the scenes and with visitors at this world-famous museum. Junior Docents receive training on the plants, animals, and geology of the Sonoran Desert region and participate in field trips and live animal encounters. Applications are accepted year-round for 12 positions. You can download the application and recommendation forms at www.desertmuseum.org or call (520) 883-3083.

rocks of all kinds and sizes. Budding scientists will love the store, where they can take home science kits, posters, books, and learning toys. Or they can look for planets, galaxies, and star clusters in the observatory's 16-inch telescope, which is open year-round 7 to 10 p.m. on clear Wed through Sat nights for free. Flandrau is open daily with varying hours. Admission to Flandrau, which includes a planetarium show, is $7.50 for adults, $4 for kids 4 to 12; kids under 4 are free. Parking can be tough here in the middle of the university, especially during evening athletic events. On weekends and after 1 p.m. weekdays, Flandrau visitors park for free along Hawthorne Street (north of the Science Center). Paid parking is available at the Cherry Avenue Garage near McKale Center and the 2nd Street Garage, located on 2nd Street west of the Flandrau.

GADSDEN-PACIFIC DIVISION TOY TRAIN OPERATING MUSEUM $
3975 N. Miller St.
(520) 888-2222
www.gdptoytrainmuseum.com

Their hours are irregular, but if your child loves toy trains, this is *the* place to go. This huge warehouse space is home to 5 table-tops of operating miniature train layouts, and each layout models a different scale environment. Kids can even operate some of the controls. From the intersection of N. Romero and W. Roger Roads, go north to Price Street and turn left (west). Go 2 blocks to Miller Avenue. Call ahead for hours of operation; admission is free, but donations are welcome.

INTERNATIONAL WILDLIFE MUSEUM $$
4800 W. Gates Pass Rd.
(520) 617-1439
www.thewildlifemuseum.org
Housed in a very cool-looking fort, the International Wildlife Museum features over 400 kinds of mammals, insects, and birds from around the world. There's just one thing—they're all stuffed! But kids seem to love this friendly, easily accessible museum nonetheless. Especially because they can touch just about everything here (a real

plus), including hairy buffalo, a life-size lion, a bear, and a crocodile. You can also watch some terrific nature films in the comfortable 98-seat theater. There's also a gift shop and restaurant on the premises. The museum is open every day except Thanksgiving and Christmas, Mon through Fri 9 a.m. to 5 p.m., Sat and Sun 9 a.m. to 6 p.m. Admission is $8 for adults, $6 for seniors, $3 for kids 4 to 12; children under 4 are free.

Ben's Bells

While you're visiting 4th Avenue, stop by Ben's Bells Studio, part of the Ben's Bells nonprofit organization, which celebrates and promotes kindness in a very unique and special way. Founded in 2003 to honor the memory of 2-year-old Ben Packard, who died suddenly of croup, this organization distributes beautiful handmade mobiles of a colorful ceramic flower and a lovely copper bell to people in Tucson who have contributed to the community in a positive way. If you and your kids would like to participate in this wonderful Tucson tradition, you can help create the ceramic flowers that decorate the mobiles and teach your kids about the value of kindness. The Studio is open Tues through Sat starting at 10 a.m. You'll find it at 816 E. University Blvd. in Geronimo Plaza. Helping create the bells is free, but donations are welcome. For more about the organization and the Studio, go to www.bensbells.org or call (520) 628-2829.

MINI-TIME MACHINE MUSEUM OF MINIATURES $$
4455 E. Camp Lowell Rd.
(520) 881-0606
www.theminitimemachine.org

This is a kids' paradise. Everyone from toddlers in tiaras to 13-year-olds on the cusp of manhood will find something to love here. Room after room is filled with miniatures and dollhouses—there are even displays under the floors! The Enchanted Tree will fascinate younger kids with its embedded mouse family vignettes and tinkling fairies who appear mysteriously inside the tree. Don't miss the echoing rotunda, with its starry sky—if you look long enough, you may see a shooting star. The other rooms will keep everyone busy looking at the hundreds of furnished contemporary and vintage dollhouses, miniature animals, snow villages, and lots, lots more. A gift shop is full of fairy-themed items and mini-mini animals so your kids can start their collection. Open Tues through Sat, 9 a.m. to 4 p.m. General admission fee is $7, kids 4 to 17 are $5, under 3 are free. Closed major holidays.

OLD PUEBLO TROLLEY $
4th Avenue and 8th Street
(520) 792-1802
www.oldpueblotrolley.org

The historic Old Pueblo Trolley is a great ride for everyone, not just kids. The restored antique electric trolleys rumble along the tracks on their route from the main gate at the University of Arizona along University Boulevard to 8th Street with lots of stops along the way (extensions to the line to take it through the downtown area are in progress). The velvet seats and wood-paneled interior complete with uniformed conductor transport you back to an age gone by. Kids love to stomp on the bell (ask the conductor). The 1-mile University/4th Avenue loop takes about 25 minutes and is a great way to explore this unique area, home to funky shops, eclectic restaurants, cafes, and the UA crowd. You can also visit the trolley car barn and museum at the end of the line at 8th Street. On your way off, take a minute to check out the lovely wrought-iron trolley stops.

One-way fares are $1.25 for adults, 75 cents for kids 6 to 12 and seniors, and free for kids younger than 6. But the best deal is on Sunday, when a ride is only a quarter. Or you can get all-day fares for a mere $3 (adult) and $2 (child) and stop, shop, and sightsee in this fascinating area. It operates Fri from 6 to 10 p.m., Sat from noon to midnight, and Sun from noon to 6 p.m.

OLD TUCSON STUDIOS $$$
201 S. Kinney Rd.
(520) 883-0100
www.oldtucson.com
Little broncobusters (and big ones, too) will be thrilled by the sights and sounds at this slightly hokey replica of an old frontier town. Kids can see spectacular stunts, musical revues, and gunfights (all pretend, of course), hear old Southwestern lore, and pan for gold. They also can ride a miniature train or an antique car (these have a varied schedule, so call ahead).

Old Tucson Studios started out in 1939 as a movie set and later was turned into a theme attraction. It's been the site for hundreds of Western movies and TV shows. There are shops, rides, restaurants, and saloons along with all the trappings of the Old West. It opens at 10 a.m. daily; closing hours vary seasonally. Gate admission is $16.95 for ages 12 and older, $10.95 for ages 4 to 11, and free under that. Discount coupons are easy to find around town at the visitors bureau and some banks and grocery stores. (See the Attractions chapter for more information.)

PIMA AIR AND SPACE MUSEUM $$
6000 E. Valencia Rd.
(520) 574-0462
www.pimaair.org
What kid isn't enraptured by flying machines? Within Pima Air and Space Museum's 100,000-square-foot building and 150 acres of surrounding land, there are more than 250 examples of nearly every type of flying machine ever invented. A 42,000-square-foot hangar is home to the Aviation Hall of Fame and rare aircraft. There's a perfect replica of the very first airplane, the Wright flyer; an SR-71 Blackbird that flies at Mach 3-plus and set the speed record; presidential airplanes; World War II bombers; helicopters; and ultralights. (The museum is fortunate to be across the street from the airplane graveyard at Davis-Monthan Air Force Base, so it can get unusual planes that are retired there.)

There are numerous hands-on exhibits for kids, including a cockpit they can climb into and work the flight controls and a control tower where they can turn on runway lights and listen to radio transmissions. The museum's Challenger Learning Center specializes in educational programs for children. Here kids can check out a training version of an Apollo space capsule, see a real moon rock, and learn all about the Phoenix Mars mission. For an extra fee, kids will love the Flight Simulator ride, located in Hangar 1 North (you must be 38 inches tall to ride).

Hours are 9 a.m. to 5 p.m. daily, except Thanksgiving and Christmas (last admission at 4 p.m.). Admission prices vary seasonally, but it's free for children 6 and under. The on-site Flight Grill serves up kid-friendly fare. (See the Attractions chapter for more information.)

TUCSON CHILDREN'S MUSEUM $$
200 S. 6th Ave.
(520) 792-9985
www.tucsonchildrensmuseum.org
Housed in the historic Carnegie Library in downtown Tucson, this museum is a real hit with kids, and although many of the exhibits are a bit weary and well worn, the kids don't seem to mind. You'll find a wide variety of hands-on exhibits, a fire engine, police motorcycle, a music room, and an Ocean Discovery Center with an underwater sea video. Kid-size computer workstations offer simple interactive software programs, and dinosaurs roam (not really) in the robotic animation exhibit. There's also a giant bubble room where kids can surround themselves with a 5-foot cylindrical bubble. Special areas include an art studio, music performance area, and the hands-on Electri-City Gallery, which shows how electricity works.

Special events take place throughout the year, and there are always fascinating kid-friendly activities happening, like making prints from a fresh apple, creating stationery with twigs and leaves, fashioning Mexican paper flowers, and making slimy bugs—all included in the price of admission.

Admission is $6 for ages 2 to 18, $8 for adults, and $6 for seniors. Hours are 9 a.m. to 5 p.m. Tues through Fri and 10 a.m. to 5 p.m. Sun. Kids younger than 16 must be accompanied by an adult. Children under 24 months get in free.

CREATURES, CRITTERS & CACTI

Kids are enthralled with things that crawl, growl, bite, and sting, so here are some great places where they can see wildlife without Mom or Dad worrying about having to administer first aid.

ARIZONA-SONORA DESERT
MUSEUM $$$
2021 N. Kinney Rd.
(520) 883-2702
www.desertmuseum.org
If there's only one place you have time to visit, this probably should be it. Don't be fooled by the name "museum"—actually it's a unique combination of zoo and natural museum that's truly world-class.

Kids will be enthralled by just about everything they see—reptiles, desert insects such as scorpions and tarantulas, and wild cats such as bobcats. The beaver and otter pond is fun to watch from above but even more exciting from below, where observers can see all the underwater antics of these furry swimmers. There's also prairie dog town, bighorn sheep climbing around their mountain caves, and huge walk-in aviaries, including one devoted exclusively to hummingbirds. "Life on the Rocks—Leapin' Lizards" is a terrific kid-friendly exhibit highlighting some of the smaller species found in rocky environments. Not all the animals here are real, see if you can tell! Volunteer docents conduct hands-on shows throughout the museum daily. Kids will like the cafeteria-style restaurant and especially the ice-cream shop located along the trail. The gift shop has lots of books and learning tools on the desert life presented at the museum.

The museum is primarily a walking experience, with 2 miles of paths on 21 acres. Strollers are available for free. It's hot here in summer, so be prepared or plan your visit for early in the day or the evening or go during Summer Saturday Nights (June through Aug), when special activities are scheduled. It's open every day, and admission prices vary seasonally; kids 5 and under are free. (See the Attractions chapter for more information about this museum.)

CHILDREN'S DISCOVERY GARDEN AT THE TUCSON BOTANICAL GARDENS $$
2150 N. Alvernon Way
(520) 326-9686
www.tucsonbotanical.org

A great way to introduce kids to nature, this tiny garden created just for them is a lovely oasis in the middle of the larger botanical garden. A giant bee and butterfly hover above touchable and edible plants, a worm farm, and a beautiful water wall made of exquisite ceramic tiles that you'll have trouble dragging your kids (and yourself) away from.

Butterfly Magic is another big draw for kids. For an extra admissions fee, you can walk through a greenhouse full of fluttering live tropical butterflies and view their stages of development from pupa on in a special exhibit, only on display October through April. (See the Attractions chapter for details on the Tucson Botanical Gardens.)

PICTURE ROCKS MINIATURE HORSE RANCH $
6611 N. Taylor Ln.
(520) 682-8009

Run by fourth-generation Arizonans Connie and Al Kazal, this working ranch is home to over 55 miniature horses and colts, 45 tiny Nigerian dwarf goats, 300 multicolored bantam chickens, and a bird sanctuary. Kids will adore this open, friendly (educational even!) place. You can feed the chickens (bring lots of loaves of cheap wheat sandwich bread) and pet the horses and goats. Bring your camera and lots and lots of space on your memory card for some great photo ops!

There's a $5 per person entry fee (all monies go to feed and care for the animals). Special rates are available for groups and schools. Open daily by appointment. Reservations are necessary, so do call ahead. There is no minimum group size, and the Kazals are happy to arrange a tour or birthday party for anywhere from 1 to 65 people. Keep in mind that morning is best (between 8 a.m. and noon), as that's when the animals will likely be awake and alert. Wheelchair accessible and walker friendly, there's a shaded picnic area and wheelchair-accessible restrooms but no restaurant facilities. Take Ina Road West and pass under I-10, go left on Wade to Picture Rocks to Taylor Lane (approximately 10 miles), then turn left on Taylor Lane.

REID PARK ZOO $$
1100 S. Randolph Way
(520) 791-4022
www.tucsonzoo.org

Though small, this well-designed zoo offers everything from long-nosed giant anteaters to lions, tigers, and rhinos—it's the perfect size for kids. There are also jaguars, pygmy hippos, elephants, zebras, giraffes, and all manner of birds in aviaries. The South American section features bears, llamas, tapirs, and the carnivorous piranha, plus a lush aviary. Kids love baby animals, so be sure to ask what's been born recently. All of the 500 or so animals here live in modern, naturalistic settings, but the restaurant and gift shop are reserved for their human guests. There are lots of special activities for kids here—you

---

Kids' Summer Theater Programs

Numerous summer theater programs are available all around town for kids of all ages. Here are just a few notable ones:

- In the foothills, the Community Schools summer program at the Catalina Foothills High School offers several choices for elementary, middle, and high school students. Overseen by the high school's drama teacher, students perform popular musicals; (520) 209-7551.

- The university area offers a great summer arts and theater camp at ZUZI Dance Company (see the Arts & Culture Chapter), where kids create the choreography and the costumes as well as dance and perform; (520) 629-0237.

- On the east side, private prep school St. Gregory School offers several theater-focused summer classes as part of their Minds Alive! summer camp, including "Musical Theatre for the Aspiring Broadway Star." If you think you have a future "Annie," call (520) 327-6395.

---

can even feed a giraffe on designated days for a small fee. The zoo sits in the middle of Reid Park, a great place to have a picnic, ride a bike, or play on the playground.

The zoo is open daily from 9 a.m. to 4 p.m. Sept through May, and from 8 a.m. to 3 p.m. from June through Aug; closed on Christmas. If you go in the summer, go early in the day when animals are active. Parking is free, which also happens to be the admission price for children younger than 2. The older crowd has to pay a modest fee—$3 for kids up to 14, $7 for adults, and $5 for seniors. Family memberships offer considerable savings. All children younger than 14 must be accompanied by an adult. Strollers and double strollers can be rented for the day. (See the Attractions chapter for more information.)

GET A LITTLE CULTURE

Introducing kids to a little culture may not be tops on their list of things to do, but it works better if the attraction is specifically geared to youngsters. So in this section we present culture your kids might actually enjoy, plus places where the little hams you have at home can take a stab at real acting.

ARTS FOR ALL/THIRD STREET KIDS
2520 N. Oracle Rd.
(520) 622-4100
www.artsforallinc.org
Although it focuses on kids with disabilities, this nonprofit performing arts group welcomes all children. Funded by grants and various charities, it offers youngsters the chance to learn and perform dance, music, drama, painting, and drawing. In addition to classes, usually held after school during the school year or via a summer camp, the organization has 2 performing components. One is the ensemble company that performs at various private functions and has traveled to Australia, performed at the White House, and appeared in a movie filmed in Tucson. The other component is open to kids who

Close-up

Skyride at Mount Lemmon's Ski Valley

For a great day trip with the kids, take a drive to Mount Lemmon's Ski Valley and ride the chairlift to the top. Just an hour from Tucson, the drive is gorgeous, the lift exhilarating, and the scenery beautiful. The kids will love every minute! Once at the top you can hike a series of trails (in summer months), and from May to October you'll see millions of ladybugs clustered all over trees, flowers, twigs—just about everywhere. The bright red, black-spotted insects hibernate here every year, and it's an incredible sight.

You can bring your own picnic feast to eat atop the mountain, or stop in the snack bar or the slightly more formal (there are real tables) Iron Door Restaurant with patio dining and a kid-friendly menu that won't break the bank. (Try the famous chili and homemade corn bread with warm honey.) The Skyride is open year-round. Take Catalina Highway off Tanque Verde Road in Tucson. Drive 4.2 miles to the forest boundary, and continue 26 miles to the Ski Valley turnoff. Turn right and drive 1 mile to the ski area. Call (520) 576-1400 for recorded information.

audition for the youth ensemble, who perform dance and drama productions that are open to the public. Watch the newspapers for information on performances, or call the organization. It provides a great opportunity for kids to learn skills in the arts and to perform.

✴STUDIO CONNECTIONS
4625 E. River Rd.
(520) 731-1559
www.studioconnections.net

DaVinci Kids (ages 7 to 12) and DaVinci Prep (ages 13 to 19) are the youth programs offered by this acclaimed theater group. The young thespians work with award-winning director Robert Encila to hone skills in stage movement, voice training, improvisation techniques, costuming, and production skills. The results can be viewed at performances of cutting-edge plays held several times a year for proud parents and guests.

TUCSON SYMPHONY ORCHESTRA
Tucson Symphony Center
2175 N. 6th Ave.
(520) 882-8585 (box office)
www.tucsonsymphony.org

The Tucson Symphony Orchestra offers 6 informal, interactive "Just for Kids" concerts designed to introduce quality classical music to children of all ages. Each concert highlights an ensemble of the orchestra in a presentation combining humor, storytelling, demonstrations, and audience participation. They're held at the Tucson Symphony Center on the first Saturday of the month from October through March. Call for the exact dates and times. There is a suggested donation of $2.

MUNCHKINS IN MOTION

You certainly don't need us to tell you that kids love to move. From roller-skating to tumbling, Tucson's got them covered.

LITTLE GYM OF EAST TUCSON
7225 E. Broadway Blvd., Ste. 150
(520) 751-1107
www.thelittlegym.com/easttucsonaz
Part of a national chain, this kid-friendly gym offers classes in gymnastics, karate, dance, tumbling, and more for tiny tots as young as 4 months. They also offer a parents' night out on select Fridays so you can drop off the kiddies and get to know each other again!

RANDOLPH SKATEPARK
200 S. Alvernon Way
(520) 791-4560
Twisting and high-flying bodies along with scrapes and bangs of skateboards are what you'll see and hear at this facility right behind the Tucson Parks and Recreation Department's Randolph Center. Kids—mostly teens—now have a 16,000-square-foot asphalt-paved area to call their own and strut their skateboarding skills. It includes 2 Bauer boxes, which for the uninitiated are platforms with ramps leading up to them and a rail along the back; 1 flat-top pyramid; and 2 grind rails. Skateboarding isn't permitted in other city areas the kids seem to gravitate to, such as downtown sidewalks and the Tucson Convention Center pavement, so this is a safe and legal alternative. In-line skating is also popular here. It's free. During the school year hours are 2 p.m. to dark Mon through Fri, 8 a.m. to 4 p.m. Sat; closed Sun.

SAGUARO AQUATICS
2045 W. Omar Dr.
(520) 638-8040
www.saguaroaquatics.com
Swimming is key in Tucson, where kids of all ages have almost 365 days of sunshine! Learn how to do it right at this year-round swim school for infants all the way up to adults. Swimming classes, swim teams, and the ever-popular kids' night out every Friday with dinner and a movie make this a popular pick. There are 3 locations in town, some open seasonally, so check in advance.

SKATE COUNTRY $$
7980 E. 22nd St.
(520) 298-4409
www.skatecountry.com
Kids who like loud music and light shows accompanying their roller-skating will love Skate Country. But it's not just for kids—entire families can have a. blast here. For starters, quad skate rentals are one price for any age: $3; if you use in-line skates, bring your own. The rink, which has good supervision, is open daily year-round, but skating hours and admission prices vary. Monday through Thursday at designated times is called Cheap Skates because it's only $4. But if the whole clan is going, Sunday Family Night may be the best deal—a family of up to 6 pays only $12 to skate from 6 to 9 p.m. Saturday mornings are reserved for "tiny tots," when kids younger than 12 skate from 10 a.m. to noon for $4. There's also an adult skate Thurs from 8 to 10 p.m. for anyone age 18 or older for $5. A video arcade and snack bar are available.

JUST ADD WATER

Water parks are great finds in Tucson's desert and in summer's heat, when the whole family needs to find a cool place.

BREAKERS WATER PARK $$$
8555 W. Tangerine Rd.
(520) 682-2530
www.breakerswaterpark.com

Kids can actually catch a wave in Tucson, but only at Breakers Water Park, which holds 1.3 million gallons of water. Unlike almost everything else in Tucson, however, water parks are summer season attractions, so Breakers is only open late May through Labor Day. But that's precisely the time a splash in the cool water is most welcome. The 20-acre park in the far northwest also has 5 waterslides and a toddler pool, so it's fun for kids of all ages. Don't forget the waterproof sunscreen.

It's open in summer Tues through Sun from 10 a.m. to 6 p.m. Admission prices vary; there is a season pass, and kids under age 3 are free. Tube and locker rentals are extra. Admission is reduced after 3 p.m. No outside food or beverages can be brought into the park.

JUST PLAIN FUN

These are our picks for places kids will love while they get to pretend to be racecar drivers, baseball champs, golf pros, or even fairy-tale characters.

FUNTASTICKS
221 E. Wetmore Rd.
(520) 888-4653
www.funtasticks.com
If your kids are way too full of energy, give them a couple of hours here and you might tire them out, at least momentarily. The stuff to keep kids entertained and exercised runs the gamut. In addition to Tucson's largest kiddie arcade, there are two 18-hole miniature golf courses, bumper boats, single- and double-seat go-karts, rookie go-karts, laser tag, batting cages, and a video arcade. These attractions usually cater to older kids and teens, but Funtasticks has lots of stuff geared to the littler ones—baby bumper boats, kiddie cars, and a small roller coaster, to name a few.

Funtasticks is open daily, but hours vary for activities. Call ahead for times. The rates for each activity also vary.

Funtasticks is located across the street from Tucson Mall and is surrounded by shopping and places to eat. It's also less than a half block from a Sun Tran bus transit center that is a major transfer point with an information booth, covered waiting area, and restrooms.

GOLF 'N STUFF
6503 E. Tanque Verde Rd.
(520) 296-2366
www.golfnstuff.com
This is a lot like Funtasticks (see above) but on the far east side. In Little Indy, kids can maneuver their own miniature racecars along a twisting track. Or they can bump around in bumper cars or bumper boats, bat a thousand in the batting cages, aim for a hole in one on the miniature golf courses, or test their skills in the huge video arcade. Older kids will love the rock climbing and laser tag. Some of the attractions have minimum age requirements, so you might want to call ahead instead of seeing the look of disappointment on little faces once you're there. It opens daily at 10 a.m. and closes at 10 p.m. Sun through Thurs and 1 a.m. Fri and Sat. Rides open at various times seasonally. Prices are per activity.

VALLEY OF THE MOON
2544 E. Allen Rd.
(520) 323-1331
www.tucsonvalleyofthemoon.com
It's wild, wacky, and weird—and kids love it. The spirit of childhood was embodied by one man in this little hidden wonder. Long

The Sporting Life

There's plenty of opportunity for kids to both watch a sport and be a sport around Tucson.

SPECTATOR SPORTS
The University of Arizona has teams in men's basketball, women's softball, baseball, football, and hockey, so there's likely to be some sort of college game going on any time of the year. See the Spectator Sports chapter for all the details, call the university (520-621-2287), or check the website at www .arizonaathletics.com to see who's playing when.

RODEO
Kids also love watching a rodeo, and Tucson has one of the best in the West— La Fiesta de los Vaqueros, held the last weekend in February. It's a several-day event complete with a major parade that kids will love, too. (See the Festivals & Events chapter for more information about the rodeo.)

GOLF
For kids who want to get in on the action, Tucson parks offer junior golf clinics in May and June; then kids have unlimited free golf at city courses after completing the clinic. Call the city's Parks and Recreation Department (520-791-4653) or see the Golf chapter for more details.

TENNIS
Randolph Park has junior tennis on Saturday for kids ages 5 to 17 that includes instruction and practice time on the courts. You must register in person, but you can get information from the Parks and Recreation number above.

BASKETBALL
Several Tucson parks have a Saturday-night teen basketball league, also called Late Night Hoops, for 13- to 19-year-olds (520-791-4870).

PARKS & REC CLASSES
Pima County Parks and Recreation (520-877-6000) offers lots of sports and classes for kids—swimming, BMX bicycle racing, gymnastics, tae kwon do, track, golf, and soccer. They're held at various times of the year and at locations around the county. Check the program guide and class catalog available at rec centers around town for details.

ago he created rock cliffs, caves, pools, and miniature gardens among the desert flora on his piece of land and called it Valley of the Moon. Then he added fantasy fairy tours and Bunnyland Theater, with trained rabbits. Playing the mysterious mountain gnome, he gave tours, told stories, and performed magic shows that captivated his young audiences. All of this happiness he gave away for free. Now operated as a nonprofit organization, the Valley of the Moon continues the tradition of entertainment with a variety of special events. Hours vary, and donations are welcome. Call to find out when activities and events are scheduled; some events have a fee. Valley of the Moon also books parties.

PICK A PARK

Parks aren't just for playing Frisbee or flying kites. Tucson has dozens of parks with tons of fun things for kids—and parents—to do. Many of the parks have swimming pools, so put on those swimsuits and jump in; some of them are open year-round, but most are especially inviting in the heat of summer. Swing, jump, climb, and slide on the jungle gym equipment. Hit tennis balls, toss footballs, or play softball. Have a family picnic under a ramada. It's all free, except for a nominal charge to swim—or perhaps use the courts. (For a complete list of parks and what they offer, see the Parks & Recreation chapter.)

✳BRANDI FENTON MEMORIAL PARK
3482 E. River Rd.
(520) 877-6000
www.pima.gov/nrpr/parks/brandi-fenton/index.htm
Great for a family outing, this 56.7-acre park is located north of the Rillito River at E. River Road and N. Alvernon Way and offers a multitude of activities for kids of all ages. Everyone loves the brightly colored splash park, a terrific way to cool off on hot Tucson days. The splash park is open April 22 to October 31 from 7 a.m. to 7 p.m. Two covered playgrounds offer slides, rock climbing walls, and bouncy, rubbery pavement. Three soccer fields, covered basketball courts, and

an equestrian arena are perfect for sports fans of all ages.

Dogs are welcome here, too, at the off-leash dog runs at the east entry to the park. You'll also find walking paths, a fitness course, and a memorial garden at the visitor center. Named for 13-year-old Brandi Fenton, who was killed in a car accident, this park is a wonderful memorial to her young life. The park is open from 7 a.m. to 10 p.m.

ENTERTAINING EATS

Finding good food for kids is always a challenge. Tucson has its share of family-style restaurants, but many upscale restaurants are offering healthy kid-friendly cuisine as well. Here is just a sampling of the kid-centric choices around town.

✳CREATE CAFE
4660 E. Fort Lowell Dr.
(520) 298-3421
www.createcafe.com
This brightly painted, low-key restaurant is one of the most kid-friendly locally owned restaurants in town. Create Cafe offers a great healthy (!) and delicious menu with tempting selections for even the pickiest eater. The kids' menu features such popular items as organic "spaghettioos" and nitrite-free hot dogs. Family nights are from 5 to 9 p.m. on Sat and feature movies and a jumping castle. Open daily for breakfast, lunch, and dinner.

CHUCK E CHEESE'S
6130 E. Speedway Blvd.
(520) 745-8800
www.chuckecheese.com
The pizza, burger, and salad menu isn't really the main draw here; it's the fun and games.

It's a madhouse with kids everywhere, and lots of noise. Young ones love crawling through the tubes and watching Chuck E Cheese in the mechanical stage show. Older ones gravitate toward the Skee-Ball or video games. Kids can win prizes, while parents can get package deals covering food and tokens (or "bags of gold," as they're known here). Chuck E Cheese's is open daily during afternoon and evening hours.

LITTLE ANTHONY'S DINER (MAIN LOCATION)

7010 E. Broadway Blvd.
(520) 296-0456
www.grandmatonyspizza.com
We guarantee moms and dads will like this place as much as, if not more than, the kids do. It'll take you back decades to the real diners that are almost extinct now, complete with oldies on the jukebox and black-and-white-checkered floors. It's got a great atmosphere, with happy servers who sing and dance and give a great rendition of "Happy Birthday" to those celebrating. At any moment someone will spring up from a booth and swing to the oldies on the dance floor. There's a video room with pinball machines, and outside you'll usually find at least one beautifully preserved auto from the '50s plus a few rides for the kids. The food choices are many and reminiscent of yesteryear's diners—from burgers, salads, and pizzas to old-time blue-plate specials such as turkey, meat loaf, and fried chicken. The kids' menu has burgers, peanut butter and jelly sandwiches, corn dogs (on a stick), and mac 'n' cheese. Little Anthony's is open daily. This busy and popular spot is behind the Gaslight Theatre.

MIMI'S CAFE

4420 N. Oracle Rd.
(520) 690-9544
www.mimiscafe.com
Finally, a chain restaurant that offers more than chicken fingers for kids! This family-friendly place has lots to choose from, even for picky eaters (their kid-size burgers are served plain—no pesky lettuce or tomato). The children's menu even offers a turkey dinner and soup and salad. Open daily for breakfast, lunch, and dinner from 7 a.m. to 11 p.m. A second location is at 120 S. Wilmot Rd. (520-747-7273).

OREGANO'S PIZZA BISTRO

4900 E. Speedway Blvd.
(520) 327-8955
www.oreganos.com
A Chicago-based chain, Oregano's offers a blob of raw pizza dough to every table with kids, which keeps them amused and happy throughout the meal. And the food is pretty good, too! You'll find lots of pizza, giant salads, onion rings and fries, toasted ravioli, garlic bread, and soup along with kid-friendly pizza slices and bowls of pasta. You'll have to drag them away!

i Look out for dinosaurs if you happen to be at the northwest corner of Tanque Verde and E. Grant Roads. Two huge dinos guard the McDonald's at this intersection, and the larger one is usually dressed up according to the season, with a Santa hat or Halloween costume. Installed by local McDonald's owners Michelle and Michael Retzer, the creatures were made by La Reata Studios in Amado, Arizona, at a cost of $55,000.

TRAIL DUST TOWN
6541 E. Tanque Verde Rd.
(520) 296-4551
www.traildusttown.com
This isn't just one restaurant but several places to chow down and shop while the kids have fun. It's a lovely little plaza of shops and restaurants in authentic Old West replica buildings surrounding a trellised courtyard. It's pleasant to just stroll around, but the kids are more likely to want to ride the narrow-gauge railroad and do the mine tunnel tour, go panning for gold, see the gunfight shows, or ride the antique restored carousel. There's an ice-cream and candy shop, a general store with all kinds of old-fashioned trinkets and goodies, a cowboy steak restaurant (Pinnacle Peak), and another restaurant with pleasant outdoor seating (Dakota Cafe). As the name Trail Dust Town implies, the theme is Western, but there's no dust here— just pretty walkways, real shade trees, and benches for watching the goings-on or the kids. Get the details on the eating establishments in the Restaurants chapter, though the kids will probably be just as happy with the ice-cream and candy shops.

TOYS & OTHER NECESSITIES

ANGEL THREADS
La Encantada Mall
2905 E. Skyline Dr.
(520) 299-3221
This lovely shop offers clothing, shoes, and accessories for young girls and boys from infant to girls 8 and boys 4, in both casual and dressy styles. You'll also find stuffed animals and a selection of diaper bags.

BABY'S AWAY
(520) 615-9754
www.babysaway.com
This business is more for moms and dads than babies, because it rents all kinds of things parents might find a need for, especially when vacationing. If you're looking for a stroller, high chair, playpen, crib, car seat, or even a tub of toys while you and baby are away from home, here's where to call. There's no retail shop, but Baby's Away delivers just about anything to help take care of baby. If you're traveling with a baby, keep this number handy.

BUILD-A-BEAR WORKSHOP
Tucson Mall
4500 N. Oracle Rd., #135
(520) 888-9218
www.buildabear.com
Everyone loves teddy bears, and what's better than making your very own! Build-a-Bear Workshop lets kids big and small pick out their very favorite stuffed animal friends, stuff it, stitch it up, and select its special outfits. It's a favorite spot for birthday parties. Open Mon to Sat 10 a.m. to 9 p.m. and Sun noon to 6 p.m.

CARTER'S FOR KIDS
Foothills Mall
Ina Road and La Cholla Boulevard
(520) 742-7501
www.carters.com
This is an outlet store for all the famous Carter's kids' clothes that have been outfitting youngsters for generations.

THE GYMBOREE STORE

Tucson Mall

4500 N. Oracle Rd.

(520) 293-2119

www.gymboree.com

This is a private-label clothing store for kids from birth to age 7 that sells shoes and accessories. The clothing is mostly casual, mostly cotton, and always bright and colorful. An additional location is at La Encantada Mall, 2905 E. Skyline Dr. (520-615-1183).

KID'S CENTER

1725 N. Swan Rd.

(520) 322-5437

www.e-kidscenter.com

Tired of giant toy stores dizzyingly full of junky stuff? Head for this terrific shop full of educational, interesting toys and tons of wonderful books and puzzles.

LIL' TRADERS

6216 E. Speedway Blvd.

(520) 881-8438

www.liltraders.com

A children's resale shop, this is a great place for quality used clothing plus toys, athletic equipment, and some furniture. Lil' Traders buys, sells, and trades.

LITTLE BIRD NESTING COMPANY

224 N. 4th Ave.

(520) 603-2694

www.littlebirdnestingcompany.com

This adorable little shop specializes in new and gently used children's clothes and select toys and accessories. Many items are locally made. You'll find lovely blankets and quilts, clothing size newborn through age 12, and lots of infant carriers and diapers. Weekend workshops for parents include a diapering boot camp—who knew there were so many choices and styles? Open daily.

MILDRED AND DILDRED

La Encantada Shopping Center

2905 E. Skyline Dr.

(520) 615-6266

www.mildredanddildred.com

Don't worry about touching in this bright, colorful toy store—it's encouraged! Chock-full of high-end specialty toys for the up-to-10 set, this place focuses on toys that encourage children to use their imagination. (Remember that?) You'll find kid-friendly play tables and a fanciful sky mural on the ceiling along with dress-up clothes, collectible dolls, old-fashioned board games, stuffed animals, books, and more at this popular kid-magnet. They also offer story times several days a week.

i Looking for things to do in town with your kids? The Tucson edition of *Bear Essential News* has tons of listings: best places for birthday parties, guide to summer camps, and coupons for just about every kid-friendly place here. This free newspaper is available around town at convenience stores, fast-food restaurants, and kiosks and online at www.bearessentialnews.com.

STARIZONA

5757 N. Oracle Rd.

(520) 292-5010

www.starizona.com

Starizona is an unusual local astronomy shop that, in addition to having a large stock of telescopes and accessories for sale, offers a slew of free viewings through its high-tech telescopes. Starting at sunset on Friday, and

Saturday nights, you can check out the incredible heavens. Best of all, it's free! This is a great way to learn the sky, how to use your new telescope, try out scopes or accessories, or just have a great time!

i Summer is here—yay! Wondering how to keep the kiddies busy? Free movies are the ticket. From May 30 to August 5, Grand Cinemas locations at Crossroads and Oracle offer a summer movie club, free to all kids 10 and under (adult tickets are only $2). Screen family-friendly faves like *Marmaduke* and *Diary of a Wimpy Kid*. Check www.movievalue.com for printable schedules. Shows start at 10 a.m.

YIKES TOYS
2930 E. Broadway Blvd.
(520) 320-5669
www.yikestoys.com
Looking for a unique gift for the person who has everything? You'll definitely find something at Yikes Toys, which specializes in eccentric toys for all ages. There are tons of little goodies here great for party grab bags, like realistic plastic and rubber animals, funky whistles, nose flutes, lots of gag gifts, jokes, tricks, and odd things like rubber monster women and a lovely selection of old tin toys.

FESTIVALS & EVENTS

For a small city, Tucson is extremely busy year-round with special events and festivals that showcase our multicultural heritage. No matter what month you plan to visit, you'll always find an interesting or unusual event to check out. From film festivals to rodeos, carnivals to bike races, golf tournaments to music under the stars, Tucson has a diverse—and fun—mix of entertaining events.

Thanks to our consistently beautiful weather—some 350 days of sunshine a year—few events will be canceled due to rain or cold (although once in a while a summer monsoon will cause an event to be postponed or canceled). In fact, the majority of events take place outdoors except during summer, when the 100-degree-plus temperatures send everyone scurrying indoors.

February and March are the busiest months, something that should be noted when making hotel reservations. February alone hosts two of the biggest events—the La Fiesta de los Vaqueros Rodeo and parade and the world-famous Tucson Gem and Mineral Show. Add a major golf tournament, an international film festival, and the Renaissance fair—just to name a few—and your slate should be quite full.

JANUARY

SENIOR OLYMPIC FESTIVAL
4208 S. Santa Rita Ave.
(and other venues throughout town)
(520) 791-3244
www.tucsonseniorgames.org
The Tucson Parks and Recreation Department (see the Parks & Recreation chapter) is known for the wide variety of programs it offers, especially those created with seniors in mind. One of the best examples in the varied slate is the Tucson Senior Olympic Festival for participants over age 50.

Modeled after the real thing, complete with a celebratory opening ceremony and lighting of the torch, the Olympic Festival brings together senior athletes from all over the Southwest for 9 days of competition and camaraderie in mid-January. The festival

attracts thousands of senior athletes competing in nearly 90 events and 33 sports at venues all over town. Competitions are held in aerobics, racquetball, swimming, cribbage, a wide variety of card games, cycling, horseshoes, bocce, and much more.

The public is invited to watch (and maybe get a little inspiration to get into shape). Watch the newspaper or call the City of Tucson Parks and Recreation Department for a complete rundown of times, places, and events. There is a registration fee to participate.

DILLINGER DAYS
Various locations downtown,
around Congress Avenue

Downtown Tucson transforms into the 1930s for this annual event commemorating the capture of John Dillinger and his gang in 1934 in Tucson. The Hotel Congress offers tours and lectures. You'll find reenactments of the shoot-out on the street corners, along with live music, walking tours, film documentaries, and food all along Congress Avenue for this event in mid-January. If you're into it, dress in 1930s clothes and join in the fun.

i Two great sources for current festivals and events are the Tucson Visitor and Convention website, www .visittucson.org, and *Tucson Lifestyle Magazine* (www.tucsonlifestyle.com). The visitor website offers comprehensive listings of festivals and events in Tucson and southern Arizona. Every issue of the monthly *Tucson Lifestyle* includes an arts and events guide that covers 50 events and exhibits in town.

JEWISH FILM FESTIVAL
Jewish Community Center
3800 E. River Rd.
(520) 299-3000
www.tucsonjcc.org
This annual festival, which runs for about 2 weeks starting in mid-January, features films by award-winning Jewish directors, producers, and writers. A wide assortment of films is shown, and pre- and postfilm receptions are held. Often the director or subject of the film will attend. Ticket prices depend on the time of the showing, with discounts available for seniors and students. (Tickets to special showings may be higher.) There is also a festival pass that will get you into all the films.

Parking at the JCC is easy and free in the front lot.

ANNUAL QUILTER'S GUILD SHOW
Tucson Convention Center
260 S. Church St.
(520) 547-5463
http://tucsonquiltersguild.com
Whether you love quilts for their historic value or enjoy the intrinsic beauty that is the art of the quilt, you won't want to miss this show. The Tucson Quilter's Guild sponsors this annual event, which features more than 200 quilts, quilted garments, quilting demonstrations, antique displays (including a short history of each quilt), product vendors, and even a raffle. Visitors to this 3-day event in the middle of the month also have an opportunity to vote for the best quilt of the show, which then receives the "Viewer's Choice" award. There is a fee for admission and parking in the TCC lot.

SOUTHERN ARIZONA SQUARE/ROUND DANCE AND CLOGGING FESTIVAL
Radisson Suites
6555 E. Speedway Blvd.
www.sardasa.com
Thousands of square and round dancers kick up their heels to calling by the finest callers, cuers, and clogging instructors at this annual event, which offers dancing for all levels, from basic to experienced to challenge. There are registration, ticket, and spectator-only fees, which change annually.

This event attracts many RVers; call ahead for special parking arrangements for your recreational vehicle. The event is sponsored by The Square and Round Dance Association of Southern Arizona, which has folk dancing classes and dances citywide just about any time of the year.

WINGS OVER WILLCOX

Willcox Chamber of Commerce
1500 N. Circle I Rd., Willcox
(520) 384-2272, (800) 220-2272
www.wingsoverwillcox.com

A must for bird lovers everywhere, this wonderful weekend event, held in mid-January, is devoted almost entirely to birding. There are so many things to do that you won't know where to begin! Among the highlights of the weekend are several opportunities to view the amazing sandhill cranes that winter in the Willcox area by the thousands. The weekend also includes lectures, field trips, tours, a banquet, and seminars by experts. You can attend a daylong photography tour, join other beginning birders and learn how to identify common bird species, explore the Dragoon and Chiricahua Mountains, or go on a hawk stalk in Sulpher Springs Valley to spot the more than 15 species of hawks, eagles, and falcons that live there. Advance registration is required for all activities. Fees vary by event.

FEBRUARY

ARIZONA RENAISSANCE FESTIVAL

US 60, 7 miles west of Florence Junction
(520) 463-2600
www.royalfaires.com

Although time travel hasn't been perfected just yet, you may want to try the next best thing: the Arizona Renaissance Festival. For 8 weekends from February through the end of March, costumed folk, be they kings or commoners, stroll the 30-acre grounds entertaining the crowds in much the same way they did at a 16th-century marketplace. This includes jousting, jesters, Renaissance music, and dancers. The food sold is much the same as it was in days of yore. Craftspersons create

and sell their wares. Bring your wallet; most rides cost extra.

The fair is held rain or shine from 10 a.m. until 6 p.m. Take Oracle Road north to Pinal Pioneer Parkway—Highway 79—to Florence Junction, where you catch US 60 for 7 miles.

Tickets prices vary; kids under age 5 are free. Discount coupons are available at all Arizona Fry's Food Stores.

COCHISE COWBOY POETRY AND MUSIC GATHERING

Buena Performing Arts Center, Sierra Vista
www.cowboypoets.com

If you're a fan of cowboy music and poetry, this is the place to be. Poets, singers, and musicians perform some of the best stuff you'll ever hear. Headliner performances take place on Friday and Saturday evenings and Sunday afternoon at the 1,300-seat Buena Performing Arts Center. Ticket prices vary. Don't miss this unique event. It's held on the first consecutive Friday, Saturday, and Sunday in February.

LA REUNION DE EL FUERTE

Fort Lowell Park
2900 E. Craycroft Rd.
www.oldfortlowellneighborhood.org

Go back in time to when the West was young! The Old Fort Lowell Neighborhood Association sponsors this free event, held in mid-February from noon to 4 p.m. that showcases the neighborhood and its fascinating history in early February. History buffs will love the cavalry drills, period reenactments, and self-guided walking tour (with free map) of the ancient Hohokam site, military camp, and historic homes and chapels. Music performances take place throughout the day, along with a series of lectures that feature local historians and experts. Food, drinks, and souvenirs are sold along Fort Lowell Road.

TUBAC FESTIVAL OF THE ARTS
(520) 398-2704
www.tubacaz.com

Art lovers will enjoy this lively festival held in Tubac, about 40 minutes south of Tucson. The town of Tubac has long been considered an arts mecca, with numerous galleries showcasing local artists from painters to ceramicists. The festival, which began in 1959 and is sponsored by the Tubac Chamber of Commerce, features live music, booths with the work of local artisans, and access to all the galleries in town. Take I-19 south to exit 40.

TUCSON GEM AND MINERAL SHOW
Tucson Convention Center
260 S. Church St.
(520) 322-5773
www.tgms.org

The Tucson Gem and Mineral Show really sparkles! Held the second week in February, this amazing event is the largest gem and mineral show in the world. Begun nearly 50 years ago, the show attracts the finest dealers, jewelers, and lapidary artists from around the world, plus thousands of visitors every year. Specialty exhibits are some of the big draws. Lectures are also an integral part of the weekend. And although it has spawned hundreds of satellite exhibits all over town—some beginning as early as the middle of January—the Gem and Mineral Show is a separate entity and is held exclusively at the TCC. It is open to the public for the entire 4 days and is not to be confused with the adjacent dealer show, which is open to gem dealers only.

Food is available at the TCC food stands. There is an admission fee and a fee for parking on-site in the TCC lot. The show runs Thurs through Sun. Check the newspaper for a comprehensive map, list of show locations, times, and costs.

THE ACCENTURE MATCH PLAY
CHAMPIONSHIP
The Gallery Golf Club
14000 Dove Mountain Blvd., Marana
(520) 571-0480, (866) 942-2672
www.worldgolfchampionships.com

The Accenture Match Play Championship takes place at the end of February at the Ritz-Carlton Golf Club, Dove Mountain, in Marana, just north of Tucson. The world's top 64 golfers participate in this exciting 5-day tournament that features a multimillion-dollar purse. This major tournament attracts all of professional golf's major players.

✳LA FIESTA DE LOS VAQUEROS
Tucson Rodeo Grounds
4823 S. 6th Ave.
(520) 741-2233
www.tucsonrodeo.com

Begun in 1925, La Fiesta de los Vaqueros (the feast of the cowboys) has been a highlight of the winter season in Tucson. Held the last full weekend in February, the festivities kick off for the public with the world's longest nonmotorized rodeo parade.

The parade begins at S. Park Avenue and Ajo Way and then travels south on Park Avenue to the rodeo grounds on Irvington Road at S. 6th Avenue. Crowds begin to line the route in the early morning—the parade starts around 9 a.m.—and parking can be at a premium, so it's best to plan ahead.

Grandstand seats are available for reasonable rates, but you can get a great view for free on any of the streets on the route. Shuttle service from various locations will take you to the parade site for a separate charge.

The parade features bands from all the local schools, local celebrities, real cowboys on their mounts, Mexican dancers, the Buffalo Soldiers from a nearby Visionquest program, horse-drawn carriages, and the requisite clowns.

Time was that so many families were involved in the rodeo that attendance at schools in the area dropped considerably during the event. Eventually the school districts conceded to the issue and closed for the Thursday and Friday of the rodeo. Happily for schoolchildren citywide, that tradition continues so that everybody can attend some or all of this event. Kiddies can join in on the rodeo fun, too, with the Mutton Bustin' competition—the littlest cowboys and cowgirls see how long they can ride on the back of a sheep—and the Arizona Junior Rodeo competition.

The rodeo itself is a 5-day event, beginning on Wed and culminating on Sun afternoon. Preliminary events are held on previous days. The public can watch such happenings as the Tucson Pro Roping contest and qualifying events for the rodeo.

Officially recognized by the Professional Rodeo Cowboy Association, the rodeo offers prize monies to the tune of hundreds of thousands of dollars.

Ticket prices vary depending on the day and the event. Parking on all days will cost you and is available on the rodeo grounds. Events usually end around 4:30 p.m. each day. You can buy tickets at the rodeo grounds or by calling (520) 741-2233, (800) 964-5662. Get your tickets in advance to ensure seating and avoid long lines.

i Open during most of Rodeo Week, the Tucson Rodeo Parade Museum, on the northeast corner of S. 6th Street and Irvington, houses over 150 vehicles, including antique buggies and wagons, along with a fascinating collection of historic photos. Call (520) 294-1280 for hours and tour information; an admission fee is charged.

MARCH

WINTER CHAMBER MUSIC FESTIVAL
Leo Rich Theater, Tucson Convention Center
260 S. Church St.
(520) 577-3769
www.arizonachambermusic.org
One week a year, in early March, the Leo Rich Theater at the TCC comes alive with the sounds of chamber music. Sponsored by the Arizona Friends of Chamber Music, the festival features top musicians and promising young talent playing everything from classic to modern pieces. A short introduction is given before each concert. The concerts are held on opening Sunday night; Tuesday, Wednesday, Thursday, and Friday nights, and the closing Sunday afternoon. A youth concert free to area students is held on Wednesday. The Gala Benefit Dinner is held on Saturday evening. Tickets are available for individual concerts, with discounts to students with ID. A package for all of the concerts is also available. The gala is priced separately. Chamber music is a part of the evening, of course. And take a little bit of the evening home with you by buying a CD of previous years' concerts. The Friends of Chamber Music also hold a series of concerts throughout the year.

CLIMB "A" MOUNTAIN
Pima Community College West Campus
2202 W. Anklam Rd.
(520) 323-4200, (800) 227-2345
www.community.acs.events.org/
ctctucson

Held the second week in March, this walk may not seem much of a challenge, but remember, most of it is uphill. Beginning at Pima Community College West Campus, this 3-mile round-trip walk allows for some of the prettiest views of Tucson. When you reach the top of "A" Mountain, you'll find a festival with food vendors, a jumping castle, massages, music, information booths, and plenty of fun. Proceeds benefit the American Cancer Society.

As part of the festivities, you can purchase a commemorative flag honoring (or in memory of) a loved one who has battled cancer. The flags are placed alphabetically along the route and can be taken home after the event. Registration begins early in the morning, followed by a group warm-up—no one wants to get injured here. Incentives are offered for those who earn the most money from pledges. There is a registration fee; all registered walkers receive a T-shirt.

SAN XAVIER WA:K POW WOW
San Xavier del Bac Mission
I-19, exit 92
(520) 294-5727

The Tohono O'odham Indians invite hundreds of Native American dancers and craftspeople from the US and Canada to gather at the San Xavier Mission grounds 12 miles south of Tucson for intertribal competitions in drum and dance techniques, including gourd, team, round, grass, hoop, and 2-step dance. Exhibitions and native crafts enrich the festival. Local families cook and sell traditional foods. Though still cameras are allowed, video cameras are not.

The festival costs $8 for adults, $6 for children 7 and up, and is free for younger ones. There is also a parking fee. All monies go to benefit the San Xavier community. (Read more about the mission in our Attractions chapter.)

TUCSON FESTIVAL OF BOOKS
University of Arizona campus
www.festivalofbooks.org

Held in mid-March, this huge event offers something for everyone and features hundreds of authors. Major national writers, local authors, workshops, speakers, movie screenings, screenwriters, food demos, food booths, face painting—it's all here. Row after row of white-tented booths take over the Main Mall at UA with readings, giveaways, and lots of books, books, books. Admission and workshops are all free.

APRIL

4TH AVENUE SPRING STREET FAIR
4th Avenue between University
Boulevard and 9th Street
(520) 624-5004
www.fourthavenue.org

If you're in town on one of the two weekends—one in April, the other in December—that the 4th Avenue Street Fair is being held, consider yourself lucky, and then put on a pair of walking shoes and head for this longtime Insiders' favorite. The 6-block area—which on any given day is a great place to shop, dine, and have fun—is closed to traffic during the fair.

Artisans and craftspersons offer one-of-a-kind clothing, handcrafted jewelry, handmade toys, pottery, unique household items, essential oils and aromatherapy goods, dried flowers, and much, much more. You can have your palm read or your face painted. You can watch jugglers do their thing, dance to the beat of a reggae band, or just enjoy some of the best people watching Tucson has to offer. Food booths on the side streets offer goodies from all over the world. Merchants stay open and sometimes have special sales or giveaways.

Sponsored by the 4th Avenue Merchants Association, this is an event not to be missed. Parking is at a premium on the side streets, but patience will pay off, even if it means a short walk to "the Avenue." (See the Close-Up in our Shopping chapter.)

COUNTRY THUNDER USA
Canyon Moon Ranch, Florence
20585 E. Price Station Rd.
(520) 868-9711
www.countrythunder.com
Over 150,000 fans head to this 4-day event, one of the biggest events in country music, taking place in early April. Headliners have included Leann Rimes, Brooks & Dunn, and Martina McBride. At Canyon Moon Ranch off Highway 79 in Florence, get ready for lots of music and food. You can camp nearby or stay at one of the limited number of local hotels. Admission is daily, or you can purchase a pass for the whole shebang.

SOUTHERN ARIZONA HOME BUILDERS ASSOCIATION (SAHBA) HOME & PATIO SHOW
Tucson Convention Center
260 S. Church St.
(520) 795-3025
www.sahbahomeshow.org
With hundreds of exhibitors and thousands of visitors, this is the home show of all home

shows in the area. Twice a year—in early April and October—the cavernous Tucson Convention Center Exhibit Hall is packed so full of exhibits and booths that it spills over onto the floor of TCC's arena. You'll find ideas for any project you may be contemplating, and some that you didn't even know existed. Exhibits can be found on landscaping, barbecuing, skylights, garage doors, kitchen projects, innovative flooring, spas, swimming pools, and much more.

You'll also enjoy guest speakers and daily demonstrations, and you may even win one of the many door prizes offered by exhibitors.

There is an admission fee, but kids under 12 get in free. Parking is plentiful in the TCC lots and will cost a fee for all day.

TOUR OF THE TUCSON MOUNTAINS
Throughout the mountains
(520) 745-2033
www.pbaa.com
More than 1,000 bicycle riders tour the Tucson Mountains west of the city in 27- and 73-mile races that start at Town Hall in Marana. This race usually takes place on a Saturday in mid-April and includes a kids' and family fun ride. Fees vary depending on which course you choose.

TUCSON GLASS FESTIVAL
Galleries, museums, and studios around town
(520) 884-7814
www.sonoranglass.org
Sponsored by the Sonoran Glass Art Academy, this festival takes you all over town to view the work of some of the most interesting and creative artists in town—glass artists. A 3-day pass ($10, kids under 5 free) includes entry to exhibits, artist studios, galleries, and

glass-blowing demonstrations. An extra fee gets you into the exclusive party at the Glass Academy where you can rub shoulders with the artists and enjoy live music and finger foods. Funds raised support the academy's Youth Development Program. The festival takes place in the beginning of April.

UNIVERSITY OF ARIZONA SPRING FLING
Rillito River Park
N. 1st Avenue and River Road
(520) 621-5610
http://springfling.asua.arizona.edu
Although the Spring Fling, the country's largest student-run carnival, attracts thousands of students, it's a great family-fun activity. You'll find carnival rides, live music, food booths, and games. Wildcat athletes can often be found shaking hands and signing autographs.

This 4-day event in early April is manned by some 3,000 student volunteers and helps raise money for the 120 clubs and organizations on campus. (Spring Fling is also the name of the nonprofit organization that puts the whole thing together.)

Thurs through Sat the event is open to midnight. On Sat gates open at noon. Sun hours are from noon to 8 p.m.

ARIZONA INTERNATIONAL FILM FESTIVAL
Various venues
(520) 882-0204
www.filmfestivalarizona.com
Film buffs in Tucson launched the Arizona International Film Festival to bring to light the talents of independent filmmakers from around the world. Founded in 1991, the festival has grown from a 4-day event with a handful of films to a 10-day extravaganza featuring dozens of films from a variety of countries.

Held in late April and sponsored by the Arizona Media Arts Center—which operates the Screening Room, 127 E. Congress St. (see the Nightlife chapter)—the event also features workshops, screenings, music, indie, family films, and the Reel Frontier Film and Video competition. Films are shown throughout the festival at the various venues around the city.

Since the first festival, it has premiered over 400 films (both world and US premieres), had 40 countries represented, featured over 150 Arizona works, and has been attended by almost 50,000 people. Films are shown on different dates at the different venues, which allows for catching the film you might have missed or getting to see a favorite another time. The sites are found all around town, so no matter where you are, a showing is just minutes away. Sites include the Screening Room, the Loft, and several other "regular" movie theaters.

Tickets for single events can be purchased 1 hour before each screening on-site. Special events, such as workshops and the Award Night Gala, and certain screenings will run you extra, depending on the event. A variety of passes are available, giving you entry into a plethora of events depending on the type of pass you purchase. Passes can be bought ahead of time (check the local papers for specific information on where to buy them). Parking, of course, varies depending on the film site.

PIMA COUNTY FAIR
Pima County Fairgrounds
11300 S. Houghton Rd.
(520) 762-3247
www.swfair.com

Annually in late April, the Pima County Fair is the biggest draw in attendance in Tucson. Each year over 400,000 people attend the fair to enjoy the farm exhibits, the food, and the nightly entertainment.

Throughout the 10-day run, you'll find the usual contests, exhibitions, games, and carnival rides—and plenty of extra touches, such as the interactive children's exhibits and a fine art exhibit, that go beyond the standard offering of a county fair.

Entertainment includes nationally known bands as well as local favorites. Local students show and sell their carefully tended livestock, poultry, and even rabbits. Ribbons are awarded for every kind of homemade goodie (or craft project) you can think of. There is an entrance fee; kids 5 and under are free.

LA FRONTERA TUCSON INTERNATIONAL MARIACHI CONFERENCE
Tucson Convention Center
260 S. Church St.
(and other venues throughout town)
(520) 838-3908
www.tucsonmariachi.org

This annual event in late April celebrates the blend of Hispanic music and culture that has influenced Tucson since its beginnings. The conference offers a chance to hear the best mariachi bands in the world, enjoy folk dancing, and observe artisan exhibits of Mexican arts and crafts. Because this is a 5-day "conference," many of the activities, such as seminars and workshops, are only for conference participants. But on the weekend following the conference, people from throughout the US and Mexico come to enjoy the events that are open to the public, many of which are free. Then there's

the Festival de Garibaldi, an all-day street fair along Armory Park with music and dance performances and booths offering crafts, souvenirs, and food.

The major draw of the conference, however, is the Mariachi Concert held at the TCC on Friday night. Concertgoers are treated to several hours of rousing music and celebrated Mexican dancers. Ticket prices vary widely, and tickets are available through the TCC or the number listed above. Other concerts take place at various venues around town. All proceeds from the Mariachi Conference benefit a local behavioral health organization.

TUCSON POETRY FESTIVAL
Various venues, Tucson
www.tucsonpoetryfestival.org

Started in 1981, this festival celebrates the beauty of language. The 4-day festival takes place in early April and includes open-mic readings and special performances featuring regional talent. Readings, workshops, and presentations by acclaimed poets also are scheduled. Call or check the website for exact times, locations, and admission prices.

MAY

CINCO DE MAYO
Kennedy Park
Mission Road and Ajo Way
(and other venues throughout town)
(520) 791-4873

This holiday—which translates as "5th of May"—celebrates the victory of the Mexican army over the French at Puebla, Mexico, in 1862. Festivities can be found citywide, especially at the many Mexican restaurants in town. You'll find music, dancing, crafts, and food at this lively fiesta.

TUCSON FOLK FESTIVAL
El Presidio Park area
115 S. Church St.
(520) 319-8599
www.tucsonfolkfest.org

This music festival, sponsored by the Tucson Kitchen Musicians Association, includes major national acts as well as continuous music featuring contemporary folk, blues, bluegrass, folk rock, ragtime, and gospel groups. Local and regional acoustical musicians play on multiple stages. Booths sell crafts and food. The free event is held the first weekend of the month.

IRONWOOD FESTIVAL
Mason Audubon Center
3835 W. Hardy Rd.
(520) 971-6238
www.tucsonaudubon.org/masoncenter

Held on the second weekend in May at the Mason Audubon Center on the northwest side of town, this 1-day festival celebrates the centuries-old ironwood trees in the park by focusing on nature and preservation. Open only by appointment during the rest of the year, this lovely 20-acre preserve provides a great opportunity to explore grounds full of saguaro and cholla cacti, grapefruit trees, and meandering paths. The festival features educational activities, interpretive walks, cultural presentations, food, music, live animal presentations, and many more activities. You'll find booths and information for most of the local and regional parks and many environmental organizations. It's a great event to take the kids to; they love touching the live snakes, desert tortoise, and lizards.

Parking is at a premium; you can park on the roadside or at nearby Tortolita Middle School and catch a ride on free shuttles

provided by Tucson Electric Power. The center is located on the southwest corner of Hardy and Thornydale Roads. There is an admission fee.

> **i** If your kiddies are getting tired of sitting still, the Tucson Folk Festival features a special children's show featuring a local performer on the Casa Cordova stage. Kids are encouraged to participate by singing, clapping hands, and dancing; www.tucsonfolk fest.com.

JUNE

JUNETEENTH FESTIVAL
Kennedy Park
Mission Road at Ajo Way
(520) 908-4544
www.juneteenth.com

In celebration of the day Texas slaves heard about their emancipation (2 months after the Civil War ended), Juneteenth festivities include athletic events, gospel music at churches around the city, and a 1-day festival at Kennedy Park (see the Parks & Recreation chapter). You can listen to gospel music and a wide variety of musical entertainment throughout the day on Saturday, plus visit an assortment of food booths, all in celebration of Afro-American culture. Take Ajo Road west to La Cholla Boulevard and watch for signs. This event is free.

HA:SAN BAK: SAGUARO HARVEST CELEBRATION
La Posta Quemada Ranch at Colossal Cave Park
(520) 647-7121
www.colossalcave.com

Saguaro cactus fruit (*bahidaj*) has been harvested by the Tohono O'odham people for centuries. Learn the details of how the harvesting is done and what the fruit is used for in workshops and demonstrations by tribal members. The event includes an all-day workshop (reservations strongly suggested), beginning at 6:30 a.m., where you get to pick saguaro fruit and prepare it for syrup making. Public activities from 11 a.m. to 2 p.m. include music, traditional dancers, craft making, and food. Workshop costs vary, and there is an entry fee per car to enter the park. Dates can change depending on the weather, so be sure to call first.

JULY

4th of July Fireworks
Various locations
Many of the major resorts tucked away in the foothills of Tucson sponsor their own well-executed fireworks, but the main event for residents is the massive light show launched from "A" Mountain, just west of downtown. This free spectacle can been seen from around the city, and many people gather for tailgate parties around the Convention Center downtown. But here is an Insiders' tip: Find someone who has a home with a flat roof (there are lots of them around here). From there you'll be able to catch not just the fireworks downtown, but probably one or more of the many other displays going on.

AUGUST

TOMBSTONE VIGILANTE DAYS
Various locations, Tombstone
(888) 457-3929
www.tombstonevigilantes.org
Any visit to Tombstone, "The Town Too Tough to Die" (see the Day Trips & Weekend Getaways chapter), means strolling down the wooden sidewalks, touring the historic buildings, and soaking up some of that Old Wild West atmosphere. During this 3-day festival, the citizens of Tombstone go all out to celebrate the history of their hometown. Along with the usual gunfights and hangings (mock, of course), you can enjoy a chili cook-off and period fashions. And if you're up to it, try the Vigilante 10K run. Take I-10 east to the Benson exit, Highway 80, and follow the signs to Tombstone.

AUGUST

TOMBSTONE VIGILANTE DAYS
Various locations, Tombstone
(888) 457-3929
www.tombstonevigilantes.org
Any visit to Tombstone, "The Town Too Tough to Die" (see the Day Trips & Weekend Getaways chapter), means strolling down the wooden sidewalks, touring the historic buildings, and soaking up some of that Old Wild West atmosphere. During this 3-day festival, the citizens of Tombstone go all out to celebrate the history of their hometown. Along with the usual gunfights and hangings (mock, of course), you can enjoy a chili cook-off and period fashions. And if you're up to it, try the Vigilante 10K run. Take I-10 east to the Benson exit, Highway 80, and follow the signs to Tombstone.

SEPTEMBER

BLESSING OF THE VINES FESTIVAL
Village of Elgin Winery
471 Elgin Rd., Elgin
(520) 455-9309
www.elginwines.com
Have you ever dreamed of stomping grapes? (Anyone remember *I Love Lucy* episode 150?)

Your dream will come true at the Elgin wine festival, where the grape-stomping competition is only one of many activities. The festivities go on for 2 days in early April and include wine tastings, lunch, music, and arts and crafts. Elgin is about 90 minutes south of Tucson. Take I-10 to exit 281, go south, and turn left onto Elgin Road. The winery is about 4 miles on the right. There is an admission fee, which gets you entrance into the grape-stomping competition and a souvenir wineglass.

MUSIC UNDER THE STARS
Reid Park
22nd Street and Country Club Road
(520) 722-5853
The Tucson Pops Orchestra began playing in 1955. Today the 50-piece group presents numerous concerts each year, and it continues a tradition of offering free concerts under the beauty of Tucson's night sky each Sun at 7 p.m. during the month. Bring a blanket or lawn chair and sample the various refreshments sold by local vendors, or come early with the family and enjoy a picnic before the show.

GREEK FESTIVAL
Greek Hellenic Community Center
1145 E. Fort Lowell Rd.
(520) 888-0505
Old-world charm meets modern-day fun at this popular event held in mid-September. (The festival has drawn upward of 20,000 people in past years.) It's easy to do because admission is nominal, with kids under 12 free.

Along with a dazzling array of Greek foods, you'll be able to learn Greek dances; sip ouzo, *metaxa* (Greek brandy), or Greek beer; buy Greek handcrafted items; or ride an assortment of carnival rides.

This is one of the area's most popular events, so parking is at a premium. It might be best to park on one of the side streets nearby and walk a short way to the festival. The Hellenic Community Center is located just off the corner of Fort Lowell Road at Mountain Road. The festival runs from Thurs through Sun nights.

MOUNT LEMMON OKTOBERFEST
Mount Lemmon Ski Valley
10300 Ski Run Rd., Mount Lemmon
(520) 885-1181, (520) 576-1400
While it isn't Bavaria, Mount Lemmon is the closest thing to it in the area and offers some respite from the lingering heat that may still be present in late September. The festival is usually held for 4 weekends in late Sept and early Oct. You'll find German food, music, and dancing at this free event. There is a charge for parking.

REX ALLEN DAYS
Various locations, Willcox
(520) 384-2272, (800) 200-2272
www.rexallenmuseum.org
The last of the singing cowboys is a native of Willcox, a large farming community about an hour and a half east of Tucson. Featuring a carnival, a rodeo and a parade, arts and crafts, and Western music and dancing, this annual event in late September hearkens back to the good old days. Rex Allen Jr. performs 2 special shows on Saturday, late afternoon and evening. There is a charge for tickets to his show and the rodeo, but just about everything else is free. Take I-10 east to the Willcox exit and head south.

OCTOBER

TUCSON CULINARY FESTIVAL
Loews Ventana Canyon Resort
7000 N. Resort Dr.
(520) 299-2020
www.tucsonculinaryfestival.com
There is no better way to experience the amazing culinary variety in Tucson than to attend this annual event. Every major chef, food vendor, and food- and wine-related retailer in town are here. For a set admission fee, you'll have access to wine tastings, food samples, seminars, and cooking demonstrations. Extras include a Sunday brunch hosted by a top chef.

✳TUCSON MEET YOURSELF
El Presidio Park
349 W. 31st St.
(520) 792-4806
www.tucsonmeetyourself.org
Despite its odd name, this 3-day festival in early October is a great place to experience the cultural diversity of Tucson. You'll find booth after booth of foods from every ethnic background: Danish, Laotian, Greek, Korean, Mexican, Southern, and Native American. Try an iced Japanese green tea, sweet potato pie, lamb kebabs, prickly pear juice, Mexican horchata, and Korean stir-fry. The variety is overwhelming, so bring a hearty appetite. The festival also features music of all types, a children's program, cooking competitions, and folk art demonstrations.

El Presidio Park is located in the heart of downtown between Alameda and Pennington Streets on Church Street. Look for the beautiful domed courthouse off Alameda Street. Paid parking can be found at the El Presidio underground garage, which can be entered off Alameda Street. There is also a public works garage at 50 W. Alameda St.

DESERT THUNDER PRO RODEO
Tucson Rodeo Grounds
4823 S. 6th St.
(520) 721-1621
www.desertthunder.com
Here's a chance to see real rodeo cowboys at work. This qualifying event runs for 2 days in mid-October and features bull riding, barrel racing, calf roping, and the like. You'll also enjoy team roping, steer wrestling, women's drill team, and, for the younger set, mutton busting, junior bull riding, pony rides, and a jumping castle. Goodies are available—you might want to purchase a real cowboy hat to take home with you. Ticket prices vary. Kids are free with 1 paid general admission ticket.

TUCSON BLUEGRASS FESTIVAL
Location varies annually
(520) 296-1231
www.desertbluegrass.org
Held at the varous locations in late October, the festival features workshops in guitar, bass, banjo, and song construction. You'll also find music and craft vendors and performers at the plaza stage. The action starts at 10 a.m. There is an admission fee; kids under 16 are free. If you're into bluegrass, this is the place to be!

NOVEMBER

EL TOUR DE TUCSON
Congress Street and Granada Avenue
(520) 745-2033
www.pbaa.org
November brings ideal cycling weather and with it this world-famous perimeter bicycling race. Held the Saturday before Thanksgiving, the ride starts in the heart of downtown and then continues around the city, returning to downtown for the finish. The route covers

dirt paths, traveling through washes, and plenty of riding up- and downhill. For the less hardy souls, or bodies, as the case may be, there are start-up points at 109, 79, 66, and 40 miles. And kiddies can join in for fun rides. This race is sanctioned by the Perimeter Bicycling Association of America, which is headquartered right here in Tucson.

Spectators can watch El Tour for free anywhere along the route. All registered riders receive a poster and a medallion.

THANKSGIVING FIESTA
Singing Wind Bookshop
700 W. Singing Wind Rd., Benson
(520) 586-2425

The indomitable Winn Bundy, former librarian and a font of information about writers, poets, and musicians in the region, hosts this annual fiesta at her delightful Singing Wind Bookshop in Benson. It attracts hundreds of book lovers. Authors read from their latest books, and there's lively music and lots of fun. It's held on the Sunday preceding Thanksgiving Day. (See the Shopping chapter for more information about Singing Wind.) Take I-10 to exit 304, and drive north 2.25 miles on Ocotillo Road. Go right onto Singing Wind Road, and follow it to the ranch house that serves as the bookshop.

DECEMBER

NACIMIENTO
Tucson Museum of Art Complex
140 N. Main St.
(520) 624-2333
www.tucsonmuseumofart.com

A *nacimiento* is a Mexican nativity scene. You'll be able to see one of the finest examples of this beloved holiday tradition at the Cordova House, which is part of the Tucson Museum of Art complex downtown.

A creation of Maria Louisa Tena—who began the nacimiento as a tribute to her mother, who always had a nacimiento in their house—the finely detailed scene includes tiny angels, animals, the manger, trees, moss, fairy lights, and even running water. Scenes from the life of Christ, Mexican ranches, African villages, and Bible stories complete this wondrous exhibit. The entire scene fills the room and even reaches the ceiling in some places.

The exhibit starts in November and runs through March. You can enjoy the terrific Holiday Craft Market at the same time. There is no admission fee for viewing the nacimiento. Parking is available in the museum parking lot or on any of the side streets nearby.

✳4TH AVENUE WINTER STREET FAIR
4th Avenue between University
Boulevard and 9th Street
(520) 624-5004
www.fourthavenue.org

Along with the 4th Avenue Spring Street Fair in April, this is the area's second-largest event in attendance, some 250,000 people a year. And it's no wonder! Artisans and craftspersons offer some of the most unique items around in early December. The musicians and performing artists are abundant. And the food . . .

The Winter Fair is a great place to find presents, whether it's jewelry, clothing, or pottery, for those special someones on your list, and while you're at it, buy something special for yourself. You can also have your face painted, take part in a political discourse, or have your fortune told—maybe you'll find out that you'll be returning to the Street Fair next year.

LUMINARIA NIGHTS
Tucson Botanical Gardens
2150 N. Alvernon Way
(520) 326-9686
www.tucsonbotanical.org
The stars of the show at this 2-day event near the beginning of the month are the more than 2,000 luminarias (candles nestled in sand inside a paper sack) that light the paths throughout the gardens. For years families have delighted in the glow of the night and the accompanying music by a variety of musical groups that perform at locations throughout the garden grounds. The candles are lit from 5:30 to 8 p.m.; admission prices vary. Come and enjoy complimentary snacks at this 5.5-acre oasis in the heart of Tucson.

TUCSON MARATHON
Start locations vary, Oracle
(520) 403-3355
www.tucsonmarathon.com
Runners in this marathon will drop 2,500 feet in elevation from the start of this race (in Oracle) to the finish line (they'll also enjoy some outrageous desert and mountain views along the way).

The majority of this race is downhill, so if you are a die-hard marathoner, you'll be delighted with your time—this is, after all, the nation's fastest USA Track and Field marathon in America. Please note, it is recommended that you train your quadriceps to avoid serious aches and pains after your downhill run. For the not-so-experienced, a half-marathon is also held, and if you can round up 4 friends, you all can enter as a relay team, with each leg of the relay a different length.

Finishers receive a medallion. Entry fees vary depending on time of registration (call the Tucson chapter of Roadrunners Club of America at (520) 326-9383 or go to www.azroadrunner.org for info on this race and many others in the area).

Both the Tucson marathon and the half-marathon are certified by USA Track and Field. Marathoners will also be happy to know that this race is a Boston Marathon qualifying race, and proceeds earned go to a local charity.

> **i** During the Christmas season you'll see many stands along the roads selling *ristras* (pronounced *REE-stras*)—ropes and wreaths made from dried red chili peppers. These make great Southwestern holiday decorations when hung from doors and windows.

HOLIDAY NIGHTS AT TOHONO CHUL PARK
7633 N. Paseo de Norte
(520) 642-6455
www.tohonochulpark.org
The lovely Tohono Chul park lights up with over a half million lights for its popular holiday event, held for 4 days in December. Walk the paths that meander through miles of beautifully landscaped gardens and get a whole new view of the park at night. Stop to listen to the fountains and music while you enjoy the soft night air and lack of snow. The Tea Room offers drinks of all kinds and delectable menu items to fortify you. There's also hot cider and wine. The gift shops are open if you haven't finished your holiday shopping, and lovely ornaments for sale if you haven't finished trimming your tree.

WINTERHAVEN FESTIVAL OF LIGHTS
Fort Lowell Road between Country Club Road and Tucson Boulevard
www.winterhavenfestival.org

This long-standing Tucson tradition is just the event to get you into the holiday spirit. For 10 days, just before and shortly after Christmas, the residents in this older, mid-town neighborhood—clearly defined by Prince Road on the north, Fort Lowell Road to the south, Country Club Road to the east, and Tucson Boulevard to the west—go all out in decorating the exteriors of their homes. Nearly everyone gets involved (rumor has it that when you move into the neighborhood, you must agree to partici-pate in decorating your home). Some folks stick to the traditional Christmas themes, but you're just as likely to find an extraterrestrial or two or a cowboy Christmas scene. Some homes also honor Kwanzaa and Hanukkah.

Admission is just a few dollars or a couple of nonperishable food items for the local food bank. You can choose to take a hayride or horse-drawn carriage tour (sepa-rate reservations and fees required; www .winterhavenrides.com), which saves wait-ing to enter the area, or ride the city buses. Certain nights are designated walk-through only (no cars). Check the local newspapers. Prepare for long waits to get in and lots of traffic. Parking is limited on the perimeter of the neighborhood but is usually free.

ARTS & CULTURE

Back in the 1860s, when Tucsonans wanted a little culture—and entertainment—they'd attend one of the many Mexican puppet shows or circuses that traveled through town. Performances would be outdoors, of course, and in order to enjoy the evening show, the audiences had to build bonfires using old cacti.

The arts scene in Tucson is quite different these days. Today you'll find symphony orchestras, jazz, bluegrass festivals, the state opera, ballet companies, folk and modern dance companies, art museums that rival bigger cities in scope, numerous art galleries, and several diverse local theater companies.

Venues have changed, too. Although we still enjoy many fine productions under the stars, Tucson audiences can attend performances at everything from a large arena setting to a small intimate theater. Indeed, Tucson has lived up to the *Wall Street Journal* calling it "a mini-mecca of the arts."

OVERVIEW

Music lovers will be thrilled at the many options available. Tucson supports annual blues, jazz, bluegrass, mariachi, Western music, and folk festivals and the UA Music School hosts numerous wonderful concerts throughout the year. Local support organizations make sure that each of these types of music can be heard year-round, many times for free. And the bar and club scene in town (see the Nightlife chapter) offers all types of live music just about any night of the week.

Tucson theater audiences can enjoy productions that range from major Broadway plays and musicals by professional touring companies to original works, experimental plays, multicultural works, and classical theater staged by local professional and community groups. The stage could be a park, a concert hall, the University of Arizona, or a small, experimental theater that seats 20 people. Pima Community College also plays an active role in the dramatic arts. The University of Arizona Theater Arts Department, with its Repertory Theatre, is one of the nation's oldest theater departments, and outdoor concerts and plays are held at the DeMeester Outdoor Performing Arts Center.

Dance offerings range from a classical ballet troupe to Afro-American/Latino, Native American, and Mexican folk dancers.

Art galleries and museums are plentiful. Many of the art galleries are located in and around downtown, but others can be found citywide. The Tucson Museum of Art, the University of Arizona Art Museum, and the Center for Creative Photography, which is located on the UA campus, boast many fine exhibitions and collections. Pima Community College's Art Museum, located at the Center for the Arts on campus, is another fine example of the diversity of sites where art is exhibited.

Tucson has long been recognized as a creative and prolific center for the literary arts. For more than 30 years, the University of Arizona Press has been publishing award-winning books. The university's creative writing program also boasts the country's largest, in size as well as scope, writing program (it's been rated among the top 10 in the nation). The UA's Poetry Center and Tucson's annual Poetry Festival have done wonders in bringing poetry out of the literary closet and into the public's ear. Tucson has fast become a haven for regional and national writers alike. The late Edward Abbey and Joseph Wood Krutch are writers from Tucson's past. Today nationally prominent writers such as Barbara Kingsolver, J. A. Jance, N. Scott Momaday, Alberto Urrea, Nancy Mairs, Tom Miller, Charles Bowden, Richard Shelton, Leslie Marmon Silko, Peter Wild, and Jane Miller are just a few of the names associated with Tucson's writing community. Many are featured at the annual Tucson Festival of Books (see the Festivals & Events chapter).

The Tucson performing arts season typically runs from September to May. During this period the University of Arizona and Pima Community College are in session, and the snowbirds—winter visitors escaping the snow of the Northeast and Midwest—become temporary residents of the Old Pueblo, making for larger audiences. In the summer major events decrease; though the literary scene remains constant, many smaller theaters continue to perform, and the art galleries and museums remain open.

What follows is an overview of the arts scene in Tucson. We have included several of the support organizations because they are extremely influential when it comes to championing local art and artists.

SUPPORT ORGANIZATIONS

ARIZONA COMMISSION ON THE ARTS
417 W. Roosevelt St., Phoenix
(602) 771-6501
www.azarts.gov
The Arizona Commission on the Arts, established in 1967, is the state agency that connects artists and communities across the Grand Canyon State. Their website includes extensive information on programs, grant opportunities, advocacy, and resources and includes both in- and out-of-state opportunities and resources in the areas of jobs, arts education, arts organizations, and artists.

ARIZONA MEDIA ARTS CENTER
PO Box 431, Tucson, AZ 85702
(520) 882-0204
www.azmac.org
This service and resource organization encourages the study, production, appreciation, and use of all forms of film and video. It has a research library and offers programs, classes, and conferences. An international film festival and art film presentations are held at the Screening Room, 127 E. Congress St. in the Tucson Arts District (see the Festivals & Events chapter).

THE CENTRAL TUCSON GALLERY ASSOCIATION
www.ctgatucson.org
This is a member-based gallery association of several top Tucson galleries. The association organizes First Saturday Art Tours in and around downtown Tucson. An Art Safari is held in February, a Summer Art Cruise in June, and The Big Picture in October.

TUCSON ARTS BRIGADE
PO Box 545, Tucson, AZ 85702
www.tucsonartsbrigade.org

This nonprofit arts and education organization supports the love of art through murals, dance, theater, puppetry, events, special projects, and community action by working collaboratively with numerous local organizations. They sponsor workshops, hundreds of temporary and permanent public art projects all around town, and special events, including the annual Water Project, billed as Tucson's synergistic water festival.

TUCSON/PIMA ARTS COUNCIL
100 N. Stone Ave., Ste. 303
(520) 624-0595
www.tucsonpimaartscouncil.org

The council, a nonprofit organization, was established in 1984 and is recognized as the official arts agency of the city of Tucson and Pima County. Recipient of the 2003 Governor's Arts Award for Service to the Community, the council provides arts and cultural development services through direct funding, technical assistance, commissions, and contracts to both individual artists and arts organizations. Numerous workshops are offered throughout the year.

VENUES

BERGER PERFORMING ARTS CENTER
1200 W. Speedway Blvd.
(520) 770-3690
www.asdb.state.az.us/berger

Known locally as "The Berger," this auditorium offers cozy seating for 496 with an elevated stage. A state-of-the-art facility, it's a favorite site for acoustic music and for Celtic, eclectic, folk, and traditional music concerts. Located on the campus of the Arizona School for the Deaf and Blind, the Berger is one of the city's premier venues for smaller, yet popular events.

CENTENNIAL HALL
University of Arizona
1020 E. University Blvd.
(520) 621-3341
www.uapresents.org

Originally the Main Auditorium, Centennial Hall, which dates back to 1937 and is listed on the National Register of Historic Places, was renovated in 1986 and rededicated and renamed Centennial Hall in honor of the 100th anniversary of the University of Arizona. The space blends the charm and formality of the old theater with state-of-the-art technical and acoustic advances. Today the facade of the building looks just as it did back in 1937, yet the back of the theater soars 5 stories high and easily accommodates big Broadway productions.

UA Presents, the university's performing arts series, offers numerous performances here between September and April. Independently produced shows, mostly in music and dance, continue at the hall year-round. On-street parking is free after 5 p.m. and on weekends, with paid covered parking available in various parking garages on the campus. Reserved parking for handicapped patrons is also available.

DEMEESTER OUTDOOR PERFORMING ARTS CENTER
Reid Park, 22nd and Country Club
(520) 791-4873
http://cms3.tucsonaz.gov/parksandrec/
specialplaces.php

The DeMeester is a most eclectic, and perhaps the most casual, performance venue in the area. Performances are year-round and include concerts, dramas, and special events. The natural amphitheater offers lawn seating, and patrons are encouraged to bring lawn chairs or blankets. Often food vendors will be on-site, but picnics are allowed.

PIMA COMMUNITY COLLEGE CENTER FOR THE ARTS
2202 W. Anklam Rd.
(520) 206-6986
www.pima.edu/cfa

Located at Pima Community College's West Campus, the Center for the Arts has several venues. The Proscenium Theater is a plush, state-of-the-art facility with box seats along the walls. With 425 seats, it's the college's largest and most used venue for both college and outside community productions and concerts. Considered to be "Tucson's finest midsize performing arts venue," its blend of high-tech equipment, superb acoustics, and classical aura is appreciated by performers and audiences alike. When events are happening at PCC, they usually happen here. Other arts organizations also use this venue.

The Black Box Theater, the college's space for experimental theater, seats 75. The stage can be manipulated into either a traditional setting, a thrust stage, or a theater in the round. Lighting and acoustics are state of the art.

Offering another intimate venue is the Recital Hall. Here the amphitheater seating offers a great view of the stone-backed stage no matter where you sit. This is an ideal spot for smaller groups to perform. The hall seats 75-plus.

The Center's Amphitheater and Courtyard allow for outdoor performances. This venue is also used for receptions.

RIALTO THEATRE
318 E. Congress St.
(520) 740-1000 (tickets)
www.rialtotheatre.com

Constructed in 1919, the Rialto Theatre was the most elegant and luxurious playhouse west of the Mississippi. Its unique architecture made it a dramatic showcase for plays, films, and vaudeville. The stage was the largest in the western states. The Sistine Choir sang from it, Ginger Rogers danced on it, and Tucson's first talking picture was shown from it. As the oldest performance theater in Tucson, its opening served notice that Tucson was on the nation's cultural map.

In 1948 the Rialto changed its name to the Paramount. For the next 15 years the theater was Tucson's premiere movie house, but changes in economics and society caused the Paramount to close its doors for the last time. A decade later, the theater where once orchestras played overtures to discriminating audiences had become a porno palace.

Known then as the Cine Plaza, the theater cleaned up its act in 1978 with a switch to first-run Spanish-language films, but a fire in 1981 and a boiler explosion in 1984 bolted its doors again. Unused for a decade and in disrepair, the Rialto was scheduled for demolition.

Concerned Tucson citizens, recognizing the importance of preserving this architecturally unique structure, negotiated the purchase of the theater property. The nonprofit Rialto Theatre Foundation was established in 1995 to raise the funds necessary for the theater's restoration.

Partially restored, the Rialto is now home to big-name acts alongside eclectic blues, rockabilly, and many trendsetting music groups.

TEMPLE OF MUSIC AND ART
330 S. Scott Ave.
(520) 884-8210, (520) 622-2823 (tickets)
www.arizonatheatre.org

This is truly the flagship of Tucson's downtown performance venues. In 1907 a women's civic organization called the Saturday Morning Musical Club decided the city needed a "temple" for music and art. It took longer than they expected, but their dream came true in 1927, when the Temple of Music and Art was completed. Over the years and through the misuse of many owners, the Temple fell into disrepair. A very vocal group set about to save it—one woman even stood between the building and the bulldozers to prevent its destruction. Her efforts and those of many others were rewarded when the demolition was called off and the restoration began. The Temple's $2.6 million restoration was completed with an official grand opening on October 13, 1990.

The Temple is the home of the Arizona Theatre Company, which performs in its 622-seat Alice Holsclaw Theater. The theater also hosts a variety of other performances, including music, dance, and contemporary rock acts.

Upstairs, along an outdoor balcony walkway, is the Cabaret Theater (which seats about 90) as well as the Temple Gallery, where various contemporary works are exhibited.

TUCSON CONVENTION CENTER
260 S. Church St.
(520) 791-4104
http://cms3.tucsonaz.gov/tcc

The arena, which seats 9,000-plus people, hosts huge events, such as ice shows, conferences, circuses, and concerts by big-name stars who make a stop in the Old Pueblo. But there are 2 more artistic venues: the Music Hall and the Leo Rich Theatre. The Music Hall seats 2,200-plus and is the home of the Tucson Symphony Orchestra, the Arizona Opera Company, and Broadway in Tucson. The much smaller Leo Rich seats 511, making it an ideal spot for chamber music recitals and concerts by contemporary and pop artists.

THEATER

ARIZONA REPERTORY THEATRE
Fine Arts Complex
University of Arizona Campus
Park Avenue and Speedway Boulevard
(520) 621-1162
www.cfa.arizona.edu/tftv/about-theatre

Arizona Repertory Theatre is the professional training company of the University of Arizona's Department of Theater Arts. One of the nation's oldest theater departments, it has offered performances to the community for more than 60 years. Plays and musicals are produced August through April, with several productions a year.

i Don't pass up performances at the local high schools. Catalina Foothills High School (4300 E. Sunrise Dr.; 520-209-8300) and Tucson High Magnet School (400 N. 2nd Ave.; 520-225-5326) have some incredibly talented students who perform in plays and musicals at campus theaters throughout the year. You may see their names in lights in the future!

ARIZONA ROSE THEATRE COMPANY
(520) 888-0509
www.arizonarose.cc

Founded in 1986, this theater company offers productions throughout the year, at various venues around town. The company is committed to presenting high-spirited and upbeat productions that offer positive statements. It also performs at local schools throughout the year.

ARIZONA THEATRE COMPANY
Temple of Music and Art
330 S. Scott Ave.
(520) 884-8210, (520) 622-2823 (tickets)
www.arizonatheatre.org
This group has been designated "The State Theatre of Arizona." Founded in 1967 as the Arizona Civic Theater, the company staged its first productions in a small hotel in Tucson for a small number of theatergoers. In 1972 the company went professional and changed its name to the Arizona Theatre Company. Later in 1978 ATC began performing in both Tucson and Phoenix.

Today ATC mounts several professional productions per year during the regular arts season, ranging from Shakespeare and classical and contemporary dramas to musicals and works by new artists.

BORDERLANDS THEATER
40 W. Broadway Blvd.
(520) 882-7406 (tickets)
www.borderlandstheater.org
This professional company presents theater and educational programs that reflect the cultural and racial diversity of the Southwest border region. Through its work, Borderlands seeks to generate a better understanding of the multiethnic diversity of the border that contributes to this region's unique character through play production and development with a focus on the Chicano/Latino voice. Education outreach programs include mentoring, school visits, and community collaborations.

GASLIGHT THEATRE
7010 E. Broadway Blvd.
(520) 886-9428
www.thegaslighttheatre.com
Tucson's only live, old-fashioned musical melodrama theater, the Gaslight is well known in the area for its lighthearted, rip-roaring comedies. Audiences can enjoy hissing at the villains, cheering the heroes, and tapping their toes to the music. The majority of these year-round productions are written by local playwrights (including the song parodies) especially for Gaslight Theatre. It's good family entertainment, where one can also dine on a wide variety of snack foods like pizza, hot dogs, and nachos, and enjoy fountain treats, beer, wine, and soft drinks. The food is provided by Little Anthony's Diner, which is located at the back of the theater. It's one of the best-run operations in town.

INVISIBLE THEATRE
1400 N. 1st Ave.
(520) 882-9721
www.invisibletheatre.com
A very visible force in Tucson's cultural community, Invisible Theatre is the city's original experimental theater (affectionately known as "The I.T."). Susan Claassen established the I.T. in 1971, and for the first few years of productions, it offered works from local writers. Since the late 1970s it has become better known as a "director's theater," presenting adaptations of classics, off-Broadway plays, musicals, comedies, and original scripts. The I.T. also supports Project Pastime, an educational program for developmentally delayed students. The 80-seat theater's season runs September through June.

LIVE THEATER WORKSHOP
5317 E. Speedway Blvd.
(520) 327-4242
www.livetheatreworkshop.org
This production company offers a full schedule at its theater on Speedway, as well as an educational program for aspiring artists and special acting classes for kids 6 to 18. Since its founding in 1994, LTW has become an important element of Tucson's community theater groups. Its 90-seat air-conditioned theater offers intimacy and comfort. LTW offers drama classes as well. Audiences appreciate the reasonably priced tickets.

STUDIO CONNECTIONS
4625 E. River Rd.
(520) 731-1559
http://studioconnections.net
Founded in 2002, this theater group and acting school is directed by professional equity actor and theater teacher Robert Encila. The small and versatile troupe of professional and nonprofessional actors, the DaVinci Players, performs everything from musicals and classics to cutting-edge plays just out of New York with great precision and skill. Performances are held at the St. Francis in the Foothills church in a small and intimate setting. Studio Connections also has youth theater groups, DaVinci Kids and DaVinci Prep (see the Kidsstuff chapter).

THIRD STREET KIDS
2520 N. Oracle Rd.
(520) 622-4100
www.artsforallinc.org
Arts for All Inc., a nonprofit organization, runs this program that began in 1985 as an after-school theater program for children with disabilities. Students ages 3 to 21 come from throughout greater Tucson and meet 5 times a week at the above address. There are also weekend workshops and art camps. The students have represented Arizona at several national and international events. (See the Kidstuff chapter.) Founder and executive director Marcia Berger has won numerous awards for her work leading this group. A day program for adults with developmental disabilities is another major part of Third Street's programs.

DANCE

BALLET ARIZONA
3645 E. Indian School Rd., Phoenix
(602) 381-0196
www.balletaz.org
No, you didn't read the address wrong. Tucson and Phoenix share the professional state ballet company, which was developed when 3 rival ballet companies joined together. Ballet Arizona creates, performs, and teaches classical and contemporary ballet, primarily in Phoenix.

BALLET FOLKLORICO TAPATIO
2100 S. 4th Ave.
(520) 622-0231
www.purotapatio.org
Swirls of colorful costumes, enthusiastic dancers, and toe-tapping Mexican folk music make this dance troupe a visual and musical delight.

A professional dance group, dancers perform all the traditional Mexican folk dances. (Each state in Mexico has a particular dance to call its own; costumes are specific to each region as well.) The dancers also perform traditional dances of the Southwest during their many shows around town.

BALLET TUCSON
200 S. Tucson Blvd.
(520) 903-1445
www.ballettucson.org

Ballet Tucson is an energetic company of professional dancers and apprentices ranging in age from 16 to 35. Many of its members have danced professionally with companies of national stature such as New York City Ballet, American Ballet Theatre, San Francisco Ballet, Ballet West, Alvin Ailey, Boston Ballet, and Dance Theatre of Harlem. The company presents classics as well as innovative contemporary works. In addition, an exceptional children's company of more than 100 performs alongside Ballet Tucson's professionals in family-oriented productions such as *The Nutcracker, Cinderella,* and *A Midsummer Night's Dream.*

**BARBEA WILLIAMS PERFORMING
   COMPANY**
Dunbar Cultural Center
325 W. 2nd St.
(520) 628-7785

This multidisciplinary community performance company promotes African-American and Latino culture. The range of the group's work spans traditional and contemporary theater, dance, music, and even poetry. Performances are held at community centers, schools, and other venues throughout the city. You can also catch this troupe at various festivals throughout the year, usually for just the price of admission to the festival. The company also promotes Afrocentric art in its gift shop, which offers hair design, gourds, and unique decorative items for the home.

✳ZUZI DANCE COMPANY
738 N. 5th Ave.
(520) 629-0237
www.zuzimoveit.org

Founded in 1998 by Nanette Robinson and Nancy Mellan, ZUZI is a nonprofit community-based dance organization devoted to the mission that everyone can dance regardless of age or ability.

ZUZI specializes in aerial dance, using a variety of trapezes in their modern dance routines. Three programs, ZUZI! Dance Company, ZUZI School, and ZUZI! Theater, are supported solely by grants and donations. The school offers nonstop classes for all ages in aerial, modern, ballet, hip-hop, and jazz dance and works closely with area schools to develop and foster an interest in dance and movement.

A summer camp program introduces kids to the beauty of dance through the exploration of the performing arts of music as well as the visual arts and costume design. Performances throughout the year include the terrfic *You Gotta Have Heart!* which showcases youth dance groups from around the city performing hip-hop, ballet, and aerial dance routines. Annual Solstice events also are extremely popular and showcase the varied talents of the ZUZI Dance Company artists. Performances are held in the historic YWCA in a lovely, intimate theater that used to be the indoor swimming pool.

REDHOUSE DANCERS
6932 E. 4th St.
(520) 419-3641
http://larryredhouse.com

This Native American cultural performing arts group was formed in the Monterey Peninsula area in 1965. The family group moved to Tucson in 1973. The group performs spectacular and colorful dances that incorporate intertribal social dances and songs at a number of festivals, fiestas, schools, and conventions throughout the area, and can be booked for special events.

UNIVERSITY OF ARIZONA DANCE DIVISION
School of Dance
Ina Gittings Building, Room 121
(520) 621-4698
http://web.cfa.arizona.edu/dance
The dance program at the University of Arizona offers the study of dance as an art form and as a performing art. The philosophy of the program is that dance leads to an understanding of human movement. Jazz, ballet, and modern dance are offered with equal emphasis so students can experience and appreciate the diversity. As a performance group, UA dancers have been recognized for their professional productions and performances at the Ina Gittings Dance Studio Theater.

LITERARY ARTS

OLD PUEBLO PLAYWRIGHTS
PO Box 64914, Tucson, AZ 85728
(520) 318-0559
www.oldpuebloplaywrights.org
Founded in 1989, Old Pueblo Playwrights is dedicated to the nurturing of fledgling playwrights and screenwriters. Members bring their first-draft scripts to weekly Monday-evening meetings at the Temple of Music and Art for feedback from other members. Many members have sold screenplays and gone on to win national theater awards or have had their works produced by one of Tucson's many theater companies. Each year

the group presents a Festival of New Plays to showcase members' works.

SOCIETY OF SOUTHWESTERN AUTHORS
PO Box 30355, Tucson, AZ 85751
(520) 546-9382
www.ssa-az.org
A nonprofit organization with more than 600 members, the society is open to poets, novelists, nonfiction writers, essayists, playwrights, and screenwriters who are published or aspire to be. The group has monthly meetings where general topics are discussed, and an occasional mixer offers a chance to network. Once a year it sponsors a large writers conference where attendees meet and talk with nationally known authors, publishers, agents, and other regional writers. Keynote speakers at past conferences have included Ray Bradbury and Tony Hillerman. There are membership fees.

UNIVERSITY OF ARIZONA POETRY CENTER
University of Arizona
1508 E. Helen St.
(520) 626-3765
www.poetry.arizona.edu
Established in 1960, this is a nationally acclaimed resource of over 50,000 books, periodicals, and audio/video recordings. The gorgeous and restful 17,500-square-foot facility at the corner of Helen and Vine Streets provides a library, a rare-book room, quiet areas for reading, audiovisual listening and viewing spaces, a gallery, a studio apartment for visiting writers, and a welcoming outdoor amphitheater for presentations and receptions. The center's mission is to provide a welcome environment that will "maintain and cherish the spirit of poetry" for students

and the community. The library and most reading and special events are free and open to the public.

MUSIC

Tucson's music scene offers everything— classical music, opera, folk, chamber music, country, bluegrass, Western, blues, jazz, and New Age. A variety of vocal groups and choirs ranging from professional to "kitchen musicians" are also active. So whether you are a professional musician, a part-time music maker, or a member of an appreciative audience, you can find fellow music lovers with ease.

It would be almost impossible to list all the support groups and music organizations in this chapter (Tucson's large mix of music offerings could be a book unto itself). Here we give you a look at some of the area's larger and more active groups. Should your tastes run to a more particular type of music, one of these groups can steer you in the right direction.

ARIZONA OPERA COMPANY
4600 N. 12th St., Phoenix
(520) 293-4336
www.azopera.com

In 1971, 15 local musicians and actors came up with the idea of founding a professional opera company in Tucson. The following spring the city witnessed its first classical production of Rossini's *The Barber of Seville*. Today it's the state's only professional grand opera company. Between October and April the company presents 7 performances of 5 productions at the Tucson Convention Center's Music Hall. Past productions have included *Aida, La Boheme, Carmen*, and *La Traviata*. This is the only opera company

in the US to perform regularly in 2 cities (Tucson and Phoenix) and is one of only a few American opera companies to have produced the entire Wagner Ring Cycle.

ARIZONA REPERTORY SINGERS
PO Box 41601, Tucson, AZ 85717
(520) 792-8141
http://arsingers.wordpress.com

This 40-plus-voice mixed ensemble brings a wide variety of choral music to venues throughout southern Arizona. Founded in 1984, the chorus specializes in a cappella choral music from numerous eras and countries. Concerts number about 20 per year. The group is known for its musicianship and beautiful, professional performances. All the concerts take place at a variety of locations.

i Opera lovers, take note! During opera season (October through April) the Tucson Opera Guild hosts weekly brown-bag opera gatherings at noon on Friday at Grace St. Paul's Episcopal Church at 2331 E. Adams St. Bring your own lunch—they provide cookies, coffee, tea, lively discussions, and singing. Call the guild, (520) 742-4935, for details and to get on the mailing list.

ARIZONA SYMPHONIC WINDS
5201 N. Rocky Ridge Place
www.azsymwinds.org

A community ensemble of some 60 musicians, the group has been performing at a variety of venues throughout Tucson since 1986. Most winter concerts are held at the auditorium of Rincon University High School. Arizona Symphonic Winds regularly presents outdoor concerts at Udall Park. This group allows emerging artists a chance to develop their talents through performance and education.

CIVIC ORCHESTRA OF TUCSON
PO Box 42764, Tucson, AZ 85733
(520) 798-0062
www.cotmusic.org
Founded in 1975, this volunteer symphony orchestra offers concerts at a variety of sites throughout the city. It also sponsors an annual Young Artists competition, a competition open to Tucson-area high school students, and conducts a musical education outreach program at area schools. The afternoon performing season runs October through May and offers several concerts.

DESERT VOICES
PO Box 270, Tucson, AZ 85702
(520) 791-9662
www.desertvoices.org
Established in 1988 as the Metropolitan Community Chorus, today the choral ensemble produces several major concerts between December and June. Though the group is dedicated to promoting a positive gay and lesbian, bisexual, and transgendered presence in southern Arizona, membership is open to anyone who is supportive of gay/lesbian and alternative lifestyles. Four major concerts are held at various venues throughout Tucson.

THE FOOTHILLS PHIL
2101 E. River Rd.
(520) 577-5090, ext. 1910
www.cfsd16.org
This philharmonic offered through the Catalina Foothills School District brings adults and students together to share their love of music and seeks to motivate students to pursue the study of stringed instruments. It offers a complete orchestral experience. The orchestra presents concerts at Catalina Foothills High School Theater, 4300 E. Sunrise Dr., in Dec and May. Tucson's own Lázló Veres conducts.

OLD ARIZONA BRASS BAND
(520) 529-2807
www.oabb.homestead.com
This terrific brass band really takes you back to the old days. Founded in 1997 by Ray Hicks, the band's mission is to provide a living representation of the military and civilian brass bands of territorial Arizona from 1872 to 1912. The music, uniforms, and musical instruments are authentic to the cavalry and town bands of this period. They perform throughout southern Arizona and at several historical celebrations and reenactments, including the annual Reunion de El Fuerte Festival, held at Fort Lowell Park (see the Festivals & Events chapter).

SONS OF ORPHEUS—THE MALE CHOIR OF TUCSON
PO Box 31552, Tucson, AZ 85751
(520) 621-1649
www.sonsoforpheus.org
A nonprofit, nonsectarian community men's choir, Sons of Orpheus includes men of all walks of life. Founded in 1991, the choir presents concerts throughout southern Arizona, nationally, and internationally that range from classical to popular and span all periods, styles, and languages. Director Grayson Hirst encourages any man who enjoys singing to join.

SOUTHERN ARIZONA SYMPHONY ORCHESTRA
PO Box 43131, Tucson, AZ 85733
(520) 323-7166
www.sasomusic.org

Established in 1979, the symphony is a blend of professional and amateur volunteer musicians who offer a rich diversity of classical performances. Critics rave over the intensity of this company's performances. Over the years the orchestra has premiered several new works by American composers in Tucson and southern Arizona, while still maintaining a balance of the classics such as works from Rossini, Beethoven, Haydn, and more. SASO performs several concerts between October and May. Performances are usually at venues around town. Season tickets and single tickets are available. Discounts are available for seniors and students.

＊TUCSON ARIZONA BOYS CHORUS
5770 E. Pima St.
(520) 296-6277
www.boyschorus.org
Founded in 1939 and known as "America's singing ambassadors," this well-established group has become internationally recognized and tours extensively throughout North America and overseas. The chorus has performed for presidents, kings, and heads of state. Dedicated to providing boys 8 to 14 in the area with an educational opportunity as well as performance experience, the group offers many local concerts in Tucson at various venues between October and May. Their Musicale Regale, Winter Holiday, and Pops concerts are truly delightful.

TUCSON GIRLS CHORUS
4020 E. River Rd.
(520) 577-6064
www.tucsongirlschorus.org
Founded in 1985, this nonprofit organization provides an environment where girls in grades 2 through 8 develop self-esteem, discipline, and music literacy. Today there are more than 200 girls involved in 4 choruses. The chorus usually offers many concerts at different venues around town.

TUCSON PHILHARMONIA
PO Box 41882, Tucson, AZ 85717
(520) 623-1500
www.tpyo.org
A full symphonic youth orchestra, Tucson Philharmonia rehearses at the Armory Park Center. It provides symphonic training and performance opportunities to southern Arizona youths in a professional environment. Membership in the orchestra is determined each year by audition (this is considered an all-star group) and currently comprises approximately 100 high school–age musicians from schools around southern Arizona. The young musicians travel from as far away as Douglas and Nogales to practice each week. Fall and spring concerts are held between November and March at various venues. The philharmonia offers coaching sessions with Tucson Symphony Orchestra musicians and scholarships for instruments and education. A sampler series of concerts takes place throughout the year at Armory Park; this series is free.

TUCSON POPS ORCHESTRA
PO Box 14545, Tucson, AZ 86732
(520) 722-5853
www.tucsonpops.org
This professional pops orchestra has been offering southern Arizona Music Under the Stars for free since 1955. The concerts take place at Reid Park's DeMeester Outdoor Performance Center, which is named in honor of the violinist founder of TPO. The orchestra offers several concerts each season that feature old favorites and popular classics.

The concerts are held in May, June, and September.

TUCSON SYMPHONY ORCHESTRA
2175 N. 6th Ave.
(520) 882-8585 (tickets)
www.tucsonsymphony.org
The oldest existing professional symphony orchestra in the Southwest, TSO was founded in 1929. During the year TSO offers world-class guest artists and several concert series, including Classics, Pops, and Masterworks. Concerts are held between September and April at the Tucson Convention Center Music Hall, Catalina Foothills High School, and many other local venues.

UNIVERSITY COMMUNITY CHORUS
University of Arizona College of Fine Arts
(520) 626-8936
http://web.cfa.arizona.edu/ucc
This exciting 100-plus chorus is made up of university students, professors, and professional and amateur singers from the community. The chorus performs several concerts a year, including a popular holiday songfest. Works range from Handel to Orff. No auditions are necessary.

UNIVERSITY OF ARIZONA COLLEGE OF FINE ARTS
1017 N. Olive Rd.
(520) 621-1307
http://web.cfa.arizona.edu
Numerous events are held during the school year at the College of Fine Arts, which has existed for more than 100 years. With the help of its world-renowned faculty (who are highlighted during the Faculty Artist Series) and its 500 music majors and 100 dance majors, the School of Music presents more than 300 concerts per year, almost on a daily

basis. Concerts feature everything from classical recitals, jazz, and opera to steel drum bands.

MUSIC SOCIETIES & ORGANIZATIONS

No matter what your musical taste, there is probably a local organization you can join, a newsletter you can receive, limited discounts on concerts you can take advantage of, or like-minded enthusiasts you can mingle with. Below is a sampling of the music societies and organizations in the area.

ARIZONA EARLY MUSIC SOCIETY (AEMS)
PO Box 44172, Tucson, AZ 85733
(520) 297-3448
www.azearlymusic.org
This nonprofit group's mission is to present concerts of early music and promote related activities such as classes about various forms of early music, including harpsichord, lute, harp, and violin. Smaller, more intimate concerts are a part of the Hausmusik series. Private homes serve as the venue. Tickets, which include a meal, are $30.

DESERT BLUEGRASS ASSOCIATION
www.desertbluegrass.org
A nonprofit group of pickers gets together once a month and produces a monthly newsletter to inform members of upcoming bluegrass music events and news. Dues are annual and include the newsletter. Pickers and players gather several times per week at local eateries to jam. Listeners are more than welcome (bring your banjo if you want to join in). These jam sessions are free. They also sponsor fall and spring festivals. (See the Festivals & Events chapter.) Membership

will get you a newsletter, info on upcoming events, and discounts on events statewide.

TUCSON FRIENDS OF TRADITIONAL MUSIC
PO Box 40654, Tucson, AZ 85717
www.tftm.org
These Tucson friends promote participation in and appreciation of traditional music and dance. The year-round calendar features concerts, dances, and workshops. With a substantial membership, it sponsors contra dances with live music and callers. Family and other memberships are available.

TUCSON JAZZ SOCIETY
100 N. Stone Ave.
(520) 903-1265
www.tucsonjazz.org
Founded in 1977, the society hosts the popular Jazz Under the Stars series at St. Philip's Plaza and brings major jazz artists to town. Family and individual memberships are available, which include concert ticket discounts.

TUCSON KITCHEN MUSICIANS ASSOCIATION
PO Box 26531, Tucson, AZ 85726
www.tkma.org
This nonprofit group's primary focus is to promote acoustic and folk music in the area. TKMA produces the annual Tucson Folk Festival, a 2-day event held each May that presents a variety of acoustic music styles by local and national performers (see the Festivals & Events chapter). It also produces or coproduces a number of other concerts year-round at venues around town and presents free music in local schools. As a member you'll receive discounts on concert tickets as well as a monthly newsletter.

VISUAL ARTS
Galleries
It's not unusual to stroll into a cafe or restaurant in Tucson and see original artwork hanging on the walls for sale, especially downtown and on 4th Avenue. Art is everywhere in Tucson, and the number of galleries and original art shops—close to 150—increases each year. Some may not hang around for long, but they are quickly replaced with others.

BLUE RAVEN GALLERY
3054 N. 1st Ave., Ste. 5
(520) 623-1003
www.blueravengalleryandgifts.com
This small, rustic gallery showcases Mata Ortiz pottery, Tohono O'odham contemporary and traditional baskets, original silk paintings, bronzes, and sculptures. The focus is on innovative work featuring Sonoran Desert culture and wildlife and Sonoran sea life expressed in various media. The gallery also offers classes. Open Wed through Sat and by appointment. Hours vary, so be sure to call ahead.

CONRAD WILDE GALLERY
439 N. 6th Ave., #171
(520) 622-8997
www.conradwildegallery.com
This gallery shows contemporary painting, sculpture, and works on paper from emerging and established artists. Open Tues through Sat; Fri and Sat only during the summer.

DAVIS DOMINGUEZ GALLERY
154 E. 6th St.
(520) 629-9759
www.davisdominguez.com

Located in the up-and-coming Warehouse District, this well-known gallery is the largest (in square footage) contemporary gallery in the city. It has been in Tucson since 1976 and features modern paintings and major sculpture. Open Tues through Sat.

✳DEGRAZIA GALLERY IN THE SUN
6300 N. Swan Rd.
(520) 299-9191
www.degrazia.org
High above the city, at a site that was once quite remote, stands this unusual gallery that celebrates the life and work of the late Ted DeGrazia. More than 125,000 people a year visit this site to view some of the more than 10,000 DeGrazia paintings that deal with Spanish exploration of the Southwest, Indian lore, legends, celebrations, rodeos, and bullfighting. DeGrazia even designed the floor tiles, light fixtures, and other decorative features throughout the gallery. Signature works are of Indian children with round faces and flowing black hair. The prolific artist also worked in bronze, ceramics, stone lithographs, serigraphs, glassware, and jewelry.

Down a path from the main building is the small, open-roofed Mission in the Sun—a chapel DeGrazia designed and built himself. The chapel's walls are decorated with DeGrazia murals.

Before his death in 1982, DeGrazia created the DeGrazia Art and Cultural Foundation to keep the site operating. Since that time the foundation has also supported other arts organizations, including public broadcasting, within Tucson.

The gallery is open daily. You can purchase DeGrazia posters, cards, and gifts at the charming gift shop located in the main building. There is no admission fee.

DESERT ARTISANS' GALLERY
6536 E. Tanque Verde Rd.
(520) 722-4412
www.desertartisansgallery.com
Desert Artisans' Gallery was founded in 1987 by local artist Sarah Rankin. The gallery is a fine art co-op gallery featuring Southwestern art from Tucson Arizona and the Southwest. It features contemporary works in oil, pastels, acrylic, photography, watercolor, ceramics, glass, and more. As a co-op gallery, they offer great values on beautiful art by allowing you to buy directly from the artists. Open 7 days a week.

THE DRAWING STUDIO GALLERY
33 S. 6th Ave.
(520) 620-0947
www.thedrawingstudio.org
Founded in 1992, this not-for-profit gallery is affiliated with the artists' cooperative the Drawing Studio. The gallery space features the work of students and professional artists in a variety of media. There are continuous year-round exhibitions here, and the studio offers weekly drawing and studio practice open to the public, a wide variety of workshops, and courses ranging from drawing to printmaking and calligraphy.

ETHERTON GALLERY
135 S. 6th Ave.
(520) 624-7370
www.ethertongallery.com
Specializing in Native American vintage photographs and classic photography, this 3,500-square-foot gallery also exhibits contemporary paintings, prints, and sculptures. Etherton operates the Temple Gallery on the second floor above the courtyard at the Temple of Music and Art as well. The main gallery downtown is open Tues through Sat.

You'll find it above Downtown Kitchen and Cocktails restaurant.

GALLERY WEST
6420 N. Campbell Ave.
(520) 529-7002
www.indianartwest.com
This gallery in the foothills specializes in Native American art. Representing many tribes, including Apache and Navajo, the collections here range from basketry to jewelry to photography. You will find some of the most beautiful and rare Navajo and Hopi textiles displayed, along with contemporary jewelry by acclaimed artisans and silversmiths.

LA PILITA MUSEUM GALLERY
420 S. Main Ave.
(520) 882-7454
www.lapilita.com
For a unique experience in one of Tucson's most historic downtown districts, head to La Pilita in Barrio Viejo, next to the El Tiradito Shrine and El Minuto Cafe (see the Restaurants chapter). A small museum and gallery, exhibits here change monthly and focus on regional history. A permanent exhibit of historic photos of early Tucson is worth a look, and don't skip the store featuring books on regional history and folk crafts. Open Mon through Sat; closed in summer.

LOUIS CARLOS BERNAL GALLERY
Center for the Arts
Pima Community College, West Campus
2202 W. Anklam Rd.
(520) 206-6942
www.pima.edu/performingarts/
bernalgallery
Housed in Pima Community College's Center for the Arts, the Louis Carlos Bernal Gallery is dedicated to a longtime PCC instructor

and celebrated photographer. The gallery features the work of international, local, and regional artists. Special exhibits highlight student competitions showing works in ceramics, drawing, fibers, metals, mixed media, painting, photography, prints, and sculpture. Open Mon through Fri.

i For a comprehensive listing of galleries in town, including helpful maps and descriptions, pick up a copy of the *Arizona Collectors Guide*. The guide is free at the visitor center and arts venues around town, and is available online at www.azcollectors guide.com.

MADARAS GALLERY
3001 E. Skyline Dr., #101
(520) 615-3001
www.madaras.com
These galleries feature local artist Diana Madaras's pastel watercolors of desert scenery. These very popular works are featured on prints, cards, and calendars available in gift shops around town. Here you can find her work all in one place along with fine art originals. A second location is at 1535 E. Broadway Blvd. (520-623-4000). Open Mon through Sat; Skyline location is also open Sun.

MEDICINE MAN GALLERY EAST
7000 E. Tanque Verde Rd., Ste. 16
(520) 722-7798
www.medicinemangallery.com
This gallery displays one of the finest collections of early American and Western art. Specialties focus on the life work of Maynard Dixon and the Taos Society of Artists. You will also find antique American Indian art, which includes Pueblo pottery, Navajo textiles, kachina dolls, and jewelry. It also offers

a wonderful assortment of antique furniture, including Stickley, Mission, Arts and Crafts, and Spanish colonial furniture. Hours vary.

METAL ARTS VILLAGE
3230 N. Dodge Blvd.
(520) 326-5657
www.facebook.com/metalartsvillage

Metal art has a long tradition in Tucson. From decorative to practical, it can be found in homes, restaurant interiors, architectural details, ranch fences, sculpture, and bridges around town. Eleven working artists' studios, a central gallery, and a sculpture garden make up this paean to the craft of metalworking. The Village offers visitors the chance to see artists at work in their studios, hammering and melding the metals that will become art. The complex is also home to stained-glass and wood artists. Artists in residence include contemporary metal designer and fabricator Steve Kimble of ART Inc., the founder and developer of the Village (Studio F; 520-975-9792); metal sculptors Al Gann (Doglix, Studio K; 520-204-6104) and Mark Wallis (Studio L; 812-360-8077); and stained-glass artist Genia Parker (Studio B; 520-325-8791). Open Mon through Sat.

i If you are interested in the work of local artists, you can view them live and in person in their studios during the Tucson Artists Open Studios event, held twice a year in the fall and spring. You can visit artists' studios all over town, browse their work, and learn about their inspirations (some folks even supply snacks!). More information and a list of participating artists and their locations are at www.tucsonopenstudios.com.

OBSIDIAN GALLERY
4320 N. Campbell Ave., Ste. 130
(520) 577-3598
www.obsidian-gallery.com

Specializing in fine contemporary crafts, works in clay, fiber, metal, jewelry, glass, wood, and mixed media are featured at this well-known gallery. Past rotating exhibits have included El Dia de los Muertos (Day of the Dead), a multimedia exhibition featuring works by more than 30 local artists. Open Mon through Sun.

PHILABAUM GLASS STUDIO AND GALLERY
711 S. 6th Ave.
(520) 884-7404
www.philabaumglass.com

This working studio and gallery is internationally known for its contemporary blown-glass pieces. Artist Tom Philabaum's works are exhibited throughout North America, Europe, and Mexico. Here at his studio you will be mesmerized by Tom and his team as they shape molten glass into sculptures. Call for specific times.

The gallery shows a wide assortment of contemporary glass art by studio artists from across the country. A featured artist exhibition changes every few months. The gallery is open Tues through Sat.

RAICES TALLER 222 ART GALLERY & WORKSHOP
218 E. 6th St.
(520) 881-5335
http://raicestaller222.webs.com

Raices (roots) and Taller (workshop) is both a gallery and a workshop. The brainchild of a group of local artists, it's the only Latino-based nonprofit cooperative contemporary gallery in the city. Located in the historic

Close-up

Louise Serpa—Rodeo Photographer

A Vassar girl, Louise Serpa never imagined that she would spend most of her adult life in dusty rodeo arenas all over the Southwest. So how did this self-described NYC debutante become the most well-known and respected female rodeo photographer in the country?

A divorced mother with two young daughters, Serpa moved to Tucson in 1960. While watching a friend's child compete in Junior Rodeo, she grabbed a camera, started taking photos, and got bitten by the shutterbug. Fascinated by the athleticism of the rodeo riders and drawn to the endless energy of the arena, she started following the circuit, taking pictures as a hobby. What started out as a hobby, however, became a necessity after one of her daughters came down with severe rheumatoid arthritis. Her first paying shots were taken with a $27 Argus C3, and she sold the photos for pennies apiece to make money to cover medical expenses. In 1963 she was the first woman photographer permitted to shoot inside any professional arena, and that was the beginning of a stellar career that has spanned several decades.

Serpa was inducted into the Cowgirl Hall of Fame in Fort Worth in 1999 and is the recipient of numerous awards. Her photographs are exhibited at museums and galleries worldwide. Her highly acclaimed book, *Rodeo* (Aperture Press), is a real insiders' look at the world of rodeo illustrated by her amazing photographs. Her work can be purchased via her website: www.louiselserpa.com.

Warehouse District, this is a terrific and vibrant art space. The gallery offers workshops in silk-screening, silver sand casting, and papier-mâché and is renowned for its unique Dia de los Muertos (Day of the Dead) exhibits. Open Fri and Sat or by appointment.

RANCH HOUSE GALLERY AT AGUA CALIENTE PARK
12325 E. Roger Rd.
(520) 749-3718
Located in the original ranch house in the Roy Drachman Agua Caliente Park, this small gallery in a beautiful setting features works by artists from Pima County with a focus on Southwest themes. The shows change every 6 weeks and have included photography, oil, watercolor, and sculpture. Admission is free. The gallery is open Wed through Sun,

Nov through Apr, and Tues through Sat, May through Oct. The ranch house itself is a piece of Tucson history, completely furnished with period antiques and wonderful historic photos of the surrounding park area.

SACRED MACHINE MUSEUM
28 E. Congress St., Ste. 123
(520) 977-7102
www.sacredmachine.com
This funky gallery showcases the work of acclaimed local artist Daniel Martin Diaz. Enter this gothlike domain to view his amazing and macabre work, reminiscent of Hieronymus Bosch with a Southwest twist. The entirely self-taught artist's paintings are in many major museums and private collections around the country, and his artwork and illustrations have been commissioned

for several feature films and album covers. The gallery also hosts special exhibits and events throughout the year that feature other artists and illustrators. Get on the mailing list!

SANTA THERESA TILE WORKS SHOWROOM
439 N. 6th St.
(520) 623-1856
www.santatheresatileworks.com
Santa Theresa artisans make one-of-a-kind handcrafted and painted tile works at this working studio. Located in the historic Firestone Building, it's amazing to see the creativity at work here—from individual custom tiles to full-scale artworks and murals in fantastic designs and colors. Here you can browse the showroom and see the works in progress at the studio. Santa Theresa has also produced several public artworks in town; ask for a copy of the guide listing locations. If you're creative, the studio offers many workshops throughout the year. Open Tues through Sat.

SETTLERS' WEST GALLERIES
6420 N. Campbell Ave.
(520) 299-2607
www.settlerswest.com
Settlers' West has been around since the early '70s and in that time has earned a reputation for beautiful and unique works that represent Arizona (wildlife and Western works predominate). Open Mon through Sat.

TOHONO CHUL PARK GALLERY
7366 N. Paseo del Norte
(520) 742-6455
www.tohonochulpark.org
Tohono Chul Park's small gallery rotates works of regional artists with about 16 changing exhibits each year. Past exhibits have included American Indian art, photography, and Mexican tile art. The desert-garden park also has a gift shop, with one-of-a-kind items by local artisans, and a restaurant with 2 outdoor patios. High tea is served in the afternoon. (See the Restaurants chapter.) There is a charge to access the gallery.

Art Museums

CENTER FOR CREATIVE PHOTOGRAPHY
University of Arizona campus
1030 N. Olive Rd.
(520) 621-7968
www.creativephotography.org
Established in 1975 and located across from the UA Museum of Art, this one-of-a-kind photographic center and museum is known throughout the world for its extensive archives and collections of works by important 20th-century photographers. The center contains more than 60,000 photographs, as well as galleries and research facilities. The museum store carries the largest selection of photography books in Arizona, along with photography-related gift items.

Southwest photographer Ansel Adams and Dr. John P. Schaefer, then president of the university, conceived this center, which now houses the late photographer's complete archives, in 1974. The other several dozen archival collections housed at the center include Richard Avedon, Ernest Bloch, Dean Brown, Wynn Bullock, Harry Callahan, Louise Dahl-Wolfe, Andreas Feininger, Sonya Noskowiak, Marion Palfi, Aaron Siskind, W. Eugene Smith, Frederick Sommer, Paul Strand, and Edward Weston. Prints of archival work can be viewed with reservations.

The center is open Mon through Fri from 1 to 4 p.m. and Sat and Sun from noon to 5 p.m. Admission and events are free.

MUSEUM OF CONTEMPORARY ART (MOCA)
265 S. Church Ave.
(520) 624-5091
www.moca-tucson.org

Founded in 1977, MOCA exhibits the work of avant-garde contemporary artists with 8 to 12 temporary exhibitions each year, some solo exhibitions, and some thematic group exhibitions. The museum offers a variety of education and outreach lectures and events designed to educate the community about issues and ideas in contemporary art. MOCA is Tucson's only public institution devoted exclusively to the art of our time. Open Wed through Sun. There is an admission fee but under 17 are free.

THE PROCESS MUSEUM
8000 S. Kolb Rd. at I-10
(520) 404-0596
www.processmuseum.org

Ever wonder about the creative process? What influences an artist as they create their work, what "mistakes" they leave behind, and how they create? You can find out here! This 71,000-square-foot "museum" collects early works, remnants, and artifacts that the artist leaves behind during the creative process. The primary focus of the museum is "to reveal the mental processes of the artist while engaged in creating work." The brainstorm of John Wells, president of the medical equipment company Wells Johnson Company, the museum houses his vast personal collection and also serves as a studio for emerging artists, who use part of the space for ongoing work. The general collection consists of several thousand art pieces that fill the hallways, offices, and conference rooms of this huge office building space. Artists represented here are the crème de la crème of Tucson: Olivier Mosset, Eriks Rudans, Chris Rush, Helmay Prinzen, David Johnson Vandernberg, and Vytas Sakalas are just a few of the established artists represented here.

A large proportion of the space is devoted to the works and life of Owen Williams, a local artist whose studio is re-created here along with his works from childhood. It's fascinating to see how his art progressed throughout his life and what influenced him. Wells has amassed dozens of notebooks cataloguing his sketches, photos, and news clippings, and all that influenced the creation of his art. This is truly an unusual and fascinating collection for art lovers and those who want an insiders' view of the creative process. The museum is open for private 2-hour tours at 10 a.m. on Tues and Thurs; reservations are required but there is no charge. The best way to make a reservation is on the website. Wells personally leads each tour, sharing his own passion and enthusiasm for the artistic process and the creation of art in its many forms, from sculpture to paintings. The private tours can last up to 3 hours, so wear comfortable shoes. Invitation-only special exhibits are mounted twice a year in an adjacent building; check the website for dates.

*TUCSON MUSEUM OF ART AND HISTORIC BLOCK
140 N. Main Ave.
(520) 624-2333
www.tucsonmuseumofart.com

Founded in 1924, the Tucson Museum of Art was housed at several sites in the city before the current museum was built in 1975 on the site of Tucson's original Spanish presidio. The complex takes up an entire city block in the heart of downtown.

Besides the modern main building, the site has towering shade trees, a bubbling fountain, outside sculptures, and courtyards. The complex also includes 5 distinctive homes built between 1850 and 1906. La Casa Cordova, a restored 1850s-era home that is believed to be the oldest house in town, replicates life during that time and contains a small presidio museum. Casa Romero House is now a pottery studio, library, and part of the museum's art school. The Hiram Stevens House, built in 1866, is now the home of the Cafe a la Carte. The historic Edward Nye Fish House houses the Goodman Pavilion of Art of the American West. J. Knox Corbett House, a 1907 restored mission revival home, is furnished with period pieces and is open for tours.

The Tucson Museum of Art houses a permanent collection of more than 6,500 works of art. The focus is the Americas, including pre-Colombian, Spanish, colonial, Western American, and contemporary American art. Each year it hosts 8 to 10 changing and traveling exhibitions of work in all media.

The noncredit Art School has operated for over 50 years and offers classes in ceramics, sculpture, painting, drawing, theater arts, mixed media, art history, and art criticism for students 5 through 105.

Inside the main building is a gift shop offering many one-of-a-kind handcrafted ceramic, wood, fabric, and jewelry items from local artists, as well as posters, books, and greeting cards from around the world. The outdoor area hosts concerts, block parties, art festivals, the fall Holiday Craft Market, the spring Artisans Market, and more. You'll also find an adorable cafe, Cafe à la C'art (see the Restaurants chapter), with outdoor seating at umbrella-covered tables or indoor seating at cheerful bistro tables.

You could spend all day here, especially if you plan on venturing off into the surrounding Historic Block, where other small artsy shops abound.

The museum is open Tues through Sat from 10 a.m. to 5 p.m. and Sun from noon to 5 p.m. It's closed on Mon from Memorial Day to Labor Day, as well as for major holidays. Admission fees vary; free to those 12 and younger. The first Sunday of the month is free.

UNIVERSITY OF ARIZONA MUSEUM OF ART
Park Avenue and Speedway Boulevard
(520) 621-7567
http://artmuseum.arizona.edu
Located on the University of Arizona campus, this museum is open to the public throughout the academic year, with limited summer hours. The permanent collection has more than 4,000 works, including Rembrandt, Pontormo, Degas, Arp, Piranesi, Picasso, O'Keeffe, and Rothko. It also houses one of the Southwest's most complete collections of art from the Renaissance to the present day, thanks to a donation by Samuel H. Kress in the 1950s of more than 50 works. Most noteworthy are the collections of European and American 19th- and 20th-century paintings and sculptures. Most of the permanent collections are displayed on the second floor and are rotated several times a year. The first floor features changing exhibits.

The museum is open Tues through Fri from 9 a.m. to 5 p.m. and Sat and Sun noon to 4 p.m. Closed on university holidays. There is a $5 general admission fee.

Murals & Public Art

Though wall paintings have been found in the ruins of prehistoric Indian kivas dating back 1,000 years, Tucson's modern mural movement began in the 1950s and 1960s when a number of local banks commissioned interior murals—painted and mosaic—featuring historic images of Tucson and Arizona. By the 1970s murals began showing up in different neighborhoods. The artists who produced them were influenced by such artists as José Orozco and Diego Rivera. Many murals rich in Mexican American images were created on the outside walls of neighborhood centers, beginning with the El Rio Neighborhood Center. Five more were created at other centers, incorporating imagery from other cultures including Yaqui, Tohono O'odham, and African-American.

During the 1980s financial support from the city of Tucson, Pima County, community service organizations, and private businesses helped create dozens more murals in the area. Today Tucson sports hundreds of murals and public art throughout the community, with more created each year. Schools, realizing that getting students involved in mural projects was great for the students' self-esteem, sought funds to create murals on playground walls, ramadas, and inside the school buildings. The Arizona Commission for the Arts responded with funding to send artists to schools to help the students create these murals, and today there are more than 66 murals at more than 40 schools.

One of the most visible pieces is Tucson artist Simon Donovan's $2.4 million **Diamondback Rattlesnake Bridge,** created for the city of Tucson. This magnificent footbridge spans Broadway just west of Euclid Avenue. A companion bridge completed in 2007, the 240-foot **Basket Bridge** spans Park Avenue where it becomes Euclid. Designed by Rosemary Lonewolf, the metalwork features designs of coyote tracks and lizards. Nearby, where the Barraza-Aviation Parkway meets E. Broadway, you'll see black-and-white historical images on ceramic tiles conceptualized by graphic designer Stephen Farley.

The fanciful Sun Tran bus stops downtown include a 1956 Chevy near the corner of E. Broadway and 4th Avenue, while the stop on N. Church Avenue and W. Pennington Street blooms with giant purple flowers. Farther uptown on N. Stone Avenue, you can't miss the 630-foot colorful mural by Pasqualina Azzarello. Many major thoroughfares in town are sprinkled with beautiful ceramic artworks, tiles, and wrought-iron sculptures of desert plants and animals, much of it funded by the Department of Transportation.

Other public art is very visible, too. From the sculpture dubbed *Sonora,* which stands in front of the downtown library, to the rock work that lines either side of Mountain Avenue, Tucsonans don't even have to cross the doors of a museum to see art. Most of the works come from the city and county One Percent for Art budget and have met with public approval. The UA campus and PCC campus also display many types of public artworks.

With numerous murals and public art scattered citywide, it's a good idea to have a guide. The **Tucson/Pima Arts Council** (520-624-0595) offers a comprehensive listing at their website: www.tucsonpimaartscouncil .org. These works have become a vital part of Tucson's art scene and heritage. Hunting down this unique art makes for an interesting and out-of-the-ordinary afternoon tour of the Old Pueblo.

HISTORICAL MUSEUMS

ARIZONA HISTORY MUSEUM
949 E. 2nd St.
(520) 628-5774
www.arizonahistoricalsociety.org
This museum is much more than dusty exhibits tracing the history of the state. Here you'll find hands-on exhibits, most notably the period rooms where you can see how Arizonans lived and worked through the decades. The museum also houses an extensive photo exhibit, a research library, and a Mining Hall, where visitors can learn about the impact this industry made in Arizona. The gift shop is great, too. The Downtown Museum, in the Wells Fargo Bank, 140 N. Stone Ave., highlights Tucson history with rotating exhibits. There are varying admission fees. (See the Attractions chapter.)

✳ARIZONA STATE MUSEUM
University of Arizona campus
Park Avenue and University Boulevard
1031 E. University Blvd.
(520) 621-6302
www.statemuseum.arizona.edu
Located on campus, just northeast of the main gate, this museum features exhibits detailing Native American life and culture in the Southwest from prehistoric times to the present. You'll find pottery, baskets, clothing, and all the other artifacts that made up daily life, all with detailed information on how they were used. The museum's collection of Southwest Indian pottery is the largest in the world and much of it is featured in the Pottery Project, a permanent exhibit, with an interpretive gallery. The building is a work of art, too, with wide marble staircases and a large lobby. The gift shop offers Native American arts and crafts. Open to the public Mon through Sat 10 a.m. to 5 p.m.

FORT LOWELL MUSEUM
2900 N. Craycroft Rd.
(520) 885-3832
www.arizonahistoricalsociety.org
This small but unique museum features exhibits about military life on the Arizona frontier and is located in the reconstructed commanding officers' quarters, which were established in 1873. You'll find it in Fort Lowell Park at the corner of Craycroft and Fort Lowell Roads. Open Fri and Sat 10 a.m. to 4 p.m. Lots of special activities take place throughout the year, including walking tours, lectures, and living history events. Admission fees vary; the first Saturday of the month is free.

THE NATURAL WORLD

ew cities on Earth have natural settings as spectacular as Tucson's. The Sonoran Desert covers approximately one-third of Arizona, from Tucson west into California and south into Mexico and the Baja Peninsula. Out of this desert grow several mountain ranges and a remarkable array of plants, animals, and natural resources—not to mention several million people in cities like Tucson, Phoenix, and Yuma and in Mexico. The Sonoran Desert floor lies 3,000 feet above sea level but rises to more than 9,000 feet in the mountain ranges surrounding Tucson. The city of Tucson occupies 150 square miles of this desert, while metropolitan Tucson covers 550 square miles.

Take a few moments to review the Pronunciation Guide. Many of the words for plants, animals, and places come from Spanish and Native American languages. Here's a sample of some you might need to know. Learning how to pronounce these strange-looking words will be of great benefit as you travel in and around Tucson and through this chapter.

PLANT LIFE

Perhaps the most remarkable aspect of our desert is its plant life. Contrary to popular opinion, the desert teems with plant life, ranging from the most majestic of them all, the saguaro cactus, to carpets of spring wildflowers. That's because, for a desert, the Sonoran is fairly wet, averaging more than 11 inches of rainfall and only 17 short-lived freezing lows a year in the Tucson area.

Cacti are perhaps the most unusual and most noticeable of the desert plants. Cacti are succulents, meaning that they have an uncanny ability to store water. They also typically have a built-in defense mechanism, thwarting predators and the curious with their almost-indefatigable needles. Some of these prickers are so tiny they appear invisible, but one slight touch and the uninitiated will painfully learn otherwise. One of the

neat things about cacti is their constancy. Day after day and year after year, they remain green and stable and sturdy.

Saguaro

Say the word *cactus* and what usually comes to mind is the saguaro. Saguaro means "giant cactus" in Latin, and it grows only in the Sonoran Desert. A protected species, it has come to be a symbol of Arizona and even the entire West. Saguaros can reach an amazing 50 feet in height and weigh more than two tons, most of it stored water. It takes 75 years for a saguaro to even begin to grow its first arm or two, and they can grow up to 20 or more arms.

The saguaro is home to a number of desert dwellers, as evidenced by the many holes you'll see in them. Hole makers include

Pronunciation Guide

agave	uh-GAH-vee	ocotillo	oak-oh-TEE-yo
Ajo Way	AH-hoe Way	paloverde	pah-lo-VER-day
arroyo	ah-ROY-oh	Pima	PEEM-ah
cholla	CHOY-ya	Rillito	ree-EAT-oh
Cruz	cruise	Sabino	sah-BEAN-oh
gila	HEE-la	saguaro	sah-WAH-ro
Ina Road	EYE-nuh Road	Tanque Verde	tank-ah VERD-ay
javelina	have-a-LEEN-uh	Tohono Chul	toe-HOE-no CHEWL
Mam-a-gah	MOM-uh-ga	vaquero	vak-CARE-oh
mesquite	m'SKEET	yucca	YUCK-uh
nopalito	no-pah-LEE-toe		

pack rats, Gila woodpeckers, and other birds. When tenants move out, others take occupancy, including elf owls, purple martins, and sparrow hawks. The saguaro's insulation keeps its internal temperatures about 20 degrees cooler than the outside air, which makes it a mighty inviting dwelling to the little ones. In April or May the saguaro cactus blooms with waxy white flowers at the tip of its arms or main trunk. The flowers eventually give way to crimson-colored fruit. For centuries Native Americans have harvested the fruit for food.

It has become quite popular to incorporate saguaro ribs into furniture or other home accessories, but anyone who does so can only use saguaros that are already dead and felled—and even then only with a permit. Landscapers and developers can obtain permits to relocate saguaros, but in truth those over 12 feet rarely survive the transplant, taking three to five years to die. Although you can see saguaro cacti anywhere in the Tucson area, including many front yards, Saguaro National Park (east and west units) has thousands, many of them giants, and is easily accessible. (Read all about the national park—actually a preserved parkland with units on either side of Tucson—in our Parks & Recreation chapter.)

Compared with the saguaro cactus, made famous in movies, paintings, and postcards, the desert's other cacti are relative unknowns. Cacti are native to the Americas and encompass over 1,000 species; in southern Arizona, we have 100 of them, each one more interesting-looking than the next.

i It's the Gila woodpecker and the gilded flicker who make those nest holes in the saguaros. The Gila woodpecker creates a new nest annually. When that hole is later abandoned, other creatures, such as lizards or even pygmy owls, move into the cool interior. Gilded flicker cavities tend to be on the north or northwest side of the saguaro.

Ocotillo

The ocotillo cactus, also called the Devil's Armchair, appears as a stand of tall, spindly sticks spreading upward and outward forming a V shape. And though the cactus may seem dead, a good rain will produce hundreds of tiny bright-green leaves up and down each of its spindles. In spring the ocotillo sprouts gorgeous red blooms several inches high at the tops of its spindles. Under the right conditions, the ocotillo is truly a beauty of the desert.

Prickly Pear

Another common cactus is the prickly pear, so named because its red fruits resemble pears. Those brave enough to tackle the fruit make it into a variety of prickly pear edibles like jelly and candy. The prickly pear cactus itself looks like a collection of green oval pads stuck on one another. These pads are a favorite Mexican vegetable, called *nopalito*, albeit quite tricky to harvest. Prickly pears can be green or a lovely purple hue.

Organ Pipe

The organ pipe cactus is so called because it sprouts a clump of tall slender arms that reach skyward, resembling the pipes of an organ. From afar, it has much the same coloration and riblike appearance of a saguaro, but its shape is different and its arms much thinner and straighter.

Cholla

Another cactus is the cholla, of which there are many varieties. Any cactus that looks like a miniature tree—with trunks and lots of squiggly little branches covered with prickers—is probably a cholla. One type of cholla is called jumping cholla because its spiny protrusions supposedly leap off and attach themselves to unwary passersby. This is quite an exaggeration, but they will attach if bumped; then it's the victim who jumps. Another is the teddy bear cholla, named because its needles resemble a fluff of teddy bear–like fleece, but don't be deceived by its appearance. Other cacti include the barrel and the hedgehog, both of which sprout brilliantly colored blossoms in springtime. Remember that all cacti have needles, some more visible and ferocious than others, so it's wise to look but not to touch.

i The nonprofit Arizona Native Plant Society is a great resource for learning more about indigenous plants. They sponsor field trips and workshops and distribute a statewide newsletter with articles on native plants, landscaping, and conservation. For more information, go to their website: www.aznps.org.

Agave

Cacti are not the only unusual things that grow in our desert. The agave, also a succulent, is another signature plant of the Southwest. It sprouts a rosette of thick, hard, sharp-tipped leaves out of the ground. But the agave's most amazing feature is a stalk that grows straight up from the center of the leaves, sometimes reaching 15 to 20 feet, with smaller branches near the top that sprout large clusters of flowers. Protruding majestically out of the scrubby desert landscape, this plant can easily be mistaken for a tree because of its mammoth height and shape. It has earned the nickname "century plant" because it takes so long for the plant to bloom—up to 30 years. Some species bloom only once after all that work and then die. Beyond its striking looks and amazing life cycle, the agave has other claims to fame—it's an ingredient in tequila, a liquor produced primarily in Mexico and made famous by a tasty frozen concoction as well as a song (hint: "Margaritaville") and a natural sweetener.

i Many plants in the Sonoran Des-ert have medicinal qualities. You can learn more from local herbalist John Slatterly, who offers herb walks, trips, and apprenticeships through his Tucson company, Desert Tortoise Botanicals (520-275-2105; www.desert tortoisebotanicals.com). His full-day, hands-on Plants of the Sonoran Desert field class will give you a detailed look at the edible and medicinal plants that surround us.

Yucca

And then there's the yucca, which looks like it might have stepped out of a science fiction movie set. Unlike the agave, yuccas have a stem or trunk on which the leaves grow—long, thin daggerlike leaves that are more often brown than green nearer the ground, giving the impression the plant is wearing a hula skirt. Nicknamed "Spanish dagger" for obvious reasons, the yucca also sprouts a stalk from its center that bears a large cluster of wheat-colored flowers in spring. Native Americans use the tough and fibrous yucca leaves for weaving baskets, sandals, and rope and its roots for soap. Although not unique to the Sonoran Desert, yuccas do seem to like it here. One of the larger and more famous varieties is the Joshua tree, which can have a life span of 500 years and is more commonly found near the California border.

Creosote Bush

One of the oldest living things on Earth makes its home in the Arizona desert—the creosote bush, which has been around for about 11,000 years. The creosote is known more by smell than by sight. Accompany-ing almost the first drop of desert rain are two distinct aromas—one is earth (or dirt or dust to some noses) and the other is the almost tarlike fruity smell emitted by the creosote that actually comes from a resinous coating on its stem and leaves. It's a smell we've grown to love and appreciate, for it signals rain.

Cereus

It may not be fair to introduce you to this next plant, because your chance of seeing it is slim to none. It is the night-blooming cereus, a nocturnal flower with delicate white petals and a baby's breath–like center of yellow stamens that blooms only during a single night in June. If you happen to be in Tucson during June, contact the Tohono Chul Park (520-575-8468) and you may be lucky enough to be there when this rare plant unfurls its flowers. (You'll find Tohono Chul Park listed in the Attractions chapter.)

i Don't miss the annual night-blooming cereus event at Tohono Chul Park. This otherwise sticklike cactus produces beautiful white, waxy flowers between May and August that bloom for only one night. The park has one of the largest collections in the world of these plants, and when there are enough of them blooming at one time, the park calls a "bloom night." The flowers have a highly unusual smell that attracts the sphinx moth. To find out when bloom nights are happening, call (520) 742-6455.

Trees

Yes, trees do grow in Tucson. Two of the most prominent native trees are the paloverde and the mesquite. The latter has become

Close-up

The Saguaro Harvest

When the beautiful white flower of the saguaro ripens in summer, it is harvested by the Tohono O'odham (desert people) who have made their home in the Sonoran Desert for thousands of years. The fruit is harvested using a pole (*kuipad*) about 12 feet long made of saguaro ribs with a pointed stick made of mesquite tied to the end. The end of the stick is used to knock the ripe fruit (called *bahidaj* in the O'odham language) from the cactus. The pod is split open to reveal the magenta flesh and tiny black seeds inside. The harvest is a very spiritual event that reflects the O'odham's respect for nature; no fruit is picked until the saguaro is asked to give its blessing to the harvest, and great care is taken to pick only the ripest fruit.

The pulp is collected in baskets, cooked, and strained to make a delicious syrup and jam, and the seeds are dried and ground to make nut butter. The O'odham also collect any sun-dried pulp (*jun*) that has fallen on the ground or stuck on surrounding trees. This crunchy sun-dried fruit is eaten like candy. The syrup is also fermented to make wine that is drunk during the annual rain dance ceremony (*jujkida*). You can participate in this unique seasonal event, held in late June, through the Arizona-Sonora Desert Museum (520-883-2702) and at Colossal Cave Mountain Park (520-647-7121). Reservations are critical.

popular among barbecue aficionados and fireplace owners as a wood with great burning qualities and a pleasant aroma. In fact, that delicious smoked steak you dined on last week in Seattle or Chicago may well have owed its distinctive flavor to an Arizona mesquite tree.

Botanically, the mesquite tree is a legume (yes, bean). It has a dark bark with twisting branches and small fernlike evergreen leaves. Many mesquites never become more than scrub due to lack of water. Like many other desert dwellers, it has been a source of food, fuel, medicine, and containers for Americans, Native and otherwise, for centuries. And the bees use the blossoms to make a delicious edible honey. It is a protected tree, and cutting is allowed by permit only. There are several bosques of mesquite around Tucson providing lovely shaded neighborhoods for the

lucky residents. (Check out our Neighborhoods, Neighboring Towns & Real Estate chapter for some tips on finding them.)

Prolific in the desert, the paloverde tree (paloverde means "green stick" in Spanish) is named for its beautiful lime-green bark. It doesn't have leaves and doesn't need them because photosynthesis takes place throughout the tree, but it does have thin needles (long or short, depending on variety). The paloverde is at its most glorious in spring when it is covered with a cascade of golden yellow fleecelike blooms. A street lined with paloverdes is a sight not to be missed in the Tucson spring.

Many nonnative trees grow here as well, often with a little help from a garden hose. Local favorites are citrus trees—grapefruit, orange, lemon, and lime. You will see at least one of these lush green-leafed beauties growing in many a back or front yard,

Close-up

Desert Harvesters

The nonprofit, volunteer, grassroots organization Desert Harvesters has been promoting sustainability and the use of desert foods since its founding in 1993. Grown out of a neighborhood project in the funky Dunbar neighborhood, the organization has developed as a major proponent of mesquite, one of the Sonoran Desert's most abundant trees and crops. The mesquite tree, once reviled by area farmers for its deep roots and tenacious grasp on the land, produces edible pods twice a year, once in the spring and once in the fall. These pods, when ground, produce a delectable flour or meal that is full of nutrients and fiber and is gluten-free. All the rage in gluten-free cooking and featured on menus in many top area restaurants, local mesquite flour is silky and beige, with a slightly sweet, graham-like flavor. Desert Harvesters was one of the first organizations to highlight this edible desert food and promote its use through neighborhood pancake breakfasts featuring their famous recipe, and by making available a hammermill to grind the pods into flour (the traditional way involves using ancient holes in the local bedrock to pound the beans). Once the bane of farmers, local landscapers, and pool owners, the lowly mesquite pod is now lauded for its flavor and versatility. Desert Harvesters holds pancake breakfasts, mesquite milling events, and more all around Tucson, and even has a lovely cookbook, *Eat Mesquite!* where you will find that famous pancake recipe among many others collected from mesquite fans and cooks all over Tucson. Visit their website, www.desertharvesters.org, for a calendar of activities and everything you ever wanted to know about mesquite.

particularly in the midtown neighborhoods like Sam Hughes and El Encanto and in some foothills areas. (See the Neighborhoods, Neighboring Towns & Real Estate chapter for a description of these neighborhoods.) These trees give Tucsonans three precious commodities—shade, undeniably the best-tasting fruit to be had, and in spring the wonderful smell of the citrus blossom.

No discussion of local plant life would be complete without mention of the desert broom. The desert broom seems to be green even when everything around it is browning from lack of water. It goes to seed around November or December, and each plant produces hundreds, possibly thousands, of fluffy white seeds. Its branches were used as brooms by the pioneers, and some Native Americans chew the stems to ease a toothache.

ANIMALS & OTHER THINGS

The first thing you should know is that our animal life is prolific, in part because the desert is relatively wet and in part because it produces so many things for the animal population to consume and live in or under. The second thing you should know is that most of the scary sagas you've heard about the animal life are quite exaggerated. Many of our four-legged and feathered inhabitants are certainly unusual, though, and will no doubt pique your curiosity.

Birds

Among the most fascinating bird dwellers of the Tucson area are the roadrunner and Gambel's quail. The television cartoon characterization of the roadrunner is not too far off base. It usually travels by foot rather than by flight; in fact, the roadrunner is the fastest American bird afoot, traveling at least 15 miles an hour when racing away from predators. It can reach 2 feet in length, mostly tail and legs with a silly-looking feathery topknot. Perhaps it comes as no surprise that the roadrunner is a member of the cuckoo family. Although you won't likely find one sprinting across a city street, they are fairly easy to spot in less built-up areas.

i The Tucson Audubon Society offers a wide variety of free day trips to get you acquainted with the birds of Arizona. Visit www.tucson audubon.org for further information.

Gambel's quail also seems to prefer feet to flight. (Fortunately for the bird and for us, this is not the quail sought after by hunters and treasured for its flavor.) Its primary mark is a reddish teardrop-shaped plume atop its head. To see how popular this bird is with the human population, just enter any Southwest or Arizona specialty shop and you will find numerous replicas of it—from mailbox flags to lawn ornaments to T-shirt art. But seeing them for real, especially as a family unit, is quite a remarkable sight. After the chicks are born in spring, the family travels around the desert on foot—an adult, followed by perhaps a dozen tiny young, followed by the other adult—all in a row. Be careful when driving along county streets lest you disturb and perhaps even injure this marvelous procession.

The Sonoran Desert has more species of birds—about 500—than any other arid region on Earth, making it a top spot for birders. You may not be a master spotter, but you will easily recognize hummingbirds, ravens, pigeonlike mourning doves, wrens, owls, and woodpeckers.

Mammals

As for furry friends, you might expect to see chipmunks and squirrels only in heavily treed areas. Don't be surprised when you see them in the desert, too. Other animals you're likely to spot in the rural environs include coyotes, 10-inch-high kit foxes, mule deer—so named because of their floppy, mulelike ears—and jackrabbits with elongated ears and legs. In higher elevations you may see bobcats, mountain lions, bighorn sheep, black bears, and a strange-looking piglike creature called a javelina. A member of the peccary family, this animal has an elongated snout and caninelike teeth and travels in herds for protection.

Reptiles

But it's the reptile population that visitors to our desert find most fascinating and often most frightening. Those squiggly, sure-footed, and speedy lizards can be as small as an inch and as large as several feet in length. The variety of lizards in the desert is almost endless, and most seem to blend in invisibly with the landscape. Some have hard spine-like intrusions covering their body, or great folds and wrinkles. The Gila monster, the largest lizard known to the US, is a protected species recognizable by its black-and-yellow beadlike skin. It definitely has the worst reputation among lizards. Despite being the only venomous lizard in the US, it is slow and

Rattlesnake Safety Tips

There are eleven species of rattlesnake in southern Arizona and it pays to be aware and cautious of this potentially deadly and quite beautiful desert creature. One of nature's most well-camouflaged animals, rattlesnakes crave warmth and sun and are most active during daytime hours in the spring and fall months. However, the snakes can also be active in the evening hours and during the nighttime, particularly during summer. You may see them stretched out on dark asphalt in the early evening absorbing the heat.

Tips

- Watch where you are walking, look ahead, look down, look around.
- Do not sit on rocks or the ground without checking the area first.
- Do not approach a snake; even if it appears to be sleeping or curled up, it can move quickly and strike. Back up slowly and give it a wide berth.
- Do not touch a dead snake; the head of the snake still contains venom and can still strike.
- Do not attempt to remove or relocate a snake yourself; call the fire department or a professional removal service (try Tucson Rattlesnake Removal, 520-425-7580; www.tucsonrattlesnakeremoval.com).
- If you are bitten, go immediately to the closest hospital.
- Call the Arizona Poison and Drug Information Center at the University of Arizona College of Pharmacy, (800) 222-1222, if you have questions or need information. The line is manned 24/7.

timid and has to chew into its victim to inject poison. Odds are you will not even catch a glimpse of this shy creature, let alone be bitten by one.

Another Arizona reptile with a bad reputation, albeit a bit more deserved, is the rattlesnake. Few people realize that rattlers can be found in nearly all of the contiguous 48 states. They're simply more visible here because we spend so much time outdoors treading in their territory. In truth, however, a human stands a greater chance of being struck by lightning in these parts than being bitten by a rattlesnake. And many snakebites happen because of carelessness or bravado

or even intoxication. The snake's rattle is a forewarning—listen up!

Pima County is home to eight venomous snakes, including seven varieties of rattlesnake, which can be found from the high mountains to the low desert (and occasionally in a homeowner's garage). The other poisonous snake is the small and rare coral snake, with colorful bands of red, yellow, and black. Snakes are most active in spring through fall but can be seen anytime of the year. They are more likely to wander into urban settings when searching for water during prolonged dry spells.

Spiders

Our desert is home to another well-known and often misunderstood type of fauna—spiders. One species of these has been the subject of horror movies and strikes fear in the hearts of most. Yes, it's the dreaded tarantula. But unless you suffer from arachnophobia, you have no reason to fear it. Their reputation is totally unfounded and no doubt exacerbated by both Hollywood's portrayal and their sheer size. They can reach a diameter of 4 inches or more and stand several inches high. But they don't jump and typically don't even sprint very far. They do have fangs but don't often bite; if they did, it would feel like a bee sting and be no more dangerous. Tarantulas are most often seen in late summer. Females stay close to the burrows they dig, so you would be more likely to see a male as it wanders around in search of a mate. In B movies the monster tarantulas only live about 90 minutes; in real life they have unusually long life spans—males up to 10 years and females up to 25.

Of all the spiders found in the desert—including the female black widow spider, whose bite is venomous and can cause complications but is not usually deadly, and the wolf spider, which can be quite large and amazingly fast but doesn't bite—the only variety whose bite can lead to really serious complications is the brown recluse, which is not unique to this area. This spider's shape is similar to a black widow's except it is brown and, other than that, not very distinctive.

Scorpions

The scorpion is another desert creature with a fearsome reputation that's largely unfounded. Its most identifying characteristics are two claws in front and a slender whiplike tail that curves upward. They come in all sizes, from quite small to 3 inches or more in length. The smaller the scorpion, the more potent the sting. While a scorpion's sting won't really hurt a human, it can be dangerous to domestic animals like cats and small dogs—and also to small children and seniors. And because scorpions like to find comfort in air-conditioned buildings during the summer heat, they often turn up in living rooms or bedrooms, contributing to a thriving exterminating business in southern Arizona.

THE MOUNTAINS

Rising from the Tucson valley floor are four mountain ranges that ring the city. (Actually, a fifth range is sometimes included, the Tortolitas to the northwest, but we don't want to overwhelm you.) Although they are within the Sonoran Desert, the mountains differ greatly from the desert floor that's nearly 6,000 feet below them. To the north are the Santa Catalinas, east are the Rincons, south are the Santa Ritas, and west are the Tucson Mountains. The stark Tucson Mountains are so close that they almost spill into the downtown business district, while the spread of Tucson's population has reached right into the foothills of the other three ranges. But even if you never actually get up into the mountains, you certainly will notice their beauty and ever-changing hues, especially at sunrise and sunset.

Because of their elevation, the mountains provide cooler temperatures as well as flora and fauna different from the desert floor's. Here you will find the southernmost ski area in the US at the top of Mount Lemmon in the Catalinas. You will also find cacti and giant century plants giving way to oak, aspen, and pine trees. And wildlife to be found here but not in the valley includes mountain lions, black bears, peregrine falcons, and bighorn sheep. You may even see some very unexpected un-wild life, such as cattle roaming the open ranges of the lower mountain elevations. The proximity of these mountain ranges to the city makes Tucson a place of wonder, delight, and diversity for residents and visitors alike. Each of these mountain ranges has its distinct characteristics and people playgrounds, so here is an overview of what you might see.

Santa Catalina Mountains

The name Santa Catalina, meaning Saint Catherine, comes from Father Kino, a famous discoverer whom you can read all about in our History chapter. The highest point of this 200-square-mile range is Mount Lemmon at 9,157 feet. The Mount Lemmon Highway, or Catalina Highway, is a dramatic road of steep canyons on one side and mammoth granite spires on the other, with many scenic stops along the way. We're not talking New England here, but the fall foliage show is still a sight, with golden aspens and red oaks displaying their vivid hues among towering green pine and fir trees. (For details on how to get to Mount Lemmon and what to do and see there, turn to the Attractions chapter.)

Also in the Santa Catalinas is Tucsonans' own "special oasis." It's called Sabino Canyon and is easily accessible from the city's northeast side. Actually, Sabino is just one of several exquisite canyons in this area of the Santa Catalinas, and if you've seen one canyon you haven't seen them all, because they are all very different. But Sabino is the closest, and it will satisfy nearly anyone's craving for a taste of the wilderness. The

canyon is a well-developed riparian woodland of cottonwood, willow, and other native trees along a cool creek (complete with waterfalls and swimming holes) and with bountiful wildlife, all meandering along the mountainside for almost 4 miles. (Details on Sabino Canyon, including tram information, are in the Attractions and Parks & Recreation chapters.)

Other attractions in the Catalinas, but not accessible by road, include rock formations known as Prominent Point, Finger Rock, Thumb, and Rosewood Point—all of which rise above the city to the north of Alvernon Way. Areas of the Catalinas that are a bit more accessible via easy hikes are Pima Canyon and the Pusch Ridge near Catalina State Park on Tucson's northwest side. (Look for details on these in our Parks & Recreation chapter.)

Rincon Mountains

To Tucson's east lie the three peaks of the Rincon Mountains, with a top elevation of 8,666 feet. Unless you are an accomplished hiker, there is no easy way to ascend this range. Because the Rincons run north to south, they do offer some spectacular sights viewed from the city: glorious reflections of the sun's colors at sunset, fierce-looking clouds rumbling toward the city during summer's monsoon storms, and a massive blanket of bright white when dusted by a rare winter snow.

The most popular way to experience the Rincons is at Saguaro National Park East (see the Parks & Recreation chapter), which offers excellent views of the mountains, not to mention its own amazing attractions and great spots to watch the sun setting over Tucson's western mountains. Another option is to take Reddington Pass, a rugged and dusty road that offers great vistas and some Arizona cattle-country scenes as well. Reddington Road is also the way to access the trail to Tanque Verde Falls. When running at full tilt after winter or summer storms, the falls in this narrow granite canyon are awesome, but the force of the water and the slippery rocks can create a dangerous combination. Watch your step!

The Rincons are also home to Colossal Cave, a massive underground labyrinth that indicates Arizona was once covered by ocean. It is one of the largest dry caverns in the world, and its end has yet to be discovered. Other than a movie theater, it also may be the only place around to experience a constant 70 degrees during summer's unrelenting heat. (Read about Colossal Cave in our Attractions chapter.)

Santa Rita Mountains

Have you ever heard of a mountain range without an "Old Baldy"? Neither have we. Ours can be found in the Santa Rita Mountains to Tucson's south. Its other name is Mount Wrightson, and it tops out at 9,453 feet. With no road, this Old Baldy is definitely best left to the serious hiker. The second peak of the Santa Ritas is Mount Hopkins, and located at its pinnacle is the Smithsonian's Whipple Observatory. Although accessible by a narrow switchback road, there is no point in driving it because the observatory is behind locked gates. Instead visit the observatory's visitor center at the south base of the mountain, and make a reservation for the bus tour to the observatory. (See the Attractions chapter for details.) A more down-to-earth and car-friendly way to enjoy the Santa Ritas is the beautiful Madera Canyon at about 5,000 feet elevation. Here you will find easy hiking, a cool stream, nature trails, and picnic spots. And the birding in Madera Canyon is exquisite, with species that are not seen elsewhere in the US. You might see elf owls, trogons, flycatchers, and up to a dozen species of hummingbirds.

Tucson Mountains

Last but not least, we visit the Tucson Mountains on the west. This range is the smallest of the four in both girth and height, but in many ways it's both more dramatic with its volcanic peaks and more people-friendly with roads, trails, and other attractions. These mountains have much to offer in rich flora and fauna. At the Mam-a-gah Picnic Area, accessible by a 20-minute hike from the King Canyon trailhead across from the Arizona-Sonora Desert Museum, you will find the Tucson Mountains' only permanent source of water. Continue downstream on the wash and you will find extensive petroglyphs—ancient carvings in rock.

The closest spot to traverse this range, however, is at "A" Mountain, the conical little mountain that overlooks downtown Tucson. Viewable from almost any high ground in Tucson and accessible by car, it derives its moniker from the big letter "A" painted on it by each year's University of Arizona frosh class. Officially named Sentinel Peak, this is also the sight of Tucson's annual July 4th fireworks, funds and weather permitting (see the Festivals & Events chapter for details). The Tucson Mountains can be accessed from three roads: from Ina Road to Picture Rocks Road on the north side, through Gates Pass Road from Speedway Road near downtown, or on the south side via Ajo Way. This is also where you'll find Old Tucson Studios, home of many Western film shoots; Saguaro National Park West; and the exquisite Arizona-Sonora Desert Museum.

Speaking of the Arizona-Sonora Desert Museum, you may find it comforting to know that you need not necessarily spend weeks, months, or even years attempting to see firsthand the vast Sonoran desertscapes described in this chapter. It's all re-created—from birds to cacti to coyotes—in magnificent form at the museum, so if your visit to our fine city is short, make this one of your first stops. (Get the details on this world-class museum in our Attractions chapter.)

THE RIVERS

Tucson boasts two "major" rivers: the Rillito and the Santa Cruz. The Rillito River runs east to west across what seems to be almost the center of Tucson. But in fact it forms the northern boundary of the city; to its north actually lies Pima County, where Tucson's population continues to spread. Rillito translates to "little creek" in Spanish (we take what we can get in these parts). The Santa Cruz River runs along what is today I-19, except the river was there first. In fact, it's been used as a transportation route between Mexico and points north for centuries; the fact that the river is usually dry just added to the convenience. The strangest thing about this river, however, is that it starts its course in southern Arizona, runs south into Mexico, then makes an abrupt turn and flows back north into Arizona near Nogales. It then continues as a north-flowing river for 180 miles until it reaches the Gila River.

About the only time water runs in the rivers is after heavy rains—the summer storms of July and August and winter rains in January and February. In the interim, the riverbeds are great for walking the dog, horseback riding, or mountain bike riding. In fact, many miles right along the Rillito and the Santa Cruz have been turned into river parks for safe and scenic fun.

In addition to the rivers, dry washes, also called arroyos in Spanish, dot the landscape. These are natural or man-made pathways for rainwater. Tucson's soil is made up primarily of sand, clay, and rock, none of which have great absorption qualities. So instead of going down, water travels along the surface, entering into smaller washes, then larger ones, and eventually into the rivers. Within several days or even hours after the rains subside, the rivers and washes again run dry. Conversely, only a few hours of torrential rain will overflow these same washes and rivers, causing flooding, road closures, and property damage.

Our dry washes and riverbeds perform a vital function beyond channeling the rain. They are home to much of our desert plant and animal life.

i The Tucson Water Department offers free, guided tours of all the city's public water projects. You'll visit the Clearwater Recharge Basins in Central Avra Valley and see the pumping station, hydro-pneumatic tanks, and pipeline that brings in Colorado River valley water. Several water treatment plants are on the agenda, offering an insiders' view of how wastewater is recycled, contaminated water is removed, and backwash water is treated. Also included is the Sweetwater Wetlands, a reclaimed area that is a model for water resource management techniques. To schedule a tour, call the Public Information Office at (520) 791-4331.

NATURAL RESOURCES

The riches of nature abound in and around Tucson, and our two most prominent natural resources are water and minerals. Stand on nearly any high ground in Tucson and look toward the southwest, beyond the buildings of the city. You will see a large expanse of light-colored earth; this is a copper-mining plateau near Green Valley. Unlike the traditional method of underground mining, pit mining requires removing all the rock layer before sifting the earth under it to mine the copper; it's obvious the growth in this industry has not come without taking its toll on the land.

Since the dawn of time, rocks and minerals have fascinated people, providing both utility and adornment. Native Americans of the Southwest gathered turquoise and other stones for ceremonies and weaponry. Spaniards came into the Southwest in search of mineral wealth, although they dug only gold and silver, overlooking deposits of base metals like copper. Gold prospectors scoured "them thar hills" looking for the precious metal, and Tombstone was founded as a silver-mining town. Arizona towns like Bisbee and Globe still thrive on copper mining. And Tucson is host to the greatest gem and mineral event in the country, and probably the world, each February—the Tucson Gem and Mineral Show (see the Festivals & Events chapter).

With an annual average rainfall of only 11 inches and nearly constant sunshine, it's no wonder that water would be a precious resource in Tucson. Our desert flora and fauna generally make do with the water nature provides—plants by storing it internally for months and animals by resting during the day and foraging at night, often for the very plants that hold moisture. But what do people do?

In Arizona two-thirds of the water people use comes from underground, and in Tucson practically all our water needs are met with groundwater. It's been said that even if Tucson didn't have a rainfall in five years, no one would have to turn off the tap. But as the population increases and we look for more ways to green up our surroundings, the supply will diminish. Billions of dollars have been spent by federal and state governments, including Arizona's, to divert Colorado River water as an alternate source of water. The Colorado River no longer reaches to its outlet in the Gulf of California—we are using it up. But for now, at least, Tucson's water supply is adequate.

The reality is that no matter where one lives, water is a precious natural resource and water conservation is a wise human practice. Unlike some other cities in the arid Southwest, Tucson's population has largely accepted desert landscaping as opposed to trying to re-create Kentucky in their backyards. Grass lawns are still visible in older midtown neighborhoods, but newer housing communities are adopting desert landscaping, or Xeriscaping, whereby native and low-water-usage plants are grouped according to their water needs to conserve water.

Natural resources have long formed the backbone of Pima County's economy, often referred to as the four Cs: climate, copper, cotton, and cattle. Climate has produced a healthy tourism industry, while the mines of Pima County now produce over 70 percent of the copper mined in the US. You may be surprised about the cotton, but drive north of Tucson, such as on I-10 toward Phoenix, and you will see acres and acres of it growing with the help of irrigation. Cattle ranching has been an important part of southern Arizona since Father Kino first introduced the tame beasts in the 1690s. The first Arizona cowboys, or *vaqueros,* were Native American or Mexican. Although much diminished from earlier days, cattle ranches, complete with the "cowboys" who tend them, still exist, mostly in higher elevations. The flavor of the cowboy West remains strong in Tucson—from cowboy boots and Stetson hats to horseback trail riding and world-class dude ranches for cowboy wannabes.

i If you are wondering how to garden in our desert landscape, don't despair. Drop your trowel and click on www.tucsonbotanical.org/desertconnections. This helpful website is a collaboration of the Tucson Botanical Gardens and Pima County Library and features a searchable plant database along with step-by-step gardening tips.

STARGAZING

Tucson is known as the astronomy capital of the world. With nights that are nearly always clear, stars as bright as beacons, and unobstructed mountain peaks to hold our formidable astronomy tools, the Tucson area offers some of the best possible conditions on Earth for viewing outer space.

Several major astronomical observatories are located near Tucson: the University of Arizona's facilities in the Santa Catalina Mountains; Kitt Peak National Observatory, 56 miles west of Tucson; and the Smithsonian Astrophysical Observatory on Mount Hopkins, in the Santa Rita Mountains; and the Mount Lemmon SkyCenter at Steward Observatory. These sites hold the most sophisticated and advanced telescopes and

tracking devices ever created, some parts of which were developed by the University of Arizona. And in a more down-to-earth location, right in Tucson, sits the university's Flandrau Planetarium. (For information on visiting these places among the stars, turn to the Attractions chapter.)

Meanwhile, as you glance upward at Tucson's star-filled night skies, remind yourself that some of the world's foremost astronomers are doing the same, trying to unravel the mysteries of endless space and perhaps our own humble beginnings.

THE WEATHER

In case you haven't already noticed or heard, Tucson has sunshine—more, it is reported, than any other place in the US. The actual count is 350 days a year. (Lest you feel deceived, this refers to any day on which the sun shines at some time rather than days on which it shines all day.) To be sure, there are days in the summer months when Tucsonans look skyward, urgently pleading for just one cloud to pass by.

The average yearly high is 82 and low is 54. The hottest months on average are June and July at 99, and the coolest are December and January at 65. If this sounds too good to be true, remember that these are averages. It is just as likely that Tucson will have a number of 100-plus (or even 105-plus) days and a number of winter nights with temperatures below freezing, at least for a few hours.

Temperatures are the subject of a lot of talk in Tucson, but so is rain. In summer a word you'll hear often is monsoon—as in "When are the monsoons getting here?" or "Here come the monsoon clouds, so where's the rain?" The climatologists say using monsoon is a misnomer; a monsoon is what

India or Southeast Asia experiences. But Tucsonans like its descriptive quality and aren't likely to give it up.

About mid-July, just when Tucsonans are sure they can't survive another day of 100-plus temperatures, months without rain, and rising humidity, the late-afternoon clouds begin building up—huge, rapidly moving white and dark gray clouds, tinged with reds and golds by the sun's rays still shining in the western sky. But these are fickle clouds. For days they may release no rain, or just a smattering of rain on some lucky sections of the mountains or valley. Eventually, they give us what we long for, along with ferocious winds, thunder, displays of lightning that are unparalleled, and maybe even a sky-sweeping rainbow or two or three. With the lightning also comes the fear of fire, particularly in the mountains and foothills that have been parched for months. As inaccessible as some of these places are, the mountain fires can burn for days or even weeks, fueled by high winds and not at all affected by dribbles of rainfall.

i According to the National Weather Service, the record high for Tucson was 117 degrees on June 26, 1990. A record low of 6 degrees was recorded on January 7, 1913.

By nightfall or shortly thereafter, the rains subside and the desert is cooled off and somewhat watered down, at least briefly. Mother Nature repeats this scene, often several days a week, through July and August and often into September. And whether on any given day she will produce rain or just its trappings, only Mother Nature knows for sure; that's the way of our monsoon season. We do get a bonus with these late-summer rains: Plant life that has seemed to all but die suddenly resurrects, and birds and animals of all sorts come out of hiding to enjoy the rain and have a feeding frenzy. It's like having a second spring.

Tucson may also have a second "rainy" season, typically in December and January, when average amounts are 0.84 and 0.75 inch, respectively. (Yes, you read those numbers right—less than an inch.) These are the rains that will sometimes produce a blanket of mountain snow and, ever so rarely, a dusting of valley snow. At Mount Lemmon, however, the average annual snowfall is 175 inches, which makes downhill and cross-country skiing possible a mere hour's drive from the city. When these winter rains are normal and are followed by rains in March and April, we can expect a great spring show of blooms from the desert that lasts into early summer.

Tucsonans boast about the dry heat that results from our very low humidity levels much of the year. And indeed it is a benefit of our climate. On even the coolest winter days, one rarely feels cold or chilled during the daylight hours. For eight months of the year—October through May—you can simply count on beautiful weather for almost any outdoor activity.

Although Tucson has many attractions that make it a great place to recreate and reside, our weather certainly tops the list. It is the weather that makes possible so much of what we do, see, and enjoy in and around Tucson.

PARKS & RECREATION

With nearly 350 days of sunshine a year and a fascinating array of recreational options, you'll find plenty of fun in the sun in Tucson! Parks and forests can be found in just about any direction—although some forests aren't quite the traditional forests you'll find elsewhere. State parks offer hiking, fishing, camping, bird-watching, and more. Pima County and the city of Tucson both maintain outstanding parks and recreation departments. Because of the location of many of the parks, there has been a great deal of cooperation among the federal, state, county, and city governments. This cooperative effort has resulted in preservation of the natural beauty of the area as well as quality service for visitors. And, if all that isn't enough, many local recreation-oriented businesses offer everything from skydiving and rock climbing to hot-air balloon rides and mountain goat pack adventures. You can even be a true city slicker by taking part in a cattle drive.

CORONADO NATIONAL FOREST

Encompassing more than 1.7 million acres in southeast Arizona and southwest New Mexico, this forest is home to many types of cacti, as well as pine tree forests in the mountainous area, known in these parts as "sky islands." A total of 12 mountain ranges with elevations ranging from 3,000 to 10,720 feet are within the boundaries of this spectacular, biologically diverse forest.

Wildlife covers everything from roadrunners and jackrabbits to mountain lions and bears. These larger wild creatures tend to shy away from humans, so don't let that deter you from enjoying the many marvelous sites within the Coronado National Forest.

The following areas are all located in the Coronado National Forest, and most are within an hour's drive from town.

Mount Lemmon

As you travel the winding highway (designated a scenic byway in 2005) to the top of Mount Lemmon, you'll notice several changes in the vegetation. In all, five climate zones exist on this mountain. That's why there is a 20- to 30-degree temperature difference between the bottom (desert) and the top (pine forest). Camping, picnicking, skiing, hiking, fishing, and bird-watching are just a few of the recreational activities available to visitors.

As a short stop, park your car at Windy Point. The view will show you where you were just a short while ago. You might also want to take another rest at Rose Canyon Lake. Here among the whispering pines, you can enjoy a picnic, a short hike, or a little bit of fishing. As you continue to the top, follow the signs that will take you to the tiny village of Summerhaven, where a community center, shops, and a general store can be found. And then continue on just a bit and visit Ski Valley, our lone skiing spot in the immediate area. The lifts are open year-round.

A day pass costs $5 per car, but if you plan on camping you might want to buy the weekly pass for $10 or a yearly pass for $20, available for purchase on the mountain or at locations around town.

If you are only traveling to Summerhaven or Ski Valley, and are not planning to camp or hike, a pass is not necessary.

The road sometimes is closed due to weather or construction. Before you go, check the Mount Lemmon construction hotline at (520) 547-7510 or the USDA Forest Service website at www.fs.fed.us/r3/coronado.

Sabino Canyon & Bear Canyon

If you were to ask a hundred Tucsonans what *the* place to take out-of-towners is, the answer would likely be . . . Sabino Canyon. Each year more than one 1 million people visit this lovely spot. Tucked into the Catalina Mountains (it's the largest of the 3 major canyons in the range), Sabino Canyon is a perfect example of the ecosystem that makes up the Sonoran Desert and surrounding area. A tour of Sabino gives you a respect and love for the desert, whether it's your first time or your 15th.

This magnificent canyon is one of the most visited spots in Tucson. Part of the Santa Catalina Mountains, it has streams, waterfalls, various desert flora and fauna, saguaros and other types of cacti, trees, and wildlife. You can access all this beauty either by foot or tram or both. The motorized covered trams have benchlike seating and will take you on a wonderful guided tour. Drivers are well versed in the canyon flora and fauna. You'll ride on roads and over bridges built in the 1930s by the Civilian Conservation Corps (CCC). Get ready for some magnificent vistas. You can also hop on and off the tram at any of the stops along the way if you want to get a closer look or just sit at one of the many picnic spots and enjoy the hot sun and the cool breeze. Take Sunrise Drive east to Sabino Canyon Road and turn left, heading north for about 0.25 mile. Parking is $5 per day per vehicle or $20 for a yearly pass. Call (520) 749-8700 for information about Sabino Canyon and the Coronado National Forest.

Near the parking area, a lovely visitor center (520-749-8700) is open weekdays from 8 a.m. to 4:30 p.m. and 8:30 a.m. to 4:30 p.m. on weekends with excellent displays about area flora and fauna and a gift shop. The helpful staff and rangers can supply maps and detailed information about hiking trails (expert, easy, and kid-friendly nature trails are available). You can also take a tram ride.

The tram service is operated 365 days a year by **Sabino Canyon Tours** (520-749-2861, recorded information, 520-749-2327, live operator; www.sabinocanyon.com). There are 2 routes: Sabino Canyon and Bear Canyon. Hours and fees vary, so check first. Only cash is accepted, no credit cards, for either tram.

i For an amazing and unusual view of Sabino Canyon, consider a nighttime tram ride. During April, May, June, September, October, and November, Sabino Canyon Tours offers evening rides 3 nights per month. Reservations are necessary; call (520) 749-2327.

Generally the Sabino Canyon tram runs every 30 minutes from 9 a.m. to 4:30 p.m.; adults cost $8, children 3 to 12 are $4. The Sabino Canyon tram takes you on a narrated 3.8-mile, 45-minute tour with 9 stops along the way.

The Bear Canyon tram is primarily for hikers; this is a non-narrated 3-mile ride with 3 stops at popular hiking trailheads. Generally this tram operates on the hour from 9 a.m. to 4 pm; $3 for adults, $1 for children ages 3 to 12.

As long as you hold on to your ticket, you can get on and off the trams at any stop along the way, so you can take a hike, play in the water, picnic, or just stroll to the next stop for pickup.

Whichever way you choose to view the canyon, you'll be awed by its raw beauty. You'll see tall crags that reach heavenward (some intrepid folks choose to climb these high tors); running water from mountain streams; stately saguaros; hundreds of ocotillo, barrel, prickly pear, and cholla cacti; and mesquite and cottonwood trees. You may even catch a glimpse of wildlife and most certainly will see all types of birds. Picnic areas are plentiful.

SAGUARO NATIONAL PARK

More than 80,000 acres of land make up the two sections of this one-of-a-kind park. The area was established as a national monument in the 1930s and then upgraded to national park status in 1992. There are hiking and nature trails throughout for all ages and abilities. You'll find thousands of saguaros, plus stands of ocotillo, cholla, prickly pear, and barrel cacti. Creosote bushes and mesquite trees are also plentiful. Both parks have a $10 entrance fee per vehicle, and a $5 fee for individuals on bicycles.

Saguaro National Park East/Rincon Mountain District

When you visit this beautiful national park for the first time, you will be amazed at the sheer number of saguaro and other types of cacti found here. Cactus Forest Drive, an 8-mile tour, is astounding. This is the older of the 2 sections, so the saguaros are mature and may be more than 200 years old. Also known as the Rincon Mountain District because it's in the Rincon Mountains, the park is made up of more than 67,000 acres of cacti, rock formations, and desert. Wildlife residing here includes javelinas, coyotes, Gila monsters, bobcats, deer, and lizards and birds galore. You may not see all of these creatures, but if you stay until sunset, you may hear the mournful serenade of the coyote population.

i For a unique adventure, take an exciting off-road jeep tour of the Sonoran Desert. These 4-wheel-drive, open-air jeeps will take you on special trails designed to give you a great feel for the desert. The experienced drivers are great guides and will tell you everything you ever wanted to know about desert flora and fauna. Most tours offer day, sunrise, and sunset tours. You can also request the driver bring along some exciting wildlife (tarantulas and snakes, for example) for closer viewing. You never know what you might see on this great ride. Be sure to make reservations in advance. Try Trail Dust Adventures (520-747-0323; www.trail dustadventures.com).

Camping and hiking are allowed, but you must have a permit, available at the visitor center. Hikers are warned that this is considered wilderness hiking, which means, in this case, that it is very rocky and steep, and elevations run from 3,000 feet to more than 7,000 feet.

Vegetation changes from desert scrub to various pine trees. Bring plenty of water and a friend. Picnic areas are also available along the Cactus Forest Drive. There is an admission fee per vehicle to the park, which is also good for Saguaro Park West. The visitor center is free and open daily (except for Christmas and New Year's Day).

Take Broadway Boulevard east to Old Spanish Trail, and then follow the signs to the visitor center, open 9 a.m. to 5 p.m. daily except Christmas. Here you can find plenty of useful information about the park. Call (520) 733-5153 for more information, or visit www.nps.gov/sagu.

Saguaro National Park West/Tucson Mountain District

There are 2 approaches to the Tucson Mountain District part of the park. The long, and not quite as interesting, way is to take Ajo Way west to Kinney Road, then head north to the visitor center (open 9 a.m. to 5 p.m. daily except Christmas). This way is for the faint of heart and those pulling trailers or driving recreational vehicles. The road is flat and only slightly winding. The other way, more beautiful and just a little challenging, is to take Speedway Boulevard to Gates Pass Road. Here's where your heart will start pumping as the road narrows and the edge drops quite a distance to the desert floor. Follow the road past the Arizona-Sonora Desert Museum for about another 2 miles. The visitor center has information about the

flora and fauna found in the park, as well as lovely exhibits and a bookstore.

Hiking trails snake through the area (see the hiking section in this chapter). The shortest of these is Cactus Garden Trail, which is only 100 yards; the longest is the Hugh Norris Trail, which is 4.9 miles one-way. Several of these trails link together or meet with longer trails in the park if you're looking for an extended day hike.

Indian petroglyphs can be found at the northern end of the park via the Signal Hill Trail. Ask for directions at the visitor center.

As in the east section of the national park, you'll find many saguaro cacti (although the saguaros here are younger than the ones in Saguaro East), beautiful rock formations, and stunning scenery. The park has wonderful hiking and biking adventures. Take the paved Bajada Loop Drive, a total of 6 miles, for a real taste of what the park has to offer. Picnic sites can be found along the way. There's no charge to enter this part of the park. Call (520) 733-5100 for more information, or visit www.nps.gov/sagu. The visitor center is open daily, except on Christmas and New Year's Day.

Every 10 years the park takes a census of its magnificent saguaro cacti. Over 300 volunteers take to the trails to count and measure the park's saguaros. According to the 2010 census, approximately 1.6 million individual saguaro plants are growing within the park.

IRONWOOD FOREST NATIONAL MONUMENT

Declared a national monument by President Clinton in 2000, this wide-ranging area about 25 miles southwest of Tucson covers 129,000 acres. Included in this amazing swath of land are the desert mountain ranges of Silver Bell, Waterman, and Sawtooth; desert valleys; and one of the richest stands of ironwood trees in the Sonoran Desert. But you'll have to be equipped with a sturdy SUV or, better yet, four-wheel drive to access these wonders of nature, as the roads are unpaved, rough, and rutted. There are no facilities of any type here, just pure unadulterated nature. There are no admission, parking, or camping fees. Camping is permitted for up to 14 days, but there are no official campground sites.

If you're a nature lover who hates visitor centers, guided tours, and lots of people, this is the place for you, and it's gorgeous any time of year. From Tucson, take I-10 west to Marana. Take exit 236, turn left on Sandario Road for 0.1 mile, then turn right on Marana Road and go west about 5.8 miles to Silver Bell Road. Continue on Silver Bell Road to travel through the national monument. You can return to I-10 at Sasco Road.

A cautionary note: Many parts of the monument are very isolated; be sure to bring adequate food and water. For more information, call the Bureau of Land Management at (520) 258-7208; www.blm.gov/az/st/en/prog/blm_special_areas/natmon/ironwood.html.

STATE PARKS

In addition to Catalina State Park, other state parks of interest in the Tucson area include Patagonia Lake State Park and Tumacacori National Historic Park (see the Day Trips & Weekend Getaways chapter). State park fees may be higher during peak seasons.

Catalina State Park

You'll find camping, hiking, picnicking, horseback riding, and some of the prettiest up-close-and-personal experiences with desert life at Catalina State Park. Located 9 miles north of the city off Oracle Road, the park covers some 5,500 acres at the foot of the Catalina Mountains. Although a state park, it's still part of the Coronado National Forest and is maintained cooperatively by the USDA Forest Service and the State of Arizona.

With its easy accessibility, over 100 picnic areas, 120 campsites, and numerous hiking trails, it's easy to see why this is such a popular spot (more than 135,000 visitors a year take advantage of the diverse recreational activities).

Birders can enjoy the 1-mile nature loop that travels through a heavily wooded mesquite stand. The area provides shelter for many birds, including golden eagles and various falcons.

For hikers, 7 additional trails lead to wooded areas through canyons, natural pools, and the ruins of a prehistoric Hohokam village. During the rainy season running water is plentiful. Elevation changes are minimal. Campers should note that wood fires are not allowed, so bring charcoal or your camp stove. Horseback riders are also welcome, but they must stay on the nature trails (see Horseback Riding later in this chapter).

Park entrance fee is $7 per car. For more information, call (520) 628-5798 or visit www.pr.state.az.us/parks/cata/index.html.

Pima County Natural Resources, Parks & Recreation

Pima County Natural Resources, Parks, and Recreation Department maintains parks and neighborhood recreation centers throughout the entire county, several of which are at public schools. In addition to the usual services, classes, sports programs, and swimming pools, the department also is responsible for a caving area (see Caving later in this chapter), operating a baseball complex, distributing a variety of health services, maintaining an archery range, overseeing a horseracing track (see the Spectator Sports chapter), and maintaining a campground and several hiking trails.

Kids of all ages can find something to do—whether it's a toddler program, the various teen-oriented programs, or the many senior programs and classes. Middle-agers need not feel left out. They, too, can grab a bit of fun or learning with the programs and services available at the neighborhood centers.

With more than 15 recreation centers and numerous parks, the county has something for everybody. Whether you want to learn how to speak Spanish, make your own holiday gifts, or trace your family tree, the county parks and recreation department has it.

Teens can learn babysitting skills, arts and crafts, or architecture. Little ones can learn social skills or just have fun.

i For an unforgettable evening, head to Gates Pass for the sunset. Tucson's desert sunsets are remarkable for their vividness and colors, and you'll get the best-ever view here. Take someone you love and a great bottle of wine, a picnic maybe.

Seniors can join the neighborhood senior centers and take classes in such things as painting or clogging. They can also join in group activities such as guided group hikes or softball. Many special activities are also planned year-round.

Aquatics, golf, boxing, tennis, archery, hiking, and numerous other recreational activities can also be found in county parks. Classes and activities vary from season to season, and not all are offered at every recreation facility. The department publishes *Leisure Times* twice a year, which includes a complete listing of all the happenings and where they are happening. Call (520) 877-6000 for more information or check the Web at www.pima.gov/nrpr.

Pima County Parks

COLOSSAL CAVE MOUNTAIN PARK
(520) 647-7275
www.colossalcave.com

Located less than 25 miles from the city, Colossal Cave was first explored by Anglos as far back as 1879 and used by prehistoric peoples long before that. It is considered a "dry" cave, which means the formations have stopped "growing" due to lack of water. The temperature is always a comfortable 70 degrees.

At the 2,500-acre park that surrounds the cave, families can have some fun with trail rides, a riparian area for some great hiking, a museum, and several picnic sites. You can tour the working La Posta Quemada Ranch, which is also part of the park. The ranch has cookouts for large groups, and little ones get the opportunity to "pan" for gold and "rope" a steer. Birders will find the riparian area a heaven on earth.

There is a fee to enter the park and fees for the various activities. Hours differ by the season, so call ahead. Take I-10 to exit 279 and then travel 6 miles north or take the Old Spanish Trail (catch it off Broadway Boulevard). (See the Attractions chapter for more information about Colossal Cave.)

RILLITO RIVER PARK
(520) 877-6000
www.pima.gov/nrpr/parks/rillito_
riverpark/index.htm

Originally constructed as part of the reclamation of the riverbanks after several years
of serious flood damage, this multi-use path
is one of the prettiest places to exercise
anywhere.

Stretching from I-10 to Craycroft Road,
this linear park is a favorite outdoor place for
many Tucsonans. It's also the site of many
"walks" for charitable organizations throughout the year.

Paved and unpaved paths run along
either side of the river, with both sides
available for skating, jogging, and walking.
Cycling is limited to the north bank, and
horseback riders are limited to the south side
(although you'll find some great riding in the
riverbed itself). The only other rules concern
right-of-way. Signs are posted along the way
to remind you who gives way to whom.
Water fountains, restrooms, picnic areas, and
parking can be found at certain cross streets,
and a few picnic areas with grills are scattered throughout. Footbridges cross the river
at various halfway points between the street
entry points.

The landscaping is complemented by
beautiful public art, mainly metal and tile
work. Midway along the route is Children's
Memorial Park, dedicated to hundreds of
area children who have died. A large plaque
engraved with the names of the children
and a statue stand in tribute. Also en route is
the lovely Brandi Fenton Memorial Park with
splash pond and off-leash dog parks (see
the Parks & Recreation chapter). Dog lovers
will adore the shady, beautiful off-leash dog
park, the Smiling Dog Ranch, hidden behind

trees on the east side of the path just before
Mehl Park's baseball fields.

Enter the park at any major cross streets.
Parking for cars can be found at the access
ways.

ROY P. DRACHMAN–AGUA CALIENTE
  PARK
(520) 749-3718
www.pima.gov/nrpr/parks/agua_
caliente/index.htm

The phrase *oasis* in the desert may be highly
overused, but in the case of Agua Caliente
Park, it rings true. Listed on the National
Register of Historic Places, this 101-acre park,
located at 12325 E. Roger Rd. in northeast
Tucson, features a natural spring that feeds
into 3 large ponds. Palm trees and beautiful
Santa Catalina Mountain views add to the
pleasures of this lovely park. Walking, wildlife
viewing, birding, and picnicking in the shade
are all activities open to the public. Some
of the large mesquite trees are thought to
be over 200 years old, and the site was first
occupied as early as 5,500 years ago. Rarely
crowded, the park is a terrific spot for a picnic
or for lounging with a great book. The lovely
Ranch House Visitor Center and Art Gallery
are open seasonally. The park offers many
educational programs and early-morning
bird-watching walks.

SANTA CRUZ RIVER PARK
(520) 877-6000
www.pima.gov/nrpr/parks/santacruz_
riverpark/index.htm

Beginning at Grant Road on the north and
traveling to 29th Street/Silverlake Road—
with a short break between Silverlake Road
and Ajo Way—cyclists, joggers, walkers, and
skaters take advantage of this linear park

along the banks of the Santa Cruz River for recreation and transportation.

Sites along the way include the Garden of Gethsemane, a huge stone monument with various religious figures (see the Attractions chapter), a disc golf course, beautiful ceramic work by local artist Susan Gamble, and Tucson's largest tree—a huge eucalyptus measuring 4 feet in diameter located just under the Congress Street Bridge. Picnic sites are also available.

At El Paseo de los Arboles, a park within a park, trees can be planted in a grove as a living remembrance of a loved one or for a special occasion. This tiny park has won national recognition for planning and implementation. Planting is done on a scheduled basis.

Parking with access to the east side of the park can be found north of Speedway Boulevard or near the 22nd Street Bridge where each street intersects the bike path. Parking with access to the west side can be found just south of Speedway Boulevard.

TUCSON MOUNTAIN PARK
(520) 877-6000
www.pima.gov/nrpr/parks/tmp/index.htm

Located west of the city, Tucson Mountain Park, a 20,000-acre desert preserve, has thick stands of saguaro cactus; great hiking, biking, and camping; and, some say, the best place in the Tucson Basin to see a sunset, at Gates Pass. Maintained by the county, the park borders Saguaro National Park West. Enter the park at Ajo Way and Kinney Road.

CITY OF TUCSON PARKS & RECREATION

The City of Tucson maintains an award-winning Parks and Recreation Department. Not only does the department operate more than 125 parks (many with swimming pools, tennis courts, and picnic areas), but Parks and Rec also has year-round classes, arts and crafts shows, a zoo, an outstanding after-school and summer program, senior programs, fast-pitch and slow-pitch coed softball leagues, adult volleyball and basketball leagues, and swimming programs. The city also runs more than a dozen rec centers that serve as neighborhood meeting places for young and old alike.

i For a lovely new hike in Tucson Mountain Park, try the 2-mile Hidden Canyon Trail. You'll enjoy lots of expansive views. Go west on 22nd Street (it becomes Starr Pass Boulevard). Just before the Starr Pass Resort, turn right onto the service drive. Wind around another 0.25 mile to the trailhead on the right. Parking is allowed along the road.

The *City of Tucson Parks and Recreation Program Guide and Class Catalog* is available at any of the city's centers or area libraries and select retailers. You can also check the Web at www.tucsonaz.gov/parksandrec for a comprehensive listing of parks, centers, and events or call (520) 791-4873 for more information.

You'll find an assortment of public art in city (and county) parks, thanks to forward-thinking local government leaders. One percent of the city's park department budget for capital improvements from bond funds is earmarked for public art. Works are chosen with the help of the Tucson/Pima Arts Council.

Programs, Classes & Leisure Activities

KIDCO
(520) 791-4873

Designed with the elementary school kid in mind, this safe, creative program will please both children and parents. Arts and crafts, games, and a citywide carnival are just a few of the elements that make up this after-school and summer recreation program for ages 5 through 12. (See the Education & Child Care chapter.)

YOUTH AND TEEN PROGRAMS

Numerous after-school and summer programs are available for kids ages 12 through 17. The after-school Junior Teen Scene for 12- to 14-year-olds provides recreation activities with special focus themes in life skills, arts and crafts, dance and music, community service projects, sports, games, and career development. Specific rec centers offer a wide variety of activities, from martial arts to tennis lessons. A Junior Leadership Volunteer Program for 13- to17-year-olds teaches kids to assist youth program staff throughout the year working with after-school and recreation programs.

SENIOR PROGRAMS
(520) 791-4873

Recognizing that many of the retirees in Tucson are anything but retiring, Parks and Rec has developed an extensive array of activities for seniors. From the Senior Olympic Festival (see the Festivals & Events chapter) to a friendly game of bridge at one of the designated senior centers, those over 50 can attend classes in everything from Tai Chi

to tennis, join a collectors club or a hiking group, or just plain socialize.

ADAPTIVE RECREATION CENTER (ARC)
1000 S. Randolph Way
(520) 791-5643

Among the many swimming pools with waterslides, splash areas, wading pools, diving boards, lap lanes, and myriad classes, the Edith Ball Adaptive Recreation Center, located in Reid Park near the zoo, is a fully accessible, state-of-the-art facility that offers both specialized and inclusive programs for people with disabilities as well as general-use participants. The facility contains 2 pools, including a heated outdoor recreational pool that is covered by an attractive tent. This pool has a zero-depth entry, a "spray-ground" water feature, 4 lap lanes, and a walking channel with a current to provide resistance during water walking exercise. The second pool is a heated indoor therapy pool used exclusively by people with disabilities.

TUCSON CITY PARKS

Tucson has hundreds of parks, maintained by the city and the county. Comprehensive listings of these and the facilities available at each are available at the websites for the City of Tucson Parks and Recreation Department (http://cms3.tucsonaz.gov/parksandrec) and the Pima County Natural Resources Parks and Recreation (www.pima.gov/nrpr). Here is an overview of some of the most popular ones.

BRANDI FENTON MEMORIAL PARK
3482 E. River Rd.
www.pima.gov/nrpr/parks/brandi_
fenton/index.htm

This lovely park has something for everyone—kids, horses, dogs, walkers, runners, you name it! The 56.7-acre park is north of the Rillito River at River Road and Alvernon Way.

The park sits on the edge of the Rillito River park and offers covered basketball courts (you will appreciate this when temps hit the 90s), 2 grassy off-leash dog parks, soccer fields, a kids' splash park, a shaded playground, walking paths, an equestrian arena, ramadas, and grills.

An antiques fair takes place on the grounds seasonally every third Sunday. The park was created in 2005 to commemorate the life of Brandi Fenton, who died tragically in an accident at the age of 13.

CHRISTOPHER COLUMBUS PARK
4600 N. Silverbell Rd.
Site of one of 3 city parks with a lake, Christopher Columbus Park offers sailboating—use the launch ramp—and fishing on Silverbell Lake (see the Close-up in this chapter; no swimming allowed). Picnic areas with grills, ramadas, and a playground are also in the park. Model airplane fans can enjoy their hobby at the park's model airplane facility.

A popular feature of this west-side park is a leash-free dog run. The 14,000-square-foot area is open from dawn to 2 to 3 hours after dusk and features a Fido fountain.

FORT LOWELL PARK
2900 N. Craycroft Rd.
A trip to this midtown lovely is more than just a walk in the park. Here you will also find a history lesson or two and see the remains of buildings that were once part of historic Fort Lowell, an outpost that guarded the town of Tucson. (See the Attractions chapter.)

Tennis courts, a swimming pool, a playground, a jogging path, an assortment of fields with and without lights, handball and racquetball courts with lights, and both sand and grass volleyball courts attract visitors all week long. A pond attracts ducks and other waterfowl. Parking and picnic spots with ramadas can also be found.

The entrance to the park and parking is just east of the intersection of Glenn Street and Craycroft Road.

GOLF LINKS SPORTS COMPLEX
2400 S. Craycroft Rd.
This wide-open recreation area is the site of many soccer games in the evening and on weekends. Four softball fields with lights are also a busy part of this park. Trees are plentiful.

HIMMEL PARK
1000 N. Tucson Blvd.
With a great number of tall, mature shade trees and a gorgeous swimming pool and kids' pool, Himmel Park is one of the "coolest" spots in town. Athletes young and old can enjoy the exercise course, the Little League and soccer fields, and the tennis courts. The courts are lit at night, and the park serves as one of the sites for the city's USTA tennis league program.

For a more leisurely choice, you can always pack a lunch to munch at one of the picnic sites or grab a book from the public library on-site (don't forget to apply for your library card first).

Located just 1 block south of Speedway Boulevard on Tucson Boulevard, Himmel Park is easily accessible with plenty of free parking.

Close-up

Urban Fishing

Rejoice, all who love to fish! Even though we live in a desert, there are several man-made lakes teeming with fish all around town. So, take your rod, your bait, lots of water, and sunscreen and head out to hook some dinner.

KENNEDY PARK

3600 S. La Cholla Blvd.
(520) 791-5909, (520) 837-8013
www.azgfd.gov/h_f/urban_lake_kennedy.shtml
A 10-acre lake smack in the middle of Kennedy Park, the lake is stocked with trout, bass, sunfish, and catfish. With a maximum depth of 12 feet, you can bring a small fishing boat or canoe, but no motor boats are allowed here. No live bait, so bring your fancy lures to catch these fishies. Open daily 6 a.m. to 10:30 p.m.

LAKESIDE LAKE

Chuck Ford Lakeside Park
8300 E. Stella Rd.
(520) 791-5909, (520) 837-8013
www.azgfd.gov/h_f/urban_lake_lakeside.shtml
This 14-acre, 35-foot-deep lake is teeming with trout, bass, crappie, sunfish, carp, and catfish. You can float under the blue Tucson skies on Lakeside Lake in a canoe or small fishing boat (14 feet and under). No live bait allowed here. If you get tired of waiting for the fish to bite, there's a lovely walking trail—stretch your legs and then go back to your fishing. Open daily 6 a.m. to 10:30 p.m.

SILVERBELL LAKE

Christopher Columbus Regional Park
4600 N. Silverbell Rd.
(520) 791-5909, (520) 837-8013
www.azgfd.gov/h_f/urban_lake_silverbell.shtml
Located in one of Tucson's oldest parks, Silverbell Lake (only 5 feet deep) is home to stocked trout, bass, catfish, sunfish, and white amur. You can take up to 4 catfish, so throw in your line and get the deep fryer ready for a fish fry! Non-fishermen can

---

JACOBS PARK
3300 N. Fairview Ave.
Jacobs Park offers all the amenities of a large city park while still maintaining the feel of a cozy neighborhood park. Located on the near west side (3 blocks south of Prince Road on Fairview Avenue), this urban green space has a new play pool, a swimming pool, a

YMCA, ball diamonds, soccer fields, swings, slides, grills, picnic areas, a small dog park, and acres of open space where the kids can frolic; or let them cool down under the shade of one of the large old trees in the park. Weekdays will find the locals enjoying a quiet respite, while the weekends are filled with soccer league games, picnickers, and spend their time at the model airplane area and model boat lake. No gas motor boats or live bait here. Open daily 6 a.m. to 10:30 p.m.

SAHUARITA LAKE

Sahuarita Lake Park
15466 S. Rancho Sahuarita
(520) 822-8896
www.azgfd.gov/h_f/urban_lake_sahuarita.shtml
Just south of Tucson in the family-friendly community of Sahuarita (see the Neighborhoods chapter), you'll find this 10-acre, 12-foot-deep lake, open sunrise to sunset. Catfish, trout, sunfish, and bass reside in the depths here just waiting to grab your line. No live bait here; small, non-gas boats are OK. If you tire of waiting for your bobbin to go under, you might find live music at the amphitheater in the park.

THE SKINNY ON URBAN FISHING LICENSES

Arizona Game and Fish Department regulations state that "a valid fishing license is required of any person, except residents or non-residents under the age of 14 (14) years and blind residents, for taking aquatic wildlife from public waters." This means that if you are 14 or over, you will need to purchase a license before putting your line in the water.

For Urban Lake fishing *only*, the following licenses are available at major sporting goods stores like Big 5 and Sports Authority and at Walmart and Kmart sporting goods departments.

1. Urban license: $18.50 for the calendar year allows you to fish in all urban lakes.

2. One-day urban license: $16.75 allows you to fish in urban lakes for 1 day only.

Be sure to specify that you want an urban license, as numerous other fishing licenses are available. For more details, call the Tucson office of the Arizona Game and Fish Department at (520) 628-5376.

The Arizona Game and Fish Department also publishes a terrific free urban fishing guidebook, available at over 330 sporting goods stores statewide. The guide includes a fish-stocking calendar, fishing regulations, and lake and park maps.

city league baseball and softball. A YMCA, which is housed in the recreation center, is the site of many senior activities.

J. F. KENNEDY PARK
Ajo Way at Mission Road
Kennedy Park is known for its well-stocked fishing lake (see Close-up this chapter). This popular south-side park also offers picnic sites with ramadas, soccer fields, multiple-use courts, Little League fields, a grassy volleyball area, a swimming pool, and lighted tennis and basketball courts, in addition to the outdoor fiesta area. Kennedy Park is easy to find. Take either Ajo Way west or Mission Road south. The park is at the southwest

corner of the intersection of Ajo Way and Mission Road.

LAKESIDE PARK
8300 E. Stella Rd.

Boaters and anglers will be pleased with the fishing and boating at this east-side favorite (see Close-up this chapter). Boating is restricted to small sailboats, rowboats, and canoes. But Lakeside Park has much more to offer than just water sports.

All fields, with the exception of the Little League field, have lights. Picnic sites, with and without ramadas, can be found. Joggers can take a turn along a pleasant path around the lake, and kiddies can spend some time on the playground equipment.

MCCORMICK PARK
2950 N. Columbus Ave.

At first glance, McCormick Park (named for Ada McCormick) may appear to be one of the many tiny parks that dot the city, but on closer inspection you'll notice a baseball field, an exercise course, a grassy volleyball area, a basketball court, a rec center, a playground, and a fair share of picnic ramadas with grills.

Located in midtown, McCormick Park is near the Central-Lighthouse-City YMCA, which houses a pool. The park is located about a block and a half south of Fort Lowell Road on Columbus Avenue.

MORRIS K. UDALL PARK, UDALL CENTER
7290 E. Tanque Verde Rd.
(520) 791-4931

One of the larger and most popular Parks and Recreation centers, Udall offers the latest in recreational facilities and a senior center. The rec center has workout rooms,

racquetball courts, an indoor track, arts and crafts rooms, meeting rooms, and a heated pool. The center offers myriad programs and activities. Hundreds of leisure classes are held here throughout the year. The center is open daily.

The park area is also top-shelf, with an outdoor amphitheater, lighted volleyball courts, a playground, off-leash dog parks, and fields for all kinds of organized sports. Take a jog on the well-maintained jogging path, or enjoy a picnic in one of the shady ramadas.

RANDOLPH RECREATION COMPLEX
200 S. Alvernon Way
(520) 791-4560

This is the city's main recreation center and will please athletes and nonathletes alike. Encompassing a gymnasium, a swimming pool, a tennis center, and performing arts and arts and crafts buildings, you can be assured there is always something going on here. Parking is plentiful.

RANDOLPH ARTS AND CRAFTS BUILDING

A complete lapidary shop, ceramics room with kilns, children's crafts room, and painting studio make the Arts and Crafts Building one of the most popular recreation sites in Tucson. The pottery shop and photo lab are located adjacent to the Arts and Crafts Building. A wide variety of classes include drawing, calligraphy, enameling, and jewelry.

RANDOLPH PERFORMING ARTS BUILDING

Dance, music, and dramatic art classes are offered here along with a dance room, music studio with piano lab, and fully equipped auditorium.

RANDOLPH RECREATION CENTER COMMUNITY BUILDING, BUILDING #1

Randolph Center's central information desk, offices, and meeting rooms can be found in this building. Dance, arts and crafts, and pottery classes are just a few of the activities held in Randolph Gym. Gymnastics classes for infants through teens take place in a well-equipped gymnastics room, along with a slew of great leisure classes. Check the *Tucson Parks and Recreation Program Guide and Class Catalog* for more details. The building is open Mon through Fri from 6:30 a.m. to 8 p.m., Sat from 8 a.m. to 4 p.m. Closed holidays.

RANDOLPH SWIMMING POOL

This wonderful pool is open seasonally. Call to check on hours and programs.

REFFKIN TENNIS CENTER
50 S. Alvernon Way
(520) 791-4896
www.reffkintenniscenter.com

The US Tennis Association (USTA) awarded the center a National Facility of the Year Award. This terrific center, the largest in the Southwest, offers 25 lighted tennis courts, a pro shop, 10 racquetball courts, and year-round instructional programs for all ages. Monthly open tournaments for all ages and levels, tennis leagues, and racquetball clinics round out the program.

REID PARK
22nd Street and Country Club Road

You'll hear old-timers (those who've lived in Tucson for more than 20 years) still calling this beauty Randolph Park. That's because until the Parks and Rec Department decided to honor Gene C. Reid, a longtime Parks and

Rec director, the park was called Randolph Park. Today the moniker Randolph is used for the Randolph Recreation Complex located adjacent to Reid Park (see separate listing above for details).

This gem in the parks department crown comprises the city zoo, a beautiful rose garden, a large pond, ball fields, picnic areas with grills and some ramadas for shade, a sports complex/baseball field, a performing arts amphitheater, and the Randolph Rec Complex.

Mature trees and plenty of grass make this an ideal spot for a family picnic. Evenings and weekends are filled with city league slow-pitch softball and volleyball games.

DEMEESTER PERFORMING ARTS CENTER IN REID PARK
22nd Street and Country Club Road
(520) 791-4873

This lovely little band shell is one of the nicest touches in Reid Park—the site of Shakespeare in the Park, numerous music concerts, and other live performances. Seating is, for the most part, on the grass. Bench seating is available for 60 to 100 people. You'll notice a molded-concrete sculpture on the band shell. The 6 figures represent all aspects of the arts, and the sculpture is appropriately named *Celebrate the Arts*. This was the first piece of public art commissioned under the city's One Percent for Art program.

HI CORBETT FIELD IN REID PARK
Randolph Way and Camino Campestre
(520) 791-4873

Located in the northeast corner of Reid Park, the lovely Hi Corbett Field is a unique vintage ballpark built in the 1920s (see Close-up in the Spectator Sports chapter). Home to the Tucson Toros, the field seats 10,000 and has snack bar facilities.

REID PARK ROSE GARDEN
22nd Street and Country Club Road
Here you'll find more than 100 varieties of roses. Cosponsored by the Rose Society of Tucson and All-American Rose Selections Inc., the garden is located west of Reid Park Lake. (Insiders know the best blooms can be found in April.)

i Reid Park Zoo offers a variety of specialized tours. One example is a behind-the-scenes tour in which you can visit the zoo kitchen and health center and other off-limits places. Check the website at www.tucsonzoo .org for current programs.

REID PARK ZOO
1100 S. Randolph Way
(520) 791-4022
www.tucsonzoo.org
Reid Park Zoo is a highlight of any visit to the park. With over 500 animals—the South American Habitat Loop features 11 habitats within 3 ecosystems—the zoo is a source of both education and fun for the whole family. Trained docents can answer just about any question posed, and an impressive graphics system acts as another source of information about the zoo and its denizens. As part of the public art-in-the-parks program, a series of bronzes that are modeled to scale is scattered throughout the zoo. Information about each animal is on the sculptures. It's also in braille.

The zoo runs a variety of special educational programs throughout the year, including summer camps and workshops; many are held at the Lee H. Brown Conservation Learning Center. During the hot summer months, Summer Safari nights on Friday from late May to early July are especially popular, as is the interactive wet-play area, which is open daily. Bring a towel!

The zoo also maintains a well-respected captive-breeding program. The giant anteater breeding program is considered the most successful of its type in the world.

Classes are also available, as is a great gift shop. Admission fees vary. The zoo is open from 9 a.m. until 4 p.m. (See the Attractions and Kidstuff chapters.)

RECREATION

Archery
Pima County operates an archery range, which is located in Tucson Mountain Park, just west of the city. Open from 7 a.m. until dusk, the range offers targets from 20 to 70 yards and three 14-target units. The more challenging units are laid out in several choices—animal, hunter, and field.

Day use is $3. Take Ajo Way west to Kinney Road. Turn north on Kinney Road and then go past Old Tucson Studios, continuing for approximately 1.5 miles.

Boating & Urban Fishing
Three city lakes offer boating (small sailboats, rowboats, and canoes only, please!) and fishing: Kennedy Lake in Kennedy Park, Lakeside at 8300 E. Stella Rd. (at the corner of Stella and Sarnoff), and Silverbell Lake in Christopher Columbus Park (see Close-up this chapter).

Stocked by the Arizona Game and Fish Department, the lakes will satisfy any angler, but a fishing license is required for people over the age of 14. All boats must also be registered if motorized. Call (520) 628-5376 for more information or check the website at www.azgfd.com.

LAKE PATAGONIA
400 Patagonia Lake Rd., Patagonia
(520) 287-6965
www.pr.state.az.us/parks/pala/index
.html

This 265-acre lake is very popular with desert folks—and with good reason. In addition to the swimming and hiking, fishers can angle for trout in the winter and a variety of other game fish in the other months.

Boaters can bring their own (only small boats are allowed), or you can rent a canoe, rowboat, or pedal boat for a fee plus a refundable deposit. Call the marina (also the retail store) at (520) 287-5545 for rates. There is an entry fee per vehicle for the park.

Boxing

BOXING INC.
1240 N. Stone Ave.
(520) 882-8788

Boxing is not just for guys—think *Million Dollar Baby*! A great way to get fit fast, these gyms offer over 42 classes a week, including kickboxing, muay thai boxing, grappling, sparring, and mixed martial arts.. Open daily except Sun; most classes are 1 hour long. There is a monthly membership fee. Not sure if boxing is for you? You can try it for just $15—they'll provide gloves and wrappings. Additional locations are at 2524 N. Campbell Ave. (520-795-3333) and 4165 W. Ina Rd. (520-744-7333).

UNDISPUTED FITNESS AND TRAINING CENTER
1240 N. Stone Ave.
(520) 882-8788
www.undisputedusa.com/tucson

This large gym with cardio equipment, weights, boxing ring, boxing bags, and wrestling mat specializes in boxing and kickboxing training. They also offer classes in jujitsu and an after-school youth boxing program. There is a membership fee and lots of specials; you can schedule a visit to check out the facility.

Caving

CAVE OF THE BELLS
Coronado National Forest
(520) 388-8300
www.fs.fed.us/r3/coronado/forest/
recreation/caves/bells.shtml

Part of Coronado National Forest, the Cave of the Bells with its underground lake is located in Sawmill Canyon at the end of a 4-wheel-drive road on the eastern slopes of the Santa Rita Mountains. The cave entrance is gated and protected, accessible only with a key that is available in Tucson at the Coronado National Forest Supervisor's Office, 300 W. Congress St. A $100 refundable deposit is required. Call for detailed directions or check the website.

COLOSSAL CAVE MOUNTAIN PARK
I-10, exit 279, Vail
(520) 647-7275
www.colossalcave.com

Colossal Cave has a colorful history, having been used by prehistoric peoples—and by train robbers. Some say the thieves' stolen booty still lies hidden deep within the cave. Tours are offered daily, but it's a good idea to call ahead, as the times change. A guided tour is a short 0.5 mile. In addition to this 45-minute tour—no reservations needed—you also have your choice of other, more "in-depth" tours. For a slightly spooky, some might say romantic, experience, try the candlelight tour. The tour is held after hours and groups vary between 10 and 20 people, so you are afforded a more personal touch. Reservations are needed for this tour because they are only given on the second and fourth Saturdays of the month. Children under 10 cannot take this tour.

Or for a more out-of-the-way experience, dare to take the Ladder Route Tour. Donning a helmet with a headlight, you'll climb ladders, cross bridges, and crawl through narrow passageways. As with the Candlelight Tour, there is an age limit here—10 years of age. (See the Attractions chapter for details on Colossal Cave.)

CORONADO CAVE
Coronado National Memorial
(520) 366-5515
www.nps.gov/archive/coro/cave.htm
Located at the end of the Coronado Cave Trail (0.75 mile one-way) in Coronado National Memorial, this is a live cave with tunnels, stalagmites, and stalactites that is easy to explore. Two flashlights per person are required; helmets are optional. To enter the cave you must get a free visitor's permit at the visitor center. Take I-10 east and exit south on Highway 90 to Sierra Vista, then south on Highway 92 to S. Coronado Memorial Drive. (From Bisbee take Highway 92 west.) Follow S. Coronado Memorial Drive 5 miles to the visitor center.

KARTCHNER CAVERNS STATE PARK
Highway 90, Benson
(520) 586-4100 (information line),
(520) 586-2283 (reservations)
www.pr.state.az.us/parks/kaca
Discovered by amateur spelunkers in 1974, this incredible living cave was kept secret for 14 years until it was opened to the public in 1988 by the Arizona State Parks Department. Now the central attraction in the 550-acre park, Kartchner is a wet, or live cave, meaning that the calcite formations are still growing. You'll see amazing 70-foot-tall ceilings dripping with many-colored stalactites and stalagmites along with rare quartz needles that form birds' nests and thin stalactites called soda straws that extend like spaghetti. You have to see it to believe it. The cave's relative humidity averages 99 percent year-round, and the temperature stays around 67 degrees. You'll also find a 23,000-square-foot Discovery Center full of exhibits. Reservations are critical. The park is about 50 miles south of Tucson on Highway 90. (See the Attractions chapter.)

Hiking

The Sonoran Desert and the surrounding mountains offer outstanding hiking opportunities. Some are user-friendly; others offer challenges that should only be attempted by experienced hikers. But no matter your status as a hiker, there are several important things you should do when you take a hike. One, always bring more water than you think you'll need. The desert heat can surprise you. Two, always tell someone where you're going and how long you expect to be there. Better yet, take a friend along—and make sure someone knows where the both of you are going! No matter how tempting it may be to spend several hours alone in the desert, it's best to ask a friend or two along. One more caveat: Stay on the well-marked trails to avoid getting lost.

Pima County maintains numerous trails throughout the area, many of which cross state and federal land. You may need to purchase a state permit to hike through some of these areas. During the cooler times of the year, the county also offers group hiking and nature walks. Your four-footed best friend is only allowed on certain trails and then only on a leash. Call the county parks and recreation department for details at (520) 877-6000, or check the website at www .pima.gov/nrpr.

Saguaro National Park's east and west divisions both have great trails that take you through various terrain from desert floor to mountaintop. The visitor centers at each part of the park have information and maps on the specific trails to be found. There are quite literally thousands of hiking areas and trails in the area, so the best bet is to stop by one of the local camping supply stores, like Summit Hut (see listing in the Shopping chapter), to purchase one of the many hiking guides available. Or contact local hiking groups and organizations (see the Insiders' tip in this chapter) for suggestions. Here are just a few of the many beautiful trails to explore in the area.

ASPEN TRAIL–MARSHALL GULCH LOOP
Mount Lemmon

Mount Lemmon offers many scenic hiking trails, including the gorgeous Aspen Trail–Marshall Gulch Loop, located just minutes from the tiny village of Summerhaven.

This hike will take you through lofty pines, lush ferns, and other cool foliage. Altitude starts at about 7,500 feet and proceeds

at a leisurely pace to around 8,000 feet. Because this is a mountain trail, the best times to enjoy it are spring, summer, and fall. Running water is not uncommon in winter.

Take the Catalina Highway north out of Tucson toward Mount Lemmon and Summerhaven. When you reach the junction with the turnoff for the ski area, continue straight for another 1.3 miles (do not take the Mount Lemmon Ski Valley turnoff) through Summerhaven, following signs to the Marshall Gulch area. The trailhead is at the end of the road. The total hike is about 3.7 miles. At the Marshall Gulch Ridge the elevation is 8,000 feet. Views along the way are spectacular.

CATALINA STATE PARK

This state park north of the city is ideal for family hikes. The elevation changes are minimal, while still offering some great views and desert scenery. Several well-marked trails can be found in the park area. The Canyon Loop Trail is a 2.3-mile loop trail from the main trailhead. It goes through some of the lower foothills of the Santa Catalinas. There are several other options, including the Romero Canyon Trail, which leads into Pusch Ridge, and the Sutherland Trail, which heads into Cargodera Canyon. (See the section on Catalina State Park at the beginning of this chapter for more information.)

DAVID YETMAN TRAIL EAST
Tucson Mountain Park

This moderately difficult trail is named for a former county supervisor who was big on desert preservation. Located in Tucson Mountain Park, the trailhead starts at the west end of Camino del Oeste near the end of Anklam Road. The trail meanders for approximately 5.5 miles through chollas,

Hiking Hookup

Looking for folks to go hiking with? Check out these local organizations.

Tucson Hiking Meetup Group
www.meetup.com/tucsonhiking
Part of a national network, this local group organizes all kinds of hikes from beginner to advanced. Members are enthusiastic and friendly and welcome newcomers. The website lists the various hikes planned, a mini map, members attending, and comments.

Sierra Club, Rincon Chapter
www.arizona.sierraclub.org/rincon
(520) 620-6401
This local chapter of the Sierra Club leads hikes almost every weekend, and you don't have to be a member to go.

Ramblers Hiking Club
www.clubs.arizona.edu/~ramblers
Open to the public, this is the University of Arizona hiking club. There is no membership fee. The club organizes a variety of activities as well as all sorts of hiking and camping trips locally and beyond.

To get to the trailhead, take Speedway Boulevard west. Notice the name change to Anklam Road. Follow Anklam Road until Camino Del Oeste and turn left, then travel to the trailhead.

FINGER ROCK

This hike in the Santa Catalinas is really 3 very different hikes ranging from very rugged to user-friendly. All 3 basically begin at the north end of Alvernon Road.

The Finger Rock Trail gives hikers, appropriately enough, a magnificent view of Finger Rock. At the 3-mile point, you will cross Linda Vista Saddle, a great place to pause and catch the *linda vista* (beautiful view). From here you can then continue 1.5 miles to a junction where you can continue to Mount Kimball (turn left/west) or head up to the Window (turn right/east). This is considered by local hiking experts to be rugged and steep.

Two hundred feet from the Finger Rock trailhead, you will pick up Pontatoc Canyon Trail. This 6-mile round-trip hike will take you to pools of cool water during the rainy season. One mile into Pontatoc Canyon Trail, you can pick up the Pontatoc Ridge Trail, which has stunning views of the city, the desert, and the mountains. It's considered an easy hike of about 3.8 miles round-trip. Elevation at the trail's end is about 6,000 feet. At the end of the Ridge Trail are several old mine holes; use extreme caution and avoid this dangerous area.

GOLDEN GATE LOOP

As you hike this easy trail, look up—you may experience déja vù. The ridges along this part of the Tucson Mountains have appeared in many a Western movie.

saguaro, and other desert vegetation. You can catch the shorter, tougher uphill climb of the John Krein Trail about three quarters of the way along. Elevation runs from 2,000 to 5,000 feet. You will cross a wash, just past the Krein Trail turnoff. Remember, if there's a lot of water, proceed with extreme caution: You don't want to get swept away. The only way back is the way you came, for an 11-mile round-trip.

The trail begins at the David Yetman West trailhead at the pullout designated G3, on the west side of Gates Road as you descend from the summit. You'll hike for about 0.5 mile and then follow the sign to the loop trail. The elevation ranges from 2,700 feet to 3,000 feet, making this an easy hike for even the novice hiker. About 0.75 mile along the way, you will come to a fork in the trail. Either direction will loop you around to where you are standing.

Views along the way are great, but vegetation stays about the same, with plenty of saguaros and other low-desert vegetation. One note: At the far end of the loop you will walk awhile along Kinney Road. Be careful of the traffic, and keep an eye out for the return trail marker.

MILLER CREEK TRAIL

The Rincon Wilderness Area rises to some 8,486 feet, offering intense hiking and some of the most beautiful views you will ever see. This 16.2-mile round-trip hike is only one of 5 that lead into the mountain wilderness. Take I-10 east to the J-Six-Mescal Road exit (exit 297), and head north on FR 35 for about 17 miles. Look for the trailhead on the left. The trail is well signed, so getting to the top will be easy to find (although the rugged hike will prove challenging for even experienced hikers). Beginning at the gate—please close it behind you—the trail follows Miller Creek into Saguaro National Park East. The terrain changes from desert to scrub to oak woods. As you pass though the oak stands, the trail begins to get steep. At the Happy Valley Saddle, take the Heartbreak Ridge Trail. Here you'll notice the change to pine forest (by this time you've climbed some 1,900 feet in a little over 5 miles).

Following the trail, you'll come to the signed junction to Rincon Peak. Follow along until you reach the top. Take at least 6 quarts of water.

PIMA CANYON

This challenging hike in the Santa Catalinas will take you close to 5,000 feet in elevation, high enough to perhaps catch a glimpse of bighorn sheep.

The northern trailhead starts at the east end of Magee Road. Although there's some public parking, it should be noted that parking on the road could result in a hefty fine. The first third of a mile passes through a subdivision, and it's best to stay in the fenced corridor. The only drinking fountain and emergency phone will be found at the entrance.

The canyon, with its rocky walls, still allows for great views of the valley. About 3 miles into the hike, the vegetation changes and you might see running water. Another 2 miles takes you to an elevation of about 2,500 feet. Hike another 2 miles and you will reach 4,500 feet in elevation. You'll be at Mount Kimball.

Camping is allowed with a permit. And to protect the bighorn sheep that reside near here, no dogs are permitted. Campsites must be set up at least 400 feet from the trail.

SABINO BASIN

A hiker's visit to Tucson isn't complete without a trip to the heart of Sabino Canyon. Whether you start at the visitor center and walk the paved road to the trailhead or take the tram to the trailhead, you will walk away from the hike enriched by a deeper understanding of the way Mother Nature has designed the area.

The hike from the trailhead has been called easy, and you will see everything from saguaro and cholla cacti to Mexican oaks, cottonwoods, and sycamores at the trail's end. You may even find some running water. About halfway through the hike, you can catch the trail to Hutch's Pool, a popular local swimming hole.

At the trail's end, in Sabino Basin, several canyons join together. You can meet up with other trails at this point, one of which leads 1.6 miles to Mount Lemmon. Choose to take another canyon trail, or turn around and hike back the way you came, for a 5-mile round-trip. (See the Sabino Canyon section at the beginning of this chapter for more information.) Contact the visitor center before you head out, as sometimes trails are closed due to wildlife sightings.

i If you're not into serious hiking, head to Tohono Chul Park for one of their Walk in the Park tours. These fascinating docent-guided tours meander through the 48 spectacular desert acres of the park and are offered at 9 a.m. and 1 p.m. on Tues, Thurs, Fri, and Sat. The pace is slow, the terrain easy and fairly flat. Call (520) 742-6455 or check www.tohonochulpark.org for more details.

SEVEN FALLS

People love this hike, and it's no wonder. Located in Bear Canyon, the trailhead is easily accessible and the 4-mile hike is doable for just about anyone with good hiking boots and stamina. The views along the way are some of the most spectacular you'll ever see.

And yes, waterfalls can really be found, along with lovely natural pools for swimming. The amount of water you'll find, though, depends entirely on the time of year and the amount of recent rainfall. Sometimes, in fact, when there is an abundance of rain or snowmelt, the water can be quite deep and fast moving. It can also be quite cold, so come prepared, and be careful.

Catch the trailhead via Sabino Canyon to Bear Canyon. Follow the well-marked trail to the base of the falls and then proceed, carefully, to the top of the falls. The hike, or climb, as it may better be called, can be tricky, so proceed with caution. For the return trip, retrace your steps. Check with the visitor center to be sure the trail is open. (See the Sabino Canyon section earlier in this chapter.)

Horseback Riding, Hayrides, Cattle Drives, & More

COCORAQUE RANCH CATTLE DRIVES
3199 N. Reservation Rd.
(520) 682-8594
www.cocoraque.com
To experience the true West, why not check out a real working cattle ranch? Family run since the 1890s, Cocoraque Ranch offers several ways to relive the life of a real cowboy. You can do the work that ranch hands and cowboys have been doing for decades by taking a 2- or 3-hour or all-day trail ride where you'll check the cattle, fences, and watering holes along the way. If you can band together 15 or more people, you can do a real cattle drive, during which you'll be in the saddle for 2.5 hours driving the herd from different pastures, then back to the ranch house for a real outdoor cookout with cowboy beans, steak, chicken, and tortillas.

PURPLE MOUNTAIN PACK GOATS
PO Box 1345, Tucson, AZ 85702
(520) 403-4056
www.azpackgoat.com

And now for something completely different . . . custom-guided hikes with alpine pack goats carrying all equipment, food, and beverages. You can bring your own food, but co-owner Tom DiMaggio has been known to serve up some delicious gourmet grub on hikes.

Each trip is planned with the customer in mind. The DiMaggios use information regarding size of party, physical capabilities, and interests to design a one-of-a-kind tour for you and your group. You can traverse any of a number of gorgeous trails in Madera Canyon, the Dragoons, and throughout the Coronado National Forest.

Prices vary and are per person per day (the cost varies depending on your choice of a prepared meal, the number of folks in your party, and distance of the trek). Bring your camera to take pictures, because friends back home may not believe you when you tell them about this adventure. As with any desert hike, don't forget your water.

PUSCH RIDGE STABLES
13700 N. Oracle Rd.
(520) 825-1664
www.puschridgestables.com

Offering a full slate of horse-related activities, this stable is adjacent to Catalina State Park and other areas of the Coronado National Forest. There are 10,000 acres here for your enjoyment, whether you decide to take the usual horseback ride with a guide or one of the many other options available. Pusch Ridge Stables has breakfast rides, which begin at dawn, so you can experience the beauty of a desert sunrise. Or opt for an evening steak ride, where your meal is cooked over an open fire in real cowboy fashion. To add a little romance, moonlight rides are also on tap. One- and 2-hour horseback rides are also available daily.

The stable's hayrides will carry you and your party over desert trails via horse-drawn carriages. At one of the stops you can enjoy a picnic or steak dinner. Entertainment, such as a hoedown or recreational games, can be included. The costs vary per person for horseback rides and hayrides; cash only, no credit cards.

Take Oracle Road north to Milepost 84, then make an immediate right turn and follow the signs to the stable.

ROCKING K STABLES
13401 E. Old Spanish Trail Rd.
(520) 647-0040

This stable on the east side offers trail rides through 6,000 acres bordering Saguaro Park East. The working ranch also hosts cattle drives complete with fireside Western cookouts. Hayrides and sunset rides are popular here. All levels of riders are welcome. Call for rates and schedule.

WALKING WINDS STABLES AT HILTON EL CONQUISTADOR RESORT
10000 N. Oracle Rd.
(520) 742-4422

Trail rides at these stables will take you through beautiful desert and mountain scenery. The ride through the national forest will afford you some of the best views of the area. Both novice riders and those with a little more experience in the saddle will enjoy rides of 1 or 1.5 hours. They also offer sunset rides for spectacular beauty.

Take Oracle Road north to the Hilton El Conquistador Resort; the stables are on the grounds.

Hot-Air Ballooning

BALLOON AMERICA
(520) 299-7744
www.balloonrideusa.com
Balloon America's pilots will float you over the magnificent Catalina foothills. The 2-hour Catalina Mountain Tour soars at altitudes from treetop level to 3,000 feet and takes you toward Sabino Canyon and the base of the Santa Catalina Mountains. After the flight, you can toast with a glass of complimentary champagne.

There's a digital camera on board so you can document your flight. Passengers must be age 3 and over. Call for prices and special packages. There are no flights during summer months.

Baggage and smoking are not allowed, but you are encouraged to bring your camera.

Early reservations are also a must. And you'll pay a fee if you cancel 14 or more days prior to your flight (any later than 14 days will result in your being charged the full price). If the company has to cancel for any reason, you will receive a full refund. The Catalina Mountain Tour is priced seasonally per person.

The balloons take off from La Mariposa Resort at N. Houghton Road between Speedway and Tanque Verde Road. Closed May through October 1.

TUCSON BALLOON RIDES
3079 W. Avenida Cresta
(520) 235-5355
www.tucsonballoonrides.com
The flight path for these 3- to 4-hour balloon rides takes you over the Sonoran Desert, Tucson Mountains, Saguaro National Park West, and the Avra Valley at between 500 and 4,000 feet. The Sonoran Sunrise cruise is followed by a champagne brunch. As part of your package, you get a picture taken from chase vehicles that follow below. Open daily Sept through May; free pickups and dropoffs from all resorts and hotels in town. Private and customized high-altitude (6,000 feet–plus) flights are also available by reservation.

Rock Climbing

With all the mountains that surround Tucson, there are plenty of sites for rock climbing, no matter your level of skill. Favorite spots include Windy Point, on the Mount Lemmon Highway; Esperero Spires, a 500-foot climb near Sabino Canyon; Table Mountain, near Pusch Ridge, north of the city; and Leviathan Dome in Oracle, also north of town.

ROCKS & ROPES
330 S. Toole Ave., Ste. 400
(520) 882-5924
www.rocksandropes.com
For all you rock-climbing hounds out there, this indoor rock-climbing gym has plenty to offer. Thirty-five-foot walls with 125 routes, measuring in various degrees of difficulty, fill the converted warehouse. Fifty-three top ropes can also be found.

Lessons are offered for newcomers. The $30 first-time fee includes lessons, use of gear, and plenty of information. Monthly memberships are also available. Nonmembers can access the gym. Hours run from 3 to 10 p.m. weekdays and from 11 a.m. until 8 p.m. weekends. The doors open to members only at noon during the week. A second location will open on the northeast side in early 2012.

Singles Organizations

EQUALLY YOKED
5125 N. 16th St.
(520) 882-9778
www.equallyyoked.com

Equally Yoked is the largest social club for Christian singles in the nation, with 30 member centers and over 35,000 members. The Tucson location organizes social activities and outings of all kinds.

TUCSON DESERT SINGLES
www.tucsondesertsingles.org
This local nonprofit organization offers a wide variety of singles activities, from hiking and concerts to happy hours and dances at venues all over town. There is a membership fee to participate; open to singles over 45.

Skiing

SKI VALLEY, MOUNT LEMMON
(520) 576-1321 (live), (520) 576-1400 (recorded information)
Ski Valley is the southernmost ski area in North America. At an elevation of 9,100 feet, skiers have their choice of 15 runs ranging from beginner slopes to expert ones. Ski Valley allows for snowboards. Lift ticket prices vary, and rental equipment is available at the ski-lift complex. You can also take a learn-to-ski lesson.

Days of operation are truly limited, and if it's been a dry winter, skiing will be minimal. Call the 24-hour recorded info line for details and conditions. If you are skiing, you will not need to pay the user fee to drive Catalina Highway up the mountain.

Skydiving

SKYDIVE ARIZONA
4900 N. Taylor Dr., Eloy
(520) 466-3753
www.skydiveaz.com
For a view of Arizona that is literally above all the rest, take the 45-minute drive north to SkyDive Arizona. There novice and veteran skydivers alike will find all levels of skydiving instruction and fun.

If you're not quite ready to solo jump, opt for a tandem dive with an experienced diver. And for those who appreciate the beauty of skydiving but would rather keep their feet on the ground, spectating is free. Prices vary on lessons and jumps.

Take I-10 west toward Phoenix and exit at Sunshine Boulevard. Turn right and go about a mile to Frontier Road, where you will turn left. Driving 2 or 3 more miles takes you to Tumbleweed Road. Turn right and proceed for another 2 miles to the school. Closed Tues and Wed.

SKYVENTURE ARIZONA
4900 N. Taylor Dr., Eloy
(520) 466-4640, (888) BODYFLY (263-9359)
www.skyventureaz.com
Afraid to jump out of a plane? Try the next best thing—indoor skydiving. Just an hour north of Tucson, this vertical wind tunnel is a terrific way to defy gravity. Just take a quick lesson, suit up, and you're flying. Open to ages 3 and up, there is a 250-pound weight limit. Be sure to make reservations in advance; they book up quickly.

Swimming

As you might have guessed, swimming is a year-round activity in Tucson. To accommodate swimmers of all ages, public pools can be found citywide. The city swim program offers free swimming lessons for children during the summer.

For older water bugs, there are also adult swim classes, adapted aquatics for those with disabilities, competitive swim leagues, aqua exercise, synchronized swimming teams, diving classes, and special times for family swims.

Hours vary from park to park and season to season, with the Adaptive Recreation Center at Reid Park, Catalina, Sunnyside, and Clements pools open year-round. It's best to call ahead to check hours and times. Full listings of all city pools are available at http://cms3 .tucsonaz.gov/parksandrec/aquatics.php.

Pools may close at the first sight of lightning during a summer monsoon. For information call (520) 791-4245.

BREAKERS WATER PARK
8555 W. Tangerine Rd.
(520) 682-2530, (520) 682-2304
www.breakerswaterpark.com
The giant wave pool is the big attraction at this fun spot. But the 5 waterslides come in a close second. Located on the far northwest side, Breakers is open during the summer season, roughly from the end of May until Labor Day. You'll find a kiddie pool and acres of running-around room as well. No outside food and beverages are allowed, but there is a snack bar. Trees and ramadas offer much-needed shade.

Open Tues through Sun 10 a.m. to 6 p.m. Admission prices vary, but anyone under age 3 gets in free. Tube and locker rentals are extra.

Racquet Sports & Handball

Tennis
Tucson has more than 200 tennis courts among the city, county, schools, private resorts, and clubs. While most of the resorts require a stay, the city and county courts are available to everyone.

Adult tennis lessons are held at Reffkin Tennis Center and Udall, Himmel, and Fort Lowell Parks. The city's USTA tennis league can also be found at these sites. In addition, multiple-use courts are available at many city parks. Fees vary. Call (520) 791-4896 for information. No reservations are accepted.

Tennis clinics are available for all ages, with the Junior Tennis Program offering competitive camps and leagues. The Junior Tennis Program has lessons and games for youngsters on Saturday and after school.

City of Tucson public courts are available at:
- **Reffkin Tennis Center:** (520) 791-4896
- **Fort Lowell Tennis Center:** (520) 791-2584
- **Himmel Park Tennis Center:** (520) 791-3276

Pickleball
Public pickleball courts are available at Clements and Udall Parks.

Racquetball
Public racquetball courts are available at Reffkin Tennis Center and Udall Park.

Handball
Tucson is also the home of the Handball Hall of Fame and the US Handball Association (www.ushandball.org). There is an annual membership fee, and with it you get a monthly magazine and information on tournaments and league play. Contact the USHA at (520) 795-0434.

GOLF

Yes, there is grass in Tucson! And you'll find most of it on the superb golf courses that dot the city. Lush green grass, mountain views, bright blue skies, and over 25 courses in the city alone make Tucson a golfer's dream come true. You can literally hit the links here 365 days a year on courses designed by top architects like Tom Fazio, Arthur Hills, Robert Trent Jones Jr., and Tom Weiskopf. You can choose from a vast variety of course types, locations, and prices—from posh resorts charging up to hundreds of dollars in peak season for a round with cart to municipal courses at less than $40 with cart. The county course and five municipal courses are maintained at standards that in most parts of the country are reserved for the best country clubs, so even if you're on a budget, you can play on truly superb courses.

OVERVIEW

Summer golfing in Tucson offers some outstanding values, with prices up to half the peak winter season rates and tee times that you don't have to scramble to get. You may not want to drive, chip, or putt golf balls in the midday heat, but courses are open sunrise to sunset, so you can play when temperatures are more bearable.

For visitors or newcomers to Tucson, the hardest part of the game may well be finding the golf course. Many of the courses have obscure addresses—they're on streets named just for the golf course, for example, and the street names give no clue as to where they really are. So to help you find the links you're looking for, we include some major cross streets or other directions that will get you there with a lot less frustration. Except for the day-trip courses at the end of the chapter (which are listed geographically), the courses are listed strictly in alphabetical order, but we tell you where in the area each is located to help you decide which to play

when. We also tell you which courses are semiprivate, meaning that you'll need to be a member of the club or guest at the resort to play them. Courses that are strictly private are not listed here.

Most Tucson courses have four seasons for determining fees. The peak season usually runs from early January to mid or late April, when the fees are steepest. Prices are lower in the fall or early winter season, usually October through December, and in the spring or early summer season (mid- or late April through May or June). Lowest rates—often more than 50 percent off the peak rates—are offered in summer, generally running June or July through August or September. Most courses offer "twilight" rates year-round, typically beginning around 2 p.m. Nearly every course is open sunrise to sunset, which means longer playing hours in summer than in winter.

If you're a golfer who prefers the old-fashioned way of golfing—walking rather than riding a cart—you'll need to select your courses carefully. Most courses in the Tucson area just aren't made for walking and won't even permit it; the desert terrain is too rocky and hilly or the courses are too long to reasonably walk them. If you're looking for a course to walk, watch for those that say traditional (although even that's not a guarantee you can walk it). The best ones would be most of the municipal courses, plus Crooked Tree, Dorado, Quail Canyon, and Green Valley's Haven and Tortuga. But not to worry, you can still get lots of walking in at other courses by keeping your cart on the cart path and walking to your shots.

TIPS ON PLAYING CITY COURSES

You may not need a golf lesson, but if you're planning to play any of the five excellent Tucson municipal courses, we offer this lesson in how best to navigate them. It's critical that you know about the reservation system, and you also may want to know some of the great ways to save money.

There are three ways to make reservations at Tucson municipal golf courses. You can call (520) 791-4336 to speak with a live customer service representative 24 hours per day, you can log on to www.tucsoncity golf.com and book a tee time six days in advance, or you can visit www.golfnow.com and reserve there.

If you are a Tucson resident, your best bet is to get a Resident Reward card for $20, which you can do by showing your Tucson driver's license and a document with a valid Pima County address to the folks at Randolph Golf Course's Pro Shop at 600 N. Alvernon Way. This resident program will

entitle you to discounts at certain times of the year and also to certain rewards.

Nonresidents can get the same discounts by purchasing a $75 nonresident reward card, entitling you to resident rates at the municipal golf course. In either case, you will need to reserve by providing a credit card number.

Another great way to save money if you're age 62 or older is the senior's card. Its discounts are slightly less than the resident's card, but you'll save a couple of bucks—even more if you have both cards. Inquire about this card at the Tucson City Golf number or office listed above or at any of the municipal courses. Senior rates do not apply January through March.

GOLF COURSES

ARIZONA NATIONAL GOLF CLUB
9777 E. Sabino Greens Dr.
(520) 749-3519, ext. 401
www.arizonanationalgolfclub.com
Robert Trent Jones Jr. designed this beauty of a classic desert golf course at the foot of the Santa Catalina Mountains to be as challenging as the rugged natural flow of the land. Instead of carving up the terrain, the design meshes with the land and its natural hills, arroyos, rocks, and stands of giant saguaro cacti. So although it tests the limits of your ability, it also offers the tranquility of spectacular scenery, including the rare beauty of 9 natural desert springs. Accuracy is a hallmark of this course. It will take your best and biggest hits to play the 625-yard number 11, for example.

From the longest of 3 tee positions, the par 71 course is 6,776 yards and rated 72.4. Arizona National Golf Club has a great driving range as well as a putting green and clubhouse. In peak season the rate is $99 on weekends for 18 holes with a cart. Take Tanque Verde Road northeast to Catalina Highway. Go left onto Catalina Highway and take a left onto Houghton going north. Take a left on Snyder and a right onto Sabino Greens Drive.

THE CROOKED TREE GOLF COURSE AT
ARTHUR PACK REGIONAL PARK
9101 N. Thornydale Rd.
(520) 744-3366
www.crookedtreegolfcourse.com
Located on the northwest side of town, this county-owned 18-hole golf course is designed to be difficult, yet friendly. Greens are true and quick, while fairways have also been upgraded. The practice facility is superb, and walkers will enjoy the scenic mountain and desert vistas. Championship tees have been lengthened and improved, leading to more challenging play for the low handicapper.

City and county amateur championships are often played here, and it's often possible to just walk onto the course without advance reservations, especially in summer. For 18 holes in peak season, the weekend cost is $50 with a cart. Seniors are eligible for a small discount on the playing rates. Facilities include a driving range, renovated clubhouse, chipping green, and putting green. The views of Pusch Ridge at the base of the Santa Catalina Mountains are a real bonus.

DELL URICH MUNICIPAL GOLF COURSE
600 S. Alvernon Way
(520) 791-4161
www.tucsoncitygolf.com
This course was redesigned, renovated, and renamed in 1996. It used to be the south course to Randolph North, and they were both known by the name Randolph. They are the most centrally located courses in Tucson if you're staying in the downtown area or anywhere nearby and want a great golf course with a midwestern feel that you can get to quickly. Both courses are accessed from Alvernon Way just north of 22nd Street, and they share facilities such as practice green, driving range, and clubhouse. As with the other municipal courses, it would be hard to find a better golfing venue for the money, or even for more money. Of the 2 side-by-side courses, the 18-hole, 6,633-yard (70.8 rating), par 70 Dell Urich is shorter and less challenging, but the renovation did add more contours. Its straightforward layout and smooth terrain make Dell Urich (pronounced YOU-rick) great for novices or a quick round of golf. Like all the municipal courses, discounts are available for residents and seniors, and you must use the automated central phone system—explained in detail earlier in this chapter—to reserve tee times.

Rates vary widely by season and residency status. Reservations are necessary during the peak season—sometimes weeks in advance.

DORADO GOLF COURSE
6601 E. Speedway Blvd.
(520) 885-6751
This par 62 public course is conveniently located on the near east side of town right off a main byway. But it's also nicely secluded in the midst of a lovely, quiet residential community. Dorado is a traditional grassy course and well maintained with bent grass greens. You can play 9 or 18 holes quickly on this executive course and only pull out your driver once or twice. Long yardage is 3,751 at a rating of 58.9. During the winter peak

season, it's best to call several days to a week ahead for reservations. The best deals at this course are reduced fees after noon, available year-round. There's a chip-and-putt area and a snack bar. The course is close to several hotels. The winter weekend rate for Dorado is $32 for 18 holes with a cart.

i The First Tee of Tucson program, intended for kids ages 5 to 17, teaches kids core life values as well as golf skills. Kids sign up for 3- or 6-week classes and have a ball. The program is funded and sponsored by the Tucson Conquistadores, so the registration fee is only $5 per 6-session class. Classes are taught year-round. To learn more, call (520) 628-1555; www .thefirstteetucson.org.

EL RIO–TRINI ALVAREZ MUNICIPAL GOLF COURSE
1400 W. Speedway Blvd.
(520) 791-4229
www.tucsoncitygolf.com
A favorite for both locals and visitors, this city course is close to downtown on the near west side just beyond I-10. Ideal for the short knocker, this par 70 course measures from 5,824 to 6,418 yards and is rated 69.6. It has a fairly flat terrain with tight fairways, lots of trees, and 2 small lakes. The greens are famous for being small and hard—a pitch-and-run setup.

Facilities include a practice green, well-lit driving range, and clubhouse. The oldest municipal course in Tucson and one of the oldest courses in Arizona, it dates back to the 1930s and was the original site of the Tucson Open. Discounts are available for residents and seniors, and tee times can be made only through the central Parks and Rec number.

For prebooked 18 holes with a cart, the winter prime time (after 7 a.m.) resident rate is $26.

FRED ENKE MUNICIPAL GOLF COURSE
8251 E. Irvington Rd.
(520) 791-2539
www.tucsoncitygolf.com
You'd have to look hard to find a better desert course than this one (pronounced *enk*—no *e*) run by the city. Located on the southeast side of town on a main thoroughfare, this is a limited turf course with substantial teeing areas, large greens, well-calculated bunkers, and tricky sand traps. It's target golf, calling for accuracy over distance. You can choose from 4 teeing areas. White tees are 6,114 yards, rated 69/125. If you play from the back tees and plan to get a good score, you'd better be a good golfer. The heavily bunkered 455-yard, par 4 number 9 hole will challenge anyone. The course offers a practice green, well-lit driving range, and a bar and grill for après golf. From a couple of spots on this course you can see the Davis-Monthan Air Force Base's aircraft boneyard, a pleasant scene if you're into flights of fancy.

Rates vary seasonally and by residency status.

THE GOLF CLUB AT VISTOSO
955 W. Vistoso Highlands Dr.
(520) 797-7900
www.vistosogolf.com
Located northwest of Tucson in Oro Valley, the Golf Club at Vistoso was voted the best public golf course in Tucson by *Golf Digest* magazine. Designed by the famous Tom Weiskopf, the longest of 4 tees plays to 6,932 yards at par 72 and a rating of 71.8. With views of the Tortolita Mountains to the northwest and the Catalinas and city to the

south, the fairways are surrounded by natural washes, giant saguaros, and mesquite trees, producing a stunning and challenging target golf course.

Each of the 18 holes is named—Prickly Pear, Double Cross, Waterfall, Hidden Green, Risky, and Sidewinder are a few that will give you a clue about what to expect as you play them. Facilities include a clubhouse, driving range, and putting green. The peak-season rate for 18 holes on the weekend with a cart is $99 before 1 p.m. Check the website for specials. You can get to the Golf Club at Vistoso from Oracle Rd. by going west on First Avenue to Tangerine and continuing on to Rancho Vistoso Boulevard. Take a left on Vistoso Highlands Drive, and watch for signs in the center divider.

HERITAGE HIGHLANDS AT DOVE MOUNTAIN
4949 W. Heritage Club Blvd.
(520) 579-7000
www.heritagehighlands.com
This Arthur Hills–designed, semiprivate course is part of a country club retirement community on Tucson's far northwest side. Set amidst lush natural vegetation, it's situated at the base of the Tortolita Mountains with views of the whole valley and every mountain range. The course is a loosely formed semicircle of long, angled fairways. With its variety of tee boxes and fairway angles, every game can seem totally different. It's almost like 2 courses in one—the front 9 are flatter and the back 9 more challenging and hilly. This par 72 championship course challenges the best without being too intimidating for the average player. The course measures 6,904 yards from the back tee at a rating of 72.2. Its signature hole is number 13 (a blind tee shot to a plateau

about 35 feet high, dropping to a long green behind an outcropping of rocks), and there are 4 challenging par 5s. Facilities include a clubhouse with bar and grill, driving range, and putting green.

A nonresident golf pass is available for an annual fee. Go west on Tangerine Road from Oracle Road (or east on Tangerine from I-10) to Dove Mountain Boulevard and head north until you come to the gated community that is home to the course.

HILTON EL CONQUISTADOR RESORT AND COUNTRY CLUB
10000 N. Oracle Rd.
www.hiltonelconquistador.com
This resort on the far northwest side (in Oro Valley) offers one 9-hole and two 18-hole courses set amid the dramatic natural landscapes and rolling elevations of the Santa Catalina Mountains. Also available is a comprehensive golf academy.

PUSCH RIDGE COURSE
(520) 544-1770
This 9-hole par 35 course gets its name from the dramatic granite ridge adjacent to the Hilton El Conquistador Resort that towers 2,000 feet above the course. The course winds around and above the resort (on the east side of Oracle Road), offering some of the best city and mountain views to be had. A tight course that golfers describe as the best 9-hole course in the area, it runs the gamut from fast greens to long driving holes to short par 3s. Yardage from the longest of three tees is 2,788 with a rating of 65.6. The course features dramatic elevation changes and some risk/reward holes that offer fun choices for players of all levels. A putting green, plus the resort's restaurants, are available to golfers.

CONQUISTADOR AND CAÑADA
(520) 544-1800

The Hilton El Conquistador's 2 18-hole courses are located not at the resort but about 3 miles away at the Country Club, 10555 N. La Cañada Dr. Facilities include a driving range, putting greens, and a restaurant and lounge.

Both the golf and the views from these desert courses are spectacular. Greens fees are seasonal; call the pro shop for the most updated information.

i The Lodge at Ventana Canyon offers weekly summer golf camps for kids starting in early June. Held Mon through Thurs, the camps offer kids group instruction from seasoned pros, lunch at the pool, swimming, and a spectacular view. Call the pro shop at (520) 577-4061 for details.

THE LODGE AT VENTANA CANYON GOLF AND RACQUET CLUB
6200 N. Clubhouse Ln.
(520) 577-4061
www.thelodgeatventanacanyon.com

The Lodge at Ventana Canyon Golf and Racquet Club is just south of Loews Ventana Canyon Resort, and both are just north of the intersection of Kolb Road and Sunrise Drive in the northeast foothills. The lodge offers 2 distinct courses (the Canyon Course and the Mountain Course, described below) nestled against the dramatic backdrop of the Santa Catalina Mountains. In a 1,100-acre enclave, half the terrain is preserved open space providing a natural habitat for deer, rabbits, Gambel's quail, and other native creatures amid the saguaros and mesquites. Winding through this secluded hideaway are two

18-hole championship courses—Canyon and Mountain—designed by Tom Fazio.

Unless you're a member of the lodge, you may play only the resort course. In peak season you can reserve only 7 days out unless you're a member or lodging guest. It's rather complex, in case you haven't noticed, so call for an explanation if you're still confused. Whichever course you do play, you'll be playing on one of the best courses around.

CANYON COURSE
Area golfers say it can easily take 6 hours to play a round of 18 on this course that offers both some incredible golfing and views amid fine desert scenery. It winds through the beautiful Esperero Canyon and incorporates the massive rock formation known as Whaleback Rock, where at night bobcats emerge from the desert to snooze along the green. The fairways are lush on this 6,818-yard par 72 course with a rating of 72.7. This is definitely a target course where many balls are lost to the desert rough. You'll be impressed by the dramatic finish on the par 5, number 18 island green, where patrons of the restaurant may offer a round of applause if you manage to keep the ball in play.

MOUNTAIN COURSE
This second course at Ventana Canyon is more difficult. The obstacles inherent in its natural desert landscape make the Mountain Course one of the most formidable in the area. At 6,926 yards and par 72, it's rated 74.2. The course's renowned 100-yard, par 3 number 3 signature hole is hit from a peak over a ravine to the green on another peak, and the tee offers a breathtaking panorama that stretches for 100 miles across the Sonoran Desert into Mexico. This is reputed to be

the most photographed hole (other than the Grand Canyon, we presume) west of the Mississippi.

OMNI TUCSON NATIONAL GOLF RESORT AND SPA
2727 W. Club Dr.
(520) 297-2271
www.tucsonnational.com
This top golf resort and spa is home to two 18-hole courses: the Tom Lehman–designed desert-style Sonoran golf course and the championship Catalina course, with yardages from 4,678 to 7,662. The par 70 Sonoran course features steep elevation changes and magnificent views of the surrounding Sonoran Desert. Lehman's design incorporates strategic fairway bunkering that requires players to place their tee shots carefully, while a set of green complexes call for thoughtful approaches and a deft short game. The par 73 (par 72 for the PGA tour) Catalina course has been home to the PGA Tour's annual Chrysler Classic of Tucson since 1976.

Facilities include a driving range, short game area, and putting green, as well as a restaurant and grill. Peak-season weekend play here is $185 for 18 holes with a cart. It's located in the northwest near the intersection of Cortaro Farms and Shannon Roads. Or from I-10, exit at Cortaro Farms Road east to Shannon Road, then go north.

QUAIL CANYON GOLF COURSE
5910 N. Oracle Rd.
(520) 887-6161
www.quailcanyongolf.com
Built by Gil Kammert in 1964, this course is the place to get your short game in shape. It's more of a recreational than professional course, with 18 par 3 holes totaling 2,311 yards. Hole number 4 is longest at 165 yards, number 7 the toughest (it's long with natural obstacles), and number 14's pond is usually home to local ducks. Rates vary seasonally. It's easy to find in northwest Tucson at Oracle and Rudasill Roads.

THE QUARRY PINES GOLF CLUB
8480 N. Continental Links Dr., Marana
(520) 744-7443
www.playthepines.com
This course is located in the far northwest, where the town of Marana is rapidly expanding southward toward Tucson. The Pines is situated in a sprawling industrial/residential development called Continental Ranch, and the course itself abuts the west side of I-10 from about Cortaro Farms Road northward. Tucson's first quarry course, the back 9 holes of this 18-hole course are built on the original 90-acre, 100-foot-deep sand and gravel quarry. The front 9 is a links-style course. The course was designed by the Phoenix architectural firm Gilmore Graves and offers a mix of dramatic elevation changes and stunning mountain views. Course length is 6,486 yards, par 71 with a rating/slope of 70.4/132. There's a clubhouse, 2 practice greens, restaurant, and full-service pro shop. The peak-season weekend rate is $74 including cart and range balls. Exit I-10 at Cortaro Road west, then to Arizona Pavilions Way north.

i Don't miss golfing at twilight, offered year-round at many courses here. The soft night air, indigo skies, and some of the most incredible sunsets are an unforgettable Tucson experience.

Golf Courses in Tucson

Tucson offers a wide variety of courses for all abilities. From top resorts and private clubs to easily accessible public courses, you'll find it all here in this increasingly popular golfing destination. Check our individual alphabetized listings for details on each course.

Municipal Courses
The following public courses are operated by the city of Tucson and Pima County:

- Crooked Tree
- Dell Urich
- El Rio–Trini Alvarez
- Fred Enke
- Randolph North
- Silverbell

Private and Resort Courses
Tucson is also home to the following select luxurious private and resort courses that are open to the public:

- Arizona National Golf Club
- Dorado Golf Course
- The Gallery at Dove Mountain
- The Golf Club at Vistoso
- Heritage Highlands at Dove Mountain
- Hilton El Conquistador Resort and Country Club
- The Lodge at Ventana Canyon Golf and Racquet Club
- Omni Tucson National Golf Resort
- Quail Canyon Golf Course
- The Quarry Pines Golf Club
- Santa Rita Golf Club
- Starr Pass Golf Resort

RANDOLPH NORTH MUNICIPAL GOLF COURSE
600 S. Alvernon Way
(520) 791-4161
www.tucsoncitygolf.com
Randolph North is the longest of Tucson's municipal courses. A favorite of locals, it's a nice course with a midwestern feel. The course features a traditional country club design and is noted for its mature vegetation, tall trees, and wide, expansive fairways. Greens vary from relatively flat to severely sloped or tiered and from large to small. Two outstanding holes are the 15th, a lovely hole of 200 yards surrounded by water, and the 18th, with 2 ponds that carry over from fairway to green. Long yardage is 6,863 with a rating of 72.5. Facilities include a well-lit driving range, practice green, and clubhouse. This is a superb course located almost in the heart of Tucson and surrounded by city parks and recreational offerings.

The prebooked 18-hole resident fee with cart is $40 in winter (Dec through Apr 15).

SANTA RITA GOLF CLUB
16461 S. Houghton Rd.
(520) 762-5620
www.santaritagolf.com

This course is at the foot of the Santa Rita Mountains on the far southeast side of the valley, about a 30-minute drive from central Tucson. Every one of the 18 holes features beautiful views of the mountains, and many offer Tucson valley views as well. The course also boasts some of Arizona's most outstanding bent grass greens. And because it's nearly 1,000 feet above Tucson, it's slightly cooler and a good choice for summer golf. Be forewarned, however, that wind is a factor here on almost every hole.

You can tee off from any of 3 teeing positions, with the longest at 6,337 yards, on this par 72 course rated 70. Five of the holes are very challenging par 3s; the 250-yard number 12 is reputed to be the most challenging par 3 in Arizona, with hazards all the way and a very narrow layout. Santa Rita has a clubhouse and full practice facilities. Rates vary seasonally and by tee times.

SILVERBELL MUNICIPAL GOLF COURSE
3600 N. Silverbell Rd.
(520) 791-5235
www.tucsoncitygolf.com
Silverbell Golf Course is a championship layout located high upon the west bank of the Santa Cruz River. Redesigned by golf course architect Ken Kavanaugh, who molded the old Silverbell course into a more demanding mix, the course has undulating fairways that meander among stands of mature pine trees, strategically placed bunkers, and 2 large lakes that come into play on 5 holes. All the holes are challenging and fun. A par 70 golf course consisting of 5 par 3s and 3 par 5s of varying lengths and strategies will test and excite golfers of all abilities from beginner to professional. Amenities include a practice green, well-lit driving range, and full-service clubhouse. In winter (Dec through Apr 15),

the cost to residents for prebooked 18 holes with a cart is $30. The course is situated close to downtown at the foot of the Tucson Mountains just west of I-10 and north of Grant Road on a main byway.

STARR PASS GOLF RESORT
3645 W. Starr Pass Blvd.
(520) 670-0400
www.jwmarriottstarrpass.com
This 27-hole Arnold Palmer signature design course is a favorite among visiting pros. Perched in the foothills of the Tucson Mountains, the rocky, cactus-covered desert terrain surrounds the lush green fairways and bent grass greens of these three 9-hole courses. The courses are kept at PGA standards all year. There are tricky but fun holes at all three courses. The Coyote course is the longest, the Roadrunner nine is the shortest, and the Rattler is considered the toughest. The desert-style layout challenges players at any level.

The golf club has great teaching facilities and practice areas. In addition to a lovely territorial-design clubhouse, Starr Pass has a great driving range and putting green. The fees vary seasonally. The course is 3 miles west of I-10 on Starr Pass Boulevard (which is actually 22nd Street for most of its length) and very close to the downtown area.

PRACTICE RANGES

If you're interested in taking a whack at some balls with your driver or putter but don't have the time to get to a golf course, you'll find several nicely equipped practice ranges around the city. All are open year-round and have hours generally from early morning to 9 or 10 p.m. but tend to close earlier in winter months. Most have clubs you can rent or just use for the practice, and some actually sell clubs and give you a chance to demo them before you buy. Some also offer lessons. Unless otherwise noted, there is a fee for a bucket of balls, depending on the size, and the putting and chipping areas are free whether you're paying for a bucket of balls or not.

LA MARIPOSA CLUB
1501 N. Houghton Rd.
(520) 749-1099
www.lamariposaresort.com
This is a membership sports and fitness center that happens to also have a golf practice range that's open to the public. You'll find a driving at this east-side spot on Houghton between Speedway Boulevard and Tanque Verde Road.

THE PRACTICE TEE
4050 W. Costco Place
(520) 544-2600
www.thepracticeteetucson.com
This northwest facility is called "upscale" by those in the know and indeed does seem to have lots to offer, starting with 100 all-grass tee stations from which you can hit to actual greens. You'll find putt, chip, and sand trap practice areas as well as lessons; clubs to rent, buy, or demo; and club repair. Ball buckets come in 4 sizes. Look for this facility behind the Costco/Home Depot where Orange Grove Road meets Thornydale Road.

ROLLING HILLS GOLF COURSE
8900 E. 29th St.
(520) 298-2401
Part of a members-only golf course on the southeast part of town near Camino Seco Boulevard, the driving range and chipping and putting areas here are open to the

public. Clubs are available for rental, and you can buy large and small baskets of balls.

DAY TRIP GOLF COURSES

Just 30 minutes down I-19 from downtown Tucson is Green Valley, a bustling and expanding retirement community that's also become a hot spot for golf. It offers beautiful scenery set in the rolling terrain of the Santa Cruz River valley plus a number of spectacular golf courses to choose from within a short distance of one another. And after you've played to your heart's content in Green Valley, just take a swing farther south down I-19 to find courses in Tubac, Rio Rico, and Nogales. You can play for days in this area south of Tucson and never play the same course twice. Good golf packages are available if you prefer to stay in the area rather than drive down from Tucson.. You'll also find a course, Del Lago, in Vail, a rapidly growing area in the southeast part of town.

i Tucson plays annual host to the World Golf Championships–Accenture Match Play Event, one of 4 World Golf Championship events. Eligibility for the Accenture Match Play Event is limited to the top 64 worldwide players. Past champions include the great Tiger Woods. The event takes place at the Gallery Golf Club at Dove Mountain each February.

HAVEN PUBLIC GOLF COURSE AND TORTUGA GOLF COURSE
110 N. Abrego Dr., Green Valley
(520) 625-4281
www.havengolf.com
This was Green Valley's first golf course, built in 1967, and is also one of the easiest to find.

Just exit from I-19 at Esperanza Boulevard (exit 65), go west, look for the large sign to the left of the Green Valley Social Center, and untrunk your clubs. Ideal for players of all skill levels, Haven is 18 holes totaling 6,905 yards (rated 71, par 72). The Tortuga Golf Course is a 9-hole pitch-and-putt course. This course is an excellent choice if some of your traveling companions are just not ready for the big 18—you can play the par 72 Haven course and your traveling companion can keep busy on the par 3 Tortuga, and everybody is happy. The Haven course is a traditional design with grass throughout and mature vegetation. In fact, you may be surprised to see large pine trees interspersed with eucalyptus and palm trees. Panoramic views of the Santa Rita Mountains may lull you into a sense of calm, but don't get too relaxed or you'll miss some shots requiring both distance and accuracy.

The facilities include a driving range, putting green, and chipping green, plus the Overpar lounge. For Tortuga the peak-season fee is $15 (no carts). Haven's peak-season rate is $41.15 for 18 holes, including use of a cart.

TORRES BLANCAS GOLF CLUB
3233 S. Abrego Dr., Green Valley
(520) 625-5200
www.torresblancasgolf.com
One could say that this course rose out of the ashes like the legendary phoenix. When developers began digging out the course in 1994, they actually uncovered a nearly complete golf course that had been abandoned due to the economic conditions of the early 1980s. Under the dirt was what course developers discovered to be a masterpiece layout by Trevino Designs that needed only an irrigation system and a few

refinements. The result is a 165-acre course with a traditional design reminiscent of the PGA Tour courses—the fairways are expansive and considerably wider than most modern golf courses. It stretches along the west bank of the Santa Cruz River and eventually into one of the state's largest pecan tree orchards. Three lakes add to the beauty and challenges of the par 72 course that plays to 7,000 yards at a rating of 69.9.

Annual and seasonal golf memberships are available; fees vary by season and time of day. There's also a full-service gourmet restaurant, the Abrego Grill. Torres Blancas is located within one of Green Valley's residential communities, Santa Rita Springs Development on the east side of I-19, and its Mediterranean-style clubhouse with a tower can easily be seen from the highway. Take exit 63, Continental Road, east to the frontage road, then south to the course.

SAN IGNACIO GOLF CLUB
4201 S. Camino del Sol, Green Valley
(520) 648-3468
www.sanignaciogolfclub.com
Designed by Arthur Hills in 1989, San Ignacio has earned accolades for its excellence. To get there, exit I-19 at Continental Road (exit 63), take the west-side frontage road south to Camino Encanto, and follow the signs. The course is an 18-hole, par 71/72, 6,704 yards with a rating/slope of 72/135.

No matter which teeing position you choose, intelligent decisions and accurate shots are de rigueur. San Ignacio was designed to use the natural terrain to its best possible advantage, and its superb layout makes it possible for golfers to see everything they will encounter from every tee, including the best route to the green. The fairways and rough are Bermuda grass, and the greens are bent grass. The signature hole is number 13, a 522-yard double-dogleg par 5 featuring elevated tees and a double lake along the left side. And San Ignacio offers dining at the Coyote Grill.

In peak season, 18 holes with a cart run $62.

CANOA HILLS GOLF COURSE
1401 W. Calle Urbano, Green Valley
(520) 648-1880
www.canoahillsgolfclub.com
This par 72, 6,610-yard course is a good 18-hole choice for anyone who wants a challenge, yet is fair to the average golfer. Surrounded by the natural terrain and stands of mesquite trees, the fairways are tight yet inviting. Accuracy in placing the ball is key here. The greens are generous, and their bent grass always in immaculate condition. Facilities include a practice range, putting green, and grill. The rate for 18 holes with a cart in peak season is $62. To get here, exit from I-19 at Continental Road, take the west-side frontage south to Camino Encanto Road, and follow the signs.

CANOA RANCH GOLF CLUB
5800 S. Camino del Sol, Green Valley
(520) 393-1966
www.canoaranchgolfcourse.com
This 18-hole course, designed by the team of Schmidt-Curley, offers gorgeous views of Elephant Head and Green Valley. You'll find dramatic elevation changes and beautiful desert surroundings. Note especially the rock wall carved right out of the mountain on hole number 2. There are 6 par 3s here—and they're tough. It's been featured in *Golf Digest* as one of the top courses in the world. Some say that if you can only play one course in the area, this would be a good choice. The Grill on the Greens is a great spot for a delicious breakfast, lunch, or dinner. Rates vary seasonally and by tee times; there are resident, twilight, sundown, and 9-hole rates.

Take I-19 south to exit 56, Canoa Ranch Road. Take the frontage road north about 0.25 mile to Calle Tres. Turn west and go 0.5 mile to Camino del Sol, then turn south and follow the road to the clubhouse.

DEL LAGO GOLF CLUB
14155 E. Via Rancho del Lago, Vail
(520) 647-1100
www.dellagogolf.net
Located about 15 miles southeast of Tucson in the fast-growing area of Vail, this Nugent Group–designed course offers 120 feet of elevation change, a combination of links and desert golf with wide sweeping fairways, and 7 lakes with spectacular mountain views. The first hole begins at the peak of the course, while other holes play down to the valley. Back tees at 7,206 yards carry a rating of 73.9 and a slope of 135; par is 72. With an elevation of 3,500 feet, it can be cooler than Tucson-area courses. The course surrounds the master-planned community of Rancho del Lago and has a driving range, practice bunker, 12,000-square-foot practice green, and a clubhouse with a full-service pro shop and restaurant. This is a Tucson gem, with a great layout and plenty of dimension that helps pull out your best golf.

From Tucson take I-10 to the Vail Road–Wentworth exit (exit 279) and go north on Vail Road for 3.5 miles; the course is at the top of the hill. Peak weekend rates for 18 holes with a cart are $89.

Tucson is host to several professional tournaments. The Chrysler Classic of Tucson, one of the PGA's longest-running tournaments (begun in 1945), is held annually at the Omni Tucson National Golf Resort in February. The LPGA Championship takes place in March of every year at the Randolph North Municipal Golf Course. Both events attract thousands of golf fans and lots of pros to town.

TUBAC GOLF RESORT & SPA
1 Otero Rd., Tubac
(520) 398-2021
www.tubacgolfresort.com

If you're a movie buff as well as a golf buff (or even just a golf-movie buff), you may recognize this golf venue as one of the sites for Kevin Costner's *Tin Cup*. In fact, the lake on the 16th hole was created just for the movie (we hope it poses less trouble to you than it did to Mr. Costner). Located south of Green Valley on the east side of I-19 at exit 40, Tubac is a traditional championship course that winds along both sides of the Santa Cruz River. At this spot, however, the dry riverbed to the north becomes a viable stream feeding the beautiful, stately cottonwood trees that contribute to this course's appeal. The setting seems more quaint and rural than Southwestern. Nine new holes, designed by local golf architect Ken Kavanaugh, were added in 2006, bringing the total to 27.

The original 18 holes were the work of pioneer golf course architect Red Lawrence.

One of its signature holes is the long par 5 Rancho #4, known as Tubac's Tin Cup Hole. You'll find a driving range, practice greens, and restaurant and lounge at the resort, plus it's just minutes away from the delightful Tubac Village (see the Day Trips & Weekend Getaways chapter). A clubhouse, golf pro shop, and practice facility round out the package.

RIO RICO RESORT COUNTRY CLUB
1069 Camino Caralampi, Rio Rico
(520) 281-8567, (800) 288-4746
www.esplendor-resort.com

Continue south down I-19 to exit 17, take a left at the stop sign, follow the large terracotta markers, and you'll find Rio Rico Golf Course, one of Arizona's lesser-known gems. Although the resort itself is on the west side of the interstate, the course is on the east side, meandering through rich pastureland. Golfers here have been known to think they actually were playing in the lush and rolling hills of Arkansas or Tennessee. Fairways are lined with mesquite and cottonwood trees. The classic 18-hole layout designed by Robert Trent Jones Sr. welcomes every player with its rolling fairways and large open greens, plus enough sand traps and water hazards to challenge the best. From its longest tees the course measures 7,126 yards, par 72, and rating of 73. Food and beverages are available at the course, as are a practice range and putting green. The cost for 18 holes on the weekend with a cart in peak season is $69. The resort also has popular golf packages.

BICYCLING

Tucson is a bicyclist's paradise. Miles of scenic trails and terrific weather year-round are just a couple reasons *Bicycling Magazine* ranked Tucson as one of the top three North American cities for bicycling. Whether you're a professional or just looking for some great exercise, this bicycle-friendly city is the place to ride.

HISTORY

Tucson has a long history of bicycle-friendly legislation and planning. At the forefront of bikeway development, the city designated its first bikeways in 1971, totaling some 8 miles. This was the nation's first community plan for a bikeway system, a series of designated bike routes designed to assist cyclists in connecting with other routes around the city.

In 1975 the first Tucson Regional Bikeways Plan was approved by the Pima Association of Governments, and over the next two years more than 56 miles of bikeways were added. The policy was so successful that the Bicycling Federation of America used it as a national model.

The next expansion of this transportation plan was completed in 1981. It called for all new road construction and reconstruction projects to include bike lanes. This direction has helped install over 630 miles of bike lanes in the Tucson region to date. To answer the growing interest in what Tucson had to offer bicyclists, the Pima Association of Governments began publishing the Tucson Bicycle Map in 1986.

All of the planning and policies paid off in 1994 when Tucson was officially designated a "Bicycle Friendly Community" by the League of American Bicyclists.

Now the city and county and Pima Association of Governors each have full-time bicycle coordinators along with a host of nonprofit bicycling groups, advisory committees, and cycling clubs. Plans to expand bike lanes, create bike boulevards, increase motorist-biker education programs, add more bicycle-friendly facilities and bike parking will only enhance this already pro-bicycling city.

HITTING THE STREETS

The free Tucson Bicycle Map can be found at all retail bike shops and public libraries around the area. This multicolored map lists shared-use paths, bike lanes, residential bike routes, and just about everything else a cyclist needs to know to peddle around Tucson. We strongly recommend getting one. That way you can pick the best way to get around town on your bicycle.

Out on the roadways, many of the official routes are marked with large green Bike Route signs, and most have 4- to 5-foot-wide sections with white lines painted to mark the bicyclist's designated roadway. On other busy routes, streets have separate bus lanes that are shared with bicyclists.

When riding within the city, remember that bicyclists have the same responsibilities as motorists. Those responsibilities include riding on the right with traffic, obeying traffic signals, having lights on after dark, and signaling before turning. There's also one additional responsibility: If you're younger than 18, you're required to wear a helmet. (And if you're older, it may not be the law, but it's a very good idea.)

In many areas, even those with good biking systems, riders still have to exercise great care when crossing major thoroughfares. However, the city has alleviated that problem in some areas. For example, the city has two bicycle boulevards that crisscross the University of Arizona and extend in each direction, providing bike commuters a safe way to get to work, school, and entertainment destinations. If you're going to campus from north of Speedway Boulevard, a main east–west thoroughfare makes crossing simple. Three bicycle and pedestrian tunnels have been installed at Olive Road, Highland Avenue, and Warren Avenue, all between Campbell and Park Avenues.

BIKE & RIDE

Sun Tran, the city's bus system, has made it easy to bicycle and ride the bus with its Bike & Bus program. Bike racks are mounted on the front of all buses. Passengers unfold the rack and mount their own bikes, but it's on a first-come, first-served basis because the racks only carry two bikes.

Sun Tran also rents weatherproof bike-storage lockers at a number of locations and all transit centers for a fee. A number of bus stop locations have bike racks for people who want to leave their bikes at the stop. All these locations are listed in the Sun Tran information guide. (See the Getting Here, Getting Around chapter.)

BIKE PATHS

As part of the effort to maintain safe and accessible bicycling for residents, the city has created a series of great bike paths. Each route has its own charm, and all are shared with walkers, joggers, and in-line skaters. As an extra bonus, you'll find many beautiful public artworks along the way.

THE BARRAZA-AVIATION BIKEWAY/ GOLF LINKS PATH

A cyclist can take the path from Escalante and Kolb all the way downtown, crossing the gorgeous bicycle and pedestrian bridges— the Diamondback and Basket. The entire stretch of path is about 10 miles long!

As you drive along the city streets, you may see white-painted bicycles out of the corner of your eye. These are ghost bikes, memorials for bicyclists who have been killed or hit on the street. Part of a national program, these memorials appear in over 150 locations throughout the world. Slightly macabre but beautiful, they are reminders to us all to share our streets.

DAVID BELL BIKE PATH

This bike path is right in the heart of the city. The 3-mile "loop" makes this a great spot for a quick jaunt either before or after work. The pathway circles a good portion of Reid Park, traveling parallel to Randolph Way on the west, Broadway Boulevard on the north, Alvernon Way on the east, and 22nd Street on the south. Access is easy from any one of these roadways. Those who choose to drive can leave their cars in any one of the park's parking lots.

MOUNTAIN AVENUE BIKE BOULEVARD

Mountain Avenue is a north–south primary collector that leads to and from the University of Arizona. The Mountain Avenue corridor was chosen to encourage and facilitate the use of alternative, nonpolluting modes of transportation. Six-foot bike lanes, separated by a rideable 3-foot buffer area, and reduced travel lanes of 11 feet for vehicles effectively make this a bicycle boulevard that provides a connection from the University of Arizona to the Rillito River Linear Park and Pima County Trail System. South of campus, the bikeway continues along Highland Avenue and connects to the Aviation Bikeway.

4TH AVENUE/FONTANA BICYCLE BOULEVARD

A 3-mile north–south route along 4th Avenue and Fontana, this bike-friendly stretch between University and Prince is the first of 40 planned boulevards to cover over 170 miles of in-town streets. Special features include bike corrals, kiosks, special signage, traffic circles, and public art.

OLD SPANISH TRAIL BIKE PATH

Another route on the east side, this one presents a little more of a challenge with its slight hills and dales. The pathway boasts some of the nicest scenery due to its proximity to Saguaro National Park, a great place to park and start your ride. This pathway has been improved with new bike lanes added to make the entire ride easier, with continuous bike lanes all the way to Colossal Cave. An underpass at Old Spanish Trail and Harrison helps cyclists and pedestrians avoid the traffic at the Target Shopping Center.

Don't miss Cyclovia Tucson in late March, when the weather is perfect for cycling. This annual car-free event gives cyclists, walkers, and runners access to a 5-mile loop from scenic downtown Tucson all the way to S. 38th Street. Entertainment and special events line the route. More info and a map are at www.cycloviatucson.org.

3RD STREET BIKE BOULEVARD

The 3rd Street Bike Boulevard is an east–west connector route that provides bicycle access to and from the university and midtown areas. It includes special arterial street crossings, traffic calming devices, and other bicyclist-friendly enhancements. West of campus, the bikeway continues along University Avenue through Main Gate Square shopping district to the 4th Avenue historic shopping district in downtown Tucson.

TUCSON DIVERSION CHANNEL BIKE PATH

At the present time these 2 bikeways are separate paths, but plans to link them are in the works. One part, which is only 1 mile long, offers beautiful desert scenery and interesting artwork along the way. The other part, which stretches for 3 miles, borders a city park and Kino Memorial Hospital. There's some up-and-down riding (on ramps) as you travel along. Sam Lena Park offers the best access and car parking from the east, although you can start at any of the overpasses along the route. Catch the western start just on the other side of I-19.

RIVER PARKS

The banks of Tucson's river systems have been in the process of being turned into recreational facilities since the first River Park Master Plan was introduced in 1976.

Since the first section of the river park was completed in 1987 along the Rillito

River between Campbell Avenue and Flowing Wells Road, the city and county have been determined to build a pedestrian, in-line skating, bicycle, and equestrian trail network. These well-marked 2-lane, 10-foot-wide minihighways will connect all the major watercourses along the Santa Cruz and Rillito Rivers, Tanque Verde Creek, Julien Wash, and Panatano Wash and serve as an alternate route for bike riders to weave through the metropolitan area.

Today two major sections of the river park system exist—Rillito River Park and Santa Cruz River Park. The parks are linked and offer an uninterrupted 23-mile stretch of paths from Silverlake to Craycroft Roads.

Both parks open at sunrise and close at sunset, and each has amenities including restrooms, drinking fountains, parking, artwork, picnic areas with bike racks, and frequent switchbacks that lead down to the sandy riverbeds. At major intersections cyclists are given the choice to go under the streets or cross them. Either way, using the river park system can be either an adventure or a tranquil way of crisscrossing the urban sprawl of Tucson.

Rillito River Park

This east–west river park runs between Craycroft Road and I-10. It's made of a combination of paved and unpaved pathways.

The north bank is designated for walkers, joggers, cyclists, and in-line skaters; the south bank is reserved for walkers, joggers, and horseback riders. Don't make the mistake of riding your bike on the south bank—the park rangers will stop you, and you could be fined. And remember: When it comes to yielding on this well-kept path, bike riders are at the bottom of the food chain and are required to yield to everybody. Parking and easy access can be found at any of the major cross streets. (See the Parks & Recreation chapter for more information on Rillito River Park.)

Santa Cruz River Park

This is a very well-kept river park and the nicest way to transit the heart of Tucson. The park runs from Grant Road, north of downtown, south through the downtown area, and around Congress Street to Irvington Road. There is a break from Silverlake Road south to Ajo Way, but it is easily bypassed and worth the temporary detour along Mission Road to pick up the river trail farther south to Irvington Road.

On the west bank of the Santa Cruz, near the corner of Riverside Drive and Huron Street, you'll pass a playground, ramadas, picnic tables, and restrooms. There's a set of arches designed by local artist Susan Gamble that tell the history of the river and its ancient inhabitants.

Farther south along the west bank is the Garden of Gethsemane, featuring religious statuary by sculptor Felix Lucero (see the Attractions chapter). The statues were made from materials found in the Santa Cruz.

As you ride south and emerge from under the Congress Street Bridge, a huge eucalyptus tree will come into view. At 4 feet in diameter, it is Tucson's largest tree. On the ride farther south are restrooms, drinking fountains, and opportunities to cut down into the riverbed to explore. (See the Parks & Recreation chapter.)

MOUNTAIN BIKING

The entire Tucson vicinity is within easy proximity to mountain and desert parks that offer great chances for off-road riding. The area's splendid scenery, moderate climate, and range of elevations, from the desert floor to the 9,100-foot-high Mount Lemmon, make the surrounding area ideal.

If you plan to enter any mountain bike races, we suggest you contact the nonprofit **Mountain Bike Association of Arizona** (www.mbaa.net). This organization sponsors many area races sanctioned by NORBA.

For maps and information on trails, check the local bike shops for a copy of the Tucson Bicycling Map. It includes designated trails in both Saguaro National Park East and West. The parks also have trail maps, which can be found at the visitor centers in each park. Keep in mind that there are trails specifically designated for mountain biking.

The most important thing to remember when spending any time in the parks is the "Leave No Trace" ethic that has kept these areas pristine. Keep your riding groups small, and stay on the trails to avoid scarring the landscape and plant life everyone comes to admire.

Here are some of the area's best and most scenic trails, which are highly recommended by Sonoran Desert Mountain Bicyclists, who have kindly provided this information and who list other trails, maps, and helpful advice on their website at www.sdmb.org.

FANTASY ISLAND

Fantasy Island is a mountain bike playground in southeast Tucson. It features over 16 miles of twisty singletrack in natural Sonoran Desert and was built by mountain bikers for mountain bikers. It is located off Irvington Road, just east of Harrison Road. Mountain bikers love this place.

Saguaro National Park East

CACTUS FOREST LOOP

Though there are more than 75 miles of trails in Saguaro National Park East (some of which head into the nearby Rincon Mountains), the 8-mile Cactus Forest Loop in Saguaro East is the only section of the park's trail system that is legal for mountain bikes.

To get there, take Broadway Boulevard east to Old Spanish Trail and follow the signs to Saguaro National Park East. You will pay a day fee of about $3 per bike. Because the trail is a paved loop, you will find the trailhead no matter which way you turn past the guardhouse. Be sure to stop at the visitor center for trail maps.

The trail heading north is one-way in that direction, while the loop heading south is two-way for bicycle traffic. Heading south, you'll hit the Javelina picnic area along a slight detour. This is the point where traffic becomes one-way again—from the opposite direction. Some riders take this 1.3-mile route, have a snack, and then head back the other way past the visitor center to travel the entire loop. Others prefer to go north and stop at this picnic area during the final leg of the trip to reflect on what they've seen over the past 7 miles.

Either way, this trip through the desert forest of cacti is enjoyable, and you're bound to see a number of desert creatures lurking in the bush. The trail is accessible to beginners, but more experienced riders will enjoy it as well.

North of Tucson

CATALINA STATE PARK

This is certainly one of the nicest, in-close areas to ride. Catalina State Park is located north on Oracle Road about 6 miles from the intersection of Ina and Oracle. Golder Ranch Road, which leads to much of the 50-plus-year-old trail and the Chutes, is around 10.5 miles north on Oracle from the intersection of Ina and Oracle Roads. Both are on the right (east) side of Oracle Road.

There is plenty of singletrack and some technical areas, along with a whole bunch of beginner to intermediate rides. This area has something for everyone. You can arrange your ride to be virtually any distance or time you would like. There is a 2-mile introductory fun ride, up to 30 miles of killer climbs, and technical challenges. All of this, and it is beautiful as well.

There is a loop of singletrack that will definitely convince people that riding is fun! Go to the parking area at the end of Golder Ranch Road and pick up the singletrack down the road on your right. There are 2 tracks, one about 50 yards down on the right and another about 300 yards along, also on the right. These will eventually join up at a dirt road. You can't miss with these trails. You can do about a 3-mile loop and will really have a ball. Watch out for the cacti, however!

Mount Lemmon

MEADOW AND ASPEN DRAW TRAIL

This is a wonderful, cool ride—7 miles, with the uphill mostly on asphalt. There is singletrack for almost all of the return downhill. This is a loop you will probably want to do twice. Ride it, eat, and ride it again. It is 30 degrees cooler than the Tucson basin and feels all of it. The elevation is 8,000 to 9,000 feet, so the air is a lot thinner and you will most definitely take notice of this. The uphill on the little-used road to the observatory is fairly tough. The singletrack has some technical challenges (logs, wet roots, tree stumps, switchbacks, etc.), but it is rideable by an intermediate who is cautious. If you are out of shape, blow this ride off.

Directions: Take the Mount Lemmon Highway to the top (Summerhaven) and park in the dirt parking area on your right as you enter the village. Get on your bike and head back the way you came in to the turn to the Mount Lemmon ski area and go left. Take this road to the observatory on the top of the mountain. Take the trail from the parking area to the left of the gate on the road to the observatory. The trail is at the west end of the lot. It's a short climb, roughly parallel to the road, and then a slight downhill. Bear to the right at an intersection, and skirt the south side of the observatory. You'll encounter some rocks and roots on the singletrack, but it's rideable. You will come out on a jeep road. Turn left and follow the road, climbing back toward the observatory. When you return to the parking area, find the trail dropping down to the south, and take it a short distance to a gate on the road that goes behind the ski area. (This is close to the road you came up.) Follow that road about 0.25 mile and look for a trail on the left. This is the Aspen Draw Trail (do not go on the Aspen Trail!).

South of Tucson (Santa Rita Mountains)

GARDNER CANYON—KENTUCKY CAMP

This area has literally miles upon miles of singletrack and 4-wheel-drive roads. You can find any type of ride that interests you. It is fairly close to Tucson, much cooler, has beautiful scenery, is well marked (mostly), has caves and lots of history—has just about everything—and some can hike while others ride.

The ride that is featured here brings into play most of the singletrack in the area, uses very little of the 4-wheel-drive roads, and passes through Kentucky Camp (an ill-fated gold-mining venture just after the turn of the 20th century with restored adobe structures). This will let you experience many different riding levels (you can walk parts if you want) and can take as long as you wish because it is an out and back.

Directions: From I-10 and the Sonoita, turn onto Highway 83, head south until you get almost to Sonoita, and go right (west) on the Gardner Canyon turnoff. Take your first right (Y in the road), and stay on that road until you get to the large parking area on your left (a couple of miles). Good maps are posted in this area. Ride up (left/west) the Forest Service road for a couple of miles to a gate on your left at the top of the ridge. Turn left and head down to Kentucky Camp.

INFORMATION, PLEASE!

Whether you need maps or information on trails, local rider clubs, or Tucson bicycle laws, the following quick reference list will help you get started.

CITY OF TUCSON BICYCLE COORDINATOR
201 N. Stone Ave., 6th Floor
(520) 791-4371
http://cms3.tucsonaz.gov/bicycle
This full-time, paid position handles the promotion and coordination of bike- and pedestrian-related projects, including the annual Bike Fest, for the city of Tucson. Call for updates on bikeways, legislation, and special events.

EPIC RIDES
2609 E. Broadway Blvd.
(520) 745-2033
www.epicrides.com
An offshoot of PBAA, this organization sponsors mountain bike gatherings in Tucson and throughout Arizona. Their comprehensive website offers listings of rides and gatherings and an e-newsletter to keep you up to date.

GREATER ARIZONA BICYCLING ASSOCIATION—TUCSON CHAPTER
www.bikegaba.org
The Tucson chapter of this state organization promotes interest and involvement in all aspects of bicycling. To this end it publishes a free monthly newsletter with comprehensive tour and racing listings, legislation updates, and other bicycling news. Their website offers a great list of local rides and maps. The newsletter is distributed by most of the bike shops listed under Retail Shops & Repair in this chapter.

i Love to bicycle but tired of pushing the pedals? Have someone else bicycle for you! Take a pedicab tour of Tucson's downtown and university areas with Tucson Pedicab and let them do all the work. You'll find them on 4th Avenue or by clicking on www.tucson pedicab.com.

THE PERIMETER BICYCLING ASSOCIATION OF AMERICA
2609 E. Broadway
(520) 745-2033
www.pbaa.com
The PBAA is a national group located in Tucson. It organizes El Tour de Tucson every November as well as a number of other

Close-up

Cycling with Others

Tucson is truly a bicyclist's paradise, with great weather and lots of scenic rides. If you're looking for a group to ride with, there are lots of bike clubs in town. Here's a sampling:

DooDah Road Club
This is a great group of people dedicated to promoting enjoyable cycling for the whole family and for all levels of cycling enthusiasts. Annual dues are $18, but it isn't necessary to join to ride with the group. For more information, contact the Head Doo at www.doodahroadclub.org.

Greater Arizona Bicycling Association
GABA rides, competitive to leisurely, are open to anyone. All riders must have a helmet, and all bikes must be in good working order. Check www.bikegaba.org for a schedule of day rides, or call (520) 760-0458.

Southern Arizona Mountain Biking Association
SAMBA organizes bike rides and related events every week. Rides are for varied skill levels in the mountains and desert country around town. Helmets are required. Nonmembers are welcome at all events. If you like what you see, then you can become a member for an annual fee. For more information, call (520) 358-4438. A detailed schedule is posted at www.sambabike.org.

smaller events. The association publishes *Tail Winds*, a full-color, tabloid-size free newspaper, 6 times a year. It's crammed with information and advertising and is distributed at area bike shops. PBAA is a membership-driven organization. Annual membership includes a year's worth of *Tail Winds* plus discounts on any PBAA-sponsored event and many other benefits.

REGIONAL BICYCLE COORDINATOR
Pima Association of Government
177 N. Church Ave., Ste. 405
(520) 792-1093
www.pagnet.org
The Pima Association of Governments (PAG) coordinates the regional bicycle planning process among local jurisdictions and produces several area bicycle maps. Contact these folks with any and all questions about biking rules and regulations.

SONORAN DESERT MOUNTAIN BICYCLISTS
PO Box 65075, Tucson, AZ 85728
(520) 290-0002
www.sdmb.org
This organization is devoted to the promotion of the sport of mountain bicycling by providing fun, safe biking experiences and social events for the mountain bicycling community.

SOUTHERN ARIZONA MOUNTAIN BIKING ASSOCIATION
2720 E. 3rd St.
(520) 358-4438
www.sambabike.org

BICYCLING

This nonprofit, locally based club schedules mountain bike rides on both weekends and weekdays for riders of various skill levels, leading rides into some of the most beautiful and remote country found in southern Arizona.

SUN TRAN CUSTOMER SERVICE CENTER
4220 S. Park Ave., Bldg. 10
(520) 792-9222
www.suntran.com
City buses are equipped with bike racks. The *Sun Tran Ride Guide* lists the times and routes of these buses, as well as other useful info for the city bike commuter. (See the Getting Here, Getting Around chapter for more information about Sun Tran.)

TUCSON–PIMA COUNTY BICYCLE ADVISORY COMMITTEE
(520) 207-5864
www.biketucson.pima.gov
Established in 1987, this joint committee of Pima County and the city of Tucson is a citizen advisory group of approximately 21 people who meet each month to provide direction in decisions affecting the bicycling community. The committee also provides a strong voice in advocating for cyclists needs.

MAJOR EVENTS

A weekend hardly goes by without some group of riders teaming up for short or long rides as a riding club. Here we list a few of the standout events that draw large numbers of people and add some millions to the local economy. Keep in mind that an industry-approved bike helmet is always required to participate in these events.

April

BIKE TO WORK WEEK
http://cms3.tucsonaz.gov/bike-fest
Taking place at the beginning of April, Bike to Work Week is designed to support and encourage bicyclists who commute to work. This weeklong event, supported by the city's Bicycle and Pedestrian program, features free breakfast stations, free bike tune-ups, raffles, and giveaways.

TOUR OF THE TUCSON MOUNTAINS
Various locations
(520) 745-2033
www.pbaa.com
Organized by the PBAA, this event draws some 1,000 cyclists of all ages and abilities to participate in the 73-mile, 27-mile, and Kids' Fun Ride events in April. Starting points vary every year. The event routes riders around the Tucson Mountains.

i Old Pueblo Grand Prix (www.old pueblograndprix.com), a 0.6-mile urban loop, brings professional and amateur cyclers downtown for an exciting race. Spectators are welcome. Check the website for specific dates and times.

September

CORONA DE MARANA MS BIKE TOUR
National Multiple Sclerosis Society, Southwest Chapter
44400 E. Broadway, Ste. 600-0
(520) 747-7472
www.nmss.org
This scenic 1-day loop tour usually takes place the last Saturday in September and starts in Marana, just a few miles north of Tucson. The event is part of a national series of rides designed to raise funds for the

Multiple Sclerosis Society. With several rides, it's a great outing for the whole family. There is a registration fee and a minimum donation required to participate. Riders receive free breakfast and lunch. This is a fully supported ride with rest stops, SAG vehicles, and a bike patrol.

November

EL TOUR DE TUCSON
The Perimeter Bicycling Association of America
2609 E. Broadway
(520) 745-2033
www.pbaa.com
Since 1983 cyclists have turned out for this tour, considered the oldest and largest perimeter cycling event in the US, that actually circles the Tucson area. El Tour is always held the Saturday before Thanksgiving. Every year the proceeds from the race are given to a different local charity.

This is a fun ride, and all participants receive medallions. There are 109-, 79-, 66-, and 40-mile routes and fun rides for adults and kids. The event is a big deal in Tucson, with strong police traffic support along the route for safety, as well as aid stations and medical personnel. More than 9,000 cyclists, ranging from celebrated athletes from around the world to casual bikers, come out to compete or at least participate. Processing and registration fees apply, depending on when you sign up. The ride begins and ends in downtown Tucson.

El Tour de Tucson has been named by *Bicycling Magazine* as one of the 10 best century courses (that's 100 miles for all you nonbikers) in America, and the city folk who come out to watch are very supportive.

RETAIL SHOPS & REPAIR

AJO BIKES
1301 E. Ajo Way
(520) 294-1434
www.ajobikes1.com
This shop promises to provide "wheels for everyone," offering a large selection of kids' trikes, BMX, freestyle, adult road and mountain bikes, and adult trikes. They are also the largest recumbent (reclining bike) dealer in the Southwest. Repairs and service are provided by master mechanics.

ARIZONA BICYCLE EXPERTS
2520 E. 6th St.
(520) 881-2279
www.abecycling.com
Not your average bike shop, this small shop is geared toward the avid cyclist. Staff research and stock high-quality products that are durable and dependable. They carry Santa Cruz, Moots, Orbea, Felt, Race Face, and Chris King; do service and repairs; and will accept and hold bikes shipped from out of town. Rentals are available here as well.

BROADWAY BICYCLES
140 S. Sarnoff Dr.
(520) 296-7819
www.broadwaybicycles.com
One block south of Broadway Boulevard on the east side, this shop has been around since 1975 and offers a full line of biking clothing, accessories, parts, tools, car racks, and expert repairs on all makes. Broadway rents mountain bikes for a 24-hour period.

FAIR WHEEL BIKES
1110 E. 6th St.
(520) 884-9018
www.fairwheelbikes.com

Located in the heart of the university area, this store specializes in pro and custom bikes—road, mountain, and BMX—and used bikes. Fair Wheel offers a complete service department and rentals with pickup and delivery. Mountain bikes and road bikes are available for daily and other rentals.

ORDINARY BICYCLE SHOP
311 E. 7th St.
(520) 622-6488
www.ordinarybikeshop.com
This shop sells new road, touring, hybrid, mountain, cruiser, and tandem bikes and a selection of used bikes. You'll find full repair services and all accessories here, too. No rentals.

ORO VALLEY BICYCLE
12985 N. Oracle Rd.
(520) 825-2751
www.orovalleybicycle.com
A family-owned business since 2001, the staff has over 25 years of experience in the bicycling industry. They offer models from Raleigh, Specialized, Lemond, Gary Fisher, Diamondback, Giant, Co-Motion, Moots, and more and carry an extensive selection of parts, clothing, and cycling accessories. Buy your bike here and get personalized service and free lifetime adjustments on any bicycle sold. They also sell new and reconditioned bicycles, take trade-ins, and offer rentals. Additional locations are at 2850 W. Ina Rd. (520-544-5999) and 4749 E. Sunrise Dr. (520-577-5511).

PERFORMANCE BICYCLES
7204 E. Broadway Blvd.
(520) 296-4715
www.performancebike.com

Part of a larger chain based in California, these stores offer every kind of bicycle imaginable, from tricycles to cross-comfort styles. You'll also find clothing, electronics, equipment, and more. An additional location is at 3302 E. Speedway Blvd. (520-327-3232).

PIMA STREET BICYCLES
5247 Pima St. at Rosemont
(520) 326-4044
www.pimastreetbicycle.com
Do you have an old bike you'd like to get rid of, or not enough cash to afford a brand-new shiny bike? This is the place for you! It's a consignment-only shop dedicated to getting you the best price for your bike, minus their 20 percent commission. Bicycles of all shapes and sizes are welcome—you set the price.

i BICAS (Bicycle Intercommunity Art and Salvage) is a nonprofit community bike shop that offers terrific rides, repair classes, advocacy, and events for bicyclists of all ages. Located at 44 W. 6th St., on the northwest corner of 6th Street and 9th Avenue, they sponsor community rides on the last Saturday of each month and a series of bike-in movies. Call (520) 628-7950 or go to www.bicas.org for details.

SABINO CYCLES
7045 E. Tanque Verde Rd.
(520) 885-3666
www.sabinocycles.com
Sabino Cycles offers a full-service repair department, parts, accessories, clothing, rentals, and bikes for all ages.

SPECTATOR SPORTS

Tucson is a terrific venue for spectator sports. You'll find just about every outdoor and indoor sport here, from minor league baseball and competitive swimming and diving to horse racing and ice hockey. The University of Arizona offers nearly every sport imaginable, including top-ranked Pac-10 teams in men's baseball and basketball and women's softball.

The university's nickname is the Wildcats, and you won't be in Tucson long before seeing signs, T-shirts, hats, or publications touting the Cats. UA competes in at least 18 varsity sports, most of which are very spectator oriented and provide great viewing and great fun for Tucsonans, who are faithful and supportive fans of their college teams. Unless otherwise noted, tickets for all UA games can be obtained at the ticket office at McKale Center, which is on National Championship Drive just west of Campbell Avenue and a block north of 6th Street (520-621-2287; www.arizonawildcats.com). Just remember that any of the ticket prices given in this chapter are subject to change.

In addition to profiling the major college sports you can watch in Tucson, this chapter covers other spectator sports offered in Tucson, such as racing and golf. We also take a slight detour to the north to tell you about the major sports teams based in Phoenix, because it's not uncommon for Tucson residents or visitors to travel there for a pro or bowl game. And finally, we also provide a primer on the major sports playing fields in both cities so you know how to get there, where to park, and what to expect.

TUCSON

Baseball/Softball

Professional

TUCSON PADRES
Kino Stadium
2500 E. Ajo Way
(520) 434-1367
www.minorleaguebaseball.com
The minor-league Tucson Padres make their home at Kino Stadium, part of the Kino Sports Complex. The Triple-A affiliate for the San Diego Padres, they play in the Pacific Coast League. The team moved to Tucson in 2010 and will play all their home games here until a new stadium is built in California. Season runs April through September.

TUCSON TOROS
Hi Corbett Field
900 S. Randolph Way
(520) 325-1010
www.tucsontoros.com
Playing on real grass at Tucson's historic Hi Corbett Field (see Close-up this chapter), the Toros are Tucson's independent

professional baseball team in the North American Baseball League. Host of the wildly popular Thirsty Thursdays and Fireworks Fridays during home games, the team is on hiatus but is expected to return to action for either the 2012 or 2013 season. The season runs late May until the first week of Sept. Check the website for up-to-the-minute information.

i Attention, sports lovers! Head to the Pima County Sports Hall of Fame, located in La Placita Village (110 S. Church St.; 520-406-0742; www.pcshf .org). Founded in 1989, the museum is devoted to the men and women who have had a positive effect on sports in Pima County. Honorees range from high school athletes to professionals and include some of the unsung heroes of sports—coaches.

College

UNIVERSITY OF ARIZONA WILDCATS— MEN'S BASEBALL
Sancet Field
640 N. National Championship Dr.
(520) 621-4102
www.arizonawildcats.com
A testimony to the quality of UA's baseball program is the fact that plenty of professional baseball players, coaches, and managers have come from the team over the past 20 or so years. With its excellent sports reputation, UA can recruit good players, and with weather conditions conducive to lots of practice opportunities, the result is a good team and fans who come out to watch the games. The Wildcat baseball players were NCAA champs in 1976, 1980, and 1986, and play fine baseball every season, which runs from February to May. Led by

Arizona head coach Andy Lopez, the Wildcats appeared in the 2004 College World Series and gained a berth in the Fort Worth Regional in 2010.

Ticket prices vary. The playing field is at N. Warren and E. Enke Drives just across from McKale Center, where tickets can be obtained. The closest parking is at the Cherry Garage to McKale Center's west or another pay parking lot just north of that.

UNIVERSITY OF ARIZONA WILDCATS— WOMEN'S SOFTBALL
Hillenbrand Stadium
E. 2nd Street and N. Warren Drive
(520) 621-4920
www.arizonawildcats.com
The women's softball team is hot, hot, hot. As winners of many national titles, including the 2007 NCAA national championship, their home games are often sold out, and they've definitely elevated the profile of the sport nationwide. The season runs from February to May, and games are played at the 2,000-seat Hillenbrand Stadium on campus. Tickets are available at the McKale Center ticket office.

Basketball

TUCSON FIESTA BOWL BASKETBALL CLASSIC
McKale Center
1 National Championship Dr.
(520) 621-2287
www.fiestabowl.org
This basketball event is played at McKale Center in Tucson. It's an invitational tournament, with the UA basketball team and 1 other collegiate program. Ticket prices vary; call for details. Buy tickets at the McKale Center ticket office, by phone, or online.

UNIVERSITY OF ARIZONA
WILDCATS—MEN
McKale Center
1 National Championship Dr.
(520) 621-4813, (520) 621-2287 (tickets)
www.arizonawildcats.com

Tucson has one of the best college teams, compliments of UA and coach Sean Miller. This Pac-10 team has been conference champions for 8 of the past 13 years, reached the Final Four in the NCAA tournament 4 times, won the NCAA championship in 1997, and was 2001 NCAA runner-up. In 2011, his second year as coach, Miller led his team to the Pac-10 championship and took them to the NCAA Elite Eight. The season runs from November to April and opens with the annual Red/Blue intrasquad scrimmage.

Home games are played at McKale Center at the university, which seats more than 14,500. Your best chance for a ticket is to befriend a season ticket holder who can't get to the game. Individual game tickets may be available at the McKale Center ticket office, online or by phone. As in all urban university towns, parking is at a premium and can be almost as tough to get as a ticket to the game. The closest option is the Cherry Garage immediately west of McKale Center, but those spots are for reserved season ticket holders.

UNIVERSITY OF ARIZONA
WILDCATS—WOMEN
McKale Center
1 National Championship Dr.
(520) 621-4813, (520) 621-2287 (tickets)
www.arizonawildcats.com

The women's basketball team was the 2003–04 Pac-10 co-champion. And their popularity is growing, with several WNBA draft picks from the team including Ify Ibekwe in 2011. They play at McKale Center from early November through early March, with the NCAA tournament games immediately after. Ticket prices vary and are available from the McKale Center ticket office.

i Low on funds but love sports? You're in luck! Admission to the following Arizona Athletics sporting events is always free—just show up: cross-country, golf, gymnastics, soccer, swimming and diving, tennis, and track and field. Call the McKale ticket office at (520) 621-4920, or go online, www .arizonawildcats.com, for schedules.

Football

UNIVERSITY OF ARIZONA WILDCATS
Arizona Stadium
E. 6th Street and N. Warren Drive
(520) 621-4917
www.arizonawildcats.com

When September rolls around in Tucson, it may not seem like fall with temperatures still hovering in the low 100s, but that's what greets the university's Wildcat football players and fans in Arizona Stadium. Sunscreen is mandatory if you're going to a day game, but fortunately most are at night. The Wildcats are in the Pac-12. The biggest rivalry each year is against our neighbors to the north, the Arizona State University Sun Devils. Ticket prices vary. Parking on or near campus can be tough, so the easiest option may be the shuttle buses from the eastern end of El Con Mall at Broadway and Dodge Boulevards and from the Tucson Mall.

SPECTATOR SPORTS

i The University of Arizona offers individual and season passes for tailgating. You can set up your grill and sip your beverages of choice with friends at various locations around the stadium, including the UA Mall, the McKale lawn, and Gittings lawn. If you want to tailgate in style with 100 or more friends, consider the reserved tent tailgating, which includes tent, tables, table covers, fencing, chairs, and trash cans. You can even bring your own UA-approved caterers and bartender! (*NOTE:* Tailgating begins 6 hours prior to kickoff. Alcohol may only be consumed during this time; all tailgating activities cease at kickoff.) Call (520) 621-2287 or (800) 452-2287 for details.

Golf

The World Golf Championship—Accenture Match Play Championship made its first appearance in Tucson in 2007. Since eligibility is limited to the top 64 available players in the world, you can count on seeing the finest golfers work their magic. Past champions include Tiger Woods, Jeff Maggert, and Steve Striker. The February match is played at Marana's Ritz-Carlton Golf Club, Dove Mountain, a Jack Nicklaus–designed 27-hole, par 36 course. Each year the tournament is sponsored by the Conquistadores, a civic group that supports local charities with the proceeds. You can purchase tickets online by visiting www.pgatour.com or by calling (866) 942-2672. (For details on the tournament, see the Festivals & Events chapter.)

Racing

Horses
RILLITO DOWNS
Rillito Park
4502 N. 1st Ave.
(520) 293-5011
www.rillitodowns.com
Rillito Downs is Tucson's only venue for horse racing, which takes place Saturday and Sunday afternoons, usually January through February, but the season length varies. The 0.6-mile racetrack is just off 1st Avenue, south of River Road, and is adjacent to the (usually dry) Rillito River, making it a pretty spot to watch the thoroughbreds and quarter horses run. And it's right next to Rillito Park, so you can take a picnic lunch and make a day of it. The racetrack features outside and inside seating with an admission fee, pari-mutuel wagering, and a full bar and restaurant. In addition to live races, there are simulcast races, and Rillito Downs races are played at several off-track betting sites around Tucson. Parking is free and usually ample.

Greyhounds
TUCSON GREYHOUND PARK
36th Street at 4th Avenue
2601 S. 3rd Ave.
(520) 884-7576
www.tucsongreyhound.com
When the horses aren't running at Rillito, and even when they are, you can still watch races of the 4-legged variety at Tucson Greyhound Park, which is open year-round (except Thanksgiving and Christmas) and has pari-mutuel wagering. Live races are run 6 days a week—Mon through Sat evenings. Greyhound Park also simulcasts races, both horse and dog. For the general admission fee, you'll

watch the greyhounds streak along from a large air-conditioned grandstand, with bars, concession stands, and a nonsmoking area, or from the trackside rail. The park also offers a clubhouse, where a full-service restaurant and bar are available; reservations are advised. Call for race schedules, post times, or clubhouse reservations. Parking is free at the track.

Cars

SOUTHWESTERN INTERNATIONAL RACEWAY
Pima County Fairgrounds
Exit 275 just south of I-10
(520) 762-9700
www.sirace.com
Throughout the year, Tucsonans can head to this drag racing track at the county fairgrounds and see everything from professional fuel cars to novice street cars race on a quarter-mile drag strip. Events at this IHRA-sanctioned facility take place at various times, including Fri evenings. Check the schedule for specifics. Spectator tickets are $5, with kids younger than 10 always free. Spectators are not allowed to bring in alcohol or any glass containers, but the raceway has a full line of concessions, including beer. Parking is ample and free.

MUSSELMAN HONDA CIRCUIT
11800 S. Harrison Rd.
(520) 245-5278
www.mhcircuit.com
Go-karts, supermoto motorcycles, ATVs, and more all use this motor sports facility near the Pima County Fairgrounds for training and racing and to learn defensive driving skills. Home of the Southern Arizona Kart Club, the track (a replica of Japan's Suzuka South Kart Circuit) is 0.07986 mile long and 43 feet

wide, with 13 turns and a 17-foot elevation change. The track hosts a youth Karting Camp in conjunction with the University of Arizona's Youth University (see Education & Child Care chapter). Services include a pro shop and rentals of karts, mini motos, ATVs, and supermoto motorcycles. Hours vary; call for a schedule.

i If you really want to get an Insiders' look at sports in southern Arizona, pick up a copy of *Daily Star* sportswriter Greg Hansen's book *Hustling to Beat Deadline,* a compilation of his columns since 1981. You can buy it online at Amazon.com or pick it up at the newspaper's offices at 4850 S. Park Ave.

Rodeo

There aren't many spots in the States where you can see an authentic rodeo, but Tucson is one of them. The biggest—also one of the oldest in the nation—is **Fiesta de los Vaqueros,** which takes place over several days in late February at the Tucson Rodeo Grounds, 4823 S. 6th Ave.. (For all the details, see the Festivals & Events chapter.) Another is the **Desert Thunder Pro Rodeo** held the 3rd week in October at the Tucson Rodeo Grounds. It's the 3rd-largest PRCA/WPRA-sanctioned rodeo and offers live music and a chili cook-off in addition to all the roping, riding, and bronco busting. Ticket prices vary but it's free for kids with 1 general admission ticket. Call (520) 721-1621 for information, or check www.desertthunder .com. Parking at the Rodeo Grounds is a fee per vehicle, or park for free on neighboring streets.

Close-up

Tucson Sports Stadiums

ARIZONA STADIUM

This is the University of Arizona's football stadium, located on E. 6th Street a couple of blocks west of Campbell Avenue. Built in 1928, the stadium originally had only 7,000 seats; after numerous upgrades, it now seats over 56,000. Spectators cannot bring in any containers or alcoholic beverages or large backpacks or bags, and no alcohol is sold here during any college activity. There are a few unusual things about this stadium that the average spectator may never notice. One is that two sides of the stadium, the south and east, actually are built over dormitories. (We hope no students are trying to snooze or study during a game.) A 420-foot "Ring of Fame" along the facade of the skyboxes on the west side of the stadium honors former football players who have been named either to All-America teams or as national players of the year, or players who have been national statistical leaders. You'll find the typical stadium concessions on all levels. If you're not lucky enough to find parking in one of the university's nearby garages, try the neighborhood streets to the south.

HI CORBETT FIELD

One of the country's most beautiful vintage baseball fields, Hi Corbett was built in 1927 and has operated under several names. The stadium's current name was bestowed in 1951 in honor of Tucson native and former Arizona state senator Hiram Stevens Corbett, who was instrumental in getting the Cleveland Indians to town for spring training back in 1947. Games here feel like the good old days of players like Mickey Mantle and Joe DiMaggio. The grass on the field is *real*, and you'll watch the game under open sky with great views of players close up—no sky-high, nosebleed bleachers here. The stadium capacity is just under 10,000, parking is free, and there is a snack bar.

Seniors

Each year the Tucson Parks and Recreation Department holds the Tucson Senior Olympics. For about one week near the end of January, seniors from all over the area gather at a variety of sites including senior centers, city parks, and adult residential communities to compete in games such as track, tennis, bicycling, boccie, swimming, shuffleboard, golf, and many more. Many of them go on to the state Senior Olympics held in Phoenix and even the nationals (in 1997 Tucson was the site of the national Senior Olympics). For information on how to participate or when and where to go to watch the games, call Parks and Recreation at (520) 791-3244, or check www.tucsonseniorgames.com. (See the Festivals & Events chapter.)

MCKALE CENTER

Named after the late J. F. "Pop" McKale, UA athletic director and coach from 1914 to 1957, this copper-roofed circular structure seating over 14,500 is home to a number of Wildcat sports, including men's and women's basketball, volleyball, and gymnastics. Located just north of 6th Street and west of Campbell Avenue on National Championship Drive, it's surrounded by other university sports fields, including the stadium, Jerry Kindall baseball field, and Hillenbrand Aquatic Center. McKale is wheelchair accessible, and entry for all spectators is on the south side facing National Championship Drive. Concession stands are on the upper levels, and no containers can be brought into the center. McKale also houses the university's main ticket office, where tickets for all sport games can be purchased. The ticket booths are outdoors on the south side facing National Championship Drive, and there are metered parking spaces right there for picking up or inquiring about tickets. Phone numbers for inquiring about or charging tickets are (520) 621-CATS (2287) or (800) 452-CATS (2287). There's a pay parking garage just to the west, but don't count on getting in during a game.

KINO STADIUM

This baseball stadium is part of a Pima County facility called Kino Sports Complex that also houses practice and playing fields for baseball, soccer, and basketball. The stadium is located on Ajo Way near I-10. It debuted for 1998 spring training and is now home to the minor-league Tucson Padres. The 150-acre complex includes an 11,000-seat ballpark, 12 practice fields, 3 practice infields, 1 major-league clubhouse, a minor-league clubhouse, batting tunnels, and pitching mounds. For baseball games there are 5 seating levels and corresponding prices ranging from lawn seating to club seats. Factoid: During a spring training game here between the Arizona Diamondbacks and the San Francisco Giants on March 24, 2001, pitcher Randy Johnson threw a pitch that knocked a dove right out of the sky and killed it. By the way, the pitch was ruled no pitch! For information about the stadium, call (520) 434-1367 or (866) 672-1343 or go to www.kinosportscomplex.com.

PHOENIX

For faithful fans of spectator sports, Phoenix isn't all that far away—less than a two-hour drive or bus trip and half that by plane. Even though most of Arizona's major sport teams are based in Phoenix, they're still considered Arizona teams; many even have adopted "Arizona" as part of their name rather than "Phoenix" to signify their statewide affiliation. So if Tucson doesn't satisfy all your cravings for sports, head on up to Phoenix.

Baseball

ARIZONA DIAMONDBACKS
Chase Field, Phoenix
(602) 514-8400
www.azdiamondbacks.com
Winners of the 2001 World Series against the powerful New York Yankees, the

Diamondbacks, a National League expansion team, play in the state-of-the-art Chase Field in downtown Phoenix. Ticket prices vary and are available for individual games, for the season, and monthly. Tucsonans can leave the driving to them by taking the D-Backs Express bus from Foothills Mall to Chase Field for $18 round-trip ($15 for kids 12 and under). The bus trip is offered only for Sat and Sun games and reservations are a must at (602) 462-4798.

CACTUS LEAGUE BASEBALL SPRING TRAINING

Arizona is heaven for folks from other parts of the country who are die-hard baseball fans and a bit sun-starved. For about a month each spring from early March to the first of April, they can watch their favorite major-league baseball teams practice and spar with other teams during spring training. Multiple teams currently practice in Phoenix and its suburbs, including the Chicago Cubs at Hohokam Park in Mesa, the San Diego Padres and the Seattle Mariners at Peoria Sports Complex in Peoria, the Los Angeles Angels at Tempe Diablo Stadium in Tempe, the Milwaukee Brewers at Maryvale Sports Complex in Maryvale, the San Francisco Giants at Scottsdale Stadium in Scottsdale, the Chicago White Sox at Camelback Ranch–Glendale, and the Texas Rangers and Kansas City Royals at Surprise Recreation Park. With each of these teams playing in town, baseball fans have hundreds of games to choose from during the month. Ticket prices vary, but vacant seats are not easy to come by, especially for the more popular teams. For information on schedules or how to get tickets for any of the games check the Cactus League website at www.cactus-league.com.

Basketball

PHOENIX MERCURY

US Airways Center
201 E. Jefferson St., Phoenix
(602) 252-9622, (602) 514-8333 (office)
www.wnba.com/mercury

The Phoenix Mercury was one of the initial charter teams in the WNBA and played their first season in the summer of 1997 at the air-conditioned America West Arena (since renamed US Airways Arena) in downtown Phoenix. And they're good—in 2007 and 2009 they won the WNBA championship. Attendance exceeds expectations, with home games averaging 10,000-plus fans who may pay hundreds of dollars per ticket. (It's a way for basketball devotees who can't get into the arena for a Suns game to see pro basketball and maybe even afford a ticket for the kids.) The season runs from September to May.

PHOENIX SUNS

US Airways Center
201 E. Jefferson St., Phoenix
(602) 379-7900 (office), (602) 379-7867 (box office)
www.nba.com/suns

This championship NBA basketball team features top players Grant Hill and Steve Nash. You may also recognize their furry mascot, "Go" the Gorilla (5 feet, 8 inches; 350 pounds), who is as athletic and entertaining as the more famous team members and has risen to dean of NBA mascots. The Suns are a winning team, so tickets to their home games during the October to June season at US Airways Center sell out quickly. They can be obtained through the Suns' ticket office or through Ticketmaster at (800) 4-NBATIX (462-2849).

Football

ARIZONA CARDINALS
University of Phoenix Stadium
Loop 101 & Glendale Avenue, Glendale
(602) 379-0101 (office),
(602) 379-0102 (box office)
www.azcardinals.com
The Cardinals, founded in 1898 and a charter member of the National Football League, are the oldest continuously run professional football franchise in the nation. The NFC West division team plays home games at the gorgeous University of Phoenix Stadium, which played host to the 2008 Super Bowl. Ticket prices range widely from single-game tickets to season tickets, and they're fairly easy to get.

TOSTITOS FIESTA BOWL
University of Phoenix Stadium
Loop 101 & Glendale Avenue, Glendale
(480) 350-0900
www.fiestabowl.com
Every New Year's Day or thereabouts, one of the major college bowl games is played outside Phoenix at Glendale's University of Phoenix Stadium. The Fiesta Bowl is usually played between 2 top college teams selected by the Fiesta Bowl Committee. This bowl is now part of the College Football Bowl Alliance, so once every 4 years it will be the site of the national championship playoff, the first of which was right here in the early days of 1999. Ticket prices vary and can be obtained from various sources.

Ice Hockey

PHOENIX COYOTES
Jobing.com Arena
9400 W. Maryland Ave., Glendale
(623) 463-8800 (office),
(623) 772-3485 (box office)
www.phoenixcoyotes.com
From September through April, Arizonans can go to the Jobing.com Arena in Glendale and watch the National Hockey League Coyotes. During the season more than 80 games are played at the arena, and fans love them. Tickets sell out fast. They can be obtained from Ticketmaster outlets at (800) 745-3000. Occasionally the Coyotes play a game in Tucson at the Tucson Convention Center, so call for information.

DAVIS-MONTHAN
AIR FORCE BASE

Since 1927, some of America's most famous (and infamous) flying machines have flown the skies of Tucson. The *Spirit of St. Louis* and its pioneering pilot were here to participate in the opening ceremonies of the air base. Bombers like the B-17 Flying Fortress, the B-24 Liberator, and the B-29 Superfortress (used to drop the atomic bomb on Japan) flew overhead during World War II.

OVERVIEW

When the jet age was ushered in around 1953, Tucsonans could glance skyward and spot a new B-47 Stratojet or a squadron of F-86-A Sabre jet fighters. And then came the cold war era with its Titan II missiles and silos and U-2 reconnaissance planes that flew global missions out of our Air Force base. Later years brought the F-4 Phantom fighter, and today A-10 Thunderbolts shine against our blue skies.

But long before "US Air Force" was even a glimmer in anyone's eye, what is now known as Davis-Monthan Air Force Base in south-central Tucson got its humble start as a municipal airfield—really just a two-man refueling station and a dirt runway. The year was 1919 when Tucson officials voted to create an airport. It all began on an 82-acre site where the rodeo grounds are today. (A plaque on the rodeo grounds on S. 6th Avenue marks the spot.) First called Macauley Field and then Fishburn Field, it became Tucson Municipal Flying Field in 1923. Tucson officials definitely had vision. Not only had they established the first municipal airport in Arizona, but hoping

that it would be selected as the site for an Army air base, they also began building it to military specifications under guidance from the Army Air Corps.

By 1927 their dreams were coming true. Col. Charles A. Lindbergh, fresh from his triumphant solo flight across the Atlantic aboard the *Spirit of St. Louis,* came to town to dedicate the air field as an Army Signal Corps base. It was the largest municipal airport in the US and the first to be converted to a military base. By this time the airfield had been relocated from S. 6th Avenue—still a good way from where the heaviest concentration of Tucson's population of 32,000 was concentrated—to a location farther southeast where city fathers had already bought up 1,280 acres of homesteaded ranch land. This was the Davis-Monthan Air Force Base of the future.

It was also at the 1927 dedication that two Tucson military aviators became immortalized when the airfield was officially named Davis-Monthan Airfield. The two young men may never have even met each other, but it would turn out they had a lot in common.

One was born in England, the other in Tennessee, but both would eventually live in Tucson. One attended Tucson High School and the University of Arizona and served in the Army at Fort Huachuca, Arizona. The other worked on his family's Tucson ranches before joining the Army. Both were military pilots when aviation was still in its infancy, and both ultimately would perish in the flying machines they loved—Lt. Samuel H. Davis in Florida in 1921 and Lt. Oscar Monthan in Hawaii in 1924. Their names would grace a municipal airport, an Army air base, and eventually a US Air Force base.

ℹ️ Initiated in December 1994, the Pilot for a Day program benefits children and their families in the Tucson community who have catastrophic illnesses. Children of all ages, military or civilian, can be a guest of the 355th Fighter Wing and one of Davis-Monthan's flying squadrons for an entire day. The full-day program starts with a swearing-in ceremony, followed by a tour, demos, simulated flights, lunch, and a visit to the control tower. The day ends with a final "Desert Lightning" salute. For more information, call the 355th public affairs office at (520) 228-3378.

For more than 10 years after its conversion to an Army Signal Corps base, Davis-Monthan Field continued to serve both military and commercial flights. Among the pilots who landed here were Amelia Earhart, Wiley Post, and James Doolittle, along with Standard Airlines, which later was absorbed by American Airlines.

During the 1930s the Army built the base's first hangar and operations building and added paved roads and runways. By the end of the decade, with war clouds building in Europe and the Pacific, the Army wanted to station some men and planes at the field. At the same time city leaders wanted the federal government to take over the field in order to get additional funds for construction and the soldiers who would be stationed there. Agreement was reached—the city would move its airport to a new site (where Tucson International Airport is today) and the Army would take over Davis-Monthan Field.

WARTIME EXPANSION

When Pearl Harbor was attacked on December 7, 1941, the population of Davis-Monthan Field was 2,175. One year later the base's military population had jumped to 9,642, and the field was being expanded to the tune of $3 million by the federal government. The base's war mission was to train light and heavy bombardment aircrews who then would be deployed overseas. It had the reputation as the best heavy bombardment station in the nation. As the base workload increased and aircraft personnel were dispatched to distant shores, women from the area took on base chores ranging from driving dump trucks to serving in the Women's Army Auxiliary Corps. And for a time, the base also held a German prisoner-of-war camp.

With the war's end, the base became a "separation center," processing nearly 10,000 returning soldiers for transition to civilian life. When that job was done, the base was deactivated and the field became a storage location for B-29 bombers and C-47 cargo planes, better known as "Gooney Birds." But this respite would not last long. With the

Close-up

☀AMARC Tour

You can tour the amazing aircraft storage and warehouse facility, known as AMARC (Aerospace Maintenance and Regeneration Center) and nicknamed the "boneyard." Home to over 5,000 aircraft, the 2,600 acres of open storage hold more than 70 types of aircraft, including post–WWII aircraft from the Korean War, B-52 bombers, helicopters, fighter jets, and much, much more. Tucson's low humidity, nonalkaline soil, and hot weather are perfect for the long-term storage of these miracles of modern engineering, and you won't see anything like it anywhere else in the world.

The tours are organized by the Pima Air and Space Museum and run Mon through Fri (except for holidays and military alerts). Starting times are seasonal, so call ahead. There are several tours a day, and they last about 1 hour. The tour takes place by bus that boards in front of the museum. Photo ID is required for everyone over 16. Due to increased security, only 1 small carry-on item is allowed, and that is subject to search. Adults $7, children 12 and under $4. No reservations are accepted, so get there early; call (520) 574-0462 for more information.

official creation of the US Air Force shortly after the war, the base was turned over to the new branch of the service and got its official name—Davis-Monthan Air Force Base—in early 1948.

In the years that followed, Davis-Monthan served as a home base for Titan II missiles, U-2 reconnaissance forces, and a series of fighter jets. Following the Strategic Arms Limitation Treaty, Russian satellites flew overhead taking photographs of the nuclear arms and aircraft dismantled by Davis-Monthan personnel and placed in open view on the base for the satellite cameras to see. Davis-Monthan planes and personnel were dispatched to serve in three more wars—the Korean War, Vietnam, and Desert Storm—as well as many real or potential trouble spots around the globe.

Today Davis-Monthan occupies 17 square miles (almost 9 percent of the city), employs military and thousands of civilian personnel, and trains thousands of pilots

and support personnel. But Tucsonans seem to either love it or hate it. For some residents the thunderous drone of massive cargo and transport planes or low-flying fighter jets is nothing more than an intrusion. For others the sound is a welcome one, signifying our nation's military might and the streamlined beauty of the world's most sophisticated flying machines. For some—like land developers—Davis-Monthan means only that valuable land cannot be turned into commercial or residential profit. For others the lost land value pales in comparison to the base's contributions to Tucson's economy, estimated to be in the millions.

Fortunately for the air base and for Tucsonans who welcome its presence here, the bulk of our residents favor it. When federal rumors of its possible closing were rampant in the early 1990s, supporters far outnumbered the picketers, and it was easy to make a case for Davis-Monthan's significance not only as a military installation but also as an integral part of the city's lifestyle and economy.

With 27,000 people connected with Davis-Monthan (including military, dependents, civilians, and retirees), it's not difficult to see the base's significance to Tucson and Arizona. They eat in Tucson restaurants, shop in Tucson stores, attend Tucson's events and art programs, hook up to Tucson's utilities, and enroll their kids in Tucson's day-care centers and schools, adding to the city's and state's tax base with every purchase or service they consume. And if the base weren't here, many of Tucson's 13,000 or more military retirees (and their pensions) might not be either. Over the years the government has pumped many millions into Davis-Monthan, often hiring local contractors for the work done on the base, from paving runways and roads to erecting hangars and housing.

Nor is the impact of the base purely economic. Davis-Monthan makes a big deal out of encouraging volunteerism. One office on the base works exclusively to help match base personnel with community volunteer assignments. Military dependents, and sometimes the military personnel as well, spend many hours volunteering in Tucson's schools, youth organizations, and other agencies. And if a natural disaster or emergency occurred in the area, you can be sure the base's people and resources would be there to help the community out.

Behind its 25 miles of fence and restricted-access gates, Davis-Monthan has everything from fast food to the Air Force's version of M*A*S*H, and from an 18-hole golf course to "the world's largest parking lot." The average visitor to Tucson, and even most residents, may only be aware of the runways, airplanes, and air traffic control tower—the trappings of Davis-Monthan that can easily be seen by driving along Golf Links Road or merely looking skyward. But these are just the tip of the iceberg.

Inside this city within a city, over 5,000 people live within multiunit and single-family housing (the rest live off base), two elementary schools are run by the Tucson Unified School District, and a base hospital serves thousands of patients annually. There are restaurants, officer and enlisted clubs, a base exchange (BX), a commissary, a post office, a youth center, and a service station. For entertainment, base personnel can choose from an 18-hole golf course, a pool, movie theater, bowling alley, parks, and sports fields, plus a library and fitness center for improving mind and body. Military retirees who call Tucson home also have access to this vast array of facilities.

✳AVIATION GRAVEYARD (AMARC)

Although much of this military complex is out of view, even the Air Force can't hide "the world's largest parking lot" from the public eye. Only it's not for vehicles; it's for aircraft (and related equipment). Perhaps you caught a glimpse of it as your plane descended toward Tucson—endless airplanes lined up in perfect rows on the desert floor, as if waiting to launch a fearful invasion. They stretch for miles—colossal B-52s and Gooney Birds; scores of helicopters; and sleek, fearless fighter jets. If the planes parked here belonged to another country, they would be one of the largest air forces in the world. But up close you could see that these are old aircraft, often partially covered with a skin of plastic to protect them from the elements. These 2,600 acres on the east end of Davis-Monthan hold over 5,000 aircraft and tons of related equipment. It's the only storage depot like it in the world.

Tucsonans tend to call it the airplane boneyard or graveyard, but officially it's the Aerospace Maintenance and Regeneration Center, or AMARC, run by the Department of Defense. In 1965 the Defense Department consolidated all US Army, Navy, and Air Force storage locations into this one. They picked Davis-Monthan because of the Sonoran Desert—the air is dry and the ground so hard and alkaline that even a 180,000-pound B-52 can be towed over it without sinking.

And what about the fate of these flying machines? A small percent are returned to flight status. Many are gradually picked over for spare parts. Some are flown to remote places and used for target practice. Some are purposely kept untouched so they could be put into battle on short notice if need be. Even several Boeing 707s banned by the FAA rest here, their powerful engines that were too noisy for commercial airports now stripped off for use in Air Force tanker planes. Some of the aircraft could be sold intact to a foreign government, but only after lots of red tape and only to "friendly" buyers. The majority of the planes are sold for scrap, but only after their navigational equipment and weaponry are removed. So the next time you lift up that can of soda or that garden rake, you may be holding all that's left of a 1950s military bomber or fighter.

It's quite a sight to see, this final resting place for Uncle Sam's warplanes. It even has its own celebrity row—a line of rare and one-of-a-kind aircraft, each with a sign designating its name—worthy of the history books and a spot in anyone's photo album. You can catch a glimpse of AMARC by driving south on Kolb Road. Or better yet, if you want to see "the boneyard" planes up close or in the lens of your camera, or see a captured Iraqi tank or some of the spiffy planes on the base's tarmac, take a tour of the base.

AMARC is only one of the many missions going on at Davis-Monthan. Nearly every major air command, the Air Force Reserve, and the Air National Guard are represented here. The 355th Wing is the base's primary activity and occupant, responsible for training pilots on the A-10 Thunderbolt, a low and slow and highly maneuverable tank destroyer. (It also happens to be a relatively quiet jet, which pleases Tucsonans who are picky about the noise level.) The 355th also conducts training for other aircrews, provides airborne command and communications, and helps with Strategic Arms Limitation Treaty (SALT) compliance. It also operates one of only five air transportable hospitals (the Air Force version of a M*A*S*H unit), which can be deployed on a moment's notice to trouble spots around the globe.

i If you'd like to see the inner workings of the base, the 355th Fighter Wing offers organized group tours with specific conditions and limitations; tours are limited to one bus load and are booked on a first-come, first-served basis to organized groups only—there are no individual tours. To schedule a tour, contact the community relations office on base at (520) 228-3378.

Davis-Monthan also houses the 12th Air Force Command and the people assigned to it, who are responsible for the combat readiness of all tactical air forces west of the Mississippi. The base is the site of an Air National Guard unit that flies the F-16 Fighting Falcon, an Air Force Reserve unit that flies search and rescue helicopters, and the West Coast Combat Search and Rescue unit. Other federal agencies using the base include the Federal Aviation Administration, the US Customs and Border Patrol, the US Army Corps of Engineers, the Air Force Office of Special Investigation, and a detachment of the Naval Air Systems Command. With one of the longest runways in the Air Force—13,643 feet—Davis-Monthan is equipped to handle just about any job in the airborne military.

DAY TRIPS & WEEKEND GETAWAYS

I t's difficult to imagine wanting to leave Tucson, but the reality is that southern Arizona has much to offer. In this chapter we give you some ideas on great day and weekend trips not to be missed!

The choices are so great that we've really only scratched the surface here. We've selected some destinations that both visitors and residents consider to be must-sees if they get the chance, plus a few others that are relatively undiscovered. Most of the weekend getaways included here are within a three-hour drive of Tucson. A few are a bit farther, but we include them because they're especially appealing destinations.

For most of the weekend getaways, we've mapped out an itinerary that highlights a number of locations, attractions, and activities. You may not get to them all, but at least you'll be informed enough to make a choice about what you absolutely can't miss and what can wait until next time. Even if you're just searching for a day trip, be sure to read the sections on getaways as well—they contain lots of ideas for day trips. Conversely, the day trips described here can easily be turned into getaways—we even give a few tips on how best to do that.

Whatever your destination or its duration, it's always best to call ahead and confirm the seasons and hours they're open, prices, and any age restrictions so that you won't be disappointed on arrival. Likewise, contact the chambers of commerce or visitor centers for your destinations; they'll provide lots of useful information, even if you're making last-minute plans. And last but not least, get a good map.

DAY TRIPS

Boyce Thompson Southwestern Arboretum

This combination state park/museum/ nature preserve is about 2 hours from Tucson and can easily be a day trip, or it can be combined with other sights east of Phoenix for a weekend getaway (we map out such a trip under Phoenix & Environs). Either way, plan on at least a couple of hours to see this site that most people fall in love with. It's a fascinating collection of arid land plants

from all over the world—3,200 different desert plants to be more exact. It's also a rich riparian habitat that supports more than 300 species of mammals, birds, reptiles, and amphibians thanks to Queen Creek, which flows through the property.

The **Arboretum** (520-689-2811; http:// cals.arizona.edu/bta) is located near the mining town of Superior and was endowed in 1924 by William Boyce Thompson, the founder of 2 major mining companies in the Superior area. He established it as a research facility, but much of it is now open to the public, along with a visitor center and gift shop, self-guided nature walks, miles of easy trails, a desert lake, a picnic area, and restrooms. It's open daily (except Christmas) from 8 a.m. to 4 p.m. Sept through Apr, and until 5 p.m. in fall, winter, and spring. Hours are 6 a.m. to 3 p.m. May through Aug. Fees are $7.50 for adults and $3 for children 5 to 12. From Tucson, take Oracle Road (Highway 77) north to Highway 79, then go east on US 60 to Milepost 223. Highway 79 is also called the Pinal Parkway, a scenic drive along which the native vegetation is identified with markers.

Safford

A great day or even a weekend camping trip, Safford in Graham County, just 2.5 hours from Tucson, is worth the drive. Take I-10 east past Willcox to US 191 north 25 miles right into Safford.

Kids of all ages will love **Discovery Park**, part of the Eastern Arizona College campus. It's open to the public from 9 a.m. to 5 p.m. Mon through Fri and 4 to 9:30 p.m. every Sat for stargazing (928-428-6260; www.eac.edu/discoverypark). You can explore 200 acres of riparian and natural habitat and peek inside a pond through a glass window. The park is also home to the world's largest camera obscura. On Saturday you can sign up for tours of the **Mount Graham International Observatory** (http://mgpc3.as.arizona.edu/tours.htm), which take place from mid-May through mid-Nov, or until weather prohibits them. The tour, which leaves the park by van at 9:30 a.m., features a trip up scenic Mount Graham, lunch near the summit, and a guided tour of the observatory facility, including the 20-inch Tinsley reflector.

When your feet get tired, head to the hidden **Roper Lake State Park** in the shadow of Mount Graham, located off US 191, 6 miles south of Safford. You'll find a beautiful, scenic lake surrounded by reeds, picnic sites, and campsites. Only small electric motorboats are allowed here, so you can swim, paddle a canoe, or sail or row a boat along the lovely shores, and there is a natural hot springs pool on the grounds. Call (928) 428-6760 for details on fees and to reserve a campsite. The park is open daily 6 a.m. to 10 p.m. For more information check the Web at www.pr.state.az.us/parks/rola/index.

If you don't like to soak in the great outdoors, Safford is home to several other hot springs that are more commercial. Check out **Essence of Tranquility** at 6074 Lebanon Loop (928-428-9312; www.azhotmineralspring.com) and **Kachina Hot Springs Artesian Mineral Spa** at 1155 W. Cactus Rd. (928-428-7212; www.kachinaspa.com).

Madera Canyon

Nature lovers will be enthralled by this spot 60 miles south of Tucson in the Santa Rita Mountains. It's a popular day trip destination for Tucsonans escaping the heat in summer and for birders all year long. About 400 species of birds have been sighted here, including hummingbirds and elf owls. There are about 200 miles of scenic trails, some of which hug the meandering Madera Creek, so there's something here for casual walkers as well as serious hikers wanting to explore the upper reaches of the mountains. At an elevation of 5,600 feet, Madera Canyon is covered with thick pines and is significantly cooler than the desert floor below.

At the entrance to the recreation area is a small visitor center, though it's usually open only on weekends. There's also a small store that may or may not be open, so it's best to have your own supplies. Nearby is a small campground with toilets and drinking water. The canyon's **Santa Rita Lodge Nature Resort** (520-625-8746; www.santa ritalodge.com) caters to birders—all cabins and casitas have bird feeders outside the windows. Madera Canyon is under the purview of the Coronado National Forest, so call the **Nogales District Office** at (520) 281-2296 for information. There is a $5 daily parking fee.

To find Madera Canyon, take exit 63 off I-19, then go east on White House Canyon Road, which becomes Madera Canyon Road. The road winds up the mountainside for about 15 miles, but it's easy to traverse by car. Just remember that this is an outdoor recreation area in the middle of a mountain, so you won't find much here beyond the bounties that nature provides.

✳Sonoita

Located in Santa Cruz County, just 48 miles south of Tucson at the junction of Highways 82 and 83, you'll find the lovely town of Sonoita. Dubbed Arizona's Wine Country for the many vineyards and wineries in the area, Sonoita was founded in 1882. At 4,970 feet in elevation, the landscape here is much different from Tucson's. The Sonoita area was the setting for several classic movies including *Oklahoma* and *Red River*, so if you're a movie buff you might recognize the rolling hills, craggy mountains, deep canyons, and golden plains that are features of the local landscape. The area is home to numerous wineries, a historic ranch, and a lovely riparian preserve.

The scenic **Empire Ranch,** located on the Las Cienegas National Conservation Area (520-258-7200; www.blm.gov), is just 6 miles north of town. Overseen by the Bureau of Land Management, the 160-acre property, originally a working ranch, dates to the 1800s. The fully restored 1870 adobe and wood frame ranch house (listed on the National Register of Historic Places) is open to the public daily. This is a great way to see how ranchers really lived and worked—exhibits and furnishings are all original. The Empire Ranch Foundation (a nonprofit organization that raises funds for ongoing restoration) hosts an annual **Roundup and Open House** event annually in October that features horsemanship and branding demonstrations, cowboy mounted shooters and border collies showing off their amazing skills at corralling sheep and cattle. There's lots of food including great tri-tip barbecue and cowboy beans, Western music, storytellers, and wagon rides (888-364-2829; www.empireranchfoundation.org). From Tucson take I-10 east to exit 281/Highway 83. Travel south 19 miles, and turn left on the gravel road between Mile Markers 40 and 39. Drive east 3 miles to the ranch headquarters.

If you fancy a taste of the grape, stop by the locally owned and family-operated **Dos Cabezas WineWorks,** (520-841-1193; www.doscabezaswinery.com) whose wine was featured at a White House dinner in honor of Sandra Day O'Connor. You can taste some too at the tasting room, open year-round, Thurs through Sun, 10:30 a.m. to 4:30 p.m.

The terrific small-scale **Sonoita Rodeo** takes place every Labor Day weekend at the fairgrounds (520-455-5553; www.sonoita fairgrounds.com). This small, family-friendly rodeo features wild horse races, barrel races, a kids' rodeo, bareback riding, roping, and bull riding. You will see the real ranching community here, not fancy cowboys, but salt-of-the-earth families who make their living ranching and whose skills are not just for show but for survival. The fairgrounds are also the location of the oldest horse show in the country, the **Quarter Horse Show,** which takes place each spring. There are entry fees for both events.

The **Sonoita Creek Natural Area** (520-287-2791; www.pr.state.az.us/parks/socr/index.html) is a gorgeous 9,000–acre-plus riparian area, home to a wide variety of wildlife including 106 species of birds, butterflies, and dragonflies. Part of the Arizona state park system, it's just downstream from Patagonia Lake State Park (see listing this chapter). You will need a permit to enter the area, available for a fee at the Patagonia State Park gatehouse (520-287-6965).

For upscale, gourmet fare, **Canela Bistro** (520-455-5873; www.canelabistro.com) chefs/owners John Hall and Joy Vargo offer delicious dishes featuring locally produced foods and wine in their cozy dining room and garden patio. Open Thurs through Sun; call ahead as hours may change. For cowboy fare, head to **The Steakout** (520-455-5205; www.azsteakout.com). A local landmark, it's been dishing up grub since the 1950s and features live music with local bands.

Patagonia Lake State Park

Water-deprived Tucsonans and their visitors will be glad to hear that the damming of Sonoita Creek more than 30 years ago created the largest recreational lake in southern Arizona. And there's more good news—it's less than 2 hours away. The 265-acre lake and the 645-acre park in which it sits combine to offer just about every type of outdoor recreation. For folks who like to catch their dinner or just fish for sport, the lake is stocked with trout in winter and with bass, crappie, catfish, and bluegill the rest of the

year. If you didn't bring your own, a concession at the general store rents paddleboats, canoes, and rowboats at hourly rates, plus deposit. The lake even has a sandy beach for swimmers and sunbathers who just want to be reminded of the ocean. You can windsurf here, as well as water- or Jet Ski, but not on weekends from May through September, because that's when desert dwellers come here in droves. There are picnic areas, restrooms, and showers, plus plenty of places for casual hikes through the rolling hills around the lake. (See the Campgrounds & RV Parks chapter for information on the campsites.) The park is also home to the Sonoita Creek State Natural Area, a riparian oasis. There is a day-use fee per vehicle. For swimming, surfing, boating, and fishing in southern Arizona, take I-10 east to Highway 83, go south to Highway 82, and continue south 7 miles on Highway 82 past the town of Patagonia. To reach the park by phone, call (520) 287-6965, or check out their website at www.pr.state.az.us/parks/parkhtml/patagonia.html.

Taliesin West

Admirers of one of the 20th-century's greatest architects, Frank Lloyd Wright, won't want to miss visiting his personal winter residence and architectural school. Located in Scottsdale (the outskirts of Phoenix), Taliesin West is only about 2 hours from Tucson, so it's an easy day trip. But there's so much else to do in this area that it could also be included in a weekend getaway (you'll find ideas for that elsewhere in this chapter). Perched on 600 acres of rugged Sonoran Desert at the base of the McDowell Mountains, Taliesin West is a National Historic Landmark. Like most of Wright's structures, it's both amazing and unique. He and his apprentices gathered rocks from the desert floor and sand from the washes to build this set of structures that includes his former residence, a school, and an architectural firm, all linked by dramatic terraces, gardens, and walkways.

If you plan to visit Taliesin West, take one of the tours. Each season, different types of tours are offered at different times of the day and for various prices, so call ahead for recorded tour information. For example, a morning panorama tour lasts 1 hour and includes the Cabaret Cinema, Music Pavilion, and Wright's private office, but not the residence. Another tour—Insights—lasts 90 minutes and includes the dramatic Taliesin West living room with furniture Wright designed and living quarters. In addition to the various scheduled tours during each season, private and group tours are available but must be arranged in advance. Walking shoes and sun protection are recommended, and toddlers must be in strollers or carried. There's a bookstore with an extensive selection of Wright books and prints, works by Taliesin artists, and souvenirs. For additional information call (480) 627-5340 or go to www.franklloydwright.org. The entrance to Taliesin West is at the intersection of Cactus Road and Frank Lloyd Wright Boulevard in northeast Scottsdale at 12621 N. Frank Lloyd Wright Blvd.

Tubac

Just 45 miles south of Tucson off I-19 at exits 40 and 34 is a lovely little village that once was the second-oldest European settlement west of the Mississippi. Today it's a sophisticated artists' colony.

Tubac and the surrounding areas are filled with history. In the 1700s the Spanish came north from Mexico and built a presidio (or fort) here, and the settlement of Tubac became the first European settlement in Arizona. Operated by the Tubac Historical Society, **Tubac Presidio State Historic Park** (520-398-2252; www.pr.state.az.us/Parks/TUPR/index.html) the site of this small fort and is open daily from 8 a.m. to 5 p.m. From October to March a living history program reenacts 18th-century life.

In the heart of Old Town Tubac (which is just east of the present-day shopping area), you'll also see **Placita de Anza,** historic **St. Ann's Church,** an 1885 1-room schoolhouse, and the **Tubac Historical Society,** which offers a research library, exhibits, and self-guided tour maps. It's difficult to visit Tubac without taking in some of the shopping opportunities, but there are plenty of alternatives if shopping isn't on your top-10 list of things to do. In addition to all the historical sites, there's a 4.5-mile trail that winds south along the Santa Cruz River, and in this part of the river, you'll actually see water flowing year-round. The trail begins at the picnic grounds south of the presidio museum in Old Town Tubac. Throughout the year Tubac conducts many events and performances featuring music, dance, song, and art. In December, for example, there's Fiesta Navidad and Luminaria Night, which celebrates the holiday season in the Mexican tradition, and in February Tubac holds its Annual Festival of the Arts (see the Festivals & Events chapter), now more than 40 years old.

Intermingled with all this history and natural beauty are shops, restaurants, and inns that occupy old adobe and newer whitewashed brick structures reminiscent of the earliest settlers' housing. Most of the artists and craftspeople who sell their wares in Tubac also live here, so it's truly an artists' colony. There are only about a half dozen small streets in this entire village, but they are lined with about 5 dozen shops carrying everything from jewelry and pottery to sculpture and clothing. The shops offer anything and everything made by Mexican and American Indian crafters and artists, plus creations in metal, jewelry, ceramics, and glass, and on canvas by local as well as internationally known artisans.

The dining choices are nearly as vast as the shopping choices. At **DeAnza Restaurant and Cantina** you can dine on Mexican food and margaritas indoors or out on a lovely patio. For a taste of Italy, try **Melio's Trattoria**. At **Old Tubac Inn,** diners can play darts or pool while waiting for their meal or for carryout food to enjoy at the picnic grounds in Old Town Tubac. Or take the footbridge to **Shelby's Bistro**. The **Chile Pepper** has cappuccino, ice cream, and fountain drinks if you're just too busy to take the time for sit-down dining. For a fancy Mexican/Southwest sit-down meal, try the upscale **Dos Silos** restaurant at the Tubac Golf Resort.

Although Tubac can easily be a day trip because it's so close to Tucson, it's also a great spot for an overnight or weekend getaway. There's certainly plenty to do in the form of shopping, gallery gazing, hiking, history learning, and golfing (see the Golf chapter). If you decide to turn your day trip into a getaway, here are a few places to bunk out. For authentic charm, try either the **Tubac Country Inn** (520-398-3178; www.tubac countryinn.com) or **Tubac Secret Garden Inn** (520-398-9371; www.tubacsecretgarden .com). Both are in the historic district and across the street from the presidio park. The Secret Garden Inn has a wall surrounding three acres of green oasis. Another spot to stay is the lovely, intimate **Tubac Golf Resort & Spa** (520-398-2211; www.tubac golfresort.com) just a quarter mile out of

town. For more information check the website at www.tubacaz.com, or call the chamber of commerce at (520) 398-2704.

i If you need to relax after shopping in Tubac, head to the Floating Stone Aqua Spa (16-18 Calle Iglesia, 520-398-3193, 800-767-2325, www .thefloatingstoneinn.com). The spa features 5 pools of differing temperatures including a 40-foot lap pool and cold plunge pools with chlorine and chemical free water all filtered by a special ionization process. Services include massages, classes and aqua therapy. The day use fee is $20 and gives you access to all the pools and routine movement classes. Spa services are priced individually. If you're too relaxed to head back home, the adjacent historic inn is a lovely place to stay.

Tumacacori

If you're going to visit Tubac, it's only a short drive to Tumacacori, pronounced *too-mah-kah-core-ee*. It's the site of a Franciscan mission built in the 1700s that was regularly besieged by the Apache Indians. The ruins that are visible today include a chapel and graveyard. Visitors can also walk through an adobe mission church built between 1800 and 1822. The site has been converted into a National Historic Park with a visitor center where you can learn all about the mission and its colorful history. This is a very picturesque and tranquil spot with lots of mesquite trees and a 0.5-mile trail. On weekends there are often cultural demonstrations.

Nearby is the **Santa Cruz Chili and Spice Company,** in business since 1943 and famous for their Santa Cruz chili paste

(520-398-2591; www.santacruzchili.com). Open Mon through Fri from 8 a.m. to 5 p.m. and Sat 10 a.m to 5 p.m., and 10 a.m. to 3 p.m. in the summer. You'll find spices, herbs, salsas, and cookbooks plus a Western museum. Just to the north of the park is **Wisdom's Cafe** (520-398-2397; www.wisdoms cafe.com), which offers Mexican fare.

Like Tubac, Tumacacori can be a day trip from Tucson, or you can stay in this area for a weekend full of history, hiking along the river, bird-watching, and shopping. Tumacacori is just south of Tubac at exit 29 off I-19, or simply take the frontage road between the two.

WEEKEND GETAWAYS

Cosanti & Arcosanti

If you're heading north to Scottsdale and beyond, these are 2 unusual attractions you might want to include in your itinerary. Because Cosanti is in the heart of Paradise Valley, a close-in suburb of Phoenix, it could be a day trip from Tucson, but there's so much else to do in the Phoenix area that including Cosanti in a weekend getaway would be a much better alternative. Arcosanti, on the other hand, is a bit too far for a comfortable day trip but could easily be combined with a weekend visit to the Prescott, Jerome, and Sedona areas (and we guide you to and around these areas elsewhere in this chapter). Both of these attractions were founded by Paolo Soleri and are now operated by the nonprofit Cosanti Foundation. Soleri is an Italian architect who moved to Arizona in 1956 and has become famous for his unusual project called Arcosanti and for his spectacular bronze wind chimes.

A state historic site, **Cosanti** is the residence and sculpture studio of Paolo Soleri and his staff. It is located at 6433 E. Doubletree Ranch Rd. (480-948-6145; www.cosanti .com) in upscale Paradise Valley (just northeast of the Phoenix city limits). Except for major holidays, it's open daily from 9 a.m. to 5 p.m., 11 a.m. to 5 p.m. on Sun, and it's free. Cosanti's essence is a gallery of Soleri art, but it's much more than that: a blend of desert landscaping of cacti, paloverde, and olive trees with earth-formed concrete architectural structures. Suspended amid courtyards, terraces, and garden paths is the work of Paolo Soleri and his artisans—a spectacular array of bronze and ceramic wind bells. Visitors can see how these art forms are crafted on-site and purchase them as well. There is also a line of "cause bells," all of which represent issues of national or global concern and sales of which go to help nonprofit organizations. (For ways to make this part of a weekend getaway, see Phoenix & Environs in this chapter.)

While Cosanti is a place, **Arcosanti** is a vision turned almost into reality. Arcosanti represents a term that Soleri coined, arcology, to describe the concept of architecture and ecology working as one integral process to produce new urban habitats. Thus this strange-looking project of ultramodern structures built into the basalt cliffs 60 miles north of Phoenix was created as an urban "city" to epitomize Soleri's concept of arcology. It combines housing (originally for 5,000 people but never fully realized), large-scale solar greenhouses, a music center, and artist workshops and galleries. Today it's a place for students and professionals to study architecture, ecology, and art in the Soleri fashion and for visitors to view this 4,000-acre experiment in urban architecture. Visitors can see the creation of Soleri wind bells and purchase them, take tours, and snack at the cafe or bakery. Be prepared to do some walking and stair climbing, because Arcosanti is built into cliffs. The access road to Arcosanti is mostly dirt and very rough riding.

For information on Arcosanti or its tours, workshops, or overnight accommodations, call (928) 632-7135 or check the website, www.arcosanti.org. It's open daily except Thanksgiving, New Year's Day, and Christmas, and a donation is suggested per person. Hourly tours between 10 a.m. and 4 p.m., and a variety of special tours are also available: agriculture, architecture, and bird-watching. Take I-17 north from Phoenix to exit 262. To make this site part of a weekend getaway, consider staying overnight in the Verde River Valley towns of Prescott or Sedona, which we describe elsewhere in this chapter.

✳ Cochise County

Southeast of Tucson is an area filled with history, beauty, and tons of things to do and see. (Both Rhode Island and Connecticut would fit within Cochise County's 6,200 square miles.) It includes the farmlands and ponds of Willcox; some of the premier birding spots in the country; Tombstone, the "town too tough to die"; and the mountains where the famous Apache Indian chief Cochise made his stronghold and where his successor, Geronimo, finally surrendered. Many of these sites could be individual day trips from Tucson, or the area can be visited in one or two weekend getaways. For one weekend getaway, we recommend taking Highway 80 south and visiting Benson, Tombstone, and Bisbee. A second getaway lies a bit farther east and takes in Willcox and the Chiricahua and Dragoon Mountains. Read on for trips that explore Cochise County.

Benson to Bisbee

About 70 miles south of Tucson is Tombstone, the "town too tough to die," which can be a day trip from Tucson or combined with the other sites outlined in the following paragraphs to make a weekend getaway. From Tucson, take I-10 east to exit 302 to Highway 90 south and watch for signs for one of the world's most interesting natural wonders, **Kartchner Caverns** (see also our Parks & Recreation chapter). Located in Kartchner Caverns State Park, the cave is a wet, or live, cave, meaning that the calcite formations are still growing. There are several sections, each more spectacular than the last. There are several tours offered: A Throne Room tour is available year-round, and a Big Room tour provides historic detail (October 15 through April 15; under age 7 not permitted). The tours will give you a close look at the variety of formations and colors. Reservations are strongly recommended, as the tours sell out very quickly. Avoid disappointment and call (520) 586-CAVE (2283) for reservations several weeks in advance. For information call (502) 586-4100.

i Today driving from Tucson to Tombstone on the interstate takes a little over 1 hour. In the 1800s travel to Tombstone was by stagecoach only. It would have taken Big Nose Kate 2 to 3 days, traveling about 3 to 5 miles per hour (assuming no Indian attacks or robbery attempts) to get from Tucson's railroad station to Tombstone to see her lover, Doc Holliday.

Tombstone

Continue about 20 miles south on Highway 90, then west on Highway 82 another 25 miles to one of southern Arizona's most popular and famous family attractions, Tombstone. This is where, in 1881, the Earp brothers and Doc Holliday battled it out with the Clanton boys near the OK Corral. But there's more to the old silver mining town than the OK Corral, including Courthouse State Historic Park, the Rose Tree Inn Museum (displaying the world's largest rosebush, planted in 1885 and covering 8,000 square feet), the Birdcage Theater, the Crystal Palace Saloon, wooden sidewalks, preserved historical buildings, and even a stagecoach ride down the main drag, Allen Street. Shops, saloons, and eateries flourish here as well. A must-see on the outskirts of Tombstone is Boot Hill, the famous graveyard where the victims of the OK Corral shoot-out are buried, along with lots of other folks. It's perhaps too commercialized now, but you'll be able to ignore that as you walk through the cemetery reading the fascinating tombstones, which range from humorous to touching.

If your visit to Tombstone is part of a weekend getaway, some good choices for lodging include the **Best Western Look-Out Lodge** (520-457-2223, 877-652-6772; www.bestwesterntombstone.com), a motel with a lot of Old West character and great views. The upscale **Apache Spirit Ranch,** just 2.5 miles outside of downtown (520-457-7299; www.apachespiritranch.com), features 17 Western-themed guest houses, a pool, a Jacuzzi, a restaurant, and live entertainment.

Stop by the visitor center at 315 Allen St. (520-457-3929) for maps, information, and ways to save a few bucks on local sights. Their website, www.cityoftombstone.com, is a good information source.

Bisbee

From Tombstone continue south on Highway 80 toward Bisbee. Along the way, the hikers and birders among you might want to detour onto Highway 90 west, then Highway 92 south to see **Ramsey Canyon Preserve,** managed by The Nature Conservancy and open daily from 8 a.m. to 5 p.m., closed Tues and Wed, Sept through Feb. The preserve attracts more than 170 species of birds and dozens of species of butterflies.

i Don't miss breakfast in Bisbee. The Bisbee Breakfast Club (75A Erie St.; 520-432-5885; www.bisbee breakfastclub.com) offers it from 7 a.m. to 3 p.m., and even food writers Jane and Michael Stern were impressed with the homemade biscuits and Blue Wally Cakes bursting with blueberries and walnuts and topped with real maple syrup. Save room for pie—fresh daily, it's not to be missed.

While you're there, stop in for a good old time at the **Arizona Folklore Preserve,** where state balladeer Dolan Ellis (a founding member of the New Christy Minstrels) cranks out a mighty fine yarn and tune. Specializing in cowboy songs and tales of the Old West, Ellis entertains just about every Sat and Sun at 2 p.m. with old-fashioned jokes, stories, and pictures in a cozy cafe setting. Tickets are $15. Call in advance to make reservations (520-378-6165), or go to www.arizonafolk lore.com.

Many varieties of hummingbirds summer here, while coatimundis and white-tailed deer are among the year-round residents. The parking lot is small (23 spaces) and available on a first-come, first-served basis. Admission is $5 per person; under age 16 free. There's a visitor center and bookstore. The **Ramsey Canyon Inn** (www.ramseycanyoninn.com) adjacent to the preserve has 6 guest rooms and 2 separate apartments. Call (520) 378-3010 for reservations. Call (520) 378-2785 for more information on the preserve, or visit www.nature.org/arizona.

After your commune with nature, continue south on Highway 80 through Mule Mountain Tunnel to the former copper-mining town of Bisbee, a pretty little town that hugs the steep mountainside. At one time this old mining camp was one of the richest mineral sites in the world, and in the early 1900s Bisbee was the largest city between St. Louis and San Francisco. Eventually the mines played out, and Bisbee became an artists' colony and retirement area characterized by its Old World charm and restored Victorian and European-style buildings. Turquoise is big here, since it's a by-product of copper mining. To get a glimpse of what mining was like, go just beyond downtown to the **Lavender Pit Mine,** a huge hole that is one of the world's largest open-pit mines. Or for a more authentic sample of mining, visit the **Copper Queen Mine** (520-432-2071; www.queenminetour.com). Plan on taking one of the tours offered daily and lasting about 1 to 1.5 hours. You'll be outfitted in miner's garb and enter the shaft via a small train like the real miners rode. (The underground temperature is a cool 47 degrees on average, so be prepared.) If the underground tour sounds a bit too scary, take a surface tour by van. And if you still haven't had your fill of mining, there's the **Mining and Historical Museum** across the street in town.

Bisbee has lots to offer besides its former industry. One of its most popular attractions is the fully restored Copper Queen Hotel, built in 1898, in the heart of downtown Bisbee at 11 Howell Ave. You need not book a room here to wander in and enjoy its grand lobby, saloon, and dining room from yesteryear. The hallways are lined with photos of the Copper Queen's early days, some depicting the celebrities who have stayed here, including John Wayne and Teddy Roosevelt. Another must-see is the historic **St. Patrick's Catholic Church** built in 1916 at 100 Quality Hill on Higgins Hill (call 520-432-5753 for hours and directions). The stained-glass windows here are considered one of the 10 best examples of Victorian glass in the nation. In fact, all over the downtown area you'll find well-preserved turn-of-the-20th-century brick buildings that today house a variety of boutiques, craft shops, and restaurants. It's easy to park the car in one spot and then see the town on foot, stopping whenever the urge strikes for a bite to eat or a memento to buy. Stop by the visitor center on Main Street any day for maps and walking-tour guides.

Although a day trip from Tucson to Bisbee is long but not impossible at 100 miles, Bisbee is also a great weekend getaway by itself or via the itinerary described earlier. Unique places to stay besides the **Copper Queen Hotel** (520-432-2216; www.copperqueen.com) include the **School House Inn,** which is just what its name indicates, a schoolhouse transformed into a bed-and-breakfast (520-432-2996, 800-537-4333; www.schoolhouseinnbb.com), or the **Letson Loft Hotel**, located in the oldest remaining commercial building in Bisbee (520-432-3210, 877-432-3210; www.letsonlofthotel.com). For a sumptuous meal, the award-winning **Cafe Roka** offers sophisticated Italian and California dishes. It's always full and hours are seasonal, so be sure to make a reservation before you go (520-432-5153; www.caferoka.com). For more information about Bisbee, go to www.discoverbisbee.com or call (520) 432-3554.

Willcox

As a great day trip or to start out another weekend getaway that will take you into the mountains of Cochise County, visit the farming area of Willcox. Willcox is about 2 hours east of Tucson off I-10, and along the way you'll go through the dramatic boulder area of the Dragoon Mountains called Texas Canyon. Be sure to stop for a close-up view, a bit of hiking, or photos amid this unusually beautiful terrain. Nearby at the Dragoon Road exit just south of I-10 is the **Amerind Foundation** (a contraction of *American* and *Indian*), a research facility and museum housed in a beautiful Spanish colonial revival building displaying high-quality exhibits that give an overview of Southwestern Native cultures. It's open Tues through Sun, with an admission fee for anyone older than 12 (520-586-3666; www.amerind.org).

Continue heading for Willcox on I-10 to exit 336 north, then take Fort Grant Road, which will lead to nearly a dozen farms where kids and parents have a great time picking all manner of delicious fruits and vegetables. If you're not into picking your own, many have already done it for you and sell it freshly harvested. Willcox is most famous for its apple crops and some of the best-looking apple pies you've ever seen, but lots of other things will entice the farmer in you, including corn, tomatoes, chilies, peaches, pecans, pumpkins, melons, and more. In other areas around Willcox, you'll find about another dozen farms, including a couple specializing in pistachios. The harvests usually run from July through October or early November, so summer and fall are the best times to head for Willcox. The farms are well marked from the road, or you can stop at the easy-to-spot **Chamber of Commerce Visitor Center** (520-384-2272, 800-200-2272; www.willcoxchamber.com), at 1500 N. Circle I Rd., exit 340 off I-10, to pick up a list of where the farms are and what they offer. The chamber of commerce will also send out a brochure on request.

While you're in Willcox, stop at the **Rex Allen Cowboy Museum** (520-384-4583; www.rexallenmuseum.org), located in one of Willcox's oldest commercial buildings. This was the famous cowboy's birthplace, and the museum focuses on his life and the pioneer settlers and ranchers who shaped the West. It's open daily from 10 a.m. to 4 p.m. Willcox also happens to be about the only place is southern Arizona where it's possible to see waterfowl such as geese, ducks, and cranes, especially in the winter months. You'll spot them at the Willcox ponds south of the interstate and west of town.

i When in Willcox, stop by Apple Annie's Orchard, where they sell fantastic sky-high apple pies, cider, and fresh apples (in season). You can pick your own, take a hayride through the orchard, grab a burger at the snack bar, and buy all kinds of apple-themed gifts at the gift shop. You'll find them 5.5 miles from exit 340, off I-10. Call (520) 384-2084 or visit www.appleannies.com for more information

The Chiricahuas

From Willcox head south on Highway 186 (the "Apache Trail") to the Chiricahua (*chee-ree-CAH-wah*) Mountains for an outdoor adventure, but don't plan on combining this with Willcox in 1 day; find a spot to stay in Willcox overnight or camp out in the mountains. Two lodging options in Willcox are **Days Inn** (520-384-4222, 800-329-7466) and **Quality Inn** (520-384-3556, 800-262-2645).

Both Willcox and the Chiricahua Mountains also have places for RVs. You can drive into much of these mountains on paved roads or well-graded dirt roads, but to really explore you'll want to do some foot travel. Your first stop might be the turnoff to **Fort Bowie,** an 8-mile gravel road that ends in a parking lot. From here you'll take an easy 1.5-mile footpath to the fort ruins, along the way passing several well-marked historic sites, including a cemetery where Geronimo's baby son is buried and a picturesque 4-foot waterfall at Apache Spring. For details check www.nps .gov/fobo.

Back on Highway 186, continue south to the **Chiricahua National Monument,** with its thousands of rock spires and stone columns reaching skyward. Travel through the park along a winding 8-mile road to Massai Point for a spectacular view of the unusual rock formations. Throughout the area you'll find streams, maybe even a waterfall, and plenty of trees, along with breathtaking views. There are places to camp and restrooms but little else in the way of modern amenities. In summer this getaway will be cooler than Tucson, but carry water and sunscreen; in winter it will probably be too cold for comfort. To continue along the Apache Trail, take Highway 181 to US 191 north to Ironwood Road, then west 9.1 miles to the campground entrance. Part of this road is rough and rocky and leads to **Cochise's Stronghold** (www.cochisestrong hold.com) in the Dragoon Mountains, where the famous Apache Indian leader and his warriors evaded the cavalry easily in the canyons and cliffs of the terrain. It's now a year-round park with picnic areas, lots of historical information, and hiking and nature trails. Admission fee for day use (hiking and picnicking) is $5. The **Cochise Stronghold Bed**

and Breakfast in Pearce (520-826-4141, 877-426-4141; www.cochisestrongholdbb.com) is a really great place to stay. This romantic retreat in the heart of Cochise Stronghold Canyon offers luxury suites, casitas, and even a secluded tepee.

For more information on the attractions in these mountains, including camping areas, call the Coronado National Forest in Tucson at (520) 388-8300 or go to www.fs .fed.us/r3/coronado. For information about the Chiricahua National Monument, call (520) 824-3560, ext. 302, or go to www.nps .gov/chir.

New Mexico

If you're looking for a getaway that not everyone else in southern Arizona is flocking to, consider crossing the border, but this time into another state. Take I-10 east to Lordsburg, New Mexico, then Highway 90 north to Silver City, a drive of about 3 hours. It's an old mining town full of history—Billy the Kid roamed the streets in his youth, and miners and merchants built elegant Victorian homes here during its mining heyday. But on this getaway we're going a bit northward, via US 180, to a place called **Glenwood** in one of the least-populated counties (Catron) in the Southwest. Its climate parallels the Arizona high country, so it's an ideal summer destination and great in spring and fall as well. This is land once occupied by gold and silver miners, Apaches, and even Butch Cassidy and his Wild Bunch.

This getaway is truly an escape and definitely leans toward outdoor fun—canyon hikes, ghost towns, and hot springs—peppered with some good old-fashioned food and hospitality. It's been called New Mexico's best-kept secret, and we're letting you in on it.

Glenwood is a pastoral community of about 200 year-round residents. For lodgings try the scenic **Double T Homestead** (575-539-2812; www.doublethomestead.com) with its fantastic views of the Mogollon Mountains. Choose from a historic restored adobe, rustic cabin, or guesthouses on the property. There's even a horse motel fully equipped with a corral and water for your equine friends. Just south of the center of Glenwood is a USDA Forest Service office where you can get maps and recreation information on the area's hiking trails, 186 miles of trout streams, riding trails, and camping sites.

A must-see attraction is the **"catwalk" of Whitewater Canyon,** about 5 miles east of Glenwood at the end of NM 174, also known as the Catwalk Road. The canyon was reportedly once a hideout for Indians and desperadoes such as Butch Cassidy, while the catwalk was built by miners in the 1800s to carry water to a remote mill site. It was rebuilt in 1961 by the Forest Service as a recreation attraction. As you walk along the very safe and easy-to-navigate metal "sidewalk" that clings to the sides of the steep canyon walls, 25 feet below you'll see Whitewater Creek as it tumbles over boulders and winds through a forest of trees. At one point on the 1-mile catwalk, stairs lead down to the creek, where you can enjoy a tiny sandy beach, a waterfall, and wading pools. Looking skyward, you might be lucky enough to spot a bighorn sheep or 2 grazing near the canyon's peaks. At several spots, trails depart from the catwalk and wind up and down along the canyon. Be sure to take a picnic along and a good book—the picnic area near the entrance offers great shade and the relaxing sound of the tumbling creek. There is a self-pay parking fee of $3.

After this visit with the beauty of nature, you might want to take a drive to the restored mountain ghost town of **Mogollon,** once the site of one of the largest gold mines in the country. But don't make this trip unless you feel comfortable navigating narrow switchback roads, because that's the only way to reach Mogollon. Traffic, however, will be almost nonexistent. No more than a few dozen people live in Mogollon today, and they've opened up shops and even a guest lodge to attract tourists. The nearby forest of the Gila Wilderness offers fishing, hiking, bird-watching, and observing the wildlife. For more information about Glenwood and surrounding attractions, check the **Silver City Chamber of Commerce,** (575-538-3785; www.silvercity.com).

Phoenix & Environs

There's no shortage of things to do and see in the Phoenix area and no shortage of places to find information on them—tourist materials abound at the airport, nearly every hotel, and the **visitor bureau** (602-254-6500; www.visitphoenix.com). Instead of reinventing the wheel, we'll concentrate on mapping out a weekend getaway that consists of some of the attractions described in this chapter with a few others tossed in. For starters, as you head northward on I-10 (actually I-10 West), take a slight detour to the **Casa Grande Ruins National Monument** (www.nps.gov/cagr), which is accessible from exit 194 heading toward Coolidge. Here you'll see the ruins of a Hohokam Indian settlement built in 1350 and learn what archaeologists and historians know today about this now-extinct tribe. (This is true desert with little natural shade, so be prepared for the sun and heat.) After this step back into history, return to I-10 toward Phoenix.

In Phoenix your first stop should be one of the most exquisite museums in the state, the **Heard Museum** at 2301 N. Central Ave. in the downtown area (602-252-8848; www .heard.org). The Heard exhibits hundreds of outstanding historic Native American works, some dating back 1,000 years and representing almost every tribal group, past and present, of the Southwest. They also have an exquisite gift shop focusing on Native American items and culture.

For a luxurious stay, consider the **Arizona Biltmore Resort and Spa** (2400 E. Missouri; 602-955-6600, 800-950-0086; www .arizonabiltmore.com). This gorgeous historic hotel, known as the "jewel of the desert," has been host to many celebrities and politicians. Built in 1929, its unusual architecture was influenced by Frank Lloyd Wright. The giant checkers and chess set, nightly s'mores parties, outdoor pool movies, and waterslide will keep the kids happy, while the perfect landscaping, poolside bar, excellent restaurants, and cushy robes will keep adults relaxed.

Scottsdale

Downtown you'll find Scottsdale's **Arts District** located on the west side of Scottsdale Road from Main to Third Avenue. This area is packed with galleries and museums featuring a wide variety of amazing art. The **Old Town District,** on the east side of Scottsdale Road, from 2nd Street to Indian School Road, is home to historic buildings and numerous shops featuring Western ware, Southwestern jewelry, and more. You'll also find the sleek **Scottsdale Museum of Contemporary Art** (7374 E. 2nd St.; 480-874-4666; www.smoca .org), featuring modern and contemporary art, architecture, and design from around the globe. Designed by award-winning architect Will Bruder, SmoCA's minimalist building (formerly a movie theater) includes a public "skyspace" by the acclaimed artist James Turrell. And don't miss Frank Lloyd Wright's incredible **Taliesin West** at 12621 N. Frank Lloyd Wright Blvd. (see the comprehensive listing under Day Trips earlier in this chapter).

To continue on our getaway, head back to the interstate (I-10) east to the Superstition Freeway, also known as US 60. In Apache Junction take Highway 88 north, aka the Apache Trail (one of several carrying this name in the state). Here you'll see the spectacular Superstition Mountains, where legend has it the hidden fortune of the Lost Dutchman Mine has yet to be discovered. Stop at the **Goldfield Ghost Town** (4650 N. Mammoth Mine Rd.; www .goldfieldghosttown.com) to see the area's only historic ghost town and try your luck at gold panning.

Farther north along the Apache Trail, you'll arrive at **Canyon Lake,** one of 3 lakes created by dams in the Salt River. This is a gorgeous spot for just admiring the water and its surrounding canyon cliffs or enjoying a lakeside picnic. Better yet, try something totally unexpected in Arizona—a cruise on a steam-operated paddle wheeler. The **Dolly steamboat** glides along the lake and its secluded inner waterways for about 90 minutes as the guide recounts legends of the Superstition Mountains. It operates daily. Ticket prices vary, with kids younger than 6 admitted free. Call (480) 827-9144 or visit www.dollysteamboat.com for tour times, and be sure to allow several hours at Canyon Lake if you plan to include the boat cruise. For the perfect finale to this getaway, head back south on Apache Trail and east on US 60 to **Boyce Thompson Southwestern Arboretum** (see the earlier listing under Day Trips).

For places to stay on this getaway, consider Scottsdale or nearby Paradise Valley as a good midpoint. For budget accommodations, there's **Days Inn Scottsdale Resort at Fashion Square Mall** (480-947-5411, 800-329-7466). Or try a resort that has great amenities, including a huge pool with a swim-under waterfall, but is more reasonable than most in this upscale area—the **Doubletree by Hilton Hotel Paradise Valley Resort** (480-947-5400, 800-222-8733). These are but 2 possibilities from hundreds of places to stay that are easy to locate in Phoenix-area tourist guides or by just driving along the roadways. For a comprehensive guide to Phoenix, log onto www.visitphoenix.com.

Florence

Instead of riding I-10 all the way to Phoenix, take a scenic detour north out of Tucson on Highway 79 (which you'll pick up past Oro Valley). Also known as the Pinal Pioneer Highway, this will take you to Florence, the 5th-oldest town in the state. Just 45 minutes northwest of Tucson, it was founded in 1866 and hasn't changed much since.

On your way you can stop at the **Tom Mix Memorial** at Milepost 116. This is the spot where Mix, Hollywood's first "King of the Cowboys," who appeared in over 300 movies, had his fatal car accident in 1940.

An unusual stop along the way into town is **St. Anthony's Greek Orthodox Monastery** (4784 N. St. Joseph's Way; 520-868-3188; www.stanthonysmonastery.org). Established in 1995, the lovely grounds, church, and chapels are open for visiting and viewing between 10:30 a.m. and 2:30 p.m. daily. Stop at the gatehouse before entering the grounds, and note that there are some dress code requirements and

recommendations. Groups of 10 or more need to call in advance. To get to the monastery, continue on Highway 79 North, turn on Paisano Drive just before Mile Marker 124, and follow it to the end. This turns into an unmarked road, which is St.Joseph's Way.

Downtown Florence has been designated an official historic district and has over 140 homes and commercial buildings on the National Register of Historic Places, more than any other town in Arizona. Some of the notable historic sites are the first and second county courthouses, both completely different in architectural style. The first was built in 1877 and is open to the public as **McFarland State Park,** home of the town's visitor center at 310 N. Main St. It holds the papers of hometown boy Ernest W. McFarland, who held the 3 highest offices in Arizona—chief justice of the Arizona Supreme Court, governor, and US senator—and was known as the "Father of the GI Bill." The second was built in 1891 of American-Victorian architecture and is still in use today. Historic buildings of note in town also include the beautifully restored **Silver King Hotel,** built in 1895 and now a marketplace, **Michael's General Store,** a restored 1890s mercantile now home to a restaurant/cafe, and the **Clark House,** a restored adobe Victorian built in 1888 that is now the town's newspaper office. Maps for self-guided walking tours of the historic district are available at the visitor center and the Historical Museum.

For a real look at life in territorial Arizona, stop by the **Pinal County Historical Museum** at 715 S. Main St. (520-868-4382), which houses an eclectic collection including information about the WWII POW camp located here (surrounded by an Army Air Corps practice bombing range), period furnishings, the first lethal gas chamber double chair, and ropes utilized in hangings. Open Tues through Sat.

For a bite to eat, head to family-owned **L&B Inn** at 695 S. Main St. (520-868-9981; www.lbinn.com) for fresh Mexican fare. For more about Florence, visit the website www .florenceaz.gov.

Rocky Point, Mexico

Unfortunately, the Mexican state of Sonora, home to Puerto Peñasco (also known as Rocky Point), has been the victim of continued drug wars and violence that have affected tourism. An April 2011 State Department advisory states that travelers are "advised to exercise caution when visiting the coastal town of Puerto Peñasco. In the past year there have been multiple incidents of TCO-related (Transnational Criminal Organizations) violence, including the shooting of the city's police chief. US citizens visiting Puerto Peñasco are urged to cross the border at Lukeville, AZ, to limit driving through Mexico and to limit travel to main roads during daylight hours."

Fans of Rocky Point continue to flock here, however, noting that they feel safe and welcome in this beautiful resort town with its azure waters, pristine white sandy beaches, some of the freshest seafood ever, a scenic downtown, a fisherman's wharf, upscale time shares, hotels, and restaurants.

If you do decide to visit Rocky Point, be cautious, and before you go, check the State Department's website (http://travel.state .gov), which lists up-to-date travel warnings and alerts, or call their toll-free number, (888) 407-4747 (Mon to Fri, 8 a.m. to 8 p.m. eastern time). Tourists are also advised not to walk on the beach areas after dark.

To reach Rocky Point via the scenic route, take Highway 86 west from Tucson to Highway 85 (at Why, Arizona) heading south, which will put you at the border. From there Mexico Highway 8 goes to Puerto Peñasco. Along the way you'll go through **Organ Pipe Cactus National Monument,** a 500-square-mile preserve of huge organ pipe cacti and lots of other desert wildlife on the Arizona side of the border.

Rocky Point is very Anglicized—English is spoken by many, US currency is accepted, and most signage is in English, so it's easy to find your way around. Because Rocky Point has really become a tourist attraction, there are plenty of hotels and other amenities. In addition to hotels, lodging choices include RV parks and rentals of condos and homes, some of them quite luxurious beachside vacation homes.

i For customs regulations and border crossing info, call before crossing the border to check for current regulations. The Mexican and US Customs offices are available 24 hours a day to answer any questions; (520) 287-1410.

The weather is about the same as Tucson's, sometimes a few degrees warmer, which means that it may not be beach weather in December or January, but spring and fall are perfect, and summer will actually feel hotter because of the oceanside humidity. But there's a solution to that problem—jump in the water. Water is all around, along with miles of white beaches, and they're all public. To the town's north is an area called **Cholla Bay.** With lots of beach, small beachfront houses, and nightlife, this area is a favorite of vacationing college students and young adults. To the town's east is more beach, miles of it, along with a gated

Close-up

Tohono O'odham Nation Cultural Center and Museum

The Tohono O'odham Nation Cultural Center and Museum is worth a stop on the way to Rocky Point or as a day-trip destination itself. Located in the tiny town of Topawa just off Highway 86, the $15.2 million facility showcases Tohono O'odham life and culture. The second-largest tribe in the US, the Tohono O'odham (Desert People) are less well known than other tribes. The fascinating exhibits at the museum offer a window into the world of these amazing people who have made their home in the Sonoran Desert for centuries. In addition to the exhibit and gallery space, an outdoor patio offers a fabulous view of sacred Baboquivari Peak. Nature trails, an outdoor amphitheater, and covered armadas are great for walking and picnicking. There are no food vendors here, so bring your own. The museum is open Mon through Sat 10 a.m. to 4 p.m. For more information call (520) 383-0201.

Signage for the museum is limited. To get there take Highway 86 to Sells, follow the business loop toward the hospital, and turn south at the sign reading TOPAWA AND SAN MIGUEL, which takes you onto BIA Route 19. Travel approximately 9 miles south and turn left onto the dirt road at the sign for Baboquivari Peak, which is Fresnal Canyon Road. The museum will be on your right about 1,000 yards ahead.

upscale community called **Las Conchas,** with homes and condos.

As for where to stay, there are numerous choices from motels and hotels to condos and time shares. Hotels range from midlevel **Playa Bonita** (www.playabonitaresort.com) to the luxe **Mayan Palace** (www.mayanpalace.com) just outside of town. There are also RV parks north and east of town. Reserving a hotel in advance is a good idea, and reserving an RV space or private rental in advance is a necessity.

Seaside, you can frolic in the salt water or on the beach, search for seashells, snorkel, fish, parasail, and scuba dive. You also can rent just about any kind of fun you didn't bring with you—personal watercraft, ATVs, parasail rides, scuba dives, and even a banana boat ride in the shallow surf. (Look for the large tourist information sign for places that rent equipment, fishing boats,

and so forth.) You can also golf, rent ATVs, take boat and deep-sea fishing trips, or explore the shoreline on kayaks.

You'll also find oyster farms just outside of town. Place your order and the oysters are brought to shore from the sea right before your eyes. Watch for signs by the roadside.

Do be sure to visit **CEDO** (www.cedo intercultural.org) in the Las Conchas neighborhood. This valuable organization conducts research, provides educational and conservation programs about the Sea of Cortez, and sponsors fascinating eco-adventures. Kids will love the fin whale skeleton and environmental exhibits at the visitor center, and they might learn something at the same time!

In town or on Cholla Bay, you can shop for all the regional goods Mexico is famous for, including blankets, jewelry, carvings, and more. But don't miss a visit to the fish market in the scenic **Old Port** area. Whether you're doing your own cooking or merely want to take some of the sea's bounty back to Tucson, you'll find large shrimp and all kinds of freshly caught fish. Seafood is a staple of many restaurants, but there's also a variety of other restaurants from small scale to upscale serving Italian food, burgers and pizza, and of course Mexican food. For more information call the visitors bureau at (602) 539-0027, or check www.cometorockypoint.com.

Verde Valley

North and a bit west of Phoenix is an area called Verde Valley (named for the Verde, meaning "green," River) that houses some of the state's most popular spots: the mountainside former mining town of Jerome, the historic and lovely city of Prescott, and the breathtaking red-rock country of Sedona. Because this area has so much to offer and is quite different from Tucson and the Sonoran Desert, we'll map out a weekend getaway to take you there, but you'll need a long weekend—3 or 4 days—to fit it in. The driving time alone from Tucson to Sedona, the farthest point of this trip, is 4 hours, and that doesn't include some must-see stops along the way.

Begin this multifaceted weekend getaway by taking I-10 west to Phoenix, where you'll catch I-17 north. For your first stop, consider **Arcosanti,** the urban habitat founded by Paolo Soleri (described previously in this chapter under Day Trips). But be sure to allow enough time to drive a bit farther up I-17, to exit 289, for **Montezuma Castle** (www.nps .gov/moca). Don't be fooled or put off by this attraction's moniker—it's not a castle, but an Indian ruin, one of the best-preserved prehistoric cliff dwellings in Arizona. If you only have time to see one Indian ruin in the southern

half of the state, this should be it. The Sinagua (Spanish for "without water") Indians built Montezuma Castle around AD 1125. A peaceful farming people, they cultivated the valley using water from the Verde River and its tributaries and sometimes built cliff dwellings as a way to live protected from the more aggressive inhabitants of the area. What today is called Montezuma Castle was such a dwelling. (Later settlers erroneously thought it was built by the Aztec Indians and, thinking it looked like a castle, named it for the Aztec leader.) Today it's a national monument and a sight to behold. After parking your vehicle and entering the visitor center, you'll still have no idea what lies ahead until you walk down a pathway with a creek coursing nearby—the same water that centuries ago provided the sustenance for this small group of cliff dwellers who disappeared. The first sight of the 5-story cliff dwelling is breathtaking, and the 500-acre monument itself is a lovely place of huge old trees and pathways lined with the story of these people. Montezuma Castle (928-567-3322) is open daily from 8 a.m. to 5 p.m. (6 p.m. in summer) and costs $5 for anyone older than 16.

If you'd like to see more examples of ancient dwellers, both Sinagua and Hohokam, take I-17 a few miles farther north to exit 293 and visit **Montezuma Well.** This is an oasis of lush vegetation, including huge Arizona sycamore trees, where you'll see remains of a Sinagua cliff dwelling and pueblo and a Hohokam pithouse. From the Indian ruins you'll probably want to find a spot to rest for the night before tackling the rest of this getaway. Prescott is the closest spot, Jerome the most difficult to get to, and Sedona the farthest, but any will do as a base from which to explore the exciting and varied Verde Valley.

Highway 69 west will take you into **Prescott,** a scenic city that combines the Old West and 1860s Victorian charm. Prescott was founded when gold was discovered in nearby hills and was the Arizona Territory's first capital. By then rowdy gold miners were frequenting Prescott's now-famous Whiskey Row, and European gentry were living in grand Victorian houses. More than 500 buildings in Prescott are on the National Register of Historic Places, so history and architecture buffs will find much to explore in this city, including the territorial governor's residence built in 1864. The downtown area is where you'll find most of the historic sites, along with Whiskey Row, museums, and a lovely square called Courthouse Plaza, where many art shows and special events take place.

> **i** The Desert Rain Cafe offers a unique and delicious menu featuring traditional Sonoran Desert ingredients like cholla cactus buds, tepary beans, and prickly pear nectar. Open Mon through Fri for breakfast and lunch, the cafe is affiliated with Tohono O'odham Community Action, a nonprofit organization dedicated to revitalizing culture and health on the Nation. The cafe is located just off Highway 86 in Sells. Call for directions and hours, (520) 383-4918, or visit www.desertraincafe.com.

Prescott is also a great place for outdoor fun. It actually has 4 seasons, but they're mild; in other words, it's minus the extreme heat of the desert in summer and the extreme cold and snow common to the north. In and around Prescott visitors can play golf, hike, climb on some of the state's best rock formations, fish, ride horses, pan for gold, watch and wager on the horse races at Prescott Downs, and see the world's oldest rodeo in July. If you choose to make Prescott an overnight stop, there are many choices of hotels and bed-and-breakfasts, among them the historic **Hotel St. Michael** (928-776-1999, 800-678-3757; www.stmichaelhotel .com) and the quaint **Hotel Vendome** (928-776-0900, 888-468-3583; www.vendome hotel.com).

Another spot you might want to consider visiting in Verde Valley is **Jerome.** Although most ghost towns in Arizona have remained just that, Jerome is one of the rare exceptions. The mines around this old mining town clinging to the side of Mingus Mountain once produced $125 billion worth of copper ore, and Jerome had 15,000 residents. For several decades it was almost totally abandoned (earning it the reputation of a ghost town), but today it is an enclave of artists and is a National Historic Landmark.

At its 5,000-foot elevation, Jerome offers some spectacular vistas of mountains, the Mogollon Rim, and the red-rock country. The downside of Jerome is the road one must traverse to reach it. This narrow and winding switchback road up the mountain, although paved, is not for everyone. But once in Jerome, you'll find a quaint and scenic village with shops, restaurants, museums, galleries, and old-time saloons. Dining options are limited in number but varied. Grills and hamburger joints join the upscale **Asylum Restaurant** (928-639-3197; www.theasylum.biz) with its spectacular views. For lodging there are several bed-and-breakfast inns, but it's best to contact the chamber of commerce (928-634-2900; www.jeromechamber.com) in advance to find out what's open and the price of a room. From I-17 take Highway 260 west to Cottonwood, then Highway 89A to Jerome.

To round out your Verde Valley getaway, we've saved what many people believe is the best for last: the red-rock scenery of **Sedona** and **Oak Creek Canyon.** From either Prescott or Jerome, Highway 89A will take you to Sedona; otherwise, from I-17 take Highway 179 to the Sedona exit. Be sure to include some time for seeing the surroundings because, although the town is picturesque and can keep you very busy, a walk in the wild here is like nothing you will experience elsewhere. That's because this pocket of the state was blessed with vibrant red sandstone cliffs and rock formations that display their dramatic spires and odd shapes amid pines, sycamores, buttes, and a beautiful rushing stream, Oak Creek.

Some highlights of the red-rock country you'll want to include in your sightseeing are **Red Rock Crossing,** which is a bit off the beaten path for most tourists and therefore a more peaceful spot for frolicking in Oak Creek or hiking along an easy trail to the base of Cathedral Rock; **Bell Rock,** a landmark formation southeast of Sedona on Highway 179, which is called the Red Rock Scenic Byway and is one of only 27 US roads designated as an All-American Highway; the Frank Lloyd Wright–designed **Chapel of the Holy Cross** at 780 Chapel Hill Rd. (www.chapeloftheholycross.com); and the popular **Oak Creek Canyon** north of town, where slide rocks at Slide Rock State Park (http://azstateparks.com/parks/slro) provide some serious rides down the creek for kids and adults alike. No matter where you may choose to drive, bike, or walk around the Sedona countryside, however, you'll be treated to nature at its finest.

Sedona is a mecca for shopping, the arts, dining, and lodging—and it all leans toward upscale. **Tlaquepaque** (pronounce it *tla-keh-pah-keh;* www.tlaq.com), for instance, is a lovely shopping center with the architecture and flavor of Old Mexico and about 2 dozen shops. Throughout Sedona you'll find shops selling everything from Southwestern items to fine clothing and home accessories. The town is dotted with scores of art galleries, while art exhibits, live theater, and music events are regular happenings here. Sedona also has a vast array of eateries, from delis and ice-cream shops to some very fine dining. And if this is where you plan to rest for a night or two, the accommodation choices are almost dizzying. There are motels, such as **King's Ransom** (928-282-7151; www.kingsransom.com) and **Sedona Super 8** (928-282-1533) that, while not cheap in this neck of the woods, are at least affordable. Or choose from among many bed-and-breakfasts, including 2 that travel writers often call among the best in the Southwest: **Grace's Secret Garden** (928-284-2340, 800-579-2340; www.gracessecretgarden.com) and the **Casa Sedona** (928-282-2938, 800-525-3756; www.casasedona.com). If you really want to splurge on a resort stay, Sedona offers some of the best. Two choices for luxurious accommodations are the **L'Auberge de Sedona** (928-282-1661, 800-905-5745; www.lauberge.com) and **Enchantment Resort** (928-282-2900, 800-826-4180; www.enchantmentresort.com).

At an elevation of 4,400 feet, Sedona is cooler than Tucson and a favorite playground of both Arizonans and tourists. It's a busy place year-round but especially in summer when desert dwellers need an escape. In addition to attracting tourists for all the obvious reasons, Sedona also is said (by those who know these things) to be a "vortex" of spiritual rejuvenation; for the uninitiated, that's something like having a mystical energy, making Sedona a mecca for meditation types. But whatever your reason for visiting Sedona—its spectacular beauty, art offerings, mystical energy, or the cool running waters of Oak Creek—you'll be enchanted.

For information contact the chamber of commerce (928-282-7722, 800-288-7336; www.sedonachamber.com) or stop by the visitor center at 331 Forest Rd. in uptown Sedona for maps, tour information, accommodations, and more. Open daily except Christmas, Thanksgiving, and New Year's Day.

Lake Havasu City

Lake Havasu City is not just about the London Bridge, although it is true that the real **London Bridge** is now located here, bought by town founder Robert P. McCullouch Sr. in 1968 at a cost of over $2 million. The 22 million pounds of granite that made up the bridge were dismantled and moved from London through the Panama Canal and then trucked 10,000 miles to Lake Havasu City. Reconstruction of the bridge took 3 years and it now spans a 1-mile man-made channel that split a piece of land from the mainland to create Havasu Island and put water under the bridge (literally!).

Lake Havasu City offers something for everyone in a remarkably scenic setting. The varied blue hues of the lake, hidden coves, and marsh grasses, surrounded by craggy mountains, make for a beautiful landscape.

About 315 miles north of Tucson, this is a terrific weekend trip, great for families and anyone looking to get away and enjoy water sports and more—and especially for Tucsonans starved for a water view. The history

of the area is quite interesting. The land was purchased in 1963 by Robert McCullouch Sr., a multimillionaire who was looking for a place to test his small boat engines. Finding the lake a perfect spot, he moved his operations to the area, conceived of and created a master-planned community that is now Lake Havasu City, and set up a fleet of airplanes to bring prospective buyers to the area from all over the country.

Home to over 55,000 residents, the city sees its population swell by 43 percent with snowbirds during the winter months. At this popular summer vacation spot, up to 10,000 additional folks head here from all over Arizona and California for the peak summer boating season.

The most direct route, west on I-10 to Quartzsite and north on I-95, will get you here in about 4.5 hours, with a few interesting stops along the way. The tiny town of **Quartzsite,** at the crossroads of I-10 and Highway 95, is the site of a funky miniature pyramid in town dedicated to Hadji Ali (known locally as Hi Jolly), a camel driver who was involved in an Army experiment to use camels as pack animals in the 1800s.

About 10 miles before you get into Lake Havasu City, you'll pass the entrance to the **Parker Dam.** Take the side road and see the beautiful Art Deco–style dam built in the 1930s that is responsible for creating the lake. At 320 feet, the dam is the deepest in the world. The reservoir behind the dam has a storage capacity of 211 billion gallons and supplies water to the Central Arizona Project, which carries water all the way down to Tucson.

Once you get into Lake Havasu City, there are lots of things to do and see. There are over 45 miles of lake, so boating and water sports are really popular here.

Boating enthusiasts will be in heaven—you can rent canoes, Jet Skis, speedboats, paddleboats, pontoon boats, kayaks, and ski boats. There are numerous companies throughout town and on the waterfront, including **Arizona Watersports** (800-393-5558; www.arizonawatersports.com), where you can rent just about anything that floats. Or if you don't want to do your own boating, go out on one of the many tours offered at the lake. **Kon Tiki** (928-855-0888) offers several tours ranging from 1 to 3.5 hours. Want a bird's-eye view of the lake? Opt for a parasail (928-302-0638; www.lakehavasuparasail.com).

Fishermen can choose from many options; rent your own boat and head out on the lake or into the many estuaries and coves. If you're boatless, head to the specially designated fishing piers in the parks, fish from the shore, or go out on a fishing excursion. (Anyone over 14 will need a fishing license, available at local sporting goods stores.)

Looking to really relax on the water? The unusual **Cabana Boats,** equipped with a full-size bed and canopy, will fit the bill. These rent for about $250 per day with a full ice chest. Call (928) 486-6951 or visit www.cabanaboat.com to reserve one.

Golfers, bring your clubs! There are 4 golf courses in town, ranging from a 9-hole to an 18-hole, par 72 championship course, **Emerald Canyon Golf Course** (928-667-3366).

Hikers can enjoy the numerous trails and paths in the city's lovely parks. Try the 2.5-mile Crack in the Mountain trail in **SARA Park** (www.lhcaz.gov/parksAndRecreation/parks/saraPark.html) 5 miles outside of town. The 2.5-mile hilly trail, rated somewhat difficult, takes you through a series of dry falls to an actual crack in the mountain at mile

point 1.4. The park is also home to a shooting range, model airplane field, and BMX track.

Even Fido will be happy with several dog-friendly hotels (check www.dogfriendly.com for full listings) and 2 beautiful leash-free dog parks (**Avalon Park** and **London Bridge Beach Park**).

History buffs should not miss the small but extremely informative history museum, the **Lake Havasu Museum of History,** located in a strip mall at 320 London Bridge Rd. (928-854-4938; www.havasumuseum.com), with displays of both the Native and more recent history of the area and its development. It's open Tues though Sat, with an entry fee.

The gorgeous **Aquatic Center** at 100 Park Ave. (928-453-2687) is worth a peek. Operated by the city, it's a vast cavern of swimmable lap and kiddie pools and a 254-foot slide. There are fees to participate, and hours and open swim times vary, so call ahead.

The very friendly and helpful staff at the **visitor center** at the foot of the bridge at 314 London Bridge Rd. (928-855-5655; www.golakehavasu.com) will be happy to guide you to other main and off-the-beaten-path sites to see in town, recommend restaurants and tours, as well as provide easy-to-read maps, walking tours, and even souvenir hats and T-shirts.

Lake Havasu has worked hard to preserve its natural beauty with numerous parks, walking paths, and trails both within the city limits and beyond.

There is a lovely path from the bridge along the channel and into **Rotary Community Park,** which features a beach, playgrounds, picnic areas, a skate park, and bocce ball court.

While walking the path, you may notice the series of **miniature lighthouses** along the water's edge. A source of much local pride, the 10 lighthouses are scale reproductions of famous lighthouses around the country and function as navigation aids to boaters on the lake. (Go to www.lh-lighthouseclub.org for a description of each one.)

Chain hotels and motels are abundant and offer rooms at all price ranges. For longer-term stays, time shares and condo rentals are also available. The visitor center and the Convention & Visitors Bureau can supply you with a comprehensive list.

If you want to be in the center of the action, the large-scale **London Bridge Resort & Convention Center** (928-855-0888, 800-624-7939; www.londonbridgeresort.com) is right at the bridge and has a pool that overlooks the waterway along with restaurants and a nightclub.

If you like a slightly more secluded place, the **Island Inn Hotel** on Lake Havasu Island (928-680-0606; www.havasumotels.com) is one of the older hotels in town. It is gently used but offers an outdoor pool and great views of the lake.

The upscale, modern in-town **Heat Hotel** (928-854-833; www.heathotel.com), with only 25 rooms, each with a private balcony, has some of the best views of the water and the bridge.

If you don't want to stay in a hotel, the lakeside and island are dotted with campgrounds and RV resorts. One of the largest is the **Crazy Horse Campgrounds** (928-855-4033; www.crazyhousecampgrounds.com) with 632 tent and hookup sites within walking distance of the bridge. The campground has 1 mile of beach, beachfront tent camping, boat launch ramp, and boat and Jet Ski rentals. The **Islander RV Resort** (928-680-2000; www.islanderrvresort.com) has 500 RV sites with beaches, a boat ramp, and boat docks. There are even special storage facilities in town for RVs, and many homes here come equipped with super-large RV garages.

There are lots of restaurants to choose from, ranging from chain to upscale. Locals and breakfast lovers flock to the **Black Bear Diner** (928-855-2013; www.blackbeardiner .com), where you get gigantic portions of buttermilk pancakes, homemade corned beef hash, and bottomless cups of joe. The enormous, family-friendly **Shugrue's Restaurant and Bakery** (928-453-1400; www .shugrues.com) offers wide window views overlooking the bridge and a ginormous selection of hand-cut steaks, seafood, and homemade desserts. More upscale fare is available at **Cha-Bones Steakhouse and Tapas Bar** (928-854-5554; www.chabones .com) where locals take out-of-town guests they want to impress. If you have a sweet tooth, head to **Scoops Old Fashioned Ice Cream Parlour & Soda Fountain** (928-453-7084; www.uptownscoops.com), where the ice cream is homemade and the soda fountain will take you back to the 1950s.

Special annual events include the **Chihuahua Race,** billed as the largest gathering of Chihuahua's in Mohave County, held at the beginning of May. The **Desert Storm Speedboating Event,** held in late April, brings in high-performance boats from all over to participate in a parade on Main Street and boat races in the channel.

Appendix

LIVING HERE

In this section we feature specific information for residents or those planning to relocate here. Topics include real estate, education, health care, and much more.

NEIGHBORHOODS, NEIGHBORING TOWNS & REAL ESTATE

Tucson is made up of a variety of eclectic neighborhoods, ranging from upscale new housing and condo developments to historic, artsy, downtown communities. You'll find a little bit of everything here.

Much like the rest of the country, the Tucson housing market has been affected by the economy, but there are some bright spots! In 2010 NBC's *Today* show named Tucson among the top 10 places for bargain homes based on home value, home size, job growth, and increase in home prices, and *Sunset Magazine* listed Tucson in its March 2010 issue as one of the West's "20 Towns of the Future," for its "fresh, innovative and environmentally sound buildings." It's a good time to buy if you're looking for a family-friendly, small city with lots of great sunshine and natural beauty.

OVERVIEW

According to the Tucson Association of Realtors, the median sale price for homes in Tucson as of February 2010 was $150,000, with an average sale price of $195,996. Although the median sales price was down compared to that of 2009, the number of homes sold was up and inventory was shrinking. Note that the prices listed in this chapter are just averages and do not include foreclosure homes, which are available in all neighborhoods in town.

However, even with the housing market slowdown, land is still scarce in the Tucson area. When the market begins to turn around, land values should continue their upward swing, so if you are thinking of moving to Tucson, now is a great time. The areas of most growth include downtown, where many new homes are being built and renovated as a result of

Rio Nuevo, a multimillion-dollar revitalization effort (see the Area Overview chapter). The northwest (Oro Valley and Marana) and southeast (Rincon Mountain) areas of town are bursting with available new single-family homes and developments, and the Green Valley, Vail, and Sahuarita areas continue to expand with luxury housing, developments, and active adult communities (see the Retirement chapter).

Tucson, unlike many cities of its size or larger, does not have suburbs in the customary sense. There's Tucson (the city) and there's Pima County (surrounding the city), and within both are numerous neighborhoods and towns, each with something a little different to offer. This chapter presents a primer on the metro area—from its fascinating historic areas to the sprawling newer ones. We try to convey the character and lifestyle, distinguishing architectural features, a few major points of interest, and what the real estate scene is like in select areas.

If you're a visitor to Tucson, you'll find great information about specific neighborhoods to visit for their historic, cultural, and design significance. If you're a new resident or plan to be, this chapter will help you get an overview of the many options Tucson offers in the more established neighborhoods and where the growth is.

NEIGHBORHOODS

Historic & Old Neighborhoods

El Presidio

The Hohokam Indians were the first human inhabitants of Tucson. Long after they disappeared, Spanish settlers arrived from Mexico and created what is Tucson's first neighborhood—El Presidio. They may not have known it, but they settled very near a Hohokam site. The first neighborhood started out as a fort (or presidio) called San Augustin del Tucson, covering approximately 12 acres and enclosing 2 plazas, a chapel, a cemetery, stables for horses, and quarters for officers, soldiers, and settlers. Gradually houses were built outside the presidio walls, and eventually the walls came tumbling down.

As with the other downtown historic areas, the neighborhood really took off with the arrival of the railroad and Anglo-Americans in the early 1880s, their Victorian, Tudor, and bungalow-style houses supplanting the Sonoran row houses of the first settlers. Meyer and Court Streets offer examples of the original Sonoran architecture, with adobe row houses built to the front property line and open courtyard spaces in the interior. In contrast, the houses along Main Avenue reflect architectural styles introduced from the East and Midwest by Anglo-Americans—these houses are set back from the street, surrounded by yards and lush vegetation, and Victorian in architectural style. The grand homes along Main and Granada Avenues and Paseo Redondo earned this area the name "Snob Hollow" in the 1920s and 1930s, coined because Tucson's movers and shakers lived there and the area was in a topographical hollow.

Designated the El Presidio Historic District in 1975, it covers a 12-block area immediately north of today's downtown, bounded roughly by Alameda, Church, and 6th Streets and Granada Avenue. The district is rich with old structures, many of which have been converted into museums or professional buildings. The oldest is **La Casa Cordova,** now housing a Mexican heritage museum. Nearby is the **Edward Nye Fish House,** a typical prerailroad Sonoran row house that now houses the **Tucson Museum of Art's Pavilion of Western Art.** The **Steinfeld Mansion** at 300 N. Main Ave. was built for $10,000 in 1899. The 12,000-square-foot **Manning House,** at 450 W. Paseo Redondo, was built in 1907 and occupied by a onetime mayor. Other historic residences are the Corbett House, Romero House, and Stevens House.

If your tour of the area makes you a bit weary of concrete and buildings, visit a lovely little oasis in the midst of it all—the **Alene Dunlap Smith Memorial Garden,** on the east side of Granada Street just north of Franklin Street. If you'd like to get in a bit of shopping or dining with your history, visit **Old Town Artisans,** an adobe-walled structure on Washington and Meyer Streets, parts of which date back more than 150 years. The half dozen shops here include items handmade by local artists and a collection of folk art. Directly across Alameda Street (the historic district's southern boundary) are **El Presidio Park** and the **Pima County Courthouse,** built in 1928 in an elaborate Moorish style with a tile mosaic dome that's a Tucson landmark.

i Many of the historic districts in and around the downtown area make for some excellent walking tours, complete with historic buildings, houses converted into museums, churches, and even a shrine. Stop by the Metropolitan Tucson Convention & Visitors Bureau at 100 S. Church Ave. for tour information and lots more on the Tucson area (including discount offers on accommodations, travel, attractions, and more).

El Presidio has been undergoing a residential renaissance as a result of multimillion-dollar initiatives aimed at revitalizing the downtown area. Historic adobes have been renovated and lovely new single-family and townhomes constructed, some designated for lower income residents. Paving projects and other roadwork are improving access and traffic flow. It's a friendly, intimate neighborhood with a strong neighborhood association committed to preserving the look and feel of this historic area. There are not a lot of services here; commercial and historic buildings are the norm. The area attracts a variety of people from artists to professionals. It might not be a first choice for families with school-age children. Homes here range from the mid-$100,000s to more than $900,000; upscale, refurbished developments like Franklin Court, a 9-unit upscale residential development at the northeast corner of Franklin and Court, start in the

$300,000s. The area falls within Tucson Unified School District, Tucson's largest school district.

Armory Park

Way back when, the area now known as Armory Park began as the original military plaza of Camp Lowell. (Later the military camp was moved to the Rillito River area and renamed Fort Lowell, discussed separately in this chapter.) From 1880, when work on the transcontinental railroad reached Tucson, until about 1920, the Armory Park area transformed into a residential area inhabited by prominent railroad executives, affluent entrepreneurs, and working-class people. Anglo-Americans began migrating in and, with the help of the railroad, imported building materials typically used in eastern housing. Also typical of the Anglo style, their houses were built in the center of lots with spacious yards all around.

Today you'll still see an eclectic mix of Victorian, Queen Anne, California bungalow, Mission, and Spanish colonial revival styles. Designated a historic district in 1974 (Tucson's first), Armory Park covers about 30 blocks just southeast of the central business district. It extends from 12th Street south to 19th Street and from about Second Avenue on the east to Stone Avenue on the west.

In addition to an actual park—named, what else, Armory Park—and a senior center adjacent to it, some of the highlights of the district are the **Temple of Music and Art,** a handsomely restored structure now housing the Arizona Theatre Company; the original Tucson Carnegie Library, now home to the **Tucson Children's Museum;** and the **Tucson Center for the Performing Arts,** formerly a Catholic church. **Safford Middle School** is an excellent example of the Mission revival style, with plastered walls, an elaborate ornamental entry, and portals.

Along with turn-of-the-20th-century hotels, converted office buildings, and even a bed-and-breakfast or two, the outer edge of this neighborhood is growing rapidly as a result of the development of **Armory Park del Sol** at S. 3rd Avenue and 16th Street. This attractive development includes 2 parks, a community garden, and landscaped common areas. The well-designed homes are energy efficient and, although modern, incorporate historic elements from the Queen Anne, Mission revival, territorial, and bungalow styles found in the neighborhood. Homes start in the mid-$300,000s.

The Armory Park area has few services and attracts primarily young professionals. Several historic buildings in the area, including a former convent and an icehouse, have been converted into upscale lofts with apartments both for rent and for sale. A lovely historic area within the Tucson Unified School District, it may not be the ideal place for families, however, because of the dense traffic, the commercial businesses intermingled with residences, and the homeless population that often occupies Armory Park.

One of the interesting residential areas on the edge of downtown and A Mountain is the **Mercado District of Menlo Park,** a 14-acre residential and commercial neighborhood with 250 adobe-style houses ranging from row houses and lofts to town houses and custom homes. This pedestrian- and family-friendly development features winding streets, wide sidewalks, 7 small plazas, and a great view of the downtown.

Barrio Historico

In sharp contrast to the contemporary concrete edifice right across the street known as the Tucson Convention Center, Barrio Historico dates from the mid-1850s. Also known as Barrio Viejo, this historic district covers about 20 blocks from Cushing Street on the north to 18th Street on the south and from the railroad tracks on the west to Stone Avenue on the east. Although working-class Mexicans were the predominant settlers, Chinese, African-American, Anglo-American, and Native American settlers made it a somewhat ethnically diverse area.

Unlike for some of the other central historical neighborhoods, the influx of Anglo-Americans and the railroad had less impact on the barrios, and they retained much of their Spanish culture and heritage, as well as the name *barrio*. What did have an impact on the barrios, however, was urban renewal in the late 1960s; about half the barrio neighborhoods in the downtown area gave way to parking lots, government buildings, the convention center, and other commercial structures. Barrio Historico is one of a handful of barrios that were saved from the bulldozers.

i For news on what's happening with real estate, new developments in the downtown area, and great neighborhood descriptions, check the website of the nonprofit Downtown Tucson Partnership, www.downtowntucson.org.

Designated a historic district in 1975, Barrio Historico is an excellent example of Sonoran style, which relied on the use of native materials—mud adobe, mesquite, and saguaro—and ingenuity to adapt to the desert climate. Houses were tightly clustered, often with shared walls, to gain protection from the desert heat. They were built close to the front property line so that interior courtyards would be protected from the sun by the surrounding structure. Another characteristic of the barrios is that they were self-contained—local merchants set up shop to sell groceries and staples, provide furniture and other craft works, and even give credit.

i The website www.zillow.com offers a great overview of home prices by neighborhood. Just type in the neighborhood you are interested in and a great map pops up with all the homes and their asking prices. You can click on a listing and get more details. The site also lists foreclosures, rentals, and open houses.

A visit to Barrio Historico is a journey back in time not only to early Tucson, but also to Mexican villages or Mediterranean villages, whose architecture strongly influenced the Sonoran style. It contains the largest and best-preserved collection of old adobes in the West. Today the restored row houses are used for residences as well as offices and studios for artists and designers. But the most unusual site in Barrio Historico may well be **El Tiradito,** meaning "the little castaway" but commonly called the Wishing Shrine.

Legend has it that this outdoor adobe shrine with a soot-scarred image of the Virgin of Guadalupe was erected for a man murdered in a love triangle before the turn of the 20th century. It is believed to be the only one of its kind in the US dedicated to a sinner buried in unconsecrated ground. Now on the National Register of Historic Places, it is said that if you light a candle there at night and it burns until morning, your wish will

come true. This makeshift shrine, common in the Mexican culture, stands as a lonely reminder of the past set amid modern paved roads and restaurants, and within throwing distance of the TCC. You'll find the shrine on Main Avenue just south of Cushing Street and right next to a more modern neighborhood landmark, yet still one of the older family-run Mexican restaurants in the city, El Minuto Cafe (see the Restaurants chapter).

This area too is being upgraded and renovated as part of the improvements to the downtown and El Presidio areas. Attractive elderly and mixed housing developments and new adobe and territorial-style homes are recent additions to the neighborhood. Home prices here are in the mid-$100,000 range. This area is in the Tucson Unified School District but may not be an ideal area for families with kids because houses have no yard areas and are very close to the street. Commercial businesses are intermingled with residences, and it's very close to the congestion and heavy traffic of the Tucson Convention Center.

West University

The 60-block area located between the University of Arizona and downtown is historically significant because it exemplifies the pattern of middle- and upper-class residential development in Tucson from 1890 to 1930. Thus it was designated a historic district by the city in 1984. Although some buildings reflect the Mexican style, the neighborhood's architecture is mostly European and California bungalow styles because it was settled by Anglo-Americans after the arrival of the Southern Pacific Railroad.

Strolling pedestrians will pass restored bungalows and Victorian-style houses on tree-lined streets, the **4th Avenue shopping** district (and Tucson's trolley line), and, just beyond the east boundary of the district, the university's first building, Old Main. The district extends roughly from 6th Street north to Speedway Boulevard and from 7th Avenue on the west to Euclid Avenue. Today it's a mixture of older homes occupied by longtime residents and more transient student rentals, peppered with a few fraternity houses, bed-and-breakfast inns, restaurants, and shops catering mostly to students. Home prices vary widely here, ranging from the mid-$100,000s to over $600,000 for renovated properties.

Middle-school kids in this neighborhood can attend the very first elementary school ever built in the state, which is now **Roskruge Middle School** on E. 6th Street, a handsomely restored building that obviously still has old-world charm and appeal. This school and the neighborhood are in the Tucson Unified School District.

i To learn more about Tucson's downtown neighborhoods, sign up for a walking tour with Kruse Arizona (520-881-1638; www.kruseari zona.com), run by local historian Alan Kruse. Not only will you learn all sorts of insider information and historic tidbits about Tucson's past, but most tours also include coffee and pastries and a take-home annotated bibliography.

Fort Lowell

There's something about the Fort Lowell area that just seems to silently shout "history." Maybe it's the ghosts of the Hohokam, or the imagined sounds of the battles between the cavalry post's soldiers and the Apaches, or the generations-old adobe homes handmade by early Mexican settlers. Or perhaps it's the juxtaposition of uniformed 6-year-olds playing soccer games on the very parkland where more than 100 years ago uniformed soldiers may have played, or where more than 1,000 years ago Hohokam Indians tilled the ground to farm. Whatever the reason, this area, located just south of the confluence of the Pautano and Tanque Verde washes, is often said to reflect where Tucson's soul resides.

Hohokam Indians first settled and farmed this area about AD 300. They were long gone by 1873, when the military began building a cavalry post to protect Arizona settlers from Apache raids—a fort that was 7 miles away from "Tucson" and connected to it by the "Fort Lowell Road." Under the safety of the fort, Mexicans migrated here to farm and ranch the fertile bottomlands, and they were soon followed by Mormons.

Only 0.25 square mile in size, the district is rich in 1,500 years of history. Fort Lowell Park contains the **Fort Lowell Museum** (part of the Arizona Historical Society), some remaining ruins of fort buildings, and even a Hohokam archaeological site. Fort Lowell Road, to the west of the park, offers some rambling Sonoran ranch adobes nearly hidden by lush vegetation. Just west of the district boundary is **San Pedro Chapel,** built in Mission revival style and designated as the city's first historic landmark in 1982 (and also on the state and national registers). Very nearby is a tiny chapel called **La Capillita,** originally built in 1915 by the Mexican settlers but reduced to a pile of rubble until a group of local volunteers led the effort to rebuild it in 1997.

The Fort Lowell Neighborhood Association opens it doors to the past once a year in February for **La Reunion de El Fuerte,** which is open to the public and free (see the

Festivals & Events chapter). The 1-day event takes its name from the Mexican settlement that grew up among the abandoned military buildings and was named El Fuerte, or "the fort." Visitors can get a rare view of the cavalry corrals and stables, or at least what's left of these fragile adobe ruins, which are now protected by chain-link fencing and metal roofs under the purview of the Fort Lowell Museum. Other events at La Reunion include cavalry drills, music, and walking tours of the district.

In recent years vacant land in this area has been gobbled up by home builders, but even the new developments seem to reflect the character of the old—mostly stucco houses with lots of vegetation that retain the sense of quiet calm of the neighborhood. Today the area contains an eclectic mix of residences, from starter and patio homes in the low $200,000s to luxury adobes selling for as much as $600,000-plus and from turn-of-the-20th-century adobe houses to contemporary architecture. The narrow and curving E. Presidio Street is lined with newer homes but feels like an old hacienda-lined street of Mexico, with walled courtyards, lush vegetation, and hundreds of mesquite trees.

Located in the Tucson Unified School District, this is a great neighborhood for families—quiet, filled with history, mostly large properties, and fairly removed from commercial businesses but within easy access of them. One of Tucson's foremost private preparatory schools, **St. Gregory,** is at the north end of the neighborhood.

i Tucson locals often drop by Rincon Market in the Sam Hughes neighborhood for breakfast on Saturday or Sunday mornings. It's a great way to meet people. Rincon Market is at 2513 E. 6th St.; (520) 327-6653.

✳ *Sam Hughes*

First there was Sam Hughes, local pioneering merchant and civic leader. Then there was Sam Hughes Elementary School. Then there was the Sam Hughes neighborhood, bounded by Speedway Boulevard, Campbell Avenue, Broadway Boulevard, and Country Club Road. Originally homesteaded by 5 landowners, this square mile east of the university was eventually subdivided into numerous housing projects and then combined under the rubric "Sam Hughes neighborhood." It contains some of the Old Pueblo's finest examples of charming Mission revival and Spanish colonial homes.

This is a neighborhood that has become very popular with upscale city dwellers—people who prefer the city life to the outskirts (and the accompanying commute), along with quiet streets, older homes both restored and still needing fixing up, the proximity of the university and all it has to offer, and friendly sidewalks and streets for jogging or bike riding. A neighborhood association was formed in 1971 to preserve the residential character of the area and fend off undesirable development. Long a Tucson treasure, the neighborhood became a national treasure with its National Historic District designation in 1994.

Highlights of the neighborhood, in addition to the many lovely homes and relative peace and quiet, include **Himmel Park** and its namesake library and the **Rincon Market** on 6th Street and Tucson Boulevard, a favorite gathering and shopping place for the residents for years.

Among the neighborhood's famous residents are Frank Borman, who lived here before going on to orbit the moon and become president of Eastern Airlines, and Hiram "Hi" Corbett, a civic leader who brought Cactus League baseball to Tucson and whose name the baseball stadium bears.

The nostalgia, the historically preserved homes, and the proximity of town combine to make Sam Hughes pricey and its residents a largely liberal mix of attorneys, professors, architects, and a surprising number of retirees. One of the biggest additions to this historic neighborhood is **Sam Hughes Square** at the southeast corner of Campbell Avenue and 6th Street. The 3-story building is home to commercial and office buildings and condominiums, a first for this area. Served by Tucson Unified schools, this is a good family neighborhood, as long as your family conforms to the association rules and preservationist philosophy. Prices range from the mid-$100,000s to upward of $1 million for the large, beautifully restored homes on 3rd and 4th Streets. Houses do go on the market here, but not many and not frequently. You can buy a whole lot more space for the same money elsewhere, but not in a central neighborhood with this kind of commitment to the past and the future.

Pie Allen

This neighborhood owes its unusual name to pies made by one of its earliest settlers. Made from dried apples because fresh fruit was scarce here then, John "Pie" Allen's pies were a big hit and started Allen on the road to becoming a local entrepreneur and eventually mayor of Tucson. Bounded by Park and 4th Avenues and by 6th Street and Broadway Boulevard, the neighborhood covers 24 blocks just west of the university. Residents formed an association in 1980, primarily to protect themselves and their historic homes from university expansion.

A building boom in the 1880s transformed the former ranch land into homes occupied largely by railroad workers. Almost every architectural style popular between the 1860s and the 1940s is represented in Pie Allen, and many have been restored. Several were designed by one of Tucson's most famous and distinctive architects, Josias Joesler. One of the area's vintage buildings, a Spanish colonial revival–style structure dating from 1928, is the **Colonial Hotel** at 410 E. 9th St.

Within the Tucson Unified School District, Pie Allen boasts the oldest high school in the state, now **Tucson Magnet High.** Today homes in this neighborhood are less expensive than, say, Sam Hughes homes and start in the low $200,000s.

El Encanto

This hidden neighborhood just west of the sprawling El Con Mall boasts some of the most elegant homes—almost mansions—in central Tucson. Sometimes referred to as the "Beverly Hills of Tucson," this neighborhood developed in the late 1920s has a strong California influence, beginning with its geometric street pattern that was a major departure from the grid pattern of all prior neighborhoods in Tucson. From a central circle, streets fan out in a diagonal pattern, making the neighborhood a bit difficult for the uninitiated to traverse. Another obvious California influence is the landscaping— hundreds of Mexican fan palms and date palms were planted during the initial layout, along with many citrus, olive, and eucalyptus trees. The street pattern, combined with the lush landscaping and many walled yards and courtyards, gives the neighborhood a sense of mystery and privacy.

Given the value of this real estate today, it's astonishing that the land was actually acquired free from the federal government by a homesteader more than 90 years ago. The first home built here and its surrounding 10 acres were purchased for $3,700 by Leroy "Jessie" James (no, not the famous outlaw), who was ridiculed for buying worthless desert land so far from town. Jessie no doubt had the last laugh when a few years later he got offers of 10 times that amount.

Today this neighborhood, bounded by 5th Street and Broadway Boulevard and Country Club Road and Jones Avenue, is city living at its finest. Emanating from the center circle, which boasts more than 150 saguaro cacti, are nearly 150 homes on 1-acre lots in styles including Moroccan, Spanish, Italian, Mexican, and early California. About 50 are on the National Register of Historic Places. Home prices here can easily reach or exceed $1.5 million, and there is not much turnover. It's in the Tucson Unified School District.

i Take a stroll through one of Tucson's secret delights, Poet's Corner. It got its name from all the streets named for poets. The area is bordered by Swan Road on the east, Columbus Boulevard on the west, 6th Street to the north, and Broadway to the south. See streets named for Poe, Burns, Whitman, and 9th Street. Oh, wait. That's not a poet.

Winterhaven

Added to the National Register of Historic Places in 2006, 2 things are most noticeable in this 0.5-square-mile neighborhood that extends from Tucson Boulevard to Country Club Road and Prince Road to Fort Lowell Road. One is the lush green grass surrounding every home, unusual in the Tucson desert; the other is the street named Christmas Avenue. The former no doubt results from the fact that a fertilizer company once occupied much of the land, its huge manure piles making for rich soil underneath. The latter signifies the neighborhood's real claim to fame—the Festival of Lights, which started in 1949, the same year the development opened, and has been held annually every Christmas since then (see the Festivals & Events chapter).

Winterhaven remains an attractive residential neighborhood with ranch-style homes, located fairly close to the university and downtown areas. It's a peaceful and comfortable middle-class neighborhood that looks like it was transplanted from back East—explained by the fact that the developer reportedly patterned it after Shaker Heights, Ohio.

In 1949 homes sold for $9,000 to $16,000. Today homes on good-size lots covered with green grass and mature vegetation start at about the low $200,000s. It has a strong neighborhood association and lies within the Tucson Unified School District boundary. More details are available at www.mywinterhaven.net.

Tucson Country Club

At one time this enclave was considered way out in the boondocks, but with continual expansion to the east, it's actually quite convenient to downtown and nearly all points in the valley. This is old-world country-club living at its finest amid mature vegetation, lots of mesquite trees, large flat lots, and some of Tucson's most prominent residents.

An exclusive, upscale neighborhood bounded by the Tanque Verde and Pantano washes on the south and west and by Tanque Verde Road on the east, Tucson Country Club is almost an island in a sea of recent development, most of it commercial. Hidden behind service stations, restaurants, and all manner of shops, the neighborhood of 300 to 400 homes begins on a street called Camino Principal and winds westward to a private golf and country club. And unless you drive through the entrance area, you'll have no idea this neighborhood exists.

Many of the club's homes were built in the 1950s. The price for resales ranges from the upper $200,000s to over $600,000. It's within Tucson Unified School District boundaries.

Other Neighborhoods

In the 1920s Tucson's population topped out at 20,000. By the '60s we were just passing the quarter-million mark. Today we're close to a million in the metropolitan area. Where do all these people homestead? In every direction they can, including up the mountainsides.

The Catalina Foothills

Today the word *foothills* designates any area rising into any one of the mountain ranges surrounding Tucson, and as the population swells, so too do the mountainside homes. But the original foothills growth was to the city's north at the base of the Santa Catalina Mountains, an area close to the city center and offering views over the entire Tucson valley. It's a very popular area that attracts wealthy retirees and families.

The Catalina foothills area extends from River Road on the south to as high or far as anyone can build on the north and from about Craycroft Road on the east to about Campbell Avenue on the west. Here you will find exclusive gated communities such as

Finisterre, Skyline Country Club, and Cobblestone; the Westin La Paloma Resort and its country club housing; many custom homes on 1-acre lots; luxury apartment complexes; kid-friendly developments; and mansions. This area is also home to famous artist Ted DeGrazia's studio on N. Swan Road. (See the Arts & Culture chapter for details on the studio and its founder.)

Catalina foothills land is scarce, and 1-acre lots can command upward of $1 million. The most exclusive homes in the upper regions of the mountains can go for millions. These desert homes are far removed from the traffic and bustle of the valley below yet close enough for a quick commute. Their appeal is bolstered by the school district. Much of the area lies within District 16, usually reputed to be the best in the metro area. Many families choose to live in the foothills just for the school district, which boasts the highest test scores in the city, and homes within the District 16 boundary (versus foothills homes in the Tucson Unified School District) typically command a higher price.

Sabino Canyon

Nestled into the lower Santa Catalina Mountains but farther east than the Catalina foothills, the Sabino Canyon area is still definitely foothills land and much in demand. And it has another major draw—the Sabino Canyon recreation area. Extending north from River Road and east from Sabino Canyon Road, it is lovely desert land on the northeast side of the metro area, much of it still being developed. Although primarily residential with very few commercial businesses, major services are within easy reach.

Homes right along Sabino Canyon Road start in the low $250,000s, while those farther east and around the world-famous Canyon

Ranch Spa can cost in the millions. This area offers choices ranging from homes built in the 1970s to high-end condos and townhomes to golf course homes. The Sabino Canyon area is a great place for families—many neighborhoods are "neighborhoody" with homes in close proximity, no big-box stores, and much of it lies within the realm of the popular District 16 schools. (Homes south of Snyder Road are in the Tucson Unified School District but within the boundary for Fruchthendler Elementary School on Cloud Road, one of that district's finest.)

i The most expensive home in Tucson in April 2011 (according to the multiple listing service) was a 24,000-square-foot, $9.999 million mansion in the exclusive foothills development The Canyons. Special features include a 15-seat movie theater, lion sculptures, and a 15-car auto gallery with rotating turntable to showcase your favorite car.

Ventana Canyon

The posh Loews Ventana Canyon Resort was the forerunner of development in this exclusive and pricey area in the foothills of the Catalina Mountains that falls between the Catalina foothills and Sabino Canyon areas and north of Sunrise Drive. This is incredible desert land with home prices that often match. For folks who can afford it, this is one of the most desirable spots in the east-side area.

Driving along Sunrise Drive near Kolb Road, you can look north into the mountains and see houses so far up, they look minuscule but in reality are contemporary mansions hugging the granite mountainside. On a more down-to-earth level, lovely patio homes and single-family homes surround the golf courses of the resort, occupied by families and retirees who appreciate the golf course views and recreation. To the east along Sunrise Drive are many developments with attractive family-oriented homes and condos starting from the mid-$100,000s and up.

Ventana Canyon offers nearly every housing choice, but they are all high-end—condos, townhomes, patio homes, single-family homes, and mansions. Many of the communities are gated, and they tend to be more affordable than the gated communities in the more established Catalina foothills. This is strictly residential land with several commercial businesses and shopping malls along Sunrise Boulevard. It's accessible to all of the east side of Tucson and about a 30- to 40-minute commute to downtown or the university. And it lies within the highly desirable District 16 for schools.

East

This area is growing by leaps and bounds, with large tracts of single-family housing developments and chain store retailers taking over what was, until fairly recently, virgin desert land. Just about anything in the vast area east of Alvernon Way and extending north to the Catalinas, east to the Rincons, and south to the Santa Rita Mountains can be considered the "Eastside." The close-in Eastside has some affordable housing, while the closer the mountains the higher the home sites and the prices.

Nearly all the neighborhoods would be considered family oriented; there are numerous housing developments in the area, particularly along Houghton Road, where new single-family homes start in the low to mid-$200,000s. Other choices include townhomes and patio homes, manufactured homes, and a multitude of apartment complexes. Most of the Eastside is served by TUSD except for the far east, which is served by the Tanque Verde School District.

Some of the more exclusive areas on the Eastside include Old Spanish Trail near Saguaro National Park, the Bear Canyon and Agua Caliente areas in the northeast, and the Reddington Pass area winding into the base of the Rincon Mountains. Here you will still find expanses of virgin desert, along with homes built on large acreages, retirement communities, luxury developments, and even some horse properties.

One of the older Eastside neighborhoods with unique lots is the Forty-Niner Country Club Estates on Tanque Verde Road just east of Tanque Verde Loop Road. Built in the '70s around a private golf course, this neighborhood features a mesquite bosque, lush vegetation due to the fertile floodplain soil, lakes, and grass. There are 4 subdivisions here, from gated communities and single-family homes right on the edge of the golf course to townhomes. Single-family homes range from the high $200,000s to more than $1 million, while townhomes start in the low $200,000s. The neighborhood is in the Tanque Verde School District, ranked one of the best in metro Tucson.

Dorado Country Club

An oasis in the midst of Tucson's close-in eastern commercial sprawl near Speedway Boulevard and Wilmot Road, Dorado is a lovely community surrounded by a wall that keeps it private and quiet yet within biking or walking distance of stores, restaurants, movie theaters, and more. At one time this was a gated community with a private golf course. The 2 gated entrances are now

purely decorative, and the golf course is open to the public. The streets wind around the golf course and are lined with a variety of home types—from roomy patio homes and townhomes to exclusive single-family homes on large lots—often situated with views of the golf course. Many retirees and professionals live here.

Housing prices start in the mid-$100,000s and go to the high $500,000s. The only rentals available are private homes.

Southeast

This region, south on Houghton Road from Old Spanish Trail to just past I-10, is growing rapidly, and housing developments are sprouting up faster than weeds. There are lots of single-family homes, manufactured homes, master-planned communities, and older ranch-style neighborhoods. Most of the new developments are south of Golf Links Road near Rita Ranch, one of Tucson's largest master-planned communities. Practically a city unto itself with its own parks, ball fields, and stores, Rita Ranch with 4,500 homes takes up a huge swath of property on the west side of Houghton. The master-planned community of Civano (www.civano neighbors.com) is also here, on the east side of Houghton Road, south of Golf Links. A huge development of energy-efficient, environmentally friendly homes built in various styles, Civano has many activities and numerous amenities. The attractive development is very popular with young families, despite its distance from central Tucson. Homes here range from the mid-$100,000s to the high $400,000s. Farther south, 7 miles past I-10, is the unincorporated community of Corona de Tucson, an older, more established subdivision. Overall, prices can range widely here, from the mid-$100,000s to upward of $400,000.

This part of town is fairly far from central Tucson, but easy access to I-10 makes it a popular area for commuters going into town. There is a shopping center with major retailers on Old Spanish Trail and Broadway This area of town is within the Vail School District.

Tucson Mountains & the West

The jagged Tucson Mountains forming Tucson's western edge are literally surrounded by real estate, even though the west side traditionally had been less popular and less populated than Tucson's east and northwest. This may be the result of the mountains themselves posing an obstacle to infrastructure development and travel. Or it may be that it's too close to downtown and some of the "less desirable" areas surrounding it. But change is in the air, and this area is starting to boom, with major developers moving in fast. With Catalina foothills lots scarce and home prices out of reach for many, the Tucson Mountains are becoming popular. All of the Tucson Mountains area is within TUSD until it reaches the Marana School District in the far north.

For a bird's-eye view, let's go first to the western base of the range, where there are several large manufactured home communities as well as both older and newer houses, some in tract housing developments and others on large rural plots. Although close to major attractions like Saguaro National Park West, Tucson Mountain Park, the Arizona-Sonora Desert Museum, and Old Tucson Studios, this area is somewhat of a trek from Tucson and accessible only by 2 roads—Ajo Highway to Kinney Road on the south end

and the narrow, winding Gates Pass Road in the middle of the range.

At the southern and southeastern tip of the mountain range our view takes in the Pascua Yaqui Reservation and the growing area around Ajo Way and Valencia Road, where housing options include modest single-family homes and apartment complexes. Traveling north to Gates Pass Road, there are more exclusive homes on large properties, many with spectacular views of the valley and the mountains. At the far north end of the mountains, around Picture Rocks Road, housing opportunities include manufactured homes, family-oriented developments with attractive tract homes, large contemporary custom homes built into the mountainside, and lots of vacant land.

Our final destination is the eastern side of the mountains, closest to downtown Tucson, and the most built-up side of this mountain range. Housing here includes the area around Silverbell and Anklam Roads and Pima Community College's west campus, where neighborhoods are older and family-oriented and homes are affordable, starting around $100,000. Here we also see the hot housing area called Starr Pass, anchored by a golf course and the Starr Pass Marriott, a major resort hotel in Tucson. This luxury residential community offers saguaros and city views from golf course villas, luxury apartments, and custom homes on sites from the mid-$100,000s to the upper $400,000s. Townhomes start in the high $100,000s, while luxury homes run to over $2 million. Starr Pass has an eclectic mix of residents, from families to retirees to vacation home owners.

Northwest

Tucson's sprawl north of the Rillito River and across 80 square miles of desert is the vast northwest. The population is growing in this area. Very little existed here before 1960, but you'd never know that driving north on Oracle Road or west on Ina Road. The number of housing developments is mind-boggling, not to mention the golf courses, shopping centers, schools, churches, retirement communities, restaurants, banks, and every imaginable kind of commercial enterprise. Much of the area considered northwest is unincorporated Pima County land, while other areas have incorporated into towns like Oro Valley and Marana.

Here you will find Tohono Chul Park, the Sheraton El Conquistador Resort, Foothills Mall, Rancho Vistoso (Tucson's Sun City), Catalina State Park and its Romero Falls, Omni Tucson National Golf Resort, Heritage Highlands Golf Club, Northwest Hospital, Miraval—Life in Balance Resort, Continental Ranch, the retirement community of Saddlebrook, and the area called Catalina that runs along US 89 to the Pima County northern boundary.

The average listing price in April 2011 for this area was in the low $200,000s, but some high-end properties reach the millions, especially in the western foothills of the Catalina Mountains. But the choices are almost infinite—golf course communities, manufactured housing, new apartment complexes, condos, townhomes, retirement communities, custom mountainside homes with fabulous views, and down-to-earth typical family-oriented neighborhoods with attractive tract homes and nearby schools.

The northwest is popular for several reasons. Land is still available for new housing, and home buyers have a broad choice among both older homes in established neighborhoods and brand-new homes. For folks who commute often to Phoenix for business or for air travel, the proximity of I-10 is a great attraction. Likewise, the proximity of the freeway for commuters to downtown Tucson and the university means not having to battle crosstown traffic each day. And the Amphitheater School District, which serves the bulk of the northwest, draws families to this side of town.

Midvale Park

This was Tucson's first completely planned community, carved out of 1,300 acres known as Midvale Farms between the Santa Cruz River on the east, Mission Road on the west, Irvington Road on the north, and the San Xavier Reservation on the south. It was designed in the early 1980s to provide a complete mix of commercial, residential, educational, and recreational offerings—shopping centers, office buildings, schools, parks, and a variety of housing styles. Groves of cottonwood and pecan trees were left untouched by the builders, and landscaped boulevards and bike paths were integral to the design.

Annexed by the city in 1983, Midvale Park is a sprawling, affordable area with single-family, multifamily, and manufactured housing options. Close to I-19, it's accessible to downtown, the airport, and major employers such as Raytheon and Burr-Brown. Homes can be purchased here for under $100,000, and kids attend either Tucson Unified School District or the Sunnyside School District. More details are at www.midvalepark.com.

TOWNS & A CITY

City of South Tucson

This is a small town surrounded by a city, a place where to be a minority is to be in the majority. It's 1 square mile of people with a strong sense of independence, pride, and perseverance. After one thwarted attempt to incorporate to prevent the City of Tucson from annexing it, area residents successfully incorporated in 1939 and now have their own political structure and emergency services. South Tucson's population of over 5,500 is over 70 percent Hispanic. Businesses tend to be small and family run. Some of the best Mexican restaurants in Tucson are in South Tucson, particularly along S. 4th Avenue. Two of Tucson's main attractions are located here—Tucson Greyhound Park and La Fiesta de los Vaqueros, or the annual rodeo, in February.

Generally, the people and Spanish-style houses of South Tucson have populated the area for generations. The residents fix up the homes, add to them, or perhaps move to better housing, usually in the same area. Much residential property has been converted into small businesses—bakeries, restaurants, and a variety of shops. Real estate is in lower demand here with growth through existing residents of South Tucson, recent immigrants from Mexico, or small-business owners. Most of the housing is small and Spanish style, typically starting in the mid-$90,000s and probably in need of repair. A renovated or new house can be had for $100,000 or less. The schools are part of the Tucson Unified School District.

Oro Valley

Home to the massive communities of Rancho Vistoso (over 4,000 housing units) and Copper Creek, Oro Valley is experiencing ongoing growth. Six miles north of Tucson's city limits along Oracle Road (Highway 77), the valley is formed by the juncture of the Santa Cruz River and Gold Creek in the Santa Catalina Mountains. Originally incorporated in 1974, the town has grown to more than 34 square miles through annexation, with a population of over 40,000. Named one of "America's Top-Rated Smaller Cities," Oro Valley has the image of being a small, sleepy bedroom community nestled in the western foothills of the Catalinas, but in reality it's a growing town in metro Tucson.

Housing in Oro Valley runs the gamut but tends toward the high end, because much of it is situated in the foothills, which is pricey property with a view. Median sale price in April 2011 was $235,000 but homes in exclusive developments go for well over $1 million. The Amphitheater School District serves this area. Check www.orovalleyaz.gov for more details.

Marana

Incorporated in 1977, Marana (Spanish for jungle) continues to grow. Once a small farming community producing mainly cotton, Marana had an airfield that was the largest pilot-training center in the world during WWII, training some 10,000 flyers. In addition, 5 Titan missile sites were located in the area. Today Marana is nearly 120 square miles with an estimated population of nearly 37,000. In the past 3 decades, Marana's population has grown 22 times over. Future plans include the construction of 2 new residential neighborhoods and a $1.3 million retail complex.

Large-scale housing developments in town include the vast master-planned communities of Continental Ranch and Continental Reserve. Very popular with young families, this middle-class community offers kid-friendly neighborhoods with wide streets and parks. Marana is also home to the luxury resort community Dove Mountain, where homes sell for as high as $1 million. More information about Marana is at www.marana.com.

Green Valley

Often called one of the most successful retirement communities in the country, Green Valley is about 25 miles south of Tucson off I-19. This isn't a city or town, but you'd never know it. It's an unincorporated area of Pima County that took off in 1970 and continues to grow dramatically. The permanent population of about 26,000 swells up to about 40,000 from January through March with the arrival of winter visitors and seasonal homeowners. It has the atmosphere of a small town but provides all the services and commercial establishments anyone would need.

Although primarily a retirement community (the median age here is 72.2) and home to several active adult communities, a number of housing developments have no age restrictions, and kids attend the Continental School District. Housing prices range from the low $70,000s to over half a million. Spanish colonial and territorial architectures prevail in Green Valley. It's famous for its golf courses (see the Golf chapter) and for its proximity to nearby attractions, including the Titan Missile Museum, Madera Canyon, Tubac, and Nogales, Mexico. (Look for more on Green Valley in the Retirement chapter.) Go to www.greenvalleychamber.com for additional information.

Sahuarita

This town (pronounced *saw-wah-REE-ta*) just north of Green Valley in the Santa Cruz Valley was established in 1994. About 20 miles from Tucson, it's also growing, with a population of over 24,000. A family-friendly community, it features 3 master-planned communities and multiple smaller neighborhoods. The major development here is the master-planned community of Rancho Sahuarita (www.ranchosahuarita.com) with 11,000 families who can enjoy a lake, recreation facilities, and hiking trails. Home prices range from the upper $100,000s on up. There are also 2 retirement communities in town (see the Retirement chapter for details). Although a bit far from Tucson proper, Sahuarita is family friendly and offers lots of recreation facilities and several retailers and grocery stores. The town is served by the Sahuarita Unified School District. Go to www.ci.sahuarita.az.us for details.

Vail

Named for the Vail brothers Edward and Walter, who arrived in the late 1870s, this area is on the far southeastern part of town. Although Vail was christened as a town in 1893, it was never incorporated and thus has no official boundaries or legal status. Still small with a population of several thousand, it is growing rapidly, attracting young families and professionals with its relatively low housing prices, sense of community, and excellent school district. Housing here is mostly new single-family developments starting in the mid-$100,000s. It's close to the University of Arizona Science and Technology Park, Raytheon, and Davis-Monthan Air Force Base but fairly distant from retailers and services. It is served by the Vail School District (www.vail.k12.az.us).

REAL ESTATE

Companies

All the major national real estate companies are represented here, and most have multiple offices across the metro area. In addition, there are a couple hundred local realty companies ranging in size from small to huge. Given the geographical size of Tucson and the size of its real estate market, it's almost a necessity to rely on a real estate professional, especially if you haven't zeroed in on a neighborhood you want or are unfamiliar with Tucson's many hidden communities.

If you select one of the major companies, you can be assured that at least one of the many agents in one of their many offices will be a specialist in a given neighborhood. The Tucson Association of Realtors at 2445 N. Tucson Blvd. (520-327-4218; www.tucsonrealtors.org) can be a resource for inquiring about real estate companies.

The many real estate publications available nearly everywhere (grocery stores, shopping centers, libraries) for free will also help you find a real estate agent. They often identify agents who specialize in, for example, adult and golf communities, the Catalina foothills, or the northwest. Another clue to finding an area specialist is the location of the office; for example, the Century 21 office at 7780 N. Oracle Rd. specializes in properties in Oro Valley and northwest Tucson. There's also a company that deals only in helping buyers find a new home in one of Tucson's 150-plus new subdivisions. You can also find real estate companies that specialize in modular or manufactured homes. And nearly every one of the major companies also has listings of lots if your choice is to build.

CENTURY 21

Centra Realty
532 N. 4th Ave.
(520) 882-0767
www.century21.com
Although affiliated with a national company, each office of Century 21 is independently owned and operated. There are 5 full-service real estate agencies in the area (see website for a list). As part of the nationwide referral network of Century 21, they all deal with relocations to or from other places in the country. The company also has an extensive rental listing, including apartments, condos, and homes.

COLDWELL BANKER RESIDENTIAL REALTY

2890 E. Skyline Dr., Ste. 250
(520) 577-7433
www.coldwellbanker.com
With offices strategically located around the metro area and beyond, this national company provides full-service real estate services to buyers and sellers across Tucson. They also represent a number of new home developments and handle relocations nationally for people moving to or from Tucson. See the website for a list of other locations.

DEL ORO REALTY

2292 W. Magee Rd.
(520) 744-1121, (800) 884-5663
www.delororealty.com
This realty company in the northwest is operated by a couple who are both brokers and owners and specialize in the northwest area of the valley. They deal in residential sales, land sales, and property management, so they also have a list of rentals available in the northwest.

LONG REALTY COMPANY
Home Office
900 E. River Rd.
(520) 888-8844
www.longrealty.com
The largest realty company in the Southwest, Long has been in business since 1926. Agents cover the entire metro Tucson area as well as Green Valley. They also provide comprehensive relocation services nationally and internationally. See the website for a complete list of offices in the area you're interested in.

NORTHWEST PROPERTIES
7632 N. La Cholla Blvd.
(520) 544-9927
www.leaseyourhome.com
As its name suggests, this agency specializes in the northwest. They offer full residential real estate services (including the multiple listing service) as well as short- and long-term rentals and property management.

PRUDENTIAL FOOTHILLS REAL ESTATE
7231 E. Speedway Blvd.
(520) 577-8333
www. foothillstucson.com
This full-service real estate agency was founded in 1989. With 100 full-time associates, they have a centrally located main office and a full-time relocation director.

REALTY EXECUTIVES OF SOUTHERN ARIZONA
Central
2251 E. Grant Rd., #103
(520) 877-4940
This national company has 5 offices around Tucson (3 of them new) plus another in Tubac and is one of the area's major realty companies. Call for additional information on area offices.

RE/MAX
11115 N. La Canada Rd., Ste. 155
(520) 461-1255
www.remax.com
The local office of this national company is independently owned and operated and offers full-service real estate, including residential, commercial, and relocation assistance through the national network.

SOTHEBY'S INTERNATIONAL REALTY
3430 E. Sunrise Dr., Ste. 120
(520) 742-1335
www.sothebysrealty.com
Specializing in high-end properties, this office of the renowned international realty and auction firm also offers comprehensive corporate relocation services.

Rentals

Apartments are as plentiful in Tucson as sunshine. And it's largely because of our abundant sunshine that Tucson attracts so many visitors and newcomers who seek rental housing. There simply is not an area of Tucson—north, south, east, or west, in the hills or in the flatlands—that doesn't have something to rent.

The average monthly rent for apartments in the metro area ranges from $550 to nearly $1,500 depending on size and location. Luxury condos in neighborhoods like the Catalina foothills or Sabino Canyon can easily approach $1,100 for two or three bedrooms. Conversely, lower priced nice one- and two-bedroom apartments can be found in surrounding neighborhoods.

But apartments are not the only option for leasing. Many privately owned condos, town houses, patio homes, and single-family homes are available for rent, often at not much more than a high-end apartment. The four best ways to find these rentals are to drive around neighborhoods and look for signs, check out the Sunday real estate section of the *Arizona Daily Star*, or contact realty companies that also handle or locate rentals. (See the following listing of real estate companies for ones handling rentals.) Also take a look at http://tucson.craigslist.org for current listings.

With the mind-boggling array of rental choices, you might need a few good places to start. First, cruise around Tucson and decide on some areas where you'd prefer to live; this will make your selection chore much easier no matter which resource you rely on. Next, read the real estate section of the Sunday *Arizona Daily Star* (the Sunday edition is most comprehensive), where rentals are broken down by type and geographic area. For another resource, look for the various apartment guide booklets, like *For Rent Magazine* (http://tucson.forrent.com) and HouseHunters (www.househuntersaz.com), which can be found (free) at most local supermarkets, major drugstores, and corner quick marts.

Here are a few of the apartment-finder services in the Tucson area to help your search.

ADOBE PROPERTY MANAGERS INC.
2122 N. Craycroft Rd., Ste. 120
(520) 325-6971
www.adobepropertymanagers.com
This agency provides strictly rentals and property management. The choices include

apartments, condos, town houses, and single-family homes but not mobile homes. Most rentals require a 6-month or annual lease and are unfurnished.

APARTMENT LOCATORS
5460 E. Speedway Blvd., Ste. B103
(520) 323-2200, (800) 955-7545
www.apartmentsarizona.com
This service is free to renters and boasts more than 45,000 apartments, condos, townhomes, and houses listed for rent, both furnished and unfurnished and month to month or longer term.

FOOTHILLS PROPERTIES
6262 N. Swan Rd., Ste. 165
(520) 299-2100
www.tucsonfoothills.com
Despite the company's name, they don't focus just on the foothills but cover the entire northern section of the valley. This is a full-service property management firm with nearly 600 properties in their portfolio. They manage unfurnished long-term rentals, as well as furnished vacation rentals. Rental costs vary.

PEACH PROPERTIES HM INC.
299 S. Park Ave.
(520) 798-3331
www.peachprops.com
Specializing in rentals, this small company headquartered in Tucson offers all sizes and styles of rentals, from the funky to the standard. Located in the Lost Barrio, the company maintains a website with extensive listings, photos, and price ranges.

RELOCATION

Welcome to Tucson! You've made a great choice. With a metro population of just over one million, Tucson was voted "friendliest city" and one of the "top ten US cities to visit" by the readers of *Condé Nast Traveler* magazine. The second-largest city in Arizona and one of the fastest-growing metropolitan areas in the country, Tucson offers low-key living in the beautiful Sonoran Desert surrounded by five mountain ranges.

There's something here for everyone. Love to golf? Tucson is consistently rated one of the best golfing destinations in the western US. Into bicycling? *Bicycling Magazine* has ranked Tucson one of the top three cities in North America for cycling. Thinking of retiring? Tucson is one of best places to retire, according to *AARP Magazine*.

There are few places that offer the sophistication of a small city with nearby wilderness areas that are still home to mountain lions, javelinas, and bears. You can attend a Broadway show or throw on your hiking gear and walk miles into pristine desert or forestland in a matter of minutes. With spectacular weather; hundreds of city, county, state, and national parks; a symphony; a ballet; and a top-rated university, Tucson has it all.

Multicultural with a strong mix of Spanish, Mexican, and Native American heritage, Tucson has a distinct personality.

Moving to any new area has its share of challenges, and Tucson is no exception. Here we aim to make things a little bit easier by offering a mini resource guide for newcomers packed with important phone numbers and local information.

UTILITIES & BASIC SERVICES

Everyone needs water, gas, electricity, and a phone. Here's who to call:

TUCSON WATER DEPARTMENT
(520) 791-3242
http://cms3.tucsonaz.gov
Services most of Tucson and Pima County. Plan to call at least a week ahead of your move-in date to set up services.

SOUTHWEST GAS CORPORATION
(877) 860-6020
www.swgas.com
Founded in 1931, Southwest Gas is the major supplier of natural gas in the area. It serves over 1.8 million households, businesses, and industries in Arizona, Nevada, and portions of California.

RELOCATION

TUCSON ELECTRIC POWER COMPANY
(520) 623-7711
www.tucsonelectric.com
Arizona's second-largest investor-owned electric utility, Tucson Electric Power Company (TEP), the principal subsidiary of UniSource Energy (publicly traded on the NYSE under the symbol UNS), serves more than 1.5 million customers in Arizona.

QWEST COMMUNICATIONS
(800) 244-1111
www.qwest.com
Handles phone service installation for Pima County.

CABLE TELEVISION

Is there life without cable? There are two major cable companies in town, Cox Communications (520-884-0133) and Comcast Digital Cable (520-744-1900), or you can splurge on satellite. (See the Media chapter for more details).

AREA CODE

Just so you know, Tucson and Pima, Pinal, Santa Cruz, and Cochise Counties all use the 520 area code.

DAYLIGHT SAVING TIME

Unlike the rest of the country (except Hawaii), the state of Arizona doesn't observe daylight saving time, so forget about spring forward/fall back. Our time is the same as Pacific daylight time (three hours earlier than the East Coast) during April through October. The rest of the year we are two hours earlier than the East Coast.

VOTER REGISTRATION

There are several organizations in town that assist with voter registration. For starters, contact the Pima County Recorder's Office voter registration line at (520) 740-4350 or check office locations online at www.recorder.pima.gov.

CITY GOVERNMENT

Got a problem or a concern? Contact the mayor's office at (520) 791-4201; http://cms3.tucsonaz.gov/mayor.

DRIVING LAWS

Be safe and follow the rules! The state of Arizona requires that all front-seat passengers and drivers have their seat belts fastened, and children under age 5 must ride in car seats. Bicycle riders 17 years old and younger must wear a helmet, and motorcycle drivers under 18 must wear a helmet.

CAR REGISTRATION

If you live in Arizona more than seven months in one calendar year, you must title and register your car here. You will need to have an emissions test, certificate of title, current registration, and proof of Arizona insurance. There are five motor vehicle divisions in town. For locations and hours, call (520) 629-9808 or visit https://servicearizona.com for online services and information.

EMISSIONS TESTING

The Department of Environmental Quality, Vehicle Emissions is located at 4040 E. 29th St., (520) 628-5395. There are three inspection locations in town. For the nearest location, current wait times, and best times to test, call (877) 629-9227, 24 hours a day, or visit the website www.myazcar.com.

HEALTH CARE

There are dozens of hospitals and more than 2,000 physicians here. In addition, Tucson is home to numerous clinics, urgent care facilities, alternate health care providers (there are more than 4,000 holistic medicine providers), and specialty practices. Check the Health Care chapter for comprehensive listings.

LIBRARIES

Looking for a good book? There are library branches all over town, and all Pima County residents are eligible for a free library card with proof of ID and residency. Just stop in at any location, or you can sign up online. For a list of library locations and other details, go to www.library.pima.gov.

MAIN LIBRARY INFOLINE
(520) 791-4010
Reference librarians will answer your questions and search for information Mon through Sat.

EDUCATION

The University of Arizona and Pima Community College are the major advanced learning centers here. You'll also find 15 school districts, many private schools, and charter schools along with several specialty (including the Arizona State Schools for the Deaf and Blind) and technical schools. Detailed listings are in the Education & Child Care chapter.

CHILD CARE

The Education & Child Care chapter provides listings of local day-care centers, preschools, and babysitting services, but here are two useful resources to have at hand:

CHILD AND FAMILY RESOURCES
(520) 881-8940
www.childfamilyresources.org
Offers a variety of referral services.

TUCSON OFFICE OF CHILD CARE LICENSURE
(520) 628-6541
www.azdhs.gov/als/childcare
Maintains records for every state-licensed child-care facility.

REAL ESTATE

As the second-largest city in Arizona, the Tucson area and Pima County continue to expand. There are many neighborhoods and towns here, all with distinct personalities and price ranges. Here are some housing resources, but for much more detail, read the Neighborhoods, Neighboring Towns & Real Estate chapter.

LONG REALTY COMPANY
www.longrealty.com
The largest commercial agency in town (and in southern Arizona), these skilled agents know Tucson and Pima County like the back of their hand. Their website also offers helpful information about relocating.

TUCSON METROPOLITAN CHAMBER OF COMMERCE
(520) 792-2250
www.tucsonchamber.org

RELOCATION

A great resource for housing and economic data about Tucson and Pima County. Non-members can get lots of information from their website.

RETIREMENT

Pima County is attracting seniors in droves, especially to the Green Valley area located just south of town. Sunny weather, great facilities, and needed support services make Tucson an ideal retirement destination. Check out the Retirement chapter for details and listings of retirement services and communities of all types, from active senior to assisted living. A terrific central resource is the Pima Council on Aging, (520) 790-7262; www.pcoa.org.

HOUSING

There are a number of ways to find out about housing in Tucson. The *Arizona Daily Star* prints a supplement in the Sunday edition that provides new home information. *Tucson*

Lifestyle publishes a free magazine called the *Tucson New Homes Guide,* also available online at www.tucsonnewhomesguide.com. *Tucson Homes Illustrated is a free magazine available at local merchants* (www.hitucson .com). The *Tucson Relocation Guide* at www .tucsonrelocationguide.com provides community profiles, facts and figures, and useful information for newcomers.

VISITOR INFORMATION

METROPOLITAN TUCSON CONVENTION & VISITORS BUREAU VISITOR CENTER
100 S. Church Ave.
(520) 624-1817, (800) 638-8350, (888) 288-2766
www.visittucson.org
The Metropolitan Tucson Convention & Visitors Bureau maintains a terrific visitor center chock-full of valuable information for visitors and residents alike. Their website also offers tons of Tucson facts and information.

EDUCATION & CHILD CARE

Managing ongoing statewide budget cuts is probably the biggest challenge the education system faces here. Nearly all of the school districts serving Pima County are financially strapped and under pressure. On top of this, Arizona spends less on education than most other states do. As a result, Tucson has a vast number of private and charter schools as alternatives to public education.

Despite underfunding of public education, however, Tucson has some fine public schools and school districts. It also has some of the nation's best private schools and leads the nation in number of charter schools.

For youngsters who are not yet ready for school, Tucson has numerous child-care options, from day-care centers operated by religious organizations or private businesses to preschools affiliated with the YMCA or local school districts. We also have resources for finding the child care that's right for you and your child.

Opportunities for higher education in Tucson are almost limitless. Whether you're looking for a degree from a top-notch university, career training, or just some courses to improve yourself, you'll find it here. We have the University of Arizona, ranked as one of the top in several fields of study, including anthropology, astronomy, pharmacy, and creative writing. We have one of the nation's largest multicampus community colleges. And we have a slew of schools that offer training and degrees in nearly every career imaginable.

Here we provide a general overview of the school districts that serve Tucson as well as some of the private schools and charter schools in the area. You'll also find profiles of colleges, universities, and other institutions of higher learning. Finally, we wrap up the chapter with a look at the child-care scene in Tucson.

PUBLIC SCHOOL DISTRICTS

AMPHITHEATER UNIFIED SCHOOL DISTRICT
701 W. Wetmore Rd.
(520) 696-5000
www.amphi.com
Its first school was a 5-room adobe building in 1893. Today the district has 22 schools and is growing by leaps and bounds along with the population of the Oro Valley and Catalina areas of the valley. The 109-square-mile

district extends as far south as Grant Road, to the north it reaches the Pima County line, on the west is Shannon Road, and east is Campbell Avenue. Over 14,000 students attend 13 elementary, 3 middle, and 3 high schools. Two of the elementary schools contain kindergarten through 8th grade.

Also within this district is a privately operated program called Community Extension Programs (520-888-2727) that offers before- and after-school programs for students in the elementary schools. It's conducted at the elementary school sites and costs include a registration plus monthly fees. The before- and after-school programs are also available at selected school sites during holiday breaks and the summer.

Amphi is known as one of the best public school districts in the valley. On standardized test scores that compare it with other districts, Amphi students score among the highest. Their high schools also have outstanding athletic programs.

Some of the schools operate on a traditional calendar year that ends in late May and starts in mid-Aug, while others are on a modified year with a shorter summer vacation and several intersession breaks.

i You will need the following to enroll your child in any school in Arizona: two proofs of residency (e .g., utility bill, lease agreement, tax return, paycheck stub) and proof of age (a child must be 5 years old before September 1 of the current school year to attend kindergarten, and 6 years old before September 1 to enter 1st grade).

CATALINA FOOTHILLS SCHOOL DISTRICT
2101 E. River Rd.
(520) 209-7500
www.cfsd16.org
Bounded roughly by the mountains to the north, Camino Seco to the east, Snyder Road and Sunrise Drive to the south, and 1st Avenue on the west, Catalina Foothills School District (CFSD), also commonly known as District 16, has 1 preschool and 4 elementary schools, 2 middle schools, and 1 high school.

Bus transportation is provided for most of the district's students.

CFSD's schools emphasize academics and the arts and have strict discipline policies. Students score in the top 10 percent of the nation and are among the highest in the state on standardized tests. The average CFSD student reads and computes 1 full year above grade level. Spanish-language instruction is provided starting in kindergarten.

The district operates an intergenerational orchestra—the Foothills Phil—open to all interested musicians. Its CARE program, based at each elementary school, is open to enrolled elementary students for before- and after-school enrichment and is especially valuable to families with both parents working. Like most of the valley school districts, school starts in early-August and ends in late May. The district offices on E. River Road formerly housed its first school designed by famous local architect Josias Joesler.

FLOWING WELLS UNIFIED SCHOOL DISTRICT
1556 W. Prince Rd.
(520) 696-8800
www.flowingwellsschools.org
Surrounded by the Amphitheater, Tucson, and Marana School Districts, Flowing Wells is geographically much smaller than the others. It covers 13 square miles between Grant and Ina Roads and the Santa Cruz and Rillito Rivers on Tucson's northwest side.

About 6,000 kids are in the district, which encompasses 1 early learning center, 6 elementary schools, and 1 junior and 2 high schools plus Junior ROTC. Numerous extension programs include before- and after-school care at select elementary schools, a Big Brothers and Big Sisters program, as well as tutorial services. In addition to the standard curriculum, vocational programs such as agriculture, fine arts, culinary arts, mechanics, and robotics are offered to enrolled students through JTED (Joint Technological Education District). Support services for families are also offered through various partnerships.

The district has a good reputation for academics, and many of its schools have won state and national awards over the years. All schools are on the traditional school-year calendar, beginning in early August and concluding in late May.

MARANA UNIFIED SCHOOL DISTRICT
11279 W. Grier Rd.
(520) 682-3243
www.az.maranausd.org
Geographically, this school district covers a large area of the west and northwest valley—550 square miles—about 16 miles northwest of downtown Tucson. It extends east from Shannon Road and the Tucson Mountains, north to the county line, and south to where the Tucson Mountains end. It encompasses the town of Marana, the growing northwest residential areas along I-10 and west of downtown, and the largely desert areas west and north of the Tucson Mountains.

Just under 13,000 students attend 12 elementary, 2 middle, and 3 high, schools. The student achievement scores are typically well above county, state, and national norms. The district has licensed early education centers for 4- and 5-year-olds during the school year, enrichment centers available year-round for K–6 students, along with gifted and special education programs and related services such as psychological testing, speech pathology, and occupational

and physical therapy. In addition, the district offers a preschool program for disabled students ages 3 to 5, and a family resource center. The district also provides a variety of resources and programs to ensure that the academic and personal needs of eligible Title I, English-language learner, migrant, and Native American students are met.

The district offices on W. Grier Road are west of exit 236 off I-10. The school year runs from early August to late May.

SUNNYSIDE UNIFIED SCHOOL DISTRICT
2238 E. Ginter Rd.
(520) 545-2000
www.sunnysideud.k12.az.us
This district covers 96.3 square miles in the south part of Tucson, including 2 miles of the Tohono O'odham Indian Reservation. More than 17,000 students attend 22 schools pre-K through 12th grade. There are 13 elementary, 5 middle, and 3 high schools, plus 1 alternative school for grades 9 through 12 and an early childhood education center. It's the second-largest district in Pima County, with a majority of Hispanic students. And like most districts in the booming Tucson area, its schools are overcrowded.

Despite the strains, it operates many good educational and enrichment programs. They include an all-day kindergarten, ELL, special education, a gifted and talented program, and middle school intramural athletics. One of its elementary schools is not a neighborhood school but instead accepts students who want a more challenging and stringent educational environment (on a first-come basis). The district also has dropout prevention, a teenage parent program, and health services.

Close-up

Ventana Vista

Ventana Vista Elementary School, located in the Catalina foothills, was designed by internationally noted architect and native of the Southwest Antoine Predock. Designed as a "children's city," the unusual structure is set against the backdrop of the Santa Catalina Mountain Range. In the architect's own words, "Spaces and elements throughout the school were designed to create unique learning environments for children. Educational icons are strategically placed throughout this children's city as landmarks and learning tools." The stunning design features a mystery light monitor, a solar solstice wall, and a natural periscope for viewing the mountains. Wonderful tiled murals and private courtyards found around every corner are complemented by desert landscaping, children's gardens, and play areas. Lucky kids! Ventana Vista is located at 6085 N. Kolb Rd., just north of Kolb and Sunrise Drive.

Other unique offerings include family literacy programs. District headquarters on E. Ginter Road are north of Valencia Road and west of Tucson Boulevard. The school year runs from early August to late May.

TANQUE VERDE UNIFIED SCHOOL DISTRICT
2300 N. Tanque Verde Loop Rd.
(520) 749-5751
www.tanqueverdeschools.org
This district (District 13) was organized in 1886, when this part of town was considered remote from Tucson. Today over 1,650 kids attend 1 high school, 1 junior high, and 2 elementary schools in the district.

Tanque Verde has the reputation of being one of the best districts in the area. Academically, students score above the norms, and the tax base for school funding enables small class sizes and top-notch instructional resources. Its boundaries encompass the upscale neighborhoods east of Sabino Canyon, the Forty-Niner Country Club, and the Redington Pass and Old Spanish Trail areas.

The curriculum includes all the basics plus Spanish (grades 1–9), fine arts, computers, and choir. Special education, gifted education, remedial reading, and speech and language therapy are offered as needed. The Tanque Verde Extended Care program offers after-school classes, summer programs, and activities. District offices are on the corner of Tanque Verde Road and Tanque Verde Loop Road. Students attend classes from early August to late May.

TUCSON UNIFIED SCHOOL DISTRICT
1010 E. 10th St.
(520) 225-6000
www.tusd1.org
Tucson Unified School District (TUSD) was one of the first public school districts established in Arizona and today is the second-largest in the state, encompassing the most populated part of the metropolitan area—it covers 231 square miles. Beset by ongoing budget cuts, the district has been forced to close and merge schools within its boundaries. Despite this, there are many excellent schools and programs. Class sizes are limited

to 28. Total enrollment in 2011 was 52,837 in 60 elementary schools (many with pre-K and all with full-day kindergarten), 14 middle schools including 2 magnet schools (Dodge and Utterback School of the Arts), 12 high schools, and 1 K–12 school.

The high school count includes 5 magnet schools and the Museum School for the Visual Arts as well as 4 alternative schools, including 1 especially for teenage parents. Certain high schools offer Air Force and Army JRTOC, career and technical courses through JTED including fire science, culinary arts, automotive, and finance, and AP classes including Latin, Chinese, and Japanese.

The district also has a dual credit program through Pima Community College where students can receive college credit for select courses. Dozens of programs and clubs at the high school level include astronomy, music theater, Future Farmers of America, forensics, and Special Olympics.

All of the district's schools operate on a traditional school-year calendar, which ends by late May and resumes in mid-Aug. Among the district's most unique and popular features are its 19 magnet schools, which offer special curricula. Examples include math and science, engineering and technology, creative and performing arts, law, international studies, health, and aviation and aerospace.

Unique schools in the district include Cholla High Magnet School, the only Pima County school that offers a 2-year international baccalaureate diploma program in addition to Arabic and Mandarin language programs, and the Ochoa Elementary School, which has introduced the Reggio Emilia educational program schoolwide.

Another unique option provided to TUSD students is the opportunity to apply to University High School, which specializes in college-prep course work for very high-achieving students. Please note that students must meet admission criteria and pass an entrance exam to be selected to attend.

A comprehensive support system for students with special needs is also available through the district. Most students receive special education services at their home school; however, there are specialized programs for students with complex needs. Gifted students in the district have access to self-contained classes for gifted and talented education, also known as GATE, at several elementary and middle schools.

Programs continue to be offered after school lets out for the summer break. More details regarding these and other TUSD programs as well as updated information on school closings can be viewed at the district's website. The district is one of the largest employers in Pima County.

VAIL SCHOOL DISTRICT
13801 E. Benson Hwy.
(520) 879-2000
www.vail.k12.az.us

Situated in the far southeast and extending east from Wilmot Road and south from Irvington Road, the Vail School District covers a sparsely populated area but one that has seen a huge increase in housing. Its eastern boundary is the Rincon Mountains, and to the south it reaches the Santa Rita Mountains. It encompasses the Rita Ranch area as well as Corona de Tucson.

Founded in 1903, the Vail School District was once a ranching community with a 1-room schoolhouse. Only 20 minutes southeast of downtown Tucson, the Vail School District is one of the fastest-growing districts in Arizona. Considered one of the best districts in the county, with relatively small class sizes and state-of-the-art technology, the district has 7 elementary schools, 4 middle schools, and 2 charter, 2 comprehensive, and 1 alternative high school, with more than 10,000 students in grades K through 12. The district projects enrollment to continue to grow rapidly.

PRIVATE SCHOOLS

In addition to the schools among the eight public school districts covered here, Tucson has many private schools, some of which have a religious affiliation, with tuition ranging from around $1,000 to $13,000 a year. So if your neighborhood public school doesn't suit your needs, there's a vast array of private schools to choose from. Some are considered among the top in the nation. Here we provide a brief profile of a variety ranging from those with special programs to serious college prep.

Unless otherwise noted, all the schools listed here operate on the same school calendar (mid-August to late May) as most Tucson schools and offer some type of financial assistance.

CASAS CHRISTIAN SCHOOL
10801 N. La Cholla Blvd.
(520) 297-0922
www.casaschristianschool.com
Started in 1970, Casas is a Christian school that incorporates Bible study and prayer into the curriculum. Its academics emphasize problem solving, critical thinking, and research skills. Emphasis is on math, science, language, music, art, and spiritual growth. The school also has Bible and computer technology classes. About 500 students attend grades kindergarten through 8 with a class size of 20 or fewer.

GREEN FIELDS COUNTRY DAY SCHOOL
6000 N. Camino de la Tierra
(520) 297-2288
www.greenfields.org
Founded in 1933 as a residential ranch school for boys, Green Fields is one of Arizona's oldest independent day schools for grades 1 through 12. Its 21-acre campus includes an extensive library, modern science labs, a computer lab, tennis, swimming, ball fields, and a center for the performing arts that seats 300. Kids here can learn desktop publishing, pottery, printmaking, drama, and darkroom photography along with algebra, calculus, journalism, Spanish, and French. They can participate in several interscholastic sports or intramural tennis. It's an outstanding college preparatory school with about 240 students and a teacher-to-student ratio of about 1 to 9.

KINO SCHOOL
6625 N. 1st Ave.
(520) 297-7278
www.kinoschool.org
Located on 10 acres just north of the city limits, Kino is a highly eclectic, loosely structured independent coed school for grades kindergarten through 12. Younger students learn language arts, environmental responsibilities, social and motor skills, and self-expression. Older kids learn to think critically and creatively, be self-directed, and take responsibility for their community. Kino considers the world to be a classroom and regularly exposes students to the environment and the arts through local and extended field trips. Students are involved in setting their own goals and evaluating their progress. Enrollment numbers about 70, with a ratio of 1 teacher to 7 students. At present,

limited financial aid is available through the school.

SALPOINTE CATHOLIC HIGH SCHOOL
1545 E. Copper St.
(520) 327-6581
www.salpointe.org
This coed school for grades 9 through 12 has just under 1,200 students representing a broad socioeconomic mix, about 24 percent of whom are not Catholic. This excellent college preparatory school requires courses in English, foreign language, math, theology, science, and social studies, as well as volunteerism. Electives include the fine arts, humanities, physical education, and practical arts. Class size is about 27, and over 99 percent of Salpointe graduates go directly to college, many on grants and scholarships. Students participate in 24 varsity sports, including baseball, basketball, cross-country, football, golf, soccer, tennis, volleyball, and swimming. Parish families get discounts on tuition. Over $1.5 million in aid is available to students who need financial assistance.

SATORI SCHOOL
3801 N. 1st Ave.
(520) 887-4003
www.satorischool.org
Satori, a Japanese word describing the pursuit of learning, offers a preschool through 8th grade program for gifted children. The 2nd through 8th grade is a charter school that is tuition-free. The school campus consists of a number of separate buildings. The self-directed curriculum, which includes math, art, dance and movement, drama, humanities, foreign language, and computers and science, is designed to challenge the intellectual, emotional, behavioral, and social needs of these children. Enrollment is

about 230, with an average class size of 10. The school also offers summer camps for children with science exploration, hands-on learning, and field trips.

ST. GREGORY COLLEGE PREPARATORY
3231 N. Craycroft Rd.
(520) 327-6395
www.stgregoryschool.org
This is a nonsectarian coed day school for grades 6 through 12 located along the bank of the Rillito River near the Fort Lowell historic area. The campus includes a theater that seats 370, a gymnasium, a 7,000-volume library with computer labs, and outdoor athletic facilities. Nearly all courses offered at the school are advanced placement or honors, and student–teacher ratio is 9 to 1. The school is also known for its strong studio art, photography, drama, and music departments.

Students are encouraged to volunteer or take internships in the community. Seniors can participate in an East African studies class and 2-week senior internship in Kenya assisting in local public schools.

During summer the school has enrichment programs of 2 to 6 weeks, some of which include studies abroad. Enrollment is about 280. Financial assistance is available, as are scholarships.

i Each year the *Arizona Daily Star* publishes an annual survey of private schools in Tucson. It offers good at-a-glance information, including tuition, so call the newspaper, (520) 573-4400. The newspaper also publishes a similar profile of charter schools.

TUCSON HEBREW ACADEMY
3888 E. River Rd.
(520) 529-3888
www.thaaz.org
Located adjacent to the Jewish Community Center, the day school for grades 1 to 8 is a modern building facing the Santa Catalina foothills. It includes an auditorium for dining and theater events, a library, outdoor courtyard, and state-of-the-art classrooms with science, computer, and art labs, and students have access to all the facilities at the community center. The general academic curriculum is integrated within a Judaic framework to provide both a secular and religious education. Enrollment averages about 200 with a class size of 14. The community center, a separate facility, operates a preschool during the regular school year that includes early-morning and late-afternoon hours.

TULLER SCHOOL
5870 E. 14th St.
(520) 747-1142
www.tullerschool.com
In operation since 1956, this private coeducational school known officially as the Abbie Loveland Tuller School, uses the Tuller Method, a "correlated pattern system devised to give all students the opportunity to achieve their highest potential." Very small classes from kindergarten to 8th grade make this an intimate school experience. The grounds are lovely with fountains and old-growth trees. Uniforms are required, as well as attendance at chapel. Tuition assistance is available.

TUCSON WALDORF SCHOOL
Presidio Campus
3349 E. Presidio Rd.
www.tucsonwaldorf.org
This private school offers grades 1 through 8, kindergarten, nursery, and parent-child classes. The early childhood classes and grades 1 through 3 are located at the Presidio campus, while grades 4 through 8 attend the River Bend Campus at 3605 E. River Rd. (520-325-5514) in the Binghampton Rural Historic Landscape District. The River Bend campus has lovely grounds, and both locations have gardens and outdoor play areas. Students are taught following the Waldorf method, which fosters creative development, wonder, and joy in learning and integrates academics and the arts. The unique curriculum includes Spanish and German, drawing, music theory, watercolor painting, and knitting, along with the 3 Rs, The school welcomes visitors and hosts monthly open houses and events. Tuition assistance is available and the school also accepts Department of Economic Security (DES) funding.

CHARTER SCHOOLS

In 1994 Arizona's legislature passed one of the nation's most lenient charter laws, and the state leads the nation in the number of charter schools. These are "alternative" schools that are allowed to operate without the rigid educational requirements attached to public schools except regarding health, safety, civil rights, special education, insurance, and student assessment testing. Essentially they are public schools under contract—or charter—from a public agency to a group of parents, teachers, a business, or others who want to create alternatives and choice in education. Charters may be granted by the state or by individual school districts. The charter school then receives a per-student allocation (equivalent to the district's average cost per pupil) for each student enrolled, plus some state monies allocated for capital needs.

The number of charter schools in Pima County continues to grow and includes a wide range of schools from small ones in temporary facilities to established Montessori schools. On the whole, parents who choose this option are pleased with both the quality and professionalism of these institutions, and public schools are finding the need to be competitive with them to retain students.

For more information on charter schools in Tucson, contact the Department of Education at (520) 628-6794, or check the website at www.ade.az.gov/charterschools/info. Here we offer just a sampling.

BASIS TUCSON
3434 E. Broadway Blvd. (Upper School)
(520) 326-3444
www.basisschools.org
The recipient of numerous academic awards and rated by *Newsweek Magazine* as among America's top 10 high schools, this charter school system has a rigorous liberal arts curriculum and high academic standards. A system of yearly comprehensive exams ensures that all students have accomplished their academic goals. The curriculum includes Latin, Mandarin, literature, history, art, philosophy, mathematics, and science. Upper-level student curriculum centers on AP subjects. Sports and fine arts courses are offered to all students. After-school sports and band are also available. All seniors participate in an internship or external study program. Their other schools include 3825 N. 2nd St. (Middle School, 520-326-6367); 11155 N. Oracle Rd. in Oro Valley (520-308-5220); and 3825 E. 2nd St. (520-326-6359).

KHALSA MONTESSORI ELEMENTARY SCHOOL
3701 E. River Rd.
(520) 529-3611
www.khalsamontessorischool.org
This school is geared to parents who want a Montessori education for their kids without the private-school price tag. The Montessori philosophy holds that teachers need to give children the tools, environment, and nurturing in which they can learn and grow. Enrollment is about 350 and there is often a waiting list.

SONORAN SCIENCE ACADEMY
2325 W. Sunset Rd. (K–12)
(520) 665-3400
www.sonoranacademy.org
The Sonoran Science Academy (SSA) schools are tuition-free public college-preparatory charter schools that emphasize science, math, and computer technology. The numerous extracurricular academic clubs include robotics, anime, chess, and drama. PE, art, and music are part of the rigorous curriculum, and free tutoring is offered to students in all subjects. Class sizes are around 20. Their other schools include Broadway Campus (K–8) at 6880 E. Broadway Blvd. (520-751-2401) and Davis-Monthan Campus (6–10) at 5741 E. Ironwood St. (520-300-5699). At the Davis-Monthan location, only grades 6 through 9 are tuition-free.

TUCSON COUNTRY DAY SCHOOL
9239 E. Wrightstown Rd.
(520) 296-0883
www.tcdcharterschool.com
One of the more established charter schools in town, the school serves students from preschool through 8th grade. The student–teacher ratio is about 1 to 25. Curriculum

includes technology, Spanish, art, music, and PE, along with extracurricular athletic teams. Summer prep courses and a summer day camp are also available. There is frequently a waiting list for most grades.

> **i** There is a special place at the University of Arizona for students with learning and attention challenges—the Strategic Alternative Learning Techniques (SALT) Center. SALT provides comprehensive academic support services including the development of an individualized education plan for each student, as well as tutoring and psychological services in a state-of-the-art facility. There is a separate application process and additional fees; call (520) 621-1242 or visit www.salt.arizona.edu for more information.

HIGHER EDUCATION

*UNIVERSITY OF ARIZONA
University Boulevard and Park Avenue
(520) 621-2211
www.arizona.edu
Although designated by the territorial legislature in 1885 (before Arizona was a state), the school existed only on paper until a saloon owner and 2 gamblers donated 40 acres. It opened in 1891 in its first building, Old Main, with 32 students in agriculture and mining. Today it's one of the top-20 public research universities in the country, with an enrollment of over 38,000 and covering 378 acres. It offers undergraduate, master's, doctoral, and professional degrees. It boasts University Medical Center, a leading research and teaching hospital.

Ranked 16th among all public universities by the National Science Foundation, the university offers students more than 300 undergraduate and graduate degrees through 20 colleges and 11 schools on 3 campuses.

It has multiple colleges, ranging from agriculture and architecture to medicine and law, and numerous schools ranging from music and dance to public administration. A number of degrees can be obtained through the university's evening and weekend program.

The school year consists of 2 semesters—August to December and January to May—with two 5-week summer sessions available.

The UA Outreach College offers regular university credit courses off campus, noncredit courses, workshops both on and off campus, and high school and university online and distance-learning courses. Call (520) 621-7724 for details. The university's library system, which is also available to the public, contains an amazing 5 million–plus print volumes and over 600,000 electronic books. In addition to the main library at 1501 E. University Blvd. (520-621-6442), there are separate science and engineering, music, poetry, and health sciences libraries, the last located at University Medical Center.

The university's athletic accomplishments rival its academic ones. Arizona Athletics is home to 500 student-athletes who compete in 19 sports. Over the years UA student-athletes have won 18 national team championships and 37 Pac-10 conference team championships. Campus Recreation offers fitness classes, intramural sports, and numerous sports clubs.

Wildcats hold national titles in men's basketball, baseball, women's softball, women's golf, and synchronized swimming.

And if it weren't for the university, Tucson's cultural and educational community would face a serious void. The school houses the Museum of Art, with one of the best collections of Renaissance art in the Southwest. Centennial Hall, a major venue for performances in Tucson, is part of the university, as is the Arizona State Museum. Flandrau Science Center and Planetarium and its mineral museum are available to Tucsonans compliments of the university. UA also houses the Center for Creative Photography.

The university's presence benefits the community far beyond its cultural offerings. The Cooperative Extension, which has offices in every county in Arizona, assists farmers and supports natural resources statewide. UA operates southern Arizona's Public Broadcasting Station (KUAT) as well as several radio stations. For kids, UA's Outreach College Arizona Youth University programs offer a variety of enrichment programs.

It's highly unlikely that you can visit Tucson, or live here, without somehow being touched by the university. Maybe you'll use the university's library, attend performances at Centennial Hall, or visit a museum. Perhaps you'll get medical care at UMC or one of several university physician clinics around Tucson. Or you might visit the Admissions Office for publications on the university. Maybe you'll take the kids to Spring Fling, a carnival on the mall featuring rides, eats, and other fun. And most likely, you'll be watching the Wildcats compete in football, basketball, and many other sports at McKale Center, Arizona Stadium, Frank Sancet Field, or Hillenbrand Stadium.

Visitors, including Tucson residents, should stop by the campus visitor center, which has an enormous amount of helpful information about UA and its facilities. Located at 811 N. Euclid Ave., on the northwest corner of Euclid and University, the center is open Mon through Fri. Call (520) 621-5130.

The center also offers a 90-minute walking tour, led by UA student ambassadors. Tours are also offered on a regular basis by the Admissions Office. Call (520) 621-3641 for schedule information. While you are on campus, remember that pedestrians have the right-of-way and that finding parking can be difficult, especially if there are special or sporting events taking place.

Prospective students interested in attending the university can contact the UA Admissions Department at (520) 621-3237 or visit http://admissions.arizona.edu for specific information about admissions policies and procedures.

i If you happen to be at UA's School of Aerospace and Mechanical Engineering at the southeast corner of Mountain and Helen, take a moment to climb the stairs and walk across the amazing bridges linking the two buildings. Held up by cables, they bounce when you walk across—kids love the sensation and you will, too!

PIMA COMMUNITY COLLEGE
4905 E. Broadway
(520) 206-4500
www.pima.edu
Opened in 1969, Pima is one of the nation's largest multicampus community colleges. The college has 6 campuses: Community Campus, Downtown Campus, East Campus, Desert Vista Campus, Northwest Campus, and West Campus. In addition, classes are offered at other sites throughout Pima and Santa Cruz Counties.

The college offers a total of 195 transfer and occupational programs leading to associate of arts, associate of business, associate of science, associate of general studies, associate of applied arts, and associate of applied science degrees and basic, advanced, and technical certificates. Pima Community College is a 2-year institution that serves residents of Pima and Santa Cruz Counties. Each year the college meets the educational needs of its students through credit and noncredit courses. All 6 campuses offer university transfer programs, occupational and developmental education, and special interest courses.

Pima students have access to free academic and career counseling, tutoring, financial aid and veterans assistance, basic skills assessment, disabled-student resources, and other special programs. Libraries are located at multiple campuses and contain a collection of more than a quarter-million multimedia items and books. Financial aid may be available in the form of scholarships, loans, grants, and part-time employment. Annual enrollment for credit and noncredit programs is over 68,000. There are multiple options and sessions for course schedules throughout the year, from 5-week to 14-week late-start classes.

In addition, the college offers summer sessions, a winter intersession, and short-term classes (8 weeks or less). Students may also choose self-paced, accelerated, day, evening, weekend, online, and televised classes. Pima offers college success courses for those wanting to improve their college experience, free workshops on subjects ranging from taking tests to career planning, and job fairs that are open to the public.

The college plays a significant role in local economic development by providing customized training and on-site classes to business and industry throughout Pima and Santa Cruz Counties. A state-of-the-art computer training center specializes in cost-effective training for employees of local companies and is available for employers to conduct their own training.

Extracurricular activities include a student newspaper and literary magazines; student chorale, jazz band, and other music ensembles; and student drama productions. Pima also offers 16 intercollegiate athletic teams, such as baseball, basketball, cross-country, football, golf, soccer, softball, tennis, track, and volleyball, along with intramural sports.

Pima's Community Education Office (520-206-6574) offers hundreds of personal development courses at learning centers throughout the area. Pima for Kids, a youth program, offers fun and educational activities and summer camps for children; call (520) 206-6579.

The college's West Campus also houses the Center for the Arts, where exhibits and performances by students, local production companies, and national troupes are presented throughout the year.

Free parking is available at all campuses, and most have cafeterias that are open all day during the week. Sun Tran buses stop at all PCC campuses.

Other Colleges & Technical Schools

Tucson has a number of smaller colleges and specialty schools that offer degrees or career training. The **University of Phoenix**'s Tucson locations at 300 S. Craycroft Rd. and 555 E. River Rd. (520-881-6512 and 520-408-8202, respectively; www.phoenix.edu) are part of the nation's largest private university. This is where working adults can get an undergraduate or graduate degree by going to class evenings and weekends and online. They have degree programs in business, education, technology, management, criminal justice, and nursing plus nondegree graduate courses and teacher certification for school educators and administrators.

The **Art Institute of Tucson** (520-318-2700; www.artinstitutes.edu/tucson), a small private college in midtown Tucson, offers degree and diploma programs in digital film, baking and pastry, culinary arts, hospitality, fashion design and marketing, graphic design, Web and gaming design, interior design, digital photography, and advertising. The classes are very small; enrollment is about 450.

Prescott College at Tucson, 2233 E. Speedway Blvd. (520-319-9868; www.prescott.edu), offers an adult degree program where students of any age can earn a bachelor's or master's degree or PhD in a unique individualized program that combines tutorial and traditional independent study. Areas of study include teacher education/certification, management, human services, psychology, counseling, and environmental studies.

Brown Mackie College, 4585 E. Speedway Blvd., Ste. 204 (520-319-3300; www.brownmackie.edu/tucson), offers bachelor's degrees in business administration as well as several associate's degree and certificate programs. Tracks of study include accounting, legal assistant, criminal justice, and computer networking and security. Students have a choice of day or evening classes, and financial aid is available.

Carrington College, 3550 N. Oracle Rd. (520-888-5885; www.carrington.com), has diploma programs for medical, veterinary, and dental assistants; massage therapy; and pharmacy technology in addition to associate's degree programs for several health-related management areas.

For a school that specializes in health fields, contact **Pima Medical Institute,** 3350 E. Grant Rd. (520-326-1600; www.pmi.edu). It offers associate's degrees in a number of health fields, including respiratory therapy and radiography, and career training in numerous medical, dental, and veterinary assistant positions.

Two other schools that offer career training in business and technical fields are **ITT Technical Institute,** 1455 W. River Rd. (520-408-7488; www.itt-tech.edu), and **Brookline College,** 5441 E. 22nd St., Ste. 125 (520-748-9799; www.brooklinecollege.edu). The former offers associate's, bachelor's, and master's degree programs in fields such as electronics, information systems, and computer drafting. The latter offers diplomas and associate's degrees in medical, business, pharmacy technician, and criminal justice.

Several schools provide career training in office skills such as word processing, computer software, legal secretarial, court reporting, and transcription.

For people pursuing a career in art, the **Southwest University of Visual Arts** at 2525 N. Country Club Rd. (520-325-0123; www.theartcenter.edu) is a design college offering associate's and bachelor's degrees and training in illustration, photography, and painting.

And if the food and beverage industry strikes your fancy, you can attend the **Bartending Academy,** 2723 N. Campbell Ave. (520-325-6300; www.tucsonbartendingacademy.com), for training in bartending during the day or evening.

i If you're looking for something to keep the kiddies occupied, head to your local public library. Pima County libraries (www.library.pima.gov) offer free classes and programs for kids of all ages, including story times for the wee ones, read to the dog for beginning readers, and video games and chess for teens.

Child Care

Like most comparable metropolitan areas, there is a significant demand for child care in Tucson because of single-parent families and households with both parents working. Schools, churches, nonprofit organizations, and private businesses all help meet this demand with a variety of day-care and preschool programs. Although there are too many to list here, we can describe some of the options available to parents and resources for tracking down others.

Day-care facilities include **Childtime,** with multiple locations and pickup services (www.childtime.com); **Kindercare,** which accepts children as young as 6 weeks (www.kindercare.com); **La Petite Academy,** with various locations around town (www.lapetite.com); and the **Sandbox,** which offers both full and after-school care from 6:30 a.m. to 6 p.m. for kids ages 1 to 8 (520-795-9595; www.sandboxtucson.com).

KIDCO is a recreation program designed for kids 5 through 12. Offered during the school year and the summer, it takes place in schools around Tucson. A comprehensive list of locations is published twice a year in the Tucson Parks and Recreation Department's program guide. Funded by Parks and Rec, this innovative program offers kids a safe, comfortable place to be after school and during the summer with a variety of activities. There is a registration fee for KIDCO. For more information and to register, call the registration line at (520) 791-4877.

Childcare Resource and Referral, 2800 E. Broadway Blvd. (520-325-5778; www.azchildcare.org), provides information and referrals on child care, sitters, preschools, and how to search for quality care as well as a child-care center. You can also search for child-care centers and providers at their website. Child and Family Resources (520-881-8940; www.childandfamilyresources.org) is a private, community-based nonprofit agency headquartered in Tucson offering dozens of programs throughout Arizona. **Parenting Arizona** (3710 S. Park Ave., Ste. 702; 520-319-1040; www.parentingaz.org) is a statewide nonprofit agency with a mission to strengthen families and prevent child abuse and neglect. The agency offers parenting classes, in-home family support services, Safe Haven—an after-school program for at-risk children—and numerous community outreach program.

i The Parent Connection (www.theparentconnectionaz.org) is a great spot for parents and kids, from newborns to toddlers. The center provides all sorts of classes and activities, as well as outreach programs at their child-friendly center at 5326 E. Pima in Tucson. You'll find organized play groups, music classes, support groups for new parents, and all sorts of resources here. Your first class is free, but after that you will need to join for a nominal fee, and there are charges for some programs. But it's a great way to meet other parents and to introduce your child to new experiences and other kids. For more information, call (520) 321-1500.

Each year *Inside Tucson Business* publishes a list of child-care providers in the metro area (www.insidetucsonbusiness .com). The *Arizona Daily Star* publishes special sections throughout the year about summer programs, schools, and special kids' activities.

Founded by Tucsonan Christina Bishop and her sister, the online service www.thesit terservice.com will find you a sitter for home or hotel or even special events. All sitters are over 18, have been interviewed, and have been submitted to a limited background check. You must apply and pay a registration free to participate in the service, then simply call or e-mail the service to request a babysitter.

HEALTH CARE

Back in 1880 when Arizona was still a territory and every small town and settlement had its neighborly doc or two (who no doubt made house calls), St. Mary's Hospital opened in Tucson, the state's first. That same year the Sisters of St. Joseph of Carondelet began their work to provide health care to the settlers of the area, eventually opening another hospital.

Things have changed a great deal since then. Today both of those early hospitals are part of the nationwide Carondelet Health Care System, and Tucson now has about a dozen hospitals, medical clinics, mental health and substance abuse facilities, hospices, alternative medical services, and health spas.

We offer here the major players, as well as some phone numbers you'll want to keep handy during your stay in the Old Pueblo. (For information on Tucson's two health spas, Canyon Ranch and Miraval, go to the Accommodations chapter.)

URGENT CARE CLINICS

Although we earnestly hope you won't need health care during your stay in Tucson, if you do, you may want to turn to an urgent care center as a first stop. These centers typically provide care for anything that's not life threatening (for which you'll want to seek an emergency room, which we cover in the hospital section of the chapter). Most are open extended hours—from about 8 a.m. to 8 p.m. or longer. Although no appointment is necessary, you may have a long wait, so it's best to call ahead.

EL DORADO URGENT CARE
1400 N. Wilmot Rd.
(520) 884-4999
www.eldoracouc.com
Open 10 a.m. to 10 p.m. daily.

NEXTCARE
(888) 381-4858
www.nextcare.com
Locations include:

6238 E. Pima
Open 8 a.m. to 8 p.m. weekdays; 8 a.m. to 4 p.m. weekends and holidays.

501 N. Park Ave., Ste. 110
Open Mon to Fri, 10 a.m. to 10 p.m., weekends noon to 8 p.m.

9525 E. Old Spanish Trail, Ste. 101
Open weekdays, 8 a.m. to 8 p.m., weekends 8 a.m. to 4 p.m.

4280 N. Oracle Rd., Ste. 100
Open weekdays 8 a.m. to 8 p.m., Sat 8 a.m. to 2 p.m., Sun 8 a.m. to 4 p.m.

NORTHWEST MEDICAL CENTER URGENT CARE

1295 W. Duval Mine Rd., Green Valley
(520) 399-2027
Open 8:30 a.m. to 7:30 p.m. 7 days a week.

ORANGE GROVE

3870 W. River Rd., Ste. 126
(520) 219-6616
Urgent care hours: 9 a.m. to 8 p.m. 7 days a week. A pediatric provider is available Mon through Fri from 5 to 8 p.m., Sat and Sun from 9 a.m. to 8 p.m.

RANCHO VISTOSO URGENT CARE

13101 N. Oracle Rd. (Oracle and Rancho Vistoso Boulevard)
(520) 818-2000
Open 7 days a week, 8 a.m. to 7 p.m.

LA PALOMA URGENT CARE & PHYSICIAN OFFICES

4001 E. Sunrise Dr. (Hacienda del Sol and Sunrise Drive)
(520) 209-7000
Open 7 days a week, 9 a.m. to 7 p.m.

CONTINENTAL RESERVE

8333 N. Silverbell Rd. (Silverbell and Continental Reserve Loop)
(520) 202-7700
Open 7 days a week, 9 a.m. to 7 p.m.

UNIVERSITY OF ARIZONA MEDICAL CENTER—SOUTH CAMPUS

2800 E. Ajo Way
(520) 694-8888
www.uph.org
Open 10 a.m. to 10 p.m., 7 days a week.

URGENT CARE ASSOCIATES

www.urgentcaretucson.com
1622 N. Swan Rd. (just south of Pima Street)
(520) 795-8888
Open 9 a.m. to 9 p.m. weekdays, 9 a.m. to 6 p.m. weekends.

9348 E. Rita Rd.
(520) 382-8000
Open noon to 8 p.m. Mon through Fri, 10 a.m. to 4 p.m. weekends.

REFERRAL SERVICES

Several agencies help consumers find medical and dental services. Keep in mind that those operated by a hospital are most likely to make referrals to medical practitioners who are affiliated with their facilities. There is no charge for using these referral services.

ARIZONA CENTER FOR INTEGRATIVE MEDICINE

www.integrativemedicine.arizona.edu/alumni.html
Find a graduate who has been trained in integrative medicine on this website for the world-renowned University of Arizona program.

ARIZONA DENTAL REFERRAL

(800) 866-2732
www.azda.org

ℹ️ The University of Arizona's Human Origins Genotyping Lab analyzes human DNA for National Geographic's Genographic Project.

BANNER HEALTH REFERRAL AND RESOURCE LINE

(800) 230-2273

www.bannerhealth.com

For physician and specialist referrals in the Phoenix area. All physicians are with the Banner Health Hospital.

PIMA COUNTY MEDICAL SOCIETY

(520) 795-7985

www.pimamedicalsociety.org

HOSPITALS

Tucson has a number of specialty hospitals, such as rehabilitation and psychiatric, as well as acute-care hospitals—those most likely to have an emergency room and a full spectrum of medical and surgical services. (Most of the hospitals listed in this section are acute care.) Many have physician office complexes; some have a hospice, psychiatric unit, substance abuse unit, or nursing home on the campus. What follows is a select but not comprehensive listing of top hospitals in town.

i The Healthy Living Connections Program at TMC's El Dorado campus at 1400 N. Wilmot Rd. offers educational classes and lectures (usually free), health screenings, consultations, a health resource center, and support groups of all kinds. Call (520) 324-1690, or check www.tmcaz.com/community/seniorservices/healthy_living_connections for details and schedules.

CARONDELET HEART AND VASCULAR INSTITUTE

4888 N. Stone Ave.

(520) 696-2328

www.tucsonhearthospital.com

This 60-bed facility, part of the Carondelet Health network, offers a total heart-care environment for cardiac patients, from prevention and wellness through surgery and rehabilitation, all with the latest technology. The emergency department, however, is ready to treat not only acute coronary conditions but also any emergency. A variety of wellness programs are offered, including screenings for cholesterol levels and cardiac risk.

CARONDELET ST. JOSEPH'S HOSPITAL

350 N. Wilmot Rd.

(520) 296-3211

www.carondelet.org

This 400-plus–bed facility on the Eastside offers a full range of comprehensive inpatient and outpatient services, an emergency room, a regional hospital eye center, a neurological institute, stroke and trauma rehabilitation services (the hospital is certified a Primary Stroke Center), and extensive women's care services including private birthing suites.

CARONDELET ST. MARY'S HOSPITAL

1601 W. St. Mary's Rd.

(520) 872-3000

www.carondelet.org

St. Mary's, the state's oldest hospital, founded in 1880, is just west of downtown. The 402-bed facility has comprehensive inpatient and outpatient services, including critical care, behavioral health, cardiovascular, chemotherapy, inpatient acute care dialysis, diagnostic and interventional medical imaging, gastroenterology lab, general medical and surgical inpatient care, neurology, orthopedic surgery, inpatient and outpatient rehabilitation, urology, and complex wound care.

Need Help?

Ambulance, Fire, or Police • 911

Alcoholics Anonymous • (520) 624-4183

American Cancer Society • (520) 321-7989

American Diabetes Association of Southern Arizona • (520) 795-3711

American Heart Association • (520) 795-1403

American Parkinson Disease Association • (520) 326-5400

Arthritis Foundation • (520) 917-7070

Autism Society of Greater Tucson • (520) 770-1541, hotline

Catholic Community Services of Southern Arizona • (520) 623-0344

Community Outreach Program for the Deaf • (520) 792-1906 (voice or TDD)

Muscular Dystrophy Association, Greater Tucson • (520) 795-3434

National Multiple Sclerosis Society, Southern Arizona Chapter • (520) 747-7472

Pima County Health Department • (520) 243-7770

Pima County Medical Society • (520) 795-7985

Planned Parenthood of Southern Arizona • (520) 624-1761

Southern Arizona AIDS Foundation • (520) 628-7223

Southern Arizona Association for the Visually Impaired • (520) 795-1331

Southern Arizona Center Against Sexual Assault • (520) 327-1171, information; (520) 327-7273, crisis

EMERGE—Center Against Domestic Abuse • (520) 795-8001

KINDRED HOSPITAL
355 N. Wilmot Rd.
(520) 584-4500
www.khtucson.com

Kindred Hospital Tucson is a 51-bed facility licensed by the state of Arizona as a specialty hospital providing long-term acute care. The hospital is certified by Medicare and accredited by the Joint Commission on Accreditation of Healthcare Organizations. Kindred Hospital Tucson offers a full range of services to medically complex and catastrophically ill patients. Most of Kindred's patients are referred from local hospitals and require acute care for an extended time. Specialized services include ventilator weaning, wound care, and rehabilitation.

NORTHWEST MEDICAL CENTER
6200 N. La Cholla Blvd.
(520) 742-9000
www.northwestmedicalcenter.com

A 300-bed hospital in the valley's northwest, Northwest Medical Center offers emergency room services and features a women's center, cardiopulmonary services, and oncology facilities. It also hosts many wellness and health classes for the local community, particularly for seniors. The medical center operates an urgent care service.

NORTHWEST MEDICAL CENTER ORO VALLEY
1551 E. Tangerine Rd., Oro Valley
(520) 901-3500
www.nmcorovalley.com
Established in 2005, this 144-bed facility offers emergency services, cardiology, orthopedics, general surgery, oncology, and an inpatient rehabilitation unit. Specialized services include high-definition, state-of-the-art radiological and diagnostic equipment and operating suites.

SOUTHERN ARIZONA VA HEALTH CARE SYSTEM
3601 S. 6th Ave.
(520) 792-1450
www.tucson.va.gov
The Southern Arizona VA Health Care System comprises a 285-bed teaching hospital in Tucson. The 83,000-square-foot ambulatory wing houses outpatient clinics, including primary care clinics, a women's health clinic, eye clinic, pharmacy, and diagnostic unit. A 45,000 square-foot Mental Health Building houses most of the mental health-related services. The Medical Center provides medical, surgical, neurological, psychiatric, geriatric, hospice, and rehabilitation services and the Southwestern Blind Rehabilitation Center. SAVAHCS is located on 116 acres of land about 6 miles south of downtown Tucson. The Tucson Vet Center, offering readjustment

counseling services, is located at 3055 N. 1st Ave. (520-882-0333). The Southern Arizona VA Health Care System operates Community-Based Outpatient Clinics (CBOCs) in Casa Grande, Sierra Vista, Yuma, Green Valley, Southeast and Northwest Tucson. Call (520) 792-1450 or (800) 470-8262 for hours and locations.

TMC HEALTHCARE—TUCSON MEDICAL CENTER
5301 E. Grant Rd.
(520) 327-5461
www.tmcaz.com
Founded as a tuberculosis sanitarium in 1927, the facility was donated to the city in the 1940s to be run as a community hospital. Today it's a full-service facility spreading over 40 acres. It operates the city's most-visited emergency department. With 642 beds, it's southern Arizona's largest hospital. Services include a pediatric emergency department, women's and maternity care (with more than 6,000 births each year), pediatric care (with intensive care units for children and newborns), and many other specialty areas—including cardiac, orthopedic, neuroscience, imaging, and senior services. The TMC campus is also home to Tucson Orthopaedic Institute, the Cancer Care Center of Southern Arizona, and the Children's Clinics for Rehabilitative Services.

UNIVERSITY OF ARIZONA MEDICAL CENTER
University of Arizona
1501 N. Campbell Ave.
(520) 694-0111
www.azumc.com
A private, nonprofit hospital, the medical center is located in the Arizona Health Sciences Center, next to the University of Arizona.

The center includes the Colleges of Medicine, Nursing, Pharmacy, and Public Health and the University Physicians medical group. These affiliations allow UMC to offer the latest treatments as well as routine medical care and wellness. University Medical Center was ranked as one of the top 50 hospitals in the country by Becker's Hospital Review in 2011. The 116-bed, state-of-the-art Diamond Children's Medical Center (www.diamondchildrens.org) opened in 2010 in partnership with the University of Arizona Steele Children's Research Center. The center features a separate 24-hour, year-round pediatric emergency department. The only facility of its kind in southern Arizona, the department has its own entrance, waiting room, and pediatric triage area, so that children are treated separately from adults by emergency physicians who specialize in pediatrics.

The Peter and Paula Fasseas Cancer Clinic, at 3838 N. Campbell Ave., is the home for clinical activities of the famous Arizona Cancer Center. UMC is also the only Level 1 trauma center in the city and is one of the most highly rated in the country.

As the primary teaching hospital for the University of Arizona College of Medicine, UMC is affiliated with several research projects, including the Arizona Cancer Center, University of Arizona Sarver Heart Center, Arizona Arthritis Center, Arizona Emergency Medicine Research Center, Respiratory Center, and Arizona Center on Aging.

UNIVERSITY OF ARIZONA MEDICAL CENTER—SOUTH CAMPUS
2800 E. Ajo Way
(520) 874-2000
www.uph.org
This is the only hospital serving southern Tucson. The 197–bed facility is open 24 hours a day, 365 days a year. This comprehensive medical center and hospital features nationally and internationally recognized clinics, programs, and UA faculty physicians. It has been ranked as one of the 100 Best Value Hospitals in the US as part of the Hospital Value Index.

Services and programs include the Arizona Institute for Sports Medicine, behavioral health services, cardiology including cardiac cath lab, dialysis, emergency/urgent care, inpatient and outpatient surgical services, intensive care unit, laboratory medical/surgical/telemetry unit, neurophysiology, outpatient primary and specialty care clinics, pharmacy, physical/speech/occupational therapy, radiology (diagnostic and imaging services including MRI, breast MRI, and mammography), rehabilitation therapy, robotically assisted surgery, and telemedicine.

Future plans include building new additions to the campus on the 70 acres surrounding the hospital and creating numerous specialty treatment centers, as well as advanced teaching and state-of-the-art research facilities.

ALTERNATIVE THERAPY & WELLNESS

Tucsonans have a unique health advantage with a large community of alternative and wellness therapists to choose from, including naturopaths, homeopaths, holistic healers, chiropractors, and integrative medicine and Eastern medicine practitioners. In fact, Arizona is considered to be in the vanguard of alternative medicine, both in the open atmosphere and in the number of practitioners. Here are a few places that promote alternative wellness.

ARIZONA CENTER FOR INTEGRATIVE MEDICINE

University Medical Center
1501 N. Campbell Ave.

The Arizona Center for Integrative Medicine has 2 clinic locations (535 N. Wilmot Dr. and on the 6th floor of the University of Arizona Medical Center at 1501 N. Campbell Ave.).

The physicians at these clinics specialize in creating integrative treatment plans for patients with medical conditions ranging from cancer to chronic conditions such as diabetes and heart disease as well as offering preventive care.

The clinics are open to the public by appointment only and are self-pay. New patient visits can run up to $350, so be prepared; patients must pay for services on the day of the visit and obtain reimbursements on their own. The center does accept Medicare.

To contact the center for general information, call them at (520) 626-6417. For information about the clinic, call (520) 626-6489. To schedule an appointment, call (520) 694-8888, ext. 500, or (800) 524-5928, ext. 500.

> ℹ The Cortiva Desert Institute of the Healing Arts is a Tucson-based massage school that opened in 1982. In addition to teaching massage therapy and bodywork, the institute offers bargain massages done by students of all levels Tues through Sat; hours vary and reservations are recommended. A 50- to 55-minute massage by any student is only $35. The student clinic is located at 6390 E. Broadway and is open Mon through Sat. Call (520) 632-2160 to make an appointment.

THE ARIZONA SCHOOL OF ACUPUNCTURE AND ORIENTAL MEDICINE

4646 E. Fort Lowell Rd., Ste. 103
(520) 795-0787

An ACAOM-accredited school of Chinese medicine, this school teaches potential practitioners skills in acupuncture, herbs, and Asian bodywork therapy. Their clinic is open to the public and offers acupuncture, Chinese herbal therapy, and TuiNa (Chinese medical massage) at very affordable rates Mon through Sat; hours vary.

ASIAN INSTITUTE OF MEDICAL STUDIES

3131 N. Country Club, Ste. 100
(520) 322-6330

This school of traditional Chinese medicine teaches Chinese acupuncture and herbal medicine, Japanese acupuncture, 5-element acupuncture, and medical Qigong. The community clinic provides high-quality traditional Chinese medicine to the public and offers a diverse and comprehensive clinical internship for the institute's students.

THE JOINT

www.thejoint.com

Part of a nationwide franchise, these walk-in chiropractic clinics offer a variety of affordable services. There are 2 locations in the Tucson area, the first is at 800 E. University Blvd., Ste. 100 (520-622-3886) and the second is at 858 E. Wrightstown Rd., Ste. 114 (520-296-8849). Check the website for additional information.

RETIREMENT

Ahhhhhh, retirement. No more punching the time clock, fighting the rush-hour traffic, dealing with office politics, or waiting endlessly for that two-week vacation to roll around. You're finally free from decades of the workday world. But what to do with all that time? Well, if you're living or wintering in Tucson, your choices are almost infinite. Stroll through the many historic neighborhoods and parks, or hike or bike along the rivers and washes. Play golf or tennis every day of the year if you want. Visit the many museums and art galleries around town. Explore fascinating attractions like Tucson Botanical Gardens, Pima Air and Space Museum, or Colossal Cave. Mingle with the wildlife at Arizona-Sonora Desert Museum or Reid Park Zoo. Go to a nearby senior center and make new friends. Volunteer at a local hospital or school. No wonder *AARP The Magazine* ranked Tucson number one on its list of Best Places to Live!

OVERVIEW

If you really want to get into the lifestyle of an active older adult, consider one of the many retirement communities for which Tucson is famous. They offer carefree living (as in "leave the driving and cooking to us"). Take your meals in elegant dining rooms, leave the housecleaning to the maids, forget about any household repairs or yard work, and simply hop on the van for weekly trips to the grocery store. But beyond that, they have activities galore—swimming; walking; playing shuffleboard, billiards, or cards; dancing; learning crafts; putting on the green; working out in the exercise room; taking a group excursion; or just finding a good book in the library—and lots of neighbors to share them with. All of this awaits you in one of Tucson's retirement apartment communities.

Or maybe you like the idea of having lots of activities and people to share them with but still want to own your own home. In that case, the Tucson area is a mecca of retirement communities and subdivisions. The Del Webb Corporation, famous for its Sun City (near Phoenix), created similar communities here, including Sun City Vistoso and Sunflower. And don't forget about Green Valley just south of Tucson. It's a huge community with most subdivisions exclusively for older adults. (And heaven if you're a golfer.)

Still another option is adult communities that feature manufactured or prebuilt homes where you buy the house, lot, and a carport or garage as a package, and pay home owner fees for maintenance of the common areas and facilities. You're still a homeowner, but the cost is usually less than buying in a regular senior subdivision.

There's even another alternative for adults who like the active lifestyle—living or wintering in your mobile home or RV. Tucson has many mobile communities exclusively for adults, complete with lots of activities and amenities to fill up your days and evenings. And if you don't own your own home on wheels, you can usually rent one of theirs.

Many seniors can no longer live independently, and Tucson has a number of residential options for them. For example, some of the independent-living apartments covered in this chapter also offer assisted living, in-home care, or other related services. So you can choose to live in a retirement apartment and still get some daily help. There are many adult-care homes and nursing homes available here as well.

Whatever lifestyle you're in search of—independent or assisted or just some ideas on how to spend your time constructively—be sure to read the Resource Roundup section of the chapter. We present some important resources for older adults—places to contact for everything from Meals on Wheels to exercise classes and from nursing homes to in-home care.

i The Tucson Prunes and Pruners are fun-loving 50+ people who put on shows for reunions or birthdays or just about any group. The Prunes and Pruners are always looking for fresh dancing, singing, and comedic talent. Call (866) 778-6372 or visit www.tucson prunes.com.

RETIREMENT HOUSING

Tucson has well over two dozen adult communities, ranging from apartments to townhomes to houses, and they are very popular.

The apartment communities differ in many ways but have many similarities as well. Some are very secure, some are not. All meals may be included in the rent or some meals or none. Rules on owning pets vary. All offer cable TV hookups but may or may not include cable TV in the rent. Rents may include all utilities (except phone) or some or none. Although one-year leases are typical, many communities rent monthly. With all the variables, be sure to ask very specific questions when considering an adult community, including minimum age for occupancy.

One thing is fairly constant across all the communities: They want residents to have an array of both indoor and outdoor activities and amenities on-site, and they make it very easy to remain active, socialize, and lead a nearly carefree lifestyle.

ACADEMY VILLAGE
13701 E. Old Spanish Trail
(520) 647-7777, (877) 647-6171
www.theacademyvillage.com
This attractive adult community (55-plus) on the far east side of town attracts active seniors with a focus on lifelong learning and community involvement. There are townhomes and single-family homes, with starting prices in the mid-$200,000 to $300,000-plus range. Like most active adult communities, they offer myriad activities and programs. What makes them unique is the on-site Academy, a nonprofit organization devoted to lifelong learning, thinking, and doing, which offers ongoing educational and cultural programs, seminars, and concerts. A wellness center, pool, and tennis courts keep the body active, too.

ATRIA BELL COURT GARDENS
6653 E. Carondelet Dr.
(520) 886-3600
www.atriaseniorliving.com
Opened in 1984 and one of 3 communities in Tucson owned by Atria, this is a luxury

resort community conveniently located near several shopping areas and major medical complexes. Accommodations include 1- and 2-bedroom apartment homes with full kitchens and an emergency call system in every apartment. A full restaurant offers daily continental breakfast and choice of a chef-prepared lunch or dinner. Amenities include a heated pool, spa, exercise rooms, and more. Rental rates vary per unit and by services.

i Active seniors can participate in Tucson's annual Senior Olympics, held in January. You don't have to be a top athlete to register; the competition includes card games like cribbage, along with bocce, swimming, tennis, badminton, and much more. Call (520) 791-3244 or visit www.tucsonsenior games.org

ATRIA CAMPANA DEL RIO
1550 E. River Rd.
(520) 299-1941
www.atriaseniorliving.com
If villa living is your cup of tea, this community may be one to consider. In addition to studio, 1-, and 2-bedroom apartments in a 3-story building, Campana del Rio has 2-bedroom villas with 1 or 2 baths. The property has a total of 190 independent apartments, plus another 64 units for assisted-living and memory-impaired residents. Although the community is not gated, security is on duty 24 hours. Fine dining, complete with linens and flowers on the tables, is another hallmark of Campana del Rio, but they're not too formal to refuse diners a doggie bag for the delicious leftovers. And a private dining room can be reserved by residents who want a special gathering of friends or family.

Monthly rent includes breakfast and one main meal daily, weekly maid and linen service, free laundry facilities, scheduled van transportation, a pool, utilities, and access to scads of activities such as aqua therapy, billiards, excursions, and exercise equipment. Each apartment is equipped with emergency call buttons, and all the assisted-living units are wheelchair accessible with sit-in showers. The apartments and grounds are comfortable and clean, and the courtyard offers a tropical setting for walking, relaxing, or swimming in the pool. The minimum age is 55, monthly leases are required, and small pets are OK.

Although Campana del Rio is in a scenic and convenient foothills area, it's also a congested area for traffic—something to keep in mind if you drive a lot. But it's also only about a furlong away from Rillito Downs if you're a horse race aficionado. The property itself is set back off River Road and hugs the north side of the Rillito "River" (for an explanation of the quotation marks here, see the Natural World chapter).

ATRIA VALLEY MANOR
5549 E. Lee St.
(520) 886-7937
www.atriaseniorliving.com
Built in the mid-1960s, this complex has undergone several transformations. Although old, the buildings are spacious with wide hallways and large patios off the 64 apartments surrounding a pleasant courtyard. Valley Manor is located on a residential street 1 block south of Pima Street and east of Craycroft Road, a close-in Eastside neighborhood with major services nearby.

Apartments range from 400-square-foot efficiencies to 1,380-square-foot 2-bedroom, 2-bath units; monthly rental fees include

2 full hot meals daily in the dining room, utilities, and scheduled transportation. Maid and laundry services are available. Pets are allowed for an additional cost.

BROADWAY PROPER
400 S. Broadway Place
(520) 296-3238
www.leisurecare.com

"The Reuben sandwich is out of this world" might be a plaudit heard from residents of this 232-unit apartment complex, who generally speak highly of the dining hall's lunch offerings. But Broadway Proper has more going for it than the eats. Housed in a peach Southwestern-style 3-story stucco elevator building are 10 floors of studios and 1- and 2-bedroom apartments surrounding a central courtyard and a beautifully landscaped 0.33-mile walking path. It isn't a gated community, but it is staffed around the clock. All of the typical retirement apartment amenities are here: an elegant dining room, emergency call system in each apartment, lots of activities, weekly housekeeping and linen services, and cable TV hookups. The staff puts out a great little newsletter that profiles all the upcoming activities for the next month or two, both on-site and excursions.

The grounds are pleasantly green and palm-tree covered, and amenities include a library, beauty salon, pool and Jacuzzi (this is Arizona), free laundry facilities, and off-street parking. A luxury air-conditioned and wheelchair-accessible 26-passenger bus takes residents to scheduled activities. And right next door is a YMCA that residents can use for free. Four-footed friends can live here with owners who are age 62 or older.

Rents are monthly and include just about everything described here plus basic utilities, breakfast, and one additional meal daily. Assisted-living services, for additional fees, are available to residents who need them.

This complex is located in a busy area with lots of shopping, churches, and hospitals nearby, but it's set back from the main roads enough to allow for privacy and quiet. The downside is that it's typically all filled up and has a waiting list of about 6 months. When you go searching for Broadway Proper, ignore the street address—it's not much help. Instead, look for the Hilton Hotel on Broadway Boulevard about 2 blocks east of Kolb Road and pretend you're going into the Hilton. It happens to be located behind the Hilton and shares the Hilton's entrance. Leisure Care Inc. owns this property along with several dozen around the country.

CASCADES OF TUCSON
201 N. Jessica Ave.
(520) 886-3171
www.cascadestucson.com

This may be one of the few privately owned, as opposed to corporately owned, retirement communities in the area. An older but well-maintained complex of 215 apartments, the Cascades offers 2 types of apartments: independent and assisted. One-bedroom apartments of 400-plus square feet with balconies are available for rent with a 1-year lease. This includes 2 meals a day in the dining room, biweekly maid service, scheduled transportation, and all on-site activities. Assisted-living apartments vary from studios to 2-bedroom, 2-bath, renting at month-to-month rates. These residents get 3 meals, daily maid service, and "lots of TLC." The apartments are small but are wheelchair accessible with wide doorways and roomy showers.

The building is 4 stories with elevators and a central entrance. Apartments have emergency call buttons, and a security guard patrols at night. Amenities include a pool, game and activity rooms, and a beauty salon. The minimum age is 62, and small pets are allowed. This is a convenient location in close-in east Tucson just off Broadway Boulevard between Wilmot Road and Kolb Road. The apartment complex is close to shopping and dining and nearly all other services but off the main road enough for quiet living. Oh, and it's very shaded—somewhat of a phenomenon in Tucson.

COPPER CREST
7700 W. Bopp Rd.
(520) 883-6670
www.coppercrest.com
This is a luxury senior (55-plus) community where you buy both the manufactured home and the lot it's on. It's much like being a home owner in Sun City or Green Valley, except the home itself is prebuilt. Opened in 1989, Copper Crest has 357 sites of various sizes on its 80 acres. Complete packages—home, lot, and carport or garage—start in the low $200,000s with a maximum size of one-fifth acre. You'll also pay a monthly home owner fee for maintenance of the common areas and facilities.

Among the facilities you'll find here for recreation and entertainment are a lap pool, spa, shuffleboard, bocce, horseshoes, library, dance floor, exercise room, billiards, crafts center, and a kitchen in the clubhouse for social gatherings. And because Copper Crest lies at the southwestern edge of the Tucson Mountains, there's plenty to do and see at the Arizona-Sonora Desert Museum, Old Tucson Studios, and Tucson Mountain Park, all of which are nearby.

COUNTRY CLUB OF LA CHOLLA
8700 N. La Cholla Blvd.
(520) 797-8700
www.lacholla.us
The name is apt for this resort-style retirement community—it's adjacent to Omni Tucson National Golf Course (in northwest Tucson), and it boasts a 30,000-square-foot clubhouse. And it's exclusively for independent active adults older than 55. Monthly rents vary in price. Lots of amenities and basics accompany the rent.

For starters, you can choose from about 200-plus bright apartments of 600 to 1,100 square feet, including casitas, but you'll need to sign a year's lease. Access is through a gated entrance that's locked at night, plus 24-hour security is on duty. The basics include breakfast and 1 meal daily, utilities, housekeeping, scheduled transportation, emergency call systems, and either a patio or balcony with every unit. Country Club of La Cholla has not one but 2 dining rooms and a sports pub, complete with Friday happy hours. Contributing to your independent and active lifestyle are a heated pool and spa, lots of on-site activities and outings, shuffleboard, a greenhouse available to residents, billiards, ballroom, exercise room, library, chapel, and beauty salon. A limited number of wheelchair-accessible apartments are available.

FAIRWINDS DESERT POINT
10701 N. La Reserve Dr., Oro Valley
(520) 498-1111
www.leisurecare.com
This is an upscale senior community nestled in the foothills of the Catalina Mountains. You'll find studio, 1-, and 2-bedroom apartments that range in size from 417 to 1,437 square feet, all on a month-to-month plan.

Dining facilities are elegant, and when the weather is right, you can even dine outside. In the mornings a full breakfast is served, and residents are offered a choice of lunch or dinner. Lots of activities here will keep you busy. They have classes, a library, lap pool, movie theater, spa, Jacuzzi, putting green, and other amenities. A full-time guest services supervisor provides a comprehensive activity program. Desert Point provides independent and assisted living in an integrated environment to those age 62 and over.

THE FOUNTAINS AT LA CHOLLA
2001 W. Rudasill Rd.
(520) 777-1413
www.watermarkcommunities.com
It would be possible to live here and never leave the 16 acres of grounds, so complete are the services and amenities at the Fountains. It also happens to be a beautiful setting—Southwestern-style buildings surrounded by the natural beauty of the desert and enhanced by lots of greenery, trees, flowers, and fountains of course. Living here is not cheap, but if you can afford the best, this is one place to find it. You can choose from over 300 apartments, including 1- and 2-bedroom apartments and casitas.

The clubhouse is elegant, the corridors are wide, and pets are not merely allowed, they're absolutely encouraged. That's because the Fountains subscribes to the "Eden alternative," which seems to prove that pets are indeed a boon to the elderly, emotionally as well as physically. But even if you don't have a furry friend, there's lots going on at the Fountains. In addition to all the standard amenities, there's a dance floor and stage, on-site banking, wellness clinic, art gallery, spa and pool, library, beauty salon, outdoor gardening, and an on-site home-health agency.

Rents at this award-winning community are monthly for independent-living apartments or casitas. The Fountains also has assisted living, called the Inn, and an Alzheimer's unit called the Gardens, with monthly rates. The Fountains at La Cholla was built in 1987 and is owned by Watermark Retirement Communities. It's in the northwest of town, with 2 hospitals and 2 nursing homes about a block away.

i If you have an elderly loved one who needs just a temporary place to stay, the lovely Cascades of Tucson retirement and assisted-living community offers a special "respite care" program. There is a special fully furnished apartment with a kitchen available for a weekly or monthly rate, with access to all the services on the property. Call **(520) 886-3171.**

THE MANOR AT MIDVALE
6250 S. Commerce Court
(520) 294-3200
Managed by Sunshine Retirement, the Manor is a retirement complex with Southwestern-style architecture and lovely landscaping. Four 2-story elevator apartment buildings and the clubhouse building form a square around a courtyard, all of which are connected with covered walkways and are wheelchair accessible. You need to be 55 plus or retired to live here but won't need to sign a 1-year lease; the apartments rent month to month. You can choose from 135 1-, or 2-bedroom apartments of 500 to 700 square feet. Rents include 3 dining-room meals daily, weekly housekeeping, laundry facilities, local transportation, all utilities,

emergency call buttons, and amenities such as exercise classes, pool, spa, and a homey and friendly atmosphere. Managers live on-site. Commerce Court is a squiggly street off Midvale Road north of Valencia Road on Tucson's southwest side and not far from I-19. One of its most desirable features is its proximity to services—major stores are a walk across the street and nearly everything else is nearby.

SADDLEBROOKE
63395 E. Robson Circle
(520) 818-6000
www.robson.com
With more than 5,000 residents and still growing, Saddlebrooke is one of the largest retirement communities in the Tucson area. Unlike most of the other retirement properties in this chapter, this is a sprawling master-planned development, and the housing is for sale rather than rent. Although only 14 miles north of Tucson, it's actually situated in Pinal County, not Pima County, and abuts the northeast end of the Santa Catalina Mountains.

Buying a home here means you're likely to have great mountain views from nearly any spot plus an elevation of 3,300 feet, where temperatures are somewhat cooler than the city to the south. Although the setting is spectacular, the location is somewhat remote, but growing rapidly. Except for the few services available in Saddlebrooke, you'll be driving about 16 miles to the nearest hospital and at least half that far for groceries, restaurants, and other services. Saddlebrooke does have a fire station with paramedics, however.

Robson Communities, the developer, labels it a resort paradise, and that it certainly is. It's been listed as one of the top 100

places to retire by *Where to Retire* magazine. A multimillion-dollar rec center offers billiards, dining, a library, indoor/outdoor lap pool, weight room, tennis courts, spa, a 478-seat theater, and even massage and facial pampering. An 18-hole championship golf course with pro shop is strictly for Saddlebrooke residents and guests. Residents can hit the links every day of the year or can pay as they play.

SANTA CATALINA VILLAS
7500 N. Calle Sin Envidia
(520) 742-0505
www.brookdaleliving.com
Rancho Sin Vacas is an exclusive gated community in the Catalina foothills on Tucson's north side, which should tell you something about this retirement complex located there. It's exclusive, pricey, and lovely. And there's almost always a waiting list to rent one of its 155 independent-living apartments that range from studios to 2-bedroom, 2-bath units.

The apartments are located in 14 two-story buildings, each with only 4 to 16 apartments, so each building resembles a villa. All have a patio or balcony, emergency call system, full kitchens, oversize bathrooms, and weekly housekeeping and linen services, but some utilities and parking are extra. All units are wheelchair accessible. The monthly rent includes 20 meals a month in the elegant dining room plus daily continental breakfast and amenities including scheduled van transportation, fitness center, free laundry rooms, pool, Jacuzzi, beauty salon, and 24-hour security. The minimum age is 62.

In addition to the independent-living facilities, Santa Catalina also offers 42 private suites for skilled nursing, 70 private apartments for assisted living, and 15 private suites for memory care. All residents have access to Medicare-certified home health and full therapy services. Santa Catalina is owned by Brookdale Senior Living Inc.

To reach Santa Catalina Villas, go north on either Campbell Avenue or Pima Canyon Road from Sunrise Drive, but be sure to call ahead. Rancho Sin Vacas is a gated area, and you'll need an appointment to get by the guard.

SPLENDIDO AT RANCHO VISTOSO
13500 N. Rancho Vistoso Blvd.,
Oro Valley
(520) 878-2612, (888) 381-8889
www.splendidotucson.com
Splendido has received not one, but two "Best of 50+" housing awards and is beautifully designed. The community offers 246 luxurious villas and terrace homes for independent living in addition to assisted living, skilled nursing, and memory support care. Amenities include 6 dining areas, a fitness and wellness center and spa, 2 swimming pools, an 18-hole putting course, cybercafe, billiards room, library, on-site health-care center, and many social activities. In addition to a rental fee, there is a monthly fee that covers a wide range of services.

SUN CITY VISTOSO COMMUNITY
1565 E. Rancho Vistoso Blvd.,
Oro Valley
(520) 825-3711
www.suncity-vistoso.com
In early 1987 Del Webb opened Sun City Tucson within the larger master-planned community of Rancho Vistoso about 10 miles northwest of Tucson in what is now the town of Oro Valley. Within 10 years the 2,500

homes covering Sun City Tucson's 1,000 acres were sold out, but resales are on the market if you choose to live here.

Del Webb is renowned for the amenities and activities they offer adults 55 and older, and Sun City is no exception. Multimillion-dollar recreation facilities include pools, 8 tennis courts, an 18-hole golf course, restaurants, and countless arts, crafts, clubs, and sports offerings available to residents who own a home there and pay homeowner association fees. And surrounding Sun City is the larger community of Rancho Vistoso, with shopping centers, medical and professional offices, shops, restaurants, churches, schools, and additional sports and recreation facilities. (Rancho Vistoso's 7,555 acres contain developments by many builders, but only Sun City has an age qualification.)

Although Sun City is a bit remote from downtown Tucson, this area of town continues to grow. Mountain views abound, as do wide streets, miles of walking paths, golf course views, and a low crime rate. If you're an active adult who still wants to own (and care for) a house, contact an area real estate agent for homes available in Sun City Tucson. To find it, go north on Oracle Road to Rancho Vistoso Boulevard.

i If you're not quite ready for a retirement community but need a little help, check out Catalina In-Home Services (520-327-6351, www.catalina-in-home.com). This private-duty adult home-care company provides services such as personal care, meal preparation, light housekeeping, transportation, companionship, and errand running from 4 to 24 hours a day, 7 days a week.

SUNFLOWER

7759 Goldbrook Dr., Marana
(520) 572-9780
www.sunflowerliving.com

The word *sun* in the community's name is a good clue it's another Del Webb venture. The company's adult development in the Tucson area is located in the master-planned community of Continental Ranch in the town of Marana to Tucson's northwest. Groundbreaking took place in late 1997, and there are 967 homes on Sunflower's 245 acres. Currently sold out, homes are available for resale only through real estate agents or homeowners.

Like its sister communities, active lifestyle is the byword. A central clubhouse area, with clusters of homes emanating from it like spokes of a wheel, offers a pool, spa, tennis, and tons of activities. The grounds are abundant with walking and bicycling paths, and the wide streets are lined with hundreds of mesquite and paloverde trees along with all the customary desert vegetation. Although Sunflower is outside the city of Tucson, both Continental Ranch and Marana are growing areas. To reach Sunflower, go west on Cortaro Farms Road from I-10 to Silverbell Road, then north to Twin Peaks Road, and watch for the entrance.

Tucson Environs

GREEN VALLEY

Southern Arizona's most famous retirement community lies 25 miles south of Tucson off I-19. Although its population of over 25,000 is not strictly older adults, Green Valley is considered primarily a retirement community and continues to grow by leaps and bounds. There are several active adult communities here, including **Robson's Quail Creek** (888-648-0332; www.robson.com) and the Meritage developments **Canoa**

Ranch and **San Miguel at Las Campanas** (www.meritagehomes.com). More developments are being built to keep up with the high interest. One unusual development is called **Park Centre Homes,** at 350 E. Morningside Dr. (www.parkcentrehomesgv.com). These 35 homes are designed for residents over 75 and feature wider doorways and bathrooms. In addition, the free-standing homes are designed to be energy efficient, with solar panels on the roofs.

Shuttle buses, golf carts, and bicycles bound about the streets, which feature specially designated "traffic" lanes. At 8 miles long and 2 miles wide, Green Valley isn't a town or city per se (it's unincorporated Pima County), but it sure seems like it. Nearly all the major services are right here—shopping, recreation, restaurants, medical and dental care—more than 400 businesses, in fact. It's also a golfing mecca, with at least 7 of southern Arizona's finest courses.

Green Valley has many appealing features for seniors. At an elevation slightly above Tucson's, the summer temperature is usually more tolerable and the rest of the year is lovely, so outdoor activities are often possible year-round. Another plus is the beautiful environment—it's desert tempered with lots of lush landscaping and spectacular mountain views. Swimming pools, tennis courts, walk and bike paths, and recreation centers throughout the community contribute to a fun lifestyle for active adults. And many older adults like this retirement area because it's not "big city" but big-city facilities and services are a mere 30-minute drive away.

You'll find many types of housing, including seasonal, rentals, single-family homes, apartments, condos, and villas (or patio homes), new and resale. Housing prices range from the low $150,000s to over half a million dollars. Many housing subdivisions are located around golf courses. The best way to locate a place in Green Valley is through a local real estate agent or the **Green Valley Chamber of Commerce** (520-625-7575; www.greenvalleychamber.com).

SAHUARITA

Sahuarita, just north of Green Valley, is booming with housing options for active adults and retirees. Communities for the 55-plus set include Del Webb's Las Brisas at Rancho resort and Sonora (www.delwebb .com), two communities with multiple home designs ranging from the low $190,000s and up, are sold out but are available for resale through area Realtors. Very popular, the town has a man-made lake for sailing and swimming, parks, and many other amenities. Find out more about the community at www.ci.sahuarita.az.us.

VAIL

Just about 20 miles from downtown Tucson, the small community of Vail is growing rapidly and attracting young families and retirees. The gorgeous Del Lago Golf Club (see the Golf chapter) and an excellent school system are the main draws.

DEL WEBB RANCHO DEL LAGO
10260 S. Blendu Way, Vail
(866) 340-9322
www.delwebb.com
The newest active adult community in the Del Webb network, this 55-plus community has a 14,000-square-foot community center, ballroom library, fitness center, arts and crafts room, and exhibition kitchen for those who aspire to appear on the Food Network's *Next Food Network Star* someday! All the usual amenities associated with Del Webb properties are here, too: a pool and spa, a fitness director, tennis courts, pickleball, and bocce. Housing options include single-story, 2-bedroom 2-bathroom homes with patios and garages. Prices start in the high $170,000's.

Mobile Home & RV Communities

Because Tucson is such a popular travel and retirement destination for older adults, many mobile home communities and RV resorts cater to this group. Retirees come here as winter visitors or permanent residents and set up housekeeping for the season or for good in one of Tucson's many mobile home or RV parks for adults. They get the benefits of a great climate without the responsibilities of maintaining a house or land and often can save money compared to renting one of the area's retirement apartments. Most of these mobile and RV parks have all the trappings of a resort and offer residents ample activities and amenities along with the opportunity to make new friends with similar interests and lifestyles.

Mobile home communities differ from RV resorts (or parks) in that the homes and the residents tend to be more permanent, while the RV parks tend to be more seasonal and more like resorts. Many of the mobile home and RV communities profiled here both sell and rent mobiles already set up on a space, or residents can wheel in their own and merely lease the space. Read on for a profile of some of the major mobile communities for adults.

FAR HORIZONS TUCSON VILLAGE
555 N. Pantano Rd.
(520) 296-1234
www.tucsonvillage.com

Far Horizons has been offering RVers age 55 and older a lovely spot to visit or winter for some 20 years. It's an excellent park on Tucson's Eastside, close to major services and attractions. More than 500 RV spaces are situated amid beautiful desert landscaping, paved streets, and views of the Rincon and Catalina Mountains. Activities include arts and crafts, hiking, miniature golf, exercise classes, billiards, Ping-Pong, and shuffleboard. For water fun, there's a pool and Jacuzzi. And if you need a break from the fun, you can always do the laundry.

There are daily, weekly, monthly, and annual spaces available at varying rates.

MISSION VIEW RV
31 W. Los Reales Rd.
(520) 741-1945
www.missionviewrv.com
This is an adult community that offers both a mobile home park and an RV park—the former is called Senior Park and the latter Mission View RV Park. (There's even a third section, but it's a family mobile home park, so we don't have to confuse you further by covering it here; suffice it to say that the adult sections are off-limits to the youngsters.) The community is located on the part of the Tohono O'odham Reservation that's called the San Xavier Reservation, although it's not operated by the Indian tribe and is directly east of the San Xavier Mission. (Hence the name Mission View, and a lovely view it is.)

The adult mobile home park has nearly 200 spaces that lease for a monthly rate plus utilities, but you're not likely to get a spot here unless you're on a waiting list and someone vacates. The RV park has 150-plus spaces that are 40 feet by 60 feet, big enough to accommodate just about anything;

they have gravel, cement patios, and picnic tables. These spaces rent daily, weekly, monthly, and annually, but the months of January through March are usually reserved by the previous September. Both the mobile and RV parks are surrounded by a fence and have a single entrance, but it's not secured. Desert landscaping and paved streets surround the rental spaces.

The 2 adult communities are for people age 55 or older and share facilities and amenities—most notably an indoor tropical pool and spa and a library with 2 Internet connections. There are shower and laundry facilities in addition to the customary clubhouse and outdoor activities.

If you'd like to check out Mission View, ignore the address. Instead, take I-19 south from Tucson to exit 92, which is San Xavier Road. Go east about a mile to the RV resort.

QUAIL RIDGE ESTATES
15301 N. Oracle Rd.
(520) 825-9088
The Catalina or Tortolita Mountains are the backdrops for the terraced homesites in this manufactured-home community situated in Tucson's far northwest on gently sloping desert land. It boasts a layout in which 91 percent of the 130 homesites are corner lots and a 1996 national award as "manufactured-home community of the year." All the homes are double-wide and are only available as resales.

To qualify for Quail Ridge, each home must have one person 55 or older and no one younger than 18. The residents are active adults who take advantage of the community's offerings—pool and spa, putting green, shuffleboard, horseshoes, crafts, and lots of social gatherings. Quail Ridge is off Oracle Road north of the Rancho Vistoso area, so it's quite a trek from Tucson. But the area of Catalina is nearby with shops, restaurants, and medical services.

RINCON COUNTRY RV RESORT EAST
8989 E. Escalante Rd.
(520) 886-8431, (888) 401-8989
www.rinconcountry.com
Located on Tucson's southeast side near the eastern end of Davis-Monthan Air Force Base, this is the smaller of the 2 Rincon Country resorts. Activities and amenities, including bingo, billiards, shuffleboard, and horseshoes, rival its sister resort on the west side. Here you will find 460 spaces that rent for weekly, monthly, and annual rates. Spaces are usually unavailable in the high season without reservations years in advance. Amenities include a pool, spa, basic cable TV, a library, and 3 laundry rooms. This resort also rents and sells park-model RVs. Don't be frightened off by the proximity to the base—the airstrips are miles away on the base's west end. But you probably will have a view of the aircraft graveyard on Davis-Monthan's eastern end.

RINCON COUNTRY RV RESORT WEST
4555 S. Mission Rd.
(520) 294-5608, (800) 782-7275
www.rinconcountry.com
This is the sister resort to Rincon Country East but is much larger, probably the second-largest RV resort in Tucson. It's on Tucson's southwest side in a still somewhat rural area but within easy reach of major roads and all the west-side attractions, including San Xavier Mission, Tucson Mountain Park, Arizona-Sonora Desert Museum, and Old Tucson Studios. Its 80 acres contain 1,100 spaces that usually are filled in the high season of January through March. Both

short-term visitors and year-round residents are welcome, but you must be 55 or older. Pets are allowed, but there are restricted areas where they can be walked. Spaces go for daily, monthly, and yearly rates, with some utilities extra. The resort has a perimeter fence, and gated entry at night is by card or code.

With Rincon Country's amazing array of amenities and activities, boredom should never be a factor. An activities director arranges crafts, classes, and special events to suit just about anyone. Or you can swim in the pool, bask in the indoor or outdoor hot tub, practice on the putting green, throw horseshoes, or play tennis, shuffleboard, or billiards.

Rincon Country rents and sells "park models," which are 400 square feet with 1 bedroom, or you can wheel in your own RV for as short or long a time as you want. Opened in 1983, it's an attractive RV park with active and community-spirited residents.

SWAN LAKES ESTATES
4550 N. Flowing Wells Rd.
(520) 887-9292
At first glance you may be put off by the neighborhood surrounding this mobile home community—it's older and definitely not upscale. But if you look closer, you'll see a lovely and well-maintained community with a beautiful lake in its center, complete with ducks and fish and maybe even a swan. And residents can fish in it, too. There are 279 spaces, but not many are available. Swan Lakes sells mobile homes but doesn't rent them and leases sites monthly for a single-wide. Utilities are extra. The community is fenced in, and a nightly security guard controls access through the entrance gate. For

fun and recreation there's an extensive social and activities calendar plus 2 heated pools and a Jacuzzi.

VOYAGER RV RESORT
8701 S. Kolb Rd.
(520) 574-5000, (800) 424-9191
www.voyagerrv.com
Voyager has been voted best in the nation and has as much if not more to offer than the poshest resort anywhere. And you need not be older than 55 to live here, just 19 or older. You can bring in your own RV or buy one of their 400-square-foot park models and lease one of the 1,500-plus spaces for the night or annually (plus electricity). As you might guess, however, Voyager is full during the high season and mighty popular the rest of the year as well.

And here are some of the things that make it so popular. Start off with 150 acres of lush landscaping, well-lighted streets and walkways, plenty of parking, and spacious lots with cement patios. Toss in a 9-hole golf course with a lake, putting green, driving range, and pro shop. Add 3 heated swimming pools; 2 heated spas; 2 saunas; 16 shuffleboard courts; lighted tennis courts; volleyball courts; square, round, and ballroom dancing with instructions; billiards; card rooms; a slew of arts and crafts; lots of special-interest clubs; and deep-pit barbecues complete with cookouts. Round it out with a restaurant and general store (in-season), chapel, library, and more. There's not much more anyone could want except possibly mountain views, and Voyager has those as well.

WESTERN WAY RV RESORT
3100 S. Kinney Rd.
(520) 578-1715, (800) 292-8616
www.wwrvresort.com
Kinney Road winds along the western side of the Tucson Mountains, and that's where Western Way is. With the mountains as a backdrop, the adult RV park offers residents and visitors a heated swimming pool, spa, ballroom (and dancing), card and game rooms, library, billiards, and bingo. Directly across the street is Tucson Estates, a huge mobile home community with 2 private 9-hole golf courses where residents of Western Way can play for a fee. Also within walking distance are restaurants, beauty salons, stores, and a post office. Nearby are some of Tucson's most popular attractions: Arizona-Sonora Desert Museum, Old Tucson Studios, and San Xavier Mission. And Tucson Mountain Park is great for desert hiking and picnicking.

RVs must be full hookups; no pop-up campers are allowed. Spaces lease daily, weekly, and monthly with water, sewage, and garbage pickup included. Annual spaces are available. Of the park's 300 spaces, however, only about 80 are not occupied by year-round renters. The busy season is fall through spring, and the peak is January through March. The park has a perimeter wall with only 1 entrance, but it's not secured.

RESOURCE ROUNDUP

Tucson has over two dozen nursing homes, at least a dozen assisted-living centers, and over 200 adult-care homes licensed by the state's Department of Health Services. Whether you're seeking a place to ballroom dance or swim in a heated pool, or whether you're in need of Meals on Wheels, housing, or in-home health care, this section of the chapter will point you in the right direction.

The **Pima Council on Aging** (520-790-7262; www.pcoa.org) is a private nonprofit agency that offers a variety of information and help for seniors. Their many services include advocacy on senior issues, legal services, respite care, Medicare insurance counseling, housing referrals, places to socialize, how to get meals delivered, and a free mature workers' placement center for those over 50. Most of their services are free (with donations welcomed) or available on a sliding scale. They have excellent knowledge of the area's senior resources and can usually lend a helping hand. Seniors needing information or assistance can also call the **Northwest Interfaith Council** (520-731-3076; www.icstucson.org), which provides caregiving services and mobile meals.

There are several private agencies that make referrals to adult-care homes, nursing homes, and retirement communities. One of these is **Adult Care Home Placement Services** (520-529-0911; www.adultcare tucson.com), which specializes in matching residents to one of Tucson's many adult-care homes. When choosing this type of referral agency, look for one that's staffed by health professionals (registered nurse or social worker, for example).

For seniors looking for a place to socialize, exercise, play bingo, learn arts and crafts, or maybe even get a noon meal, both the City of Tucson and Pima County operate senior citizens programs (or centers) around town, and they're free. Your best source for locating one of these senior programs and finding out what it offers is the **Pima Council on Aging** (520-790-7262; www.pcoa.org).

The nonsectarian **Handmaker** (520-322-7035; www.handmaker.com) operates an adult-care home, assisted-living apartments, day programs, a nursing home, and home health services. **Home Instead** (520-770-9943; www.homeinstead.com) is one of a number of Tucson agencies providing a variety of in-home services for people who still live independently but need assistance with daily or weekly activities of a non-medical nature. The Pima Council on Aging provides numerous resources and programs including the Neighbors Volunteer program, which connects volunteers with elderly clients to help them with rides and groceries, and to offer support and friendship (www .pcoa.org/neighbors-care-alliance).

MEDIA

Tucson has an astonishing number of free or inexpensive publications covering all manner of topics, from poetry to music to parenting to bicycling, not to mention a slew of papers devoted to tourism and entertainment. This is good news, because wherever you are you'll find something to help you enjoy Tucson. If you prefer listening over reading, there's a radio station geared to every taste.

This chapter covers the major papers, magazines, and radio and television stations available in Tucson. The list is fairly complete, but remember that things change: Publications come and go, radio stations switch formats, and cable companies get new names.

NEWSPAPERS

Dailies

ARIZONA DAILY STAR
4850 S. Park Ave.
(520) 573-4400
www.azstarnet.com
Considered the state's first daily newspaper, the roots of the *Star* date back to 1877 when the *Daily Bulletin* began publishing with a firm Democratic slant. After going through a triweekly stage, the paper became known as the *Arizona Daily Star* in 1879. It is now a product of Lee Enterprises.

The newspaper is published 7 days a week, with a Thursday "Caliente" section that serves as a weekly arts and entertainment guide. The Sunday edition includes home, travel, book review, and editorial comment sections. Watch for regular supplements geared toward everything from wedding planning to senior health. It also operates *AzStarnet*, the Web version of the paper and home to many other local sites. The paper is 75 cents on the street, but the *Star* offers a variety of subscription packages for weekly,

monthly, and annual issues and daily and weekend editions. Daily circulation is more than 200,000, higher on Sunday.

ARIZONA DAILY WILDCAT
University of Arizona
(520) 621-3551
www.wildcat.arizona.edu
First published in 1899, this daily (Mon through Fri) college paper has a following off campus as well. It can be found around the university area. The *Wildcat* is free and contains well-written articles and editorials on local, state, and national politics as well as campus news. It's also a great source for information and schedules regarding games, seminars, and concerts at the university.

i Savannah Guthrie, coanchor on the *Today* show and a former Court TV and White House correspondent, is a graduate of the UA School of Journalism.

THE DAILY TERRITORIAL
3280 E. Hemisphere Loop, Ste. 180
(520) 294-1200
www.azbiz.com

This is Pima County's legal newspaper of record and contains some business and legal news. But primarily it's a list of legal notices filed within the county. The paper was started in 1966 and currently has a circulation of 1,000. A year's subscription is $115, or you can purchase a single issue at newsstands or newspaper boxes for $1.

TUCSON CITIZEN
4850 S. Park Ave.
(520) 573-4614
www.tucsoncitizen.com

This is a Web-only compendium of blogs published by Gannett in partnership with Tucson newspapers. It covers real estate, dining, politics, and a wide range of other topics.

Other Papers—Weekly, Semiweekly, Semimonthly, Monthly

ARIZONA GOURMET LIVING
1877 N. Kolb Rd.
(520) 721-1300
http://arizonagourmetliving.tripod.com

Published locally 4 times a year and available by subscription and at select restaurants and gourmet stores, this magazine focuses on the local dining scene, offering in-depth profiles of local chefs, restaurants, and recipes.

ARIZONA JEWISH POST
3822 E. River Rd.
(520) 319-1112
www.jewishtucson.org

Published since 1946, this biweekly Jewish-interest paper keeps the community up to date on events, news, and people. The *Post* is only distributed through patron contribution in lieu of subscription, but newcomers can receive 3 months for free on request.

AZTEC PRESS
Pima Community College
2202 W. Anklam Rd.
(520) 206-6800
www.aztecpressonline.com

Aztec Press is the student-run weekly paper printed 8 times a year at the city's community college. It's free and covers news pertinent to the campus.

BEAR ESSENTIAL NEWS
1037 S. Alvernon Way, Ste. 150
(520) 792-9930
www.bearessentialnews.com

This lively free monthly is a great kids' publication, especially if your child likes to work puzzles, play games, enter contests, or actually write articles. Parents will find a lot of useful information about day care, events, and even places to eat with the little guys. There is also a section that is written mostly by middle-school students and by members of a local Young Reporters Program. This paper can be found all over town at eating establishments, bookstores, and the Children's Museum.

DESERTLEAF
3968 E. Fort Lowell Rd.
(520) 881-5188
www.desertleaf.com

Targeting the Catalina foothills and northwest communities, this monthly magazine is delivered free to more than 50,000 households in that area as well as distributed free at select bookstores, libraries, restaurants, and coffee shops. The regular features include travel, arts, nature, history, people, restaurant listings, gallery listings, and desert gardening. People outside the distribution area can subscribe for a yearly fee via bulk mail.

DOWNTOWN TUCSONAN
E. Pennington St., Ste. 150
(520) 837-6504
www.downtowntucson.org
Published by the Tucson Downtown Partnership, a nonprofit corporation charged with improving business conditions downtown, this free newspaper comes out the first of every month. It covers the arts, entertainment, business news, and events happening in the rapidly developing downtown area.

EL IMPARCIAL
www.elimparcial.com
This daily Spanish-language newspaper, published in Mexico, covers Tucson, Nogales, and Douglas. Only $1 a copy, it can be found at supermarkets, newsstands, and local merchants, primarily on the south side of town. Subscriptions are also available.

EL INDEPENDIENTE
PO Box 210158B, Tucson, AZ 85721
(520) 621-7556
www.elindenews.com
This free English/Spanish newspaper covering the city of South Tucson is published monthly by the University of Arizona Journalism School students. Political, community, and sports articles of interest to South Tucson and the Latino community are included, as well as a helpful list of community resources. You'll find it in South Tucson government offices and retail outlets and online.

GOOD NEWS
5151 E. Broadway Blvd.
(520) 745-4403
www.goodnewstucson.com
Published by Good News Media, this Web-only Christian e-magazine focuses on local issues related to family spirituality and wholesome entertainment. Copies are available at all major grocery stores, libraries, places of worship, and retail locations around the city.

INSIDE TUCSON BUSINESS
3280 E. Hemisphere Loop, Ste. 180
(520) 295-4201
www.insidetucsonbusiness.com
Inside is the weekly business publication of professionals in Tucson. The paper is the only one devoted entirely to business news. It costs $1 from street boxes, convenience stores, or at newsstands. A 1-year subscription is $50.

LA ESTRELLA DE TUCSON
4850 S. Park Ave.
(520) 573-4419
http://azstarnet.com/laestrella
This Spanish-language newspaper is published by Tucson Newspapers, which also publishes the *Arizona Daily Star*. Distributed weekly on Friday to certain zip codes, the papers is also available on some newsstands.

THE NORTHWEST EXPLORER
7225 N. Mona Lisa Rd., #125
(520) 797-4384
www.explorernews.com
This weekly community newspaper targets the residents of the fast-growing northwest corridor, providing a local focus of news, politics, reviews, and meeting updates as well as a variety of columnists, both local and national. The paper is primarily delivered

by subscription, but you can buy individual copies at libraries, restaurants, and City Hall.

TAIL WINDS
2609 E. Broadway
(520) 745-2033
www.perimiterbicycles.com/TailWinds/TailWinds.html
Published 6 times a year by the Perimeter Bicycling Association of America, this upbeat newspaper covers everything related to biking in Arizona and neighboring states, including races and equipment. You can find it free at most bicycle shops.

TUCSON WEEKLY
3280 E. Hemisphere Loop, Ste. 180
(520) 294-1200
www.tucsonweekly.com
Tucson's free alternative weekly paper is published on Thursday, distributed through street boxes and various retail stores, and contains articles on local politics as well as music reviews, club listings, and restaurant guides and reviews. The *Weekly* also publishes an annual reader's poll of the Best of Tucson each September. A 1-year subscription is available for $110.

MAGAZINES

FITNESS PLUS
4474 E. 5th St.
(520) 881-6696
www.fitplusmag.com
As the title suggests, this free monthly magazine covers all aspects of keeping fit, including nutrition and health. Packed with ads from fitness clubs, the publication is very advertiser-driven but contains a full range of articles covering the fitness lifestyle in Tucson. It's available at hundreds of retail locations and through a paid annual subscription.

SOUTHERN ARIZONA TEE TIMES
PO Box 115, Cortaro, AZ 85652
(520) 792-6650
www.gogolfarizona.com
Arizona's only bimonthly golf publication, this magazine highlights golf throughout southern Arizona, including golf vacations and resorts. An annual subscription is available, or you can pick up a complimentary copy at area golf shops and resorts.

TUCSON GUIDE
1650 E. Fort Lowell Rd., Ste. 100
(520) 322-0895
www.maddenmedia.com
From the largest magazine-publishing house in Arizona, Madden Media, *Tucson Guide* is a classy, full-color quarterly guide to the city that has excellent feature articles, such as a regular "101 Things to Do" column and a "Festivals and Fiestas" calendar. The publication is $3.95 at newsstands and anywhere magazines are sold. A 1-year subscription is $13.95.

TUCSON HOME MAGAZINE
1650 E. Fort Lowell Rd., Ste. 100
(520) 322-0895
www.tucsonhomemagazine.com
This quarterly magazine, published by Madden Media, focuses on home and interior design and offers tips and articles about gardening and home decorating trends. A handy resource directory offers contact information for local businesses ranging from caterers to accessories. Annual subscriptions are available; the publication is also available at many book and grocery stores citywide.

TUCSON LIFESTYLE MAGAZINE
7000 E. Tanque Verde Rd.
(520) 721-2929
www.tucsonlifestyle.com
Owned by Conley Magazines, this monthly "City Book" covers Tucson's lifestyle, real estate, fashion, and society-related topics. A regular feature is the city guide "Where to Shop—Where to Dine—What to See." The annual "Newcomers" edition is very handy for residents and transplants alike. Annual subscriptions are available and also include 6 issues of the companion publication *Tucson Lifestyles Home & Garden*.

ZOCALO MAGAZINE
PO Box 1171, Tucson, AZ 85702
(520) 270-3213
www.thezmag.com
This glossy and informative publication covers urban news, arts, entertainment, living, and events in downtown and central Tucson. Independently published, it's available free all over town or by subscription 11 times a year.

TUCSON'S FILM INDUSTRY

The film industry has had a solid foothold in Tucson with Old Tucson Studios, dubbed "Hollywood in the Desert." Since it was built in 1939 as a re-creation of 1860s Tucson for the movie *Arizona*, the 160-acre site has been the location of more than 200 movies, TV shows, and commercials (see the Attractions chapter).

The **Tucson Film Office** (520-770-2151; www.filmtucson.com) coordinates filming activities and offers professional support services for filmmakers. Top-grossing productions set in the Tucson area include Michael

Bay's *Transformers: Revenge of the Fallen* and Sam Mendes's *Away We Go*.

Tucson has an active independent film community with its own **International Film Festival** (see the Festivals & Events chapter); art films shown regularly at the Loft, 3233 E. Speedway Blvd. (see the Nightlife chapter); and several popular film series at the University of Arizona.

TELEVISION

Present-day KOLD, Tucson's first TV station, went on the air February 1, 1953, as KOPO. The station was owned by Gene Autry, and the population of the city was 48,774. It took a while for the unrefined electronic stranger to catch on in Tucson. At the time TVs were selling for between $199 and $599, not much different from today until you consider a solid middle-class income was $5,000.

Today Tucson not only has a full complement of network affiliates and independent stations, but also several cable operators that provide the means to view the local stations as well as numerous national ones. Here are the television stations operating in Tucson:

KGUN Channel 9 (ABC)
KHRR Channel 40 (Telemundo)
KMSB Channel 11 (Fox)
KOLD Channel 13 (CBS)
KQBN Channel 14 (Telenoticias)
KTAZ Channel 34 (Telefutura)
KTTU Channel 18 (My Tucson TV)
KUAT Channel 6 (PBS)
KUVE Channel 5 (Univision)
KVOA Channel 4 (NBC)
KWBA Channel 58 (CW)

In addition to all the typical television offerings, Tucson boasts one of the best public-access production facilities in the country **Tucson Community Cable Corporation**

(Access Tucson), at 124 E. Broadway Blvd. (520-624-9833; www.access.tucson.org). The station is a training ground for up-and-coming TV and video producers, offering classes, digital editing booths, sound stages, and even equipment loans to members. However, its future is uncertain due to city-wide budget cuts that have put this great community asset in limbo.

Cable Companies

The cable TV companies serving Pima County have their own distinct geographical areas, so depending on where you stay in town—or where you choose to live—you'll be somewhat limited as to which company will serve you.

COMCAST DIGITAL CABLE

8251 N. Cortaro Rd., Marana
(520) 744-1900
www.comcast.com
Servicing Pima County residents, including Marana and Oro Valley, Comcast offers cable, digital cable, and high-speed Internet access.

COX COMMUNICATIONS

1440 E. 15th St.
(520) 884-0133
www.cox.com
The nation's 4th-largest cable provider, Cox services residents of Tucson, South Tucson, Davis-Monthan, Patagonia, Green Valley, and parts of Sahuarita. Cox offers broadband, digital cable, cable and Internet services, and PPV along with several local specialty channels, including the City of Tucson channel and several public-access channels.

RADIO

Tucson is unusual in that, for a city this size, there isn't much format-war-type competition among radio stations. That's because for each major format—rock, Top 40, country hits, etc.—there is usually only one station, or at most two or three.

For those desiring an alternative to the commercial, KAMP-AM, a student-run station at the University of Arizona, offers eclectic fare, as does the community station KXCI-FM. The University of Arizona also runs a professional public radio jazz station and a classical station, both of which also broadcast National Public Radio programs.

Here is a complete list of the stations on the dial in Tucson.

Adult Contemporary
KCEE 690 AM
KHYT 107.5 FM
KGMG 104.9 FM
KMXZ 94.9 FM
KSZR 97.5 FM
KWMT 92.9 FM
KZPT 104.1 FM

Christian
KFLT 830 AM
KGMS 940 AM

Classical
KUAT 90.5 FM

College Radio
KAMP 1570 AM

Community Radio
KXCI 91.3 FM

Country
KIIM 99.5 FM

Hip-Hop/R&B
KOHT 98.3 FM

Jazz
KUAZ 89.1 FM and 1550 AM (plus NPR)

Latin
KQTL 1210 AM
KTKT 990 AM
KTZR 97.1 FM
KXEW 1660 AM
KZLZ 105.3 FM

News/Talk
KCUB 1290 AM
KFFN 1490 AM (sports talk)
KJLL 1330 AM
KNST 790 AM (plus sports and UA games)
KTKT 990 AM (Arizona Cardinals)

Oldies
KGMG 106.3 FM
KGVY 1080 AM
KSAZ 580 AM
KTUC 1400 AM
KWFM 1450 AM

Rock
KFMA 92.1 FM (alternative)
KLPX 96.1 FM (classic)

Top 40
KRQQ 93.7 FM

INDEX

INDEX